Kosovo

the Bradt Travel Guide

Gail Warrander   Verena Knaus

www.bradtguides.com

edition
2

Bradt Travel Guides Ltd, UK
The Globe Pequot Press Inc, USA

KEY
Capital city ■
Main city ●
Town ○
Airport ✈
Main road
Other important road
Track (4x4, etc.)
Railway
Border post ✕
International border
National park
Cave/rock shelter ⌂
Monastery ✝

SERBIA

MONTENEGRO

PRISHTINA

MITROVICA

Leposavić

Banjska

Zvečan

Zubin Potok

Prekaz

Skenderaj

Gllogovc

Vushtrri

Podujeva

Battlava

Gračanica

Sitnica

Prishtina

Istog

Klina

PEJA

Drini i Bardhë

Novo Brdo

Kamenica

Badovc

Gračanica Monastery
page 137

Kullas in Isniq
page 179

Rugova Valley
page 167

Peć Patriarchate
page 167

GJILAN

Kllokot

Vti   Letnica

Kaçanik

Hani i
Elezit

ⓜ Gadime

FERIZAJ

Štrpce
Brezovica

Shtime

Suha Reka

Malisheva

Velika
Hoça

PRIZREN

Rahovec

ĐAKOVA

Hiking in Dragash
page 219

Prizren
page 195

Dragash

Brod

Restelica

Kodoniq

Visoki Dečani Monastery
page 171

Kullas in Dranoc
page 184

ALBANIA

MACEDONIA

N

Bradt

0   30km

0   20 miles

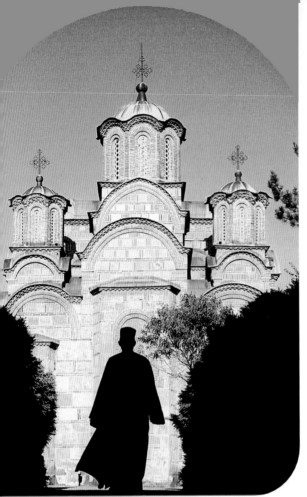

Kosovo Don't miss...

Gračanica Monastery
One of the best preserved examples of late Byzantine architecture in the world
(D/DT) page 137

Rugova Valley
A paradise for sporty types and nature lovers, with gorges, waterfalls and beautiful mountain scenery stretching all the way to the Montenegrin border
(GW) page 167

Kullas

Peja is home to a number of beautifully restored *kullas*, traditional stone fortified towers with barns for cattle below and living quarters above
(GW) page 149

Prizren

Its skyline dotted with the remnants of its Ottoman past, the city sprawls out on either side of the fast-flowing Bistrica River
(ISA) page 195

Visoki Dečani Monastery

Set in the forest of the Dečan Canyon, this is a stunning example of Orthodox monastic architecture and has survived a long history of conflict
(GW) page 175

above   The Junik Highlands offer fantastic walking and climbing country, with alpine meadows and peaks over 2,500m, including Gjeravica, Kosovo's highest mountain (MO) page 184

below   Zubin Potok, Kosovo's largest lake, has a number of beaches and is popular for swimming in the summer (GW) page 279

AUTHORS

Verena Knaus is a founding member of the European Stability Initiative (ESI), a non-profit think tank with offices in Prishtina, Istanbul, Brussels and Berlin. Before joining ESI, she studied modern history at Oxford and international relations and economics at The Johns Hopkins University.
She first came to Kosovo in summer 2001 to set up a Lessons Learned and Analysis Unit, a joint project of ESI and the UN administration in Kosovo. During those years, she researched and published extensively on Kosovo's postwar economy, international governance, minorities and migration.
In 2004, she moved to Turkey, where she researched and published on Turkey's Europeanisation. After a short stint at Yale as a World Fellow, she returned to Kosovo in January 2007, just in time for independence. Austrian by nationality, she is a passionate skier, camper, marathon runner and traveller. For many years, she led academic and biking tours across Europe. She speaks fluent German, Albanian, French, Italian and some Turkish.

Gail Warrander was a lawyer in the City of London and then for Reuters. On a commuter train she was drawn by an ad in *The Economist* and left 'the big smoke' to help with the EU-funded economic reconstruction effort in Kosovo. After three years working on infrastructure and privatisation projects she switched to working directly for the business community of Kosovo, running her own commercial law firm in Kosovo and working extensively with foreign and local investors. She then returned to the UK to attend London Business School's Sloan Fellowship programme. She is a keen mountain biker and snowboarder and speaks fluent German, French and Albanian and basic Serbian. She has travelled extensively throughout the Balkans.

AUTHORS' STORY

We did not know each other prior to writing the book although we had a lot in common, including many mutual friends, a fascination with the Balkans, Kosovo and knowledge of the Albanian language. Whilst travelling through the neighbouring countries, we both used the Bradt guides to Macedonia, Bosnia and Albania, but back in Kosovo we had to rely on word-of-mouth and trial and error in exploring the country's rich culture and nature. This spurred on each of us to coincidentally write to Bradt and lobby for a guide dedicated to Kosovo as we felt that just a chapter at the end of the Serbia guide was not sufficient. Bradt were responsive and have given us the freedom to shape the guide as we saw fit.

For a small place, Kosovo has a complex history and a rich ethnic mix and it is precisely this that made writing the guide so fascinating and at the same time difficult without offending someone. We hope that readers will bear with us if there is something that they disagree with, or which upsets their sensitivities, or if we have made any errors with regard to names or missed something out.

Our goal is simply to enlighten international visitors and Kosovar residents alike by revealing some of the hidden secrets or lesser-known facts about Kosovo's sights and people. We also want to make Kosovo more accessible for the genuine tourists, such as the adventurous backpackers who are increasingly venturing into Kosovo.

PUBLISHER'S FOREWORD *Hilary Bradt*

Bradt guides have always been good at overturning perceptions of a country or region. Kosovo is a prime example. All my imagery of the place is of war and of a nation dominated by religious divides. Verena and Gail show me how wrong I was. They tell me, for instance, that Muslims and Christians traditionally shared many beliefs and respected each other's holy places, and that this spirit of co-operation prevails. Most inspiring of all, Kosovo shares the concept of the Balkans Peace Park with its neighbours Albania and Montenegro, thus at one stroke providing glorious mountain scenery, environmental protection, carefully controlled income to the rural communities and a symbol of international brotherhood. For this alone Kosovo would be worth a visit.

Second edition published November 2010
First published 2007
Bradt Travel Guides Ltd, 23 High Street, Chalfont St Peter, Bucks SL9 9QE, England.
www.bradtguides.com
Published in the USA by The Globe Pequot Press Inc, PO Box 480, Guilford, Connecticut 06437-0480
Text copyright © 2010 Gail Warrander & Verena Knaus
Maps copyright © 2010 Bradt Travel Guides Ltd
Photographs copyright © 2010 Individual photographers (see below)
Project editor: Maisie Fitzpatrick

ISBN-13: 978 1 84162 331 3
British Library Cataloguing in Publication Data
A catalogue record for this book is available from the British Library

Photographs Ivan S Abrams (ISA); Musa Chowdhury (MC); Dreamstime: Dozet (D/DT), Fbprizren (FBP/DT); FLPA: Michael Krabs, Imag (MK/FLPA), Mike Lane (ML/FLPA); Konrad Wothe/Minden, Pictures (KW/MP/FLPA); Verena Knaus; Laurence Mitchell (LM); Mark Ofila (MO); Asdren Rrahmani (AR); Shkumbin Saneja (SKS); SuperStock (SS); Gail Warrender (GW)
Front cover Rugova Gorge, western Kosovo (AR)
Back cover Gračanica Monastery (D/DT); Prizren (GW)
Title page Peppers on sale in Prishtina (ISA); colourful door in Junik (MO); glasses of *raki* (SS)
Maps Maria Randell, David Priestley (colour)

Typeset from the authors' disc by D & N Publishing, Baydon, Wiltshire
Production managed by Jellyfish Print Solutions and manufactured in India

Acknowledgements

Both of us would like to thank Gunther Fehlinger for spurring us on to write the book and promising us that it would be a *sukses i madh* (Albanian for 'a big success'), and Louise Carvalho for her thoughtful and detailed feedback on the manuscript and her general support.

We are also grateful to the museum directors, the Kosovo Institute for Monuments, Cultural Heritage without Borders for sharing their knowledge with us and all the taxi drivers, hoteliers, restaurateurs and KFOR soldiers for their practical help.

We would like to thank Bradt for putting up with the ethnic complexities of Kosovo and their patience with the project.

VERENA KNAUS

Without Hil Nrecaj, this book would not have been written. He looked after me throughout the writing process and brightened up my life with his humour and endless patience. I am eternally grateful to him for sharing his personal insights with me and introducing me to Kosovo's history and culture.

I would also like to thank all my friends and colleagues at ESI and the EU Pillar who made my time in Kosovo such a rewarding experience. Eggert Hardten with his tireless quest for facts and provocative debate, Duska Anastasijević for explaining Mitrovica and my brother Gerald for introducing me to Kosovo in the first place. Special thanks also go to Judith Safar, Alexandra Fehlinger, Dominik Zaum and my old friends in the EU Pillar transport and security team. Thank you especially to all my friends in Kosovo and abroad who kept encouraging me and listened patiently to my thoughts on Kosovo. But really, with this book I want to thank all the countless families, businesses and officials in Kosovo who never tired of answering my questions and continued to invite me to their homes and offices. It is because of them and for them that I decided to write this Kosovo guidebook.

GAIL WARRANDER

Particular mention and thanks to Moni (Osman Gojani) and Bedia Rraci in Gjakova for taking tremendous time out to find source material, show me their city and for inspiring me with their dedication to restoring Kosovo's monuments. Thanks also to Parim Kosova in Prizren, Shehj Musa Shehu in Gjakova and the Sheh in Rahovec. Note should also be made of Mr Hoxha in Rahovec for the detailed background information and his pride in his city.

To Driton Krasniqi and Arben Kelmendi, my former employees, for their assistance with the first edition in particular with tracking down phone numbers, street names and opening hours, and for their patience with me in the office and to Bekim Gashi for helping with the second edition index. I have Maeve

O'Connell to thank for her practical assistance with Prizren for the second edition and I am grateful for the support from all my friends (inside and outside Kosovo), the frisbee crew, my legal clients, my family who embraced the idea from the start, and to Anton for joining me on biking trips. I am grateful to those legal clients and AUK who were so enthusiastic about the first edition that they bought in bulk for their own clients – particularly Ardian Shehu from Asseco and Philip Sigwart from ProCredit. Most of all I would like to thank Sabri Maloku for trailing round Kosovo, up and down muddy tracks trying to find the best route to monasteries, and for sitting in the kitchen late at night helping me create maps from scratch and going out and doing photocopying or chasing things down for me. He has continued to be a great support with the second edition – helping me check and find phone numbers, opening hours and bus times. I couldn't have done this without his great sense of humour, which makes the work worthwhile.

NOTE ABOUT MAPS

Several maps use grid lines to allow easy location of sites. Map grid references are listed in square brackets after listings in the text, with page number followed by grid number, eg: [201 E5].

FEEDBACK REQUEST

We would welcome any updates. Please send your comments to Bradt Travel Guides, 23 High Street, Chalfont St Peter, Bucks SL9 9QE, UK; e info@bradtguides.com.

Contents

Introduction

Few people think of Kosovo as a tourist destination. In recent years, most 'tourists' were people like us who came to Kosovo as part of the UN mission, diplomats, soldiers or development consultants. Only the lucky few who ventured out of their offices in Prishtina or took a detour on their way to Greece know Kosovo's many secrets and scenic nature. Packed into a relatively small place, Kosovo has breathtakingly beautiful mountain peaks, waterfalls and wildflower meadows, fascinating cultural treasures, Ottoman-era buildings, stone houses, churches, mosques and medieval fresco paintings. There are rivers for fishing, lakes for swimming and fabulous walking and mountain-biking trails.

We wrote this book for all those who come as tourists, stay for work or business or call Kosovo their home. It is written for travellers eager to discover an unknown part of Europe, adventurers looking for unspoilt nature off the beaten track, and for the diaspora and their children who come back on their summer vacation. With this book we hope to share Kosovo's secrets with you and put Kosovo and its people back on the European map.

Kosovo is an intriguing place and full of paradoxes and surprises for any first-time visitor. How come landlocked Kosovo has such a Mediterranean flair and vibrant outdoor café culture? By what twist of fate has Kosovo become the place with the best coffee anywhere outside Italy? Don't be surprised to find a deeply entrenched *raki*-drinking culture in a majority Muslim country. The answer is simple: beer and raki – as most Kosovars will quickly point out – just aren't alcohol! It will also take you only two days to understand why this country in the heart of Europe has its main streets named after Bill Clinton, celebrates the 4th of July and flies the American flag. The Kosovar majority remain eternally thankful to the US for its role in the 1999 war and its support for Kosovo's independence. European travellers may be pleasantly surprised to find that Kosovo's official currency is the euro without it being a member of the European Union (at least not yet).

The speed of change in recent years has been mind-boggling for all of us experiencing it first-hand. Kosovo was in a shambles only 11 years ago yet today there are few visible traces of the past conflict. Who would think that Kosovo is one of the safest countries in Europe? Kosovo and its people are sure to surprise you in a good many ways as you set out to discover this unknown corner in the heart of the Balkans.

Owing to its strategic position at the centre of the Balkan Peninsula, Kosovo has always been an important through-road and attractive spoil for its conquerors. Illyrians – the ancestors of modern-day Albanians – settled here long before Romans, Bulgars or Byzantines came to rule this region. The name Kosovo (derived from the Serbian word *kos* meaning 'blackbird') was first mentioned after the famous Kosovo battle dating back to 1389. Legends and romanticising epic songs secured it a special place in Serb national identity and Kosovo became an important spiritual centre and seat of the Serbian Orthodox Church. For nearly

500 years Kosovo was an Ottoman province *par excellence*, enjoying stability and the peaceful coexistence of its different communities and religions. As the Ottoman Empire disintegrated, Kosovo was trapped on the fault lines of competing national claims. The 20th century was marred by wars and destruction, and whereas other parts of Yugoslavia prospered, Kosovo remained poor and underdeveloped. In June 1999, after 78 days of NATO bombardment and the mass flight of nearly 800,000 refugees, Kosovo passed under direct UN administration. For nine years, its people were part of a unique state building experiment in the heart of Europe. Now finally independent, Kosovo is on the eve of yet another new and exciting era.

The traces of its complex and rich history make Kosovo a unique travel destination. To this day, towns like Prizren are trilingual, with signs in Albanian, Serbian and Turkish. Women in traditional Terbesh costumes are not an uncommon sight. Western Kosovo is home to the Visoki Dečani Monastery and the Patriarchate in Peć (Peja) – true marvels of medieval Serb Orthodox church building. These Orthodox monasteries form as much part of Kosovo's cultural heritage as does the impressive Fatih Sultan Mehmet Mosque in Prishtina (built years before the conquest of Constantinople), the dervish lodges and traditional town houses in Gjakova, and the traditional Albanian stone *kullas* (tower houses) in Isniq or Dranoc. This mix of cultures and traditions also lives on in the oven-baked stews (*tavas*), delicious lamb and pork dishes, stuffed peppers, nettle pies, honey-sweetened desserts and, last but not least, the home-brewed plum or grape *raki*.

A good place to start is Prishtina, the vibrant young capital. What makes Prishtina special is certainly not its beauty, but the pulse of life that you feel as you walk the streets thronged with young people and order your third macchiato coffee in a street-side café. Prishtina is busy and bubbly, but then there is also quiet and rural Viti and Gjilan, with Tuscanesque rolling hills and villages brightened up by colourful wood-carved doors. Tucked away in the southwesternmost corner, the Dragash Mountains offer a perfect hideaway, wildflower meadows and panoramic views amid fantastic alpine scenery. In winter, you can try your luck on one of the black runs in Štrpce boasting snow from late November to April, or venture west into the Rugova Gorge and rent a little ski chalet up in Bogë. One minute there is a big 4×4 on the road, the next moment you find yourself trailing behind a horse and cart. In one shop you hear a traditional pipe song, another plays the latest Albanian rap tune or turbo-pop. This is also the place where experiments were made, with mobile-phone numbers from Monaco and an airport previously licensed by Iceland.

The best thing about Kosovo – you will quickly agree – is the people you meet who make travelling and living in the country so special. The biggest source of pride for a Kosovar family is to host a guest and to offer a warm welcome. Thanks to the thousands of foreigners who lived here as part of the UN mission, Kosovars have been exposed to different cultures and English or German is spoken even in the remotest corners. As one backpacker on a tourist website put it, 'the Kosovo border guards seemed almost as excited as me about me entering Kosovo'. You will find the people you meet to be friendly, curious and welcoming. Don't be surprised to be invited into someone's home and offered coffee, tea and most likely a full meal. Just savour the moment and enjoy Kosovo's hospitality!

A NOTE ABOUT NAMES

Place names are the subject of much debate and change in Kosovo and signs for places are often the subject of political graffiti (whereby the opposing ethnic group's spelling is painted out). The authors of this guide have followed international etiquette in all the headings of the places, which is to first put the name used by the majority of the population in that place and then follow it with the minority name for the place. For example 'Peja/Peć' (majority Albanian) or 'Štrpce/Shterpcë' (majority Serb). To avoid overloading the text and maps only the majority name is used in the body of the maps and text itself except where this might be inappropriate, for example where a Serb monument is referred to, such as the Peć Patriarchate, then the Serbian name is used. In Albanian, place names decline according to their usage in the sentence. This can cause yet more confusion, eg: you may see reference to both Pejë and Peja. We have generally used the nominative version.

With some places, there has been a new naming frenzy, eg: Albanians have recently renamed Podujeva 'Besian', Kamenicë 'Dardan' and Obiliq 'Kastriot'. We have used the most common name which for now is still the old name, although where appropriate we have also indicated the new names.

Kosovo street names have changed a lot. So far as possible the names you see on the signs have been used in the text and maps, but some of the old names can stick in the locals' heads, so where appropriate they are indicated in the text to help visitors.

The inhabitants of Kosovo we have referred to collectively as the Kosovars but the text also refers to Kosovo Albanians and Kosovo Serbs. The terms Kosovan and even Kosovarian have started creeping into international lingo but are not used here.

A NOTE ABOUT TELEPHONE NUMBERS AND ADDRESSES

As there is far from complete fixed line coverage in Kosovo, many of the telephone numbers given are mobile numbers. These often belong to the individual waiter in the restaurant and so many change, particularly because the turnover of restaurants and businesses in Kosovo, especially in Prishtina, is high. Therefore please bear with us if a restaurant, shop or hotel no longer exists or the number is wrong. You may be lucky and find the number you are looking for by dialling 998 from a fixed line within Kosovo. This is the official telephone information service of Kosovo.

If dialling from a foreign phone (including a foreign registered mobile in Kosovo):

For Kosovo land/fixed lines with 038, 028, 029 – dial +381 38, etc.
For numbers indicated in the guide with 044 or 045 – dial +377 44, etc.
For numbers indicated in the guide with 049 or 043 – dial +386 49, etc.
For numbers indicated in the guide with 063, 064 or 065 – dial +381 63, etc.
To dial out from some fixed line phones you may need to dial 99 first or 00.

Note at the time of writing the illegal Serb mobile masts had been partially dismantled and we are assuming that Serb mobiles will not work in enclaves south of the Ibar in the future, but that they will continue to do so in the north. This means that there are a few places in the Serb enclaves without phone numbers listed.

X

Part One

GENERAL INFORMATION

Area 10,908km^2

Highest point Gjeravica 2,656m

Population 1.9 million (estimate)

Population density 200 per km^2

Percentage of population under 27 70%

Ethnicities Albanian 88%, Serb 7% and 5% other (including Bosniaks, Turks, Roma, Ashkali, Gorani)

Religions Approximately 90% Muslim, 7% Serb Orthodox, Catholic 3%

Capital city Prishtina

Population of capital city 300,000 (estimate)

Other major cities Peja, Prizren, Gjakova, Gjilan, Mitrovica, Ferizaj

Official languages Albanian, Serbian and, in the Prizren area, Turkish

Currency Euro; Serbian dinar also used in some areas (100 dinars were £0.79/€0.96 in August 2010)

Electricity 220V (but fluctuates)

Time GMT/BST + 1

Public holidays See pages 65–6

Natural resources Zinc, lead, silver, copper, lignite, kaolin, marble, chrome, magnesite, nickel and other ores

International telephone codes +381 landline, +377 (Vala) mobile, +386 (IPKO) mobile, and +381 (Serbian mobile)

Head of state President

Municipalities 36 (+2 more planned)

Flag Royal blue with country outline topped by six stars in yellow

I

Background Information

GEOGRAPHY

Kosovo has a surface area of 10,908km². It is ringed by mountains, with a central plain divided into two valleys, with the Kaçanik Gorge running down the centre. The mountains are as high as 2,000m on the Macedonian and Albanian borders. The highest mountain is Gjeravica near Deçan which is 2,656m and the lowest point is Vermicë in Prizren at 295m. Prishtina itself is at just over 600m.

Around 41% of the cultivable land is forest. The remainder is arable. Crops grown include barley for the beer, some wheat, and vegetables (peppers, potatoes, carrots).

There are two main valleys – the Dukagjini Valley, which has better irrigation and is slightly warmer so is better for growing vegetables and vines, and the Kosovo Valley, which is good for potatoes and orchards in the southeast.

Kosovo is unusual for a place of its size in being almost entirely self-sufficient in water. Its rivers run into the Aegean Sea, the Black Sea and the Adriatic. The main rivers in Kosovo are Drini i Bardhë (122km long) in the Peja region, Sitnica (90km), Bistrica e Pejës (62km), Morava e Binçës (60km) in the Gjilan area, Lepenci (53km) near Ferizaj and Kaçanik, Ereniku (51km) near Gjakova, Ibar (42km) near Mitrovica and Bistrica e Prizrenit (31km) near Prizren. There are five lakes over 2.5km²: Battlava Reservoir in the north which supplies Prishtina, Badovc also outside Prishtina, Zubin Potok in the north near Mitrovica, Radoniqi outside Gjakova and Vermicë on the border with Albania beyond Prizren.

The mountains are a mixture of glacial and volcanic in origin, with glacial lakes in the Macedonian Sharr Mountains in Dragash and Brezovica and also in the Rugova and Deçan areas.

Sadly Kosovo is suffering from environmental damage in terms of mineral seepage, illegal quarrying, illegal woodcutting and, most obviously to the visitor, large-scale rubbish dumping. Plastic bags and bottles clog up the streams and many fields are covered in fly-tipped waste. It is hoped that when the economy improves and with the continued involvement of the European Union in Kosovo attention will turn to this area.

As yet no attention is paid in Kosovo to global warming or energy saving, with no incentives for house insulation. Kosovo's main power plant, powered by lignite, is also a significant polluter of the environment.

CLIMATE

Kosovo has a continental climate, with hot summers and cold winters. Snow can fall as early as November and as late as April. July and August are invariably hot, although May and June can be too. The night-time/daytime temperature differential is generally greatest in September and October.

The average daytime temperature in January is −0.9°C and can reach −15°C on a bad night, while the average daytime temperature in July is 21.5°C but temperatures can go as high as 35°C. Temperatures differ little across Kosovo – just a couple of degrees. In autumn, the average monthly rainfall is 177mm, whilst in summer it is 129mm. Rainstorms can be heavy and, due to an absence of storm drains and poorly designed roads, streets can quickly turn into floodstreams.

Spring is short in Kosovo and some of the internationals refer jokingly to there being only two seasons – the mud season (autumn/winter/spring) and the dust season (summer) with perhaps a third being the frozen season (parts of winter). The absence of asphalt on some roads and widespread construction dust also causes dust clouds to form. The Kosovars will explain that their reason for watering the roads and pavements with hosepipes is to keep the dust down, although they seem to get carried away with this and the watering of the streets can seem a frustrating waste of water when water cuts are common.

NATURAL HISTORY AND CONSERVATION AREAS

FLORA AND FAUNA Kosovo's **flora** includes typical European plants such as silver birches and pines, as well as alpine plants. The Dragash area is best known for herbs and includes a wide variety of wild flowers. The fact that many fields have remained uncultivated for more than ten years due to ownership disputes or because their owners have left Kosovo has meant that you can see wild flower meadows in Kosovo which are almost an unknown sight in heavily cultivated western Europe. The best time for the flower meadows is April–May.

Walnut and chestnut trees can be found around the Deçan area; calendular, juniper berries and St John's wort can be found in Dragash.

In terms of **fauna**, you cannot fail to notice the ubiquitous blackbirds of Kosovo which gather ominously and noisily, particularly in the evenings, like a scene out of Alfred Hitchcock's film *The Birds*. A much nicer bird which is not uncommon to spot and which is the Albanian national symbol is the eagle. Apparently KFOR (the Kosovo Protection Force) has been breeding eagles and releasing them into the wild and many of them have been sighted even fairly close to Prishtina in the fields beyond Gračanica towards Janjevo. Kosovo's wildlife is quite varied and if you take more than three walks in the countryside proper you are almost bound to see a tortoise, a brown snake or an eagle. While driving back at night through the Dukagjini Valley, eg: on the road back from Montenegro, you may see the bright eyes of a fox.

An avid international walker in Kosovo since 1998 claims to have encountered brown bears on two occasions, but this requires a real excursion into the wilds of the Peja or Sharr mountains or the border areas. Deer are also present, especially around Lipjan and the Gjilan area, but again they are quite rare to catch. Slightly less rare, perhaps because Kosovar Muslims do not generally eat them, are wild boar or wild pigs, as they are referred to locally. The best location to see these is Blijanes Park in Lipjan (see *Lipjan*, page 144). The movement of large parts of the population away from villages to the towns has in fact left large tracts of the countryside uncultivated and unhunted and many villagers will now testify that there are now more wild animals than before 1999, particularly close to the border areas with Serbia. Until August 2006 (when a new hunting law was passed) hunting licences were not issued due to UNMIK's (the United Nations Mission in Kosovo) concern about arms (see *Chapter 3, Sports and activities*, page 114).

NATIONAL PARKS Kosovo's main official national park is the Sharr Mountains National Park, which also straddles the border with Macedonia. This covers Štrpce and the Brezovica ski resort and the hills around the Zhupa Valley (see *Chapter 6, South Kosovo*, pages 229–34). There are, however, almost no wardens left.

Antonia Young

For 40 years the Iron Curtain, a 900-mile military barrier, divided Europe into western and eastern sections. Within this area, no activity was allowed. When the Curtain fell in 1989, what remained was a belt of land running the entire length of Europe, within which no disturbance or development had been permitted – a strip of ecologically virgin land. The man with primary responsibility for the ending of the Iron Curtain – Mikhail Gorbachev – was one of the originators of the proposal to create, from this symbol of division, a new symbol of reunification, an ecological 'green belt', a series of protected areas and national and transnational parks, running from the Baltic in the north, between Finland and Russia, across Germany, between the Czech Republic and Austria and Hungary, and down through the Julian Alps, between Slovenia and Italy, to the Adriatic Sea. An eastern section would follow a route around the former Yugoslavia – between Hungary and Serbia, running south to follow the border between Bulgaria and Yugoslav Macedonia. Once again, there would be a western and an eastern split: the western green belt would run along Greece's northern border with Yugoslav Macedonia, and then bifurcating once again to encompass the entire Albanian border; the eastern section would run between Bulgaria and European Turkey to end at the Black Sea. Kosovo, as part of the former Yugoslavia, was of course never behind the Iron Curtain, but non-aligned in the Cold War.

Many sections covered by these belts are already protected areas. The Julian Alps National Park, on the borders of Slovenia and Italy, is already well established, and the Balkan Peace Park Project (BPPP) together with the active Balkan Peace Park Coalition (BPP) have well-advanced plans for a transnational ecological peace park across the borders of Albania, Kosovo and Montenegro. The great Balkan lakes – Prespa, Ohrid and Skadar – are already protected and there are plans afoot to extend and consolidate that protection. The World Conservation Union (IUCN) has been one of several groups and agencies supporting such initiatives.

Importantly, the green belt is now a symbol not of division but of unification; countries would now not be isolated one from another, but would co-operate to preserve natural wilderness areas. The former division of one sphere of influence from another would become an ecological common treasury running through the middle of the continent. The demilitarisation of this divide, in particular de-mining efforts, was a practical aspect of this now virtually complete transformation.

The green belt idea has been driven forward by a loose grouping of ecological organisations, national and international (involving 23 countries, of which Kosovo is one of the three Balkan Peace Park countries). It is divided into three sections – the northern Fennoscandian Belt, from the Barents Sea down to the Gulf of Finland; the Central European Belt, from the Baltic down to the Adriatic, and the more complicated Balkan Belt, along the barriers which once divided the Balkan countries.

It follows divisions that go back further than the Cold War: for example, the borders of Albania left half of the Albanian population outside those borders since 1912. The Balkans Peace Park is opening frontiers for peaceful travel, at the same time as maintaining ecological preservation. An aspect taken up by some of the cross-border projects is the opening of border crossing points – even roads – some closed since 1945, some for even longer. Most importantly, the entire area of the green belt is no longer seen as the boundaries of empires, but as the centre of a continent and an expression of its commitment to peace, integration and the preservation of biodiversity, as well as the increasing linkage of people and transnational issues.

For further details of the Balkans Peace Park Project, see www.balkanspeacepark.org

In addition, there have been proposals to make the Rugova Valley (see page 167) a national park, and the same has been mooted for Dragash. This would seem essential to cut back on inevitable illegal building. Part of the Kopaonik National Park (*www.kopaonik.net*) also juts into northern Kosovo. The forest areas of Kosovo fall under the Kosovo Forestry Authority, a well-intentioned governmental body that suffers from underfunding and under-resourcing (it has 300 staff), to tackle a major problem with illegal logging, which is popular because of high energy prices.

HISTORY

ANCIENT HISTORY The territory of Kosovo has been inhabited for more than 8,000 years and its soil is rich with archaeological finds dating back to the Bronze and Iron ages. Most of the finds are still to be uncovered, with several archaeological projects only just starting. By the 7th century BC **Illyrian tribes**, sharing a common Illyrian language, emerged as the dominant force in an area covering modern-day Albania, Kosovo and the Dalmatian coast. Illyrians built fortified towns, minted coins and produced beautiful jewellery made of silver and copper. Power rested in the hands of a close-knit ruling caste. The Illyrian tribes along the Adriatic coast were seafaring and traded intensively with their ancient Greek neighbours. The **Ardiaeans** were one of the most prominent coastal tribes and from the 3rd century BC Shkodra (in Albania) became their capital. In 229BC, during the reign of the Ardiaean queen Teuta, the **Roman Empire** launched its first attack on the Illyrian territory. The Illyrian navy was crushed decisively, but it took the Romans 61 years to establish a proper foothold on Illyrian soil. In 168BC, the last Illyrian king, Genti, surrendered to the Romans. The inland tribes residing in what is present-day Kosovo were able to resist the Roman onslaught for another 100 years before being finally defeated by the troops of Emperor Augustus. A new Roman province by the name of Illyricum was then founded. In 56BC, Julius Caesar visited the province on one of his campaigns to the east.

All through antiquity Kosovo was an important trading crossroads. A Roman military road wound its way from the famous fortress town of Shkodra in northern Albania across to western Kosovo running along the Drini i Bardhë (White Drin) River to Prizren. For centuries, Prizren was an important commercial centre supplying the entire region. Later a second trade route opened up with what is today known as Dubrovnik in Croatia (then referred to as Ragusa). Trading links extended as far as Bosnia and Herzegovina to the west, Novi Pazar to the north and Thessaloniki to the south. The Romans also mined silver in Kosovo's eastern region. In the 3rd century AD, Illyricum was a peaceful and prosperous Roman province. In AD284, Emperor Diocletian made Naissus (modern-day Niš) the capital of a Roman province named **Dardania**, after the resident Dardani tribe. Ulpiana, near Prishtina, was the economic and cultural centre of Dardania province (see *Chapter 4*, page 135).

With the split of the Roman Empire in AD395, Kosovo stayed in the eastern half of the Roman Empire and under the Eastern Church. Constantinople then became the source of artistic inspiration. Under the reign of Emperor Justinian, from AD527 to 565, the Balkan region was put under **Byzantine control**. Justinian also ordered the reconstruction of Ulpiana after its destruction by an earthquake in AD518.

The first major influx of **Slavic tribes** into present-day Kosovo took place in the middle of the 6th century. Croat and Serb tribes were invited by the Byzantine emperor to fight off the marauding Avar armies. The Serbian tribes then settled in the territories abandoned by the Avars in the area of Rascia (present-day Raška), to the north of Kosovo. In AD850, the Bulgars established a foothold in today's

Kosovo and set up a bishopric in Ohrid, Macedonia. For almost two centuries, Kosovo remained under **Bulgarian rule** before reverting to the control of the Byzantine Empire under the rule of Basil, the 'Bulgar killer'.

There have been numerous highly politicised debates about the origin of the **Albanians**. The most recent Western school of thought is that the ancestors of the modern Albanians are the ancient Illyrians. The first mention of a tribe called Albanoi was by Ptolemy in one of his maps produced in the 2nd century. By the 6th century, the Illyrian-speaking peoples were known as Albani and their language Albanian. A Byzantine record dated AD1043 mentions Albanian troops fighting alongside Greeks in the army of a Byzantine general. In 1281, an Italian record mentions an Albanian by the name of Duca Ginius ruling over an area in north Albania. He is believed to have been the founder of the noble Dukagjini family. Linguists even believe that the term 'Alb' may derive from an Indo-European word for a mountainous area, the same word as 'Alps' still in use today. The origin of shqipta' (pronounced 'shiptar'), the term used by Albanians to describe themselves, is unclear.

MIDDLE AGES The nucleus of the medieval Serbian state was based in Rascia, to the north of Kosovo. There Stefan Nemanja, founder of the **Nemanjić dynasty**, laid the foundation for the medieval **Serbian Empire** that would eventually rule Kosovo for 250 years. In 1184, he successfully extended his power base from Rascia southwards into Kosovo and into what is present-day northern Macedonia. He abdicated at the peak of his military career, and joined his youngest son Sava on Mount Athos. Venerated as Simeon, Stefan Nemanja achieved the ultimate accolade – he became the first Serbian saint. His son Sava was in turn not only a pious monk, but also a skilful diplomat, and in 1217 he arranged the crowning of his brother Stefan by a papal legate, securing him the title of 'First Crowned'. In 1219, Sava persuaded the patriarch in Constantinople to grant independence (autocephaly) to the **Serbian Church**.

In the early years, the centre of Serbian monasticism remained concentrated in the Rascia region, and did not include any territory in present-day Kosovo. The monastery of Ziča near Kraljevo was chosen as the first seat of the Serbian Orthodox Church. Stefan Nemanja's remains were buried at Studenica in Serbia. Sava became the first archbishop of the Serbian Orthodox Church and like his father he was quickly canonised soon after his death in 1235.

In the late 13th century the Nemanjić ruler Milutin, later known as Uroš II, rapidly expanded the Serbian territories. Skopje, capital of present-day Macedonia, became the new capital of the Serbian kingdom stretching all the way to Durrës on the Adriatic coast. Uroš II spent much of the wealth generated from the Kosovo mines on a major church-building programme. Serbian art had benefited greatly from the exodus of fresco painters following the raid of Constantinople in 1204 and many of them sought employment in the Balkans and deployed their skills as part of this church-building programme. The Gračanica Monastery (see page 137) near Prishtina, for example, was founded at that time.

It was Milutin's son Stefan Dečanski (Uroš III) who commissioned the building of the Visoki Dečani Monastery in western Kosovo. His son **Dušan** came to the throne in 1331 after making arrangements to imprison his father in Zvečan, ordering him to be strangled and then burying his remains at the Dečani Monastery. During Dušan's reign the Serbian kingdom expanded spectacularly to include today's southern Albania and northern Greece. In 1346, Dušan raised the Serbian archbishop to the rank of patriarch (head of the Church), cutting all remaining ties with the Greek Orthodox Church. Dušan then went on himself to be crowned Tsar Dušan by the new patriarch. In 1349, as one of his last acts he

KOSOVO IN 1196, 1335 and 1389

SLOVENIA   HUNGARY

■ ZAGREB

CROATIA   VOJVODINA   ROMANIA

BOSNIA AND   ■ BELGRADE
HERZEGOVINA

SARAJEVO■

KEY

Boundaries of Serbia
— — — — 1196
· · · · · · · · 1355
— · — · — · 1389

Montenegro   KOSOVO ● Prishtina   ■ SOFIA

PODGORICA ■   BULGARIA

Adriatic Sea   ■ SKOPJE

TIRANA■

ITALY   ALBANIA

TURKEY

GREECE

Aegean Sea

0 ———— 100km
0 ———— 100 miles   ■ ATHENS

introduced a comprehensive new legal code, known as **Dušan's code**, regulating religious practice and matters of daily life. His sons inherited the most powerful empire in the Balkans, but family quarrels led to its rapid decline. One claimant to the throne was killed in battle on the Marica River in 1371 against the advancing Ottoman armies. The rightful heir, Uroš IV, died the same year without a son. The Nemanjić dynasty came to an end and the territory was quickly carved up among different ruling families. One of these rulers was Lazar Hrebeljanovic, the later hero of the Kosovo battle. He ruled over eastern Kosovo from his power base in Kruševac, Serbia.

THE BATTLE OF KOSOVO The common myth that the Ottoman victory on the Kosovo battlefield destroyed the Serbian medieval empire and that Serbs were immediately placed under Turkish rule is not quite true. The Serbian Empire had already started to disintegrate after Dušan's death in 1355, while smaller Serbian statelets continued to survive for another 70 years under Ottoman suzerainty. The last Serbian fortress, Smederevo, fell to the Turks in 1459.

Of particular importance – even today – is the Battle of Kosovo in 1389; the military significance of this battle, however, is widely disputed. An earlier Turkish victory in the battle on the Marica in Bulgaria in 1371 had already opened the door for the Ottoman conquest of the Balkans. The Kosovo battle was only a specific campaign to avenge an earlier defeat by Sultan Murat at the hands of the Bosnian king Tvrtk. As was common for feudal armies at that time, Greek and

Serbian vassal troops were fighting on the Turkish side, and Albanian and Hungarian mercenaries were fighting under Prince Lazar's command. To apply modern-day notions of a 'national struggle' between Serbs and Turks ignores the complexities of the disputes in the 14th century.

When the two armies met on the Kosovo fields on the morning of 15 June 1389 (not 28 June as popularly thought), Murat's army may have numbered around 30,000 troops and Lazar's 20,000. Only one fact is certain: both Lazar and Murat were killed in action, though the exact circumstances of their deaths remain unclear to this day. Murat's son Bayezit rushed home as soon as possible to secure his own succession. Prince Lazar's widow, on behalf of her 15-year-old son Lazarević, agreed to become an Ottoman vassal in 1390, paying an annual tribute and committing to supply troops in the event of war. To demonstrate his political allegiance to the sultan, Lazarević married off his sister Olivera to Sultan Bayezit in a grand ceremony.

It took another 70 years after the Battle of Kosovo before the entire territory was brought under **Ottoman control**. The Ottomans only slowly established a foothold in Kosovo: in 1399, a Turkish garrison was placed in Zvečan to guard the north, and in 1423, an Ottoman court was established in Prishtina and Ottoman customs officials controlled the road between Prishtina and Novi Pazar. The Ottoman conquest could be regarded as having been fully completed only in 1455 when the valuable mining town of Novo Brdo surrendered to Sultan Mehmet after a 40-day-long siege.

OTTOMAN KOSOVO The traditional Balkan view on the Ottoman period is one shaped by 19th-century nationalism. Indeed, everything Ottoman is commonly rejected as backward, alien and oppressive, and 500 years of intense cultural exchange are reduced to a 'Turkish yoke'. A closer look reveals a more nuanced picture of the Ottoman era. Far from imposing an entirely new governing system, the Ottoman Empire absorbed and adapted the existing Byzantine and Serbian ruling systems. It brought peace and stability to the region and a steady expansion of urban centres, in particular the two administrative centres Vushtrri and Prizren. The 'golden age' of the empire is often associated with the reign of **Sultan Sylejman the Magnificent** (1520–66).

The sultan's main concerns were how to source sufficient troops to fight wars and how to secure the funds to pay for them. **Military service** was reserved for Muslims only. Non-Muslims, mostly Christian peasants (*raya*), were excluded from military service, but expected to pay taxes. Non-Muslims paid a fixed annual tax, plus a share of their produce and a poll tax levied on every male head of a household. In 1490, Ottoman officials recorded 64,328 tax-paying households in the territory of Kosovo.

Compared with other European states at the time, the Ottoman Empire was tolerant of other religions. Christianity and Judaism were generally recognised as religions of the Book and protected. Believers were allowed to practise their faith and to run their own religious institutions, as witnessed by the churches built during the Ottoman era. The exception was the Albanian Catholic minority, which was more problematic, due to the Catholics' allegiance to foreign powers – the Vatican, Venice and Austria, who were all sworn enemies of the sultan.

A *kadi*, or judge, was responsible for an administrative area called the *kadilik*. A group of kadiliks formed a *sançak*, or military-administrative district. In turn, an *eyalet* was formed by a few sançaks and presided over by a *beylerbey*. Kosovo was part of the eyalet of Rumeli and was itself divided into the sançak of Vushtrri, which included Prishtina and Kosovo's eastern half, whereas the sançak of Prizren stretched all the way to Novi Pazar, and the sançak of Shkodra included the region

9

around Peja. Gjakova at times was part of the Dukagjin sançak and Kaçanik was joined with the sançak of Skopje.

A much talked-about feature of the Ottoman Empire was the feared **Janissary Corps**, the sultan's elite troops. In the early days, the Janissary Corps was formed of slaves captured at war times. Slavery, however, had already existed under the Christian emperors and slave trading was widely practised throughout the Byzantine Empire. Later, recruitment to the Janissary Corps was done via the *devşirme*, the forceful recruitment of young Christian boys every seven years. Several of the Christian boys pressed into the sultan's elite army corps advanced to the highest positions in the imperial household. For some, the devşirme provided a real career opportunity and it ensured that the Ottoman elite reflected the multi-ethnic character of its empire.

Contrary to popular perception, forced conversions to Islam were extremely rare. Islam spread slowly and for a long time remained just a localised phenomenon, primarily among the urban elite. Catholics continued to practise their belief, particularly in the mountainous regions, and Orthodox church building continued. The Serb Orthodox Patriarchate was re-established in Peć in 1557 and continued to function, with short interruptions, until 1766. For economic reasons, in particular to avoid paying the poll tax levied on the household heads, male heads of households would convert to Islam while their families remained Christian. These families were referred to as **crypto-Catholics** and they continued to practise both faiths at home. Turkish was the language of both administration and commerce, so the city-based elite of Albanian or Slav descent conversed fluently in Turkish on the street and in their homes. It is said that many Albanian families who converted to Islam became so fully Ottomanised that the distinction between Albanian and Turkish became blurred. Even today, some families who consider themselves the urban elite in Prizren and Prishtina speak both Turkish and Albanian in their homes.

The prized asset of Kosovo for the Ottoman Empire was its mineral wealth. Kosovo's silver mines in Novo Brdo and Trepça were a major contributor to the sultan's treasury. Kosovo's main exports in those days were leather hides and wool, exported to western Europe via Ragusa (modern-day Dubrovnik). Ragusan merchants also controlled all imports of luxury goods. Western Kosovo, meanwhile, was renowned for its fruit, saffron and silk worms.

In many respects Kosovo was the Ottoman province *par excellence* and the Albanians actively influenced the empire's history. A total of 42 grand viziers, the highest imperial office, were of Albanian origin. On matters cultural, Kosovo also contributed significantly: **Prishtinasi Mesihi** (1470–1512) wrote the first humorous poem in Turkish literature; the Albanian-born **General Sinan Pasha** conquered Yemen before building the fort and mosque in Kaçanik; **Mehmet Akif** (1873–1936), the son of an Albanian villager from Peja, became a schoolteacher and poet in Istanbul and in 1921 wrote the Turkish National Anthem known as *Istiklal Marsi (The Independence March)*; the grand vizier who led the second siege of Vienna in 1683, **Mehmet Köprülü**, was also from a well-known Albanian family.

The failed siege of Vienna in 1683 marked a turning point for the region and the start of a period of instability. The Austrian imperial army under the leadership of Count Piccolomini pushed the Ottoman forces back as far as modern-day Macedonia. In 1689, the territory of Kosovo fell under Austrian control, but the **Austrian occupation** was short-lived. On 1 January 1690, the Austrian army was routed at Kaçanik and hastily withdrew from Kosovo. The Patriarchate in Peć (Peja) was ransacked and the patriarch himself fled in haste. In Serbian national history this turn of events is remembered as the **'Great Migration'** (Velika Seoba). But contrary to the depictions in paintings romanticising the era, the patriarch Arsenije had already left the territory of Kosovo ahead of the Austrian defeat and he did not guide his flock to safety. Furthermore, a large number of Kosovo's Serbian population remained in Kosovo. According to letters written by Arsenije himself, the number of Serb refugees ranged between 30,000 and 40,000, most of whom settled near Budapest. Those who stayed behind, including both Serbs and Albanians, faced the hordes of plundering Ottoman and Tatar troops who wrought brutal revenge on the local population.

In the course of the 17th and 18th centuries, the sultan's grip over his European possessions weakened, as increasing pressure to finance military campaigns gradually eroded the existing administrative and feudal system. More and more military estates (*timars*) were sold off for ready cash and turned into private holdings. The power vacuum was filled by prominent Kosovar families who often retained large private armies, including, for example, the Begolli family in Peja, the Rotuli in Prizren, and the Gjinolli family in Prishtina and Gjilan.

The first half of the 19th century was marked primarily by violent local **revolts and instability**. Many violent revolts, particularly in western Kosovo, were sparked by efforts to introduce a new conscription system or to disarm the local population. In 1831, a Bosnian rebel leader, Husein of Gradačac led his troops all the way to Lipjan and routed the Ottoman army. In an effort to reform, the Ottoman administration tried unsuccessfully to rein in the privileges of the local ruling families. Temporarily, Prizren and Peja were placed under direct military rule. The empire's reform programme was far-reaching and included the disbandment of the Janissary Corps, the introduction of state education and the granting of equal rights to non-Muslims. In 1856, the *Porte* (government of the empire) declared full freedom of religion and deserting Islam was no longer punishable by the death penalty.

The empire was also slowly catching up with **industrialisation**. By the 1860s, the first telegraph lines connected Prizren, Peja and Prishtina with Istanbul and Thessaloniki. In 1874, the first railway line connecting Thessaloniki to Mitrovica was opened, effectively eliminating Prizren's long-standing and cherished status as Kosovo's commercial centre. Instead, Prishtina, Ferizaj and Mitrovica emerged as new economic centres. The first nascent industries, a few sawmills and motorised flour mills, were all founded in eastern Kosovo.

Midhat Pasha, the energetic governor of the eyalet of Niš, developed an ambitious reform agenda, effectively restructuring the Ottoman administration. Larger units called *vilayets*, each governed by a *vali* (governor) replaced the old eyalets and in 1868 the new vilayet of Prizren was created. In 1877, Prishtina became the centre of the newly created vilayet of Kosovo. Thus, for the first time in nearly 500 years, most of Kosovo was united under a single administrative unit.

NATIONAL AWAKENING The popular view on the different nationalist movements in the Balkans is that of subjugated peoples who finally threw off the Turkish yoke. In this regard, the defining moment was 1912. For Serbs, 1912 symbolised the liberalisation of historical Serbian lands and the long-awaited revenge of 500 years of Ottoman occupation. The myth of the Kosovo battle formed the essence of the Serbian national movement as it developed in the 19th century. For Albanians in Kosovo, 1912 brought the collapse of the Ottoman Empire and the declaration of **Albanian independence** in Vlora (present-day Albania) on 28 November. The year 1912 thus marked the beginning of a century-long struggle aimed at recognition of their Albanian identity.

Albanians were, arguably, rather late in developing a national identity. As they included Muslims, Orthodox Christians and Catholics, they lacked the unifying factor of one shared religion. There was no single institution taking the lead in fostering a national identity comparable to the Serbian National Church. On the contrary, the Muslim majority saw in the sultan not only a political figurehead but also a religious one. Loyalty to the caliphate was perceived as a religious obligation. Without Albanian-language education, the language of the educated Albanian elite was Turkish. While Austria-Hungary occasionally intervened in favour of the Albanian community, Albanians lacked a consistent external patron to play a role similar to Russia's bolstering of the Pan-Slavic alliance. Well-endowed Albanian landowners and clan leaders, traditionalists out of self-interest, also had no interest in destabilising the political and economic system.

It could be said that the Albanian national movement was eventually split into three very different and distinct interest groups: Tosk-speaking feudal landowners in Albania's south; an Istanbul-educated, intellectual elite; and the Gheg-speaking northern Albanian clansmen and ruling families in Kosovo. To rally such a diverse community behind one common goal required patience, determination and a little twist of fate.

Like most national movements, the Albanian **Rilindja Kombetare (National Renaissance)** also had its birth in the Albanian diaspora. In 1876, the first Italian Albanian Committee for the Liberation of the Albanians in the East was set up in Milan, and soon afterwards the first national propaganda literature was produced. A year later, in 1877, Abdyl Frasheri set up a secret 'Albanian Committee' in Ioannina, present-day northern Greece. A first national memorandum was sent to the Ottoman government in 1877 calling for the creation of a single vilayet uniting all Albanian-populated provinces to be administered by Albanians and with military service limited to the defence and control of the Albanian territory.

The **Serbian National Awakening**, meanwhile, took a slightly different turn. In 1815, the sultan had already agreed to grant a degree of self-administration to an area around Belgrade under a Serbian prince. It was in this semi-autonomous area and among the Serbian exile communities in Western capitals that the recognition of Kosovo as Serbia's religious and historical heartland was transformed into a gripping national agenda.

In 1876, Serbia and Montenegro jointly attacked the Ottoman troops in an effort to conquer the area around Novi Pazar; however, this offensive was crushed decisively. The Ottoman troops then proceeded further north into Serbian territory until the Russians intervened, imposing an armistice. A year later, on Bulgarian soil, Russia declared war against the Ottoman Empire. A weakened Ottoman Empire was caught by surprise by a second Serbian attempt to seize the town of Niš. Serbian troops advanced as far as Podujevo and Gračanica, but were forced to withdraw following the **Treaty of San Stefan** between Russia and the Ottoman Empire in early 1878.

This important treaty created a large Bulgarian state and divided up the Albanian-populated areas between Serbia and Bulgaria. Serbia was granted administrative authority over Niš, Vushtrri and the area around Mitrovica. The signing of this treaty alarmed the Albanian national movement as well as other European powers. Within months, the great European powers called for a revision of the treaty and instead imposed the **Treaty of Berlin**. Under this second treaty, Macedonia and Kosovo remained within the Ottoman Empire. In turn, the mostly Albanian-populated area around Gusinje (in present-day northern Montenegro near Plav on the Kosovan border) was handed over to Montenegro, and Bosnia and Herzegovina was put under an Austrian protectorate. Serbia was allowed to keep the area around Niš. After this treaty was signed, Serbian troops burnt down villages and expelled more than 100,000 Albanian Muslims from the newly liberated Serbian regions. About 50,000 of these *muhaxhirs* (meaning 'refugees' in Turkish) moved from Niš to Kosovo. More bloodshed ensued. In Gjakova violent resistance to the redrawing of the Ottoman–Montenegrin border left 280 people dead. As the news of these killings spread, for the first time the Albanian national question caught the attention of European capitals.

In the meantime, Abdyl Frasheri, an Istanbul-educated intellectual, had called for a meeting of Albanian clan leaders in Prizren. At a historic meeting on 10 June 1878 the 300 delegates agreed that Albanian interests were best served by obtaining a degree of autonomy within the Ottoman Empire. The delegates' first significant decision was the formation of a defensive 'League' – remembered in history as the **League of Prizren** – to prevent the occupation of any Albanian-inhabited territory. Far from being a secessionist movement, the League solemnly declared its loyalty to the sultan and was widely seen as both traditionalist and religious. Their proposal centred on creating a single Albanian vilayet administered by Albanian officials, the application of Albanian customary laws in the courts and the introduction of Albanian-language education.

The League struggled to square its own ambition to protect the populated territories, with its demands for more autonomy and self-rule and its interest in preserving the Ottoman Empire, so its requests were hedged. For a brief spell in

KOSOVO IN 1912

KEY
— · — · — Boundaries of 1912
●●●● Bulgarian aspirations
▨▨▨▨ Greek aspirations
✦✦✦✦ Rumanian aspirations
■ ■ ■ ■ Serbian aspirations

1880, the League was in *de facto* control of modern-day Kosovo. It administered Prizren, and Sylejman Voksh – chief commander of the League – occupied Prishtina. Not being completely secessionist in its original demands, the League was initially tolerated by the Ottoman administration. In the spring of 1881, however, the Ottoman authorities decided that the League posed a separatist threat and started to act. Abdyl Frasheri and 4,000 others were imprisoned and Sylejman Voksh was sentenced to death. Within a few months, the League of Prizren was crushed.

The situation in Kosovo remained highly unstable with the occasional local revolt, tax riot and uprising gripping different parts of the territory. Haxhi Zeka, a Muslim cleric and member of the League of Prizren, took a leading role in reviving the Albanian national movement, and in 1899 he summoned a gathering of 500 Albanian delegates at his home in Peja. The delegates swore to suspend all blood feuds and agreed on a 12-point programme calling for a unified Albanian vilayet with the power to enforce both the *seriat* (Islamic law) and Albanian customary law as well as Albanian-language education.

COLLAPSE OF THE OTTOMAN EMPIRE In 1908, a new force appeared on the Istanbul stage, which directly impacted Kosovo's destiny. The movement of the **Young Turks**, particularly strong among the Ottoman officer corps, hoped to save the empire from separatist nationalist movements by imposing radical modernisation and 'Ottoman nationalism'. For a brief period, Kosovo enjoyed the liberalising spirit of the Young Turks: 25 Albanian deputies were elected for the Ottoman Parliament and a dozen new papers were published. This honeymoon period, however, did not last long.

The news that the sultan had been deposed in spring 1909 turned a revolt against higher taxes into an all-out rebellion against the regime of the Young Turks. The Young Turks quelled the rebellion with a force of 5,000 troops. In the course of this crackdown, more than 60 *kulla* (traditional Albanian fortified towers) were destroyed in Peja and Gjakova, two years of taxes were forcibly collected, and arms confiscated. In 1910, another tax revolt in northern Kosovo ended in a crushing defeat of the rebels near Ferizaj by a 16,000-strong Ottoman army and the brutal hanging and internment of the rebel leaders. Isa Boletin, one of the masterminds behind this revolt, managed to escape (see page 277). As a sign of goodwill, Sultan Mehmet V came to Prishtina in 1911 to declare an amnesty for all those who had taken part in the 1910 revolt.

Two years later, another revolt erupted in western Kosovo. At a meeting in Junik (near Deçan), the leaders of the revolt swore a general truce from all blood feuds and took an oath to overturn the Young Turk regime. Hasan Prishtina, Isa Boletin, Bajram Curri and Nexhip Draga were among the representatives at the Junik meeting. A list of demands known as the 'Fourteen Points' of Hasan Prishtina was presented to Istanbul. As before, the demands were not part of a separatist agenda, but a reformist one. The rebellion spread and within weeks Prishtina, Mitrovica, Vushtrri and Prizren were in the hands of the rebels. The leaders mustered a force of 25,000 armed men in Prishtina and another 20,000 in Kosovo's southeast. On 18 August 1912, Istanbul finally conceded and accepted an Albanian statelet within the empire. Triumphantly, Hasan Prishtina ordered the troops to go home. The struggle for recognition of Albanian national aspiration had reached its zenith. At the same time the rebellion sent a strong signal to Kosovo's neighbours that the Ottoman Empire was weak. A mere six months later, the hiatus of relative stability suffered a new blow.

On 18 October 1912, Serbia, Bulgaria and Greece declared war on the Ottoman Empire. Within just four days, Serbia managed to take control of Prishtina. Prizren surrendered without a fight, and the Ottoman armies beat a hasty retreat south into present-day Macedonia. The Serb victory was celebrated like a long-overdue revenge for its defeat in 1389. Conscious that its territorial acquisition required approval by the Great Powers, Serbia quickly set out to change the ethnic composition of the area to better strengthen its 'ethnic claim' over the territory of Kosovo.

Years of instability and the attraction to migrate to liberated areas in Serbia had reduced the numbers of Kosovo-resident Serbs to less than a quarter of the Kosovo population by 1912. Serb paramilitaries and parts of the Serb and Montenegrin army embarked on a violent rampage, burning down villages and forcing conversions from Islam to Orthodoxy. Meanwhile in Vlora, Albania, the declaration of Albanian Independence encompassed Kosovo. The diplomatic poker began in December 1912 when the Great Powers met in London to discuss the situation unravelling throughout the Ottoman Empire. Belgrade sent a memorandum claiming that it had both a moral right to the region and that it was a more civilised people; asserting a historic right by referring to the Patriarchate; and an ethnic right by citing the 'recent invasion' of Albanians. Serbia's overriding strategic goal was to gain access to the Adriatic by securing the port of Durrës, a move Austria-Hungary adamantly opposed. The London conference ultimately produced a peace package in March 1913, ignoring the Albanian demands and allocating the area of western Kosovo – Peja, Deçan and Gjakova – to Montenegro, while the remaining territory was considered 'liberated' by Serbia.

On 28 July 1914, Austria-Hungary declared war against Serbia. Bulgaria joined the Axis Powers and occupied Kosovo's southeast. Serbian troops attempted a flight over impassable mountain roads into Montenegro. A large number of Serb soldiers died and about 150,000 Serbian soldiers were captured by the advancing Austrian army. Kosovo was divided into an Austrian zone of occupation, including Mitrovica and Peja, and a Bulgarian zone in the south, including Prishtina and Prizren. About 3,000 Albanian volunteers willingly joined the Austrian forces. The Austrians actively promoted Albanian-language education, established schools, teacher-training centres and set up a special commission to standardise Albanian spelling.

By the summer of 1918, the Allied armies were fast advancing from Thessaloniki. In September, Bulgaria signed an armistice and on 1 October 1918 the Austrian-Hungarian troops were ordered to withdraw north. By the end of the month, French forces had taken Prishtina and Mitrovica and Italians had entered Prizren. In the wake of the defeat of the Axis Powers, Serbian troops occupied Kosovo for a second time in four years and on 1 December 1918, the Kingdom of Serbs, Croats and Slovenes was proclaimed under the new Serbian king Aleksandar Karadjordjević. In 1919, the kingdom was officially renamed **Yugoslavia**.

At least on paper, the Treaty for the Protection of Minorities signed in 1919 provided for primary education in minority local languages. In contravention of the treaty, however, Yugoslavia did not recognise Albanians as a national minority and refused to grant the right to Albanian-language education.

THE INTER-WAR PERIOD The inter-war period in Kosovo was dominated by Serbian colonisation, the Kaçak Rebellion and the large-scale exodus of Turkish-speakers from Kosovo.

The Serb colonisation programme had a political and a strategic military motivation. Politically, it was in Serbia's interest to tip the demographic balance in favour of Serbs and Montenegrins. Strategically, it was important to secure the main north–south Balkan communication route passing through eastern Kosovo and to settle the Albanian border region with loyal Serbs. In an effort to entice them to move to Kosovo, Serb and Montenegrin settlers were promised 9ha per family, with an additional 2ha for every adult male, free transport to Kosovo, and tax breaks. According to a new Law on the Colonisation of the Southern Regions passed in 1931, settlers were offered up to 50ha of land. Using the pretext of non-recognition of Ottoman land titles, Albanian lands were easily expropriated. More than 330 new settlements and villages and 32 churches were built for the settlers with government funds or by Serbian charity organisations. The colonisation programme also changed the ethnic composition of major towns like Ferizaj, Peja and Prishtina, where hitherto only few Serbs had lived. The programme ultimately attracted about 70,000 settlers, or about 10% of Kosovo's then population, but many who came left again soon for more fertile lands and greater political stability in inner Serbia. In Istog, about a quarter of the new settlers had left by 1935.

The single biggest threat to the colonisation programme came from the **Kaçak Rebellion** (from the Turkish word *kaçak*, meaning 'fugitive'). The centre of Albanian resistance to Serbian rule was based in Shkodra, Albania. The Committee for the National Defence of Kosovo, also known as the Kosovo Committee, gathered there under the leadership of Hasan Prishtina. Its main activity was to lobby internationally for the Albanian national cause and to direct the Kaçak resistance movement inside Kosovo. Protest letters were sent from Shkodra to bring the Albanian question to the attention of States meeting at the Paris Peace Conference, but the Albanian government was not invited to Paris. The main targets of the Kaçak's rebels were Serb and Montenegrin settlers, especially those who had been settled on properties of Kaçak rebels along strategically important routes. The Kaçak Rebellion was strongest in the mountainous region of western Kosovo and around Drenica. The biggest military heroes of the Kaçak revolt were Azem Bejta and his wife Shota from Galica village. The Kaçak revolt was eventually crushed by the Yugoslav government with the help of Ahmet Zogolli – the later Albanian king Zog. Azem Bejta was killed in July 1924 but his wife Shota continued fighting until she was fatally wounded in 1927 (see page 172).

Along with the Serb colonisation policy, the Yugoslav government also pursued a policy of forced emigration of Turkish-speaking Albanians. In 1938, Turkey and Yugoslavia signed an agreement to 'repatriate Turks'. Under this agreement, the newly founded Republic of Turkey agreed to take 40,000 families and pay Yugoslavia 500 Turkish pounds per family. The land of emigrants was quickly transformed into state ownership. Figures vary but between 90,000 and 150,000 people are believed to have left Kosovo in the inter-war period.

WORLD WAR II On 7 April 1940, Italy under Mussolini invaded Albania with 30,000 troops and created a personal union with the Italian monarchy. Meanwhile, it took the German army only one week to conquer the whole territory of Kosovo. On 17 April 1941, Yugoslavia signed an unconditional surrender. Kosovo was divided into Italian, German and Bulgarian occupation zones. The Germans reserved themselves the right to control the mines of Mitrovica and the railway line passing through Kosovo. Mitrovica became the head of an Austrian infantry division. The lion's share of Kosovo's territory was joined with Albania and governed by the 'Ministry for Liberated Areas' under Italian control. For the first (and last) time, Albania and Kosovo were united in a single unit and Albanian became the language of education and local administration.

More than 200 new primary schools were established across the territory and an Albanian gendarmerie force policed the area. Italian and German efforts to recruit Albanians into regular armed units met with limited support. The economic situation worsened dramatically in the Italian zone. Food shortages became a daily problem. With the Albanians having regained the upper hand, the former colonists became targets of revenge actions by Albanian mobs. It is estimated that by April 1944, 40,000 Serbs and Montenegrins had been expelled from Kosovo.

The **Albanian resistance movement** was founded in 1942 by the name of Balli Kombëtar (National Front). It was originally opposed to Italian occupation in Albania but bitter rivalries between the Serb-dominated communist or 'partisan' resistance movement and the National Front pushed the National Front into the collaborationist camp. On 8 September 1943, Italy capitulated and all of Kosovo was included in the German zone of occupation. The German policy was simple: it promised Albanian independence in return for support. A total of 6,491 Albanian fighters were recruited into the famed 'Skenderbeg Division'. This division was of no military value but it became infamous for its role in the deportation of 281 Kosovo Jews in the summer of 1944 shortly before Germany started its withdrawal from Kosovo.

Kosovo's partisan liberation only really started once the German troops had left and partisan units moved into the towns as the German army vacated them. Overall, the Communist Party's influence was extremely weak in Kosovo, with only a few activists in the Trepça mines. It was widely seen as a Serbian organisation and drew little other local support. By 1940, the Communist Party had 239 declared members, of which just 25 were Albanian and the remainder Serbian. From the start, the communist movement in Kosovo struggled over how to reconcile demands for Albanian self-determination with the notion of 'Yugoslavia'. The Bujan Declaration proclaimed at a meeting of the National Liberation Committee in January 1944 promised the right of self-determination and secession for Albanians. But soon after, partisans banned the use of the Albanian flag and partisan talk of Albanian self-determination ceased. In July 1945, the Kosovo Communist Party voted to annex Kosovo to Serbia. Of the 142 delegates, 33 were Albanian, representing no more than 2,250 Communist Party members in Kosovo. On 3 September, Serbia's assembly declared the 'Autonomous Region of Kosovo-Metohija' (Metohija meaning 'land of the church or monastic estate') to be a constituent part of Serbia. In an effort to cover up the bitter rivalries between the Albanian National Front and partisans during the years of occupation, the communists actively promoted a historical fiction of a multi-ethnic partisan movement.

COMMUNISM Under communist rule, Kosovo faced serious oppression for 31 out of 54 years. The most difficult period was under **Aleksandar Ranković**, Yugoslav Minister of Interior and chief of the Serbian-dominated secret police (UDB). Under his authority, police repression, regular weapons searches, executions and confiscations were state policy. Ranković fuelled suspicion against Kosovo Albanians within the Yugoslav Communist Party by portraying Albanians as potential 'fifth columnists'. In those years, the UDB stored files on some 120,000 Albanians, or about half the male population.

In the early years, there was much talk of a communist Balkan federation uniting Albania, Yugoslavia and Bulgaria. Many Kosovo Albanian communists hoped for unification with Albania under communism, but Tito's break with Stalin in 1948 dramatically changed the course of events. With Yugoslavia expelled from Cominform (the Communist Information Bureau), the border between Albania and Yugoslavia became one of the worst in the Cold War period and an iron curtain divided many families.

Meanwhile Turks (or Turkish-speakers) were recognised by Yugoslavia as a national minority and the authorities permitted Turkish schools. As a result, the number of registered Turks jumped from 1,313 in 1948 to 34,343 in the 1953 census. In 1953, Yugoslavia signed a second agreement with Turkey, resulting in another exodus of around 100,000 mainly Turkish-speaking Kosovo Albanians to Turkey.

The situation in Kosovo started to improve dramatically with the fall of Ranković in July 1966. In spring 1967, Tito visited Kosovo for the first time in 16 years, and November 1968 saw the first of many student protests demanding a Kosovo Republic. Amendments to the 1963 constitution granted more rights for the autonomous provinces in Yugoslavia including the right to have a Kosovo police, a supreme court and the right to fly the Albanian flag. The addendum 'Metohija', not in favour with the Albanians because of its reference to Church estates, was also dropped from the province's title in that year. Albanian and Turkish became official languages and for the first time there was Albanian-language secondary schooling. In 1969, the decision was taken to establish the **University of Prishtina**, attracting around 30,000 students over the next few years. Kosovo was also declared a priority for the Yugoslav Development Fund. Between 1970 and 1980, Kosovo received around 34% of all Yugoslav development funds, making up around 70% of total investments.

GOLDEN YEARS The new Yugoslav constitution of 1974 marked the zenith of Kosovo's autonomy within Yugoslavia. It defined Kosovo as a 'constituent' element of the Yugoslav federation with rights and responsibilities equal to the other republics. Kosovo had its own representatives and a veto on the rotating Yugoslav presidency, its own constitution, a quasi-national bank and its own court system. Kosovo enjoyed all the rights of a republic except, most crucially, the right to secede. The legal argument was that republican status can only be granted to a nation, and Albanians were only a nationality. By population size, however, Albanians outnumbered both Montenegrins and Macedonians, who each had their own republic.

The 1970s were a period of cultural and national renaissance for Kosovo Albanians. The newly founded University of Prishtina, Prishtina Radio and TV and the Rilindja Publishing House were the driving forces of this cultural revolution. The university created a new Albanian elite of state officials, industrial managers, university lecturers, policemen and television personalities. The period from 1968 to 1981 saw a rapid Albanisation of Kosovo's public administration and industries. For the first time in 1981, the majority of members of the Kosovo League of Communists were Albanians. The change was also felt strongly in the police and security forces, which by 1981 were about three-quarters Albanian. As a result of compulsory education in both Albanian and Serbian, a large number of people became perfectly bilingual, especially in socialist towns like Prishtina and Mitrovica. Close and friendly relations developed between Albanians and Serbs sharing the same factory floors, working in the same public administration and living side-by-side in socialist apartment blocks. Intermarriage was rare, but it was quite common to have a boyfriend or girlfriend from the other community.

Economically, however, Kosovo continued to fall further behind Yugoslavia. In 1954, the per-capita income in Kosovo was 48% of the Yugoslav average. By 1980, it had fallen to 28%. The unemployment rate in Kosovo was more than double the Yugoslav average. Kosovo's labour market was flooded with educated youngsters with no prospect of finding a job. In the mid 1980s, official unemployment in Kosovo stood at 36.3% compared with the Yugoslav average of 14.2%.

A BITTER FORETASTE On 11 March 1981, a student in the Prishtina University canteen found a cockroach in his soup. The initial protest was ultimately dispersed with tear gas and arrests, but unrest spread quickly to other towns. On 2 April, Prishtina was sealed off by the Yugoslav army and a general curfew was imposed. The official death toll was 11; reports by Amnesty International speak of 300 casualties. Between March and June 1981, 1,700 people were arrested, with many sentenced to 15 years' imprisonment. Student numbers were cut back to reduce the pool of politicised youngsters. Politically the 1981 protest had sent shockwaves across Yugoslavia.

In its wake, the Albanian communist leadership was purged and Mahmut Bakalli, President of the Communist Party, was expelled. Advocates of a Kosovo republic were labelled Enver Hoxharists (referring to the communist dictator in Albania) or separatists. Suspicion between the communities increased. Almost 600,000 Kosovars were arrested or interrogated between 1981 and 1988.

At this time of heightened economic and social crisis, parts of the Serbian communist leadership resorted to reviving the historical myth portraying Serbs as the martyred people. In pamphlets and speeches Albanians were portrayed as rapists even though inter-ethnic rapes were extremely scarce. Much was made of the higher birth rate of Albanians with pejorative remarks such as that they were 'breeding like rabbits' and the old national myth that Albanians had come 'over the mountains' gained currency again. Extracts of a memorandum drawn up by the Serbian Academy of Sciences in 1985 were circulated, claiming that Serbs in Kosovo were suffering physical, political and cultural genocide. The federal communist leadership, holding up the old Yugoslav motto of *Bratstvo i Jedinstvo* (Brotherhood and Unity), wanted to publicly denounce these nationalist claims but they were dissuaded by Slobodan Milošević.

Milošević had realised that while Yugoslavia's economy crumbled, a new form of populist nationalism could replace the socialist ideology. He skilfully mastered the art of reviving Serb nationalist myths set in Kosovo and stoking nationalist fears at a time of great economic uncertainty.

THE RISE OF MILOŠEVIĆ On 24 April 1987, Slobodan Milošević, a Communist Party apparatchik, was invited to address a crowd in Kosovo Polje (Fushë-Kosova) on the battlefield of the 1389 Battle of Kosovo. When police responded with batons to Serb protestors hurling stones, Milošević appeared on stage and in front of the TV cameras made his famous statement 'nobody should dare to beat you', alluding to the historical Turkish defeat. Presenting himself as champion of the Serbs and protector of Kosovo, Milošević emerged overnight on the Serbian political stage. In the coming years, he successfully exploited the Kosovo issue for his own personal and political gain.

The myth of the Kosovo battle was a perfect rallying cry at a time of economic crisis and political transition. Starting in 1987, Milošević loyalists organised popular rallies and demonstrators were bussed across Serbia to attend 'spontaneous meetings of truth'. These public protests helped Milošević win the power struggle within the party establishment. In autumn 1988, he forced Azem Vllasi and Kaqusha Jashari to resign from the Kosovo party leadership. In their place, he appointed Rrahman Morina, deeply unpopular for his role in crushing the 1981 demonstrations. In protest against these changes, the miners of Trepça marched from Mitrovica to Prishtina on 17 November 1988. With pictures of Tito in their hands, they called for the defence of the 1974 constitution. Ignoring the Kosovo Albanian miners' demands, on 20 February 1989 Milošević presented a list of constitutional amendments to the Serbian Assembly. By the stroke of a pen Kosovo lost its constitutional right to run its own courts, police and defence and its rights to determine its own official languages and economic or educational policy. Again, the miners of Trepça took the lead in the protests. This time they locked themselves in the mines and started a hunger strike. Schools and factories across Kosovo shut down in a general strike. After eight days, Serbia declared a state of emergency, sent in troops and hundreds of protestors were arrested. On 23 March 1989, Kosovo's provincial assembly 'passed' the constitutional amendments, abolishing Kosovo's autonomy. Tanks surrounded the assembly building and security forces supervised the voting. The new constitution became known as 'the Constitution of the Tanks'. In June 1989, Milošević seized the opportunity of the 600-year anniversary of the Kosovo battle to stage another highly politicised celebration and to present himself as the protector of the Serbian people. On 26 June 1990 and thereafter, another set of 'temporary measures' prepared the ground for mass dismissals of more than 80,000 Albanians from public sector jobs. A system of loyalty oaths was rolled out whereby workers would only be retained if they signed such an oath – in Cyrillic – to the Serbian State. Albanian doctors were sacked from the Medical Faculty and clinics were closed down. The main Albanian newspaper *Rilindja* was banned and Radio and TV Prishtina shut down. A further 'colonisation' programme used funds collected from Social Enterprises and the newly established 'Serbian Development Fund' to encourage the settlement of Serbs and Montenegrins in Kosovo, some coming from the wars in Croatia and Bosnia. Milošević also introduced a special Kosovo supplement on public sector salaries, sometimes 100% of the normal salary, to keep Serbs in Kosovo. In the 1990s, a Serb doctor in Prishtina earned twice as much as a doctor in Kraljevo in inner Serbia. As Milošević rose to power on the back of the 'Kosovo problem', he ushered in the end of Yugoslavia.

A POLITICAL ALTERNATIVE In the meantime, the Association of Writers, with its president Ibrahim Rugova, had become the nucleus of a new political force, bringing together disaffected politicians and intellectuals, most of them former members of the communist establishment. In December 1989, alluding to the League of Prizren of 1878 (when Albanian national demands were formulated for the first time) the **Democratic League of Kosovo (Lidhja Demokratike e**

In spring 1999, there were approximately 20,000 troops of the Yugoslav army (VJ) and 30,000 police, volunteers and paramilitaries stationed in Kosovo. The 52nd Corps based in Prishtina was subordinate to the Third Army with its headquarters in Niš. Regular units were topped up with reservists mobilised from within Kosovo and neighbouring areas. Until spring 1998, VJ units had not been involved in any operations in Kosovo. Overall control rested with the forces of the Ministry of Interior (MUP). The 5,000-strong 'People's Militia' under MUP command was easily recognisable by their blue camouflage uniforms and light machine guns. They were used in operations against the Kosovo Liberation Army (UÇK) and to man checkpoints. The State Security Service sent a force of about 3,000 to Kosovo to collect information on UÇK structures. Volunteers were often given tasks such as the laying of mines. They were paid by and subordinate to VJ command. Paramilitaries often worked under the command of the intelligence services led by 'Frenki' Simatovic. He was known to recruit and organise different paramilitary units. A group called 'Frenki's' was recognisable by their green and cream-coloured uniforms and jeeps. Another unit called the 'Republika Srpska Delta Force' came from the Ministry of Interior in Republika Srpska and operated mostly in the area around Gjilan. 'Arkan's Tigers' were one of the most infamous paramilitary units under the command of Zeljko Raznjatovic (nicknamed 'Arkan'). Arkan's units are believed to have worked in conjunction with the intelligence services. They were given certain areas of operation or lists of houses to loot, and operated mainly in the area around Mitrovica, Peja, Gjakova and Prizren.

The UÇK was originally formed around smaller village units often associated with one family responsible for the defence of its village. Recruitment was done either through political groupings often with strong left-wing leanings, especially among the diaspora, or at village level. The looting of Albania's state weapons depots in 1997 after the collapse of the pyramid schemes in Albania gave a major boost to the UÇK. Most of the AK-47s came from Albania, but the UÇK was always short of weapons and ammunitions. In the early days, the UÇK concentrated on police ambushes. The first larger operation took place in summer 1998 in Rahovec, but the UÇK was unable to hold the town and there were large civilian and military losses. The UÇK tried a combination of guerrilla hit-and-run tactics with trench warfare. The latter failed disastrously under VJ bombardment. A central UÇK command structure was only imposed at the end of 1998 and the UÇK divided into seven zones: Drenica (central), Pashtrik, Dukagjin (west), Shale, Llap (northeast), Nerodime and Karadak (southeast). Agim Çeku, a Yugoslav army-trained general who had served in Croatia during the war of independence, took over the general command of UÇK in April 1999.

During the NATO aerial bombing campaign Serbian security forces initially concentrated on securing the lines of communication and disrupting the UÇK's weapons supply. Villages along strategic roads like the road to Serbia through Podujevo or the pass through Suha Rekë were shelled. The Serb forces also focused on areas with a high UÇK presence such as Rahovec, Deçan, Peja, Malisheva and Drenica – these were probably the worst-affected areas. There was less fighting in the eastern half of Kosovo and Yugoslav forces there concentrated on securing the border. A common tactic was to shell villages before surrounding them from three sides. Attacks usually involved a mix of police, paramilitaries, VJ and armed civilians. Villagers were often given only a few minutes to leave their homes. Fleeing villagers were then robbed of their belongings and in many instances men were separated from women and children.

Background Information   HISTORY

Kosovës – LDK) was founded. LDK quickly developed into a cross between a political party and a mass movement and enjoyed unrivalled public support.

On 7 September 1990, 111 delegates met secretly in Kaçanik and proclaimed a 'Republic of Kosovo'. This marked the beginning of a long and arduous struggle for international recognition.

The Kaçanik Declaration was confirmed in a public referendum organised soon after its signature. The Kosovo Albanian population stood firmly behind the LDK leadership. With a turnout estimated at being 87% of the Kosovo Albanian population, 99% voted in favour of an independent Republic of Kosovo. However, neighbouring Albania was the only country prepared to recognise Kosovo as independent. The Kosovo Albanian leadership formed a provisional government and in May 1992, the first parallel elections were organised in private homes. Serb police forces stood by. Without any opposition, LDK won most of the 130 seats of the 'constituent Republican Assembly' and Ibrahim Rugova was declared President of the Republic of Kosovo. His strategy was to internationalise the Kosovo issue, while avoiding any provocation to violence. The LDK leadership had been watching closely as the wars in Croatia and Bosnia Herzegovina unfolded. Ibrahim Rugova hoped to avoid similar atrocities committed by Serbian paramilitaries, while still building up international support for independence.

PARALLEL LIVES For seven years, the Albanian struggle for independence took on the form of passive and non-violent resistance. In the face of discrimination and exclusion, Kosovars set out to organise their own parallel society. The most symbolic struggle was that over education. In 1990, Serbia imposed a new nationalist Serbian curriculum. Teachers who refused to teach the new curriculum faced beatings and arrests. In 1991, the state stopped paying the salaries of those teachers. The real showdown came at the start of the 1991–92 school year. Serbian police blocked the entrance of schools and students and teachers were not allowed to enter the buildings. Peaceful protests by parents, teachers and students were broken up violently by the police. The Albanian community organised itself at an impressive speed. In early 1992, teaching resumed secretly in private homes, barns or garages converted into classrooms. In February, the authorities had to concede Albanians the right to primary school education as it was guaranteed by the constitution. Most primary schools reopened for the second term, but segregation continued. Walls were erected between classrooms and a shift system kept Serb and Albanian children strictly apart. Secondary schools and the University of Prishtina remained closed for Albanian students. Despite the heroic efforts by teachers and parents, education standards were slipping. There was a shortage of textbooks, and teaching became highly politicised. In rural areas, children often had to walk for kilometres to get to school. Police harassment also continued unabated. There were high drop-out rates in secondary school, especially among girls.

Education was central to the resistance movement. It consumed the lion's share of the voluntary taxes raised by the parallel government. Two-thirds of tax revenues were collected inside Kosovo with the remaining one-third raised abroad among the Albanian diaspora. The most important contributions came from smaller businesses in Kosovo. With these funds, the parallel government paid the salaries for 18,000 teachers and kept 330,000 pupils at school. It also financed the studies of about 14,000 university students in makeshift faculties of the parallel Prishtina University.

Besides education, parallel structures extended into all spheres of life. Albanian medical staff were also dismissed from state institutions and clinics were closed down. The already grave health situation in Kosovo got worse. As vaccination rates dropped, diseases like polio reappeared. A first parallel clinic was opened in Prishtina in 1992. It was operated by the Mother Theresa Organisation, a Kosovo-based humanitarian organisation involved in the distribution of humanitarian aid. Over the years, a network of 91 clinics across Kosovo offered free medical treatment and medicines.

The shutdown of the Albanian-language state media in 1990 led to a plethora of private initiatives. In the early years, the two most important media outlets were *Bujku*, originally a specialist agriculture paper, and *Zeri*, a political weekly. In 1993, leading Albanian journalists started a hunger strike in protest against new measures to crack down on Albanian-language media. Almost every journalist in Kosovo served a prison sentence. In 1994, *Koha* started out as an independent weekly. Other sources of information were the Kosovo news bulletins broadcast on Radio Zagreb, the BBC Albanian Service and the Voice of America. TV programmes in neighbouring Albania also included Kosovo news on its satellite programme.

THE COST OF RESISTANCE In the face of economic hardship, families had to rely on subsistence agriculture, small businesses and migration. Small shops and cafés opened up at every corner, but without production Kosovo remained heavily dependent on imports from Serbia. Smuggling was part of economic life, especially in times of sanctions. With hyperinflation raging in the early 1990s, monthly salaries became worthless in less than a day. A complex barter system developed and Albanians started using the Deutschmark. What kept families afloat was the money sent home from family members working abroad. In March, the Kosovo government-in-exile estimated the number of Albanians living abroad at 217,000, with Germany and Switzerland the most popular destinations. By 1998, the number of Albanians abroad had more than doubled. Dozens of buses were leaving Kosovo every day. For many young men migration was the only way to avoid conscription into the Yugoslav army which was fighting unpopular wars in Croatia and Bosnia, and for most families migration of one or more family members was the only way to survive. Around DM200 million (about €100 million) was sent home every year by Albanian migrant workers. These funds helped to alleviate poverty and finance the parallel system, but they could not fully stem economic decline. Without maintenance and investment, Kosovo's infrastructure was slowly falling apart. The majority of rural households had no access to a telephone or sewage system. To survive, families depended on subsistence agriculture, but not everybody was lucky enough to own a cow or a few hectares of land.

Thousands of Kosovo Albanians lost out on years of salaries, social and pension contributions. The federal budget also 'saved' on state allowances for nearly 250,000 Albanian children. Perhaps the harshest move was the confiscation of private bank accounts. In a spectacular example of state theft more than 66,000 individuals lost all their hard currency savings. Forced mergers with Serbian companies, shady privatisation deals, looting and outright asset stripping of Kosovo's industries was another source of income for the Milošević regime. By 1998, the Kosovo economy was on its knees. Local LDK branches set up solidarity funds and organised food distributions and assistance for needy families. More than 350,000 individuals depended on humanitarian aid distributed amongst others by the Mother Theresa Organisation.

THE SLIPPERY SLOPE TO WAR Rugova's policy of peaceful resistance had pinned its hopes on a final settlement in Bosnia and Herzegovina. The November 1995 **Dayton Peace Accords** did little to help Kosovo because while they ended the war in Bosnia and Herzegovina they ignored the Kosovo issue and Milošević gained credence internationally, being perceived as open to brokering peace deals. Amongst the Kosovo Albanians there was growing disappointment with Rugova's strategy of non-violent resistance. The monopoly position enjoyed by LDK had also bred discontent. There had been no break with communist patterns of authoritarian and top-down decision making. All power was concentrated in a small clique and no culture of democratic debate had developed within the party. With LDK in control of most media outlets, access to objective information was limited. Students were the first to express their discontent and major student protests organised in Prishtina on 1 October 1997 were crushed brutally by the police. On placards posted across Prishtina, students were asking 'Europe, where are you?'. There were no signs that Kosovo was any closer to international recognition and the situation on the ground had not changed for the better.

On 28 November 1997, a new force entered the political stage. At the funeral of an Albanian schoolteacher killed during a police raid in Drenica, the **Kosovo Liberation Army** (Ushtria Çlirimtare e Kosovës or UÇK) made its first public appearance. Many assaults on Serb police followed. All signs pointed to an escalation of violence. On 28 February 1998, Serbian authorities launched an attack on two villages using military helicopters and armoured personnel carriers, leaving 16 people dead. Days later, a military assault on the compound of the Adem Jashari family in Prekaz village in Skenderaj municipality left 56 people dead. Half the victims were women, children and the elderly. Mass protests in Prishtina were calling for an end to violence. UÇK forces meanwhile increased their attacks on Serb forces and police, leaving Kosovo Albanian civilians exposed to retaliation. About 300,000 villagers took flight to the forests to escape retaliatory attacks by Serb forces. On 24 September 1998, NATO issued a first ultimatum to Serbia threatening air strikes. On 16 October, US diplomat Richard Holbrooke agreed with Milošević to deploy an unarmed OSCE mission (known as the Kosovo Verification Mission or KVM) to verify the ceasefire. By the end of 1998, the death toll had reached 1,934. News of another massacre hit the international headlines on 15 January 1999. William Walker, head of the OSCE mission, confirmed the killing of 45 civilians in Raçak village. On 6 February 1999, a peace conference was called in Rambouillet near Paris. Kosovo Albanian delegates agreed to the disarmament of the UÇK, the deployment of a NATO protection force for a three-year period and the establishment of joint Serbian–Albanian civilian institutions. The **Rambouillet Agreement** also promised a referendum on a final settlement for Kosovo at the end of the three years. The Serbian Parliament rejected the agreement and on 24 March 1999 NATO forces began their **bombing campaign**.

Aggressive action by Serbian police, army and paramilitary resulted in the mass flight of more than 800,000 Kosovar Albanians to Montenegro, Albania, Macedonia and the West. In turn, in the early months after the ceasefire, the Kosovo Serb community and other minorities became targets for revenge actions, with many killed or driven from their homes. An estimated 70,000 Serbs were displaced and around 80 churches were looted or burnt, including 15 churches dating back to the Middle Ages (see box *Serb displacement*, page 24).

The 1998–99 conflict was devastating for Kosovo. The total death toll was about 12,000 and another 5,977 were reported missing. As of April 2010, 1,862 of these missing were still unaccounted for. A study by IMG (International Management Group) after the conflict identified more than 120,000 houses and 2,000 religious, cultural and public buildings either damaged or destroyed. As many as 225 of Kosovo's 607 mosques and more than 30 churches were damaged or destroyed during the conflict.

THE ERA OF UNMIK (THE UNITED NATIONS MISSION IN KOSOVO) On 10 June 1999, NATO suspended its aerial bombardment and the UN Security Council adopted Resolution 1244 that placed Kosovo under transitional **UN administration**. The resolution foresaw that all Serbian military, police and paramilitaries had to withdraw and the Kosovo Liberation Army was to be demilitarised. A 50,000-strong joint NATO and Russian peacekeeping force was to oversee its implementation and provide security for the safe return of all refugees and displaced people. The resolution, however, did not say what Kosovo's future status should be. It reaffirmed the sovereignty and territorial integrity of the Federal Republic of Yugoslavia, while at the same time calling for a political process to determine Kosovo's status. The key difference between the Rambouillet Accord and Resolution 1244 was that the latter did not set a time limit on the international civilian administration and did not specifically mention a referendum on the final status.

On 13 June 1999, the first international administrator, Sérgio De Mello, arrived in Prishtina (until the declaration of independence, Kosovo had been governed by seven UN Special Representatives of the UN Secretary-General (SRSGs) from five different countries). The international community faced an enormous reconstruction and humanitarian relief challenge. More than 800,000 people had been displaced internally or had fled to other countries. The 1999 harvest was destroyed and almost all livestock killed. All major utility providers, from electricity to water, were in shambles after years of neglect, theft and conflict-related damages. The winter was approaching fast and people were still camping in tents without roofs or stoves to keep warm.

The international community, led by the UN, rolled out an impressive emergency and relief programme. It was estimated by the International Monetary Fund that Kosovo received more than €5 billion in total assistance up until 2005. The single biggest donor was the EU working through the European Agency for Reconstruction (EAR), contributing more than one-third of all aid in Kosovo. A large part of the total international assistance – 42% – was spent on international salaries. The UN's operation in Kosovo has been the largest international peacekeeping mission ever undertaken, in terms of staff and budgets involved. At its peak in 2001, the UN alone employed around 6,500 international staff and 5,300 Kosovars.

The UN civilian administration was structured in four pillars. Pillar I, responsible for refugee return, was managed by the UN High Commissioner for Refugees (it was later transformed into the Justice Pillar responsible for the judiciary and police). Pillar II was led by the UN and in charge of setting up a civilian administration. The OSCE assumed responsibilities for democratisation and institution-building (Pillar III), and organised elections. The EU via Pillar IV was given the difficult task of overseeing the reconstruction effort and kick-starting Kosovo's economy. The UN administration took time to build up and there was a power vacuum between the withdrawal of the Serbian administration in June 1999 and the establishment of the UN mission. In Peja region, for example, there were only seven international police officers in August 1999. Since KFOR did not assume policing or civilian responsibilities, the vacuum was filled by local strongmen of the Kosovo Liberation Army. The UÇK fighters established so-called **'interim administrations'** across towns in Kosovo and self-appointed mayors started collecting arbitrary taxes and assumed executive authority. Former UÇK fighters and other opportunist criminals occupied private properties and seized key public premises. In those chaotic first months, the Kosovo Serb community was exposed to **revenge actions** and arbitrary killings at the hands of UÇK fighters. Most of the destruction of Orthodox monuments in Kosovo actually happened during the summer of 1999 (and then later in March 2004) rather than during the aerial bombardments. There was also a lot of score-settling among the Albanian community, and several high-profile LDK activists were targeted by renegade UÇK criminals.

UNMIK faced the task of establishing an entirely new administration from scratch. There was no police, no customs service and no judiciary in place. The very first institution to be up and running was the UNMIK customs service. In September 1999, newly trained customs officers started collecting the first duties at Kosovo's borders. By summer's end the UÇK was officially disbanded and many demilitarised veterans joined the newly formed Kosovo Protection Corps (Trupat Mbrojtëse të Kosovës – TMK), a civilian emergency service but widely seen as the nucleus of a future army. The first KPC commander was General Agim Çeku, who was later to become Prime Minister of Kosovo (in spring 2006). Post independence, the Kosovo Protection Corps became the **Kosovo Security Force (KSF)** as foreseen in the Ahtisaari Agreement. The OSCE established a police school in Vushtrri and trained a force of nearly 7,000 officers for the **Kosovo Police Service (KPS)**. In early 2008, Kosovo Serbs and other minorities made up about 15% of KPS officers.

Over the years, the UN, with heavy donor assistance, has laid the foundation for a new public administration and governance system. As foreseen by Resolution 1244, governance responsibility was gradually transferred from the UN to Kosovo-run authorities. In October 2000, Kosovo held its first post-war elections, returning a landslide victory for Rugova's LDK. On 15 May 2001, the Constitutional Framework for the Provisional Self-Government of Kosovo came into force. It was not called a 'constitution', but it had the same purpose as it provided the legal basis for the establishment of functioning – albeit provisional – self-government in Kosovo.

RETURNS AND PARALLEL STRUCTURES There has been much focus by the international community since 2000 on assisting the return of Serb, Roma and

SERB DISPLACEMENT

The claim that more than 200,000 Serbs have fled Kosovo since 1999 has been one of the most persistent myths created in post-war Kosovo. Repeated by Serbian government officials and international organisations it has become something of an orthodoxy, but a closer look at official data – including Serbian government sources – confirms that it is not true. According to the official Yugoslav census in 1991, there were 194,000 resident Serbs in Kosovo. The 1990s saw a steady net outflow of Serbs from Kosovo due to the deteriorating economic and security situation, despite all government efforts to offer financial incentives or to resettle Serb refugees in Kosovo. In 2003, the Kosovo Co-ordination Centre, the main government body responsible for Kosovo, published a report about Serbs in Kosovo. According to this report, 129,474 Serbs were still living in Kosovo. Contrary therefore to popular perception, two-thirds of the pre-war Kosovo Serb population actually remained in Kosovo. This is also confirmed by the number of Serb primary school enrolment figures in 2004. The number of Serb displacements is thus probably closer to 70,000. An analysis of Serb primary school enrolment figures also disproves another important myth. Only one-third of Kosovo Serbs live in the north of Kosovo (in the municipalities of Mitrovica, Zvečan, Leposavic and Zubin Potok). Two-thirds of Kosovo Serbs live south of the river Ibar, mostly in rural areas and mixed communities around Gračanica, Lipjan, Viti, Gjilan, Kamenica and Štrpce.

For more information on the Serb community in Kosovo, you can read the ESI report *The Lausanne Principle: Multi-ethnicity, Territory and the Future of Kosovo's Serbs* on www.esiweb.org.

other minorities to their places of origin. Many Serbs face major barriers returning to their homes, especially in war-afflicted areas, and prefer settling in other Serb-majority areas. A Protocol of Co-operation on Returns was signed in 2006 by Prishtina and Belgrade, recognising the returnee's right to freely choose where to live and to receive greater assistance in that regard. As of December 2009, 19,827 minorities had returned voluntarily to Kosovo, a low number given the funds and efforts spent on this programme. Another 19,670 are still internally displaced within Kosovo, including 10,342 Serbs who are displaced mainly in the Mitrovica region. A number of organised return projects are underway in villages in Ferizaj, Istog, Klina, Prizren, Lipjan and Shtime regions and displaced Roma families are returning to the Roma quarter in south Mitrovica.

By far the biggest obstacle to return, besides emotional barriers, is the lack of economic opportunities, with high unemployment in all communities. For Serbs who had worked in the public administration in Kosovo, there is now little reason to return whereas for those who have always been farmers the changes are less dramatic.

Crime rates in Kosovo have fallen steadily from 291 murders in 2000 to 60 in 2008, which is below the EU average and well below that of Stockholm, a town generally perceived to be 'safe' and secure. Contrary to perception, there are in fact very few incidences of inter-ethnic crime. In 2006, of 56 murders, five were Serbs and one Gorani, all other victims being Albanians.

It should be noted that the Serb community still operates a system of parallel structures including education, post, telecoms, court and even police structures which report directly to and are paid by Belgrade. The Serbian government has consistently called on the Kosovo Serb community to refuse to recognise Kosovo institutions – even recommending Serbs not to pay their electricity bill as this might amount to recognition of the Kosovo Electricity Company (which the Serbs regard as being part of the Serbian entity). The Serb government also called on Serbs not to adopt the KS number plates (which were deliberately designed by the international community to be ethnically neutral by not indicating the city of origin). Fearful of upsetting the Serbian minority, UNMIK did little to address this situation of parallel structures, and these structures have contributed to the lack of integration of the two communities and once established are proving difficult to disband.

STANDARDS BEFORE STATUS A key milestone in Kosovo's political history was the Standards before Status policy launched in 2003. A set of eight standards was designed – covering key areas of development from human rights to economic policy – to benchmark Kosovo's progress and to buy time for the UN before finding a solution to Kosovo's status. Meanwhile, the economic situation was taking its toll, privatisation was stalled in a legal and political quagmire, and frustration with the UN grew as it was increasingly seen as a holding operation and not willing to bring a final and lasting solution for Kosovo's status. At a time when tensions were already running high, Kosovo Serbs put up a roadblock on the main Prishtina–Skopje highway to protest against the shooting of a young Serb. For days traffic on this main transport route was blocked.

Frustrations came to a head on 17 March 2004. Sparked by a false rumour that Albanian children had been chased into the Ibar River by Serbs, Albanian mobs across Kosovo attacked Serb monuments and homes. In what seemed like a co-ordinated action, riots broke out in Mitrovica, churches were set on fire in Prizren and Prishtina, and a mob marched towards Çaglavica (south of Prishtina) to break the roadblock. KFOR and Kosovo police were entirely unprepared for this kind of violence. In the absence of rubber bullets and tear gas and with confusion about what their peacekeeping mandate meant in practice, with only some notable exceptions, KFOR effectively stood by watching while Serb churches were torched. Two days of violence left 19 people dead (11 Kosovo Albanians and eight Kosovo Serbs), several hundred police officers and others were injured, approximately 3,600 Kosovo Serbs and other minorities were displaced and dozens of Serb churches destroyed along with homes, schools and businesses. All progress made since 1999 to bring the two communities closer was wiped out.

ROADMAP TO FINAL STATUS The March 2004 riots served as a wake-up call to the international community that Kosovo's final status could not be put on hold forever. The political and economic costs of a limbo state were just too high. In the wake of the riots, the UN developed a new roadmap leading to a negotiated settlement. The Standards before Status policy was beefed up and a regular review mechanism put in place. In July 2004, the UN released the *Eide Report* (named after its author Kai Eide, a Norwegian diplomat) promising a comprehensive review of Kosovo's governing system and the start of negotiations on a future status by mid 2005. In November 2005, the Contact Group (consisting of the US, UK, Germany, France, Italy, Russia and the EU Foreign Minister) issued a set of ten 'Guiding Principles for a Settlement of Kosovo's Status'. It called for a negotiated solution and specifically ruled out a return to the pre-March 1989 situation, a partition of Kosovo's territory and any unification with other countries. In plain English, the Contact Group made it clear that Kosovo will not be governed by Serbia again, cannot unite with Albania and that any unilateral action, including a proclamation of independence by Serb-majority municipalities in the north of Kosovo, would not be accepted.

Martti Ahtisaari, a former Finnish president and an experienced negotiator, was appointed by the UN Secretary-General to lead the negotiations between Prishtina and Belgrade. Over a period of 14 months, Ahtisaari's office organised 17 rounds of direct talks and 26 expert missions to Prishtina and Belgrade. In March 2007, Ahtisaari presented a package solution for Kosovo's final status to the UN Security Council. Without mentioning the word 'independence' directly, it grants Kosovo all the attributes of an independent state – from a national flag to passports and an army – while providing for substantive minority rights through decentralisation and some effectively irrevocable legislation and special provisions for the protection of Serb Orthodox Cultural Heritage. After yet more negotiations and diplomatic manoeuvres, Kosovo announced independence on 17 February 2008. The US, most EU member states and other supporting countries immediately recognised Kosovo. By August 2010 69 countries had recognised Kosovo and the young state had become a member of the World Bank and the IMF. Membership of other international organisations was being negotiated on a case-by-case basis. While there were some angry scenes in Belgrade and some violent protests by Serbs in north Mitrovica right after the declaration, threatened sanctions did not occur. From 15 June 2008, UNMIK took a back seat as Kosovo's supervised independence and its newly drafted constitution entered into full effect. On 22 July 2010 the International Court of Justice in The Hague ruled 10–4 that the declaration of independence in 2008 did not violate international law, Security Council Resolution 1244 or the previous UNMIK constitution. Although positive news, this has yet to lead to Kosovo's recognition by the remaining four EU states or UN membership.

The International Civilian Office (ICO) financed by the EU had the role of supervising implementation of the Ahtisaari Agreement, and after a sputtering start the EU rule of law mission known as EULEX is now in place. As of January 2010, EULEX had about 1,560 international staff on the ground, but the jury is out on its effectiveness in delivering the rule of law across the entire territory, including the Serb-populated area north of Kosovo.

Kosovo is a multi-party democracy with proportional representation in a 120-member Kosovo Assembly. There is a plethora of registered political parties, but the parties drawing most votes are the Democratic League of Kosovo (LDK), the Democratic Party of Kosovo (PDK), the Alliance for the Future of Kosovo (AAK), the Alliance for new Kosovo (AKR) and LDD (a splinter group of LDK). LDK enjoys support as a result of its legendary leader Ibrahim Rugova and its role in the parallel Kosovo government during the 1990s. PDK emerged in summer 1999 as the UÇK's political wing and is led by Hashim Thaqi, prime minister at the time of independence. The Alliance for the Future of Kosovo (AAK) was founded by Ramush Haradinaj, a former UÇK commander in Deçan region. AKR is led by construction millionaire Beghet Pacolli who earned part of his fortune in Russia during the Yeltsin era. There are at least two parties wooing the votes of Kosovo Serbs, as well as several other minority parties representing Turkish, Roma or Gorani interests.

In January 2000, the LDK government-in-exile, in existence for nearly a decade, officially ceased to exist. The Constitutional Framework for the Provisional Self-Government of Kosovo cleared the ground for Kosovo's first national elections in autumn 2001. Ibrahim Rugova's LDK emerged as clear winner, followed by PDK. After months of deadlock, the newly constituted Kosovo Assembly elected Ibrahim Rugova (LDK) as president and Bajram Rexhepi (PDK) as the first post-war prime minister. In the following months, ten ministries assumed their new roles and responsibilities.

On 23 October 2004, Kosovo held its second national elections and a new coalition government was formed by LDK with the AAK as junior partner. Ibrahim Rugova was re-elected president and Ramush Haradinaj became prime minister. Haradinaj proved an extremely dynamic prime minister, but his mandate was cut short in March 2005 by the International War Crimes Tribunal in The Hague. Indicted for war crimes, Haradinaj had to step down and face trial. He was succeeded by Bajram Kosumi, a relatively weak prime minister, who had to resign in a government reshuffle in spring 2006. Agim Çeku, a former Yugoslav army general and commander of the Kosovo Protection Corps, became Kosovo's fourth prime minister. Fatmir Sejdiu was elected President of Kosovo in February 2006 after the death of Ibrahim Rugova caused by lung cancer. General elections were held in November 2007. The PDK emerged as winners and Hashim Thaçi was appointed prime minister, forming a coalition with LDK. The coalition has remained in place despite the open secret of some inevitable wrangling, particularly as a result of the local elections held in 2009. The next general election is expected in 2011.

ECONOMY

Kosovo has always been the poorest part of Yugoslavia. Per-capita income in Kosovo continued to fall behind the other Yugoslav republics and by 1980 stood at 28% of the Yugoslav average. Unemployment even in the 1980s was at around 40% and remains above this level today. GDP per capita (on a non-PPP basis) is estimated to be about €1,000–1,200. This means that even if Kosovo grows at an optimistic annual rate of 7% it will take ten years to reach the living standards of Macedonia in 2010.

Kosovo has traditionally been an agricultural economy, dominated by small family farms producing largely for their own needs. There are 115,000 farms in Kosovo today with an average size of 0.88ha. Most farms are loss-making, but agriculture continues to be the largest employer in Kosovo. Agricultural production is insufficient to meet internal needs and Kosovo is reliant on imports. Subsistence agriculture, however, provides an important safety net for Kosovo's rural communities, which make up about 60% of the total population.

Kosovo's industrialisation came late and mainly focused on the development of natural and mineral resources. Most of Kosovo's industries were capital-intensive. The largest and most important company in the Yugoslav era was the Trepça conglomerate comprising lead and silver mines, zinc smelters and various other subsidiary companies. At its peak, it employed more than 22,000 people and was a highly inefficient, vertically integrated industrial giant. In the 1970s, Kosovo became a priority region for the Yugoslav Development Fund. Investments, however, were more often guided by political motives than economic rationale. A Croatian company, for example, invested in a textile plant in a Croatian-populated area in the southeast or spare parts for the car-manufacturing plant in Kragujevac would be produced in Peja, at a distance of about 200km. The overriding priority for Yugoslav development planners was the creation of employment, when necessary at the expense of economic efficiency.

Many of these enterprises could not compete in a global market and in common with other socialist enterprises they had too many unproductive and poorly trained staff. The social decline sparked ethnic unrest which manifested itself on the factory and mine floors. The social enterprises operated on a system of self-governance via workers' councils elected by the workers. In theory, workers 'owned' the factories in a system of 'self-management'; in practice, however, municipal governments and the Communist Party intervened regularly and key appointments were traded as political favours. In the early 1980s, these councils were ethnically mixed, reflecting the workforce. By the late 1980s, with less cash to go round and spurred on by Serbia's nationalist propaganda, the workers often divided on ethnic lines and decision making was not always in the best interests of the factory.

In 1990, the Serbian Assembly, pointing to unrest on the factory floors, passed the Law on Acting in Special Circumstances, allowing it, amongst other things to remove the workers' councils and nominate their cronies in key positions. A new aggressive labour law enabled large-scale dismissals of Albanian staff for failure to sign loyalty oaths to Serbia. Enterprises also had to meet ethnicity targets and employ resettled Serbs and Montenegrins and sometimes refugees from Croatia or Bosnia. After the mass expulsion of Albanian miners, Trepça even had to bring in Polish workers. Throughout the 1990s, asset stripping of Kosovo companies was widespread. The wars waged by Serbia and UN sanctions bred hyperinflation at hundreds of percent and a complex barter system plus use of the Deutschmark replaced the valueless dinar. The crisis was further compounded by the collapse of the Yugoslav banking system. While the rest of Eastern Europe was reforming and catching up, Kosovo was trapped in a deteriorating economic and social crisis.

When UNMIK arrived in 1999, it took some time to assess the historical economic mess. UNMIK believed that as it was a temporary body, it could not make long-lasting decisions over ownership or economic strategy so adopted a 'sticking plaster' solution consisting of international grants to prop up public enterprises like the electricity plant, short-term leases of some social industries and a package of legislative reforms. The US government was keen to put social enterprises into private hands and allow long-term capital investment, even at the risk of upsetting Serbia. After much legal wrangling, the Kosovo Privatisation Agency (KTA) was set up in 2003 with the mandate to grant 99-year leases of social enterprises. The majority of the proceeds of privatisation (80%) would be

A visitor to Kosovo cannot help but notice the large number of unfinished buildings in often unlikely locations. It does sometimes seem that Kosovar Albanians have an obsession with building. Contrary to some myths that circulate amongst international circles, the reason the buildings are unfinished is for none other than the obvious reason of finance and cash flow, rather than anything to do with taxation. The bricks and roof are the cheapest parts. The electrics, plumbing and fittings (including windows and doors) are more expensive so it takes time to raise the cash for them. A house without the electrics is quite logically known in local lingo as 'a black house', and many families in Prishtina who live in flats will tell you they have a black house out of town that they hope to move into one day. With the mortgage market in Kosovo only just beginning, most families are reliant on remittances to complete their building. What comes as a particular surprise to a visitor to Kosovo is the large scale of the Albanians' building. However, it should be remembered that the extended family usually lives in the house – with the parents on one floor and the sons on the floors above. It is also worth bearing in mind that Kosovo's population is continuing to grow and the younger generation will be increasingly reluctant to share the same flat and will expect their own floors. Kosovo is and has been for more than a century the most densely populated part of southeastern Europe – with population per square metre twice that of either Macedonia or southern Serbia.

The main problem, however, in Kosovo is not so much the number of buildings as rather that they are mostly built without any planning permission and with no controls or standards. While there are supposedly requirements for parking, garages and green space and limitations on numbers of floors, for example, these are ignored and of course no-one consults the utilities such as the electricity or sewage companies which can lead to excess demand and outages, never mind issues of schools or other services. The problem is particularly acute in the cities which have seen post-war population booms. Furthermore, there are no safety standards, including none for earthquake protection, and no respect for old or historical buildings.

The lack of planning enforcement is widely lamented by the average Kosovar – although he may be building his own house without permission at the time. The reason for the lack of enforcement is a mixture of incompetence, corruption (officials can be easily persuaded when the average sale price for a flat in a good area of Prishtina has reached €1,000 per m² – on a par with Belgrade), and fear (in 2000, Prishtina's first urban planner, Rexhep Luci, was killed). In Tirana, the mayor did eventually take matters into his own hands and bulldoze illegal builds in the centre to create green spaces and manageable road systems. It remains to be seen whether anyone in Kosovo will be brave enough to do this.

put on a trust account pending future determination of owners and creditor claimants, while the remaining 20% would be paid to the workers. By the end of 2009, more than 400 privatisation contracts had been signed and around €450 million had been collected as a result. Most of the buyers have been local property speculators who made money during the post-1999 construction boom and are now buying into other industries such as hotels or factories. Despite best efforts, there have been few international investors – the nickel plant, the flour mill in Xërxë and the Çikatova quarry being notable exceptions. Potential industrial engines like the Trepça complex with its potentially valuable mines, however, remain paralysed. In addition to international expenditure the post-war economy has also been largely propped up by remittances from the diaspora. Remittances sent home from Kosovars working and living abroad fluctuated from a post-war high of €610 million to €505 million annually today. Diaspora Albanians have also been keen investors in Kosovo's privatisation process. (See box *The fabled diaspora*, page 35.)

From 1999, private industry did grow although it was primarily trade-based, with 97% of businesses registered being sole traders. Many Kosovars returned with high hopes of building new businesses and some succeeded in taking advantage of the post-war construction boom, picking up lucrative contracts with NGOs. The most common businesses set up were petrol stations, car washes, mini markets, construction goods imports, restaurants and hotels. Kosovars were quick to spot opportunities to serve the international community.

Owing to its relative economic isolation and low integration in the global economy, Kosovo, with the exception of its mining companies, did not feel the chill winds of the global 2008–09 recession. The subsequent slowdown in investors' interest in Eastern Europe will also affect Kosovo and its already stagnant economy. There is little industry to speak of and hardly any exports besides scrap metal, electricity and galvanised steel. Regular electricity outages (the result of mismanagement, a lack of investment and Kosovars' extremely low payment record) put a major brake on industrial development. Kosovo also continues to run a massive trade imbalance of almost €1 billion. Close to 70% of Kosovo's budget – approximately €1.1 billion in 2009 – is collected in import duties at the borders. The entire public administration is thus highly dependent on the continuation of trade flows into Kosovo.

The 2004 riots triggered a realisation that the UN had focused too much on peacekeeping and not on economy building. Ultimately there are only so many construction companies, car washes or restaurants that a small place can absorb. In 2006, Kosovo and international development planners started to focus on the tender for building a new power plant and lignite mines with export capability. It was hoped that this would remedy Kosovo's electricity problem and generate much-needed export revenues. This project has in the meantime been scaled down radically.

When extolling the virtues of investing in Kosovo most Kosovars and the international community will point to EU-compliant laws that have been passed, an absence of exchange or capital controls and to linguistically skilled young people. There are renewed hopes of a service-orientated economy with call centres or IT centres, or even low-cost, low-skill assembly work drawing on the skills of Kosovo's young population. The laws do not always match enforcement (the copyright law being a case in point), bureaucrats are not always in tune with the simplicity of the laws and the erratic electricity supply does not encourage industrial investors. There is a need to improve the business bureaucracy to match certain aggressive reforms in Macedonia. In short, some dramatic measures will be needed and the next few years will be the acid test of whether the economy can indeed turn around.

Yet, not all is a disaster. The reconstruction effort was a success and in a number of areas Kosovo is benefiting greatly from modern legislation and new institutions that have been set up since 1999. There is a thriving private banking and insurance sector, albeit with high loan rates, supervised and regulated by the Central Banking Authority of Kosovo. The Customs Service enjoys a good reputation. A tender for the second mobile-phone provider was awarded in 2007 with a view to improving infrastructure and costs and the incumbent telecoms provider is also likely to be privatised. In 2006, Kosovo joined the Central European Free Trade Area – a market with 20 million people. The euro provides for stability. Domestic tax revenue, although weak in some areas, has been steadily increasing.

Kosovo's real economic asset is its European future. Kosovo already participates in the EU's Stabilisation and Association Process and progress in key development areas is subject to regular review as part of the European partnership process. In the past, the EU has been the single-biggest bilateral donor and will continue to have a major stake in Kosovo's economic development. Kosovo could experience a similar economic recovery to Romania and Bulgaria, provided the EU gives it the support that is needed – not just rhetorically – along the road to full European integration.

PEOPLE

Diverse communities have been living in Kosovo for millennia. Kosovo, like all other territories in the Balkans, has always been an ethnic patchwork. It has become what it is today because of its unique melange of peoples, languages and cultures, all adding their bit to Kosovo's cultural heritage. Too much ink and blood has been spilt in futile efforts to argue over who has an exclusive right to claim Kosovo.

An Austrian study conducted in the 1890s gives an interesting snapshot of Kosovo's ethnic makeup in the last years of the Ottoman Empire. According to this study, two-thirds of the population were Muslim and one-third non-Muslim. Ottoman statistics listed 500 Jews, between 2,000 and 3,000 Vlachs, a few thousand Orthodox Roma and 11,000 mostly Albanian-speaking Catholics. The Muslim majority was predominantly Albanian, but also included about 10,000 Muslim Roma, 6,000 Circassians and maybe around 5,000 ethnic Turks, not including soldiers stationed at the Ottoman garrisons. In addition, smaller pockets of

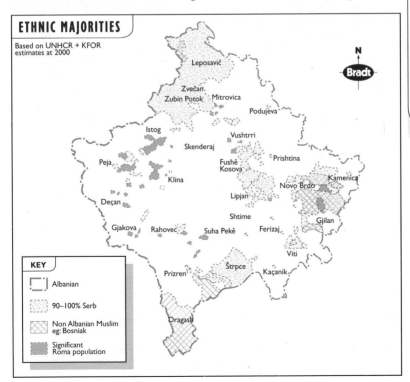

ETHNIC MAJORITIES

Based on UNHCR + KFOR
estimates at 2000

N

Bradt

Leposavić
Zvečan
Zubin Potok Mitrovica
Podujeva
Istog
Vushtrri
Skenderaj
Peja
Fushë Kosova
Prishtina
Klina
Kamenica
Novo Brdo
Deçan
Lipjan
Shtime
Gjilan
Gjakova Rahovec Suha Pekë Ferizaj
Viti
Prizren Štrpce Kaçanik
Dragash

KEY

☐ Albanian

▨ 90–100% Serb

▨ Non Albanian Muslim
eg: Bosniak

▨ Significant
Roma population

Slav-speaking Muslims or Gorani were to be found in around 30 villages south of Prizren. Ottoman sources wrote that they converted to Islam out of neglect by the Greek clergy after the closure of the Serbian Patriarchate in 1766. There were also smaller communities of Slav-speaking Muslims in Prizren and Prishtina. This turn-of-the-century snapshot of Kosovo's ethnic makeup shows just how diverse Kosovo has always been. The almost exclusive and highly politicised focus on Albanian–Serb relations today takes too limited a view of Kosovo's historic diversity.

The last official census with Albanian participation dates back to 1981. Much has changed in Kosovo since. Owing to a lack of reliable statistics, controversies over Kosovo's present-day population have been raging with a vengeance. A new population census is planned in 2011. For the moment, we have to rely on various best estimates. There are believed to be 1.9 million residents in Kosovo today. Albanians are by far the largest group. They make up an estimated 88% of Kosovo's population. The second-largest community, with a share of 7%, are Kosovo Serbs. About 130,000 Serbs remained in Kosovo after 1999; the vast majority is living in mixed rural communities south of the Ibar River. The remaining 5% of the population are split into Ashkali, Roma, Egyptians, Bosniaks, Gorani, Croats and Turks.

The Roma moved to the Balkans in the 13th century. Over the centuries, most adopted Islam as a faith and Albanian as their language. Many refer to themselves now as Ashkali. A second group tracing their ancestry back to Egypt is called Egyptians. There are an estimated 35,000–40,000 Roma, Ashkali and Egyptians believed to be living in Kosovo today. Some 78% declare Albanian to be their mother tongue, and 22% speak Romani at home. The vast majority are Muslims. Since 1999, all three groupings are officially recognised as minorities and generally referred to as RAE (Roma, Ashkali and Egyptians).

In 1961 Yugoslav statistics, Slav-speaking Muslims were able to identify themselves for the first time as 'Muslim in the ethnic sense'. Since 1999 some of this group adopted the name Bosniak, indicating that they speak Bosnian as distinct from Serbian or Croatian. There are between 35,000 and 57,000 Bosniaks in Kosovo today. The Gorani form another Slav-speaking Muslim group to be found in the mountainous Gora (Dragash) region mostly south and east of Prizren. They number around 6,000 today (see page 195). There is also a small Catholic Croat minority concentrated in Janjevo, a former mining town in central Kosovo, and Letnica, a well-known pilgrimage site in Viti municipality in Kosovo's southeast.

The origins of Kosovo's Turkish minority date back to the 14th century when Turkish officials and soldiers took posts in Kosovo. Today, the Turks number between 12,000 and 50,000 and live mostly scattered in the Prizren area and in a few larger towns. A pilot project has recently created a separate municipality in Mamusha, a Turkish majority village. It is difficult to pin down what makes a Turk in Kosovo. In the past, many Muslim Albanian families were so Ottoman-ised that the distinction between Albanian and Turkish has blurred. Turkish was recognised as one of the official languages in the 1974 constitution. Today, national radio and television broadcast news in the Turkish language and the Turkish-language daily *Yeni* is available in most towns. To this day, all Turks in Kosovo are bilingual.

Kosovo's historical Jewish population has all but disappeared. Numbering a few hundred in 1941, many were killed during the Holocaust and the survivors left for Israel right after World War II. The Vlachs constitute the second minority that has vanished over the years. Most Vlachs assimilated and became Serbs with the result that no-one in Kosovo today identifies themselves as Vlach.

One of the biggest myths in Kosovo concerns the famous Kosovo diaspora. You will hear figures ranging from hundreds of thousands to millions, depending on who you ask. Without doubt, the Kosovo diaspora is hugely important for individual families and the economy at large. Having 'a brother abroad' is like having social security, especially in times of hardship.

The earliest guest workers left Kosovo in the late 1960s. They were mostly single young men who went to Germany and Switzerland to escape rural poverty. They worked back-breaking jobs and returned twice a year for holidays. The money they sent home was used to pay for a tractor, a child's education or a family wedding. During the 1990s, especially after the mass dismissals and at the time of the Bosnian War, many more young men left Kosovo to escape Yugoslav military service and to keep their families afloat economically. They were received as political refugees and in the case of Germany were granted a legal status called *Dulding* (toleration). In March 1992, the Kosovo government-in-exile estimated that 217,000 Kosovars were living abroad. The most popular countries were Germany with 82,348, Switzerland with 72,448, Sweden with 15,652 and Austria with 12,300. By the late 1990s, about half a million Kosovo Albanians were living abroad, nearly a quarter of the population. During the war in 1999, thousands more escaped to Germany, Sweden, the US and Canada. The year 1999 marked a turning point also for Kosovo's diaspora. When the war ended, 180,000 Kosovars in Germany lost their legal status. Since then, 90,000 were assisted to return, 20,000 were forced to return and an unknown number returned voluntarily. The number of Kosovars living in Germany has dropped to fewer than 200,000 today. The Kosovo diaspora in Switzerland numbered 195,000 in 1999. It was easier for Kosovar asylum seekers in Switzerland to obtain residence permits and few have returned in the last few years. There are now between 150,000 and 180,000 Kosovars living in Switzerland. The Kosovo diaspora in Austria is estimated at about 70,000. There is also a sizeable diaspora in the UK. The most active and vocal diaspora outfit is certainly the National Albanian Council based in New York.

There are not only disputes over the numbers of Kosovo Albanians living abroad, but also great disagreement about how much money they send home. In the 1990s it was estimated that the government-in-exile collected around US$125 million in voluntary taxes, one-third of which came from the diaspora. According to the Central Bank, in 2010 remittances were around €500 million per annum, with 38% from Germany and 22% from Switzerland. Millions of euros of hard-earned savings were repatriated to Kosovo after the war to finance the reconstruction of homes and farms. The largest 'donor' after the war was the Kosovo diaspora, and the majority of destroyed homes were rebuilt with private money saved abroad. Since 1999, however, the level of remittances sent back to Kosovo has fallen dramatically. This is a direct consequence of the sharp drop in the number of Kosovars living abroad. With every person returned from Germany or another country, a family in Kosovo lost access to remittances. For the first time in decades, net migration from Kosovo is negative today. The only way 'out' at the moment is through marriage or family unification application or an illegal/black-market visa or passport. A household survey done in 2004 estimated that the annual level of remittances had dropped to €123 million. A survey by UNDP in 2009 revealed, however, that 50% of Kosovo's under-25s would leave Kosovo if possible.

For more information on migration, you can read the ESI report *Cutting the Lifeline: Migration, Families and the Future of Kosovo*, published in September 2006, on www.esiweb.org.

Kosovo has two official languages – Albanian and Serbian, and in Prizren municipality there is a third: Turkish. Some Bosnians claim that their language is a different branch from Serbian but in practice the difference between it and Serbian is small. English is used as an official language by parts of the administration that are still run by internationals but is otherwise no longer an official language.

The Albanian and the Greek languages are the only surviving ancient Balkan languages belonging to the Indo-European family. Unfortunately, not a single text in the Illyrian language has survived so tracing the direct relationship between Albanian and Illyrian is difficult. A number of place names point to a link between Albanian and Illyrian, and so does the structure of the language. The purest Albanian vocabulary can be found in expressions related to mountain life, shepherding and basic food products. It was in the high altitudes that the language survived, while the Illyrians living along the coast and in the plains were Romanised. When it comes to Christian practices and beliefs, the Albanian vocabulary borrows heavily from Latin, pointing to the fact that it was Latin-speaking missionaries who brought Christianity to the Albanian people.

There are two distinct dialects in modern Albanian. The dialect spoken in northern Albania and Kosovo is called Gheg. Most of the early Albanian literature was written by Catholic priests in the Gheg dialect.

In South Albania, people speak Tosk. In 1972, when literary Albanian was standardised, it was more closely based on Tosk than Gheg. This was no surprise, as Enver Hoxha, then dictator of Albania and the patron of a conference on standardisation of the language, was a Tosk himself. The difference between Ghegs and Tosks is mostly linguistic, but partly cultural. Ghegs lived in the northern, mountainous regions enjoying relative autonomy. Out of reach of the Ottoman – and later communist – administration, Ghegs continued to practise their own customary laws. Gheg society was traditionally organised around the clan (fis). The system is strictly patrilinear: families are identified by their sons. In the northern highlands, each clan had their own territory and grazing lands. In the plains of Kosovo, the importance of the clan was quickly eroded and replaced by the extended family. The reality of Tosks was very different. They lived in the plains under feudal landlords, fully integrated into the Ottoman system. Gheg and Tosk are mutually intelligible, but differ greatly in pronunciation. It is somewhat comparable to the difference between Austrian and German or between Scottish and English. For many Kosovars, reading Albanian literature written in Tosk feels strange. A movement around Migjen Kelmendi, a well-known Prishtina-based journalist, has been lobbying for the adoption of Gheg as it is spoken in Kosovo as a literary language in its own right. It remains to be seen what will become of this initiative in an independent Kosovo. In addition many Kosovo Albanians will use words borrowed from Serbian, Turkish or, more recently, German or English.

Serbian is one of the variants of the central-southern Slavic language that in the Yugoslav era was known as Serbo-Croat. It has links with other Slavic languages like Czech, Russian or Polish. Serbs living in Kosovo because of their long association with the Ottoman Empire also use numerous Turkish words. Serbian uses both a Cyrillic and a Latin alphabet. The Cyrillic alphabet is often regarded as the official one by institutions and most nationalist papers and politicians will use this. The Cyrillic alphabet was developed in the 9th century by St Cyril and refined by St Clement in Ohrid, in present-day Macedonia.

For practical details on learning Albanian, including the Gheg derivative, and Serbian see *Appendix 1, Language*, page 282.

Religious affiliation roughly corresponds with the ethnic makeup of Kosovo today. About 90% of the population is Muslim, 7% Serb Orthodox and 3% Albanian Catholic. In recent years, there has also been a small but growing group of Protestants of different denominations. Given their own mix of religions, Albanians have always been tolerant when it comes to religious beliefs. The League of Prizren coined the saying that the faith of the Albanians is Albanianism. The national hero *par excellence* is a good example. Gjeorg Kastrioti (Skenderbeg) was born an Orthodox, raised as a Muslim at the Ottoman court and returned to Kosovo as a Catholic. (For more about Skenderbeg, see page 123.)

The Ottoman Empire was also tolerant of different faiths. Christians and Jews were considered *zimmi* – protected people. They were subordinate to Muslims, but enjoyed legal protection. The Orthodox Church in Kosovo, especially after the re-establishment of the Patriarchate in Peć (Peja) in 1557, enjoyed a privileged position. It was in the sultan's and the patriarch's interest to sustain good relations. As a token of respect, the patriarch paid an annual gift to the sultan. This practice gradually developed into outright simony, and patriarchs had to pay the sultan for their appointment.

Kosovo is the spiritual seat of the **Serb Orthodox Church**, and is sometimes referred to as the 'Serbian Jerusalem'. The seat of the Serbian Patriarchate was originally located in Serbia proper and today it is based in Belgrade, but throughout history the Peć Patriarchate, the Gračanica Monastery and the Visoki Dečani Monastery have been of particular importance as burial grounds for Serb saints, archbishops and patriarchs, as centres of monastic learning and as living examples of the close relationship between the Nemanjić dynasty and the early Serb Church.

The **Catholic Church** was generally worse off than the Serbian Orthodox Church because of its allegiance to a foreign power – the Vatican. For most of the period, Kosovo's Catholics were under the Archdiocese of Bar (in Albanian, Tivar) in present-day Montenegro. But the Catholic Church in Kosovo suffered from neglect and a severe lack of priests. Partly due to this lack of priests, the Catholics in Trepça, for example, joined the Orthodox liturgy. The bishopric in Prizren was reinstated in 1618 and in 1656, Kosovo was placed under the Archdiocese of Skopje and Pjeter Bogdani was appointed as second archbishop. A first Albanian catechism was published in 1618, and Frang Bardhi printed a first Latin–Albanian dictionary in 1635.

Islam spread slowly and forced conversions were rare. By 1560, there were only four mosques in the towns of Vushtrri, Prishtina, Trepça and Novo Brdo and the total Muslim population was only 496 families. In the early Ottoman period, the growth of Islam was almost exclusively an urban phenomenon and closely tied to religious-charitable foundations. The Ottoman Empire allowed for rich families to endow their wealth – tax free – to a charity organisation, often managed by family members. Many of these charity organisations looked after mosques, constructed *hammams* or ran soup kitchens. By the late 16th century, 90% of the population of Peja was Muslim. Other major towns were as follows: Vushtrri 80%, Prishtina 60%, Prizren about 60%, Novo Brdo 40% and Mitrovica/Trepça 20%. Towns with large mining communities were slower to convert to Islam, perhaps because the tax implications were less significant. Sufi dervish missionaries spread a more mystical version of Islam. Several **Sufi orders** that set up lodges in towns were closely linked to certain craft guilds. The most influential orders were the Bektashi order (also strong in Albania) and the Halveti order. The Bektashi order was the official order of the Janissaries, the sultan's elite army corps. Bektashi do not fast during Ramadan and drink wine freely. (See box *Dervish and tekke*, pages 214–15.)

Most of the time, the decision to convert was economically motivated or was concerned with social status. The immediate advantage of conversion was to be freed of the *cizye*, the poll tax levied annually on every non-Muslim adult male. The rapid increase in the poll tax in the late 17th century led to a wave of conversions. Often the men converted to Islam while their wives remained Christians in the home. In the 1670s, for example, there were 300 Christian women in the Has region but no Christian men. This phenomenon is referred to as **crypto-Christianity**. It was more common in villages out of sight of vigilant Muslim clerics. In 1845, to avoid military conscription around 150 crypto-Catholics publicly declared they were Christians in Gjakova.

There was little hostility between the different faiths practised in Kosovo. On the contrary, Muslims and Christians alike often shared the same folk beliefs. Baptism, for example, was believed to secure a longer life, so it was commonly practised among Muslims as well. The Sokolica Virgin near Zvečan (see page 274) and the Black Madonna in Letnica (in Viti municipality) (see page 253) were equally venerated by Serbs, Albanians, Muslims and Christians. Traditionally, it was Kosovo Albanian families who acted as guardians of the most important churches and monasteries, including the Patriarchate in Peć and the monastery in Deçan.

EDUCATION

The first state Turkish-language education system was introduced in the 1830s. The first two Serb-language primary schools were opened in Prizren in 1836. There were also Catholic Italian-language schools in Prizren, Gjakova, Peja, Janjevo and Stublla. From 1856 onwards all communities had the right, in theory, to set up their own language public schools.

The first Albanian-language school inside Kosovo did not open until 1889, in Mitrovica. More than 300 Albanian-language schools were opened during the Austrian occupation in World War I. In breach of the 1919 Treaty of Saint Germain on the Protection of National Minorities signed by the First Yugoslavia, Serbia closed down all Albanian-language schools again in 1919. Teaching and publishing in Albanian were declared illegal.

At the outbreak of World War II there were 252 schools in Kosovo, teaching only Serbian. During the German and Italian occupations Albanian-language teaching expanded massively to 392 primary schools and 279 Albanian secondary schools. There was a real shortage of teachers in Kosovo so teachers from Albania were invited to teach. Despite these efforts, in the 1950s the illiteracy rate was still 94%.

The expansion of Albanian education continued under Yugoslav socialism with the introduction of eight-year primary schools in the 1960s and large-scale school building programmes in the 1970s. Traditional resistance in rural areas to sending girls to school was broken with a successful campaign in the 1960s declaring that 'only in education there is a future'. By the 1970s illiteracy rates had dropped to 30%. Today the illiteracy rate for the population has dropped to 2% for the under-30s. The expansion of Kosovo's public administration and industry raised hopes that education would be the key to lifelong state employment. The economic crisis of the mid 1980s, however, shattered these hopes. The gloomier the prospects for employment became, the higher was the drop-out rate from education, especially among girls.

The numbers of university-educated Albanians increased dramatically with the establishment of Prishtina University in 1969 which offered Albanian-language tertiary education in Kosovo for the first time. The university's 13 faculties churned out thousands of graduates every year and Kosovo's labour market was swamped.

Prishtina University has always been a centre of protests and political thought and was perceived by the Serbian regime to be a centre of Albanian separatism. For this reason Albanian employees were dismissed in large numbers in the 1990s and a new management was put in place by decision of the Serbian Parliament. In February 1992, a parallel Albanian University started to operate in private homes, funded by informal Albanian taxes. A last-ditch attempt to broker an education agreement between Ibrahim Rugova and Slobodan Milošević in September 1996 failed. In autumn 1997, the parallel Prishtina University took a leading role in organising a series of student demonstrations. Serb police responded with a violent crackdown on the demonstrators.

EDUCATION TODAY Today's Kosovo education system is sadly lacking in many respects, suffering not only from low salaries and underfunding, but also from the legacies of the underground and ad hoc nature of the Albanian school system during the difficult 1990s. Learning is traditional-style rote and fact-based learning, rather than analytical or skill-based. The new textbooks are better and brighter and many schools have access to computers and class sizes compare well with the West, with on average 30 children in a class. Extra-curricular activities such as sports or music are, however, very rare.

There was a large-scale school rebuilding programme funded by international donors right after the war, however there remains a shortage of buildings in towns, primarily due to urbanisation. For this reason, schools in towns operated on a shift system, with up to three shifts a day, starting at 06.00 and ending at 22.00. To remedy this problem, the Ministry of Education initiated a second wave of school constructions, reducing the number of shifts to two per school.

The Serb and Albanian education systems are separate, with the Serb system following Serbia's curriculum and the teachers usually being on the Serb government payroll. There are almost no integrated schools although one is being mooted in Lipjan. The Gorani minority, who are Serbian-speakers, have been leaning towards the Serbian system on account of their need for textbooks and access to higher education in their language.

Under Kosovo law schooling is compulsory from age six to 15. From the age of 15 to 18 it is possible to specialise and go to a technical school or gymnasium. In recent years, Kosovo-wide exams known as *Matura* have been introduced for secondary schools across the country. Schools are run by municipalities.

There is only one government-run public university in Kosovo – Prishtina University, which provides teaching in Albanian. Most facilities are in Prishtina (with the agricultural faculty on the road to Fushë-Kosova), but there are two technical faculties in southern Mitrovica and Ferizaj and a business faculty in Peja. There are about 24,000 registered students, including Albanians from Macedonia or Serbia. A second public university is being planned in Prizren.

There is a Serb-language university in north Mitrovica run by the Serbian government (regarded by the Serbian population as the displaced 'Prishtina' University). The physical training and teacher-training faculty is in Leposavić. In total, about 1,200 students from Kosovo and Serbia attend.

There are formal entrance exams for **Prishtina University** and undergraduate students must pay nominal university fees of €60 per semester. The standard of education at Prishtina University is generally low, with no real staff monitoring, no anonymous marking and many rumours of the need to pay favours in kind – or in person – to pass exams. The rector, Enver Hasani, made much of his plans to reform the university so that it can be recognised under the Bologna Process.

Each year there is an internationally funded Summer University with foreign professors. For further information, see the university's website, www.uni-pr.edu.

Keen to capitalise on a huge young population and the shortcomings of Prishtina University, private universities have mushroomed since 2005. The best of the bunch by far, albeit not cheap, is the **American University of Kosovo**, which is affiliated with Rochester University of Technology and therefore the only one with any form of genuine international quality control. The others have loose affiliations with some universities, such as Vienna. Again, even the private universities have an arts bias with arguably far too many courses in public administration, international relations or English and no engineering, geology or science courses which might be appropriate to the mining potential of Kosovo. Prishtina University has produced on average, every year since 1999, 314 economists and only 30 graduates from the engineering, mining or metallurgy faculties.

For telephone numbers and contact details of some universities see *Chapter 3, Prishtina*, page 122.

Vocational training in Kosovo is weak and hugely lacking. There is no programme of night or day-release schools. There has been some recent donor support to improve this sector from the EU and from bilateral donors like Norway, and as a result specialised vocational training schools are being established in Mitrovica, Skenderaj, Lipjan, Malisheva and Suha Rekë. The pre-existing gap has been filled to some degree by the private sector in relation to IT (there is a Cisco academy which runs courses in IT networking) and languages.

LANGUAGE SCHOOLS Kosovars, but especially Albanians, are keen to learn languages; the young in particular are eager to learn English or German. There is an unquestioned recognition that English is essential to get on in life. English is taught as a second language in all schools, as is often German. Both subjects are offered at Prishtina University. Other languages are rarer but you will find plenty of interpreters for Dutch, Swedish, Finnish, French, Danish and Italian; less so for Russian. These often arise because of diaspora contacts and work experience abroad.

Owing to their desire to learn languages there are language schools all over Kosovo. The best known are the Cambridge School and the Oxford School (see page 120). There is almost invariably one or the other in every town. They also teach other languages such as French or German and foreigners can join in such classes, although you may struggle with the explanations in Albanian.

INTERNATIONAL SCHOOLS Some international schools have sprung up to serve both the international community and wealthy Kosovars. Again, the best known of these are the American School of Kosovo, the Mehmet Akif or Gulistan School teaching in English and Turkish, the Prishtina High School, the International Learning Group (for children aged three–ten), and Quality School International (QSI). For more details of these, see page 122.

CULTURE

Art is usually a good souvenir, although it is hard to find paintings of Kosovo scenery or anything typically Kosovar. For details of galleries, see page 111. What there is in terms of art generally tends to be concentrated in Prishtina around the university.

Film-making is a high-budget, high-risk industry in the best of places, so not surprisingly there are few Kosovo-made films. The few that have been produced focused on violence and war. The most famous film made in Kosovo since 1999 was *Kukumi* by Isa Qosja. It won the special jury prize at the Sarajevo Film Festival.

ABC Cinema in Prishtina is the only cinema left operating in Kosovo and astoundingly manages to operate legitimately despite widespread piracy of DVDs. It runs fairly regular film weeks in conjunction with the French, UK or German liaison offices. The Dokufest Film Festival (*www.dokufest.com*) in Prizren each August is now turning into a festival of Europe-wide renown focusing on the showing of documentaries and culminating in a series of awards. Prishtina now also hosts its own Prishtina International Film Festival (*www.prifilmfest.org*).

The main **theatre** – Kosovo's National Theatre – is in Prishtina, and there is a private theatre (Oda Theatre – often used for live bands) and the Dodona Theatre for children, but there are also theatres in Peja, Gjilan and Gjakova. Again there are theatre weeks with visits from outside Kosovo and also regular plays in Albanian. There is a newly established ballet and the Opera and Ballet House is being built in the Sunny Hill area of town, near the Technical Faculty.

MUSIC The classical music scene is pretty well limited to the Kosovo Philharmonic and there is currently no opera. There is a lively bar and coffee-house culture and some local live bands that play, but much to the regret of the young population few of the major international bands tour Kosovo; the closest they get is Skopje. However, Kosovo has a thriving contemporary music scene and its artists sell records not just in Kosovo but also to the diaspora and to Albania. The internet is teeming with Albanian music websites full of Kosovar artists. An Albanian satellite/cable TV channel, MyMusic, shows local and international music and a material percentage of the bands playing will be Kosovo Albanian.

Kosovo's traditional music is folk music. In the past, epic poetry in Kosovo and northern Albania was sung on a *lahuta* (a one-string fiddle) and then a more tuneful *çiftelia* was used which has two strings – one for the melody and one for the drone. There were also wind instruments and a *lodra* – a big drum. These instruments can still been seen played at special events and the drum is a traditional accompaniment to weddings.

Serbian music was heavily dominated by church music, although it also had its share of sung epic poetry. *Novokomponovana* was a Serbian urbanisation of folk music including a clarinet.

Both Albanian and Serbian music were influenced by Turkish music and in this regard there is some overlap. Of particular significance also is Roma music with its brass bands and trumpets. Music dominates the Roma culture and Roma bands are often still chosen to play at weddings.

Current singers of old-style Albanian folk music include Shkurte Fejza, Shyrete Behluli, Remzije Osmani, Sabri Fejzullahu, Dani, Xeni and Sinan Vllasaliu. The scene includes singers of the busty, glamorous type including Leonora Jakupi and Adelina Ismajli who straddle the old and new.

A new blend of music that started in the early 1990s is known as *tallava*, or turbo-folk music, which is a fast-paced, aggressive music with a blend of techno and garage. This was adopted in particular in Serbia with performers like Ceca (notorious war criminal Arkan's widow), and it took on nationalist lyrics. Nonetheless, an Albanian named Meda sold more than 100,000 copies of his own version of turbo-folk, which was particularly popular in Switzerland.

Well-known contemporary rock bands whose CDs can easily be picked up in town and who sometimes also play are Gjurmët, Diadema, Troja, Votra, Humus, Asgjë sikur Dielli, Kthjellu, Tek, Glasses, Dizzies, The Freelancers, Cute Babulja and Babilon. Amongst the younger population Albanian rap is extremely popular. This is largely unintelligible to any foreigner, even one who speaks Albanian well. Popular Albanian rap artists include NR, Daliks, DJ Blunt, Bardool, Tingulli 3, Unikatil, Etno Engjujt and Mad Lion or Skills.

Modern Serbian rock bands include Van Gogh, Night Shift, Disciplina Kitschme and Bajaga Instruktori.

LITERATURE Kosovo Albanians read very little compared with across the border in Albania. For most families books are prohibitively expensive, but there is also no culture of reading (even from libraries) and Kosovo Albanian literature developed late because of the restrictions on Albanian-language education lasting well into the 1960s. As a result, the development and mass publishing of Albanian literature in Kosovo also did not occur until then. There is a general bias towards poetry when it comes to famous Kosovar authors. Kosovo Albanian authors whose works are translated into English include Rexhep Qoshja, Ali Podrimja and Sabri Hamiti. Most Serbian literature, on the other hand, is focused on writers based in Belgrade and of course the Battle of Kosovo was a trigger for famous Serbian epic poetry.

2

Practical Information

WHEN TO VISIT

The best time to come to Kosovo is spring, eg: late April, May or early June when the fields are bright green but there is still some snow on the tops of the mountains and the flowers in the meadows come out. There is a risk of heavy rain in late April but it is rare for this to last more than a day or so.

In July, August and early September the flights and roads are busy with the diaspora returning, so travelling is not quite as easy or cheap and the weather can be too hot to explore, although September generally offers pleasant weather. In the winter there is a risk of ice and fog on the roads and in practice it will be difficult to see much due to the snow.

HIGHLIGHTS

Different visitors to Kosovo will have different windows of time available. As a rule of thumb, on Sundays museums are generally closed and towns tend to be dead, so Sunday is a good day to do monasteries, waterfalls or mountains.

BACKPACKERS If you are exploring the Balkans, four to five days is probably sufficient to 'do' Kosovo, with more time needed if you wish to do some hiking. Unless you are big on nightlife, to keep costs down and have a more genuine and personal experience, you might want to spend just one night in Prishtina and from there visit Gračanica, Gadimë, the Battle of Kosovo site, Mitrovica, Zvečan and Prekaz (total two days) and perhaps base yourself in Gjakova or the Dranoc Kulla to see Gjakova, Dečan, Isniq, Dranoc, Peja and Prizren (three days). For Dragash, because of the distance you need to allow a full day and possibly stay overnight in Prizren or Dragash itself. If travelling by car or taxi then make sure that on the Gjakova/Prishtina journey you stop off at the Mirusha waterfalls (two-hour diversion) or consider a two-hour stop-off in Rahovec or diverting to Velika Hoča (one–two-hour diversion), and on the Skopje/Prishtina leg you could stop off at the Gadimë Cave (one-hour diversion) or visit the Kaçanik Mosque (half-hour diversion).

ONE-DAY OR WEEKEND VISIT If you are visiting friends in Kosovo and only have a long weekend then we would recommend one day out to Dečan Monastery and the *kullas* in Dranoc, perhaps driving back to Gjakova and staying overnight there or in Prizren. The next day you can do Prizren and drive back if you have time via Prevalac on a scenic route passing through Brezovica and the Sharr Mountains to Prishtina.

If you are relying on buses then you need to set off from Prishtina early and go from Prishtina to Peja, explore Peja and the Patriarchate on foot and catch a 13.00–14.00 bus to Dečan. Then carry on to Gjakova for an overnight and catch the morning bus to Prizren. The Prizren buses will take the main road back to Prishtina and not the picturesque Prevalac mountain route.

DAY TRIPS The most common request received when writing this book was for suggestions for one-day trips based out of Prishtina. The following suggestions are tailored for international development workers, and others based in Prishtina with weekends and time on their hands to explore Kosovo.

- Prishtina–Isniq–Dečan including Dečan Monastery.
- Prishtina–Mirusha falls (late lunch at Guri i Zi), Gjakova.
- Prishtina–Rahovec–Gjakova. If you have a car, then divert from Rahovec to see Velika Hoča. Late lunch or dinner in Gjakova.
- Prishtina–Peć Patriarchate and Peja old bazaar quarter–Drini i Bardhë waterfalls for lunch or dinner–Te Arrat Restaurant opposite the turn-off for the falls (by car you could also have dinner at Kosova Park Hotel in Banja e Pejes).
- Prishtina–Prizren. Drive back via the Monastery of Archangels, Gornje Lubijne village, Prevalac Pass, Štrpce. Lunch or evening dinner stop at Villa Park or Ljuboten Restaurant, Brezovica.
- Prishtina–Gračanica–Novo Brdo–Kamenicë and surrounding churches. Back through Gjilan. Evening dinner stop at Planet Restaurant on the road from Bujanovac/Kamenicë to Gjilan.
- Prishtina–Banjska and Sokolica monasteries–Zvečan Castle. Dinner on Ibar River just outside Mitrovica in one of the fish restaurants.

SIDE TRIPS FROM PRIZREN
- Zym and, if you have extra time (one-hour side trip from Prizren), you can also drive to Bishtazin.
- Vermicë. Evening dinner stop at Vermicë restaurants.
- Zym, Bishtazin scenic loop road.
- Rahovec and Velika Hoča.

HALF DAYS FROM PRISHTINA
- Gračanica and Ulpiana
- Kosovo Battle Memorial Complex and Sultan Türbe
- Janjevo
- Novo Brdo
- Gadimë Cave
- Berisha Hill and Kosova e Lirë radio station
- Adem Jashari Memorial in Prekaz
- Battlava Lake
- Banjska/Sokolica monasteries and Isa Boletin's house
- Bajgora Mountains/restaurant

WINTER TRIPS (only with 4×4 or chains in winter)
- Brezovica
- Bogë in Rugova Valley

SUMMER TRIPS
- Zubin Potok Lake
- Battlava Lake

HIKING TRIPS (see relevant sections)
- Štrpce/Brezovica
- Bajgora (between Podujevo and Mitrovica)
- Dragash
- Rugova Valley

- Deçani Canyon
- Zubin Potok

TOURING THE BALKANS There is a lot to be said for combining Kosovo with visits to other Balkan countries. For more details see the Bradt guides to Albania, Macedonia, Bosnia & Herzegovina, Montenegro and Serbia.

If you are flying, you can arrange open-jaw flights with British Airways into Belgrade, Dubrovnik, Prishtina or Tirana and then depart from another city. Skopje Airport is only 45 minutes from the Kosovan border or one hour 40 minutes from Prishtina. Travelling from Belgrade is feasible as it is just five hours. Recent road improvements have made it much easier to travel in and out of Albania and Montenegro. The new road from the Albanian coast to the Kosovan border through the Kalimash Tunnel (with toll) has reduced the journey time from Tirana to Prizren to about four hours from a previous eight hours of stomach-wrenching switchbacks. An alternative feasible option at the moment if you are coming from northern Albania or southern Montenegro is to take the 09.30 ferry at Koman (an hour from Shkodra). From May to August a second ferry leaves at 16.00. This takes two hours with stunning scenery. Then travel the newly asphalted road, taking you to Gjakova in 45 minutes but make sure you are at the ferry in sufficient time; it is a good 45-minute trip from Shkodra. The Prishtina–Tirana route via Lake Ohrid in Macedonia takes six to seven hours.

TOUR OPERATORS

There are a couple of UK operators who have started offering trips to Kosovo – see below – and some fledgling organisations have started doing so within Kosovo. Aside from the ones the authors know such as Rugova Experience, we are not aware of the details of the others so cannot give any information on the quality of the particular Kosovo trips or what sights you may see – check the itineraries. With the Kosovar operators it is best to be quite specific about what you wish to visit and how much hiking or other activity you want to do, quality of hotels, etc, so that they can tailor the trip appropriately for you.

UK

Regent Holidays Mezzanine Suite, Froomsgate House, Rupert St, Bristol BS1 2QJ; ☎ 0845 277 3317; e regent@regent-holidays.co.uk www.regent-holidays.co.uk
Undiscovered Destinations PO Box 746, North

Tyneside NE29 1EG or The Old Post Office, 63 Saville St, North Shields, Tyne & Wear NE30 1AY; ☎ 0191 296 2674; e info@undiscovered-destinations.com; www.undiscovered-destinations.com

KOSOVO

Be in Kosovo Ulpiana P4, S-1, nr 3, Prishtina; m 044/049 385 109; e hasanaj.ardian@gmail.com; Young, educated Kosovars who put together tailored trips for 1 or more persons, or arrange guides or hotels for cities.
Era ☎ 039 423 122; m 044 337 601/161 844; e info@era-group.net; www.era-group.net. Environmental & hiking NGO. Will organise trekking in the western Kosovo, Montenegro & northern Albania triangle. Local NGO for the Balkans Peace Park.
Gëzuar NGO www.gezuar.eu. Organising a 'Tour de Kosovo' 3-day road bike ride in Sep 2010 &

potentially future years as well as some motorbike treks.
Kosovo Tourism Group ☎ 038 552 167; m 044 241 035; e info@ks-tourismgroup.com; www.ks-tourismgroup.com. Arrange trips & packages in particular for Prishtina & Prizren, & also package tours.
Rugova Experience Rr Mbreteresha Teuta, Peja; m 044 348 831; e info@rugovaexperience.org, rugovatour@yahoo.com; www.rugovaexperience.org. Created by the initiative of an Italian organisation called the 'Trentino Kosovo Roundtable' & dedicated to the promotion & development of ecotourism in

2

Peja region. They organise trips in Rugova Valley, Deçan, Junik, Peja area, including hiking, climbing, visits to sites, agricultural trips, snowshoeing, etc. **Sabri Maloku** ☎ 038 221 730; m 044 151180; e sabri_maloku@hotmail.com. Sabri, who helped significantly with this guide & has now explored

almost every corner of Kosovo, is also happy to take tourists round Kosovo & the Balkans by car, on foot or by mountain bike.
www.kosovoguide.com or www.experiencekosova.com Trips & events advertised on these USAID-supported websites.

EUROPE If you want group bookings for flights or other types of travel organised, you can either try the travel agents listed in *Chapter 3*, page 88, or one of following German- and Swiss-based agents:

Eurokoha Various offices throughout Germany & in Zürich: Münchener Str 47, 60329 Frankfurt; ☎ +49 0 69 25 66 760; e bookingfra@eurokoha.net; www.eurokoha.net; Konrad-Adenauer-Platz 10, 40210 Düsseldorf; ☎ +49 0 211 17 39 930; e bookingdus@eurokoha.net; Hirsch Str 18, 70173 Stuttgart; ☎ +49 0 711 87 03 06 90; e bookingstr@eurokoha.net; Adenauerallee 10,

10097 Hamburg; ☎ +49 0 40 30 39 47 58; Bahnhofplatz 9, 8001 Zürich; ☎ +41 0 1 315 5959; e bookingzrh@eurokoha.net
Kosova Reisen Löwenstr 69, 8001 Zürich; ☎ +41 0 1 215 2020; m +41 0 79 815 2020; Zürich Airport Terminal 2; ☎ +41 0 43 816 5934; e info@kosovareisen.ch; www.kosovareisen.net, www.kosovareisen.com

RED TAPE

VISAS At the time of writing, no visa was needed to enter Kosovo. This may, however, change as Kosovo is expected to align its visa policies with those of the EU in return for visa liberalisation for Kosovo citizens. Citizens from EU countries, the US, Japan, Canada, Australia and New Zealand citizens as well as EU candidate or neighbouring countries will also not be required to possess a visa in the future. Kosovo is also likely to adopt practices similar to those in Montenegro, whereby anyone from a third country, eg: India, who possesses a valid Schengen visa is permitted entry. In practice visitors from countries regarded as high risk for illegal immigration, eg: parts of Africa and Asia, already face entry problems and have been turned back. After legal entry visitors can stay for 90 days. If you stay longer than that, you must register with the police. If you are staying for medium- to long-term business, consultancy or similar, then it is worthwhile getting a temporary Kosovo resident's card/permit which will facilitate all manner of business and avoid the need for Kosovo stamps in your passport. This is obtained by presenting your passport and contract, eg: consultancy, employment or business registration certificate for a Kosovo business, at the police station. They then take your home address, a fingerprint and a photo. The Prishtina police station which is responsible for registration of foreigners is on Rr Luan Haradinaj (also known as Police Avenue), opposite Café Arte on the left-hand side when walking from Boro Ramiz Stadium towards town. The door is a stiff white metal one.

SERBIAN STAMP At the time of writing and possibly for the foreseeable future, Serbia does not recognise the internationally managed borders of Kosovo. Therefore in the eyes of the Serbian authorities if you enter Kosovo directly via Macedonia or Albania or Prishtina Airport, then you have entered illegally. This means that you cannot then later cross into Serbia from the north of Kosovo or even from Montenegro as the border guards will note that you do not have a valid Serbian entry stamp in your passport. The guards will usually send you back to Kosovo. If therefore you wish to enter Serbia, you must go out into Macedonia or Montenegro and enter Serbia.

If you flew into Belgrade or entered via a 'legitimate' Serbian border, eg: the Hungarian or Croatian borders, then you are OK in the eyes of Serbia, so long as you do not then cancel out your entry stamp by going out through either Macedonia, Montenegro or Albania.

This political problem has given rise to what the internationals term 'a stamp run'. A stamp run is a trip that you do specifically to get a Serbian entry stamp. It usually involves going to Skopje and then on to Kumanovo, into Serbia and back into Kosovo via Bujanova in Serbia and across the border into Gjilan. This round trip takes about four–six hours in total, depending on traffic and the time of year. This means you then have the necessary stamp to later go across the border in the north.

The Serbian stamp lasts 90 days in most passports, unless you cancel it out by going over the Macedonian border or by receiving a stamp at Prishtina Airport (which can sometimes be avoided on request). The Serbian authorities will also write the word 'cancel' over any Republic of Kosovo stamps in your passport. The benefits of having two passports can be seen at this point and many passport authorities will issue a second one if you work in the region.

CUSTOMS (038 540 350; http://www.dogana-ks.org) You are allowed to bring into Kosovo your personal effects, plus up to €175 gifts, 200 cigarettes or 250g tobacco and one litre of alcohol or two bottles of wine and 60cc/ml of perfume or 250cc/ml toilet water. Above this you should pay customs duties. (See also *Getting your belongings to Kosovo*, page 80.)

EMBASSIES AND LIAISON OFFICES Many countries which have recognised Kosovo now have embassies in Prishtina and many also issue visas (eg: Swiss, German, Greek, UK, French, Bulgarian). Otherwise you might need to go to Skopje, Belgrade or even Zagreb for a visa. Liaison offices may not carry out all the functions of an embassy. The liaison offices will, however, usually help if you have lost your passport or money.

Albania Rr Mujo Ulqinaku 18, Prishtina; 038 248 368/9/517 831; e embassy.prishtina@mfa.gov.al, mission.kosova@mfa.gov.al

Austria Rr Ahmet Krasniqi 22, Prishtina; 038 249 284; e prishtina-ob@bmeia.gv.at

Belgium Rr Kuvendi i Bujanit (Taslixhe I) 23a, Prishtina; 038 517 698; m 043 734 734; e pristina.ob@bmeiva.gov.at; www.diplomatie.be

Bulgaria Rr Ismail Qemali 12, Prishtina; 038 245 540; e office@diplobel.fed.be

Canada Str Kneza Milosa 75, 11040 Belgrade, Serbia; +381 11 306 3000

China Tresnjim Cvet 3, Belgrade, Serbia; +381 11 22 1525; m +381 63 716 2473

Croatia Rr Mujo Ulqinaku 47, Peyton; 038 223 978; e croemb.pristina@mvpei.hr

Czech Republic Rr Ismail Qemali 31, Arbëria; 038 246 676; e pristine@embassy.mzv.cz

European Commission Rr Kosova 1, Prishtina; 038 513 1200;

Finland Rr Eduard Lir 50, Prishtina; 038 243 098; e office@fin-kos.org

France Rr Ismail Qemali 67, Arbëria, Prishtina; 038 2245 8800; e admin-etrangers.pristina-amba@diploma-tie.gov.fr

Germany Rr Adem Jashanica 17, Arbëria II, Prishtina; 038 254 500/514; e info@pristina.diplo.de

Greece Rr Ismail Qemali 68, Arbëria II, Prishtina; 038 243 013; m 044 505 051; e grpristina@mfa.gr

Hungary Rr 24 Maji 23, Arbëria, Prishtina; 038 247 763;

India Str Ljutice Bogdana 8, 11040 Belgrade, Serbia; +381 11 266 4127; e indemb@eunet.rs

Italy Rr Adem Jashanica 5, Prishtina; 038 244 925; e segreteria.pristina@esteri.it

Japan Rr Rexhep Mala 43; 038 249 995; e jplopr@yahoo.com

Luxembourg Rr Metush Krasniqi 14, Arbëria, Prishtina; 038 226 787; e lux_kosovo@ipko.net

FYR Macedonia Rr 24 Maji 121, Arbëria, Prishtina; 038 247 462

Malaysia Partizani 12, Prishtina; 038 243 467/8; e mwprishtina@mwprishtina.org

Netherlands Rr Xemajl Berisha 12, Velania, Prishtina;
✆ 038 224 610; ✆ 038 516 101;
e pri@minbuza.nl
Norway Rr Sejdu Kryeziu 6, Peyton, Prishtina; ✆ 038
248 010; e emb.prishtina@mfa.no; www.norway-kosovo.no
Romania Rr Adem Jashanica 25, Arbëria II, Prishtina;
✆ 038 246 272; e rooffice.kos@gmail.com
Russian Federation Rr Eduard Lir 20, Prishtina;
✆ 038 247 112; e ruschanemb@kujtesa.com
Slovakia Rr Ismail Qemali 63, Arbëria, Prishtina;
✆ 038 240 140; e roman_holben@mfa.sk
Slovenia Rr Anton Çetta; ✆ 038 246 255;
e nmpi@gov.si

Sweden Rr Perandori Justinian 19, Peyton Prishtina;
✆ 038 245 795 ext 9;
e swedishoffice.pristina@sida.de
Switzerland Rr Ardian Krasniqi 11, Prishtina;
✆ 038 248 088–90 (for visas);
e vertretung@pri.rep.admin.ch
www.eda.admin.ch/pristina
Turkey Rr Ismail Qemali 59, Prishtina; ✆ 038 548
545/57; e turkemb.prishtina@mfa.tr
UK Rr Ismail Qemali 6; ✆ 038 249 559;
e britishembassy.pristina@fco.gov.uk; www.fco.gov.uk
USA Rr Nazim Hikmet 30, Arbëria, Prishtina;
✆ 038 5959 3000; e PApristina@state.gov;
www.pristina.usmission.gov

GETTING THERE AND AWAY

✈ **BY AIR** **Prishtina International Airport** *(for schedules, departures & arrivals:* ✆ *038 595 8160; flight information:* ✆ *038 595 8301/9159/9160; www.airportpristina.com – also details of flight arrivals online)* This is well served by scheduled flights and handles more than a million passengers each year, primarily diaspora and internationals. British Airways usually has four direct flights a week from London Gatwick. There are almost daily flights to Istanbul on Turkish Airlines; five to seven (depending on the time of year) on Austrian Airlines to Vienna; almost daily flights to Ljubljana with Adria Airways and three or four a week to Tirana with Belle Air. Croatian Airlines operates flights to Zagreb several times a week. There are also daily flights to Montenegro. Adria and Montenegro airlines provide a good connecting route to other destinations such as London or parts of Scandinavia. (See below for contact details for all airlines.)

There are also charter flights to Frankfurt, Hamburg, Cologne, Munich, Zürich, Düsseldorf, Copenhagen and Stockholm, with the largest charters being Kosovo Airlines *(www.kosovairlines.com)*, which operates with LTU International, Hello AG, Air Berlin *(www.airberlin.com)*, Germanwings *(www.germanwings.com)* and also AirPrishtina *(www.airprishtina.com)* which flies to/from Verona, Zürich and sometimes even New York, and which works with Edelweiss Air *(www.edelweissair.ch)* and Air Meridiana *(www.merdiana.it)* to different Italian destinations. Atlasjet *(www.atlasjet.com)* also flies to Turkey

In the summer there are even more charter flights than scheduled flights as companies vie for the diaspora trade. Germany and Switzerland are the most popular destinations. This can be a cheap way to get to Kosovo, although the charters are inevitably less reliable in terms of punctuality. The charters seemingly are not fully computerised with their booking systems (which can lead to overbooking) and there can be an aura of mild chaos when you arrive to check in. Be sure to get your ticket stamped at one of the travel agent bureaux at the German or Swiss airport of departure before you queue up to check in as otherwise you will be sent back. Lost luggage numbers *(lost and found luggage;* ✆ *038 595 8175/9)* can also be found on airport websites under 'airlines'.

Skopje Airport *(www.skp.airports.com.mk)* in Macedonia is two hours' drive from Prishtina and so is a viable alternative and offers some more direct flights to Italy, Hungary or the Czech Republic. **Belgrade Airport** *(www.beg.aero)* is a five-hour easy drive away – mostly by motorway (but be careful of the stamp issue if you fly out – see *Serbian stamp*, page 46). Also there are less convenient bus connections to/from Belgrade than with Skopje. **Tirana Airport** *(www.tirana-*

airport.com) is a similar distance away as Belgrade – about five hours' drive in the summer, traffic permitting. **Podgorica Airport** is really only viable if you also wish to stop off and sightsee as it is more than a seven-hour, winding drive.

If you do intend doing a Balkan round trip from the UK it is worth investigating British Airways' open-jaw tickets which would enable you to go in/out of Belgrade, Tirana, Dubrovnik or Prishtina for reasonable prices. You can then travel overland in between.

Airline contact details

Adria Airways Rr Qamil Hoxha Pristina; ✆ 038 246 746; www.adria.com/ www.adria.si; ⏰ 13.30–16.30 daily

Austrian Airlines ✆ 038 548 435 (airport), 038 242 424/233 814; www.aua.com; ⏰ 05.30–07.00 Mon, Wed & Fri, 11.30–17.00 daily

Belle Air Rr Luan Haradinaj nr 4/1, Prishtina; ✆ 038 225 571/2; e belleair.kosova@flybelleair.com; www.belleair.it. Direct flights to Tirana almost daily to Zürich, Düsseldorf, & then various Italian cities (usually via Tirana). They do have a rather disconcerting occasional tendency to cancel flights at the last minute, however.

British Airways ✆ 038 548 661; www.ba.com; Prishtina Airport desk ⏰ 10.00–18.00 Mon, Wed & Fri, 08.00–18.00 Tue & Thu

Croatian Airlines Alta Via Travel, Rr Luan Haradinaj; ✆ 038 233 833; www.croatiaairlines.com

Montenegro Airlines MCM Travel; ✆ 038 242 424; www.montenegroairlines.com

Turkish Airlines ✆ 038 502 052; www.turkishairlines.com; ⏰ 13.00–14.30 Mon & Wed, 09.30–10.15 Fri & Sun

Please note that Prishtina Airport can sometimes suffer from fog, particularly in February, so be prepared for rerouting, mainly via Skopje or even, in a worst case senario, for cancellation of your inbound or outbound flight. After an unusual two-day fog spell affecting both Belgrade and Prishtina airports in January 2007, President Tadić of Serbia and Prime Minister Çeku of Kosovo both ended up at Skopje Airport, leading to an impromptu diplomatic meeting in the arrivals lounge!

BY CAR You can drive your car into/through Kosovo with no problem and it is very common to see foreign cars in Kosovo.

The Green Card insurance is, however, not valid in Kosovo so that foreign-registered cars (other than those with Albanian or Macedonian plates – countries with whom Kosovo has an agreement and sometimes Serbian plates) must pay €50 at the border for a two-week third-party liability insurance policy. At the time of writing payment was possible in cash only (no credit cards). The insurance policy can be renewed for longer periods at the Association of Kosovar Insurers on Rr Enver Maloku in Bregu i Diellit/Sunny Hill 28 on the left-hand side of the main road beyond Furra Qerimi and S&B Computers (✆ *038 245 115;* e *info@iak-ks.org; www.iak-ks.org*), making payment using the Association form that you can obtain from any local bank. The current price for cars for 15 days' cover is €45; one month's cover €60; two months €100; six months €200; one year €350. The payments are reimbursable in the event of an accident or if you pay the customs fees for your car and buy local insurance. Prices for minibuses are about four times as expensive and for buses six times as expensive.

Note that if you intend to hire a car in Bulgaria, Bosnia & Herzegovina, Croatia or Montenegro, etc, you need to check that the car-hire company will let you take it to Kosovo. Zoran Demovski (who speaks English) runs a reliable taxi service on demand to/from Bulgaria or Macedonia to Kosovo (✆ *+38 970 273 916;* e *zdimac@yahoo.com*). Prices from Skopje Airport to Prishtina are about €70.

WARNING! It is not advisable or safe to drive a car with Serbian number plates, particularly Belgrade plates, around Kosovo generally, even though you may see such plates in Serbian areas. Outside Serbian areas they might possibly be prone to targeting by extremists.

Exceptions are the following Serbian plates which are recognised by Albanians as being from Albanian-populated or Albanian-friendly areas in Serbia: VR −Vranje, NP − Novi Pazar and NS − Novi Sad. Plates from Montenegro are generally safe to drive in Kosovo.

Macedonian, Bulgarian, Croatian, Albanian or Bosnian plates are no problem at all.

BY TRAIN It is now possible to get to Kosovo by train, but this is a slow route and trains are infrequent and less reliable than buses. The trains do not currently cross directly/connect from Raška in the north, ie: from Belgrade, although this may change. For now you have to catch a taxi/bus. In summary, it may be much quicker to get a *bus* directly from Serbia!

The trains do, however, connect into the south of Kosovo from Skopje. There are sleeper trains to/from Athens, Thessaloniki and Skopje. At the time of writing the Skopje–Prishtina train departs from Skopje at 15.35 and arrives in Prishtina at 18.25, and the Prishtina–Skopje train departs at 07.22 and arrives at 09.55. This may well change, however, so check the website or call Kosovo Railways (see below). While considerably slower than the bus, the route from Skopje to Kaçanik runs through a gorge along the river, is incredibly scenic and so worth the journey if you have plenty of time. It is also possible to use another slightly faster train route through Serbia and get off the train in Serbia at Bujanovac and catch a bus into Gjilan in Kosovo.

For information on train travel from Western Europe, eg: London to Serbia or Macedonia, see www.seat61.com/Serbia.htm; for Serbian train times see www.zeleznicesrbije.com.rs or contact e putnik.info@srbrail.rs. Unfortunately the Macedonian site (*www.mz.com.mk*) is now only in Cyrillic and there is no published timetable. For tickets internationally see www.europeanrail.com.

Ticket prices within Kosovo are zone-based and never more than €3. For an up-to-date train schedule, see the Kosovo Railways website (*www.kosovorailway.com*) or call ☏ 038 536 619 or 038 536 355.

BY BUS This is the cheapest way of getting to Kosovo and there are a lot of international buses from as far afield as Sweden, and in particular, plenty from Germany. The number goes up in the summer.

To/from Skopje 05.30 until 17.00 (approximately every hour). Various companies.

To/from Belgrade Bus company **Dura** (☏ *038 6364 544;* m *+049 379 794;* ☺ *09.00–17.00*) runs minibuses between Gračanica and Belgrade via Kraguevac (Serbia), departing near Dolce Vita Restaurant at 04.30 and 15.00 every day, and 13.00 on Friday only. The return journey departs from Belgrade at 06.00, arriving in Gračanica at 11.30, and there is a second bus leaving Belgrade at 11.00 arriving at 16.00. The fare is about €10 one way and slightly less for a return.

Adio Tours (☏ *038 226 643;* m *044 344 200/238 783; Gračanica numbers* ☏ *038 65 538;* m *+381 63 4855 3308; Belgrade numbers* ☏ *+381 11 328 8707;* m *+381 64 855 3315/38 63 877 8032; bus drivers' numbers* m *+381 64 855 3305/6*) runs buses from Dragash to Belgrade via Mitrovica. They leave Prishtina at 05.00, 11.00 and 23.00. They leave Dragash three hours earlier, Prizren two hours earlier, and Gračanica one hour before the Prishtina times, and depart

Mitrovica one hour after departing from Prishtina. The return times of Adio Tours from Belgrade are 12.00, 14.00 and 21.30. The one-way fare is €18, €25 return.

Another bus company runs buses at 12.00 and 22.00 from Belgrade.

Sarajevo via Novi Pazar A direct bus from Sarajevo via Novi Pazar (Serbia) leaves at Sarajevo 18.00 every day.

Tirana–Prishtina Leaving Tirana at 16.30, 17.00 and 18.30 every day.

Preshevo Leaving Prishtina at 11.45, 14.05, 15.45 and 17.05 every day.

Bujanovc Leaving Prishtina at 11.05 and 15.50 every day.

Switzerland Leaving Prishtina at 07.00 and 08.00 on Saturday and Wednesday only.

Sweden Leaving Prishtina every two weeks at 09.30 on Saturday.

Italy Leaving Prishtina at 05.30 and 07.00 on Saturday.

BY BICYCLE It is possible to cycle around Kosovo but the main roads are not ideal due to a combination of drivers unused to cyclists and pot-holes. Kosovo is, however, ideal for mountain biking on the side roads, or off-road. (For details of the Tour de Kosovo, see *Tour operators*, page 45.)

HEALTH *with Dr Felicity Nicholson*

At the time of writing, health insurance was not compulsory in Kosovo (there were various parliamentary proposals being discussed), although having such insurance is a good idea. Kosovo runs a health service subsidised by the general budget. This means that you do not pay for the medical staff themselves in the centres. You will, however, be expected to pay for X-rays, tests, bandages or medicines. Generally speaking these are not expensive. Receipts are issued on request. If you have to use the hospital beds, then you need to bring your own sheets, toilet paper, soap and food. Prishtina University Hospital is poorly resourced: there is, for example, no hot water on many wards for patients to take showers.

Most UK travel insurance policies will now cover Kosovo as it is no longer on the list of places prohibited by the UK Foreign Office, but do check the small print. Note that policies invariably exclude demonstrations and violence. Foreign clinics like Euromed and Rezonanca (see page 121) are used to working with insurance companies.

PHARMACIES AND HEALTH CARE PROVIDERS There are lots of pharmacies around Kosovo who will sell not just Kosovar, Yugoslav and Macedonian medicines but also Greek and sometimes UK or US brands. As there are no prescription requirements for medicines it is possible to get antibiotics and even stronger medicines over the counter. This means that in practice self-diagnosis or over-the-phone diagnosis with your doctor back home can be an option to fall back on, particularly if you lose confidence in the local diagnosis. One option is to do some of your own internet research using medical websites such as www.nhsdirect.co.uk, www.healthline.com or www.fda.gov. Of course, this all has its own risks and drawbacks, including the risk of wrong diagnosis.

Contraceptives are widely available in Kosovo over the counter at the pharmacies, although you may struggle matching your own brand to those sold. The morning-after pill is also available at larger pharmacies. Tampons are generally not sold in supermarkets and shops, but most pharmacies keep a stock of international brand non-applicator tampons.

The hospitals around Kosovo, including Gjilan, Prishtina and Peja, have an emergency centre which is your venue for out of hours' injuries. For routine items you should go to the local health centre. Like all national health services you may need to be prepared to wait and remember this is Kosovo so do not expect high standards. There is very limited English or German spoken at hospitals or medical centres, so try and bring an interpreter with you.

There are KFOR health centres (the best are US Bondsteel and German KFOR in Prizren) but you should not rely on these as options as access is highly restricted.

There are now several private clinics and for details of private health care see *Chapter 3*, page 121. Most hospital doctors operate a private clinic with higher standards of service. Prices are not unduly prohibitive.

DENTISTS There are many good dentists in Kosovo who have trained abroad. Prices are very reasonable, although tourism for dental surgery has not yet picked up! See page 119 for a couple of recommendations.

ILLNESSES/VACCINATIONS Tap water in Kosovo is chlorinated and generally safe to drink, although if you are a first-time visitor you would be wise to only use it for boiling and to avail yourself of the ample supplies of bottled water (Peja, Rugove, Bonita, Dea and Klokot all being local brands).

Many visitors to Kosovo might suffer a mild stomach upset from time to time. Care needs to be taken if there are substantial power cuts in hot weather as restaurants and wholesalers might not take the step of throwing away the thawed frozen meat.

Hepatitis B International medical assessments have determined that hepatitis B is endemic in Kosovo. Hepatitis B is a liver infection which can lead to scarring and ultimately failure of the liver. It can only be passed on by exchange of bodily fluids; however, many people carry the disease without showing symptoms and it is 100 times more infectious than HIV – only small quantities of a wider range of bodily fluids are needed to transmit the virus. Realistically the main risks are through unprotected sex and through exposure to contaminated needles or through blood-to-blood contact. Given the fact that you never know when you might end up in a local hospital, eg: following a car accident, or where you might inadvertently come into contact with the disease, given its consequences, you would be wise to be vaccinated against the disease especially if you are working in a health care setting, with children or if spending four weeks or more in Kosovo. The vaccine comprises a course of three injections and ideally this should be given over a six-month period. However, the minimum time allowed (Engerix only) is over 21 days and other brands can be given over two months. It is wise therefore to visit your doctor or travel clinic in plenty of time before you travel. Some of the private clinics in Kosovo carry the vaccine.

Tetanus It is recommended that your tetanus vaccine is up to date. This is now given as an all-in-one vaccine containing tetanus, diphtheria and polio (Revaxis) and lasts for ten years.

Hepatitis A Vaccination against hepatitis A is also recommended (this is less prevalent in Kosovo but is transmitted through food). The first dose gives protection for a year and can be boosted from any time after six months up to around eight years to give 25 years' cover.

Rabies Rabies is carried by all mammals and is passed on to man through a bite, scratch or a lick of an open wound. It is present throughout the country. However, the chance of exposure is usually small for those who can avoid contact with carnivorous animals, especially dogs. You must always assume any animal is rabid, and seek medical help as soon as possible. Meanwhile scrub the wound with soap under a running tap or while pouring water from a jug. Then pour on a strong iodine or alcohol solution of gin, whisky or rum. This helps stop the rabies virus entering the body and will guard against wound infections, including tetanus.

Pre-exposure vaccination for rabies is ideally advised for anyone who is likely to come into contact with animals and/or is likely to be more than 24 hours away from medical help. Three doses should be taken over a minimum of 21 days, and contrary to popular belief these vaccinations are relatively painless.

If you are bitten, scratched or licked over an open wound by a sick animal, then post-exposure prophylaxis should be given as soon as possible, though it is never too late to seek help, as the incubation period for rabies can be very long. Those who have not been immunised will need a course of five injections and rabies immunoglobulin (RIG) which is a human blood product, hard to come by and very expensive. Another good reason to have the vaccine before you travel as you will then not need this product and only two doses of vaccine given three days apart. And remember that, if you do contract rabies, mortality is 100% and death from rabies is probably one of the worst ways to go.

Tick-borne encephalitis Travellers planning to visit the more rural parts of Kosovo from late spring to autumn should take ample supplies of insect repellent, and are advised to take precautions against tick-borne encephalitis. It is prevalent in central Kosovo (around the Berisha, Gllogovc, Malisheva and Suha Reka areas). As the name suggests, this disease is spread by the bites of ticks that live in long grass and the branches of overhanging trees. Wearing hats, long trousers tucked into boots, and applying tick repellents can all help. It is important to check for ticks each time you have been for a long walk, remembering not to forget the head, especially for children. The ticks are most usually found behind the ears. Checking for ticks is more easily done by someone else. If you find a tick then slowly remove it by using special tick tweezers that can be bought in good travel shops. Failing that you can use your fingernails by grasping the tick as close to your body as possible and pulling steadily and firmly away at right angles to your skin. The tick will then come away complete as long as you do not jerk or twist it. If possible, douse the wound with alcohol (any spirit will do) or iodine. Irritants (eg: Olbas oil) or lit cigarettes are to be discouraged since they can cause the ticks to regurgitate and therefore increase the risk of disease. If in doubt and you think you may leave the head of the tick stuck in then get yourself to a local hospital or a health clinic where they are well practised in speedy and effective tick removal.

Pre-exposure vaccine against tick-borne encephalitis is available in the UK (Ticovac) and two doses given ideally at day 0 then between 1–3 months will give good protection and a further vaccination after 6 months will extend coverage to 3 years. If time is short then the second dose can be taken at 2 weeks with good results. It is also available in a paediatric form for those aged 1–15 using the same time schedule . However, taking the preventative measures as described above is also very important. Go as soon as possible to a doctor if you have been bitten by a tick (whether or not you have been vaccinated) as tick immunoglobulin may be needed for treatment. This is available in Kosovo hospitals (in particular at the Prishtina Emergency Unit) but would be given only if you develop signs of the disease and not for every tick bite.

OTHER MORE COMMON HAZARDS In Kosovo, smoking is a national habit. There are no clear statistics but it seems like more than 80% of the adult population smokes. Children under 18 will commonly peddle cigarettes and phonecards. There are almost no non-smoking areas in bars or restaurants. Smoking in work meetings is still common and until recently people even smoked in the hospitals. The only place where a no-smoking ban really seems to be enforced is on buses. Under donor pressure, in early 2007 Kosovo adopted a tobacco law which requires warnings on packets and restricts advertising and direct sales and a new 2010 law will require ventilation and no-smoking areas in bars. As with similar laws in Montenegro and Serbia, there is little real enforcement. Many Kosovars in Prishtina excuse their habit with a reference to the polluted air in the capital city. This is indeed another hazard, although just how much damage is done by car fumes and KEK (the power company) no-one really knows.

Traditionally Kosovars have squat toilets, like those in Turkey, and you may still find these in many places. Typically toilet paper is not used in the countryside, so carry your own.

Owing to power shortages (which affect the water companies' ability to operate their pumps) and water repairs, it is very common for the water to be turned off for parts of the day or night, particularly outside of Prishtina. Therefore be prepared for this by having bottles filled with water to hand which can be used for impromptu standing showers or just for washing your hands. When out and about, avoid feeling a fool – check the water is running before you put soap on your hands. In any event carry wet wipes with you, particularly in the summer. Handy packs of wet wipes can be found in most mini-markets.

TRAVEL CLINICS AND HEALTH INFORMATION A full list of current travel clinic websites worldwide is available from the International Society of Travel Medicine on www.istm.org. For other journey preparation information, consult www.tripprep.com. Information about various medications may be found on www.emedicine.com.

SAFETY

Kosovo is very safe for internationals. While it always pays to take care of your belongings, street crime and petty theft in Kosovo are low and violent crime rates are much lower than in many Western cities. Most internationals, especially women, not only *are* very safe but also *feel* very safe in Kosovo. Homes of internationals are of course a target for burglars and it is possible to buy burglar alarms and metal doors/grilles. You may also want to bring a cheap smoke alarm with you (in particular if you live in a communal block).

Kosovo is still a former conflict zone and demonstrations or violence occur sporadically. Usually such events can be foreseen and you should always avoid an area where a demonstration is announced (often there will be posters ahead of the event) or where a large crowd is gathering. Gun ownership in Kosovo is still quite high so again it is strongly advised to keep away from any scuffle or argument. For the same reason be aware that it is still the Balkan culture to shoot into the air by way of celebration, including at weddings and on New Year's Eve. There is also no control on the sale of fireworks and before New Year and Independence Day on 17 February Kosovo's streets are flooded with stalls with cheap fireworks which would more than likely be banned or restricted elsewhere in Europe. These are all let off without any control or consideration. For this reason, it is best to take extreme care or, of course, you can safely watch the gunfire and fireworks from indoors or from a balcony.

While Kosovars may like to talk politics, there is a time and place for everything and it may not always be sensible to voice your views loudly in a heated situation.

If riots or unrest do develop in Kosovo, then it is possible that the mobile-phone networks will be shut down, as they were previously used in the March 2004 riots by the rioters to co-ordinate their activities. Shops will also close to avoid looting. It is worth bearing this in mind to ensure that you have enough food and an alternative means of contact or messages, eg: access to a landline or the internet.

All in all these risks are statistically incredibly rare and overall more internationals are injured from car accidents or potholes. Many manhole covers are stolen for scrap metal and therefore open drains are a common hazard and are easily missed in daylight hours, let alone on a dark night. The story of the international who fell down a hole is all too common.

LAND MINES AND UNEXPLODED ORDNANCE (UXO) Another hazard to bear in mind if out walking or biking is land mines or cluster-bomb remnants. Cluster-bomb remnants are found usually on the tops of hills or near former Yugoslav army buildings, eg: in Germia Park. Damaged trees are a tell-tale sign of the bomb. The main problem with cluster bombs is that they are extremely hard to clear as the bomb shatters into small fragments. They are usually yellow and may resemble a drinks can or part of it, but many still detonate below soil.

Land mines are usually even better disguised, often being camouflage colours, and they may also shift with the soil movements during heavy rains or snow melt. Most land mine areas are now well known and there will usually be signs. These can be anything from a formal sign (as in Germia) to a string or fencing, red paint or more rarely even simply a row of carefully placed rocks.

In any area that is known for mines it is not a good idea to deviate from well-worn tracks. Areas known to have been mined in the past include Shtime, central Kosovo (including Berisha, Gllogovc and the Skenderaj area), the borders with Albania, Montenegro and the Sharr Mountains on the Macedonian border, and even Germia Park in the north of Prishtina. Some minefields are still not cleared, especially in the border areas. If you wish to walk in the meadows, choose a safer area. The local adults will generally know if the area is mined so if in doubt ask them (or to be totally safe ask more than one person) about a path or an area. All roads (even non-asphalted ones) are cleared.

If an area cannot be entered owing to high fencing, this is usually for an extremely good reason, eg: because the area is too difficult to clear of unexploded ordnance. Do not attempt to go near such areas. This applies also to ruined buildings. One side or other in the conflict may have deliberately placed unexploded ordnance or mines in the buildings to deter returnees. You should never go into a ruined building for this reason as many of them will not have been cleared or even if they have, they might have been re-mined as an act of vengeance. Take your photos of war-damaged buildings from a distance.

If you believe you've spotted a mine, stand still. If you absolutely need to move, then retrace your steps carefully as you may have already walked through a mined area. Call either the Kosovo Police Service (KPS) or KFOR for help (see below) or if you do not have those numbers with you, contact someone who can call them or the Kosovo Protection Force. Make it clear on the phone where you are and that you believe you have spotted a mine and it should be treated with the utmost priority. Land mine sightings are now so rare that it is likely help will be scrambled within minutes, possibly using a helicopter to sight you.

If you plan to do a lot of off-the-beaten-track exploration you can contact KFOR to obtain the mine map and more detailed information about each specific region. They will be very happy to help.

OTHER POTENTIAL HAZARDS **Stray dogs** can also be a problem in Kosovo. KFOR and the Kosovo Police Service do try and round them up regularly but they still gather in groups in many areas, and are more aggressive in winter when food is scarce.

Kosovo is in an **earthquake zone**, but earthquakes are rare. In 2002 there was a small earthquake in Gjilan which resulted in several buildings being destroyed and while there was another in March 2010, it resulted in no substantial damage.

KOSOVO POLICE (KP) The KP is generally regarded as one of the success stories of the new state. They are not perceived to be very corrupt and are generally helpful and friendly. Having said this, from a Western perspective you may find any visit to the police confusing and rather bureaucratic with many pieces of paperwork with puzzling purposes, and it may be best to take or arrange for your own interpreter if your visit is planned. If you come into contact with the police, as with anywhere the key is to show respect and co-operation and this will get you a long way.

USEFUL TELEPHONE NUMBERS

KFOR ↘ 038 503 603 2939 (HQ Deputy Commander), 038 503 603 2849; www.nato.int/kfor
Police ↘ 92 (landline), 112 (mobile – from Vala); Central Police Station ↘ 038 542 092

Fire brigade ↘ 93, 038 548 005/515 944
First aid ↘ 94
PTK directory enquires ↘ 988

GAY AND LESBIAN TRAVELLERS Although changing slowly, Kosovo remains a conservative society and homosexuality/lesbianism is not openly discussed or demonstrated and is still regarded as taboo. This is not to say that there are not clubs or meeting places and there is a definite underground scene, particularly in Prishtina, Peja and Gjakova. More than anything you should be aware that while it may be fine for internationals to 'come out', this is not yet a feasible option for many Kosovars where the family pressure is strong. Exposing the clubs or bars just now may harm them rather than help them.

Like parts of the Middle East and Turkey, you may see men walking arm in arm. This is a sign of friendship rather than homosexuality so be careful of the consequences of misinterpreting it. (See also *Cultural etiquette*, page 73.)

CHILDREN IN KOSOVO Kosovars simply adore children and the streets are full of them playing on their own outdoors. Taking your child to a restaurant is not taboo. There are several international kindergartens and an English- or German-speaking dedicated nanny working from 09.00 to 17.00 only costs around €300 a month. You will almost never have to worry about finding a babysitter as your landlord or colleague will magic one up from somewhere.

There are now plenty of shops selling nappies and good baby-food brands (including baby milk), buggies, car seats and other baby gadgets. We have included some details of shops in *Chapter 3*, page 112.

WHAT TO TAKE

With power cuts common in Kosovo and sporadic street and hallway lighting even when the power is on, in order to see the frescoes well in the monasteries or churches, a good **torch/flashlight** is essential. A headtorch can also be useful as this leaves your hands free to struggle with the keys or similar. Torches can be bought in Kosovo but they tend to be heavier than the modern travel types found in Western Europe.

While the Kosovar women have perfected the art of walking even on the muddiest and iciest roads in high heels and emerging immaculate at their destination, rather like learning Albanian this is not a skill that an international visitor can easily master. Instead you will quickly find the backs of your trousers gain a new look – the Kosovo mud-splatter. Therefore a good pair of **shoes**, preferably with non-slip soles, is essential, as are machine-washable trousers when the weather is wet or it is muddy or slushy underfoot. In winter thermals, gloves, woolly hat and fleeces are recommended. In severe weather internationals will dress down even in the office. In summer consider a sunhat if planning on hiking or sightseeing.

In the summer mosquitoes are common; their arrival and departure is unpredictable but painful. **Mosquito repellent** is still not common in Kosovo, so it is definitely preferable to bring your own supplies. It is possible to buy plug-in anti-mosquito devices and their refills in the bigger supermarkets.

You should also bring three- to two-pin **plug adapters** if you do not live in a European two-pin plug country.

Contact lenses and **contact lens solution** are hard to buy in Kosovo, as are applicator tampons, so bring your own. Non-applicator **tampons** can be found in pharmacies. The choice of **suncreams** in Kosovo is more limited and pricey, so bring your own. Also, bring your own blister plasters or antiseptic cream.

The choice of **sportswear and hiking gear** in Kosovo is limited and expensive so it's best to bring your own whether it is skiing, biking, football footwear or equipment or fishing tackle.

If you intend **biking** you should bring a complete set of spares as almost none of any value are available in Kosovo. You also cannot hire or buy good mountain bikes.

$ MONEY

Kosovo's currency is the euro, although in some Serbian areas you can alternatively use the Serbian dinar.

The banking sector in Kosovo is well developed and user-friendly, with English-speaking staff and all but the smallest towns having plenty of cash machines where international cards such as Visa, Maestro, Electron and MasterCard can be used. It is also possible to get international transfers arranged from your home bank account to the bank in Kosovo, although this costs a bit more than a transfer within the EU. Raiffeisen and ProCredit Bank in Prishtina and possibly other branches accept international travellers' cheques. Using a bank card is definitely cheaper. Bank opening hours are generally 09.00 to 16.30 Monday to Friday and 08.00 to 14.00 Saturday, with the exception of all Prishtina and main city branches which open until 17.00 or 18.00 weekdays. If you want to be sure, the opening hours are listed on each bank's website.

If you are in Kosovo for several months it will be cheaper to open a bank account than use a foreign card, and this will enable you to obtain a debit card, and potentially a credit card, and run e-banking. You will require some ID to do so and some form of contract or explanation, but otherwise it should take only ten minutes. Raiffeisen, TEB and ProCredit are used to international residents opening accounts and the forms are available in English. There are also many branches of Western Union.

Kosovo society is, however, still very much cash-based and therefore you should expect to pay in cash for your restaurant meals and for smaller hotels outside Prishtina. The larger out-of-town supermarkets do take cards, as do Prishtina's hotels.

The Central Bank of Kosovo (*www.cbak-kos.org*) regulates the banks, insurance and pension companies and takes its duty seriously. In 2006 it put a locally owned bank (one of the five main banks) into liquidation for irregular lending practices.

BUDGETING It is possible to 'do Kosovo' on a low budget of under €35 a day total if you travel by bus (maximum €5 per day), carefully choose the cheaper hotels/guesthouses (€15–20 per day) and eat in the cheaper *qebaptore* (kebab shops) (€2) or local restaurants, etc (€8–15 per day).

If, however, you want to make the most of the country and travel by car to get to the more outlying areas, given the petrol and insurance costs involved in bringing your own car to Kosovo, you need to consider car hire (€35–60 per day) and petrol, better hotels (€25–50 per day), bars and restaurants (€20–25 per day). If you travel in a group of say four then this reduces prices for the car and hotel accommodation significantly.

Coffee in a Prishtina bar is €1, outside of Prishtina about €0.50. Beers are €1.30 to €1.70 in Prishtina bars and €1.00 outside. Bread is €0.35, a litre pack of imported Tetra long-life milk is €0.85 and bottled water (1.5l) €0.50. Five *qebap* sausages/meatballs are €1.20 in Prishtina and less outside. Mini pizzas are €1.50 in Pristina. Imported food items are just slightly above western European prices with some Turkish biscuits and snacks being cheaper.

GETTING AROUND

BY CAR AND RENTAL CAR If you do not have your own car, it is possible to rent one in Kosovo. There are several international franchises and also some independent chains. Prices are now dropping, making the exercise more reasonable (they are now from €20 per day for a small car to €75 for a 4×4). For more details see *Chapter 3*, page 91.

Driving around Kosovo is like driving around much of the Balkans. Be prepared for anything and in particular for reversing the wrong way up a street and for some aggressive overtaking. Although there is a general relaxed pace to life in Kosovo, the same cannot be said of the driving. What are the drivers rushing for – another *macchiato*? Roads in Kosovo are of mixed quality. Be prepared for potholes even on the main roads. They come as a standard feature on the side roads. In an effort to humorously highlight the problem, *Koha Ditore*, a local newspaper, ran a competition in 2006 for the biggest pothole in Prishtina that it would name after the city's mayor. There were dozens of entries but the winner was a hole which was more than 50cm deep and several metres long.

As yet there are no toll roads in Kosovo. In 2010, work will start on a much-desired toll road from the Serbian border at Merdare to Prizren via Prishtina to join up with the highway from the border to Durrës in Albania. The Albanian side is already nearly complete and has cut down what was once a ten-hour Prizren–Durrës journey to a much more bearable three to four hours.

One rule you need to be aware of when driving in Kosovo is that if you have an accident it is an offence to move the cars (even if they are in the way and likely to cause another accident!) until after the police have come. All accidents must be reported to the police, which can be a time-consuming procedure with much paperwork. It is usual to have a civil fine in court for causing an accident. The court cases tend to come up quickly, within a few days. If you have to leave the country you may be able to find a local lawyer to represent you. For information on local lawyers see www.oda-ks.org.

There is also a law requiring you to keep your lights on during the day (as in Montenegro and Macedonia). Furthermore, you are required to carry snow chains in the winter and a warning triangle, a yellow jacket and tow rope.

BY TAXI Given the high cost of renting a car, getting around by taxi can be a viable option. Trips within towns typically cost €2–3. For longer trips you can choose either to do the journey on the meter or negotiate a price; the latter is preferable if you wish to stop to take photos. The following are guideline prices at the time of writing. Expect to pay more if you are making a longer day of it.

Prishtina to Blace border €40	**Prishtina to Prizren return** €60
Prishtina to Skopje Airport €70	**Prishtina to Gračanica return** €10–15
Prishtina to Mitrovica €25–30	**Prishtina to Peja, Brezovica, Deçan or**
Prishtina to Gadimë return €40	**Gjakova return** €50–70

BY BUS Buses in Kosovo are frequent, quite fast, reliable and reasonably priced and they cover most of the country. The only time you will struggle with connections is between Kosovo Serb and Kosovo Albanian areas, eg: buses to Štrpce are not frequent. The buses are heavily used by Kosovars and are a very feasible way of getting around. The drivers are welcoming and patient with foreigners. Even though they themselves may know little English (try German), they will find someone who does, such as another passenger. Sign language, pointing at maps and writing times and places on paper may also help. They will even allow you to put your bicycle in the bottom of the bus for no extra charge. Beware, however, that the buses still run to Yugoslav working day timetables, which means that they start early and the last bus may depart early, even as early as 16.00 or 17.00. Furthermore, there are far fewer buses (usually about half) on Sundays. Generally the bus will also stop on request if your destination is halfway along the route, eg: Mirusha or the Gadimë Cave turn-off. If you are flagging down the bus, make sure the driver will be able to see you and that he will have time to stop. Buses are one of the few places in Kosovo where they do respect the rule on no smoking (often with the exception of the driver!). See the bus timetable below for information on the major routes. For other routes, see the relevant chapters in Part Two of this guide.

Bus timetable No bus trips within Kosovo are more than €5 – most trips are around €2 or €3. Times shown on page 60 are the times the buses depart from the shown town. Arrival times are not shown. Some buses may not terminate at the destination, eg: some buses from Peja to Gjakova may go on to Prizren. Journey times are very approximate and will depend on time of year and traffic or road conditions.

BY TRAIN The use of trains within Kosovo is only really a viable option if you wish to go a reasonable distance, eg: Prishtina to Peja, and/or you are lucky enough that the time suits you. Otherwise, even if/when the north–south line restarts (it is currently suspended), trains are generally slow and infrequent.

Ticket prices within Kosovo are zone-based and never more than €2.50 – usually more like €0.50. For details of the timetable see www.kosovarailway.com or ❧ 038 536 619 355; e info@kosovorailway.com. Trains are, nevertheless, warm and comfortable, if not deluxe.

The Prizren line is not likely to be renovated for years to come as it needs so much work. Plans to expand into Albania are just dreams for now.

MAPS Kosovo generally appears only at the bottom of maps of Serbia. Better maps of Serbia include the *Reise Know How Verlag Map* (scale 1:400,000) or the Freytag and Berndt map. They are all around €13. Try Stanfords (*www.stanfords.co.uk*) or their store in London's Covent Garden for purchases. The best map of all is the *Gizi Map* dedicated to Kosovo (scale 1:250,000; ISBN-10: 978 9630039206 and ISBN-13: 978 9630039208), but this is incredibly hard to track down. The United Nations Standards Co-ordinating Committee (UNSCC) in Kosovo produced its

KOSOVO MAIN BUS STATIONS TIMETABLE

	To Prishtina	To Prizren	To Peja	To Mitrovica	To Gjakova	To Gjilan	Ferizaj
From Prishtina ☎ 038 550 011 and 038 541 517	N/A	Every 25mins 06.50–19.45 Duration 2h	Every 20mins 07.00–20.40 (€4) Duration 1½–2hrs	Every 15mins 06.30–20.30 Duration: 45mins	Every 30mins 08.00–21.00 Duration 1hr 45mins	Every 20mins 06.30–20.20 Duration 45mins–1hr	Every 15mins 07.45–17.45 Duration 45 mins–1hr
From Prizren	Every 15mins (30mins Sun) 05.45–18.00 (06.15–18.00 Sun) (€4)	N/A	06.45, 09.00, 09.40, 10.40, 11.40, 17.45	17.00 (€4)	Every 30mins 06.00–16.00 Duration 1hr (€4)	13.15 (€5)	05.30, 09.00, 13.15
From Peja ☎ 039 432 573	Every 20mins 06.40–18.20 (€4) Duration 1½–2hr	08.45, 09.45, 10.30, 13.15, 13.30, 14.45, 17.05 (€5) Duration 2hr	N/A	08.15, 09.25, 10.00, 11.15, 12.25, 13.30, 16.30, 18.25 Duration 45min–1hr	Every 15mins 06.45–18.25	N/A	N/A
From Mitrovica ☎ 044 722 713	Every 15mins 05.45–19.15 (€1.20)	Every 15mins 06.00–19.00 (€2)	Every 15mins 06.15–19.00	N/A	N/A	N/A	N/A
From Gjakova ☎ 039 020 803	Every 30mins 06.00–18.00 (€3.50)	08.00 only	N/A	N/A	N/A	N/A	N/A
From Gjilan	Every 20mins 05.00–19.35 (€1.50)	N/A	N/A	N/A	N/A	N/A	Every 20mins 06.00–20.40 Duration 45mins
From Ferizaj	Every 15mins 06.30–20.00 (€2)	11.10, 13.00, 17.30 (€3)	N/A	N/A	N/A	Every 20 mins 07.00–19.30 (€2)	N/A

Note: times/prices subject to change. Reduced services and later starts on Sunday.

own maps which, while not brilliant, are quite workable and the best available in terms of scale unless you can get hold of the KFOR maps. KFOR has some good 1:50,000-scale maps of Kosovo which seem to be based on old Yugoslav army maps. They are €9 for a sheet which broadly covers two municipalities. These are ideal for planning biking and walking routes. To buy them you need a KFOR entrance card for Film City and so unless you know someone who has a KFOR ID card, buying them may be out of the question.

See also the University of Texas maps online for Kosovo and Yugoslavia (*www.lib.utexas.edu/maps*).

You can also pick up basic road and wall maps of Kosovo and of Prishtina city centre from the stalls outside the Grand Hotel in Prishtina and in Prishtina's bookshops (see page 111).

ACCOMMODATION

Kosovo has plenty of accommodation in terms of hotel and motel beds. Hotels in the cities are, however, surprisingly expensive, being geared towards the development set and consultants. There are almost no formal budget-range hostels or bed and breakfasts. However, asking around is probably a good idea as with word of mouth you are likely to find an informal arrangement.

There are many motels just outside the cities on the main roads which we have tended not to list in this guide. Rumours abound as to the purpose of these establishments. Furthermore, renting of rooms by the hour or for the day for the conduct of affairs or paid-for arrangements is not uncommon. As a guest you may actually remain oblivious to any such goings-on, although you may have some qualms about supporting institutions involved in trafficking or prostitution. Having said all this, it seems that most motels are probably just trying to tap into the lorry and diaspora trade and in reality a greater risk in winter is that the motels are of a poor build and badly insulated, and either without heating or reluctant to turn it on, so the room may be quite cold.

Camping is not so popular in Kosovo. The only sites are in the Rugova Valley, Brod in Dragash and Prevalac (see the relevant sections later in this guide). Camping unofficially for a day or two in areas like Dragash is not likely to cause any major upset so long as you are not obstructing the farmers, damaging crops or scaring cattle.

If you plan to stay somewhere for more than a month then it would be cheaper to rent an apartment than stay in hotels as apartments can be found for €200 a month upwards, even in Prishtina. The costs of a short-term let are naturally higher than a long-term one and you may find the family reluctant to move out their belongings which can intrude on your privacy somewhat. If your budget does not stretch to an apartment and you don't mind the company, you could arrange to stay with a family. Kosovars are keen for the extra income and naturally hospitable, so you will find it easy to make such an arrangement.

ACCOMMODATION PRICE CODES FOR DOUBLE ROOM

Upmarket	$$$$	€70+
Mid-range	$$$	€40–70
Budget	$$	€20–40
Shoestring	$	<€20

You will not be disappointed by the food in Kosovo. The choice and offerings of restaurants in Kosovo is truly outstanding and service in Kosovo is widely accepted by internationals and even locals visiting from Serbia and Albania to be the best in the region. The Kosovars really do take pride in and seem to enjoy serving you. Many chefs and waiters have worked in the UK, Germany or elsewhere in Europe and have brought their skills back with them. You can eat a meal which rivals some of the better-end establishments in London for a quarter of the price. The average price of a main course in sit-down smarter restaurants outside Prishtina is around €4. Pizzas are €2.50–4 depending on size and the restaurant surroundings. Prices in Prishtina establishments are always a few euros higher, with some main courses at luxury establishments at around €8–9 (€10 maximum). Across Kosovo it is possible to eat kebabs 'qebabi', meatballs or hamburgers and accompaniments for €1 and to eat in budget-end establishments for €2–3. It will be apparent from the restaurant description what the price bracket is and we have not categorised the restaurants (with the exception of luxury restaurants in Prishtina).

Serbian restaurants have less exposure to internationals' requirements, and service can sometimes be a little surlier.

It is not at all taboo in Kosovo to bring children to restaurants, although there are rarely high chairs so you may need to improvise. The waiters will dote over the little one and the restaurants will happily make special versions of dishes or heat up milk.

Albanian food is not widely known as a speciality but there are some truly delicious dishes. In particular try the *tavë*, or oven-pot dishes, which may include meat, tomatoes, aubergine or meat in yoghurt/egg sauce (the latter is known as *tavë elbasan*). Invariably excellent restaurants which specialise in traditional Albanian dishes are Pishat, Tiffanys, Ultra and Symphony in Prishtina, Te Jupave in Gjakova, Te Gjyla in Ferizaj and Planet outside Gjilan.

Meat in Kosovo is generally good but try in particular the lamb (*kingji*) and veal (*viqi*) dishes (the calves theoretically get better treatment than those which used to be eaten in the UK). Veal escalopes are found almost everywhere, as is *biftek,* which is steak from the shoulder or loin. For pork you have to go to the Serbian areas where meat is generally grilled and served in enormous portions, with few accompaniments.

The meat in the many *qebaptore* is usually of good quality. The kebabs are not usually served on a skewer but are put in a flat bread bap. You can say how many you want. A *komplet qebap* is one with all the trimmings of cabbage, cucumber, tomato, mayonnaise or mustard.

Pleskavica, a Serbian word also used by Kosovo Albanians, is a larger flatter piece of minced beef which is grilled. Sometimes it is stuffed with cheese.

Kosovo is also abundant in **trout** which are now also bred commercially. In the restaurants you will also find sea fish brought in from Albania.

Albanians and Serbs alike love **peppers** – green, red, yellow and spicy (*djeks* in Albanian) or not (so long as you know which you are getting!), grilled, oven baked or pickled. Try the stuffed pepper dishes in the restaurants. Come September and the outlying streets and markets fill with vans with large packs of peppers of all colours and the odour of peppers fills the flats as Kosovo goes into industrious pepper-pickling mode for the winter. Autumn is also the best time to try the homemade *ajvar*, a pepper dip which is bottled for the winter.

Whereas in local homes pickled **vegetables** may be the only winter vegetable option, unlike a few years ago it is now possible even out of season to find salads and vegetables in Prishtina and upmarket restaurants. In season the abundant tomatoes and cucumbers from Kosovo itself are extremely tasty as they are not factory grown. A popular salad is the *shopska* salad with cucumber and tomatoes and grated cheese on top. Salads in all the good restaurants will be pretty safe to eat unless there is some unusual water situation.

In terms of **cheeses** try the Sharr cheese from Prizren and the Dragash cheeses. These are soft feta-type cheeses from cows and in the case of Dragash, sometimes sheep. They may be stored in a vinegar-type sauce to protect them. If this is the case the cheese should be rinsed lightly before eating.

The local **yoghurt** is also good. You will see large cartons or bottles of white yoghurt in the supermarkets. This is generally much runnier than the Bulgarian or Greek yoghurt, although also very tasty. You can mix it with fruit or honey if you have a sweet tooth.

As a snack, or rather a meal in itself across the Balkans, *burek* is popular and most usually served in the morning as a breakfast or mid-morning snack. Traditionally in the Balkans the factories and work in the fields started early and workers went straight there, stopping to eat burek or an equivalent at around 10.00 or 11.00.

Burek is a sausage-shaped fried filo pastry filled most commonly with meat or soft white cheese and in some places with spinach. You can eat it on the go in wrapped paper or sit down to eat it – usually chopped up into small pieces on metal plates. It is commonly served with white, unsweetened drinking yoghurt in the pot or in a glass. It is a Bosnian speciality and the Bosniak *burektore* remain the best in Kosovo, with perhaps the tastiest burek of all being in Dragash.

Another pastry speciality, *pita*, is effectively a pie (although it can sometimes be sold as a sausage). The pie may contain meat, pumpkin, cabbage or root vegetables and even boiled nettles (*hitha* in Albanian).

Mantija is also a meat-filled pastry, again when cooked it is served with a yoghurt sauce.

Out of all the pastry arrangements, the most typically Albanian is *flija*. This is traditionally cooked in a large broad covered pan over an open fire and consists of a tart made of pancake layers which are each added every two to three minutes one by one. As flija takes some effort to make, it is not something you find in all the bakeries (try Furra Lumi in Prishtina if you want to sample it). Owing to the time it takes, inevitably the making of *flija* is a sociable exercise and for many Kosovars, now stuck in the city, going to the village at the weekend to make *flija* is a way of reconnecting with their past.

Sarma is a Balkan speciality of cabbage stuffed with rice or similar and is commonly eaten by Albanians at home. At home Albanians eat a lot of beans or *pasul*, not as sweet as baked beans but smaller than broad beans.

Homemade *çorbe* or **soups** can be very tasty and filling. They contain what is available: generally vegetables and meat. Mushrooms were not traditionally widely used in Albanian cooking.

Most of the **bread** sold in the bakeries is rather tasteless budget-end white bread made with cheap flour imported from Serbia. In some of the restaurants, however, you will find much more adventurous Turkish-style bread with seeds, sometimes stuffed with cheese. It is made with a heavier flour and served hot. Try *pogaqe* if you can find it on a menu (try Symphony or Liburnia restaurants in Prishtina). The Pishat Restaurant in Prishtina also has a wide range of breads (see page 104).

Large volumes of strawberries can be found in the shops around April from across the border in the Albanian parts of Macedonia and from May Kosovo has its own strawberries. Cherries follow suit in May and grapes in September.

Kosovo is not strong on desserts. The restaurants will commonly serve a tiramisu. Local cakes tend to be rather sickly sweet, particularly the most common local dessert of *baklava,* which is sweet pastry deep fried and covered in syrup. Baklava, which you may know from Turkey or Bosnia, is eaten at all times of the year but particularly after the Ramadan fast.

In terms of **drinks** *raki* is a clear spirit made by all ethnic groups from grape juice and drunk at all times of the day (except by some devout Muslims) – as a morning pick-me-up, aperitif, or after a meal. In the villages most raki will be home brewed. *Slijvovica* is the Serbian homebrew made from plums and is drunk in the same way as raki.

The most popular Kosovo **beer** is Peja beer which is available on tap (preferable) or in the bottle. It has just been revamped after investment and the taste is even better. Foreign beers, eg: Slovenian or German, are also available.

Kosovo **wines** are a mixed bunch but improving. Traditionally Kosovo produced large volumes of low-quality wine – mostly red, which is generally preferable to the vinegary white. Avoid the big cheap bottles in the supermarkets which are the large-volume socially owned enterprise variety and which, believe it or not, are often drunk mixed with Coca-Cola. The Stone Castle label is excellent, the Eko and Minnea labels are also generally better than others, although there is much investment and change going on, meaning that new labels will come out (see *Rahovec*, pages 223–4, for more information). If in doubt, it is safest to stick with the Montenegrin Plantaze variety which is reasonably priced and widely available (in almost every restaurant). The red Vranac is good, as is the Sauvignon and the white Chardonnay and Krstac. Vranac ProCorde with the red on the label is the top-end Vranac and therefore a little pricier, but query whether the difference merits the extra price. Make sure in any event that you buy the genuine yellow-label Plantaze and not the fake white-labelled wine, which is Kosovo wine rebottled. Other good regional wines are those from the Macedonian vineyards of Alexandria and Bovin (this one is slightly better quality) and the Slovenian Vipava. The Albanian wine from Korça is good but hard to track down.

There are plenty of **soft drinks and juices** in Kosovo, including from local companies who produce them from concentrates. Coca-Cola (including the Light/Diet variety), Red Bull, ice teas and Sola are all widely available. There are dozens of bottled water varieties – both *me gas* (sparkling) and *pa gas* (still). Those with better reputations are Rugove and Dea.

Other drinks of Turkish origin available in Kosovo are *ayran* (a yoghurt-type drink) and *boza* (made from wheat, with a slightly alcoholic taste).

Coffee is an integral part of Balkan life. Over coffee deals are done and politics, love and day-to-day life are discussed. Coffee goes hand in hand with cigarettes. In fact, cigarettes go with everything and there is little or no awareness of non-smokers. In villages and homes you will be served Turkish coffee which is the grainy type (don't gulp it!). You will be asked how strong you want it – *mesme* means 'medium'. If you do not want sugar, say so early on enough that they can make it without it. In the towns macchiato (espresso with foamed milk) is common, as is espresso or cappuccino (usually served with a very sweet chocolate sauce squirted on the top). If you don't like the foam on the macchiato order *pa skum* – without foam. Reflecting the Turkish influence, **tea** is also widely drunk in the home in Kosovo, more so than in Albania or Serbia and particularly in the Prizren area. The tea is served in Turkish-style small glasses on a silver or metal tray with much ceremony. English-style tea has caught on in the restaurants serving internationals, although if you want milk you have to ask for it and specify whether you want it cold (as otherwise they may think you want it hot). Herbal tea is also widely available, in particular hibiscus and chamomile and mountain tea (literally in the form of bunches of herbs) can be bought in bunches in the Dragash and Štrpce areas. It will be recommended by locals that you drink herbal tea if you are ill.

In restaurants tipping about 10% is customary, although not compulsory. If you eat a large meal and order many drinks or are a frequent customer, the restaurant may volunteer to provide coffee *kafe prej shpise* – 'on the house'.

PUBLIC HOLIDAYS AND FESTIVALS

OFFICIAL HOLIDAYS At the time of writing public holidays in Kosovo had still not been finalised.

Below, therefore, is the list of anticipated holidays including those likely to be observed in Serb majority areas. These are, however, subject to change. There is no central place where they are published.

1 January	New Year's Day
6 January (2011)	Orthodox Christmas
27 January	Sv Sava Day – holiday in Serb areas
17 February	Independence Day
9 April	Constitution Day
25 April (2011), 9 April (2012), 1 April (2013)	Christian Easter Monday
25 April (2011), 16 April (2012), 6 May (2013)	Orthodox Easter Monday
(The previous Friday is also a holiday in Serb areas)	
1 May (or nearest Monday)	Labour Day
9 May	Victory Day – holiday in Serbia/Serb areas
28 June	St Vitus Day (Serb areas only)
15 August	Orthodox Assumption
31 July–1 August (2011), 20 July (2012), 9 July (2013)	Start of Ramadan
30 August (2011), 17 August (2012), 8 August (2013)	Bajram (end of Ramadan)
28 November	Flag Day/Day of Albanians
16 November (2010), 6 November (2011), 26 October (2012), 15 October (2013)	Kurban Bajram
25 December	Christian Christmas Day

OTHER SPECIAL EVENTS/FESTIVALS

14 February	St Valentine's Day – particularly celebrated in Catholic areas. Many Kosovars now also take their girlfriend or spouse to dinner.
8 March	International Women's Day – it is traditional to give flowers to women at work

REGIONAL FESTIVALS/EVENTS (see also regional chapters)

January	Flaka e Januarit in Gjilan
5–7 March	Epopeja Day in Prekaz (see page 262)
March–April	Dam Festival of young musicians (*www.damfest.com*)
May (usually second weekend)	Run for Peace and Tolerance half marathon, Prishtina
May	Book Fair, Prishtina
June	Freedom Festival – 2-day rock, rap and pop festival, Prishtina (*www.freedomfestivalkosova.com* or Facebook site)
August	Dokufest, Prizren (*www.dokufest.org*)
14–15 August	Letnica Festival, Assumption of the Virgin
September (second week)	Rahovec Wine Festival

Practical Information PUBLIC HOLIDAYS AND FESTIVALS

2

September (second or third week)	911 Film Festival (*www.911fest.org*) and Prishtina Film Festival (*www.prifilmfest.org*)
September	Tour de Culture bike ride and Tour de Kosovo bike race (*www.tourdekosovo.eu*)
October	Infest Theatre Festival, Prishtina (*www.kosovainfest.com*)
14 October	Stefan Gjecovi Poetry Festival, Zym
November	Prishtina Jazz Festival (*www.jazzprishtina.com*)
December	Skena Up Film and Theatre Festival (*www.skenaup.com*)

Do not worry yourself unduly that if you are in Kosovo on a festival or holiday that everything will be closed completely. With the exception of the first day of Bajram, in true entrepreneurial fashion many shops and restaurants will remain open.

The methods of celebrating festivals may be different from other places. For example, whereas in western Europe and the USA Christmas is celebrated primarily in the home and with the family, for Catholic and Muslim Kosovars alike it is a very social event. The idea is to go to church and be seen and to meet people. The first night of New Year is spent with the family. This does not, however, mean there are not lots of fireworks. The same applies to the end of Ramadan. It is traditional to go out on the second night of Bajram at the end of Ramadan. In fact, Bajram consists of much visiting and eating of baklava with relatives.

Activities and anniversaries in Kosovo reflect the weather. In practice, through force of nature all armies and even modern-day protesters will generally down tools during the winter season (starting in November). Many people have commented on how everything happens in March in Kosovo and there is a lot of truth in this – most likely as this is when the weather warms, snow melts and people can move about again. As for protests, the pent-up aggression from the winter can be expended. In terms of March anniversaries, student riots broke out in 1981, Kosovo's autonomy was revoked in March 1989, the NATO bombing started in March 1999 (and with it many of the massacres whose anniversaries are remembered in the papers), the UÇK Epopeja is in March, former prime minister Haradinaj was indicted in March 2005 and his proper trial began in March 2007, and the 2004 riots were on 17–18 March.

🧺 SHOPPING

Until three or four years ago, the advice to anyone coming to Kosovo long-term would be to not rely on purchasing goods on arrival; however, recently the situation has changed dramatically. There are now out-of-town malls in Prishtina (Grand Store and Albi shopping mall) and even smaller malls being built in Peja and Prishtina and several hypermarkets in all the major cities. In *Chapter 3, Prishtina*, we have listed a selection of shops favoured by internationals and specialist shops which might be harder to find.

It is now possible to buy most things in Kosovo, although the choice of good-quality reasonably priced clothing is not that good. Clothes seem to be either budget-end Turkish or overpriced designer. Some notable exceptions where you can buy mid-range clothes are Ben-Af's larger stores in Prishtina and Prizren and some of the larger shopping centres such as Grand Store, City Park or Albi. You can also buy 'rip-off' skiwear and sturdy caterpillar-type boots at the Mini-Max store near KFOR Film City Base which is about 4km outside Prishtina on the road to Mitrovica; turn off right after Maxi.

For cosmetics try EBC, which has a major branch in Grand Store, Prishtina, and on the main road up beyond Raiffeisen up from the Ombudsperson and the Mensa or the in-house cosmetic store at the ETC supermarkets. If you need to buy household goods, such as crockery or cutlery, hoovers, TVs or DVD players, then try the major hypermarkets – Maxi, Era, Albi, Ben-Af or ETC. They also sell some DIY tools and basic car kits such as jump leads, de-icer and triangles.

The best shops for more modern and less fancy furniture are JYSK, Lesna and Mobi Inn which are opposite each other on the road to Fushë-Kosova; nearly all major Kosovo towns have a Mobi Inn. For cheaper goods try the stores near Prishtina Old Town which make their own wooden furniture although many of the goods here may be a bit ornate or ungainly for Western tastes. JYSK and Lesna are also ideal for duvets, towels and bedding.

While imported goods in Kosovo are subject to a 10% customs duty, making them more expensive than at home, labour is cheap in Kosovo and visitors should turn this to their advantage at the same time as helping the Kosovo economy. Therefore Kosovo is an ideal place to get a suit, dress or skirt tailor-made or to do those alterations that you have been meaning to get done. Many internationals have had their wedding dresses and ball gowns made in Kosovo. You can bring your own material or shop around the markets. There are plenty of tailors or *Rrobaqepes* around, although they are usually tucked away off the main thoroughfares in their flats and you will have to follow the signs to find them. Prishtina is obviously more expensive than elsewhere – other cities with good traditions of textile factories and therefore tailors are Gjilan and Gjakova. With prices for turn-ups or alterations at just a few euros, there is no reason to ever do your own sewing in Kosovo. You can also get a spare set of your house keys cut, your shoes re-heeled, your passport photos done and that watch repaired or the zip on your bag replaced – all at less than half the price and with much better service than in Western Europe.

Carpentry skills are also good in Kosovo and you can commission articles to your own design – be they boxes, cribs or furniture. Do not expect modern designs or creativity from the craftsmen – it is better if you bring your own.

While in Kosovo why not treat yourself to a bargain haircut or beauty treatment? Many of the hairdressers have trained in the major salons in London. There are plenty of beauty parlours, again tucked away, for a leg/bikini waxing or manicure or head massage at a fraction of the price you would pay at home.

Kosovars are also good car mechanics; many are trained in Germany, so if you are driving around Europe or the Balkans this is one of the best places to stop and get your car overhauled.

With the exception of the out-of-town hypermarkets which open late and on Sundays, shops in Kosovo open from about 08.30 and close generally around 18.00 to 19.00 in Prishtina and are closed on Sundays. Banks are usually open from 09.00 to 17.30 Monday to Friday and open from 09.00 to 14.00 on Saturdays. They close on the national holidays.

SOUVENIRS In terms of souvenirs there is very little choice, particularly if a metal picture or mini statue of Skenderbeg is not really your taste. Perhaps the best souvenirs of Kosovo are a copy of the red *Leke Dukagjini* or *Dukagjini Code,* costing about €35 in both languages, which can make for an entertaining read, one of the small Illyrian replica statues from the museum, or filigree jewellery. Some tourists like to buy the wool Albanian hats (*plis*).

Kosovo is famous for its filigree jewellery, although increasingly in the shops this is being replaced by modern, equally attractive designs. All jewellery is generally well priced compared with the West, although if you are looking for something more traditional, the delicate lattice of the filigree work is hard to beat. The filigree is made by painstakingly soldering each individual silver wire. Prizren is the best place for filigree, although there are also some good shops in Prishtina and Gjakova.

Ariadne Van Zandbergen

EQUIPMENT Although with some thought and an eye for composition you can take reasonable photos with a 'point-and-shoot' camera, you need an SLR camera if you are at all serious about photography. Modern SLRs tend to be very clever, with automatic programmes for almost every possible situation, but remember that these programmes are limited in the sense that the camera cannot think, but only make calculations. Every starting amateur photographer should read a photographic manual for beginners and get to grips with such basics as the relationship between aperture and shutter speed.

Always buy the best lens you can afford. The lens determines the quality of your photo more than the camera body. Fixed fast lenses are ideal, but very costly. A zoom lens makes it easier to change composition without changing lenses the whole time. If you carry only one lens, a 28–70mm (digital 17–55mm) or similar zoom should be ideal. For a second lens, a lightweight 80–200mm or 70–300mm (digital 55–200mm) or similar will be excellent for candid shots and varying your composition. Wildlife photography will be very frustrating if you don't have at least a 300mm lens. For a small loss of quality, tele-converters are a cheap and compact way to increase magnification: a 300 lens with a 1.4x converter becomes 420mm, and with a 2x it becomes 600mm. Note, however, that 1.4x and 2x tele-converters reduce the speed of your lens by 1.4 and 2 stops respectively.

For photography from a vehicle, a solid beanbag, which you can make yourself very cheaply, will be necessary to avoid blurred images, and is more useful than a tripod. A clamp with a tripod head screwed on to it can be attached to the vehicle as well. Modern dedicated flash units are easy to use; aside from the obvious need to flash when you photograph at night, you can improve a lot of photos in difficult 'high contrast' or very dull light with some fill-in flash. It pays to have a proper flash unit as opposed to a built-in camera flash.

DIGITAL/FILM Digital photography is now the preference of most amateur and professional photographers, with the resolution of digital cameras improving the whole time. For ordinary prints a 6 megapixel camera is fine. For better results and the possibility to enlarge images and for professional reproduction, higher resolution is available up to 16 megapixels.

Memory space is important. The number of pictures you can fit on a memory card depends on the quality you choose. Calculate in advance how many pictures you can fit on a card and either take enough cards to last for your trip, or take a storage drive on to which you can download the content. A laptop gives the advantage that you can see your pictures properly at the end of each day and edit and delete rejects, but a storage device is lighter and less bulky. These drives come in different capacities up to 80GB.

SPORTS AND ACTIVITIES

For details of most sports societies based out of Prishtina, see *Chapter 3*, pages 114–15.

With the exception of a passion for football and basketball, Kosovars are not sporty types. In particular few women play any sports and school sports are not organised.

The **basketball league** in Kosovo (*www.eurobasket.com/kosovobasketball.asp*) is very well organised attracting some serious sponsorship and even players from abroad. The main teams are Trepça, Peja and there are two Prishtina teams. Games are fun and supporters are lively.

There is also an organised **football league** (*www.ffk-kosova.com/eng*) with the better teams being the two Prishtina teams and Drita Gjilan. There are several

Bear in mind that digital camera batteries, computers and other storage devices need charging, so make sure you have all the chargers, cables and converters with you and take the opportunity to charge while you can, remembering power cuts are common in Kosovo. Most hotels have charging points, but do enquire about this in advance. When camping you might have to rely on charging from the car battery; a spare battery is invaluable.

If you are shooting film, 100 to 200 ISO print film and 50 to 100 ISO slide film are ideal. Low ISO film is slow but fine grained and gives the best colour saturation, but will need more light, so support in the form of a tripod or monopod is important. You can also bring a few 'fast' 400 ISO films for low-light situations where a tripod or flash is no option.

DUST AND HEAT Dust and heat are often a problem. Keep your equipment in a sealed bag, stow films in an airtight container (eg: a small cooler bag) and avoid exposing equipment and film to the sun. Digital cameras are prone to collecting dust particles on the sensor which results in spots on the image. The dirt mostly enters the camera when changing lenses, so be careful when doing this. To some extent photos can be 'cleaned' up afterwards in Photoshop, but this is time-consuming. You can have your camera sensor professionally cleaned, or you can do this yourself with special brushes and swabs made for the purpose, but note that touching the sensor might cause damage and should only be done with the greatest care.

LIGHT The most striking outdoor photographs are often taken during the hour or two of 'golden light' after dawn and before sunset. Shooting in low light may enforce the use of very low shutter speeds, in which case a tripod will be required to avoid camera shake.

With careful handling, side lighting and back lighting can produce stunning effects, especially in soft light and at sunrise or sunset. Generally, however, it is best to shoot with the sun behind you. When photographing animals or people in the harsh midday sun, images taken in light but even shade are likely to be more effective than those taken in direct sunlight or patchy shade, since the latter conditions create too much contrast.

PROTOCOL Kosovars generally do not object to photos but it is polite to ask. If resistance is shown, don't try to sneak photographs as you might get yourself into trouble. Even the most willing subject will often pose stiffly when a camera is pointed at them; relax them by making a joke. and take a few shots in quick succession to improve the odds of capturing a natural pose.

Ariadne Van Zandbergen is a professional travel and wildlife photographer specialising in Africa. She runs The Africa Image Library. For photo requests, visit www.africaimagelibrary.co.za or contact her on ariadne@hixnet.co.za.

members of the Kosovar diaspora in foreign teams, including in the English and German leagues and most recently even in the Swiss national team (World Cup 2010).

Boxing and martial arts are also very popular in Kosovo and combatants are of a high standard, with Luan Krasniqi, now based in Germany, being the most famous Kosovar boxer. Kosovo almost grinds to a halt when one of his big fights is on. A Kosovar woman, Majlinda Kelmendi, became world junior judo champion in 2009.

Some Kosovars run as a hobby and running in general has become increasingly popular in Germia. Kosovo has a **half marathon** (slightly inaccurately known as 'the marathon') of 22km which is held on the first or second weekend of May each year and has now been run since 2001. It is known as the Run for Peace and

Tolerance. It does offer cash prizes and so attracts runners from Bulgaria, Albania and even Kenya. In recent years a fun run of 10km has been added. There is water along the route but the organisation can sometimes be lacking and surprising, especially if you are used to running at more formal events. The marshals can lose enthusiasm and wander off and although the roads are supposed to be kept clear of traffic this only really applies in full to the first tranche of runners. If you are a bit further back you may find yourself running in amongst some cars. The route does not seem to vary each year and to the astonishment of new competitors takes you up the road to Fushë-Kosova and directly past the belching smoke of Obiliq, just as you get to the tricky 13km point, and then up the Mitrovica road. Running this is nevertheless an experience in itself and you can exchange comments with the KFOR soldiers and humanitarian workers. Do not be deceived by the fast pace that the local Kosovar men set off at – this soon slows down. Just keep plodding on.

Kosovars are keen on fishing and run lots of fishing programmes on television. The **Fishing Society of Kosovo** is currently run by secretary Remzi Llapashtica (m *044 307 126*) and Burim Rexhepi (m *044 161 105*). Fishing permits can be bought from them (or via contacts at the local fishing societies who are known to any local fishing equipment shop). A yearly permit costs €20 for an adult and €10 for children or pensioners.

There is a keen **caving society** called the Aragonit Speleo-Association from Peja which runs various projects exploring caves in Kosovo. For more information check their website (*www.aragonit-speleo.org*). For more details, see *Rugova Valley*, page 167.

There are expat **rugby clubs** and even a laid-back, sociable **ultimate frisbee** group. As people come and go the best route to contact them may be through Facebook or Bar 91 (see *Chapter 3, Prishtina*, page 108). There is a **horseriding** ranch 3km north of Prishtina in the direction of Mitrovica at Mazgit with 20 horses (m *044 400 590/555 063*; ⊕ *08.00–23.00*). Costs are €10 an hour. Courses cost €200 for 20 hours and include several hours of theory. They have floodlights and operate during the winter. A much nicer ranch is Vali Ranch 5km outside Gjilan in Përlepnicë (see page 246).

There is an energetic and quite well-equipped **paintballing** company (m *044 505 409/263 020, 049 505 409*; e *info@paintball-kosovo.com; www.paintball-kosovo. com/English/index.html*) about 45 minutes out of Prishtina on the road to Peja about 15 minutes' drive after the airport turn-off before Kroni i Mbretit. There are two courses, including two buses, and they can accommodate up to 20 with masks and overalls. Cost is €7 per player with reload at €5 per 100 balls or €80 per 2,000 balls.

The grossly underfunded **Kosovo Cycling Club** (*Rr Sylemani, Ferizaj;* m *044 224 473*; e *kastrioti-bike@hotmail.com*), run by its president, Avni Nuha, competes in competitions outside Kosovo with a focus on road bikes rather than mountain bikes. It would welcome internationals to join in training. If you do so, please contribute something financially to the club. Kosovo is ideal for mountain biking on the side roads and off-road tracks. Germia National Park has some good tracks, including a single-track section, which has some challenging stretches. Particularly suitable areas for mountain biking are the undulating areas near Gjilan, Kllokot, Kamenicë, along the Bajgora Ridge between Mitrovica and Podujevo and between Battlava and Gjilan, but there are many other places to explore. Try to get hold of the KFOR 1:50,000 maps.

There are some good **climbing** areas in the Peja area. Contact Vyryt Morina at **Marimanga Climbing Association** (m *044 217 741*), who can arrange climbing in the Rugova Valley. The **Kosovo Mountain Federation** (Federata Bjeshkatare e Kosovës) (*Rr Andrea Gropa;* m *044 175 174*) has been in existence since 1948.

The enthusiastic Beni (m *044 182 219;* e *hikingnjeri@gmail.com; www.njeri.net* – for further contact details, see Prishtina Tennis Club below) also goes hiking on summer weekends with groups, covering more than 30 mountains as well as being a key organiser of snow/skiing events. **Skiing Beni** (e *snownjeri@gmail.com*) also has a skiing club in the winter – Kosovo's largest. For additional skiing events, search for 'Brezovica' sites on Facebook.

There is also a **Hunters' Association** (*Kaprolli, Rr Nazim Gafurri 18;* \ *038 230 432;* e *sh_gjkaprolli@hotmail.com*).

For **paragliding**, try Aeroklub Prishtina (*Pallati i Rinisë;* m *044 140 918/ 112 928/ 112 283;* e *kaloti@hotmail.com*).

There is also a **tennis** club in Prishtina (*Prishtina Tennis Club;* \ *038 221 870;* m *044 123 647/ 182 219;* e *snownjeri@gmail.com; www.tenniskosova.com*).

ℓ MEDIA AND COMMUNICATIONS

TELEVISION Kosovo has three terrestrial home TV channels which are also on cable and satellite. The public broadcaster is RTK, which also has advertising. It broadcasts mostly in Albanian but also has Serbian, Turkish and Bosnian programmes. It has a good website (*www.rtklive.com*) in several languages.

TV21 was supported by the US government and, very unusually for a Kosovar firm, has a woman manager. It broadcasts some US shows and in the past has shown an edited version of *Sex in the City*.

Koha (*www.kohavision.net*), founded in 1994, is part of the Surroi media conglomerate that includes the newspaper *Koha Ditore*. It has a bias toward sports and films. Kosovo is one of the few places left in Europe that still gets special rights to broadcast international football events, so unlike Western Europe it was possible to see the World Cup and English Premier League matches without paying extra for them. Many Italian league games are shown on local television. Before the advent of satellite television, working on low budgets the terrestrial companies purchased cheap Latin-American soap operas from Brazil and Argentina. Despite the poor-quality acting, the high-drama love and family politics stories proved popular with bored unemployed Kosovars, particularly women stuck at home, and the actors became celebrities in Kosovo and have even visited the country. The programmes have also resulted in young children picking up and using Spanish phrases they have learnt on-screen. These *telenovelas* still fill up a lot of the screen time.

Kosovo also has its own homemade soap operas on the TV channel RTK, of which the two most famous are the comedies *Familja Moderne* and *Kafeneja Jonë*. *Familja Moderne*, which resulted in the first major copyright law decision in Kosovo, is based on the life of several generations of a modern family living in a flat in central Prishtina, with members with jobs in the Kosovo Police Service and even with international organisations! In a move which the local Kosovars took in good humour, the former UN Secretary-General's Special Representative (SRSG), Søren Jessen-Petersen, has even appeared on the programme. The storylines in *Familja Moderne* have included an unplanned pregnancy and a failed marriage to an Irish international amongst the usual family scandals. *Kafeneja Jonë*, as the title suggests, is based in a coffee bar. For a non-native speaker, the dialogues in local Gheg slang are very hard to follow. The Kosovo version of *Crimewatch* seems to have now ceased but the local equivalent of *Big Brother* (*Shpija* – house) is incredibly popular, as is the Kosovar version of the series *Who wants to be a millionaire*.

Aside from football, *telenovelas* and the news, there are two other common programme types. One is an audience show with lots of singers performing.

2

Singing starts young in Kosovo and involves much hip wiggling from the age of three upwards which can look a bit perturbing to a Western eye. The other show type is a discussion forum usually on politics or a similar topic, involving senior politicians or well-respected figures. The participants are always invariably highly opinionated besuited men. Occasionally they may have a female interviewer. Such forums can seemingly go on for hours on prime-time TV.

Cable TV   Since the arrival of cable TV in the main cities there are now more new channels on cable – Klan TV is a more recent arrival with the most popular morning show and there are some other channels from media magnates such as Dukagjini, with more in the pipeline (it seems to be the latest vogue of Kosovar business magnates to have their own channels). There are over 30 international channels and four channels of high-quality films with Albanian subtitles, sports' and kids' channels and a documentary channel translated into Albanian, is dramatically changing the Kosovo media landscape and provides tough competition for the viewing time of the Kosovars who can now flick between Albania's TV channels as well as those of western Europe.

There are satellite dishes all over Kosovo; however, in the major towns there is now a shift to using the cable TV providers who have tied up with the internet companies, Kujtesa and IPKO (see below). At the time of writing, in the main cities for €19.95 a month, a household can receive internet and over 20 TV channels, including CNN, BBC World, Explorer, Sat1, Raiuno, TV5, Sky News and Eurosport. (For more information, see *Internet*, below.)

RADIO   Kosovo has many different radio stations, including some initially aimed at the KFOR troops but which are now also popular with the local population, such as the British Forces Radio. The following are FM stations available in Prishtina (frequencies outside Prishtina vary): 88.6 Deutsche Welle, 95.2 Turkish, 95.7 Radio Kosova (traditional radio station for the older generation), 96.2 Voice of America, 96.6 Radio KFOR (modern music but also minority programmes), 97.7 Blue Sky (part of RTK group, aimed at the young population), 98.6 BBC World Service, 98.7 Radio Dukagjini (mostly modern music), 101 French radio, 102.2 Radio Plus, 103.5 Urban FM (hip, modern music and chat including foreign chart music).

NEWSPAPERS   Kosovo has more newspapers than the market can take and most are probably losing money, particularly as the statistics show that relatively few people actually read them. At the time of writing there were more than 11 titles. The main ones are:

Koha Ditore (*www.koha.net; online version available only by subscription*) founded by Veton Surroi, a journalist who operated throughout the 1990s. It is now edited by his sister since he went into politics and founded the Ora Party. It is regarded as a serious, long-standing paper with detailed news coverage and is the only one which is not really politically biased.

Zeri is another heavyweight which operated in the 1990s as a weekly paper and now also competes for top-end readers. **Kosova Sot** takes more of a tabloid stance, as does **Lajm**, which is funded by the magnate and politician Beghet Pacolli. Other newspapers come and go.

Owing to the number of diaspora, online news is increasingly popular. Good websites are referred to in *Appendix 2, Further Information*, page 304.

✆ TELEPHONE   Telephoning is somewhat complicated as Kosovo does not have its own country code as it is not recognised by the International Telecommunication

Union (ITU). Vala therefore uses Monaco's international code and IPKO uses Slovenia's. This may confuse your friends and relatives when they get their bill as they will swear they never called Monaco or Slovenia. It's even more confusing knowing what number to key into your phone if you are on roaming. If roaming you may sometimes pick up the signals of other illegal operators, eg: strong signals from Macedonia, Albania or even Montenegro which ITU does not police.

Where numbers appear in this book with 044 or 049, 045 or 043, this is the number to dial when calling *within Kosovo* from a Vala or IPKO phone. If you are calling from another mobile provider you need to enter +377 44 45 or +386 49.

Where the number appears with 038, 028 or 029, then this is again the number to dial when calling from a fixed-line phone within Kosovo. Otherwise dial +381 38 first.

Land/fixed-line phones PTK is the publicly owned provider of telecom services. There are other companies licensed to provide fixed-line services, eg: IPKO but in practice for a fixed line for anything other than large offices you will probably need to speak to PTK. Installation costs €10 and the wait is only a day or two. Illogically, transferring a phone from another person's name costs the same as a new installation. Inside Kosovo when you are calling from another PTK landline you just dial the town code, eg: 038 for Prishtina, 029 for Prizren, etc. Otherwise you need to dial +381 first. Itemised bills do not currently come automatically but can be obtained at the post office (in Prishtina at the Dardania headquarters customer service centre). To dial internationally from a PTK fixed line in Kosovo you must first dial 99 or sometimes 00 and then the country code. For example for the UK you need to dial 99 44. However, with the advent of VoIP (Voice Over Internet Protocol) and mobile-phone technology, unless you intend to make a lot of local calls or to run an office the fixed line may not be necessary.

You can also make international calls from the phone shops scattered across town. These are usually significantly cheaper for international calls than ordinary fixed-line calls. Some operate via pre-purchase of broadband and others through VoIP. Payment is made at the end of the call.

Phonecards can also be bought at post offices for different denominations for the fixed-line yellow kiosks scattered around Kosovo.

To subscribe to the fixed-line and pre-pay SIMs from PTK go to the local post office (in Prishtina you need to go to the customer service centre at the PTK headquarters). For post-pay you need a larger post office (in Prishtina, you have to go to the one on Rr UÇK). English is widely spoken by PTK staff, including at the over-the-phone help desk, and contracts are also in English.

For more prices and information, see www.ptkonline.com.

2

PHONE NUMBER REMINDERS

International PTK land/fixed line +381
Vala +377 44 or +377 45
Z Mobile +377 45 (from IPKO to dial Vala or Z mobile you can just key in 044 or 045)
IPKO and D3 +386 49 or +386 43 (from Vala you can just key in 049 or 043)
Serbian mobiles +381 63 or +381 64
Dial internationally from Kosovo land/fixed lines 99 or in a few instances 00

Mobile phones Mobile services are good but MMS/internet on your phone is sometimes only available on a post-pay basis. There are two main providers: Vala (incumbent – part of PTK) and IPKO. Z Mobile is a subsidiary provider on the Vala network.

Vala and IPKO have roaming agreements with most European network operators (although Vala has none with Serbia). A SIM card can now be bought for €5. Top-up credit can be purchased at any post office and ProCredit ATMs. Scratchcards are also available. For IPKO mobiles (*www.ipko.com*), get a SIM from one of the IPKO shops (📞 +386 43 700 700 for more information). For Z Mobile, you again need to go to a Z Mobile shop.

If you are going to be a heavy mobile user in Kosovo for a period of six months or more or need a phone for business, consider subscribing to post-pay contracts which provide cheaper block rates and an itemised bill.

Serbian operators still work in Serb enclaves – including 063, 069 and 064 numbers. Their SIM cards have to be purchased from a shop in a Serb enclave.

ⓔ INTERNET Internet services, while not quite up to Western broadband standards, are also improving. In most cities it is now easy to obtain cabled internet in your home (in the villages internet is still through satellite antennas). There are two main providers: Kujtesa and IPKO. IPKO is majority-owned by Telecom Slovenia. It has an interesting history as it was originally set up as a quasi-NGO post conflict, with US government funding. Kujtesa is now also foreign owned.

IPKO Rr Nëne Terezë, Prishtina; 📞 043 700 700 (sales), 038 20 304 051 (support); ⓔ info@ipko.com; www.ipko.com
Kujtesa Rr Pashko Vasa 18, Prishtina, next to the Prishtina, Dion & Pejton hotels; 📞 038 248 740/3, 038 225 599; ⓔ sales@kujtesa.com, ⓔ info@kujtesa.com; www.kujtesa.com
PTK or TK (Telekom Kosovo) Dardania pn, Prishtina; 📞 038 556 556; www.ptkonline.com. PTK offers high-speed, high-quality internet access. You can also use dial-up from your PC if you have dial-up software by using a PTK fixed line by dialling 90 90 90 & entering ptk under 'password' & 'login name'. This is obviously pricier as it costs the same as a fixed-line local call but it is a good fallback if you are stuck in someone's home who has no internet & are desperate to log in.

'KEK' AND ELECTRICITY Although the situation has improved dramatically in Prishtina, electricity is a common topic of conversation in Kosovo, in particular because of the frequent, mostly scheduled, power interruptions. A whole language has developed around KEK with phrases such as '4:2' meaning four hours of power, two without.

The Kosovo power station at Obiliq outside Prishtina is famous and Kosovo is one of the few places in the world where children know the power company's name, 'KEK'. This high brand-name recognition does not equate with quality so much as poor performance. Although Kosovo has some of the largest lignite reserves in Europe, it is a net importer of power since its current capacity is insufficient. This is being improved through the repair of the old (1960s built) Kosovo A power stations and in the long term through a tender for an internationally managed power plant and mining concession. This power is desperately needed by industries such as Ferronikeli. The largest units, Kosovo B1 and B2, were repaired with EU and Kosovo government funding from 1999. To the embarrassment of the donors, one of the units was struck by lightning in 2001 and the subsequent fire destroyed much of the repair work done.

KEK faces many problems, including old infrastructure, limited high-quality staff, overstaffing and fraud but the biggest are probably illegal connections and non-payment (a problem faced also by other utilities). It is estimated that about

70% of electricity used is billed (the rest being technical losses and illegal connections, even at the sub-station level and sometimes with the support of corrupt KEK staff). Out of this, payments received vary between 40% and 70% of the billed total. Payment is low in the Serbian areas as the Serb official line is that KEK is not to be recognised (it having been merged by the Serb Assembly with Electricity of Serbia in 1991). The main problem is lack of enforcement both in terms of adequate manpower and also judicial enforcement with cases taking several years and then being dismissed on technicalities. There have been countless projects to improve this situation, with little success. The use of international experts has not always been a success either. In 2002, an international manager from Germany was found to have stolen about €4 million, which was fortunately recovered after successful prosecution by the German authorities.

On account of insufficient funds to pay for imports, KEK has to run a load-shedding regime, which means that it deliberately cuts power for set periods on a rotating basis. In 2005, KEK introduced the 'ABC' regime which was designed to encourage higher payment by rewarding higher-paying areas with more power (on a good day Zone A areas should receive 24-hour power, when power is short five hours on, one off (5:1), whereas Zone C may be on 4:2, or on a bad day 3:3). Most of Prishtina's core areas are within Zone A. The same applies to other major city and town centres and more upmarket residential districts. If choosing somewhere to live you would be foolish to consider anywhere other than a Zone A area – you easily forget the major inconveniences of not having electricity until you experience it. Any novelty of power cuts soon wears off. In times of power restrictions, the Kosovo mood adjusts and people are grumpy because of inability to wash their hair/clothes, and refrigerated food going off. In the winters of 2008–10, power was much improved but it is not known if the budget will continue to sustain such large electricity imports and privatisation will take a while.

The voltage in Kosovo is theoretically 220V. Therefore a surge protector is essential, as is an uninterrupted power supply unit (known as a UPS) if you plan to run a desktop computer. Both can be bought easily in Prishtina computer shops.

POST The Kosovo postal system which is run by PTK is improving rapidly in efficiency. It is hampered only by the constant illegal building which results in houses and offices springing up in different places and changes to road names. PTK sends mail out of Kosovo by Austrian Airlines. When addressing mail to Kosovo, do not make reference to 'Serbia' as this can cause the mail to go via Belgrade which may mean delay and maybe even loss. In European countries, the USA and Canada it suffices simply to put 'Kosovo' at the bottom of the address. There are now new area postal codes, eg: Prishtina is '10 000', although these are not widely used. These are all listed on the PTK website (*www.postaekosoves.net*).

Provided the address is easy to find, post mailed to Kosovo does generally arrive. The exceptions are packages which are perceived to be valuable and therefore such goods should not really be sent. If you are sending photos, whether by DVD or hard copy, it is worth stating so on the outside of the envelope to deter the curious. The time letters take to arrive depends on the sending country. From the UK, they may arrive within three to ten days. Letters sent to the UK take seven days on average. If you order books from Amazon.co.uk or Amazon Germany, they will arrive if you use Albania as the drop down and list Kosovo as the town. PTK runs its own philately (stamps) and these are collectors' items with varying designs, eg: the countryside, buildings and artists. There have been more than 20 sets of stamps/first day covers produced. The Philately Department has its offices at the Rr UÇK building – near the Bata shoe shop, opposite the Qafa building (✆ 038 540

013/246 770; e *ptkfilatelia@ptkonline.com, info@postaekosoves.net*). You have two main choices for sending letters: either ordinary or *me rekomandim*, which means 'recorded delivery', whereby a signature is required and a trace will be made if the letter does not arrive after four days. This gives you documentary evidence that something has been sent/arrived. This costs about €1 within Kosovo and €3.40 to the EU for letters under 1kg. Ordinary post is less than €1. Postcards are about €0.20.

COURIERS There are also several major courier services who have offices in Kosovo, including TNT, DHL, UPS and FedEx. Prices are between €39 and €50 to send 0.5kg of documents to the UK's main cities.

DHL Rr Nëne Terezë near the theatre or Rr Rexhep Mala parallel to Pjata Restaurant; 038 245 245; m 044 245 545; e pleurat.hoti@dhl.com; www.dhl.com; 08.00–17.00 Mon–Fri, 09.00–15.00 Sat (Rexhep Mala office only). Also offices in Gjilan, Prizren, Gjakova, Peja & Mitrovica. See individual cities for details.

FedEx Rr Ekrem Qabej 137/145, Prishtina, & Rr Haki Myderizi, Gjilan; 038 550 870; www.fedex.com/ks; 08.00–17.00 Mon–Fri

KOEX call centre m 044 812 812; www.korier.com. KOEX is an internal Kosovo courier company collecting & delivering door to door across Kosovo.

TNT Rr Garibaldi (opposite Grand Hotel above Metro); 038 247 247; e tntkosova@hotmail.com; www.tnt.com

UPS Rr Qamil Hoxha 12; 038 242 222; www.ups.com

BUSINESS

In some respects, doing business in Kosovo is easier than in its neighbouring countries because Kosovar laws are currently also published in English (see www.unmikonline.org for laws to 2008, and www.ks-gov.net or www.gazetazyrtare.com), and until August 2006 English was the official language of administration. Furthermore, many businesses converse easily in English or German.

There are no restrictions on foreign investment or property ownership and an updated law on foreign investment was passed in 2006. Residence permits are easily granted to investors for renewable one-year periods. Work permits are required and are available at the Ministry of Labour for foreign investors or those working with NGOs or international organisations.

It is not 100% clear whether foreigners can directly purchase real estate in their own name. In any event they can do so easily through a company.

Limited liability companies, branches of foreign companies, joint stock companies and partnerships can be registered in about ten days for €20. For now, registration cannot be done online but the basics of the register are available at www.arbk.org.

There are no restrictions on opening bank accounts (other than EU-type money laundering checks) or on bank transfers of capital or funds and no withholding taxes on transfers out of the country. Hiring and firing is on paper (and generally in practice) simple – with redundancy payments capped at three months' salary maximum and union powers are limited.

Kosovo charges 16% VAT (paid at the border on imports), 10% corporation tax and a phased income tax which rises from 5% to 10% after the first €450 of monthly earnings. There is no national insurance or social security. Annual property taxes are about 0.01% of property value. There are no financial incentives for foreign investors. Customs charges are 10% with some exceptions for importation of products for agricultural production and machinery.

Initial appearances can be slightly deceptive, however, and in common with the rest of the region, the Kosovo institutions have not yet moved out of a socialist, rule-based mentality where the administration is superior to all, into the service culture of helping businesses. This general attitude, coupled with a slack worth ethic, low levels of education and hiring in the public sector often based on nepotism and low salaries which demotivate staff, can lead to extreme moments of frustration on the part of all businesses as the official will often find a fictive petty fault in your document, tell you that they don't know the answer or are not responsible and you have to go somewhere else, or tell you to come back in a few hours, tomorrow. Sometimes you are just met with a 'Balkan shrug'.

Another problem is that the administration is new and sometimes unintentionally they will say no to something different or to a complex Western structure, rather than research and embrace it. Furthermore there are huge delays in the courts, making debt enforcement difficult and the property title situation (see Economy, page 29) is unclear. This was reflected in Kosovo's poor rankings in the World Bank Doing Business report. (For more details, see www.doingbusiness.org.)

The applicable law is also not as obvious. There is a declining scale of priority laws starting with post-2008 laws, then post-1999 regulations, then those in force as at 1989, and finally, if there is still a gap, laws between 1989 and 1999 if they are not discriminatory. .

There is little obvious open corruption but plenty exists under the surface. Most local businesses in desperation reluctantly resort to the age-old Balkan ploy of a payment to speed up the process, but most international businesses can and do operate without any such payments. There is no evidence, however, that Kosovo is any worse than its neighbours as regards corruption.

It is, in any event, essential to 'know people' and the whole culture in the Balkans works on this basis of introductions and trust. Kosovo is a small society so someone will ask around to check out who or what you are. Business, as in all the Balkans, is done face-to-face over coffee or a meal and takes time. Emails exist but the culture of efficient business at a distance has not caught on. This can be exasperating if you have a long list of things to do in the day and don't have time to while away discussing politics over coffee. There is nothing else to do but take a deep breath and go with the flow and adjust your own pace for the sake of your blood pressure. At least the coffee and the food are good. In addition, a business colleague will think nothing of introducing a family or friend as a possible business contact. They almost regard doing business with family as an obligation, irrespective of the poor service or product that may result and the awkward situations that can ensue. Here it is a question of gently introducing some criteria and open competition, perhaps citing insurance or banking requirements to exclude the inexperienced family member that you feel uncomfortable about.

It is clear there are bargains to be had in the current privatisation process and there is doubtless money to be made for the persistent patient investor, especially in the areas of mining and energy.

Any foreign business should join one of the business associations rather than go it alone. Both the Kosovo Chamber of Commerce and American Chamber are open to foreigner membership, although AmCham is by far the more dynamic of the two and positively welcomes foreigners.

OTHER USEFUL DETAILS

American Chamber of Commerce Rr Tirana/Fehmi Agani 36; ℩ 038 246 012; e info@amchamksv.org; www.amchamksv.org

British Chamber of Commerce mob: ℩ 045 947 947; www.bcck.co.uk

Deloittes Rr Bedri Pejani; ℩ 038 245 582

Grant Thornton Rr Gazmend Zajmi 13; ℩ 038 247 771

Independent Commission for Mining and Minerals www.kosovo-mining.org. Awards mining licences.

Investment Promotion Agency e mustafe.hasani@ks-gov.net; www.invest-ks.org

Kosovo Chamber of Commerce Rr Nëne Terezë 20, next to Dukagjini bookshop; ☎ 038 224 299; e info@oek;kcc.org; www.oek-kcc.org
Kosovo Privatisation Agency ☎ 038 500 400; www.pak.org. Responsible for the privatisation & liquidation of social property.

KPMG Rr Sylejman Vokshi 14; ☎ 038 246 771
Ministry of Energy and Mining www.ks-gov.net/mem
PWC Str Mujo Ulqinaku 5, Ap 4, Qyteza Peyton, 3rd Fl, Prishtina; ☎ 043 722 555
Tax Administration www.mfe-ks.org

CULTURAL ETIQUETTE

Kosovars shake hands when meeting for the first time and on leaving and greeting people they already know. Close friends and relatives, men and women, also exchange kisses. The longer you have not seen each other, the more kisses are exchanged. As a sign of respect or to express happiness at seeing a person, men sometimes place their left hand on their heart and bow forward a little while shaking your hand. Kosovars may also hold on to your hand while asking how you are or where you come from.

To indicate 'yes', Kosovars move their head up and down, as it's done in most western European countries. A sudden raising of the whole chin, however, indicates a strong 'no'. It is sometimes accompanied with a click of the tongue. It can get confusing when they slowly shake their heads horizontally to show that they are listening or to express disbelief. In those moments you may hear a repeated clicking of the tongue or *kuku* – a real expression of surprise or disagreement. In the countryside, a certain huffing sound, similar to the sound of slurping, can also indicate a 'yes'.

When you enter a private home you are expected always to take off your shoes at the entrance. You will be offered a pair of slippers and it's wise to accept them as the floors might be very cold. Don't be surprised to find your shoes arranged in perfect order as you are leaving and sometimes, especially in the countryside, a member of the family might have even cleaned the shoes for you. Generally, you will notice that Kosovars pay great attention to their shoes. They are always clean and well looked after, despite the dust and dirt on the roads. A respectable person is expected to have clean shoes.

It is common to bring presents when you are invited as a guest to someone's house. In traditional Albanian culture, however, it is the guest who receives a present from the host as he or she is leaving. Hosting guests is a sign of honour, and being able to offer presents to your guest expresses high social status. You may be given some chocolate or other sweets, but also underwear or small towels. It is rude to refuse such a present, as this would indicate that you don't think that the host can afford it.

The same goes for food and drinks. When you visit a home, you will always be offered at least coffee (mostly Turkish coffee) or tea, and very often food as well. It is considered rude not to drink and eat, so save some appetite before visiting a Kosovar home. In the past, a family's wealth was measured by the amount of sugar one could offer a guest. Don't be surprised if your coffee or tea is extra sweet; it's just a sign of respect. If you do not want your Turkish coffee too strong ask for '*te mesme*' in Albanian which means, literally, 'medium'.

When you are entering a room, every person present will ask you how you are doing, how your family is doing and if you are tired. If there are more people in the room, you might be asked the same questions over again. Telephone conversations with Albanians usually also start with a long and repetitive question–answer session – how are you doing, how is your family – bounced back and forth between the two interlocutors. It's a communication ritual, so just be patient and play along.

Kosovars are generally very keen to find out about your private life, your family and your marital status. The first question is often where are you from, followed by a question about your married life and if you have children. In a country where few women over 30 are unmarried, where divorce is still rare and where family life is considered the purpose of being, these questions are not meant to be intrusive.

Smoking is widespread and the concept of non-smoking areas practically non-existent. In theory, smoking is prohibited in public buildings or offices, but most people will be puffing happily while sitting next to a non-smoking sign. Smokers are expected to offer cigarettes to others, so don't be upset if you are repeatedly offered a cigarette even as a committed non-smoker. This tradition goes back to the old days when guests were offered tobacco in the men's room and conversation only started once everyone had their cigarettes lit. Unfortunately, smoking is still allowed on some overnight international coaches.

Blowing your nose or sneezing loud in public is considered extremely rude, especially in a restaurant or at the dinner table. It's best to leave the room if you need to blow your nose.

In restaurants, bars or taxis, foreigners are expected to leave a small tip, while Kosovars often don't. When toasting say 'gezuar' (in Albanian) 'na zdravlje' or 'živieli' in Serbian and to start a meal you wish everyone a 'ju bofte mire' in Albanian or 'prijatno' in Serbian.

When visiting mosques, try and dress appropriately, although most Kosovars are not orthodox Muslims and will tolerate foreigners, so don't be deterred completely from visiting a mosque you wish to see if you have a skimpier outfit on than might be wished. There is no problem with women wearing shorts when cycling.

Funerals are important social occasions in Kosovo. Among Muslims it is traditional to have a wake for up to ten days after the occasion. Close relatives must remain in the house to greet the friends and relatives who come during that period to pay their respects. The notice of death is posted up on the house and on surrounding lampposts. Green edging means Muslim, black is Christian and blue is used for children. You will also see an empty chair with a towel attached to it outside the house where the person has died or where the wake is held, sometimes with a pot of flowers on it. Towels are used a lot as gifts and as symbols in both weddings and funerals. Both Serbian and Albanian widows traditionally wear black after their husband has died, although in practice this is most closely adhered to by Serbian women.

As with any Muslim-dominated country, during Ramadan you may have to work around your hosts' or colleagues' arrangements a bit more and be respectful when it comes to eating in front of those observing the fast.

LIVING IN KOSOVO

It is likely that many readers of this book will be reading it with a view to living in Kosovo for a period of time as a consultant, aid worker, military worker or diplomat. For this reason we have included a specific section on living in Kosovo. The number of resident expats or internationals is unknown, although KFOR has 10,000 staff in Kosovo. In addition to them, the number of internationals is believed to be between 5,000 and 10,000.

There is a wide choice of flats in Kosovo, although finding a quality one can be harder. Prices for one- or two-bedroom flats in Prishtina vary from €150 to €700 per month, depending on standards and whether heating is included or not. It is not usual to have to pay a deposit. Make sure you will not inherit a large unpaid electricity bill before you move in as this could cause you problems later and lead to you being cut off or dealing with unwanted enforcement measures. Clarify with your landlord who will pay the bill. If you pay money to your landlord to do so then check he really is paying it as otherwise you may be cut off. Many houses are illegally connected and only around 50% of households pay their bills. The same applies to your water and rubbish collection bills. A written agreement is recommended. If you are paying the rent from a legal entity then you must withhold 9% tax on the landlord's behalf.

To find flats look in the weekly ad magazine *Oferta dhe Suksesi*, which can be found in the mini market newsstands, and is also available online (*www.ofertasuksesi.com*), or scour the small ads in *Koha Ditore* or *Express*. There are also various agents around town who may save you the difficulties and time of calling and narrow your search down. They usually take a commission (about a month's rent) from the landlord. For more details see *Chapter 3*, page 119, for Prishtina agents. It can also pay to just walk around or ask around in the local cafés and restaurants in an area you want to live as word of mouth is often the best route and this can save the month's commission which will mean your rent is cheaper. When house-hunting, remember that electricity is not 100% guaranteed and in more remote areas or less smart parts of town, is likely to be more erratic. If looking at a house or flat in summer, remember also that you may have to live there in the colder seasons, so bear in mind issues such as heating and insulation.

To make life more bearable with power cuts, landlords may use either a generator (which can be time-consuming and difficult to switch on, noisy and smelly) or an inverter. An inverter charges a car battery when the power is on and you then discharge it to power low-consumption items such as your TV, a light, DVD player (but not cookers or heaters), when the power is off. They do require some maintenance of the battery fluid. Inverters cost about €100–150 to purchase.

GETTING YOUR BELONGINGS TO KOSOVO If you are planning to come to Kosovo for a long period then you will probably want to bring more of your personal belongings with you. Transport costs to Kosovo are not incredibly cheap so work out what it is worthwhile bringing as many general goods, all electrical and technology goods, and even passable modern furniture can now be bought here. DO bring your sports gear, eg: bicycle, ski gear, climbing and fishing equipment, etc, as good equipment is hard to come by and extremely expensive.

Even if you do not have diplomatic status, Kosovo's customs law does allow you to import your personal effects provided you have used them for at least six months before coming to Kosovo and you should not have problems provided there is nothing worth more than €500 (excluding perhaps a used laptop which they should permit you to import). You should not have more than one bottle of alcohol or perfume. You cannot sell on your personal effects after arrival unless you have paid customs duty and VAT on them. For more details see www.dogana-ks.com.

There are several cargo/removal companies serving Prishtina. The main cargo company is Austrian airlines/MCM, although contact the airline you intend to fly with for details of the Prishtina cargo service. In addition AGS, Allied Pickfords, MoveOne and Interdean provide door-to-door removal services from your home to Prishtina and elsewhere in Kosovo. They are overland services so may be cheaper.

Cargo contact details

AGS Kosovatex, Industrial Zone, Prishtina; ☎ 038 545 851; e manager-kosovo@agsmovers.com; www.ags-worldwide-movers.com

Allied Pickfords Kosovo Industrial Zone, Veternik, Prishtina; ☎ 038 548 264; e movers@alliedpickfords-ko.com; www.alliedpickfords-ko.com

Interdean Interconex Rr Elbasani 4, Dragodan Fidanishte, Prishtina; (the contact person is in Skopje)

☎ +389 232 153 40; e pristina@interdean.com

MCM Cargo (via Austrian Airlines) N Tereza, Prishtina & airport; ☎ 038 594 000; e mcmcargo@mcm.travel

Move One ☎ 038 566 354; m 044 500 995; e moving@moveonerelo.com

Prishtina Airport ☎ 038 595 8174/6/7; e cargoprn@airportpristina.com

Unless you are with a recognised international institution such as the EU, UN or OSCE, which each have their own number-plate system, a foreign-registered car can theoretically only be run in Kosovo for six months. Thereafter you should re-register it in Kosovo. However when you do so, you need to pay 10% customs tax, €500 excise duty, plus VAT which is 16% of the total value including such customs tax (as determined by price guide) as VAT. You also have to give up the foreign plates. With KS plates you have to swap your plates at the Serbian border temporary ones for a fee.

TIME

Kosovo time is the same as that in Germany and France, ie: one hour ahead of GMT or BST, as relevant. It gets dark in the winter at about 17.00.

TRAVELLING POSITIVELY

After the conflict Kosovo probably had more NGOs (Non-Governmental Organisations) per head of population and per square metre than anywhere else in the world. Although many of the disaster-relief NGOs have long gone, others remain with longer-term projects, particularly in civil society or minority support. Hopefully more work will be done in the future on environmental projects. Many NGOs are now entirely locally run but reliant on funds from outside Kosovo.

As Kosovo remains poor, particularly in the rural areas, and there is a skills deficit and insufficient investment in education, health, social care or environment, there is much work to do, so if you have time on your hands and the inclination, there are plenty of opportunities. As a result of a lot of co-operation in the past with international NGOs Kosovars are familiar with working with internationals. This applies whatever your background, whether you wish to contribute in terms of work with the disabled or minorities, social work, medical work, teaching, course design or even financial, legal, and management work. The only resistance and concern you are likely to encounter is from others who may see your involvement as a threat to their job.

In terms of physical gifts, these should be organised carefully to avoid them being wasted on the wrong people or going to the wrong areas. Kosovo has plenty of 'haves' as well as 'have-nots'. Many of the local or international NGOs can give guidance. There are also issues of sustainability to consider. Giving large equipment without any plans as to how it can be maintained may be a waste of funds.

Do not send shipments of aid without first planning and contacting people locally as there is a real chance of having to pay 26% of the value in customs duties and VAT at the border. Only pre-cleared, true humanitarian relief sent through the formal multilateral donor organisations such as USAID, SIDA or DFID is exempt from the border VAT and customs.

The concept of voluntary work amongst Kosovars has not yet caught on. They will still expect to be paid for any environmental or other projects.

The following is a selection of NGOs:

Balkan Sunflowers Rr Luan Haradinaj, Pallati i Rinisë Hall 114, Prishtina; ☎ 038 246 299; www.balkansunflowers.org. There is a form & information for volunteers on their website.
HandiKos, Dardania 4/7, D-2, Prishtina; ☎ 038 550 834/548 326; e handikos@ipko.org. This is Kosovo's main organisation focusing on the rights & needs of people with disabilities.

Kosovo Institute for Policy Research and Development Bregu i Diellit, Rr III, LI 39, Prishtina; ☎ 038 555 887; e info@kipred.net; www.kipred.net. Research institute focusing on political-party training, local administration & current policy debates (working language English).

2

Kosovo Stability Initiative Rr Garibaldi H11/6, Prishtina; ☏ 038 222 321; e info@iksweb.org; www.iksweb.org. Non-profit think tank providing up-to-date policy briefs on social & economic trends in Kosovo & interested in interns from abroad.

Kosovo Women's Network Rr Hajdar Dushi C-2/II-8 , Prishtina; ☏ 038 245 850; e info@womensnetwork.org; www.womensnetwork.org. An umbrella group of women NGOs & a good entry point if you are interested in gender-focused work.

REC Kosovo (Regional Environmental Centre) Kodra e Diellit, Rr Enver Maloku 28, Kati I V të, Prishtina; ☏ 038 225 123; e info@kos.rec.org; http://kos.rec.org. Good contact for anyone looking to find out more about NGOs & projects in the field of environmental protection.

The Ideas Partnership m 045 322 938; e theideaspartnership@gmail.com. Cultural, educational & environmental projects whose initiatives have included greetings cards incorporating silver filigree funded through a microfinance project & supporting rural women, a Prizren filigree co-operative, twinning the Ethnological Museum in Prishtina with a museum in Cambridge, UK, English clubs run by international volunteers in local schools, & a campaign against plastic bags.

Women for Women Rr UÇK (opposite BpB Bank, Prishtina; ☏ 038 248 417; www.womenforwomen.org. This is a Washington NGO with a lot of projects in Kosovo. It is in particular moving into supporting women in business & has therefore worked with MBA students, for example in assisting companies with business plans.

For work in Kosovo try OSCE (*www.osce.org/kosovo*) or UNDP. See also the UN Volunteers Concept (*www.unv.org*) which is aimed at bringing experienced professionals into UN projects on a paid basis. It is possible to do an internship for example where basic expenses are paid and this can be an ideal entry route into development work. For more development jobs try www.developmentex.com or www.reliefweb.int.

For donations of clothes or household goods by internationals in Kosovo, consider the Kosovo Red Cross (☏ *038 522 284*) or the Protestant church (☏ *038 225 330*) or donating them to the Roma camps in the north of Kosovo or to Roma returnees in south Mitrovica. Alternatively, check www.stuffyourrucksack.com which contains lists of charities and small items that you can carry in your backpack and drop off before starting your travels.

STUFF YOUR RUCKSACK – AND MAKE A DIFFERENCE

www.stuffyourrucksack.com is a website set up by TV's Kate Humble which enables travellers to give direct help to small charities, schools or other organisations in the country they are visiting. The idea is to bring small items which will be of use and can be fitted in the rucksack. The charities get exactly what they need and travellers have the chance to meet local people and see how and where their gifts will be used.

The website describes organisations that need your help and lists the items they most need. Check what's needed in Kosovo, contact the organisation to say you're coming and bring not only the much-needed goods but an extra dimension to your travels and the knowledge that in a small way you have made a difference.

www.stuffyourrucksack.com
Responsible tourism in action

Part Two

THE GUIDE

3

Prishtina/Priština

Prishtina is not a city you fall in love with at first sight. It is messy, with centuries-old Ottoman heritage competing with communist designs and recently built architectural monstrosities. This humble-jumble of new and old, Ottoman and communist, innovative and traditional, gives Prishtina a unique urban feel. A century ago, Prishtina was a multi-cultural and vibrant trading town with a colourful bazaar at its centre and a population conversing fluently in Albanian, Turkish and Serbian. Mosques, Catholic and Orthodox churches adorned the city's skyline and a small Jewish community ran its own schools. The forceful transformation from an Ottoman trading town to a communist capital, from Yugoslav socialism to parallel Albanian self-rule and from Milošević to UNMIK rule has left many marks of destruction. Only now, as capital city of an independent state, is Prishtina starting to reassert a new urban identity.

Prishtina has always been a city in flux, with people coming and going. In different waves of migration Prishtina lost its Turkish-speaking urban elite, its Jewish and more recently its Serbian population. The arrival of thousands of international administrators, policemen, NATO soldiers and NGO activists from all corners of the world since 1999 has added a cosmopolitan flavour to the town. The city's sudden exposure to the outside has made it open for change, new cuisine and different ways of life. Today, Mexican, Nepalese and Japanese restaurants are vying for customers alongside the old *qebaptore* (kebab shops) and smoke-filled tea houses.

Prishtina is certainly no beauty, but there are many well-hidden secrets. The best thing about the city is the people you meet. A closer look with an open mind makes Prishtina a good place to explore and a fun place to live in.

HISTORY

The area in and around Prishtina has been inhabited for nearly 10,000 years. Early **Neolithic findings** were discovered dating as far back as the 8th century BC, in the areas surrounding Prishtina, ie: Matiqan, Gračanica and Ulpiana. During the Roman period, Prishtina was part of the province of Dardania and nearby Ulpiana was considered one of the most important Roman cities in the Balkans. In the 2nd century AD, Ulpiana became a Roman municipium. The city suffered tremendous damage from an earthquake in AD518. The Byzantine emperor **Justinian I** decided to rebuild the city in great splendour and renamed it Iustiniana Secunda but with the arrival of Slav tribes in the 6th century, the city again fell into disrepair.

The first historical record mentioning Prishtina dates back to 1342, when the Byzantine emperor Johan Kantakuzen described Prishtina as a 'village'. In the course of the 14th and 15th centuries, Prishtina developed as an important mining and trading centre thanks to its proximity to the rich mining town of Novo Brdo, and due to its position on the Balkan trade routes. The Old Town stretching out between the Vellusha and Prishtevka rivers, which are both covered over today, became an important crafts and trade centre. Prishtina was famous for its annual **trade fairs** (*panair*) and its goat hide and goat hair articles. Around 50 different crafts were practised from tanning to leather dyeing, belt making and silk weaving, as well as crafts related to the military – armourers, smiths, and saddle makers. As early as 1485, Prishtina artisans also started producing gunpowder. Trade was thriving and there was a growing colony of Ragusan traders (from modern-day Dubrovnik) providing the link between Prishtina's craftsmen and the outside world.

The **first mosque** was constructed in the late 14th century while still under Serbian rule. In the early Ottoman era, Islam was an urban phenomenon and only spread slowly with increasing urbanisation. The travel writer Evliya Çelebi, visiting Prishtina in the 1660s, was impressed with its fine gardens and vineyards. In those years, Prishtina was part of the Vushtrri *sançak* and its 2,000 families enjoyed the peace and stability of the Ottoman era. Economic life was controlled by the guild system (*esnafs*) with the tanners' or the bakers' guild controlling prices, limiting unfair competition and acting as banks for their members. Religious life was dominated by religious charitable organisations often building mosques or fountains and providing charity to the poor.

During the **Austrian–Turkish War** in the late 17th century, Prishtina citizens under the leadership of the Catholic Albanian priest Pjeter Bogdani pledged loyalty to the Austrian army and supplied troops. Under Austrian occupation, the Fatih Mosque (Mbretit Mosque) was briefly converted to a Jesuit church. Following the Austrian defeat in January 1690, Prishtina's inhabitants were left at the mercy of Ottoman and Tatar troops who took revenge against the local population as punishment for their co-operation with the Austrians. A French officer travelling to Prishtina noted soon afterwards that 'Prishtina looked impressive from a distance but close up it is a mass of muddy streets and houses made of earth'.

The year 1874 marked a turning point. That year the railway between Thessaloniki and Mitrovica started operations and the seat of the vilayet of Prizren was relocated to Prishtina. This privileged position as 'capital' of the Ottoman *vilayet* lasted only for a short while. In 1912, Prishtina came under Serb rule, then briefly under Bulgarian occupation before reverting back to what then became the 'First Yugoslavia'. The **inter-war period** saw the first exodus of Prishtina's Ottomanised (Turkish-speaking) population. Under German occupation in the 1940s, a large part of Prishtina's already small Jewish community was deported, with Albanian collaboration. The few surviving families eventually left for Israel in 1949. As a result of these wars and forced migration, Prishtina's population dropped to 9,631 inhabitants.

The communist decision to make Prishtina the capital of Kosovo in 1947 ushered in a period of rapid development and outright destruction. The communist slogan at the time was 'destroy the old, build the new'. In a misguided effort to modernise the town, communists set out to destroy the Ottoman bazaar and large parts of the historic centre, including mosques, churches and Ottoman houses. A second agreement signed between Yugoslavia and Turkey in 1953 led to the exodus of several hundred more Turkish-speaking families from Prishtina. They left behind their homes, properties and businesses. Few of the Ottoman town houses survived the communists' **modernisation drive**, with the exception of those that were nationalised like today's Emin Gjiku Museum (see page 127) or Kocadishi House (see page 126).

As capital city and seat of the government, Prishtina creamed off a large share of Yugoslav development funds channelled into Kosovo. As a result the city's population and its economy changed rapidly. In 1966, Prishtina had few paved roads, the old town houses had no running water and cholera was still a problem.

Hasan Prishtina was born in 1873 in Vushtrri. His real name was Hasan Berisha, but he became known as Hasan Prishtina after his election to the Ottoman Parliament representing Prishtina in 1908. Educated at the French school in Thessaloniki, he and Abdyl Frasheri represented the liberal, intellectual wing of the Albanian national movement. Disappointed with the Young Turks, Hasan Prishtina became a key figure in the Albanian national struggle. He took a firm stand condemning the brutal crackdown on the Albanian rebels in 1910 and campaigned actively for Albanian-language schools. In 1913, he was a minister in the Albanian government of Ismail Qemali. Together with Kadri Prishtina and Bajram Curri, he established the Committee for the National Defence of Kosovo. He was also one of the main organisers of the Lushnja Congress in 1920. In 1921, during a brief interlude as Prime Minister of Albania, he tried to dismiss Ahmet Zog from the post of Minister of Interior. He resigned in the face of Zog's march on Tirana. Two months later, Hasan Prishtina and Bajram Curri brought their own troops to Tirana. From then on Zog became the sworn enemy of the Kosovo national movement. In February 1923, Hasan Prishtina and Bajram Curri organised a last uprising of Albanians in Kosovo. Zog responded by sending troops to Junik to deal a fatal blow to the rebels known as 'kaçak'. Zog also co-operated with Yugoslav border troops to prevent kaçaks from crossing back into Albanian territory. In 1924, Zog himself was driven out of Albania by his opponents. He took shelter in Belgrade. Hasan Prishtina fled to Vienna where he first survived an attempt on his own life. Upon Zog's instigation, Hasan Prishtina was condemned to death in absentia. He was imprisoned in Belgrade for a period, but released in 1931. In 1933, he was killed by an Albanian in a café in Thessaloniki on the orders of King Zog and the Serbian government.

Prizren continued to be the largest town in Kosovo. Massive investments in state institutions like the newly founded Prishtina University, the construction of new high-rise socialist apartment blocks and a new Industrial Zone on the outskirts of the city attracted large numbers of internal migrants. Within a decade, Prishtina nearly doubled its population from about 69,514 in 1971 to 109,208 in 1981. This golden age of externally financed rapid growth was cut short by Yugoslavia's economic collapse and the 1981 student revolts. Prishtina, like the rest of Kosovo, slid into a deepening economic and social crisis. The year 1989 saw the revocation of Kosovo's autonomy under Milošević, **the rise of Serb nationalism** and mass dismissals of ethnic Albanians. During the 1990s, poverty and hardship spread and migration tore families apart. Albanian schools and universities were forced to operate secretly in private homes, whilst underfunded and poorly equipped private clinics struggled to substitute for public health care. Albanian public life in the capital – from theatre and art exhibitions to music concerts – came to a complete halt.

Prishtina was spared large-scale destruction compared with towns like Gjakova or Peja that suffered heavily at the hands of Serbian forces. For their strategic importance, however, a number of military targets were hit in Prishtina during NATO's aerial campaign, including the post office, police headquarters and army barracks (today's Adem Jashari garrison on the road to Fushë-Kosova).

The majority Albanian population fled the town in large numbers to escape Serb police and paramilitary units. The first NATO troops to enter Prishtina in early June 1999 were the Brits, although to NATO's diplomatic embarrassment Russian troops arrived first at the airport. Apartments were occupied illegally and the Roma quarter behind the city park was torched. In summer 1999, most urban Serbs and

Roma fled Prishtina for fear of reprisal acts. The last official census conducted in the city in 1991 put the Serb population in Prishtina municipality at 26,893. By 2002, the number of Serbs in Prishtina had dropped to 12,405, mostly living in surrounding villages such as Gračanica, Laplje Selo and Çaglavica (which now make up a separate municipality), with fewer than 50 in Prishtina Town.

Within weeks of the **UN resolution**, the town was flooded with refugees unable to return to their destroyed rural homes, NATO soldiers and UN officials, relief workers and returnees from around the world. A popular myth has circulated in the local and international communities that Prishtina is a city of half a million inhabitants. Recent estimates, based on primary school enrolment figures, utility connections and studies on the quantity of bread consumed put the resident population at a much more modest 250,000.

As a capital city and seat of the UN administration (UNMIK), Prishtina benefited greatly from a high concentration of international staff with disposable incomes and international organisations with sizeable budgets. The injection of reconstruction funds from donors, international organisations and the Albanian diaspora has fuelled an unrivalled, yet short-lived, economic boom. A plethora of new cafés, restaurants and private businesses opened to cater for new (and international) demand. On 17 February 2008, Kosovo's declaration of independence made Prishtina the capital city of Europe's youngest state. The main roads were clogged with celebrators dancing and waving the old Albanian and new Kosovar flag. It truly was a historic moment and marked the beginning of yet another era for this politically battered town.

GETTING THERE AND AWAY

BY AIR See *Chapter 2, Getting there and away*, page 48.

Airport transfers Since there is not yet an airport bus service out of Prishtina International Airport, a **pre-arranged taxi collection** is the most economic method of travel into the city. If you know your arrival time, you can book a pick-up service with one of the Prishtina taxi firms (for contact details, see page 94). A ride into Prishtina from the airport costs about €15, plus a €2 airport parking fee. Alternatively, you may share a ride to town with other passengers through one of the airport taxis outside the arrival hall. While these taxis are sometimes more costly, you should not pay more than €20 per person. Traffic volumes vary during the day (peaking between 16.00 and 17.30) but the trip to the centre should take between 20 and 40 minutes.

Before you speed off from the airport take a bit of time to consider the changes that have occurred here. In the 1990s, this was a Yugoslav army airport only; then you may also remember the airport from the news in 1999 when, after the NATO and Russian intervention against Serbia, there was a minor diplomatic incident when Russian forces arrived at the airport before the joint NATO forces (the Russian KFOR troops have since left Kosovo altogether). Subsequently, during the UNMIK era, the flag of Iceland was flown here; with Kosovo not being a country at that point the airport could not be licensed by the international authorities, so UNMIK contracted with Iceland (rather like the way in which the mobile-phone code was contracted to Monaco on account of the absence of a country code). With the advent of Kosovo's independence, the airport finally received its own licence and now the Kosovar flag flies.

BY BUS The most economical way to reach Prishtina from other towns is by bus or long-distance coach. Prishtina's central bus station (\ *038 540 142/ 550 011*) is just minutes away from the central Rr Bill Clinton; about seven minutes from the centre by taxi, or roughly 20 minutes on foot. Unfortunately, none of the city bus lines connect with the bus station directly. Your best bet is bus No 1, although the bus stop for No 1 is a five-minute walk from the bus station, across two busy roads, so a taxi is certainly more convenient if you are carrying luggage! Taxis entering the bus station parking area are required to pay a €1 entrance fee, so you might be tempted to make your way just outside the entrance barrier and flag down one of the many passing taxis. All buses in Kosovo are run by independent travel companies. Times may vary and therefore for long-distance buses it is worth double-checking the time by asking someone to call or even dropping by the bus station to check. Buses to/from Sarajevo, Belgrade, Tirana and other more far-flung towns may also get fully booked so consider buying your ticket in advance. For more details of buses to cities in Kosovo, see the timetable in *Chapter 2*, page 60, or the relevant city section, eg: for buses to Prizren, see *Prizren*, page 199. For buses to international destinations, see *Chapter 2, Getting there and away*, page 48.

BY RAIL See *Chapter 2, Getting there and away*, page 48.
Prishtina's railway station (\ *038 518 449*) is no more than a small house – a sleepy and forlorn place to arrive at (in fact be careful that you don't miss it – it is about 1km out of town at the foot of Dragodan Hill). The traditional main station is Fushë-Kosova (Kosovo Polje) located 7km west of Prishtina. There is a regular bus schedule (No 1) operating between Prishtina city centre and Fushë-Kosova/Kosovo Polje train station.
    The connection with Leshak, a small town bordering Serbia in the north, is temporarily out of service. There is a train leaving Prishtina at 07.50, arriving in Peja at 09.47, and a later one departing at 16.30, arriving in Peja at 18.25. The trains from Peja to Prishtina leave daily at 05.30 and 11.10. For an up-to-date train schedule, including the trains to the south and Skopje, it's best to check the Kosovo Railway website (*www.kosovorailway.com*) or call \ 038 536 619. The website is in Albanian, Serbian and English.

BY CAR Arriving in Prishtina by car requires patience and strong nerves. The main roads leading to the city centre quickly become congested. There are no signposts directing you to the city centre, so orientation can be rather challenging at first. If you are **arriving by road from Skopje**, the first sign of Prishtina approaching is the Grand Store shopping centre on your left-hand side. As you approach the crest of a hill soon after, a replica of New York's Statue of Liberty and a large flag on a roundabout will be in your line of sight as you descend. At the bottom of the hill, keep right and head towards the main roundabout. The statue is on your left, and you just continue straight ahead onto Rr Dëshmorët e Kombit, an extension of Rr Nëne Terezë, or turn right at the roundabout to head up to the university area.
    If you are **arriving from the northeast**, from Niš or the Merdare border crossing, you just stay on the main road that leads straight into town. As the street becomes more alive with people, cars and shops you know you are getting closer to the centre. If you are heading for the Old Town or Germia National Park, continue straight at the first roundabout and turn left at the first traffic light. Rr Nëne Terezë is now closed to traffic and most of the surrounding streets get jammed quickly, and finding parking is difficult. To avoid stress, it's best to park your car at the main public parking facility, behind the Boro Ramiz Sports Complex. To get there, keep to the right at the first roundabout and turn left at the first traffic light. Continue straight along Rr Luan Haradinaj until you pass the yellow 'Newborn Sign' on your right. Turn right at the traffic light; the main parking facility is on your right-hand side – about 50m from the turn. It is open 24/7

Few citizens or visitors give much thought to the meaning of the names of different quarters of the town. A curious traveller, however, may wonder about the meaning of 'Tauk Bahqe', 'Ulpiana' or 'Lakrishte'.

In translation, Prishtina's quarters tell an almost fairytale-like story. Ulpiana was named after the nearby Roman city and later seat of a bishopric, and Dardania, a socialist housing settlement, is named after the Dardani tribe that also gave its name to the Roman province. The Dragodan Hill translates to 'good day' and the housing area of Bregu i Diellit is nothing other than a 'sunny hill'. Peyton City, one of the most vibrant areas in town, is named after a television series from the 1970s. Throughout the Ottoman period, cannonballs were stored in Tophane (from *top*, meaning 'cannon', in Turkish), at a safe distance from the old part of town. At one point in history, there must have been chickens running around the area of Tauk Bahqe, as its name literally means 'chicken garden'. Cabbage fields gave their names to Lakrishte, a block of apartments facing Dardania. Last but not least, Kodra e Trimave is 'the hill of the braves' – a title of honour awarded to the inhabitants of this quarter for their role in the 1981 demonstrations and throughout the difficult 1990s.

(receipts only between 06.00 and 22.00). The fare for up to 12 hours' parking is €0.50 and €1 for 24 hours. If you lose your ticket the standard fare is €5. There is also 'Liberty' covered parking located underneath the stadium. Short-term parking here (up to 12 hours) costs €1 and €2 for 24 hours.

Arriving from the west, from Montenegro, Peja or the airport, it's even easier. Simply follow the two-lane road passing through Fushë-Kosova that eventually turns into Rr Bill Clinton as you enter the city (go straight over the large roundabout/flyover). Take a left on Rr Dëshmorët e Kombit at the second traffic light after winding up a little hill. This road leads directly to the Hotel Grand at the first traffic-light intersection on Rr Nëne Terezë.

Once in town, watch out for other cars and youngsters criss-crossing the streets at all times and seemingly everywhere. The **parking** situation has improved recently thanks to several new private and public parking facilities. The standard fare at private parking places across town is €1 for both short and longer stays. There are several private parking places either side of Rr UÇK and near the OSCE headquarters, for example, but none of them offer night-time guarded services. This may be a factor in choosing a hotel, although car crime in Prishtina is relatively rare.

Be warned: the municipality earns good income from **traffic fines** and the police are quick at dismantling the licence plate of an illegally parked car. In case your licence plate or entire car is no longer where you left it, you are best advised to check at the central police station on Rr Luan Haradinaj. Kosovo police have a good reputation for being nearly corruption-proof, so do not try to buy influence! The standard traffic fine is €35 and must be paid directly at the bank (closed Sundays), although if you are lucky you may be presented with a POS terminal to pay by card immediately which will save you time. The police are permitted to retain your licence or car documents until you pay.

GETTING AROUND

The biggest challenge in Prishtina is the relative chaos when it comes to street names. For decades the naming of streets has been highly politicised and names have changed as often as the regimes have tumbled. What is today Nëne Terezë Street was once proudly called Marshal Tito, Bill Clinton Boulevard was previously named after Lenin, and Rr Tirana replaced Rr Belgrade. It can even happen that one street has three names: Dubrovnik (its former name), Gazmend Zajmi (its current name) and San Francisco – the name used by some internationals to describe it owing to the steep slope. Confusing as this might be at first glance, the favoured method for giving directions is by reference to landmarks. It's not uncommon to use 'police avenue', referring to the area near the main police station, or to refer to streets by their better-known restaurants, petrol stations or shops. Don't worry, even taxi drivers struggle at times to find their way, but don't hesitate to ask – most Kosovars will be very happy to help you and you will be surprised just how many passers-by will speak foreign languages. If they do not speak English, you can always try your luck with German or Serbian.

ON FOOT   The centre of Prishtina is easily accessible on foot since most historic sites, bars, restaurants and hotels are within walking distance of each other. With Rr Nëne Terezë closed to traffic, it is easiest to simply walk around central Prishtina. Be sure to wear comfortable shoes. Be aware, however, that moving around with a baby pushchair is not easy! Also watch out for the occasional pothole, especially late at night. Walking in Prishtina is generally safe, even at night-time, compared with other European capitals, but it's still a good idea to take a torch with you if you are not too familiar with the city. Most streets in the centre are well lit nowadays and usually busy till late at night, but in case there is an unexpected electricity outage it's better to play safe than to rely on your memory of previously seen pot-holes!

BY BUS AND MINIBUS   The Urban Transport Company of the municipality (\ *038 603 574;* m *044 361 310*) has its headquarters in the parallel street behind the bowling alley near Garden Restaurant, and operates Lines 1 to 4 of the local bus services. Others are operated by private companies.

Do not expect to get any orientation from the maps inside the bus or external electronic signs since most buses are donated or bought from Western countries, so you may be surprised to find instead external signs to 'Berliner Platz' or guidance on how to connect with the Paris metro! The buses are not really equipped for pushchairs and are not capable of accommodating wheelchairs.

The fares on all buses are €0.30 and payable to a conductor on board, except with some newer buses where you may find you need to pay at a turnstile when you enter. Keep your ticket as inspections may occur. If you are not sure when to get off, simply ask a fellow passenger.

At the time of writing there was no clear published timetable. There are seven bus lines operating in Prishtina. A useful bus route is No 4 which runs from Matiqan to Germia Park, running down past the roundabout and Baci Hotel, then on past the PTK headquarters to the Grand Hotel, down 'police avenue' or Rr Luan Haradinaj past the old UNMIK headquarters (back of the Grand Hotel), and on to OSCE, Rr UÇK, the Old Town/museum and mosques and right up to Germia Park. There are buses every five to ten minutes during the day from 06.00 until about 18.00, after which they are only every 15 to 20 minutes, with the last at 21.00. Another useful bus route is No 1, which runs from the Technical Faculty near the hospital to Rilindja and up to Fushë-Kosova. This bus connects with the train station in Fushë-Kosova. No 6 buses go to the EULEX headquarters.

Buses can get full and it may be that you can't get on. Because of this and the long waits between buses, some cars ply the main part of the most popular route – No 4, starting from the bus stop outside Fellini and Lounge at Tre Kapelle and ending in Sunny Hill. They take four passengers from the bus stop and charge €0.40 each. You can identify them by the fact they indicate the number by putting up four fingers.

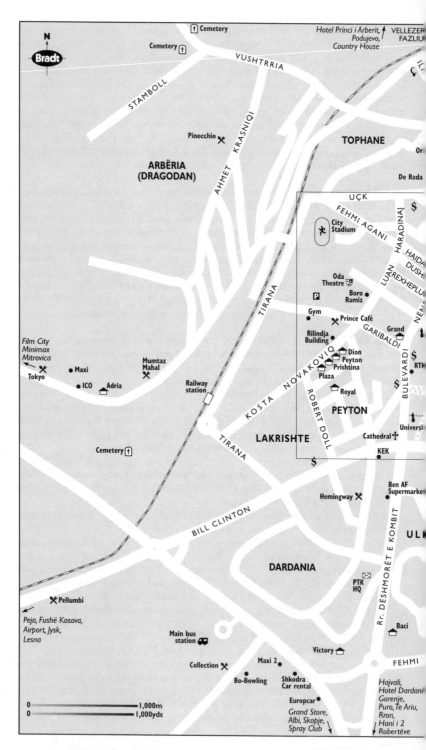

N

Brad†

Cemetery †

Cemetery †

VUSHTRRIA

Hotel Princi i Arberit,
Podujevo,
Country House

VELLEZER
FAZLIU

STAMBOLL

AHMET KRASNIQI

Pinocchio ✕

ARBËRIA
(DRAGODAN)

TOPHANE

Or

De Rada

UÇK

FEHMI AGANI

HARADINAJ

HAIDA

City
Stadium

DUSH

LUAN ZREXHEPLU

Oda
Theatre

NËN

Boro ●
Ramiz

P

Gym
●

✕ Prince Café

GARIBALDI

Grand
●

Rilindja
Building

■ Dion
● Peyton
■ Prishtina

BULEVARDI

$

RTK

Plaza ■

$

TIRANA

Film City
Minimax
Mitrovica

✕
Tokyo

● Maxi

● ICO   Adria

Mumtaz
Mahal ✕

Railway
station

KOSTA NOVAKOVIQ

ROBERT DOLL

Royal ▯

PEYTON

Universi

Cathedral †

$

Cemetery †

TIRANA

LAKRISHTE

KEK

$

Ben AF
Supermarke

Hemingway ✕

Rr. DËSHMORËT E KOMBIT

ULK

BILL CLINTON

DARDANIA

PTK
HQ

Baci
▯

✕ Pellumbi

Peja, Fushë Kosova,
Airport, Jysk,
Lesna

Main bus
station 🚌

Victory ⌂

FEHMI

Collection ✕

● Maxi 2

Bo-Bowling   Shkodra
Car rental

Europcar ●

Grand Store,
Albi, Skopje,
Spray Club

Hajvali,
Hotel Dardani
Gorenje,
Puro, Te Ariu,
Rron,
Hani i 2
Robertëve

0   1,000m
0   1,000yds

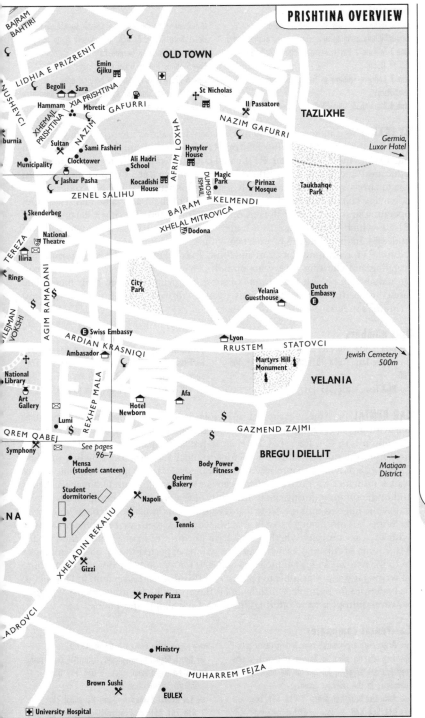

PRISHTINA OVERVIEW

OLD TOWN

TAZLIXHE

Germia,
Luxor Hotel

BAJRAM
BAHTIRI

LIDHIA E PRIZRENIT

Emin
Gjiku

Begolli

Sara

XIA PRISHTINA

Hammam

NAZIM GAFURRI

Mbretit

St Nicholas

Il Passatore

NAZIM GAFURRI

NUSHEVCI

XHEMAJL
PRISHTINA

NAZIM

burnia

Sultan

Sami Fashëri

Clocktower

Municipality

Jashar Pasha

ZENEL SALIHU

Ali Hadri
School

AFRIM LOXHA

Hynyler
House

Kocadishi
House

DUMOSHI
ISMAIL

Magic
Park

Pirinaz
Mosque

BAJRAM KELMENDI

XHELAL MITROVICA

Dodona

Taukbahqe
Park

Skenderbeg

National
Theatre

TEREZA

Iliria

Rings

AGIM RAMADANI

City
Park

Velania
Guesthouse

Dutch
Embassy

TLEJMAN
VOKSHI

Swiss Embassy

ARDIAN KRASNIQI

Ambasador

National
Library

Art
Gallery

REXHEP MALA

Hotel
Newborn

Afa

Lyon

RRUSTEM STATOVCI

Martyrs Hill
Monument

VELANIA

Jewish Cemetery
500m

Lumi

QREM QABEJ

Symphony

See pages
96–7

GAZMEND ZAJMI

BREGU I DIELLIT

Matiqan
District

Mensa
(student canteen)

Body Power
Fitness

Qerimi
Bakery

Student
dormitories

Napoli

NA

XHELADIN REKALIU

Tennis

Gizzi

Proper Pizza

ADROVCI

Ministry

MUHARREM FEJZA

Brown Sushi

EULEX

University Hospital

Bus routes

Line 1 Technical Faculty then behind Boro Ramiz/Rilindja building near the gym to Fushë-Kosova
Line 2 As Line 1 but starts at Bregu i Diellit/Sunny Hill to Obiliq
Line 3 Kodra e Trimave to Sunny Hill Medical Centre (ambulant)
Line 4 Matiqan & Sunny Hill via roundabout (Baci Hotel) along Rr Dëshmorët e Kombit to RTK, Grand Hotel, Boro Ramiz, Rr UÇK, municipality & up along Rr Nazim Gafurri to Germia Park
Line 5 Sunny Hill to Sofali (turns right at AUK)
Line 6 Arbëria (Dragodan) to hospital area
Line 7 Kolovice, along Rr Agim Ramadani to Kosovatex in Industrial Zone

BY TAXI There are several clearly marked taxi stops across town, including one just opposite the Grand Hotel [96 D5] on Rr Nëne Terezë, another one across from the OSCE headquarters on Rr Luan Haradinaj, one next to the Ministry of Education and Science near the University or opposite the post and telecom headquarters on Rr Dëshmorët e Kombit in Ulpiana. In addition, you can wave down any taxi you see on the street or call one of the many radio taxi companies operating in town. Almost all taxis operate with meters showing a starting fare of €1.50 (which may increase to €2 after 22.00). Most trips across town will cost under €4. In the event you board a taxi without a meter, do agree on a fare between €2 and €3 for any inner-city start and finish. In contrast to neighbouring countries, haggling and cheating is very uncommon. Drivers can produce a formal receipt on request; simply ask for a *facture* or most can print one from their meter. The latest hit are the new London taxis (seating up to five) – an unusual sight on Prishtina's streets.

Taxi numbers

- **Beki** ☎ 038 540 820; m 044 503 603
- **London Taxi** ☎ 038 703 703; m 044/049 300 300
- **RGB Taxi** ☎ 038 515 151
- **Roberti Taxi** ☎ 038 500 006; m 044 111 999
- **Titanic Taxi** ☎ 038 232 322; m 044 232 324
- **Velania Taxi** ☎ 038 225 325; m 044 503 703
- **VIP Taxi** ☎ 038 500 044; m 044 333 444

CAR RENTAL Previously, car rental in Kosovo was almost prohibitively expensive, but with increased competition prices are dropping fast. They vary from €20 per day upwards to €70 for a 4×4. Several car-rental companies are based around the road from the bus station to the Victory roundabout (near Bo-Bowling or Maxi 2). Note all providers charge a €2,000 insurance excess and it is not possible to buy waiver insurance for this. Rental cars can get booked up around holiday weekends and in the summer during the return visits of the diaspora, so book ahead. Expect to pay the full cost upfront. Note that few of the cars available can be used to travel to Serbia but most can go to Albania, Macedonia, Croatia or Montenegro. Check with the car company whether they have pre-paid insurance (often the case for Macedonia or Albania), or whether you will be expected to pay border insurance (€15 for two weeks for Montenegro and €30 for a month for Bosnia). At the time of writing it was not possible to take a car in Prishtina and drop it off in Dubrovnik or Podgorica for example, which hampers the possibility for using open-jaw flights; however, Europcar were offering this service for Skopje and Tirana.

Car-rental companies

- **Argus** www.argusrentals.com. International pick-ups/drop-offs. No office in Kosovo as such. It seems they just act as agent for one of the other companies in the relevant country.
- **Auto Lux** Near Europcar; ☎ 038 551 365; m 044 566 668; e auto.lux@hotmail.com; www.rent-autolux.com; ⊕ 08.00–19.00
- **Bosch Global Development** Industrial Zone, Fushë-Kosova Rd (right-hand side); ☎ 038 534 055; e info@gdkosova.com
- **Car Rental Kosovo** Rr Luan Haradinaj 18; ☎ 038 241 841; www.carrentalkosovo.com. Operated

by Eurosky Travel Company. Allows for a one-way drop-off in Skopje.

🚗 **Europcar** e info@europcar-ks.com; www.europcar-ks.com. 3 offices in Prishtina: Arbëria, near Film City; ✆ 038 222 122; Bus Station Rd (Lagjia Emshirit) near Maxi 2; ✆ 038 594 101; ✆ 038 541 401; Prishtina Airport; m 044 116 746 (24hr & emergency number). Special offers for weekend & long-term hires & chauffeur services. With Bosch Global Development (see above) probably the most professional & friendly of the car-hire companies.

🚗 **Hertz** Inside Grand Hotel ground floor; m 044 811 549; e hertzkosova@yahoo.com

🚗 **MCM Rent** Rr Fehmi Agani 9/2 (near Amelie Espresso Bar); ✆ 038 240 024; e info@mcmrent.com; www.mcmrent.com. Minimum age restriction 21 years.

🚗 **Shotani** Bus Station Rd (just down from Hotel Victory on the opposite side); ✆ 038 544 224; m 044 286 286/049 218 793; e info@rentacarshotani.com; www.rentacarshotani.com

TRAVEL AGENCIES

Travel agencies in Prishtina are used to visitors from around the world in need of quick, reliable and good advice. The staff almost invariably speak very good English and are extremely helpful.

Alta Via Rr Luan Haradinaj 19 (in front of police station No 1); ✆ 038 543 543; e info@altaviatravel.com; www.altaviatravel.com; ⊕ 08.30–19.00 Mon–Fri, 09.00–16.00 Sat. Phenomenally helpful staff offering very good service. Centrally located.

Eurokoha Rr Garibaldi (to the side of the Hotel Grand); ✆ 038 235 235/245 998; e info@eurokoha.net; www.eurokoha.net; ⊕ 08.00–20.00 Mon–Sat. Partners of Kosovo's (designated) national airline Kosova Airlines & agent for Air Berlin & Germanwings.

Eurosky Rr Luan Haradinaj 18; ✆ 038 241 841; e info@eurosky-travel.com; www.eurosky-travel.com; ⊕ 09.00–19.00 Mon–Fri, 10.00–15.00 Sat. Now part of the Hogg Robinson international travel group.

MCM Travel Rr Nëne Terezë/Dëshmorët e Kombit, just along from the Grand Hotel next to the new ProCredit Bank headquarters; ✆ 038 242 424/233 814; e info@mcmtravel.net; www.mcmtravel.net; ⊕ 09.00–20.00 Mon–Sat. Local partners of Austrian Airlines & also agents for Montenegro Airlines.

WHERE TO STAY

Prishtina's hotel scene has been catching up fast. A large international clientele of diplomats and consultants has driven up prices and standards – most hotels now offer generator-powered electricity 24/7 (a real plus, especially in winter), free en-suite and wireless internet access, satellite TV, air conditioning and sometimes even some drinks on the house. The luxury hotels offer saunas, jacuzzis and good restaurant menus. Expect to pay around €100 for a luxury room; the standard price for a single is €45–60. There are also some hotels now for more budget-conscious travellers, but at the lower end still expect to pay €15 a night for minimal comfort. With some exceptions, most hotels are within walking distance from the most important sights. All prices include breakfast unless otherwise indicated.

UPMARKET $$$$

🏠 **Gorenje Hotel** (18 apts) Veternik; ✆ 038 557 700; e info@hotel-gntc.com; www.hotelgorenjenititiki.com. Built in 2005 by a Kosovar partner of the Slovenian white-goods producer Gorenje, this hotel is a luxury alternative for guests with their own transport. Located in Veternik, the commercial zone which is to the south of Prishtina, the rooms offer comfort, internet access, laundry services & a view from the restaurant terrace on the top floor. The top-end business centre seats 65 & is fully equipped with a video beamer & a sound system can be hired for €150. There are also smaller business rooms to hire for €100. The location isn't perfect if you want to be in the heart of the city as walking is really not an option. However, it's ideal for heavyweight business negotiations or a conference or generally if you have your own wheels & really want top-end facilities rather than in-town convenience. AC & internet access come as standard. To get to the hotel enter the lobby & take the lift immediately on your left up to the top floor.

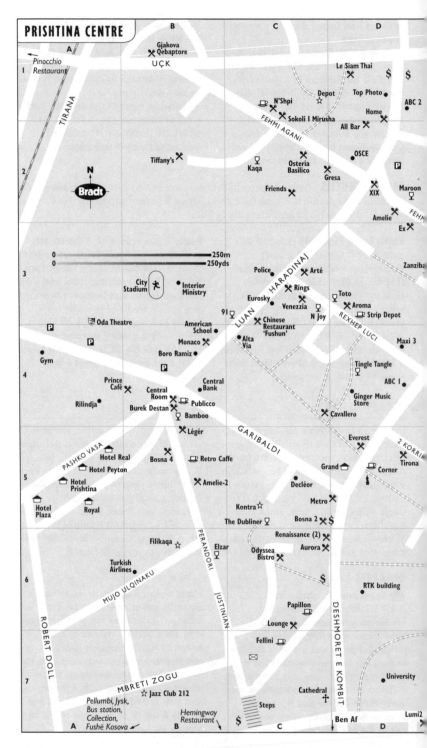

PRISHTINA CENTRE

Pinocchio Restaurant

Gjakova X Qebaptore

UÇK

Le Siam Thai X

N'Shpi

Depot ☆

Top Photo

ABC 2

FEHMI AGANI

Sokoli I Mirusha

Home

All Bar X

Tiffany's X

Kaqa

Osteria Basilico

Gresa X

OSCE

XIX X

Maroon

Friends X

Amelie X

Ex X

Bradt

N

0   250m
0   250yds

City Stadium

Interior Ministry

Police

Arté X

Zanziba

Oda Theatre

Eurosky

Rings X

Toto

Aroma X

Strip Depot

Venezzia

N Joy

91

Chinese Restaurant 'Fushun'

Maxi 3

American School

Alta Via

Gym

Monaco X

Tingle Tangle

Boro Ramiz

ABC 1

Prince Café

Central Room

Central Bank

Ginger Music Store

Rilindja

Burek Destan

Publicco

Cavallero X

Bamboo

Légér X

GARIBALDI

Everest X

2 KORRIK

PASHKO VASA

Hotel Real

Bosna 4 X

Retro Caffe

Grand

Corner

Tirona

Hotel Peyton

Hotel Prishtina

Amelie-2 X

Decléor

Metro X

Hotel Plaza

Royal

Kontra ☆

The Dubliner

Bosna 2 X

Filikaqa ☆

Elzar

Renaissance (2) X

PERANDORI

Odyssea Bistro X

Aurora X

Turkish Airlines

MUJO ULQINAKU

JUSTINIAN

RTK building

Papillon

DESHMORET E KOMBIT

ROBERT DOLL

Lounge X

Fellini

University

MBRETI ZOGU

☆ Jazz Club 212

Cathedral

Pellumbi, Jysk, Bus station, Collection, Fushë Kosova

Hemingway Restaurant

Steps

Ben Af

Lumi2

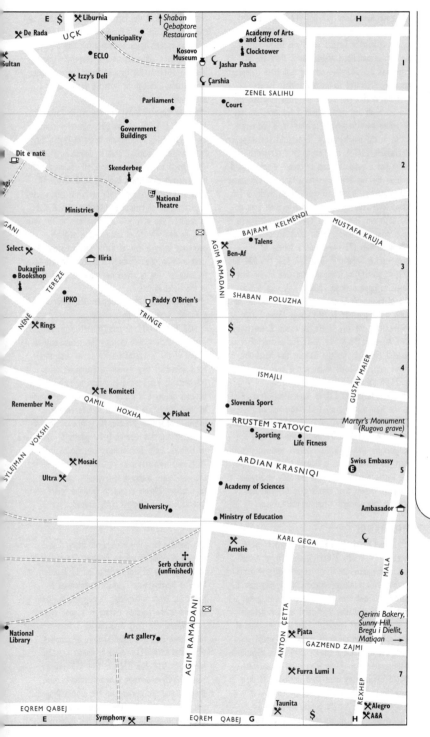

E $ ✕ Liburnia   F ↑ Shaban Qebaptore Restaurant   G   H

✕ De Rada

UÇK

● Municipality

Academy of Arts and Sciences ●

Clocktower ●

Sultan

● ECLO

Kosovo Museum

Jashar Pasha

1

✕ Izzy's Deli

Çarshia

ZENEL SALIHU

● Parliament

● Court

● Government Buildings

Dit e natë

2

Skenderbeg

GANI

agi

Ministries ●

National Theatre

BAJRAM KELMENDI

MUSTAFA KRUJA

Select ✕

Iliria

AGIM RAMADANI

✕ Ben-Af

● Talens

3

Dukagjini ● Bookshop

TEREZE

$

SHABAN POLUZHA

● IPKO

Paddy O'Brien's

TRINGE

NËNË

✕ Rings

$

ISMAJLI

GUSTAV MAIER

4

✕ Te Komiteti

QAMIL HOXHA

Remember Me ●

✕ Pishat

● Slovenia Sport

$

SYLEJMAN VOKSHI

RRUSTEM STATOVCI

Martyr's Monument (Rugova grave)

✕ Mosaic

● Sporting

Life Fitness ●

Swiss Embassy

5

Ultra ✕

ARDIAN KRASNIQI

University ●

● Academy of Sciences

Ambasador

● Ministry of Education

KARL GEGA

6

✕ Amelie

Serb church (unfinished) †

AGIM RAMADANI

MALA

Qerimi Bakery, Sunny Hill, Bregu i Diellit, Matiqan →

ANTON ÇETTA

✕ Pjata

GAZMEND ZAJMI

National Library

Art gallery ●

✕ Furra Lumi I

REXHEP

7

EQREM QABEJ

Taunita ✕

✕ Alegro

E   F ✕ Symphony   EQREM QABEJ   G $ H ✕ A&A

⌂ **Hotel Ambasador** [97 H5] (12 rooms, 6 apts) Rr Ardian Krasniqi 1; ☎ 038 248 300/400; e info@hotel-ambasador.com; www.hotel-ambasador.com. Hotel Ambasador is truly one of Prishtina's top addresses offering high-class comfort, tastefully decorated rooms & first-class service. Centrally located just beside the Swiss embassy, you can reach all key sights within a few mins on foot. All rooms have free Wi-Fi, satellite TV, 8 courtesy drinks in the minibar, & AC. Generators ensure power is available 24/7 & the beautifully decorated b/fast buffet has a good selection of cheese, meats, eggs & fruit. At the top-floor hotel restaurant you can savour Italian starters, traditional oven dishes, steaks & fish. Sauna lovers can also enjoy the relaxation area in the basement. The sauna is open to outside guests upon prior reservation. Credit cards accepted.

⌂ **Hotel Baci** (22 rooms, inc 5 suites) Rr Dëshmorët e Kombit; ☎ 038 548 356; m 044 888 882; e hotel@bacicompany.com. One of the first hotels to open back in 2000, & still regarded as one of Prishtina's better establishments. Located on a main traffic junction (*rrethi*) about 15mins' walk southeast of the city centre, all rooms & the lobby have AC, cable TV & free Wi-Fi. The overall décor is tasteful. Unusually for the Balkans this hotel also allows pets. The hotel restaurant is open from 07.00 to 24.00 daily.

⌂ **Hotel Iliria** [97 E3] Rr Nëne Terezë (next door to the National Theatre). Under communism this was Prishtina's luxury address. Marshal Tito himself stayed twice in Apt 104. During the 1990s, it was temporarily used to house refugees from the Yugoslav wars. Thereafter it was a budget location. Following the hotel's privatisation, it is currently undergoing a complete facelift & is expected to be renovated to at least international 4-star standard. Thanks to its

central location & the fact it is being renovated by the owner of the Swiss Diamond Hotel in Lugano everyone expects it to become again one of Prishtina's top addresses once it reopens – most likely in 2011. At the time of writing it was under construction, although at least 50 rooms are anticipated.

⌂ **Hotel Royal** [96 A5] (14 rooms) Rr Pashko Vasa 3; ☎ 038 220 902; e info@royalhotel-pr.com; www.royalhotel-pr.com. In the heart of Peyton City, a fast-changing & popular area in downtown Prishtina, Hotel Royal offers elegant rooms, all equipped with free internet connection, heating, AC & digital TV, some with jacuzzi/sauna. From here it's only a few steps to some of Prishtina's trendiest bars & clubs. In summer, you may also dip your toes in the small outdoor pool. The hotel restaurant is stylishly decorated using a mix of earth-coloured stone & steel, with an open chimney & outdoor terrace for the summer. The b/fast is not quite as good as that in the Hotel Prishtina.

⌂ **Hotel Victory** (42 rooms) Rr Dëshmorët e Kombit, near the main roundabout; ☎ 038 543 267/77; e info@hotel-victory.com; www.hotel-victory.com. Sporting the second-biggest replica of the Statue of Liberty on its roof, this hotel added its own flavour to Prishtina's urban silhouette. It has been a long-time favourite for business guests & a major hub for diplomats coming to town. Prices are hefty, but include ensuite, internet connection, minibar, AC, central heating & jacuzzi. It also has free Wi-Fi for guests & visitors in its business suite. Fax facilities are also available. With your own transport or a taxi you can be in the city centre within a few minutes, on foot it takes about 20mins to get to Rr Nëne Terezë. Reservations can also be made online.

MID-RANGE $$$

⌂ **Grand Hotel** [96 D5] (368 rooms) Rr Nëne Terezë; ☎ 038 220 210/11; e info@grandhotel-pr.com, for reservations; e reception@grandhotel-pr.com; www.grandhotel-pr.com. Undergoing slow & partial refurbishment at the time of writing but still with rooms available, the Grand Hotel is definitely one of Prishtina's landmarks. Under communism it was only the *crème de la crème* who would stay here, but its glamour quickly declined as Yugoslavia disintegrated. During the war, some of the most-feared paramilitary units used the hotel as their base. In the years since, it has served as a temporary home for UN police, diplomats & international officials. Its very central position makes

it a popular for conferences (with more than 5 venues) & public festivities. On special occasions like the anniversary of independence on 17 February, the lobby is buzzing with journalists, diplomats & politicians. Wi-Fi is available throughout the building. In summer the outdoor terrace is a good meeting point. Whether it truly deserves its '5 stars' remains to be seen once the refurbishment is complete.

⌂ **Hotel Adria** (23 rooms) Rr Ahmet Krasniqi, Arbëria; ☎ 038 226 222; m 044 355 366; e hoteladria@yahoo.com; www.hoteladria-ks.com. Useful if you are working on the Arbëria/Dragodan side of town, near ICO, the embassies or USAID, or if you have to get to Mitrovica as this hotel is close to the road to Mitrovica & KFOR Film City. It is about 300m from the housing district of Arbëria. AC, cable TV & internet in all rooms. It's a 5min taxi ride to get downtown.

🏠 **Hotel Afa** (70 rooms) Rr Ali Kelmendi 15, Aktash; ✆ 038 227 722/244 919; e office@hotelafa.com; www.hotelafa.com. Hotel Afa is a good alternative to the more expensive locations downtown, situated about 15mins' walk from Rr Nënë Terezë uphill in a residential neighbourhood, with a nice quiet outdoor terrace at the back. All rooms include a laundry service & come with bath, AC, cable TV, free Wi-Fi, telephone & a minibar. Conference rooms can also be hired for meetings. The hotel generally gets glowing reports for customer service.

🏠 **Hotel Dardania** (12 rooms) Veternik; ✆ 038 602 330; m 044 160 713. On the left-hand side of the road towards Gračanica after the Gorenje building. Internet, cable TV, AC. Restaurant with traditional food. Indoor pool.

🏠 **Hotel Luxor** (14 rooms) Rr Nazim Gafurri; ✆ 038 517 888; e reservation@hotel-luxor.net; www.hotelluxor.net. You can't miss this high-rise glassy building sticking out against the hilly, green background. Situated on the main road to Germia National Park, close to the American University, it's a good location for early-morning joggers or if you want some fresher air during the dusty summer months. Good service & modern, with fresh white duvets; spacious singles with balconies. A regular bus service (No 4) takes you to the centre in less than 15mins or you can order a taxi.

🏠 **Hotel Newborn** (12 rooms) Rr Mark Berisha 27; ✆ 038 227 120; e info@hotel-newborn.com; www.hotel-newborn.com. Located in a quiet area off Gazmend Zajmi to the back of Pjata Restaurant below Hotel Afa. Look for the yellow & red neon sign. 10 nice & clean sgls & 2 dbls, heating, Wi-Fi throughout, TV, minibar but no AC. Very reasonable prices – especially if there's just one of you in a single room. B/fast included.

🏠 **Hotel Ora** (35 rooms) Rr Anton Çajupi 4; ✆ 038 720 181; m 044 157 835; e info@hotelora.eu; www.hotelora.eu. Centrally located just around the corner from the government building behind a branch of ProCredit Bank & near

Liburna Restaurant with good facilities in a quiet area. AC, cable TV, ensuite bath & Wi-Fi in each room. Popular with guests of the European Commission office. Friendly staff.

🏠 **Hotel Peyton** [96 A5] (12 rooms) Rr Pashko Vasa 14a; ✆ 038 222 204; m 044 308 080; e info@hotelpejton.com; www.hotelpejton.com. A 2min-walk from the Boro Ramiz Youth & Sports Centre & former UN headquarters, this hotel is next door to Hotel Prishtina & is a good launching pad for short stays in Prishtina. All rooms have free Wi-Fi, cable TV & AC. Ask for one of the 2 rooms with a jacuzzi.

🏠 **Hotel Plaza** [96 A5] (12 rooms) Rr Pashko Vasa 22; ✆ 038 222 009; e info@hotelplaza.com; www.hotelplaza.com. All rooms have internet, AC, telephone, TV & bathrooms. The owner is a friendly former UK resident.

🏠 **Princi i Arberit** (24 rooms) Kodra e Trimave (direction of Podujevo); ✆ 038 244 244/442; m 044/049 244 244; e info@hotel-princiiarberit.com; www.hotel-princiiarberit.com. A very good hotel in utterly the wrong place. Not only is it the hotel outside Prishtina, it is also situated in an area where there is nothing else around apart from poorer housing, whereas at least the Gorenje has other restaurants & offices nearby. Having said that, there are excellent facilities & very pleasant modern rooms. The hotel has an indoor swimming pool, health club/gym, sauna & solarium & perhaps in an attempt to attract clients has installed a small bowling alley & games, eg: billiards, table football. There is also a 100-person conference hall.

🏠 **Hotel Prishtina** [96 A5] (40 rooms) Rr Pashko Vasa 20; ✆ 038 223 284; e reservations@ hotelprishtina.com; www.hotelprishtina.com. This family-run hotel in the Peyton area is centrally located & well equipped. The rooms are modern & cosy, including internet connection, AC, & a few drinks on the house. A small in-house fitness studio also caters for the sporty sort; a sauna has recently been constructed. Small outdoor pool. Excellent b/fast.

🏠 **Hotel Real** [96 A5] (9 rooms) Rr Pashko Vasa 14a; ✆ 038 245 270; e hotelreal@yahoo.com. Next door to the Hotel Pejton & run by the brother of the owner of that establishment. With internet in all rooms, cable TV & AC.

BUDGET $$

🏠 **Hotel Begolli** (11 rooms, 5 apts) Rr Maliq Pash Gjinolli (former Rr Bihaqit 8a); ✆ 038 244 277; m 044/049 308 093; e hotel_begolli@ hotmail.com; www.hotelbegolli.com. In the heart of

the Old Town, just around the corner from the city's green market, this family-run hotel offers good value at a great location. Free internet, cable TV & AC in all rooms. The luxury room has a jacuzzi. Almost half the price of many other hotels.

🏠 **Hotel Lyon** (15 rooms) St Rrustem Statovci (formerly Robert Gajdiku); ☎ 038 220 997; m 044 245 082; e hotel_lyon@hotmail.com. Hotel Lyon is located just across the street from the Rugova Memorial up on Velania Hill – about 20–25mins' walk out of town. Rooms are simple but modern, with all basic amenities, including shower, cable TV, heating, AC & Wi-Fi. The very basic hotel restaurant is open till 22.00 daily. B/fast is a little sparse. Ask for a room at the back as the ones at the front suffer from the noise of traffic speeding up & down the hill.

🏠 **Hotel Sara** (33 rooms) Rr Maliq Pash Gjinolli; ☎ 038 236 203; m 044 238 765; e info@hotelsara-medi.com; www.hotelsara-medi.com. Next door to Hotel Begolli. All rooms with AC, internet & cable TV. Again bargain prices.

SHOESTRING $

🏠 **Velania Guesthouse** (16 rooms) Velania 4/34; ☎ 038 531 742; m 044 167 455. A bit out of the way but a real bargain for budget-conscious travellers. Run by the friendly 'Professor', this private guesthouse is about 25mins' walk up the hill in a neighbourhood known as Velania, once a posh residential area inhabited mostly by university professors-turned politicians. President Rugova's residence was just around the corner. Rooms are simple (sgles, dbles, trpls & 4-bed, the last the cheapest at €10 pp). Central heating, free cable TV & internet. There is a communal kitchen on each floor with free tea & coffee & a free laundry service.

✖ WHERE TO EAT

It may come as a surprise to many first-time visitors just how many restaurants and trendy cafés there are. Prishtina is unique in the region featuring an exceptionally large choice of creatively designed bars and international cuisine from Thai and Nepalese curries to Japanese sushi and Mexican fajitas. The presence of the international community certainly added 'exotic flavour' while creating sufficient demand to sustain such a high number of great bars and restaurants. In a few cases the owners themselves are former international staff who spend much of their entrepreneurial talent ensuring fresh supplies of lemon grass or seaweed. Keeping track of what's 'in' is difficult, as stylish new bars and restaurants open constantly. Bars that used to be populated with UN staff now cater mainly to the large crowd of EU personnel working for the EU-funded Rule of Law Mission. But increasingly a new urban class of young professional Kosovars, earning good incomes in Prishtina and aspiring to a modern European lifestyle, set the local scene.

There are also a couple of excellent, inexpensive restaurants specialising in local cuisine. Traditional Albanian cuisine is really underrated – it's definitely worth a try!

LUXURY DINING

✖ **Collection** Opposite Bo-Bowling alley near Maxi 2 & the Rent-a-Car offices; ☎ 038 551 970; m 044 800 845; ⏰ 08.00–24.00 daily; 07.00–24.00 in summer. Stone/glass restaurant serving contemporary European dishes with good desserts. Overlooking a smart lawn with trees making it a popular summer venue thanks also to its summer outdoor grill.

✖ **Hani i 2 Roberteve** Hajvali Lagjia (right-hand side on the main road to Gjilan, just before Gračanica); m 044 112 609/117 219; e galleryhani@yahoo.com;www.hani2roberteve.com; ⏰ 11.00–23.00 daily. Hani i 2 Roberteve recently moved to this new location 3km outside Prishtina. In log-house style with several open fireplaces, table grills for small & large groups & an open kitchen, this is truly a new addition to Prishtina's restaurant scene. Besides good food, there are also regularly changing exhibitions of local contemporary artists.

✖ **Il Passatore** Taxlizhe 2; m 044 200 508; ⏰ 12.00–16.00 & 19.00–23.00 Mon–Sat. Tucked back off Nazim Gafurri (difficult to find – ask for the school) in Tazlizhe residential district on the left-hand side on the road to Germia. Plenty of parking. The restaurant is literally set in someone's house & there is a lovely relaxing garden in the summer. The owner is an Italian, Antonella Giorgioni, who has been known to lots of the expat community for some time. True Italian dishes. The antipasto buffet is the speciality. Not somewhere to go if you are in a hurry as service is strictly Mediterranean pace.

✗ **Le Siam Thai** [96 D1] Qafa Gallery (entrance on Rr UÇK); m 045 243 588; e lesiamthai@ gmail.com; ⊕ 11.00–14.00 & 17.30–22.30 Mon–Thu, & 11.00–23.00 Fri–Sun. A real exception in town: Le Siam is entirely non-smoking. Nice atmosphere (if you ignore the Qafa corridor outside which is a bit communist in style) & excellent Thai food. The menu includes specials like Le Siam Platter for starters, a great choice of soups, salads, curries & more extravagant meat & seafood dishes like 'crying tiger' (marinated beef) or 'drunken prawns'. Main courses €8–11, so a bit pricier than most restaurants.

✗ **Pinocchio** Rr 24 Maj 115 (Dragodan, now Arbëria); m 044 202 952; ⊕ 11.00–23.00 daily. A bit out of the way (unless you are staying/working in the area) but certainly worth the drive or hike up the Dragodan (Arbëria) Hill. Here you can pamper yourself in a nice interior with great servings of excellent Italian cuisine while enjoying a good view over the city. Free Wi-Fi. As an alternative to staying in a hotel, you can also stay in one of Pinocchio's in-house apartments. For prices & availability ask in the restaurant.

✗ **Pjata** [97 G7] Rr Gazmend Zajmi (formerly Rr Dubrovnik) 1; ℡ 038 220 739; m 044 426 625; www.pjata.com; ⊕ 11.00–23.00 Mon–Sat, 15.00–23.00 Sun. A match for London restaurants with the chefs having worked in places such as Atlantic Bar & Grill. Modern European-standard upmarket well-presented cuisine with prime ingredients. Homemade carrot & spinach soup, shrimps, avocado, minute steak, pork chops, liver & a good selection of fish. Try the lemon tarte & chocolate ganache desserts. Consistently popular with the diplomats & top UN officials (less so with the locals) & on some nights you may need to book ahead.

✗ **Puro Restaurant** Veternik (Hajvali); ℡ 038 602 099; e info@puro.in; www.puro.in; ⊕ 11.00–23.00 Mon–Sat, 18.00–24.00 Sun. Puro is one of Prishtina's chic 'in' places opened in early 2007. It's a spacious glass structure, modern in design, with an exquisite menu from starters to desserts. It's a real pleasure to see the beautifully decorated plates, but at the same time they do not compromise on the quality of the food. The steaks in particular come recommended. To get there take the road to Hajvali (towards Gračanica) & take the first left after the Gorenje building. Guarded parking outside.

✗ **Restaurant Gorenje** Veternik (Hajvali); ℡ 038 557 700; ⊕ 07.00–24.00 daily. Follow the Gjilan signs. Set back beyond Albi shopping centre, on the top floor of the Gorenje Hotel building complex out of town (take the lift straight to the top of the building). Good views of Prishtina, including a summer terrace. Modern cuisine. Good service. Generally regarded as one of the smartest places to eat, if a little bit out of town.

✗ **Rron Restaurant** Veternik (Hajvali); ℡ 038 602 450; m 044 347 777; e info@rron-ks.com; www.rron-ks.com; ⊕ 09.00–23.00 daily. Located in a dead-end road in the commercial zone southeast of Prishtina, it's relatively easy to find. Follow signs for Gjilan & take a right turn soon after the Gorenje building. Rron has long been a favourite hangout of former prime minister Ramush Haradinaj. Its elegant design, attentive service & great choice of starters & Italian-style main courses make this a great getaway for people with taste. Nice outdoor garden for mild summer evenings.

✗ **Vila Germia** Germia Park; ℡ 038 517 741; m 044 296 395; e info@vilagermia.com; www.vilagermia.com; ⊕ 18.00–24.00 daily. Beautiful setting in the Germia National Park only a few mins' drive from downtown Prishtina, this privatised restaurant features a modern mix of almost Japanese-style simple décor, with stone & artsy elements creating a cosy setting. On weekends, it's a favourite place for family meals & tends to get very crowded. There is also a large playground for children & a shaded outdoor terrace for the summer. The food is high quality at decent prices. The Skenderbeg Steak — a fried beef roll coated in breadcrumbs with cheese filling — & the trout fillet are particularly good. If it is too crowded the Lira next door & Freskia are good alternatives.

MID-RANGE

✗ **A&A** [97 H7] Rr Rexhep Mala; ℡ 038 239 535; m 044 161 713; e restaurant_aa@hotmail.com; ⊕ 08.00–23.00 Mon–Sat. Set in the Aktash district across the road from the Mensa & near the new Raiffeisen headquarters. Mixture of fish & meat dishes. Pleasant ambience.

✗ **All Bar** [96 D2] Rr Fazli Grajqevci 22; m 045 402 501/044 209 090; e info@allbar.com; www.allbar.com; ⊕ 08.00–24.00 daily. Tucked away behind Home Restaurant & near Era City market, allBar sports a stylish interior with white wooden panels & satin cushions. Italian-style cuisine including mozzarella salads, homemade pasta & ciabatta breads for starters. Free Wi-Fi.

✖ **Allegro** Rr Rexhep Mala; m 044 149 431; ⏱ 08.00—23.00 Mon—Sat. Next door to A&A, Italian-style mixed meat dishes & pleasant service. Good salads. Free Wi-Fi.

✖ **Aroma** [96 D3] Rr Rexhep Luci 10/1; ☏ 038 244 125; ⏱ 08.00—23.00 Mon—Sat, 10.00—23.00 Sun. Modelled on a typical London sandwich bar, Aroma is a good address for sandwiches, pizza or salads. You can handpick your choice of filling from tuna to chicken or roasted veggies. It's a popular place, so it unfortunately tends to get very smoky at lunchtime when it's buzzing with guests. Business is going well — 2 smaller outlets have opened recently in other, smaller locations. They also home-deliver larger orders, in case you plan a picnic or brown-bag luncheon.

✖ **Arté** [96 C3] Rr Luan Haradinaj 32; ☏ 038 249 709; ⏱ 07.00—24.00 Mon—Fri, 10.00—23.00 Sat/Sun. Italian restaurant that knows how to cook pasta with an outdoor terrace on the main so-called 'police avenue' intersecting with Rr Rexhep Luci.

✖ **Brown Sushi Bar and Restaurant** m 049 311 411; ⏱ 07.00—24.00 daily. Next to EULEX headquarters in the Farmed area of town (near the hospital) catering to an international clientele with a karaoke bar on Fri/Sat from 12.00. Also take-away & free delivery services.

✖ **Cavallero** [96 C4] Off Rr Nëne Terezë (on a little alley right next to the former UNMIK headquarters, now used by EULEX); m 049 619 375; ⏱ 08.00—24.00 Mon—Fri, 10.00—23.00 Sat/Sun; Spacious restaurant spread over 2 floors, ideal for larger groups (ask for the 10% discount on group bookings). Great burritos & sizzling fajitas, as well as cocktails & Mexican beers.

✖ **Central Room** [96 B4] Rr Garibaldi 63; m 044 810 000; www.central-room.com; ⏱ 07.00—24.00. Opposite the Rilindja building. Always lively & great for coffee or meals. Try the gnocchi or the pancakes. Free Wi-Fi.

✖ **Chinese Restaurant 'Fushun'** [96 C3] Rr Luan Haradinaj (opposite the main police station); m 044 384 928/164 032; ⏱ 11.00—23.00 every day. Popular Chinese take-away & eat-in restaurant. The spring rolls are great, & besides seafood (including squid) & chicken, you can also find various dishes containing pork. No home deliveries, but food to order.

✖ **De Rada Brasserie** [97 E1] Rr UÇK 50; ☏ 038 222 622; ⏱ 09.00—24.00 Mon—Sat. Named after a 19th-century Albanian romantic poet, de Rada Brasserie is one of Prishtina's recently opened stylish venues that could just as easily be found in Berlin or London. Its red-brick walls, old photographs & various traditional art pieces scattered around the room exude a warm & homely atmosphere & you can also go here just for a drink. The crowd is a mix of internationals & wealthy Prishtinali, both from the arts & media scene, as well as young entrepreneurs. At lunchtime De Rada offers various Italian-style sandwiches, salads & pasta. In the evenings, try the 'meze plate' for starters — a mix of dips & greens served with grilled breadsticks — or one of the seafood & vegetarian pasta dishes. Free Wi-Fi

✖ **Everest** [96 D5] off Nëne Terezë m 044 402 265 ⏱ Mon—Sat 9.00 til 23.00 Sun 11.00-21.30 Nepalese Ghurka restaurant.

✖ **Ex** [200 D3] Rr Fehmi Agani 3/8; m 044 157 039/557 700; ⏱ 07.00—23.00 Mon—Sat, 16.00—23.00 Sun. Wood interior with tasty food from curries to pasta & hefty meat dishes. Good prices. Every week a different lunch menu for about €5.

✖ **Gizzi Grill** m 044 655 966; www.gizzigrill.com; ⏱ 24/7. 2 branches, one located at the Grand Store shopping centre (out of town on the road to Skopje); Very popular with hungry night owls & clubbers. The food is nothing special, but the place has an American feel & is usually busy with shoppers at Grand Store. A rarity in Prishtina, there are also high chairs for toddlers. The other branch is located in Sunny Hill opposite the student residences.

✖ **Gresa** [96 C2] At the OSCE end of Rr Fehmi Agani; ☏ 038 245 841; m 044 112 391; ⏱ 10.00—23.00 daily. A popular place with internationals (particularly the older consultant crowd) at lunchtime for the friendly & fast service & its central location near the OSCE. Huge selection of meat & fish dishes. Enormous portions.

✖ **Home** [96 D1] Rr Luan Haradinaj; ☏ 038 224 041; m 044 336 336/049 814 514; e home@prishtinanet.com; ⏱ 07.00—23.00 Mon—Fri, 11.00—23.00 Sat/Sun. A pricey but cosy venue, serving really excellent dishes. A real hit is the Greek chicken on a skewer, the balsamic vinegar chicken & the couscous salads. If you don't mind the calories, you can also taste the homemade tiramisu. In summer it's nice to sit in the shady garden. Special 3-course brunch menu on Sun for €8.50 pp. Owing to its central location, just next door to what was at the time of writing the OSCE headquarters, it mainly draws an international crowd. Also has a no-smoking section in the back conservatory. Free Wi-Fi.

✗ **Légér** [96 B5] Rr Perandori Justinian 2, Peyton; m 044 221 829; ⏲ 08.00–24.00 Mon–Sat, 09.00–24.00 Sun. Set in a spacious garden in a trendy neighbourhood, Légér attracts a hip, late 20-something crowd. Its décor is a combination of stainless steel & glass, brightened up with the occasional deep red. A great lunchtime venue, serving generous portions of different salads, including a warm pasta salad & a choice of sandwiches. Try the haloumi salad – it's filling & very tasty. In summer, the shady garden is another real plus. Free Wi-Fi.

✗ **Lounge** [96 C6] Next to Fellini & Papillon; ☎ 038 226 215/738 475; m 043 737 475; www.lounge-prishtina.com; ⏲ 08.00–24.00. Good salads. Try the homemade pasta, tarte tatin or the lemon tarte. Sat/Sun brunch. Possibly the best & most powerful café Wi-Fi & extremely friendly waiters.

✗ **Metro** [96 D5] Rr Garibaldi 3/1 (opposite Grand Hotel); m 044 113 000/858 585; ⏲ 07.00–22.00 daily. You can tell immediately that the owner has spent a few years in London. The interior is modern & friendly, & the sandwiches – from curry to avocado chicken or vegetarian – are all served with a generous serving of pasta salad. The cappuccino is another good reason to choose Metro for your Sat-morning brunch or as a meeting place in the afternoons.

✗ **Monaco Restaurant** [96 B4] Pallati i Rinisë, Rr Luan Haradinaj, opposite former UN headquarters (now housing EULEX); ☎ 038 227 490; m 044 557 644; ⏲ 07.30–24.00 Mon–Fri, 09.00–24.00 Sat, 10.30–24.00 Sun. With a half-day delay, Monaco Restaurant stocks the best selection of international dailies & foreign-language papers in town. A good place for people watching & catching up on world news, especially when you can sit outside. Pasta & steak dishes. Can be smoky and a little lacking in atmosphere indoors. Free Wi-Fi.

✗ **Mumtaz Mahal** [96 D1] Ahmet Krasniqi (Arbëria, right-hand side going uphill); m 044 114 726; ⏲ 07.00–23.00 daily. Serving traditional Indian food for eat-in & take-away.

✗ **Napoli Pizzeria** Rr Xheladin Rekaliu (near Qerimi Bakery in Sunny Hill); m 044 785 411; ⏲ 11.00–23.00 daily. Along with Proper Pizza (see below), the closest you get in Prishtina to a real thin-crust Italian pizza. The place itself is very basic, but the pizza is just great. For groups up to 15 there is a separate large table with wooden benches. Free delivery to your home at a minimum order of €4.50.

✗ **Odyssea Bistro Bar** [96 C6] Sejdi Kryeziu, Peyton;

m 044 556 444; www.odyssea-group.com; ⏲ 11.30–03.00 Mon–Fri, 08.30–03.00 Sat, 08.00–late Sun. Definitely one of the best spots for smart dining & exquisite cocktails. Owned by the same Israelis as the Odyssea Bakery. Very lively on w/ends, especially when live bands perform. See Facebook for more details – Odyssea Group. The Sun brunch is also very popular (€8pp, without drinks). The buffet includes hot & cold dishes & Mediterranean specialities like chickpea salads, aubergine purée & fried zucchini. A new fusion-style menu has just been introduced. Another big plus is the non-smoking section!

✗ **Osteria Basilico** [96 C2] Rr Fehmi Agani 29/1; ☎ 038 225 401; m 044/049 276 276; e samir.salihu@basilico-ks.com; www.basilico-ks.com; ⏲ 08.00–23.00 Mon–Sat. Good Italian food in a nice atmosphere. Can get crowded at lunchtime.

✗ **Prince Café** [96 B4] m 045 563 562; ⏲ 07.00–23.00 daily. Situated in a prime spot next to the Rilindja government building below the offices of *Zeri* newspaper. An airy sophisticated café with a large terrace & set back from the road. It could easily be a Starbucks or Costa (except for the smoke) with a mixture of tables, sofas, biscuits, muffins & brownies. Serves a wide variety of fruit smoothies & this alone makes it worth visiting. Free Wi-Fi.

✗ **Proper Pizza** Agim Ramadani 24, near the Technical Faculty in Sunny Hill; ☎ 038 542 182; m 044 131 310; www.properpizza.com. People travel from across Prishtina to taste the thin-crust pizzas. They also have vans & bikes that deliver pizzas & drinks across town. You can order online too.

✗ **Rings Restaurant** [97 E4] Rr Nëne Terezë 16; m 044 247 999; e reservation@restaurantrings.com; www.restaurantrings.com; ⏲ 08.00–23.00 daily. The latest addition to the Rings Restaurant chain (there are 4 other outlets across town) is a central venue on Rr Nëne Terezë. Its modern & stylish interior makes you feel like you are in London or New York. In summer, the outdoor terrace on Rr Nëne Terezë is a popular meeting point & great for people watching. The menu includes pizza, seafood salads & various meat dishes. Good location also for official meetings. The ground-floor conference room seats up to 80 (for €100), the business room fits 12 (for €50). On special request, the chef will do a bespoke menu. Free Wi-Fi & 2 computer terminals for guests.

✗ **Select Bistro** [97 E3] Rr Fehmi Agani 1/1; m 044 694 811; e selectbistro@gmail.com; ⏲ 07.00–12.00 daily, 16.00–23.00 Sun. Pizza,

3

pasta & meat dishes. All-day b/fast on Sat including specials like buttermilk pancakes with maple syrup & French toast.

✘ **Te Komiteti** [97 E4] Rr Qamil Hoxha 5/2; ☎ 038 247 886; m 044 784 147; ⏱ 09.30–23.00 Mon–Sat, 10.00–23.00 Sun. An outlet of Prishtina's long-time Pjata favourite, Te Komiteti caters more to the young professional crowd. The lunchtime foccacia sandwiches & creamy vegetable soups are a real delicacy.

✘ **Tokyo Asian-Japanese Restaurant** Rr Ahmet Krasniqi (Dragodan, near Mitrovica roundabout); m 044 988 578/373 537; e tokyoinkosovo@yahoo.com; ⏱ 11.30–14.30 & 17.30–22.30 Mon–Sat. Recently opened new Asian restaurant catering mainly to the international crowd working for KFOR, ICO or the embassies in Dragodan. Serving a mix of Chinese kitchen with sushi & Philippine specialities. Take-away available.

NATIONAL CUISINE

✘ **Country House** m 044 656 054/049 393 965; ⏱ 10.00–23.00 daily. 5km outside Prishtina in a village called Bernicë e Epërme. Take the road to Podujevo & turn right after about 5km (Bermicë straddles the road so make sure you take the correct turning). Beautiful location overlooking the Bajgora Mountains. Local specialities included.

✘ **Hemingway Restaurant** Kroni i Bardhe 9 (Ilaz Kodra); m 044 145 637. This is definitely the best address for fish in Prishtina with a feel-good & cosy atmosphere. The owners Shpresa & Skender recently expanded & redecorated the place, but it has lost none of its charm. You still find Skender busy preparing the salad platters, grilled sea bass or Hemingway's delicious seafood risotto (not always available). If you plan a get-together of about 10 friends, ask for the large table in the corner. With Albanian & international *chansons* in the background it's the ideal place to stay warm throughout Prishtina's long winter nights. Now also open for b/fast & lunch.

✘ **Liburnia** [97 E1] ☎ 038 222 719; m 044 891 000; ⏱ 08.00–24.00 Mon–Sat, 11.30–24.00 Sun. Tucked away on a cobbled side street (Rr Baholli) between the City Travel travel agent & a ProCredit branch across the road from the EU headquarters, the restaurant comprises 2 tastefully renovated old Ottoman-style houses straddling the road with the traditional walled courtyard & pots of bright geraniums in the summer. A good address for traditional Albanian food including *tavë* & heated meat plates as well as Italian-style cuisine. Try one

✘ **Vila Corona** Rr Nazim Gafurri; ☎ 038 517 000; m 044509 590; ⏱ 07.00–24.00 daily. The location of the former Rio. If you are in the mood for fresh fish or seafood of different sorts & have time to go across town then try this establishment on the road to Germia on the left-hand side near the Hotel Luxor about 500m before the park entrance. Outdoor garden with artificial stream & trees which provide good shade in summer.

✘ **XIX** [96 D2] Rr Luan Haradinaj 2; ☎ 038 248 002; m 044 300 002; www.xixonline.com; ⏱ 07.00–24.00 daily (until 02.00 Fri/Sat). Despite what everyone thinks, the name of this restaurant is 'XIX' or 'Spark' & not '19'. Sometimes a little lacking in spark, however, its real draw are its brick-oven pizzas & the fact that it will deliver. Visit them to get your flat details put on their database & their motorbikes will whizz round to your residence.

of the local *raki* (*grappa*)! Very atmospheric.

✘ **Mosaic** [97 E5] Just across from Ultra set back from the road; ☎ 038 247 634; ⏱ 07.00–23.00 Mon–Sat. Popular with local politicians & known for its hefty meat platters. Wi-Fi pending.

✘ **Pishat** [97 F4] Rr Qamil Hoxha 11; ☎ 038 245 333; m 044 245 333; ⏱ 08.00–24.00 Mon–Sat, 12.00–24.00 Sun. One of the most popular restaurants mostly frequented by Prishtina's intellectual & political elite. Its interior is cosy, especially in winter when the Christmas light decoration is on. It's also a great place to try some Kosovo meze – platters of warm & cold starters served with freshly baked bread – or one of the traditional meat dishes served. On a cold day, ask for their special soups. If you are really in the mood for authentic Albanian food, try the homemade *flija*, a layered pie of pastry & cream traditionally cooked over an open fire.

✘ **Renaissance (2)** [96 C6] Rr Dëshmorët e Kombit; m 044 118 796. One is tucked away on a little alley behind ProCredit headquarters near Grand Hotel; the other is smaller, down the side road after Fellini on the left-hand side – look for the wooden door. This secret treasure of a restaurant is a good place for quiet dinner conversations over a variety of Kosovar specialities, from *meze* (traditional starters) to grilled meats or fish. There is no menu, so trust the owner's advice. It's best just to let him bring plate after plate of starters, including dips, grilled vegetables & salad, before choosing between the daily specials. The fixed-price menu including drinks is about €15pp. A glass of *raki* (grappa) is almost obligatory. Call to make a reservation first! No fixed opening times.

✗ Restaurant Old House Pellumbi (formerly Pëllumbi); 📞 038 548 713; 📱 044 238 400; 🕐 08.00–23.00. On the left-hand side of the main road as you are leaving town towards Fushë-Kosova. A mix of authentic & kitsch décor gives this place a very special feel. Start your meal with a drink & a platter of starters seated around a *sofra* (a traditional round, low table) next to the open fireplace. For main courses, it's best to try the bread-coated meat stew (*tava*) or the *pogaqe*. Stay clear of the local wines; they are usually not very good.

✗ Symphony [97 F7] Rr Ekrem Qabej, Ulpiana, behind the Ombudsperson's offices; 📞 038 548 271; 📱 044 501 882; www.codexsymphony.com; 🕐 07.30–24.00 daily. Truly the best place to try *pogaqe*, a traditional homemade bread served hot with cheese, spreads & salad. Besides *pogaqe*, the menu features a long list of local meat dishes, as well as pizza & pasta. Another plus, the locally brewed Peja beer is served on tap. If they don't bring it automatically, ask for the roasted, warm hazelnuts (*lejthija*) – great to nibble with a cold, fresh beer. Wi-Fi. Can get a bit smoky.

✗ Te Ariu Veternik; 📱 044 202 304; 🕐 10.00–23.00 daily. Traditional fare as well as pizzas. Caters particularly for families with huge outdoor area & mini zoo. Popular with Kosovar families. On leaving Prishtina, take the Gjilan exit right beyond the Grand Store & Te Ariu is about 150m after the turn-off before you go under the main road.

✗ Tiffany's [96 B2] Off Rr Fehmi Agani; 📞 038 244 040; 📱 044 700 237; 📧 tifany@gmail.com; 🕐 09.00–23.00 Mon–Sat, 18.00–23.00 Sun. Turn left towards the stadium passing Kaqa (or 'Outback') Bar. This has long been a favourite of internationals & locals alike (particularly politicians) because of its delicious Albanian dishes & some of the freshest salads in town with beetroot, carrots & onions. There is no printed menu. Try the dips for starters, stuffed cabbage leaves, *mantija* (pastry & meat), Elbasan *tava* (chicken or lamb in yoghurt sauce), & top it off with homemade baklava. The best place to take visiting guests to savour Kosovo's local cuisine.

✗ Tirona [96 D5] Rr 2 Korriku 8; 📞 038 223 337; 📧 info@tavernatirona.com; www.tavernatirona.com; 🕐 08.00–23.00 Mon–Sat. On a little side street off Nënë Terezë. There is nothing special about Tirona, except that it feels like the most authentic local restaurant in town. The owner is a well-known & passionate connoisseur of strong *raki*. It's not a good place for vegetarians – the menu is all meat in different shapes & forms. Look out for the old photographs of Prishtina to get a sense of what the city once looked like before the communist leadership set out to destroy the Old Town.

✗ Ultra [97 E5] Rr Sylejman Vokshi; 📞 038 225 155; 📱 044 246 335; 🕐 08.00–23.00 Mon–Sat, 14.00–23.00 Sun. Set a few metres back on a little through alley not far from Te Pishat. A stunning restaurant in the centre of town popular with politicians & known for its oven-baked meat dishes & steaks. Run by a Gjakovar, so very popular with the Gjakova diaspora in Prishtina. No Wi-Fi.

FAST FOOD (ALL BUDGETS) If you want to spend wisely while tasting some of the local cuisine, it's best to stay away from the upmarket restaurants and to try instead one of the local *qebaptore* for a good serving of meatballs (*qebabi*), go to one of the bakeries serving *burek* (meat or cheese pies) and *manti* (square-shaped pastry filled with meat) or, if you really want to mix with a local crowd, try one of the so-called *kuzhina popullore* (people's kitchen) where you can try home-style beans and meat stew.

✗ Aurora Pizza [96 C6] Rr Dëshmorët e Kombit (next door to ProCredit Bank headquarters); 📱 044 420 101; 🕐 24hrs. Ideal for a quick pizza-to-go & other fast food or even steaks & lasagne for bargain prices & speedy service at any time of the day. Aurora caters in particular for students & night owls. The pizza is quick, tasty & cheap – for only €1.50. Their *burek* is also very nice.

✗ Ben-Af [97 G3] Musine Kokallari 1 (Dardania) & Rr Agim Ramadani; 📱 044 111 274; 🕐 08.00– 23.00 daily. The first Ben-Af shopping centre & fast-food restaurant that opened in Prishtina is tucked away from the main road near the main traffic light on Bill Clinton Bd. There is also another one on Agim Ramadani directly up from the National Theatre with a whole upstairs floor. It is one of the cheapest addresses in town for food offering a choice of more than a dozen different hot dishes, including pizza made to order, a Kosovo version of *shnitzla* (*Wiener Schnitzel*) & other traditional dishes like *musak me* *mishe* (potato meat gratin) or *tava fasulye* (oven-baked beans). Prices are unbeatably low — a full meal, including drinks & a fresh serving from the salad bar will cost you less than €3. You can also order for take-away.

✗ **Bosna 2/Bosna 4** [96 C5] Rr Perandori Justinian (Pejton City) & also Rr Nëne Terezë near the ProCredit headquarters & tall RTK building. The best place in town to try a traditional *burek*, a pastry-made dish similar to a salty strudel filled with cheese, meet or spinach. It's best served with a yoghurt drink. Be aware: it's extremely filling for little more than €1.

✗ **Burek Destan** [96 B4] Along with Bosna possibly the best *burek* in town, including spinach *burek* which is often not available elsewhere. A kiosk near Bamboo at the bottom of Peyton City.

✗ **Friends Sandwich Bar** [96 C2] Rr Fehmi Agani 23; m 044 141 050; e friends.kos@hotmail.com; ◷ 07.00–17.00 Mon–Fri. London-style sandwich bar.

✗ **Gjakova Qebaptore** [96 B1] Rr UÇK; m 044 193 203; ◷ 07.30–16.00 Mon–Fri, 07.30–17.30 Sat. Ranked by many as possibly the best *qebaptore* in Prishtina. 5 meatballs for €1. Extremely popular.

BAKERIES AND SWEET SHOPS

✗ **Fellini** [96 C7] ☏ 038 220 065; m 044 171 406; ◷ 07.00–24.00 daily. Close to Papillon Café on the other side of the university grounds in the district referred to as Tre Šessira. They also make special birthday cakes to order.

✗ **Furra Lumi I** [97 G7] Rr Anton Cetta I; ☏ 038 229 752; m 044 115 386; e furra_lumi@yahoo.com; ◷ 07.00–21.00 Mon–Sat, 07.00–18.00 Sun. The original bakery is tucked in a dead-end side road parallel to Agim Ramadani, on the other side of the road to Pjata Restaurant. Second branch on Rr Ekrem Qabej opposite the Albanian Faculty. One of very few places in Prishtina in which you can find wholemeal & brown breads, French bread & foccacia. Also walnut & chocolate muffins, croissants, apple tarts, & cakes made to order. House specials include lasagne & *flija*. This is also the only place in Prishtina that makes bagels. The place is especially busy around Ramadan & other festivals.

✗ **Qerimi Bakery** Rr Enver Maloku; m 044 500 406; ◷ 06.00–24.00 daily. A little out of the way,

✗ **Izzy's Deli** [97 E1] Rr Andrea Gropa 38; ☏ 038 716 006; ◷ 08.00–22.00 Mon–Fri, 08.00–20.00 Sat. Great London-style sandwich bar tucked away in a side street behind old the post office/government building, which is open for b/fast & lunch. Daily specials, including soups, & rare spices for sale. Takes phone orders for take-away & delivery in the area.

✗ **Shaban Qebaptore** Corner of Rr Ilir Konushevci & Tregu e Gjelbërt (Green Market St). If you are in the mood for real Kosovo *qebabi*, this is the place to go. The quality of the meat is good, the servings are huge & the *qebabi* are delicious. The place tends to really fill up at lunchtime & serves both to eat in or take-away (please note there are no toilet facilities).

✗ **Taunita Foods** [97 G7] Rr Anton Cetta; ☏ 038 248 502; m 044 198 962/403 803; ◷ 08.00–23.00 Mon–Fri, 09.00–21.00 Sat, 09.00–23.00 Sun. Just across from the Mensa near Furra Lumi's original branch. Another excellent budget & express alternative with self-service buffet with main courses from €1.50 & salads for €0.50. Will also deliver with at least 40mins' notice. Also great fish restaurant downstairs.

but with your own wheels it's definitely worth the drive up to Sunny Hill as this is one of the best bakeries in town — fantastic bread, especially the little rolls stuffed with meat & the warm corn bread topped with vegetables. At lunchtime you can also indulge in their *burek* or *mantija*, with meat or cheese filling. Personalised birthday cakes are also made to order.

✗ **Sultan** [97 E1] Rr UÇK; m 044 661 201; ◷ 07.00–23.00 Mon–Sat. Next to Raiffeisen & with another branch on Rr Nazim Gafurri, just after the Mbreti Mosque. Original Turkish sweets & desserts & for sure the best address for baklava anywhere outside Prizren.

✗ **Venezzia** [96 C3] Rr Rexhep Luci; ◷ 07.00–23.00 Mon–Sat. Right downtown, Venezzia sells possibly the best (& largest) croissants in Prishtina. You can choose between walnut filling, apple or poppy seed: they all taste delicious. If you prefer something salty, try the *burek* or pizza. Their pizza is another cheap option for a quick bite.

CAFÉS AND BARS
Prishtina's café and bar scene is vibrant and ever changing. Even though Prishtina is just half the size of Skopje or Tirana, easily competes with other European cities. Thanks to the creativity and entrepreneurial drive of many Kosovars, artistically designed and trendy new bars keep opening up almost every other week. Some of the hippest bars tend to close and reopen, so don't be too

disappointed if your favourite is closed temporarily. Depending on your mood, you can opt for a cosy lounge-like feel, a modern steel–glass design or just a shady outdoor terrace where beer and peanuts are being served. Given that half the population is under 20, no wonder that there is a huge demand for cafés and bars where you can hang out, flirt, chat and sip a coffee. Most of the larger cafés nowadays also provide free Wi-Fi. Muslim or not, most young Kosovars do drink alcohol and there are only a few places that do not serve it. It's very rare to see Kosovars drunk, however, and especially for women it's frowned upon to drink too much. The only downside, as almost everyone smokes, is that bars get extremely smoky, especially in winter. Trendy bars tend to cluster in certain parts of town, with many of the most popular hangouts being concentrated in Rr Rexhep Luci (known as 'ABC Cinema Street'), Rr Fehmi Agani (popularly known as 'Kafja e vogel' Street) and the area around Peyton City. Prishtina is small, so bar hopping is very easy.

Around Nëne Terezë and Rr Rexhep Luci (known as 'ABC Cinema Street')

Amelie [97 G6] [Rr Fehmi Agani 10 (with big terrace), Rr Perandori Justinian & Agim Ramadani on opposite side of road to unfinished Serb church; m 045 265 600; e odysseagroup@gmail.com; www.odyssea-group.com; ⏱ 08.00–23.00 daily. Great chain of espresso bars serving sandwiches, smoothies, sweets, pancakes & hot dishes. Its stylish white interior makes it a popular place for late morning brunch & coffee throughout the day. Self-service at the counter. Free Wi-Fi.

Corner [96 D5] Rr Nëne Terezë; m 049 550 955; ⏱ 07.00–24.00 Mon–Sat, 08.00–24.00 Sun. Great location (right on the corner near Grand Hotel, hence the name), with nice outdoor seating on the now pedestrianised Rr Nëne Terezë. Ideal for people watching & parents with kids. The menu contains the usual pizza, pasta & salads.

dit e natë Bookshop & Café [97 E2] Rr Fazli Grajcevci 5; m 049 256 326; e info@ditenat.com; www.ditenat.com; ⏱ 07.00–22.00 Mon–Sat, 10.00–22.00 Sun. This great addition to Prishtina's café scene, tucked away in a little street opposite the Red Cross office, is owned by young musician Genc Salihu. With walls covered in books, including probably the best selection of English & Albanian books in town, including political science classics, philosophy, a good collection of children's books & a section featuring artistic films. With jazzy music in the background, dit e natë is a great place to hang out, meet friends or work (thanks to free Wi-Fi). Serves also a few fresh ham & cheese sandwiches at lunchtime. There are regular readings by local authors, & at 18.00 every Sun, free movie screenings.

Gagi Café [97 E2] Rr Blodin Gagica (behind the Ministry of Public Administration); m 044 160 665/049 522 511; e gagicafe@gmail.com; ⏱ 07.00–24.00 Mon–Sat. 3-floor modern café popular with the young professional crowd. Different lunch menu every day. Free Wi-Fi.

Strip Depot [96 D3] Rr Rexhep Luci 6; ✆ 038 222 888; e reservations@stripdepot.com; www.stripdepot.com; ⏱ 08.00–23.30 daily. The young owner, Petrit Selimi, is well known & extremely well connected. Upon his return from Norway, he has been actively involved in the arts, media. But above all, he is a passionate fan of comic strips, so among the daily papers you can also pick up copies of comics while enjoying a cup of real Illy macchiato. The place has recently been expanded, but without losing any of its eclectic charm. Dark wooden tables & comfy leather & velvet sofas make Strip Depot the perfect place to meet with young politicians or artists or just to hang out with friends. On sunny days, the small terrace gets crowded quickly. Free Wi-Fi. No food served.

Toto [96 D3] Rr Rexhep Luci; m 045 222 442; ⏱ 07.00–24.00. In the early days, Toto was famous for being the first bar in Prishtina with only women waiters. This no longer holds true, but it's still a popular destination for coffee & drinks. In summer, Toto's little outdoor terrace is nice & cool. Toto is a good place to try Albanian flija (layers of pasta-like pastry), but there are also salads if you are watching your waistline.

Around Rr Fehmi Agani (known as 'Kafja e Vogel Street')

Kaqa [96 C2] ⏱ until the early hours. In a little side street off Rr Fehmi Agani. A long-time favourite with internationals & Kosovars alike, Kaqa is still one of the best addresses for an outdoor beer after work & in the evenings. Its official name is 'Outback', but it is generally known as Kaqa. For a while, it was also nicknamed 'election bar' because of the high number of OSCE election observers & election officers hanging out there. Today, the crowd tends to be more Kosovar. It is at its best in the summer, but even in the winter Kaqa's sofas & tap beer are inviting.

⌖ **N'shpi** [96 C1] m 044 627 641. Tucked away behind Rr Fehmi Agani, this is an inviting new café decorated with antiques & green tapestry, giving the whole place the cosy feel of your grandmother's

living room. Special happy hours from 07.00 to 10.00 with coffees for only €0.50 & beers & raki for €1 between 16.00 & 19.00. House specialities include traditional corn bread & Turkish coffee.

⌖ **Sokoli e Mirusha** [96 C1] m 044 360 320; ⊕ until the early hours. Stylish interior in modern Baroque style. Named after a ballet composed by Akil Merk Koci. Serves salads & pasta. Nice outdoor terrace.

Some very smart new bars have opened underneath the football stadium not far from Kafja e Vogel Street.

Area around Peyton City

(most cafés are open until about 24.00, with some closed on Sundays)

⌖ **Bamboo** [96 B4] Near the TMK barracks around the cnr of Rr Garibaldi 17; m 044 430 840. A popular wine bar with a cosy interior. It's a nice alternative to the more lounge bars in Peyton City. It can get very busy at night.

⌖ **Elzar** [96 B6] Rr Parandori Justinian. Relaxed bar in single-storey old house with a lot of outdoor seating at the back. Sometimes there are live bands. Serves salads at lunch; cocktails & smoothies are planned.

⌖ **Publicco Café** [96 B6] Rr Garibaldi (on the corner opposite Central Bank). Cosy & popular café attracting mainly a local crowd, especially during summer on the outdoor terrace.

⌖ **Papillon Café** [96 C6] Rr Dëshmorët e Kombit

52A; m 044 103 310; e info@cafepapillon.com; www.caffepapillon.com. An old-time popular hangout for the young & hip, especially in the early evenings or w/end weekends. The crowd is mostly Kosovar, young & well travelled internationally. Papillon also serves sandwiches, pizzas, nachos & chicken wings. The music tends to be more rock than the usual Buddha Bar-style. As a new feature Papillon also delivers coffee-to-go or freshly squeezed orange juice; just call!

⌖ **Retro Caffe** [96 B5] Rr Perandori Justinian 7; m 045 260 332; e info@retrocaffe.com; www.retrocaffe.com. Popular café & bar in an eclectic retro style. With outdoor terrace at the back.

⌖ **The Dubliner** [96 C5] Rr Johan v Hahn (near Hotel Grand); m 044 207 067. An Irish-style pub close to the real thing. Serves salads & burgers.

Across town

⌖ **91** [96 C3] Rr Luan Haradinaj; ☎ 038 221 991; m 044 919 191; ⊕ 07.00–24.00 daily. Comfy pub, serves food, including English-style b/fast. Popular with international beer lovers especially. Serves Guinness & a popular location with international clientele to watch rugby & other sports matches. Free Wi-Fi & copies of the UK's Daily Mail newspaper.

⌖ **Paddy O'Brien's Irish Bar** [97 F3] Rr Tringa Smajli, m 045 420 900; www.PaddyOBriens.com; ⊕ Daily 07:00–late. Set back a bit just behind Hotel Iliria (under reconstruction). Cosy Irish Pub in a beautiful old-style wooden house, with a little garden at the

back. Serving Irish b/fast, burgers & salads. Popular place to watch important football games. Free Wi-Fi.

⌖ **Tingle Tangle** [96 D4] ⊕ 08.00–24.00 or later. Right in the centre but tucked away in a car park behind the flats – behind Cavallero Restaurant & Alta Via/Eurosky travel agencies. This is one of the hippest addresses in Kosovo. Plays alternative music & sometimes hosts live bands.

⌖ **Vertigo Bar** Top floor of Grand Store shopping centre (Veternik, along Skopje highway); m 044 620 618. Stylish interior & the best summer rooftop terrace in town. Serving pizza, pasta & salads.

ENTERTAINMENT AND NIGHTLIFE

Prishtina is not a city you would visit for its cultural life. Yet, it is definitely one of the liveliest towns in southeast Europe when it comes to hip cafés, outdoor bars and nightlife. The high number of young people and the post-war injection of cash have assured Prishtina a lively bar scene, with new cafés and pubs opening every other month. As the bar scene is in constant flux, it's best to ask around for the latest 'in-place', or recent openings at the time of your visit. Be warned, popular bars tend to get extremely crowded, at least until 24.00. Bars also tend to concentrate in a few areas across the town centre (see above).

While the bar scene is thriving, 'classical' cultural life in Prishtina, and in Kosovo in general, is limited to a few shows, concerts, exhibitions and festivals a year. A combination of budget constraints (the annual budget of the Ministry of Culture is ridiculously small), human resource constraints (the philharmonic orchestra for example lacks wind instruments) and the low priority generally accorded to arts and culture means that much of Prishtina's cultural life depends on private or international initiatives. To find out about upcoming events check the culture sections of the daily papers (*www.dardamedia.com*), or look out for billboards along Rr Nëne Terezë or check for flyers in some of the trendier cafés in town. You might be lucky and catch a play at the National Theatre or a show or concert at the Oda Theatre, the only private theatre in town.

A few festivals a year, including the November Jazz Festival hosted at the Oda Theatre and the Kamerfest (Chamber Music Festival), also liven up the cultural scene. In previous years Prishtina also hosted Skena Up, an international student film and theatre festival, featuring a packed programme of local and international film and theatre productions (*www.skenaup.com*). ABC Cinema occasionally hosts international film festivals sponsored by the French, German or UK governments. For more information, it's best to check out the ABC Cinema website (*www.kinoabc.info*).

THEATRE AND CINEMA

🎭 **Dodona Teatri** Rr Xhelal Mitrovica (keep going up Rr Bajram Kelmendi or take a taxi to find it); ☎ 038 230 623; e dodona86@yahoo.com. Dodona has been the municipality's theatre for youth & children since 1986. The building has recently been restored & hosts children's plays every Sat at 15.00 as well as the occasional show during the Skena Up Film & Theatre Festival. The plays & puppet shows sell out quickly & can be standing room only so get there in time.

🎭 **Oda Teatri** [96 A3] Pallati i Rinisë e Sporteve 111 (side entrance opposite the stadium); ☎ 038 246 555; e oda@teatrioda.com; www.teatrioda.com. This is Prishtina's only independent theatre, founded on 1 March 2003, featuring Albanian & English plays as well as concerts from jazz to Albanian rock. Keep a lookout for the annual jazz festival hosted in

November (*www.jazzprishtina.com*) & the occasional jamming session attracting local talents. Information about upcoming events can be found on the Albanian & English website. Bookings can be made by phone.

🎭 **Teatri Kombëtar (National Theatre of Kosovo)** Rr Nëne Terezë 21; ☎ 038 224 406; www.teatrikombetar.eu. Originally founded in Prizren in 1946, the National Theatre later moved to its current building in Prishtina. Plays start at 20.00. Tickets for €3 can be purchased at the ticket booth in the entrance hall.

🎭 **ABC Cinema** [96 D4] Rr Rexhep Luci 1; ☎ 038 243 117; e kinoabc@yahoo.com; www.kinoabc.info. Every night there are 3 shows & a choice of 2 films. Popcorn & drinks can be bought in the café. Tickets €3. Now the only cinema left in Prishtina. Often participates in festivals when films may even be free.

GAMBLING There are now lots of roulette and slot-machine places which open and close so quickly we have not included them. You will also find plenty of places for sports betting, frequented mostly by young males.

MUSIC

🎵 **Academic Ensemble (Ansambli Akademik)** ☎ 038 246 884. Specialising in national Albanian songs, this ensemble is also performing regularly at local & international festivals.

🎵 **Kosova Kamerfest** ☎ 038 244 689; e kosovakamerfest_artistic_direct@yahoo.com.

The Musical Foundation Ars Kosova was founded in 2003 with the purpose of promoting chamber music & classical music in Kosovo. In recent years, the foundation has organised promotional concerts for talented young musicians & organised the Kamerfest, bringing together well-known international & local musicians for a week of chamber music.

♫ **Kosova Philharmonic** Rr Sylejman Vokshi; ☏ 038 244 938/9. Today's 90-member Kosova Philharmonic originated in the Symphonic Orchestra of the former Radio and Television Prishtina. Plans to construct a new opera building are still in their early stages.

♫ **National Shota Ensemble (Ansambli Kombëtar Shota)** Rr Luan Haradinaj (behind the Prishtina Stadium); ▥ 044 222 263; e info@ansamblishota.org; www.ansamblishota.org. Founded in 1948, the National Shota Ensemble was officially recognised as a professional dance ensemble in 1964. Its current director Agron Shala is trying his best to revive its past fame. In previous decades, the National Shota Ensemble has performed at well

over 4,000 international folk festivals & concerts.

♫ **Xixëllonjat** ☏ 038 540 813; www.xixellonjat.com. A children's choir group for 5–14 year olds regularly performing at local & international music festivals & charity concerts. If you are interested, contact Drita Rudit on ▥ 044 500 761.

♫ **Youth and Sports Palace** [96 B4] Pallati i Rinisë, Rr Luan Haradinaj; ☏ 038 295 430; www.pallatirinise.com. Also known as Boro Ramiz, this is Prishtina's prime cultural & sports complex. Founded in 1975, it regularly hosts classical concerts, fairs or special events in the Red Hall (Salla e Kuqe). The spacious atelier (atelie) is also used for events, debates or ballroom-dancing lessons. For an up-to-date programme of upcoming events check the website.

Live music and clubs
For the best live rock bands to catch, see *Chapter 1*, *Culture*, page 40.

☆ **Cube Club** Rr Johan V Hahn 2 (opposite the Faculty of Arts near Hotel Grand); ▥ 044 124 584. Nightclub.

☆ **Depot** [96 C1] off Rr Fehmi Agani. An old favourite, & not too chic. Live rock bands.

☆ **Filikaqa** [96 B6] Rr Perandori Justinian (Peyton City); ☏ 038 244 288; ▥ 044 788 888; e reservations@filikaqa.com. Karaoke bar with huge screens on all walls & mini screens on the table sides primarily to watch football. Serves burgers, potato skins, fries & milkshakes.

☆ **Jazz Club 212** [96 B7] Rr Sejdi Kryeziu, Peyton; ⏱ until 03.00 Sat or until the guests go. A cosy & smoky club featuring live jazz or other live bands several nights a week. Dancing possible.

☆ **Kontra** [96 C5] Rr Johan V Hahn; ▥ 044 182 681. Popular with live bands, particularly during festivals.

♀**Maroon Pub** [96 D2] ⏱ until 02.00 most nights. Opposite a branch of the Amelie coffee chain (see page 107). Often crammed with young people. Live music on most Sat nights.

🎭 **Oda Theatre** [96 A3] See *Theatre* above.

☆ **Peppermint Club** Rr Nëne Terezë; ☏ 038 552 555; ▥ 044 866 444; e info@gizzigroup.com; www.peppermint-ks.com; ⏱ from 22.00 daily. At the moment *the* place to go for late-night drinking & some (but not much) dancing. House, R'n'B, Latino,

hip-hop & occasionally live music. Check the website for an updated weekly programme. The entrance fee (payable by girls also) includes 1 drink. Gets crowded on w/ends.

☆ **Spray Club** Veternik (near Fortesa Ceramics along Skopje highway); ▥ 049 660 066; e bersant@sprayclub.com; www.sprayclub.com; ⏱ till the early hours. This castle-like venue is located in a sprawling wild commercial zone known as Veternik just 2km outside Prishtina. To get there turn left off the main Prishtina–Skopje highway or just grab a taxi; everybody will know the way. Spray Club is certainly Prishtina's most renowned clubbing venue attracting international DJs & sometimes really excellent live bands. For an update on special events or to download some live remix check out their website.

☆ **Tingle Tangle** See *Cafés and bars* above.

☆ **Zanzibar** [96 D3] Rr Hajdar Dushi; ☏ 038 152 155; ⏱ until 02.00 or until the last dancer goes home. Hidden in a shabby basement in central Prishtina off Rr Nëne Terezë, Zanzibar is generally packed on Fri/Sat when local bands play loud & good-fun rock music. Most often it is the Zanzi band. Without any ventilation, the air is thick with smoke & it can get a little crammed. Often frequented by politicians & famous for being the venue where the Kosovar government collapsed for about 1hr one night in 2009 – with the discussion leaking onto international TV.

Summer specials
From June to September, Prishtina's streets resemble Munich or Zürich, and feels as if every single Kosovar living abroad has decided to come back at the same time, clogging up the streets with posh and expensive cars sporting German, Swiss, Austrian or Swedish number plates. Occasionally you can also spot

Gallery V Rr Qamil Hohxa 65, near Pishat Restaurant; 📞 038 228 212; 📱 044 114 304; 📧 veliblakcori@gmail.com; www.veliblakcori.com; 🕐 09.00–21.00 daily; entrance free. Gallery V was founded in 2002 by Veli Blakçori, an independent artist & former art teacher & cartoonist. His son Ilir Blakçori (📞 *038 235 886;* 📱 *044 686 888; www.molostudio.com*) now also has his own studio. Both also give occasional art classes.

Kosova Art Gallery Rr Agim Ramadani 60; 📞 038 227 833; 📧 gak@ipko.org; www.kosovaart.com; 🕐 10.00–18.00 but closes 1hr earlier on Sun; entrance free. Hosting regular exhibitions of contemporary art & photography.

Portet Art Gallery/Bashkim Imi Gallery 📱 044 174 678; entrance free. Just along from the Hemingway Restaurant tucked away next to a phone shop. The artist was trained in Germany & produces oil paintings of traditional Kosovo scenery, people & portraits, along with commissions & art classes. Ring in advance to check if it's open.

the odd American and even Alaskan plate. Deprived of much fun in their European home countries where many young Kosovars do backbreaking jobs all year round, the summer holidays back in Kosovo are the highlight of the year. Nightlife in Prishtina is also cheap compared with Zürich or Stuttgart, where many young Kosovars live. Summers are the time of the year to spend and have fun and, ideally, meet your future spouse. There are several new clubs or outdoor venues that open for the summer only. It's best to ask around to see what is new. In July and August, open-air concerts and discos are often held at the outdoor swimming pool up near Germia Park. For details look at the posters around the university or Peyton area..

SHOPPING

BOOKS, MAGAZINES, NEWSPAPERS, CARDS AND FLOWERS The cheapest places to buy books are the makeshift stands outside the Grand Hotel selling books translated and imported from Albania. Bill Clinton's autobiography can be found amidst literary grandees like Gabriel Garcia Marquez. Books, however, are expensive in Kosovo. You can buy birthday cards too at most of these venues.

Buzuku Behind Rr Nëne Terezë towards the former UN headquarters; 📱 044 238 738; www.librariabuzuku.com. Small book & card shop, with a limited foreign-language section.

dit e natë See *Cafés and bars* on page 107.

Dukagjini Bookshop Rr Nëne Terezë 20; 📞 038 248 143/244 031; www.dukagjinibooks.com; 🕐 08.00–20.00 Mon–Sat. The best bookshop in town with a small but well-stocked English-language section featuring books on Kosovo's history, the region as well as some fiction. Good also for maps, dictionaries & language books. Sells some magazines & *The Economist*.

Kadabooks Rr Hajdar Dushi 2; 📞 038 220 174; 📱 044 151 293; 📧 kadabooks@gmail.com. Located in a side street off Nëne Terezë near Dukagjini Bookshop. Can order foreign books.

Labi-N Rr Qamil Hoxha; 📱 044 220 009/167 526; 🕐 09.00–21.00 daily. Flower & plant shop.

Remember Me Rr Qamil Hoxha 3; 📞 038 245 345; 📱 044 283 344; 📧 info@dergoniulule.com; www.dergoniulule.com; 🕐 08.00–20.00. Flowers, chocolates & little gifts, beautifully wrapped & for delivery anywhere in Kosovo. Not cheap, but stylish. Also possible to order online & via email.

Talens Rr Bajram Kelmendi 6; 📞 038 245 635; 🕐 08.00–20.00 daily. A great place for stationery, pens, gift wraps, cards & anything you may need to live out your artistic talent. Most of the items are tastefully selected goods made in Turkey.

International newspapers Available outside Monaco Restaurant (see listing on page 103).

CLOTHES AND SHOES

Babycenter On the main road to Fushë-Kosova, on the left-hand side as you come from the city centre. The best collection of toys & clothes & anything you may need from buggies to bottles & bathtubs for babies. There is also an outdoor playground. Special offers for members.

Bata Shoe Shop Rr UÇK (opposite traffic lights on Rr Luan Haradinaj); ⏱ 09.00–20.00 Mon–Sat. Good selection of original Bata shoes. Credit cards accepted.

Divina ⏱ 10.00–20.00 Mon–Sat. 2 branches: one opposite 91 Pub, the other on Rr Garibaldi. Discounted designer/brand-name clothes.

Junior's Rr UÇK (near ProCredit Bank); ⏱ 09.00–20.00 Mon–Fri, 10.00–19.00 Sat. Clothes & shoes (mainly imported from Turkey) for kids aged 0–12yrs.

Kid's Planet Rr UÇK (near Pro Credit Bank); ⏱ 09.30–19.30 Mon–Sat. Toys & bags for kids.

Krenare Rugova Rr Garibaldi 17 corner (above Café Publicco); m 044/49 116 536, 044/49 176 092; e info@krenare-rugova.com; www.krenare-rugova.com. Kosovar designer trained in New York. Get your wedding or ball dress designed & handmade.

T&T Rr Agim Ramadan (near Ben-Af); ⏱ 09.00–20.00 Mon–Sat. Maternity wear.

FURNITURE
There's a couple of good addresses if you are on the lookout to furnish your flat or office:

Jysk Scan Colour On the road to Fushë-Kosova on the right-hand side after the Industrial Zone turn-off; ☎ 038 601 665; http://www.scan-color.com; ⏱ 09.00–21.00 Mon–Fri, 09.00–20.00 Sat, 10.00–18.00 Sun. Modern furniture, Scandinavian/IKEA style.

Lesna On the left-hand side on the main road to Fushë-Kosova; ☎ 038 854 0183; m 044 779 977; e info@lesna.net; www.lesna.net; ⏱ 09.30–20.00 Mon–Fri, 09.30–21.00 Sat. Great collection of houseware, from pots to bed sheets & lamps, as well as furniture. Here you find everything you need to furnish a new home, including furniture for kids. Free home delivery.

Mobi Inn Further along the Fushë-Kosova road on the left-hand side; ☎ 038 534 039; ⏱ 08.00–20.00 Mon–Sat. Tasteful, quality & well-priced German furniture. Mobi Inn also has a small branch in town at the intersection of Rr UÇK with the Podujevo road.

Less modern, heavier-style wood and other furniture can be found in shops on the main road to Fushë-Kosova and north of the Old Town bazaar market in the area adjacent to, but set back from the Podujevo road. It is also possible to commission pieces.

IT AND TECHNOLOGY
There is a cluster of shops in an area of Prishtina near the university and higher up the hill on Rr Ekrem Qabej towards Sunny Hill (Kodra e Diellit) where you can go to compare prices which are now quite competitive (despite the 10% customs duty in Kosovo). They sell Hewlett Packard, Fujitsu and Dell laptops, PCs, digital cameras, hard drives, routers, printers, cables and surge protectors – pretty much everything you're likely to need. They also provide servicing of PCs or laptops for a much lower price than back home.

Asseco/Pronet Veternik, tucked behind Albi supermarket; ☎ 038 557 799; www.pronet-ks.com, www.asseco-see.com; ⏱ 08.30–17.30 Mon–Fri. Specialises in top-of-the-range HP/Compaq computers, peripherals & software & Kosovo's best software development. Not a place you really drop in on but they may arrange to service your HP/Compaq.

Bo-tek Rr Agim Ramadani Objekt C; ☎ 038 245 625; e info@bot-ek.com; www.bo-tek.com. Larger PC store, specialising in Dell. Also does repairs.

Comtrade Rr Ekrem Qabej; ☎ 038 222 695; ⏱ 09.00–18.00 Mon–Fri, 09.00–15.00 Sat. In the Albanology building. Fujitsu Siemens specialist.

Daxa Electronics Rr Ekrem Qabej; ☎ 038 244 016; m 044 503 183; ⏱ 09.00–18.00 Mon–Fri, 09.00–16.00 Sat. Broad range of IT, phone & digital-camera goods, & Brother printers. Competitive prices.

Power PC IT Rr Ekrem Qabej/Hajrullah Abdullahu 140; ☎ 038 244 431; e info@ppc-computer.com; www.ppc-computer.com; ⏱ 09.00–17.00 Mon–Fri, 10.00–15.00 Sat. Dell & others.

Toshiba Rr UÇK 105/1; ☎ 038 246 222; e info@toshiba-ks.com; www.toshiba-ks.com. Sales & repairs.

MARKETS The **main green market** (⏲ *08.00–20.00 daily*) and the wholesale vegetable and food market (together with some clothes and household goods) has moved to the road to Fushë-Kosova behind the UN and is worth a trip for the experience alone. However, a more convenient market can be found down the cobbled road in the Old Town behind Shaban Qebaptore.

The **secondhand car and tool market** is held every Sunday on the road to Podujevo about 3km out of town. There are literally hundreds of cars for sale and you may get a bargain, but 'buyer beware', and remember the importance of paperwork. Driving a car with forged customs papers is a strict liability offence in Kosovo.

MUSIC AND DVDS Prishtina's streets are lined with CD shops selling the latest pirate copies of international albums and DVDs. The fact that it is illegal does not seem to bother anyone. International police and soldiers are regularly seen stocking up their private music and movie collections. Be warned that you may get into serious trouble in your home country if caught with bags full of pirate CDs.

Ginger Music store [96 D4] (sign 'Music and films that matter') m 044 126 305; e contact@ginger-embargo.com; ⏲ 11.00–late. Tucked next door to the Cavallero Restaurant near the former UNMIK (now EULEX) building (next to Grand Hotel), this store is a jewel for alternative-music lovers on the lookout for classic music & movies at bargain prices compared with anywhere else in Europe. Of course, all are pirate copies. It's also one of the few places selling alternative Albanian music; not only the latest hit charts. You can also pick up flyers on music & other events.
Minimax Outside KFOR headquarters/Film City; ⏲ 08.00–23.00 daily. This yellow-&-red building is

visible from nearly 1km away in the Dragodan side of town off the road to Mitrovica, & comprises 4 floors of goodies (mostly pirate), the first floor being DVDs, CDs, watches & wallets. There are usually more than 15–20 KFOR soldiers present at any one time & hence the aisles are organised by reference to major language groups, eg: French, German & English. The DVDs can be tested. This is one of a cluster of shops found round KFOR headquarters (each KFOR has led to a cluster of DVD, CD & watch shops & even massage parlours springing up around them). Upstairs is skiwear, outdoor clothing & some semi-designer wear.

PHOTOS, STATIONERY AND FRAMING Kosovo is a great place to get passport photos done for a cheap price and with photographers that take time to make you look your best.

Art Foto Rr Nënë Terezë (opposite Grand Hotel); ☎ 038 225 752; ⏲ 08.00–23.00 Mon–Sat. Good & quick photo developing for all needs, including passport pictures.
Canon Foto Studio Rr Agim Ramadani (opposite National Theatre); m 044/049 146 050; ⏲ 08.00–20.00 Mon–Sat. Photo studio & developing. Good passport studio.

Europrinty ☎ 038 242 110; ⏲ 08.00–17.00 Mon–Sat. Enormous range of office supplies at excellent prices. Much cheaper than Talens.
Top Photo Rr Migjeni 6b; e topfoto1@hotmail.com; ⏲ 09.00–18.00 Mon–Sat. Near OSCE. High-quality photos, including studio, passport, enlargements, adaptations & framing. Friendly management.

SHOPPING CENTRES AND HYPERMARKETS Until fairly recently Prishtina had limited shopping and for smarter clothing you had to head for Skopje, but this is no longer the case as several large supermarkets and shopping centres have opened. Many of them have their own minibuses. At all of them parking is free and Maxi 1 and Albi have crèches where you can leave the kids so you can shop hands-free. There are effectively two main locations – the Industrial Zone which is about 3km west of town stretching out on both sides along the road to Fushë-Kosova, and the top of the road to Skopje (an area known as Veternik or Hajvali).

Albi shopping centre On the left-hand side as you leave Prishtina for Skopje; ☎ 038 500 202 ext 100; ⏰ 07.30–23.00 daily. As with Grand Store but also with furniture & an excellent supermarket with in-store bakery with various types of nutty breads, croissants, the best cheese selection in Kosovo (including foreign cheeses) & a meat counter with a selection of pork.

Ben-Af [97 G3] Slightly set back on Rr Dëshmorët e Kombit & also on Agim Ramadani; ⏰ 08.00–23.00 daily. Downstairs small(ish) super-market. Good clothes selection upstairs & toy store.

Era Hypermarket City Park Industrial Zone; ☎ 038 558 800; & also in town under the Qafa building; ⏰ 08.00–22.00. Good choice of food & clothes. The best for 'exotic' vegetables & specialities like Mexican spice mix or sun-dried tomatoes. Set back from the road. Turn off right after ETC.

ETC On the right-hand side before the Industrial Zone as you are heading to Fushë-Kosova; ☎ 038 545 164; ⏰ 08.00–22.00. Huge car park.

Grand Store On the right-hand side as you leave Prishtina for Skopje; ⏰ 09.00–22.00 daily except 1 Jan. Designer clothes, cosmetics & electronics. Buses every hour from Prishtina centre to Grand Store (& return) at 07.35, 08.40, 09.40 then at 25mins past the hour until 22.25. Last bus 23.15. There is a children's playground & day-care centre on the top floor, so you can leave your child in good care & take time out to shop or have a coffee.

Interex Industrial Zone. On the left-hand side of the Fushë-Kosova road after the turn-off to Maxi & nearly opposite Jysk; ⏰ 08.00–22.00 daily. Competitively priced hypermarket.

Maxi 1 Industrial Zone, turn off right after ETC & turn left; www.maxiks.com (e-shop); ⏰ 08.00–22.00 daily. The original hypermarket founded back in 2000 when it was known as the Norwegian PX. Electricals, budget-end clothes & food. Good for household equipment & crockery if you are kitting out your flat. Complete with ice rink & restaurant. You can also do online shopping for more than 2,000 items and have the groceries delivered to your door. Cards accepted.

Maxi 2 Near the bus station, so closer to town; ⏰ 08.00–23.00 daily

Maxi 3 [96 D4] Rr Rexhep Luci (opposite ABC Cinema); ⏰ 08.00–22.00 daily. In-town shopping.

Maxi 4 Near the Lesna new apartment complex as you come into town from Skopje on the left.

FISH

Taunita Josip Rela 2; ☎ 038 248 502; m 044 169 579; e taunita_fish@hotmail.com; www.taunita.com; ⏰ 09.00–19.00 Fri/Sat, 10.00–13.00 Sun. Best shop for fresh fish, seafood & wines.

Trofta Rr E Shkupit Emshir, near the bus station & Maxi 2; ☎ 038 723 293; m 044 714 238. Sells fresh trout from the Istog trout farm.

SPORTS AND BIKE STORES

Bekim Bilali Rr Nazi Gafurri, just after Sami Frasheri school, opposite the technical school; m 044 160 433; ⏰ 09.00–19.00; in summer until 20.00. Good for repairs. A few spares & a few older bikes for sale.

Bike Tomos Rr UÇK 26; m 044 154 755; ⏰ 09.00–19.00 Mon–Sat. Bike & motorbike repairs & a few secondhand bikes for sale. Very few spare parts.

ErVi Sports Various branches, including Lidhja e Prizrenit, off Rr Bill Clinton & branches at Maxi 1 & Albi shopping centre.

Slovenia Sport/Megasport Rr Agim Ramadani 59; ☎ 038 223 442; e info@megasport.org; www.megasport.org; ⏰ 09.30–20.00 Mon–Fri, 09.30–16.00 Sat. Everything from running machines, weights, volleyballs to tennis & some ski items.

Sporting Rr Rustem Statovci, on the right-hand side off Agim Ramadani on the way up to Rugova's grave; ☎ 038 220 029; m 049 419 920; e info@sportingks.com; www.sportingks.com. A branch of the Prizren & Gjilan shops. The best selection of bikes for sale in town. Distributor of Scott & Aprilla touring & mountain bikes, bike helmets, inner tubes & other spare parts, also a good selection of weights & exercise machines, table tennis, football & other equipment. Very helpful & friendly staff.

SPORTS AND ACTIVITIES

ACTIVITIES FOR CHILDREN In the summer the outdoor swimming pools in each direction out of Prishtina are an option, although they are somewhat crowded and the hygiene standards might not be quite up to scratch. The best one to head for is probably the one in Gračanica as this is less crowded.

Adventure playgrounds in public parks are sadly lacking, with the exception of some swings and ropes in Velania district (up from the crossroads near the road to Germia) and thanks to the Italian government, the **City Park (Parku Qyteti)** has been revived as a pleasant inner-city park with a playground for children, flowerbeds and outdoor cafés (summer only) where you can sip a tea or coffee under the trees. A couple of marked paths criss-crossing the park are also suitable for children's buggies.

Some of the restaurants have installed their own swings in the garden (see below).

Magic Park Rr Ismajl Dumoshi 27 (ask locals – it's near the old people's home); ☎ 038 517 755; m 044 384 295/375 707; ⊕ 11.00–21.00 daily; entrance €1.50 for children all day. The park is a favourite in winter, with an ice-skating rink Nov–Apr. There is also a children's playground with coloured balls, climbing frames & trampolines, & a restaurant pizzeria for the adults.

Qamerlia Lukare, 5km outside Prishtina; m 044 112 067/159 102. Has a zoo, horseriding, tennis, volleyball as well as a big restaurant. Take the road to Kerqekolle (turn right before the railway crossing on the road to Podujevo), continue until Lukare & turn left after the petrol station.

Te Ariu See *National cuisine* above. With a zoo & playground.

Villa Germia and Freskia In Germia, restaurant with children's playground & Freskia has a mini zoo.

BALLET m 049 382 788/044 411 269; e bardhaneziri@gmail.com, b_norraa@msn.com. For children aged four–14.

BASKETBALL Yugoslavia always had strong basketball teams, but Kosovo has seen a real basketball boom in recent years. Privately sponsored local teams compete with international players, mostly from the US, and basketball games are generally well attended. You can watch some real quality games and it's a fun experience to watch and listen to the enthusiastic fan clubs. Tickets for basketball games cost €2 and can be purchased at the door at the Youth and Sports Palace (see page 130). The two local teams are called AS Prishtina and Sigal Prishtina, Kosovo champions in 2002, 2003 and 2005. The open-air swimming pool (see page 117) has a small basketball court.

BOWLING AND BILLIARDS

Billiardo Club Rr UÇK (opposite petrol station); ⊕ 08.00–24.00. 2 billiard tables for late-night players.

Bo-Bowling Emshir neighbourhood, near Rent-a-Car & behind Maxi 2; ☎ 038 500 060 (for bookings); m 044 241 251; e info@bo-bowling.com; www.bo-bowling.com; ⊕ 16.00–01.00 Mon–Sat, from 14.00 Sun. Look for the large sign on the ring road for the turn-off. A state-of-the-art bowling hall. Great fun to go with a group of friends. On w/ends booking is essential as it can get very busy. The bar serves drinks & snacks. Limited car parking.

Princi i Arberit Hotel (see page 99) Out of town on the Podujevo road, take the turn-off as per signs. Alternative, smaller bowling alley with less atmosphere. Good games including billiards, table football.

CHESS

Prishtina Chess Club Dardania 3/2 No 3; m 044 115 409/10

CLIMBING AND HIKING

Beni e hikingnjeri@gmail.com; www.njeri.com. Hiking group.

Kosova Mountain Federation (Federata Bjeshkatare e Kosovës) Rr Andrea Gropa; m 044 175 174. In existence since 1948.

FISHING AND HUNTING Krapi (which means 'carp' by the way) is the name of the Prishtina-based Association for Sport Fishing currently run by secretary Remzi Llapashtica (m *044 307 126*) and Burim Rexhepi (m *044 161 105*). Their main activity today concerns the cultivation and protection of Kosovo's fish stock as well as the promotion of sport fishing. Krapi has about 650 members.

Hunters' Association Kaprolli Rr Nazim Gafurri 18;
\ 038 230 432; e sh_gjkaprolli@hotmail.com

FLYING
Aeroklub Prishtina Pallati i Rinisë; m 044 140 918/112 928/112 283; e kaloti@hotmail.com; www.areoklubiprishtina.com. For the real adventurist — this club organises paragliding courses.

FOOTBALL The first football match ever played in Kosovo took place in Prizren in 1912 between two Austro-Hungarian teams. Soon after, the next 'international' match was played in Mitrovica between two teams of English soldiers. Today's football club KF Prishtina dates back to 1922.

City Stadium [96 B3] Between the Pallati i Rinisë & Rr Fehmi Agani; \ 038 226 968; e kfprishtina@yahoo.com
KF Flamurtari m 044 505 605 (for Ekrem), 044 410 041 (for Agim) to negotiate a booking for the pitch.
KF Kosova \ 038 245 334. Also has a women's team & organises football training for all ages.
KF MK m 044 426 290; ⊕ 08.00–22.00

Mon–Sat. The first fully private football club. Its training field is located near Santiago Bernabeo at the Herta commerz site, in the Fushë-Kosova Industrial Zone.
KF Prishtina Competes with KF Flamurtari, founded in 1968 & run by a group of volunteers who lovingly tend the grass (their stadium is down the road off the right from the Llapi Mosque below the railway on the road to Keqekolle or Lukare).

If you can get your own team together there are numerous fields and domes around town (whose tops may get stripped off in summer), for example, Yili football field near KFOR, with two fields and a dome (m *044 372 605*). The going rate is about €25 for an hour in the evening and less during the day.

GOLF
Driving range and minigolf Çagllavica village; m 049/045 343 433; www.prishtinagolf.com; ⊕ daily. Situated about 3km outside Prishtina; take the left-hand fork after the roundabout, in the direction of Ciao Restauarant. Good practice-swing venue out in the open air. They may be getting floodlights so call to check opening hours. Golf clubs to hire €5, 50 balls €5, 100 balls €8, shoes €2, glove €2.

GYMS AND FITNESS CENTRES
Body Power Fitness Rr Ilmi Rakovica; m 044 405 888; ⊕ 10.00–22.00 Mon–Sat. In Bregu i Diellit, opposite Ismajl Qemali primary school/tennis courts. Fully equipped modern gym (previously opposite the ABC Cinema). The opening hours are somewhat frustrating, however. Monthly cost €20, day membership €3.
Circuit training/personal trainer Emin Osmani; m 044 555 573; www.karate-ks.com. Runs classes as well as one-to-one arrangements.

Flori Rr Eduard Lir; m 049 169 192; ⊕ 09.00–12.00 & 14.00–22.00 Mon–Sat. Pleasant gym with modern equipment in central Dragodan (second street up) in basement of yellow flats, but again with frustrating opening hours. Monthly cost €25.
Gym Pallatit i Shtypit, Rr Luan Haradinaj, Riljinda; www.gym-ks.com; ⊕ 24/7 throughout the year except 17 Feb. Brand-new gym with large fitness studio, 6 showers & modern equipment (including 8

treadmills), sports massage & some aerobics/box aerobics classes. Monthly cost €25 for members, payable through direct debit, €38 per month or €15 weekly for non-members, €5 daily or €20 corporate (min 20 people). Pre-payment €200 per year (including 4 months' discount).
Life Fitness [201 G5] Rr Rustem Statovci 24 (on right hand side on way up to Rugova graves direction Velania); m 044 19 7257. Brand new gym with 4 treadmills, new equipment, sauna but more restricted opening hours. 🕐 08.00–23.00 Mon-Sat and 16.00–22.00 Sun. 1 month €30, 3 months €80, 6 months €150 and 1 year €300. 1 month sauna €20, single sauna use €5.

RUNNING AND BIKING
Germia Park Well suited for running & biking provided it is not too wet & muddy. There is a series of tracks. See the map, page 132, for more details. Keep to the paths as the areas between the paths were heavily mined (theoretically cleared, but one can never be sure), as there once was a Serbian army barracks in the area. If you are with less energetic companions then they can wait in one of the 3 restaurants, one of which has a zoo & adventure playground.

SKATING
Ice rink (Maxi Market) Outside Maxi 1, Industrial Zone; 🕐 winter 08.00–20.00. Technically not made of ice but of skateable plastic. A great place for children.

SWIMMING
Open Air Swimming Pool Germia Park; 🕐 09.00–18.00 daily from the day it gets filled with water (usually early May–mid-Sep). It's best to go early in the morning before it gets packed. There is also a small basketball court. The only indoor swimming pools near Prishtina are at Hotel Madrid (in Veternik) on the way to Vushtrri at the Swiss Wellness Centre (m 044 510 059 – see *Vushtrri*, page 260).

TABLE TENNIS
Ping Pong Club 'Art Foto' Aktash III 43. Founded in 2000.

TENNIS
Prishtina Tennis Club 📞 038 221 870; m 044 182 219; www.tenniskosova.com. Contact the enthusiastic Beni who also runs hiking & snow/ski trips (e *snownjeri@gmail.com; www.njeri.net*). Also check out his Facebook page.

Tennis courts Near the Ismail Qemali primary school, Sunny Hill/Bregu i Diellit & at the Velania-Tazlixhe crossroads; 📞 038 221 870; www.tenniskosova.com; m 044 123 647. Membership only. This is €150 for the season, €20–25 per hr. Lessons available for €20–25 per hr.

VOLLEYBALL Beach volleyball at the back of the Germia swimming pool. Great for mild summer evenings. There are two volleyball courts, not quite a 'beach' but close. Spectators can hang out on the benches or have a drink at the little café right next to the courts. Bring your own volleyballs.

Volleyball Club Zenel Hajdini School; m 044 112 013/313 500; e kvprishtina@hotmail.com; www. kvprishtina.com. There are volleyball clubs of both sexes.

OTHER PRACTICALITIES

At present there is no tourism office in town, so finding out about sights and events is quite a challenge. One of the best **cultural weekly listings** is in *Zeri* newspaper or for longer-term events try *Java* newspaper or the online media sites. For **maps** you can try the Dukagjini Bookstore on Rr Nëne Terezë.

3

The best compilation of useful **phone numbers and business-related information** can be found in the weekly *Oferta & Sukses*, which is available in newsagents and comes out each Wednesday. See also www.oftertasuksesi.com.

BANKS AND ATMS You never have to walk too far to find an ATM in the centre of Prishtina. There are five international banks operating in Kosovo today: ProCredit (German), Raiffeisen (Austrian), NLB (Slovenian owned), BKT (Albanian) and TEB (Turkish-French). They cream off the largest share of deposits. There are also two local banks – BpB (Bank for Private Business) and Banka Ekonomike (Economic Bank). ATMs operated by the international chains will accept any debit card with a Maestro sign as well as Visa and MasterCard. All banks are closed on national holidays. For more details on banks see *Chapter 2, Money*, page 157.

$ **Banka Ekonomike** Rr Luan Haradinaj on the corner with Rr UÇK; ☎ 038 244 394; ◷ 08.00–18.00 Mon–Fri, 09.00–14.00 Sat. Includes Western Union services.
$ **BpB** Rr Nëne Terezë (opposite Grand Hotel) and Rr UÇK; ☎ 038 244 666; www.bpb-bank.com; ◷ 08.00-18.30 Mon–Fri and 08.30–14.00 Sat
$ **NLB Prishtina** Rr Rexhep Luci 5; Rr Bill Clinton; Qendra Tregtare, Bregu i Diellit; Rr Nazim Gafurri, Nëne Terezë; ☎ 038 234 111/744 111; ◷ 08.00–17.00 Mon–Fri, 09.00–14.00 Sat
$ **ProCredit** Rr Nëne Terezë; Rr Dëshmorët e Kombit (near Grand Hotel); Rr UÇK; Rr Bill Clinton (top end near the crossroads); Sunny Hill trade centre; Rr Nazim Gafurri; Tazlixhe; & Rr Gazmend Zajmi (top of

the road); ☎ 038 555 555; www.procreditbank-kos.com; ◷ 08.00–18.00 Mon–Fri, 09.00–14.00 Sat
$ **Raiffeisen Bank** Rr UÇK 51; Ekrem Qabej, opposite Mensa; Rr Bill Clinton; Rr Nena Tereza (next to Fellini) ☎ 038 222 222; www.raiffeisen-kosovo.com; ◷ 08.00–18.00 Mon–Fri, 09.00–14.00 Sat
$ **TEB** Rr Agim Ramadani 15; Rr Bill Clinton, Rr Bvd Deshmoreve; ☎ 038 230 000; e info@teb-kos.com; www.teb-kos.com; ◷ 09.00–18.00 Mon–Fri, 09.00–14.00 Sat
$ **Western Union** Rr Agim Ramadani 16/1; ☎ 038 223 166; www.westernunion.com; ◷ 08.30–18.00 Mon–Fri, 08.30–14.00 Sat. Services also offered inside several of the banks.

BEAUTY SALONS

B Beauty Armend Daci 12, Sunny Hill/Bregu i Diellit (next to Oaza market opposite the tennis courts); ☎ 044/049 120 808. Facials, waxes & eye treatments, body treatments, massage, aromatherapy massage. The hot-stone massages are especially popular.
Decléor Rr Garibaldi; ☎ 038 226 789; ☎ 044 158 234; ◷ 10.00–20.00 Mon–Sat. Best to make an appointment ahead of time as it gets crowded after

work hours. Treatments include facials, waxing & aromatherapies.
Passion Rr Bill Clinton Objekti E; ☎ 038 554 433; Rr Zija Shemsiu C13; ☎ 038 553 366; Qafa tower in the centre, Rr UÇK; ☎ 038 222 221; ☎ 044 222 222; or Bregu i Diellit, Rr 2 Lamela 8; ☎ 038 555 559; ☎ 044 334 455; e info@bepassion.com; www.bepassion.com; ◷ 08.00–20.00. Passion beauty salons is a chain which operates throughout Prishtina.

CAR REPAIRS

Autoservice Vali Industrial Zone, Fushë-Kosova; ☎ 038 500 200; ☎ 044 122 107; e info@asvali.com; www.enasvali.com; ◷ 08.00–18.00 Mon–Sat. Land Rover specialists.
Baki ☎ 038 551 599; ◷ 08.00–18.00 Mon–Fri, 08.00–14.00 Sat. VW, Skoda, Seat, Audi.
Eurogoma Service Industrial Zone, Fushë-Kosova; ☎ 038 545 800; ☎ 049 504 425;

e eurogomaservice@yahoo.com. Biggest tyre sellers in Kosova. Also batteries, oil, hubcaps.
Kaçandolli Industrial Zone, Fushë-Kosova; ☎ 038 601 600; ☎ 044 115 745 ◷ Mon–Sat 08.00–18.00
Porsche Kosova 3km on the Prishtina–Skopje road; ☎ 038 551 599; ☎ 044 120 188; e info@porsche-kosova.com; www.porsche-kosova.com; ◷ 08.30–18.00 Mon–Sat

COBBLERS

Kepuce The main branch, Kepuce, can be found halfway up Ardian Krasniqi, on the right-hand side. There is also Student Kepuce just off the passageway

between Rr Sylejman Vokshi & Rr Agin Ramadani as you go up the steps on the left-hand side, in the flats.

COMMUNICATIONS The headquarters of the **central PTK office** is located in Dardania district along Rr Dëshmorët e Kombit. The Customer Service Centre on the intermediate level handles enquiries for fixed-line telephones and pre-pay (scratchcard) mobile phones. Here you can purchase a SIM card and enquire about transfer or replacements of numbers if you lose your phone. For post-pay contracts you have to go the Vala headquarters, which is on Rr UÇK near the traffic lights and the Bata shoe shop.

For **IPKO** internet or SIM cards there is an IPKO shop on Rr Nëne Terezë and another on Rr Perandori Justinian. Note that ProCredit and TEB machines allow you to make Vala and IPKO mobile-phone top-ups electronically.

Kujtesa's headquarters (for cable TV and internet) is next to Hotel Prishtina.

DENTISTS

Ditta Dental Rr UÇK 6/1; m 044/049 123 813; e dittadent@hotmail.com. Dr Aferdita Zeqiri speaks English.
Doni Dent Rr Ekrem Qabaj 7; ☏ 038 229 880; e migjend@yahoo.com; ⊕ 09.00–13.00 & 16.00–20.00 Mon–Fri, 09.00–16.00 Sat
Gopal Dent ☏ 038 512 192; m 044 283 645/049 100 345; e info@gopaldent.com; www.gopaldent.com. Located behind the Ministry of Trade & Industry near

Eulex Farmed. Take the turn to the hospital & continue, then turn left again. A new clinic opened in 2009, mostly used by the diaspora, for whom the cheaper but still EU-standard treatment is worth the trip. They do dental implants at half the price of Germany, teeth whitening, fillings & chipped teeth replacements with white ceramic. They work with Vanbreda & other major insurers. Waiting room with plasma TV & Wi-Fi. The staff speak fluent English.

DRY CLEANERS

Etileni Rr Ekrem Qabej, opposite the Languages Faculty; ☏ 038 543 083; Rr Perandori Justinian 8 (behind Tre Sheshirat); ☏ 038 227 714; m 044 161 910; ⊕ 08.00–20.00 Mon–Sat

ESTATE AGENTS

Capital Ring Rr Kosta Novakoviq (opposite Hotel Prishtina); ☏ 038 552 928; m 044 210 542; www.ringks.com. Professional estate agent, with English-speaking staff, for rentals & sales. One of the few with properties searchable online.
Eco-Impex Kosovë-Prishtinë, Rr Fehmi Agani 9/1; ☏ 038 249 263/4; e ecoimpex@hotmail.com, ecoimpex_es@yahoo.com
Immobilia Rr Qamil Hoxha; ☏ 038 227 456; m 044 155 933/197 650; www.immobilia-kosova.com —

properties for sale online. Also valuations, surveys.
Omega Rr Rrustem Statovci 7, near Slovenia Sport; ☏ 038 226 678; m 044 755 859; e omegaprishtina@gmail.com; www.omega-ks.com; ⊕ 09.00–18.00. Properties searchable online.
Miloti Milot Sejdiu; ☏ 038 244 898; m 044 130 615; e milotsplus@hotmail.com
Pajtesa Rr Bill Clinton 36; ☏ 038 224 189; m 044 224 189.

GYNAECOLOGIST

Deni Ulpiana D1/VII, 1st Fl (opposite Albi Market); ☏ 038 542 317; m 044 218 802. Dr Mirsada Behluli offers all kinds of check-ups, tests & treatments.

HAIRDRESSERS

Menda Rr Luan Haradinaj (opposite main police station); ☏ 038 227 800; m 049 227 800; www.menda.info; ⊕ 10.00–19.00. Artistic Director Dren trained abroad & makes you feel like you are in Berlin or London although the prices are not cheap.

Valon Hamza Rr Hajdar Dushi; m 044 209 003; e valonhamza@hotmail.com; ⊕ 09.00–20.00 Mon–Sat. Tucked behind Rr Luan Haradinaj (just behind Café Arte). Valon speaks perfect German (& English) & is a fully certified professional hairdresser.

INSURANCE

Association of Kosovo Insurers (insurance for cars without KS plates) Rr Enver Maloku 28, Bregu i Diellit (beyond Qerimi Bakery on main road); ✆ 038 245 115; e info@iak-ks.com; www.iak-ks.com; ⏰ 08.00–16.00 Mon–Sat

Croatia Insurance Rr Luan Haradinaj; ✆ 038 246 956; e teuta.xhoci@crosig.com; www.crosi.hr

Dukagjini Rr Dëshmorët e Kombit 67; ✆ 038 543 575

Insig www.insig-ks.com

Sigal/UNIQA Rr UÇK 60; ✆ 038 240 241; e info@sigal-ks.com

Sigkos Rr Ekrem Qabej; e info@sigkos.com

Siguria Rr Luan Haradinaj; ✆ 038 248 848; www.siguria.info

INTERNET CAFÉS/CALL CENTRES Internet cafés and international call centres in Prishtina are mostly a little bit away from Rr Nëne Terezë. Some of them open and close quickly, so keeping track is a little difficult. There are always a few on Rr Agim Ramadani opposite the half-built Serb church on the university campus. Most cafés now offer Wi-Fi access for free or for a small fee, including all of the hotels. Provided you have your own laptop with you, it's relatively easy to get online.

LANGUAGE SCHOOLS

Cambridge School Boro Ramiz; ✆ 038 249 273/4; e schoolpr2002@hotmail.com. Offers Albanian-language classes but also French & other major languages.

New Age School Off Rr Agim Ramadani near the copy shops & Rest Pjata; ✆ 038 246 100; ⏰ 7.00–22.00 Mon–Fri, 07.00–15.00 Sat

Oxford Studio Bregu i Diellit Rr 3.3; ✆ 038 454 657; Dardania ✆ 038 245 453; e oxford_studio@hotmail.com. Good Albanian teachers for foreigners. English- & Albanian-language classes for groups and one-to-one tuition. On demand Oxford Studio can also arrange special Turkish or German courses.

LIBRARIES

Hyvzi Sylejmani Library Rr UÇK 10 (from 2011, may move to new building in Dardania); ✆ 038 245 523; ⏰ 08.00–19.00 Mon–Fri, 08.00–13.00 Sat. Also a branch in Ulpiana & in Tazlixhe at the crossroads on the road to Germia. Anyone can join with ID. Must bring a passport photo for membership. Smaller library with a more friendly selection of books. Costs €5 for adults, €3 children.

National Library Sheshi Hasan; www.biblioteka-ks.org; ⏰ 07.00–21.00 Mon–Fri, 07.00–14.00 Sat. Again, anyone can join, but to do so you will need ID. Reference library only. Not possible to take books out of the building. Photocopying facilities in the building. Also access to electronic databases. Costs €12 for 12 months or €6 for 6-month membership.

LOCKSMITH

Kiki Rr Garibaldi (opposite Grand Hotel); m 049 293 023/044 286 288; ⏰ 09.00–20.00. Good for key cutting.

Servis Celsa Corner of Rr Luan Haradinaj & Rr Rexhep Luci (ground floor); m 044 358 309; ⏰ 09.00–20.00 Mon–Sat. For emergency copies of keys & photocopies.

MASSAGE

Sun Life Chinese Massage Rr Ardian Krasniqi 13 (next to Swiss embassy); m 044 738 610; ⏰ daily. The best place for a professional massage or acupuncture.

The place is clean, & even though Dr Hou Shu Ying's English is not the best, she is good at picking up where the pain comes from.

MUNICIPALITY

Prishtina Municipality ✆ 038 230 900; www.komuna-prishtina.org; ⏰ 08.00–12.00 & 13.00–16.00 Mon–Fri. In 2010, the municipality moved to new offices further out on the way to Film City, near ICO & Hotel Adria.

OPTICIANS

Oculo Optika Rr Agim Ramadani 52;
⊕ 09.00–20.00 Mon–Fri, 09.00–15.00 Sat.
Does contact lenses as well as modern glasses.
Good rates compared with the West.

PET SHOP AND VETERINARY SURGEON

Crazy Pet Rr Nazim Gafurri 121 (left-hand side on the road to Germia); ☎ 038 518 333; m 044 248 780/049 248 780; e crazy.pet@live.com;

⊕ 09.00–18.00 Mon–Fri. Live pets & supplies. Dardan Pozhegu is also a trained veterinary surgeon & runs a small veterinary clinic.

PHARMACIES There are lots around town. Try:

Barnatore A Rr Gazmend Zajmi. Mrs Karahoda here speaks good English & trained in Zagreb.
Barnatore Valeriana Rr Luan Haradinaj 18 (near former UN headquarters); ⊕ 07.00–22.00 Mon–Sat,

07.00–20.00 Sun. Pharmacist Hyrmet Nebiu speaks good English & trained abroad.
Viva Pharmacie Rr Dëshmorët e Kombit (near the PTK headquarters); ⊕ 24hrs

PHOTOCOPYING SHOPS These are mostly clustered near the university, particularly on Ekrem Qabej and along Rr Agim Ramadani, and are geared up to copy complete books as unfortunately copyright is unheard of in Kosovo.

Ricoh Rr Agim Ramadani, opposite the unfinished Serb church; ⊕ 08.00–20.30

Speed Rr Agim Ramadani, opposite the unfinished Serb church; ⊕ 09.00–21.00

POST OFFICES There are several in Prishtina. One is behind the theatre on Rr Agim Ramadani, another is further up this street, another in the basement of the PTK headquarters (Dardania building), another upstairs near Restaurant Rugova and one tucked away near Café Papillon or Lounge on Rr Perandori Justinian closer to Rr Dëshmorët e Kombit.

For more information on postal and telcom services available, go to www.ptkonline.com (also available in English). For general postal services call ☎ 038 555 222, for mobile-phone queries call m 038 500 555.

PRIVATE CLINICS

Euromed Clinic Rr Prishtinë, Fushë Kosova (on the left-hand side before the first ProCredit Bank in Fushë-Kosova); ☎ 038 534 072; e euromed_klinik@yahoo.de. The nearest Kosovars will get to Western-style medicine in Kosovo at the moment is this private clinic run by a doctor who worked for 14 years in Germany. 10 doctors specialising in radiology, cardiology, stomach surgery, orthopaedics, urology, plastic surgery & gynaecology. Many people fly in for a few days from Austria or elsewhere for consultations.
German Eye Clinic Rr Ekrem Qabej 11 (up from Mensa on left-hand side); ☎ 038 246 842;

e info@kgjs.net; www.klinikagjermaneesyrit.com; ⊕ 08.00–23.00 Mon–Fri, 08.00–14.00 Sat
Lindja Hajvali/Gračanica; ☎ 038 767 333; m 044 166 980; www.lindja-hospital.com. Infertility & IVF treatment, obstetricians/gynaecologists, paediatric & neonatal care. Opened in Mar 2009 & mostly staffed by employees of Prishtina General Hospital, but with infinitely superior surroundings; certainly the rooms are beautifully decorated with oxygen supplies & even Wi-Fi.
Rezonanca Peyton (near Club 212); ☎ 038 243 801; e atije_idrizaj@hotmail.com; www.rezonanca.com; ⊕ 24hrs

RELIGIOUS SERVICES

Catholic church Rr Karposhi 41, Ulpiana; ☎ 038 549 861. Masses at 11.00 & 15.00 on Sun in St Anthony Church, Shen Ndou, Ulpiana, 5mins' walk from the PTK building.

Islamic Community of Kosova Rr Bajram Kelmendi 84; ☎ 038 224 024; www.bashkesiaislame.net. The main office is near Dodona Theatre. Fri noon prayers take place at all mosques but the main mosque is Mbretit

Mosque, or 'Big Mosque' (Xhamia e Madhe), 5mins' walk from the parliament building toward Germia (near the National Museum).

Kosova Protestant–Evangelical church Rr Rrustem Statovci 9; ☎ 038 225 330; www.kosovachurch.net, www.kishaprotestante.org. The main church service is on Sun at 11.00 at the headquarters address above & the church is a 1min walk from Slovenia Sport, up the road toward Velania. There are another 2 churches in the city that have services every

Sun morning: one is in Peyton & the other in Rr Nazim Gafurri, towards Germia on the right-hand side.

Serbian Orthodox church Rr Shkodres 2 (formerly Valjevska 4); www.spc.org.rs. St Nicholas Church (The Diocesan Exarchate of Prishtina), as part of the Rashka–Prizren diocese, is located on your way to Germia (Rr Nazim Gafurri), about 15mins' walk from the parliament building up a steep paved road.

SCHOOLS AND KINDERGARTENS

American School of Kosova Pallati i Rinise (Boro Ramiz complex), Rr Luan Haradinaj; ☎ 038 227 277; www.askosova.org

Gulistan Education Centre Veternik; ☎ 038 540 151; e isp_ka@hotmail.com; www.ispkosova.com. A private education company, the Mehmet Akif College Secondary School, which has moved some of its facilities to Lipjan. Teaching is in English, Albanian & Turkish.

International Learning Group (ILG) Rr 'Mbreteresha Teuta' 46, Sofalia (continue straight after the Velania/Tazlixhe crossroads & then take the next main

right & continue up the left fork); ☎ 043 722 994; m 049 206 014; e ilgkosovo@yahoo.com. International school popular with EULEX & ICO families, catering for pre-school & primary school kids. All teaching in English, mainly by international teachers.

Prishtina High School Matiqan; ☎ 038 258 358; www.phs-asi.org. US run with American curriculum. A good 5km out of town.

Quality School International Dragodan; http://kst.qsi.org/. Caters for children 5–13.

TAILORS There is a cluster of small tailors on Rr Ardian Krasniqi: prices for small repairs, hems, buttons €1–2.

Anisa Rr Ardian Krasniqi 2; m 044 262 658; ⊕ 08.00–20.00 Mon–Sat

Shtepia e Modes 'AS' m 044 216 823/131 937; e shtepiaemodes_as@hotmail.com; ⊕ 09.00–

19.00 Mon–Fri, 09.00–15.00 Sat. 2 brothers who worked in Germany run a good tailors' business used to dealing with international clients in a tiny room through the tunnel behind the theatre.

TRANSLATION AGENCY

Trankos ☎ 038 242 455; e admin@trankos.com; www.trankos.com. A very efficient network of translators of Serbian, Albanian, Turkish, German

& English, who do contract work for the UN, EU & others. Payment can also be made into a UK bank.

UNIVERSITIES

American University of Kosovo Rr Nazim Gafurri; ☎ 038 518 542; e info@aukonline.org; www.aukonline.org

Prishtina University ☎ 038 244 183; e info@uni-pr.edu; www.unip-pr.edu

In addition there are dozens of private universities and colleges that have opened up since the war. The quality of education at these new private institutions varies greatly, however.

UTILITIES

City Central Heating Termokos, Rr 28 Nentori, Dardania; ☎ 038 543 210; e info@termokos.org; www.bebaime.com. Online reports (also in English) about when/why/where the city's central heating system is not working.

KEK Distribution Centre ☎ 038 543 421, 038 543

458 (Customer Relations Centre); www.kek-energy.com
Rubbish/waste-disposal company Pastrimi; ☎ 038 554 143

Water company Rr Tahir Zajmi (out of town on the road to Fushë–Kosova); ☎ 038 603 010; e info@kur-prishtina.com; www.kur-prishtina.com.

Turn first left after Pellumbi Restaurant near Garden Restaurant.

VIDEO/DVD RENTAL AND PURCHASE
Saba Video Club Rr A Frasheri 23, off Gazmend Zajmi (former Rr Dubrovnik); m 044 158 750/113 170; e sami_kutlovci55@hotmail.com; ⏲ 11.00–23.00

Mon–Sat. DVDs to rent for €0.50 & to purchase for about €1.50.

WHAT TO SEE AND DO

Depending on what you are after, Prishtina has a number of well-kept secrets. If you want to concentrate on the historical zone where most Ottoman-era monuments and buildings can be found, allow at least an afternoon. If you have more time and want to explore Prishtina's more recent past, the city offers both an open-air museum of Yugoslav communist town planning and an exciting history of civil resistance, conflict and international state-building efforts. The Rugova Memorial up in Velania or Dragodan Hill offer the best viewpoints of the city.

SKENDERBEG

'Skenderbeg' stands for Lord Alexander, the Turkish name of Gjergj Kastrioti, the most prominent Albanian national hero. Gjergj Kastrioti's father was a powerful lord based in Kruja, in present-day Albania. In 1415, Kruja Castle fell to the Ottoman armies and Gjergj Kastrioti was sent to Istanbul to be brought up at the sultan's court as part of a deal that allowed his father to continue to rule northern Albania as a Turkish vassal. As an adult, Gjergj Kastrioti returned to Kruja in 1438 – now renamed Skenderbeg – to take up an Ottoman administrative post. In 1443, at the height of a Hungarian campaign led by Janos Hunyadi against the sultan's armies, Kastrioti seized the moment and started his revolt. In a skilful diplomatic move, he united all the northern Albanian clans in the famous Besa (solemn oath) of Lezha. For almost a quarter of a century Skenderbeg challenged the sultan's authority and posed a threat to his European possessions. Skenderbeg also repeatedly appealed to European powers to send troops and weapons to help the Albanian revolt to push back the Ottoman forces. In 1448, Sultan Murat II assembled a large army to crush the revolt of Skenderbeg, but found himself fighting an advancing Hungarian army on the Kosovo fields. Skenderbeg wanted to come to the Hungarians' rescue, but when his troops arrived in Kosovo on the third day of the battle the Hungarian armies had already been dispersed in all directions. In 1466, the Ottoman forces returned with 150,000 troops. Heavily outnumbered, the Albanian troops under Skenderbeg's command were forced to surrender. Two years later, in 1468, Skenderbeg died in Lezha, leaving behind a son too young to take over the father's command.

Skenderbeg's armour has been taken to Vienna where it is on display in the Military Museum. The last fortress to be lost to the Ottomans in 1479 was Rozafa Castle in Shkodra, Albania. Legend tells that Skenderbeg himself led a group of Albanians over the Adriatic to southern Italy. These 15th-century migrants became known as Arbrësh. To this day you can occasionally hear an archaic form of Albanian being spoken in southern Italy and central Sicily.

The historic building across the road directly opposite the Skenderbeg Statue was once known as the Union Hotel and at the time of writing may be in the process of being restored despite two fires which occurred under rather suspicious circumstances. In the 1930s, it was Prishtina's top address. Next to it is the National Theatre which was restored after the war.

There are no organised walking tours, but Kemajl Luci, the chief archaeologist at the Kosovo Museum, sometimes takes visitors around after special arrangement (see page 125). With the money paid for the tour he buys equipment for the archaeological atelier in the museum's basement.

HISTORIC WALK The **Skenderbeg Statue** [97 F2] on Rr Nëne Terezë is a good starting point for a tour of the Old Town of Prishtina. This copy of an original statue put up in Kruja (Albania) by the Albanian sculptor Janaq Paco was put up symbolically on the Albanian National Day, 28 November 2001. Besides the occasional Kosovo tourist who stops to take pictures, the design of the square is not really inviting. The funds to pay for the Skenderbeg Statue came from the 'Bukoshi fund', named after Bujar Bukoshi, the former prime minister-in-exile of the parallel government. This was money left over from the parallel Albanian tax system put in place during the Milošević regime. The building rising up to the sky just behind Skenderbeg is the new **government building** [97 F2] , housing several ministries including the prime minister's office. It was originally built for the Bank of Kosovo (Bankkos). For years, it was a stark reminder of the war. In 1999, it suffered collateral damage caused by the bombing of the nearby post office. All the windows were broken and its structure was severely damaged. The orange-painted building to the left was originally designed as Prishtina's first socialist department store and was the very first – and only – building with an escalator. The UN moved in after the war before handing it over to the Ministry of Public Administration.

Further along from Skenderbeg, behind a white fence (with photos of the missing) at the road junction with a blue glass frontage facing the mosque is the **Kosovo Parliament** [97 F1] , an unattractive building but with an exciting and turbulent past. On 23 March 1989, surrounded by tanks and in the presence of Serbian security forces, the delegates of the Kosovo Assembly were forced to pass the constitutional amendments designed by Milošević effectively to revoke Kosovo's autonomy. From then on the Kosovo Assembly practically ceased to exist. Ten years later, in summer 1999, the tide had turned. The UN administration moved in and stayed until the first national elections held in autumn 2001. It then vacated the offices for the first president Ibrahim Rugova and Kosovo's first post-war prime minister Bajram Rexhepi. On 12 December 2001, the newly elected parliament held its first constitutive session. For the first time since 1989, the parliament was back in the hands of democratically elected deputies representing the Kosovo people. The renovation of the building inside (which if you can get beyond the security screens is quite fancy in parts) was partly done by Beghet Pacolli, a member of the Kosovar diaspora, who supposedly made some of his money renovating the Kremlin. The parliament includes state-of-the-art donor-funded electronic voting. Sessions of the parliament are open to the public so theoretically you can go in and watch, although almost no-one does spontaneously so if you wish to do so you would be best trying to arrange a visit in advance. The parliament is also regularly broadcast on television as it makes for low-budget programming and maybe incentivises the parliamentarians to stay awake.

Into the old town Continue east towards the old part of town. **Çarshi Mosque** [97 G1] (literally 'Bazaar Mosque'), on your right across a rather dangerous pelican crossing, marks the beginning of the Old Town. Built in the early 15th century by Sultan Bajazid to commemorate the victory of the Ottoman forces in 1389, it is the oldest standing building in Prishtina. Many subsequent changes and repair works have changed its original look, but the unique stone-topped minaret has survived for more than 600 years. Because of it, the mosque is also nicknamed 'Taş Mosque', meaning 'Stone Mosque'. In the past, Çarshi Mosque overlooked the old bazaar and a Turkish bath (*hammam*) stood where the parliament building is today. As a trading town on the Balkan trade route Prishtina's bazaar was a busy and bustling place. Traders and craftsmen were selling jewellery, tailored suits, leather hides or welded pots in more than 300 shops. Ragusan merchants negotiated import and export deals between the ports of Ragusa and Thessaloniki. The noises of hammers, street vendors, ox carts and street kids were mixing to a lively tune. All this was lost under communism. The planners at the time felt that an Ottoman-style bazaar was not worthy of a modern, communist capital. Unlike in Sarajevo or Skopje, no efforts were made to preserve the historic heart of the city. They wanted to make a clean break with the city's Ottoman past. In a concerted 'action', teams of volunteers dismantled the bazaar's shops. In its place they put a rather bizarre-looking tall white spiky **monument in the name of Yugoslav Brotherhood and Unity**.

Turn off into Rr Nazim Gafurri where the mosque and yellow museum is and this road will take you into the Old Town.

The decorated marble **fountain** (*shadervan*) between Çarshi Mosque and the yellow Kosovo Museum building is the only one in Prishtina that has survived modernisation. In the past, Prishtina had more than 50 fountains and springs that would provide fresh water for refreshment or ablution (the ritual washing required for Muslims before praying). Across the road, opposite the museum, is a small open-air archaeological park with a few tombstones and a mosaic dating back to the Roman period.

The **Kosovo Museum** [97 F1] (*Rr Nazim Gafurri;* ⊕ *10.00–20.00 Mon–Sat; entrance free or minimal charge*) is housed in the large yellow building next to the mosque. It was once the seat of the Kosovo vilayet. It was here that the governors (*vali*) of the Kosovo province would be based. The building itself dates back to 1898. It has changed hands several times in the last six decades. From 1945 until 1975, it served as headquarters to the Yugoslav National Army. In 1963, it was sold to the Kosovo Museum and in 1999, it became the Kosovo headquarters of the European Agency for Reconstruction, the largest donor in Kosovo. No surprise perhaps, as it was certainly the most attractive building in town at that time. For three years, only the basement floor of the museum was open and instead of Bronze-Age or Illyrian artefacts, the upper floors were packed with computers and donor reports. In 2002, the building was finally returned to its proper use. The museum is definitely worth a visit. The most prominent piece in its extensive collection of archaeological and ethnological artefacts is a small terracotta statuette, no more than 30cm tall. The *Goddess on the Throne* is believed to be 6,000 years old. It was found at a site near Prishtina in 1956. A few months before the last war, she was 'kidnapped' and taken to Belgrade for an exhibition along with 1,247 artefacts, including some of the museum's most valuable exhibit pieces. In May 2002, after high-level intervention by the UN, the *Goddess on the Throne* was returned to Prishtina. You can find her prominently displayed on the first floor as part of the museum's permanent collection and explanations of archaeological digs during 2000–04. None of the other stolen artefacts have yet been returned. The Ahtisaari plan presented to the UN Security Council includes their return as a condition, but Belgrade has been dragging its feet successfully. Visitors can take a short walk and learn more about the earliest civilizations inhabiting the territory of Kosovo or wonder why so many of the figurines resemble extraterrestrial creatures. All information is in English also, but if you are keen to learn more it's best to ask for Kemajl Luci, the museum's chief archaeologist and former director. He sometimes organises private tours for visitors to the museum or takes you around the old part of town. The museum's temporary exhibitions range from photography to thematic exhibits; just try your luck and see what is downstairs under the main steps.

The road running between Çarshi Mosque and the Kosovo Museum takes you to the **Kocadishi House** which before nationalisation in 1954 was the home of the Kocadishi family. The family emigrated to Turkey under a special Yugoslavia– Turkey agreement signed in 1953. Wealthier families, like the Kocadishi who spoke both Albanian and Turkish at home, were exposed to a lot of political and economic pressure to declare themselves as 'Turks'. Under Aleksandar Ranković, then Yugoslav Minister of Interior, the authorities pursued an anti-Turkish policy aimed to 'repatriate' large numbers of Muslim citizens to Turkey. About 100,000 Kosovars, including several hundred families from Prishtina like the Kocadishi family, left their private properties and businesses behind and started a new life in Turkey. The long-time Mayor of Izmir, an important town on the Turkish coast, was called Ahmet Prishtina, for example. The house survived whereas its next-door building was razed to the ground and replaced by the school.

About 50m further beyond the Çarshi Mosque on Rr Nazim Gafurri is the **Jashar Pasha Mosque** [97 G1] which was constructed in 1834. The original portico was demolished to give way for an expansion of Rr Nazim Gafurri. Jashar Mehmet Pasha was a high-ranking Ottoman official from a wealthy Prishtina family. In 1843, he was governor in Skopje.

A further 70–100m on the same side on the right as the pavement narrows is the former building of the **Kosovo Academy of Arts and Sciences** [97 G1] (⊕ *08.00–16.00 Mon–Fri; entrance free*). The academy itself has recently moved to a new building on Rr Agim Ramadani, next door to the Ministry of Education. Go inside if you can and take a look at this beautiful example of Ottoman architecture. The academy was founded in 1975 at the zenith of Kosovo's autonomy within Yugoslavia.

Just beyond the academy, across a small side road is the **clocktower (Sahat Kulla)** [97 G1] which dates back to the 19th century. The original tower burnt in a fire and bricks have been used for its reconstruction. The original bell came all the way from Moldavia to Kosovo, with an inscription reading 'this bell was made in 1764 for Jon Moldova Rumen'. It is not clear how the bell initially came to Prishtina, and it is even more mysterious who stole the original in 2001.

Next door to the kulla is **Sami Frashëri Grammar School**, which is one of the oldest grammar schools in Kosovo and still one of the schools with the best reputation. It is named after the Albanian diaspora who came from Istanbul and started the League of Prizren (see *Chapter 1, History*, page 210, and *Chapter 6, Prizren*, page 195). Now the children in their black-and-white uniform hang out in the playground and also upstairs in the Sultan Café opposite. This part of town is also one of the areas where you may still find Turkish spoken among the minority population of Turks here. There are also still lessons held in Turkish in the school.

Facing the clocktower is **Mbretit Mosque** (also known as **Fatih Mosque** or Xhamia e Madhe – literally the big mosque), Prishtina's largest and most prominent mosque, with beautiful blue-and-white paintings. The great sultan Mehmet II built it in 1460–61, eight years before his conquest of Constantinople. Its cupola was once the biggest in the region. The square in front of Mbretit Mosque has always been a popular meeting point and you can still find elderly men sitting together to discuss the latest gossip of the town. During the Austrian occupation in 1689, the mosque was briefly converted into a Jesuit church dedicated to Francis Xavier. If you are lucky, you might meet the official guide (you can recognise him by his badge), who will be more than happy to take you on a tour of the mosque. The mosque you see today was restored in 1682–83 under the reign of Sultan Mehmet IV, and the minaret had to be repaired after earthquake damage in 1955.

The building just across from Fatih Mosque is the **Great Hammam**, dating back to the 15th century. Years of neglect and destruction have reduced it to an ugly shop front and a few walls resembling the structure of a *hammam*. The shop front facing Fatih Mosque was added illegally after a fire in 1994, effectively closing off the old entrance. Today, little more than a few damaged walls are left, most of the time covered in rubbish and overgrown with trees, but restoration is slowly underway. It is hard to imagine that it was once Prishtina's prestige *hammam*, constructed around the same time as Fatih Mosque. Legend tells that Sultan Mehmet II ordered the construction workers hired to build Fatih Mosque to take daily baths in the *hammam*.

Unfortunately, the Islamic Community Archive was torched on 13 June 1999, and almost the entire collection of Ottoman records and deeds dating back more than 300 years was lost. The archive was housed in a building next to Fatih Mosque.

Take the little road that winds to the right behind Fatih Mosque. It takes you to one of Prishtina's treasures, the **Emin Gjiku complex** (⏱ *10.00–18.00 Mon–Sat; entrance €2*), set in a beautiful Ottoman town house. Hidden away in a dead-end street, it is a must-do for anyone visiting Prishtina. Here you can really get a flavour of what Prishtina was like in the past. The Emin Gjiku complex once belonged to the Gjinolli family, one of Prishtina's most prominent families. In 1957, the building was nationalised and turned into an ethnological museum. The name derives from Emin Gjinolli, a member of the family, whose nickname was 'little Emin', or in Turkish Emincik. Traditionally, high walls and gardens surrounded typical Ottoman town houses. The stone building on your left, as you enter the courtyard, is the only building that survived the destruction of the old bazaar of Prishtina. It was moved here in 1963 and is believed to have served as a storage house. There are also rumours that it might once have served as a synagogue for the town's small Jewish community. Today it houses an arts studio. The building on the right was the servants' dwelling. The most impressive building is the former guesthouse on the far left. The wooden veranda and the richly decorated guest room on the first floor were reserved for men only. It was deemed inappropriate for women of the family to be serving other men; male members of the family would serve the coffee and food prepared in the ground-floor kitchen. Both the guesthouse and the family home – now home to a carefully designed permanent ethnological exhibition – are open to visitors. The museum guides at the site are more than happy to take you on a tour and introduce you to Albanian and other national folk costumes, funeral and wedding rites or show you typical household items, from wedding garments to guns and jewellery. Allow at least an hour to visit the whole Emin Gjiku complex.

From here you can either venture back to Rr Nazim Gafurri or take a stroll in the neighbourhood of the Emin Gjiku complex. You may find the occasional Ottoman-style building hidden beside a horrid modern construction covered in glass façades. The complete failure by the municipality to control urban planning and to rein in illegal constructions after the war may come as a shock for any first-time visitor. On paper, the Old Town is a protected historical zone, but this law is just a dead letter. What you see today is a chaotic humble-jumble of modern and old, big and small, side by side. What has remained of the 'bazaar' quarter – Prishtina's green market and a smaller covered market – is today crammed in around Rr Ilaz Agushi and Rr Zija Prishtina, nevertheless it is still a fun experience to just walk through this neighbourhood.

Another interesting mosque is located on Rr Ismail Dumoshi. To get there, turn into Rr Afrim Loxha (a right turn from Rr Nazim Gafurri), passing the **Hynyler House**, another beautiful example of a typical Ottoman *konak* (town house), although somewhat dilapidated and recently the subject of a Facebook campaign to save it. Then turn left into Rr Ismail Dumoshi. **Pirinaz Mosque** is on your right a few blocks down the road. It is built of the same stone as the Mbretit (Fatih) Mosque but its construction started 100 years later. Its founder was a man called Piri Nazir who served as *vezir* (a high official) under two different Ottoman sultans. Also

3

On a bitterly cold day in January 2006, Kosovo lost its most prominent leader. The death of Ibrahim Rugova marked the end of an era. For nearly two decades, Rugova had been the key figure in Kosovo's long struggle for independence. In a twist of fate he lost his final battle against lung cancer, just days before the first meeting was scheduled to negotiate Kosovo's final status. He never saw his big dream of an independent Kosovo come true.

Rugova was born in Cerrce village in western Kosovo in December 1944, just weeks after the German withdrawal. Partisans executed his father and grandfather. In 1976, he spent a year exploring literary theory at the Sorbonne in Paris and in 1984 earned his PhD degree in literature at the University of Prishtina. As a Fellow of the Institute for Albanian Studies, he wrote several books and edited various academic journals. In 1988, Rugova was elected President of the Kosovo Association of Writers.

In 1989, Rugova entered the political ring as one the most vocal opponents of Slobodan Milošević. The Association of Writers had become a nucleus of politically discontented communists, thinkers and intellectuals. In response to Milošević's political manoeuvres, Rugova spearheaded an initiative to protect the rights and freedoms promised to Kosovo in the 1974 constitution. On 23 December 1989, Rugova was elected President of the Democratic League of Kosovo, a new party created in memory of the Prizren League of 1878 that had defended Albanian national interests against the Ottoman Empire.

Under Rugova's political leadership, a Republic of Kosovo was proclaimed on 7 September 1990. His course of action was confirmed in a referendum that returned a 99% vote in favour of independence. In May 1992, LDK won an outright majority in an election organised secretly under the strict surveillance of the Serbian police. Rugova was elected president of a government-in-exile that had to shuttle between Germany, Switzerland and Albania.

He became the international face of Kosovo. He travelled to most European capitals, lobbying actively for international support in solving the political deadlock over Kosovo. Meanwhile, his government raised taxes, financed a parallel education and health system and kept the fiction alive that Kosovo was de facto independent. With his pacifist approach he won several international peace awards, including the Sakharov Prize by the European Parliament.

for Prishtina's Serbs this mosque has always been very special. It is believed that Prince Lazar's remains were buried on the location of today's Pirinaz Mosque with the permission of Sultan Bajazid, son and successor of Murat, who died in battle on the Kosovo fields in 1389. Lazar's remains were later moved to Ravanici Monastery in Serbia proper. Local legend also tells that Prince Lazar was beheaded on the actual 'Stone of Lazar' located in the garden of Pirinaz Mosque. The real circumstances surrounding Lazar's death, however, remain shrouded in mystery. If you continue straight on Rr Nazim Gafurri towards Germia National Park, take a left on Rr Shkodra up a steep hill with a paved road with central guttering. The attractive building on your right used to be the residence of the Serbian Orthodox archbishop during visits to Prishtina. It was nationalised under the communists and converted to a museum. Today it houses the Ministry of Environment and Spatial Planning. Continue a few metres uphill to get to **Saint Nicholas Church**, which was the only active Serbian Orthodox church in Prishtina. The area around Saint Nicholas Church had always been the Serbian quarter of Prishtina. The first Serbian-language primary school was also set up here by a wealthy trader in the 19th century. In 2004, the church was attacked by a violent mob who hurled stones and set the church on fire by throwing Molotov cocktails. The building itself had only been constructed in the 19th century. The greatest and irreversible loss was the burning of the

Albanians who had supported Rugova's non-violent resistance strategy through the difficult years of repression and harassment were shocked to find that the 1995 Dayton Peace Accord, which ended the war in Bosnia, did not solve the Kosovo problem. After all these years, Kosovo was not one inch closer to independence. Rugova was accused of passivity and political naïvety. His tight grip on LDK and his monopolisation of politics were also criticised increasingly. When news broke of a Kosovo Liberation Army operating in Kosovo in 1997, Rugova dismissed it as a trick by the Serbian police to discredit his policies. The lowest point in his political career was during the bombing campaign, when he was seen on Serbian television together with Slobodan Miloševic. Many commentators and UÇK fighters-turned-politicians had written him off politically, but he made an astounding comeback in the first post-war elections in October 2000, when LDK won 58% of the vote. In March 2002, the Kosovo Assembly elected Rugova as president and in December 2004, he was re-elected for a second term. As the years passed and Kosovo remained trapped in a legal limbo over its future status, more and more Kosovars were getting restless with his leadership. He was being ridiculed for his trademark scarf and his unusual habit of offering precious stones and minerals to foreign visitors. His role within the party was so overpowering that it seemed difficult to imagine an LDK without him, and yet, he seemed to lack the vision and political drive to take Kosovo further. Anyone who had written off Rugova, however, was proven wrong – the reaction to his death was unprecedented. In the freezing cold, thousands of people queued for hours in front of the parliament to say goodbye to their president. Busloads of Albanians came back from Germany and Switzerland and special charter planes landed in Prishtina Airport. Up to half a million people turned out on the day of his funeral to watch the procession of Rugova's coffin and the burial on Martyrs' Hill in Velania. It was a solemn moment; in a sign of respect people were crying and throwing flowers in silence. Dignitaries from more than 50 countries were present at the funeral service. The only one missing was the Serbian president: he was not invited. Søren Jessen-Petersen, the SRSG at the time, expressed in his speech what many were thinking: 'Rugova has been the defining element of politics in Kosovo for so long that it is hard for us to imagine Kosovo, and Kosovar politics, without him.' Rugova's funeral was an impressive moment of a state in the making.

iconostasis, a masterpiece of Serbian art from 1840. The church has now been restored to some degree. The area above the church has always been one of the more middle-class districts of Prishtina, Tazlixhe 2, and according to KEK statistics has the highest electricity-payment rate in Kosovo.

OTHER LANDMARKS The **Jewish Cemetery** is located on top of Tauk Bahqe Hill, near Velania. It is about a 20–30-minute stiff walk from Saint Nicholas Church. To get there you need to go back down the hill from the church, continue up Rr Nazim Gafurri to the crossroads, then past the electricity substation and school playground and turn right up the hill into the Velania district. If you are feeling tired at this point, get a taxi. The graves are above the tennis courts and fair.

About 90,000 Spanish-speaking Sephardic Jews escaped the Spanish 'Reconquista' and settled in the Balkans. The coastal trade in Albania, for example, was largely handled by Jewish families and the port city of Vlora had a Jewish majority in the 16th century. By the end of the Ottoman period, 305 Jews were living in Prishtina. The darkest moment came in summer 1944, when 281 Prishtina Jews were arrested by Albanian collaborators and handed over to the Germans. The few remaining families left Kosovo for Israel right after World War II. There is no functioning synagogue in Kosovo today. The only reminders of Prishtina's Jewish past are the 57 tombstones scattered between thorny bushes and high grass. The cemetery dates back to the 19th century. It is in a desolate state today, but still worth a trip.

Not far from the Jewish Cemetery is the **Martyrs' Hill**, in the neighbourhood of Velania. If you want to get here from the centre of town, you need to walk for about 15 minutes uphill on Rr Rrustem Statovci which passes the Hotel Lyon. From the green park on the hill you have a nice view of the city and you can savour some of Kosovo's recent political history. The bitter rivalry between the pacifist leader Ibrahim Rugova and his political opponents in the Kosovo Liberation Army lasted even beyond his lifetime. In the days between Rugova's death on 21 January 2006 and his funeral, a dispute broke out between the LDK leadership and the War Veterans' Association over the location for Rugova's tomb. The veterans were opposed to Rugova's tomb sharing the same park with the graves of UÇK fighters buried on Martyrs' Hill. The dispute was resolved and today you can visit both the UÇK graves at the lower part of the park and **Ibrahim Rugova's memorial** on the top (Rr Isa Kastrati). Typical for Kosovo, the graves are decorated with large round platters of plastic flowers, a rather unusual sight. Trees surround Rugova's white marble tomb. It was constructed in the space of a few days in the freezing cold. Rugova, who was born a Muslim, is rumoured to have converted to Catholicism in the last decade of his life. Religious dignitaries of all faiths attended the state funeral, but it was strictly non-religious.

The Youth and Sports Palace [96 B4], also known as **Boro Ramiz**, dominates Prishtina's downtown urban silhouette with its strangely shaped copper roof covered by an oversized poster of Adem Jashari, Kosovo's answer to Che Guevara.

Boro and Ramiz were two partisans, one Serb and one Albanian, who fought and died during World War II. In the Yugoslav spirit of 'Brotherhood and Unity' they were joined together for life in the name of the Youth and Sports Palace. Constructed in the 1970s, this communist pet project has always been a popular hangout and meeting point for youth and it is certainly the most vibrant sport and cultural venue around. On weekends the cafés and bars in the ground floor are full, and sporting events, especially basketball games, tend to attract large crowds. There is a concert hall inside. A few months after the war, Prishtina's citizens watched in horror when parts of the stadium and the complex burnt down. A damaged electric heater had caused a fire, and there were no fire extinguishers and no fire brigade to come to Boro Ramiz's rescue. Funds left over from the parallel government were pooled to finance the repair works. Boro Ramiz's future ownership is the subject of a dispute between the municipality and the privatisation agency of Kosovo. It remains to be seen if the two partisan heroes will after all be 'privatised'. In a move which could be seen as uniting the new capitalism with the promotion of youth activities for which the centre was built, the privately funded American School of Kosovo has become one of the more recent tenants of the Boro Ramiz complex. In front of Boro Ramiz is the iconic **Newborn Monument**, unveiled with Independence. Adorned with appreciative graffiti, it's a popular photo spot.

In 1969, the decision was taken to turn the handful of satellite faculties of Belgrade University into a fully fledged **University of Prishtina** (Rr Dëshmorët e Kombit). The first foreign teacher, Mary Motes, observed back in the 1960s that there were still more oxen than students to be seen on the university green. Over the next ten years, the university grew rapidly to about 30,000 students. For the first time, Albanians could pursue higher education in their language. This made Prishtina a magnet for Albanians living in south Serbia and Macedonia. The libraries are still short of books, journals and IT infrastructure today. The biggest challenge, however, is not the repair of the hardware – the buildings and classrooms – but the mentality of the teaching body, the professors and the administration.

Unfortunately, the legacy of authoritarian thinking, corruption and the lack of a service culture lives on. It is better in some of the new faculties, like political science, which were set up after the war. The most popular subjects are economy and law. Every year the university churns out thousands of graduates. The highlight of the year is the Prishtina Summer University which attracts students and professors from abroad.

See www.uni-pr.info/zmj.

Kosovo Academic Service Centre National Library; ☏ 038 248 887; e news@ussac.org; www.ussac.org. This centre, which is immediately inside the National Library & to the right-hand side, provides information on American universities, exchange programmes & fellowships. It is also an internationally certified test centre for TOEFL, SAT & GRE tests.

World University Service www.wus-austria.org/prishtina. The Austrian-run World University Service established its first Prishtina office in 1998. The programme is actively involved in university reforms & helps Prishtina University to tap into international initiatives & programmes. The WUS office also provides student, career & scholarship advice.

The **National Library** [97 E7] is one of the architecturally most interesting buildings in Prishtina, although not necessarily to everyone's taste – a 2009 website classed it among the ten most ugly buildings in the world! According to urban legend, the head of the Communist Party asked one of his aides at the official inauguration ceremony why the scaffolding had not been taken down. It sits right in the middle of the university campus, reachable on foot from Rr Agim Ramadani or by cutting across the green park on the intersection of Rr Dëshmorët e Kombit with Rr Ekrem Qabej. In the early 1970s, the decision was taken to construct a new National University Library of Kosovo. The actual construction was completed in 1981, with a six-year delay. There are in fact 99 small cupolas or domes to let natural light into the library, sometimes thought to be built to look like the traditional Albanian *plis* hat. The different names of the library reflected the political changes. In the 1960s, the library was called 'Provincial Library' and then, for a brief moment, it was named after Kosovo's most famous partisan fighter, Miladin Popović. With the new constitution of 1974 it was no longer appropriate to name a library after a Serbian partisan, and it was renamed 'National Library'.

For almost a decade, the Albanian Faculty and its students were not allowed to set foot inside the national and other libraries in Kosovo. Parts of the National Library building were turned over to a Serbian Orthodox religious school. During NATO's bombardment the Yugoslav army used the National Library as a command and control centre. During their occupation about 100,000 books and rare volumes were stolen or burnt, the reading room furniture was smashed and hand grenades and uniforms were strewn on the floor. Parts of the Law Faculty's collection were found stacked in boxes ready for shipping to Serbia. Most of the 600,000 volume-strong central collection has survived. The library is accessible for visitors. See page 120 for more details.

Construction of the **Serbian Orthodox church** (the large brick building on the green behind the library towards Rr Agim Ramadani) was started in the 1990s under Milošević. It was meant to be the biggest church in Kosovo. Construction was halted in 1999, and the future of the building is uncertain.

The Prishtina City Library, or **Hyvzi Sylejmani Library** is tucked away in a little side alley off Rr UÇK (close to a ProCredit Bank branch) although there are plans to move to a new building in Dardania in 2011–12. The little pink building dates back to 1930. Its claim to fame is Miladin Popović, the former leader of Kosovo's Regional Committee of the Communist Party, who was accommodated in this house in 1944. Miladin Popović was killed on 13 March 1945. Since 1948, the building has housed the Prishtina City Library. Again, membership is open to all (see page 120).

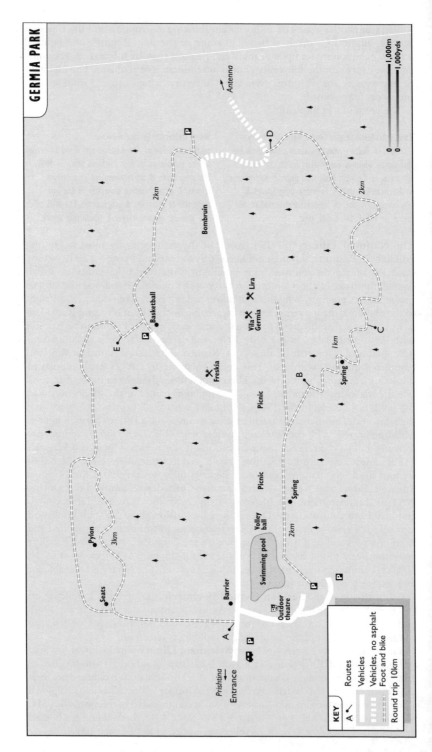

GERMIA PARK

KEY

A. Routes

Vehicles

Vehicles, no asphalt

Foot and bike

Round trip 10km

Prishtina
Entrance

A

Barrier

Seats

Pylon

3km

Swimming pool

Outdoor theatre

Volley ball

Picnic

Spring

2km

Picnic

Freskia

Basketball

E

P

2km

Bombruin

P

Spring

1km

B

Vila Germia

Lira

Spring

C

D

Antenna

2km

0 — 1,000m
0 — 1,000yds

GERMIA PARK

Getting there The No 4 bus goes up to the park from the centre of town from 06.00 until 23.00. It takes the early-morning walkers right up to the restaurants (Villa Germia and Villa Freskia) from 06.00 to 09.00. At other times the buses stop by the barrier. They leave about every ten minutes until about 20.00 and about every 15 minutes thereafter. If you wish to take your car into the park it costs €1 (funds previously went to war veterans but they might now go towards the upkeep of the park). Alternatively you can bear round to the right up the hill, park your car for free there and walk along the side path into the park.

Touring the park This park north of Kosovo is the green lung of Prishtina. There is a huge open-air pool (*entrance €1.50*), beach volleyball and a small arena used for concerts. About 1.5km into the park itself there is a basketball court. The park consists mostly of woods and extends over a wide area. While the flat, green, grassy centre can get thronged with picnicking families and piles of rubbish (especially on 1 May), if you walk a bit further out you can almost have the network of footpaths to yourself (although you may stumble on an amorous couple in a steamy car, given as they mostly live at home this is one of the few places young unmarried couples can get away from their parents). A popular remedy prescribed by Prishtina doctors is that the patient should take up early-morning walking so you will see many elderly out first thing. As late as 2004, the park had not been cleared of land mines and you could see children play on a slide just 5m from red land-mine tape. Most mines have now been cleared by TMK and Handikos but you should play safe and stick to the footpaths. The reason for the mines was that the JNA (Yugoslav National Army) was camped out in the barracks up here. The barracks building is just up from the Villa Germia Restaurant and should not be explored although it is now being cleared. The telecoms mast on the hill is next to a cluster-bomb site where care should also be exercised. Otherwise make the most of the c15–20km network of paths which are suitable for walking, jogging or biking. There used to be a small ski lift here but it was never rebuilt after the war. In the spring the furthestmost paths are full of primroses.

There are several possible walking and biking routes. One is to start from above the swimming pool (point A on the map) and walk up to the Vila Germia Restaurant and back down either along the road or the parallel lower path. This takes about 40 minutes but is somewhat dull. If you have more time either take the left-hand narrow, quite-steep path up immediately by the barrier from point A to E. This single track (which makes for great technical mountain biking) curves round through thick forest and you can walk for about 45 minutes to an hour emerging near the basketball courts at point E. From there cut down the road, a round trip of about one hour 20 minutes.

For a longer slightly more strenuous walk go from point A to point D including a steep uphill at point B to C but you can stop off at the benches along the way. You can then either cut back down the road or continue on to point E and come down, depending on time.

The full round trip on a bicycle (A, B, C, D, E, A) takes just over 1½ hours and it is more like 2½ to three hours to walk the full loop.

From point D you can also continue up a long uphill but broad road to the antenna. Do not stray off the road here as there are potential cluster-bomb fragments. If you take a left 200m before the antenna and go downhill, this road also eventually leads you back into Germia but that walk requires more time.

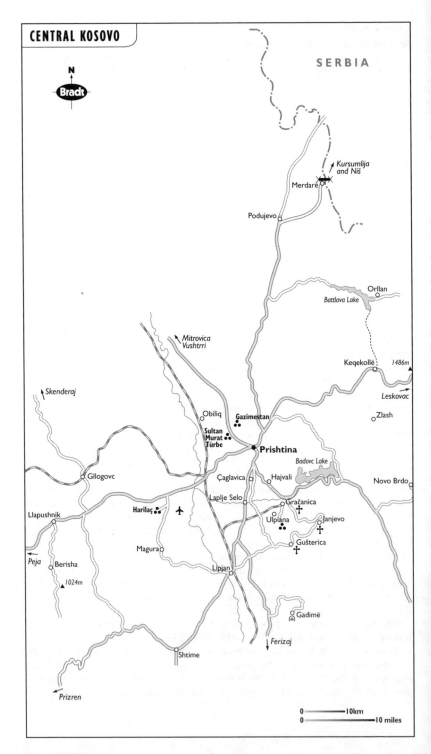

CENTRAL KOSOVO

N

Bradt

SERBIA

Kursumlija
and Niš

Merdarė

Podujevo

Orllan

Battlava Lake

Mitrovica
Vushtrri

Keqekollë   1486m

Skenderaj   Leskovac

Obiliq   **Gazimestan**   Zlash

**Sultan
Murat
Türbe**   **Prishtina**

Gllogovc   *Badovc Lake*

Çaglavica   Hajvali   Novo Brdo

Laplje Selo

Harilaç   Gračanica

Magura   Ulpiana   Janjevo

Llapushnik

Peja   Berisha   Gušterica

1024m   Lipjan

Gadimë

Ferizaj

Shtime

Prizren

0 ———— 10km
0 ———— 10 miles

4

Central Kosovo

The highlights of central Kosovo are undoubtedly the Gračanica Monastery with its stunning 14th-century frescoes, the Kosovo Battle Memorial complex north of Prishtina and the Gadimë Cave near Lipjan. On a free afternoon you can also set out to explore the countryside around Janjevo on horseback or take your swimsuit and relax on the shores of Battlava Lake. Another option is to hike to the top of Berisha Hill from where you can see all of Kosovo and visit the war-time Kosovo e Lire radio station.

All the sites in central Kosovo can easily be reached by car, bus or taxi from Prishtina. We recommend that you make Prishtina your base given that there is a much better selection of accommodation, more exciting nightlife and a good choice of dinner venues in the capital compared with any of the surrounding towns.

GRAČANICA

Gračanica is a small village, home to about 13,000 Kosovo Serbs, just 10km from Prishtina. As part of the decentralisation process foreseen in the Ahtisaari Agreement, Gračanica is one of the newly created Serb-majority municipalities, with its own Kosovo Serb mayor elected in November 2009. The new municipality includes several Serbian villages, including Çaglavica and Laplje Selo on the outskirts of Prishtina. In the past, Gračanica was a sleepy place built around a large agricultural co-operative and home to Serb farmers and miners working in the nearby Kishnica mines. After the war in 1999, Gračanica developed into a satellite outpost for Prishtina's displaced Serbian community. In the span of just a few weeks in summer 1999, most of the approximately 30,000 Serbs and Montenegrins who had lived in Prishtina before the war left the town for fear of reprisal actions by the returning Albanian population. Many have left Kosovo altogether to start a new life in Serbia, but some, especially those with jobs working for the international community, settled in Gračanica. With Serbian government funding, Gračanica was gradually upgraded into a service centre for Kosovo Serbs with a Belgrade-financed health centre, Serbian banks and various Serb government outlets providing a range of services from issuing Serbian passports and birth certificates to business registration. Fortunately, the days when Gračanica was a guarded enclave are long gone. Today, Albanians and Serbs can be seen mixing casually on the streets and in some of the restaurants in the area, and Gračanica's recently elected Serbian mayor is increasingly asserting the rights of Kosovo Serbs in an independent Kosovo. A visit to the Gračanica Monastery is a definite must for anyone staying in Prishtina for more than a day. It is a prime example of 14th-century Serb Orthodox art. For archaeology fans, the nearby remains of Ulpiana (see page 138), an important Roman and Byzantine town, also deserve a quick visit. If you have more time you can continue on to Janjevo (see page 142) or even Gadimë Cave (see page 145).

GETTING THERE AND AWAY   From Prishtina, take the main Skopje highway and as you are descending the hill turn right, following the signs for Gjilan. You double back on yourself via an underpass into the new industrial zone of Veternik (Hajvali) and after a few more kilometres you are in the centre of Gračanica with its speed bumps.

There are regular **buses** from Prishtina to Gjilan stopping on request only (let the driver know you want to get off) in Gračanica. For times see the bus timetable on page 60. By **taxi** from Prishtina, it takes only ten minutes and costs about €7. It's easy to know that you are in a Serbian village as most writings are in Cyrillic and the public buildings fly the Serbian flag. The monastery is on the left side of the main road, just after the municipality surrounded by a long wall which was built in 2004–05 by the Greek government following the March riots. The entrance is just before the road bears left.

There are **minibuses** leaving from the centre of Gračanica to Belgrade via Kragujevac (Serbia) (see page 50).

The return journey departs Belgrade at 06.00, arriving in Gračanica at 11.30, and there is a second bus at 16.00 arriving in Gračanica at 20.30. These buses are run by minibus company **Dura** (✆ *038 64 544/049 379 794;* m *+381 63 64 544;* ⊕ *09.00–17.00*) near Dolce Vita Restaurant.

⌂ WHERE TO STAY
⌂ **Motel Europa** (8 rooms) 800m from the police station; m 044 537 988. The motel has 5 dbls & 3 sgls. $$

You may be better off staying in Prishtina which has a wider choice.

✖ WHERE TO EAT   There are several decent venues along the main road in the vicinity of the monastery. If you've missed your pork on your journey so far, this is the place to have some.

✖ **Bar Klub S** Live music on Thu–Sat.
✖ **Café Matrix** Opposite the monastery entrance with a CD shop downstairs.
✖ **Café Pizzeria 'Dolce Vita'** Between ProCredit Bank & Raiffeisen on the entrance to Gračanica from

Prishtina; ✆ 038 64 304. Live music Fri–Sun. Lots of young people on the upper floor.
✖ **Restoran Ognjite** ⊕ 08.00–22.00. Goulash is a speciality.

OTHER PRACTICALITIES
Banks
$ **NLB** ✆ 038 65 277; ⊕ 08.00–16.00 Mon–Fri, 09.00–14.00 Sat
$ **ProCredit** On the left-hand side after the municipality; ✆ 038 64 947; ⊕ 08.00–16.00

Mon–Fri, 09.00–14.00 Sat
$ **Raiffeisen** ✆ 038 222 222 ext 450; ⊕ 08.30–16.30 Mon–Fri, 10.00–14.00 Sat

Internet café
Poslovni Centar 'Zavet' ✆ 038 65 074; ⊕ 09.00–17.00

Post offices
✆ 038 65 007; ⊕ 07.00–18.00. Affiliated with Serbia Post. Near the municipality & the new police station on the first major left-hand turn after

entering from Prishtina.
PTK There is also a branch of Kosovo Post in Gračanica.

Sports

Billiard Club Master ⊕ 08.00–24.00. With 2 pool tables; very relaxed, pleasant atmosphere.

Swimming pool ⊕ Jun/Jul–end-Sep 07.00–22.00; entrance €2. The pool outside Gračanica is one of the nicest outdoor pools in Kosovo as it is less crowded & well maintained. Driving from Prishtina towards Gjilan, when you get to the end of the monastery wall, take the first right on the other side of the road & continue up this road until the houses cease. The swimming pool is about 600m after the houses, or 2–3km after the turn-off from Gračanica.

WHAT TO SEE AND DO

Gračanica Monastery (⊕ *open to visitors. For group visits the resident nuns prefer to be informed beforehand. Admission free.*) Gračanica really is a must-do; it is one of the finest examples of late Byzantine architecture with one of the best-preserved cycles of 14th-century frescoes. As you approach the monastery, you will see its cupolas emerging from the recently restored walls surrounding the monastic complex. In the past a Swedish battalion was guarding the site, but access is free and the monastery is open to visitors. Take a torch if you want to look closely at the frescoes as it can be a bit dark inside.

The present-day church was built on top of an older Byzantine basilica. Parts of the lower structure date back to the days when Gračanica was the episcopal seat of Ulpiana, from which it inherited the seat of the Bishopric of Lipjan. The monastery church is one of the most beautiful endowments of King Milutin, a militant and powerful ruler of the Nemanjić family. As a shrewd politician and *bon vivant*, he married five times. Under his reign (1284–1321), the Serbian kingdom extended all the way to the Adriatic coast, with Skopje as its capital. He spent some of the great wealth collected from the Kosovo mines on a major church-building programme. Before succeeding his brother, Milutin made an oath to build a new church for every year he remained in power. Throughout his 42-year-long reign, he is believed to have built 42 churches, securing him the place as greatest builder of Serbian–Byzantine architecture.

Byzantine influences reigned strong at Milutin's court. His second wife Simonida was the daughter of the Byzantine emperor Andronicus, and through her, Milutin assembled a court school of fresco painters and architects acquainted with the latest trends from Constantinople.

Construction of the present-day church began in the last years of Milutin's reign and it was completed on the orders of Archbishop Danilo in 1322. The Church of the Assumption has the shape of an inscribed cross, topped with five cupolas. The unknown architect designed an architectural jewel combining classical Byzantine features with **Gothic elements**, including elongated cupolas and several upwards-pointing arches. The construction techniques and combination of stone and brick used for the outer walls are typical of the Byzantine Empire. The eastern façade of the church displays the best examples of stonemasonry. The front narthex was added in 1383 to protect the frescoes on the outer wall. The original outer narthex was destroyed during one of the first Turkish raids. New frescoes were completed in 1570, dedicated to the Virgin Mary. In the lower part the whole genealogy of the Serbian National Church is painted, starting with the first, Archbishop Saint Sava, to the last, Patriarch Makerija.

The exceptionally well-preserved **frescoes** in the interior of the church are the product of a team of painters assembled at King Milutin's court. The exquisite style and creative detail is attributed to two famous Byzantine painters from the Thessaloniki school: Mihailo and Evtihije. On the eastern wall of the outer narthex you can see the *Last Judgement* elaborately decorated featuring all kinds of animal creatures. The old King Milutin himself and his young wife Simonida are depicted on the main arch of the entranceway. This fresco was probably done in the last year of Milutin's reign in 1321. Dressed in imperial garments, the king holds a model of Gračanica church in his hands. High above, Christ blesses the royal couple and angels are offering crowns to them. The message to the viewer is that of a ruler by God's will. The inscription next to the young queen reads 'Palaeologina, daughter of the Emperor Andronikos Palaeologos'. Another interesting fresco painted in the narthex is the Nemanjić family tree. Milutin took great care to position his own family branch above that of his older brother Dragutin, who had abdicated in his favour. Instead of Jesse, Stefan Nemanja is depicted at the bottom of the tree, with Milutin at its top and a painting of Christ blessing the tree. The other frescoes depict portraits of different Serbian archbishops and patriarchs. On the northern wall the founding charter and all the monastic possessions are listed. A painting of Christ the Pantocrator looms high in the central dome above depictions of the Divine Liturgy, prophets and evangelists. The nave is decorated with scenes of the life of Christ and the Virgin. The narrow staircase near the entrance led directly to a royal lodge on the upper floor.

Successive raids and fires destroyed the old monastic buildings and large parts of the treasury, apart from an interesting collection of 16th- to 19th-century icons. In the old days, Gračanica Monastery was a renowned centre of learning and in 1539, it had one of the first printing presses in Serbia. In 1993, the monastery church was inscribed on the tentative List of UNESCO World Cultural and Natural Heritage.

AROUND GRAČANICA

LAPLJE SELO AND ÇAGLAVICA These two Serb villages are just outside Prishtina on the way to Gračanica. In fact with the expansion of Prishtina, Çaglavica is now more like an outer surburb of Prishtina divided by the newly expanded Skopje–Prishtina highway. Laplje Selo is more village-like and is set back from the road. Coming from Prishtina it is beyond Çaglavica and reached by turning off immediately after the Orthodox church visible from the road. There is also a road direct from Gračanica to Laplje Selo which runs parallel to the main road.

Where to stay If you are looking for a cheap place to stay, you can try:

⌂ **Motel Beli Dvor** (15 rooms) Near the main road in Çaglavica. $

⌂ **Motel Vod** (3 rooms) ☏ 049/038 81 577;

m +381 64 432 1085/049 440 213. On the road from Laplje Selo to Çaglavica, with 1 tpl room, 1 dbl & 1 sgl. $

Where to eat
✕ **Café Pizzeria Tropicana**
✕ **Ciao Restaurant** Popular with Serbs & Albanians alike. Hefty meat dishes, pleasant atmosphere.

ULPIANA (*The site is unprotected, so entrance is free.*) If you ask a Kosovar for Ulpiana you are more likely to be directed to the housing area in Prishtina by the same name, but the real Ulpiana was once one of the most important Roman cities in the Balkans and an Episcopal seat of the Byzantine emperors. After the defeat of the Illyrian tribes by Emperor Augustus in 28BC, Kosovo became part of the Roman province of Illyricum. The Pax Romana brought stability and growth to the region. Positioned on a crossroads connecting the Danube with the Aegean, and surrounded by fertile agricultural land, Ulpiana developed from a provincial backwater into an economic powerhouse. The nearby mines and mineral riches added to Ulpiana's wealth. An epitaph on a gravestone found near Leposavić describes Ulpiana as a 'marvellous and splendid city' (*Municipi Splendidissimi Ulpianae*). By the 2nd century AD, the city had become the economic, cultural and political centre of the Dardanian province. In recognition of its importance it was granted the status of a *municipium*, with its own independent administration. The city expanded in all directions with new public buildings, a military garrison and a wall surrounding the city being added over time.

Disaster struck in AD518: a major earthquake destroyed large parts of the city. The Byzantine emperor Justinian I (AD527–65), ordered the city's reconstruction. A new city was built on top of the rubble. It was renamed Iustiniana Secunda, after its patron Justinian I, but its revival was short-lived. Avar and Slav tribes had already started moving south into the Balkan Peninsula, posing a serious threat to the Byzantine Empire. Sitting on an open plain, protected only by the Drenovac Hill and the Gračanka River, Ulpiana was easy prey for the invaders. The city declined and, like elsewhere in the Roman Empire, its buildings and stones were plundered for the construction of other towns and settlements.

The Kosovo Museum started the first archaeological excavations back in 1954. For lack of funds, excavations stopped and little more than a few building structures, some tombstones, and traces of walls and of a temple are visible today. Since 2004, the Kosovo Museum has organised multi-ethnic youth camps in Ulpiana to nurture interest in archaeology in future generations (for more information you can contact Kemajl Luci at the Kosovo Museum). The sorry state of the site makes it hard to imagine Ulpiana's past splendour but with luck Ulpiana may become Kosovo's Pompeii in the future.

Getting there Ulpiana is located 11km from Prishtina or 2km from the main bus stop in Gračanica. If you are **driving**, follow the signs to Gjilan and turn right after the bus stop in the centre of Gračanica. By **bus**, head to Gjilan and get off at Gračanica Monastery. It's a 2km walk along a country road to reach Ulpiana from Gračanica. The site is hard to spot and there are no signs telling you where to turn right. After 2km look out for a little track leading into the field on the right; after about 250m you stumble across the first excavations. The main buildings are all close together; to reach the tombstones head straight into the field at a 90° angle from the road. Be ready to fight your way through bushes and wild overgrowth!

MEMORIAL COMPLEX OF THE BATTLE OF KOSOVO (GAZIMESTAN)

GETTING THERE It's impossible to miss the memorial complex of the Battle of Kosovo located on the main Prishtina–Mitrovica highway. After about 10km coming from Prishtina, on your right, you can spot the turquoise roof of the Bajraktar Türbe and the Memorial Tower on the hilltop. Take a right turn (follow the yellow sign) straight to the Memorial Tower. There is free parking in the field. If you are travelling by bus, you can catch any bus heading to Mitrovica or Vushtrri. Just ask the bus driver to drop you at the bus stop near Gazimestan. All three sites that form part of the memorial complex – the Memorial Tower, the Bajraktar Türbe and the Sultan Murat Türbe (located a bit further north left off the main road) – are within walking distance, although the Sultan Murat Türbe is a good half-hour walk from the Memorial Tower. Allow a good two hours or more to visit the Memorial Tower and the Sultan Murat Türbe to include the walking to and from the main road to the *türbe*.

MEMORIAL TOWER This imposing tower was built in 1953 to pay tribute to Serb national folklore and the myths surrounding the famous Battle of Kosovo. For a

A MYTHICAL DATE – 28 JUNE

The official national holiday of Serbia celebrated on 28 June, the day of Saint Vitus, is a magical date in Serbian history. Everything important seems to have happened that very day, except the actual Battle of Kosovo. Historians confirm that the day the armies under the command of Sultan Murat and Prince Lazar met on the Kosovo plains was 15 June, and not as told in legends and folksongs, 28 June. Historical inaccuracy of that sort is not unique to Serbian (or any) national history – who really knows the exact birthday of Christ? But there is more to 28 June than just the commemoration of the Kosovo battle. On that day in 1914, the Serb nationalist Gavrilo Princip assassinated the Austrian archduke Franz Ferdinand on a bridge in Sarajevo. This tragic event dragged the region into the first true world war in history. Seven years later, on 28 June 1921, the Yugoslav constitution was ratified giving birth to the First Yugoslavia formed out of a union of Serbia, Croatia and Slovenia. The same day in 1989, Slobodan Miloševic gave a fiery speech to crowds assembled on the Kosovo plains on the occasion of the 600-year anniversary of the battle. He warned the cheering crowds that: 'today, six centuries later, we are again fighting a battle and facing battles.' Maybe Europe should have picked up on this before letting Yugoslavia slide into war and conflict.

long time, the tower was guarded by KFOR troops and visitors needed to show their ID cards at the entrance gate. The presence of tanks and bored-looking soldiers greeting you as you entered the premises added a sombre feel to the entire complex. Now the Kosovo Police Service has taken over. You may still need ID, however.

The tower itself is about 25m high and stands on an elevated platform surrounded by concrete benches and steps. Its design captures the mood of the communist leadership at that time. The inscription in Serbian at the bottom of the tower is a stark reminder of the patriotic duty expected of any Serb to sacrifice his life in defence of Kosovo. The readers are reminded that:

Whoever is a Serb or of Serb birth,
And of Serb blood and heritage,
And comes not to fight in Kosovo;
May he never have the progeny his heart desires;
Neither son nor daughter,
May nothing grow that his hand sows;
Neither dark wine nor white wheat,
May he rot in rust as long as family's knees exist.

More than 100 steps take you up to the viewing platform on top of the tower. The view is worth the climb to get a feel of the Kosovo plains. Let your mind play tricks on you as you are looking at the smoking chimneys of the Kosovo power plant to the northwest and Prishtina to the south, and imagine what it must have been like when Sultan Murat's 30,000-strong army faced the troops assembled under Prince Lazar's command on the morning of 15 June 1389.

It was 19th-century nationalist writers like Vuk Karadžić who transformed the myth of Kosovo into a gripping national ideology. The emerging Serb national identity was defined in sharp contrast to the Ottoman Turks. The historic moment of a defeat at the hands of the Turkish armies was used to present the Serbian nation as one of hero-martyrs rebelling against the Turkish oppressors. Reviving the cult of Lazar was also a useful tool to prepare the population for the proclamation of a

KOSOVO BATTLE

The Battle of Kosovo was a source of inspiration for folk songs and stories that live on in place names across Kosovo to this day. Places like Obiliç or villages like Devet Jugovica and Lazarevo near Prishtina were named after heroes of the Kosovo battle by Serbian colonists moving here at the behest of the Serbian government in the late 1920s.

The Death of Lazar tells the story of Prince Lazar as a hero-martyr renouncing wordly temptation for a heavenly kingdom. The purity of Lazar's character is presented in sharp contrast to Vuk Brankoviç, his main partner in the field. Vuk Brankoviç was a feudal lord ruling over a large part of Kosovo. He contributed a sizeable contingent of troops and took partial command during the battle. The Brankoviç legend is a classical stabbing-in-the-back story. Legend tells that Brankoviç was selling out to the sultan and thus contributed to Lazar's defeat. In fact, Brankoviç resisted until 1392 before becoming a Turkish vassal. He was eventually deposed by the Turks and died in prison. An unlikely career for a sultan loyalist. The song called 'The Death of Murat at the hands of Milos Kobiliç' describes Sultan Murat's assassination. The underdog-turned-hero Milos Kobiliç, spurred by a dispute, becomes the hero of the day. As told in the songs, Vuk Brankoviç and Milos Kobiliç have a dispute before the battle, during which Brankoviç accuses Kobiliç of disloyalty. To prove him wrong, Kobiliç vows to assassinate the sultan. Kobiliç, in a smart move, announces that he will join the Turkish camp and visits Murat in his tent. As he kneels down to pay tribute, he pulls out his dagger and assassinates the sultan. Besides Kobiliç (whose name was later changed to Obiliç by an 18th-century writer), there is also the story about nine brothers killed during the battle after heroic fighting. The nine brothers are the sons of the brother of Queen Milica, Prince Lazar's wife. The legend of the nine brothers lives on in the Serbian name of Devet Jugovica village, located north of Prishtina.

new Serbian kingdom in 1882. Maybe a small but interesting point to note: the earliest chronicles written right after the Kosovo battle actually describe the battle as a victory of the Serbs over the Turkish army.

BAJRAKTAR TÜRBE A few hundred metres from the Memorial Tower there is a white, round-shaped building with a turquoise cupola standing in the middle of the fields. The Bajraktar Türbe – a mausoleum – was built in honour of Sultan Murat's standard-bearer (in Turkish *bajraktar*), who was killed during the battle in 1389. The tomb is an important sanctuary for the followers of the Sadije dervish order, of which Sultan Murat's standard-bearer is believed to have been a member. The Sadije dervish order has a small group of followers in Prishtina, who look after the building and try to keep it from further decay. The building is in a bad state. It was heavily damaged during the conflict and the walls are suffering from dampness and cracks. The entire lead roofing was stolen in 1999 and to this day you can see bullets stuck on the outer walls.

SULTAN MURAT TÜRBE (SULTAN MURAT MAUSOLEUM)

GETTING THERE A large yellow sign on the main Prishtina–Mitrovica highway points in the direction of Sultan Murat's mausoleum. Turn left off the main road and keep driving for 200m until you get to the little car park at the entrance of the museum complex. On foot, it's only a short walk from the bus station dropping you off at the main road.

VISITING THE COMPLEX (⏰ *10.00–16.00 Tue–Sun; entrance free*) The recent restoration works financed by the Turkish government mean the mausoleum and its adjacent buildings make an attractive cluster. You enter the complex through an arched gate facing the former guesthouse built originally to house visitors of the mausoleum. For a while it was converted into a training school for Communist Party apparatchiks. It is currently being refurbished with plans to open a new museum.

The location of the actual mausoleum is believed to be on the same spot where the tent of Sultan Murat was located and where he died in the course of the Kosovo battle. As the exact circumstances of Sultan Murat's death are not known, how and when he died remains the subject of legend. The only witness of the battle is the mulberry tree at the entrance of the mausoleum, looking back on a 700-year-long life. If only trees could talk! The actual remains of Murat have been sent to his imperial mausoleum in Bursa, the first capital of the nascent Ottoman Empire. The present-day mausoleum was reconstructed in 1850 by Hurshid Pasha. For generations the duty to guard the mausoleum has been passed from father to son within the Türbedari family. You are likely to meet Sanija, who speaks Turkish and Bosnian, or her husband Fahri Türbedari. Their home is right next to the mausoleum. Look out for the tombstones of Rifat Pasha and Mehmet Hafiz Pasha, former governors of Skopje.

JANJEVO/JANJEVË

This small town, home to a Croatian minority, with its older-style houses nestles in a dip between rolling hills. It merits at least a half-day trip from Prishtina. It seems that here time has stood still. There are almost no modern buildings and certainly no high-rises. The old houses are crumbling and abandoned and children run around the *kalldrem* (old cobbled and mud streets) just as they did 20 years ago and Roma music echoes around the valley walls.

The style of the houses, in particular some of the ornate decoration on them, shows that this was once a town of considerable wealth, generated through mining which drew in the workers from Dubrovnik.

The wealth of the past is a stark contrast to now where there is almost no income generation and the town feels (like Novo Brdo) like a ghost town with the doors of the empty houses swinging open. Less than a third are occupied. The base of the houses was traditionally used as the stable and the large Roma community still keeps horses here.

GETTING THERE To reach Janjevo there are only two **buses** a day from Prishtina – one at 11.20 and one at 18.30. You have another two options by public transport. The easier is probably to take the Gjilan bus and get off in Gračanica. There is a turning in Gračanica to Janjevo. To get to Janjevo from here you will probably need to walk a few kilometres or negotiate a local Serbian ad hoc unlicensed taxi from Gračanica. Expect to pay about €6, or €12 return. The road is very bumpy and poor. The alternative is to get a bus to Ferizaj and get off at the Laplje Selo turn-off which is the Serbian village nearest the road. From here it is about 7km to Janjevo in a taxi. It is also possible that there are infrequent minibuses from Lipjan to Janjevo.

There is also a signed turning off to Janjevo from the main Prishtina–Ferizaj high road but the town is then a further 12–15km and there are no set buses, so this route is only feasible by car. In fact it is the smoothest car route. You have to go through Donje Gušterica, a Serbian village (see below), to get to Janjevo.

🏠 **WHERE TO STAY AND EAT** There are three cafés in the centre of town – one named 'Bas Çarshia', which means 'at the market' – but they all serve pretty much the same food (sausages) so you may want to take a packed lunch. Overall, if your needs are for sleeping accommodation or good email connections, you are better off back in Gračanica or Prishtina.

OTHER PRACTICALITIES There are no banks, no proper pharmacies and only a small mini market.

There is a PTK office as you come into town from Donje Gušterica and a police station and municipality building on the far valley slope.

WHAT TO SEE AND DO The **Catholic church** is the one modern building in the whole town, situated on top of one of the hills. To get there you follow the only paved road round to the top of the hill. The church is usually locked but you can obtain the key either from the man at the kiosk or by knocking on the gates of the main building adjacent to the church.

Higher up the hill, and accessed by the top gate to the church immediately on the right-hand side as you exit the steps at the church gate, is the small renovated **house of Stefan Gjeçovi Kryeziu** (1874–1929), which dates from the 19th century and which will be made into a museum in due course (although at the time of writing the house had already been damaged from post-renovation neglect). His work is linked to that of the Albanian national movement of the Prizren League. He was an academic, Albanian-language teacher, art historian, archaeologist, ethnologist, historian and translator who studied also at the University of Leipzig. Gjeçovi's collection of museum pieces was kept in a private museum in Shkoder, Albania.

Across the hill you can see the newly renovated **school** and below this a typical **Albanian *kulla*** (fortified tower). This is abandoned although in fairly good repair. Its history is unknown.

In the lower part of town is the **old mosque** with its simple blue décor. Slightly up the road on the way to the police station and municipality is an old store, now abandoned with yellow ancient lettering.

To get an impressive view of the town you need to climb the hill opposite to the church via the mud road to reach a flat viewing area.

If you fancy a walk out of Janjevo you could walk uphill to the **Velentin Hill** 2km northeast past the town of Shashkovc (named after the 'Saxons' or Germans who came to mine in the area) to the village of Tekke (which itself is the name of a place of worship – see box, pages 214–15), where there is a *turbë* or mausoleum – visited by hundreds of believers, particularly on 5 May each year – in the process of restoration by an NGO, Balkan Initiatives. It contains the grave of the Saint 'Baba Isak' who was a dervish soldier of the Ottoman army believed to have died during the Battle of Veletin in the 14th century, having gone from the battle to drink water at the well in the village. The rich of Janjevo chose to be buried near the holy shrine and you can also see their graves. The whole area is believed to be rich in archaeological finds with a fortress at the Velentin Hill, which has not yet been explored.

To get to the *tekke* continue straight from the post office in Janjevo (do not follow the main street to the right into the town) until after the small bridge at which you turn to the left until the next river crossing. There again, cross the river and bear left following the road to the top of the hill.

LIPJAN/LIPLJAN

Lipjan is a mixed municipality, with approximately 9,000 Serbs or 12% of the population who live mostly in the villages. Approximately 300 Serbs in Lipjan Town were displaced in March 2004 – mostly to the surrounding villages. There are also a few thousand Ashkali and Roma in the towns and villages and a significant Croat population in Janjevo (see above). Lipjan municipality allocated land for a Serb secondary school in the town, with the plan that it would become multi-ethnic. Under the decentralisation plan, the borders of the municipality would be redrawn significantly to put more Serbian villages under the new proposed Gračanica municipality.

The name 'Lipjan' is believed to be a derivative of Ulpiana (see page 138) – the neo-Latin form 'Lypenion' for the city occurs for the first time in a Greek text from AD1018. Lipjan is also thought to be the birthplace of Lekë Dukagjini (1410–81), writer of the code of ethics who replaced Skenderbeg as leader of the Albanian resistance against the Ottomans following Skenderbeg's death in 1468. (See *Chapter 5, Western Kosovo*, pages 176–7.)

Lipjan is a simple town which had two main industries: the bottling factory (formerly known as the 'Coca-Cola factory') but which lost its Coca-Cola licence some time ago, but is now making other types of fizzy drinks; and the cardboard factory, which used to make boxes and packaging but is now abandoned. The main reason to visit Lipjan today is for its church and perhaps to visit the quiet outlying villages to gain a glimpse of Serbian country life.

WHAT TO SEE AND DO There are two churches which stand side by side – a modern one and the old one, Notre Dame, which is really worth the trip. It dates from the 13th–15th centuries and aside from the traditionally scratched-out eyes, the paintings are well preserved, dating from the 16th century (the church was damaged in a fire in the 15th century). To access the church ask the man at the kiosk who has the key.

In addition Lipjan can boast the spectacular Gadimë Cave within its municipality (see page 145).

The most significant change in Lipjan is that the nearby woods of Blijanes have been reopened to the public after having been closed for more than 50 years. At the time of writing, however, the guards still would not let you in without a permit from the Ministry of Environment, but with some lobbying this situation may not last for ever, so we hope that in the future this bureaucratic requirement will have been lifted. Blijanes is the only place in Kosovo where they raise deer, but where also wild boar, fox, wild chickens and rabbits can be found. There are also 33 small lakes there. The municipality told us that there are plans to build a government retreat in the woods which will extend to several hundred hectares. It seems rather a shame to spoil such undamaged wild nature with a building, so we suggest you get there before they start work. We have also heard that the trails in the woods would make for good mountain biking but it may be worth checking first with someone local to make sure you don't get lost!

Outside Lipjan is a modern prison which is slightly more open-plan than the higher-security Dubrava Prison. There have been a lot of archaeological finds from the 3rd–4th centuries AD in the Lipjan area, which remains ripe for exploration.

GETTING THERE Lipjan is 11km from Prishtina. There are two routes to get there – either go to the airport and take a left turn immediately afterwards or go down the route to Skopje and take the right-hand turn which is signed. With both routes Lipjan is about 4km from the main road. There are **buses** from Prishtina to Lipjan departing at 05.15, 10.15, 12.40, 13.45, 14.10, 16.10 and 18.45. There is also a **train** station in town.

WHERE TO STAY AND EAT There are lots of motels on the second turn-off from the Prishtina–Skopje main road to Lipjan after the large former Irish camp/chicken farm on the left.

⌂ **Motel Agi** (8 rooms) 2km out of town on the way into Lipjan. $$

⌂ **Motel Restaurant Arber** (20 rooms) m 044 271 491. Sells oven pizzas. $$

There are some restaurants in town but nothing really worth stopping off for.

OTHER PRACTICALITIES There is a Raiffeisen Bank (*Rr Ramiz Sadiku;* ☏ *038 580 190*), ProCredit Bank (*Rr Shqiperise, opposite the police station;* ☏ *038 580 303;* ⏱ *09.00–18.00 Mon–Fri, 09.00–14.00 Sat*), and NLB (⏱ *08.00-17.00 Mon-Fri*) near the municipality building.

OUTSIDE LIPJAN

The **Golesh/Magura Mine** is to the west of Lipjan, a magnesite mine which closed in 1999. Before 1990, the Golesh operation produced 110,000 tons of magnesite, 22,000 tons of sintered magnesia and 10,000 tons of caustic calcined magnesia per annum. Now the mine is a redundant hulk awaiting privatisation. Golesh village is very mixed, inhabited by both Roma and Ashkali, and is also very poor.

As mentioned, it seems the whole area around Lipjan has a long and early history. The first archaeological site which is being explored is **Harilaç** which is 3km down a turn-off on the left-hand side if you continue on the main road to Peja after the airport. This is a former inhabited fortress, currently explored by an archaeological team from Tirana and Italy working with the Institute of Monuments and the Kosovo Museum. If you are interested in archaeology then contact the Prishtina Museum or Institute of Monuments (☏ *038 390 27 028;* e *bedirraci@yahoo.com*), or Kemajl Luci from the Kosovo Museum as they may accept volunteers and will be happy to show groups around the site by prior arrangement.

EAST OF LIPJAN – SERBIAN VILLAGES There is a cluster of Serbian villages off the main road to Janjevo and there is a nice off-the-main-road drive across fertile fields from Lipjan, through Dobrotin, Donje Gušterica and then back to Prishtina through Laplje Selo.

Donje Guterica Within the village there is a stone church dating from the early 20th century with a fresco on the outside, and the yellow decaying former Serbian Elementary School, dating from 1888.

SHPELLA E GADIMËS (CAVE OF GADIMË) The cave (⏱ *09.00–15.00 daily; small entrance charge*) is in the village of Gadimë which is a mixed village of Ashkali, Roma and Albanians. The cave is large with dozens of stalactites and stalagmites of differing colours. It was discovered in 1969 by Ahmet Diti when doing work on his house nearby and was opened to the public in 1976 after exploration by Yugoslav speleologists. The cave is 1,200–1,500m long, with a 500m section open to tourists; tours take about 40 minutes.

The cave should be considered as one of the top ten sights of Kosovo, as it is quite spectacular. The cave managers will provide you with a tour guide who will point out the stalactites that resemble an eagle, the shape of Kosovo, and other interesting formations.

This is a socially owned enterprise so opening times are unfortunately subject to change at short notice. Saturday is a good day to go as there are often groups from Kosovo visiting, so you have a good chance of getting in. If the cave is closed ask in the cafés across the road as someone may know someone who has the key. Do not expect to get in immediately, so allow enough time for some hanging around before you get shown aroundround the cave.

GETTING THERE Gadimë is equidistant from Lipjan and Ferizaj on the east side of the main Skopje road.

To reach the cave you will need to ask for directions. The turning to Gadimë is on the road to Skopje (if coming from Prishtina it is after the Lipjan turn-off but before Ferizaj, if coming from Skopje, it is signed). You then have to carry on following the road for about 2km. The cave itself is not visible from the outside; there is just an unassuming car park indicating its presence.

There are 13 **buses** a day from Prishtina to Gadimë, departing approximately every hour but with a two-hour gap after the 12.45 departure. The cost is less than €3.

Buses from Ferizaj to Gadimë leave the Ferizaj bus station at 12.00, 14.00, 17.00 and 18.30 and cost €1. You can also get a taxi from Ferizaj to Gadimë and negotiate a waiting time.

GLLOGOVC/GLOGOVAC

Gllogovc is in the Drenas/Drenica region, the poorest in Kosovo with high illiteracy and poverty rates and a reputation for militancy. The population is entirely Albanian as was the case before the 1999 conflict.

Gllogovc is primarily an industrial town. Rising out of the plain with its blue buildings and roofs is Ferronikeli, an open-pit nickel mine and the town's main company. It started production in the mid 1980s, reaching its maximum level in 1989. In 1991, enforced Serbian measures resulted in the resignation and dismissal of the Albanian workers and as a result production was much lower until 1999 when it was bombed by NATO. It was purchased in privatisation by IMR/Alferon (an Indian/UK company) in 2006 for €29 million and with a commitment to employ 1,000 workers and to invest a further €20 million, making it Kosovo's most successful privatisation to date as the nickel also makes up more than half of Kosovo's exports by value. Ferronikeli has started using the Prishtina–Fushë-Kosova railway for freight with renovated trucks. This section of the railway was built by French engineers. Apparently the French were quite taken with the local spring water from the village of Poklek 6km away which allegedly has healing properties. The other mineral water in the area – Vërbovc – has a bitter taste.

The other main employment in town is Çikatova Quarry which produces limestone and products for road building. It has been bought by an Austrian company.

There are supposedly chrome and lignite resources in the Drenas/Drenica area, particularly near Tërstenik, magnesite in Dobroshevc and iron ore in Suka and Dushkaja. In Tërstenik and Baks villages stone engravings have been found (the date of which are unknown). The surrounding villages all survive on agriculture, in particular wheat and maize. As there is limited water supply in the area, the agriculture is heavily reliant on the irrigation systems put in by the irrigation company Iber Lepenc.

In 2004, the trade centre in Gllogovc with shops and offices was completed but it was built on the flood plain and is hence prone to flooding.

GETTING THERE Gllogovc is reached by turning right off the main Prishtina–Peja road and continuing for 5km. There are fairly regular buses from Prishtina. On the right-hand side of the Prishtina–Peja road before you turn off to Gllogovc is Kosovo's first business park. At the time of writing the tenants had not yet moved in.

The road to Gllogovc continues on to Skenderaj/Srbica (see page 261).

WHERE TO STAY If you need somewhere to stay, a trip back to Prishtina or Fushë-Kosova is in order (or continue on to Klina/Mirusha), although there are some second-rate motels at Kroni të Mbretit on the main Peja–Prishtina road.

WHERE TO EAT

✖ **Restaurant Kalaja** No phone. An appealing restaurant which is housed in the old stone railway station dating from 1930, probably one of the most attractive buildings in Gllogovc.

OTHER PRACTICALITIES The post office and police station are located in the centre of town, near the municipality.

AROUND GLLOGOVC

There is little to see in the area, which is largely reconstructed since the 1999 conflict and which still bears some of the signs.

BERISHA HILL AND KOSOVO FREE RADIO From this hill, it is possible to see most of Kosovo as it is a central high point. It is worth coming up here for the views on a good day. It is best known as the location of the Kosova e Lire radio station during the 1999 conflict. After two to three months of setting up, they first broadcast on 4 January 1999. Initially they broadcast from a house but this became unsafe and an underground bunker was built. The venue of the radio station has now been made into a small **museum** that it is possible to visit. The telephone number of the guard is usually written on the poster on the door. The station continues to broadcast, now legally. To reach Berisha, turn left after Lapushnik Town on the main Peja–Prishtina road and head directly uphill. The road is not well asphalted but is passable in an ordinary car in the spring and summer.

For more information see their website (*www.radiokosovaelire.com*). If you do not speak Albanian then click on *galleria* for pictures of the building of the station and the conflict period.

Golesh Hill at 1,019m, above the airport is, on the other hand, out of bounds as it houses not only the airport radar but also KFOR radar.

BATTLAVA LAKE

Battlava Lake offers a pleasant excursion or day trip, being only 33km from Prishtina. Geographically the nearest city is **Podujevo**, a town which to be frank can be safely omitted from your tourist itinerary as it was heavily damaged in the conflict and even the old mosque has little to write home about.

Battlava is an artificial lake built to supply Prishtina and its surrounds with water. It also has a hydro-electric dam owned by KEK which is barely working. As it is the only large lake where Kosovo Albanians can swim, it is extremely popular in the summer and hordes of families line the beaches at the eastern end. There are plenty of *qebap* (kebab) stalls. If you are lucky to have a spring or autumn day when the weather brightens, you can have the lake to yourself and it is bliss. The water is muddy at the lake's edge but if you can get past this the swimming is great. It is also possible to hire a boat and if you have a permit you can fish (the local fish from the lake is known as *shtuke*). The surrounding woods are good for walking if you stay on the paths.

GETTING THERE From Prishtina you must head out towards Podujevo and continue for about 15km and turn off right at the sign where all the restaurants are posted before the bridge. The lake is not signed but 'Orllan' is. Continue along the road for at least another 6–8km, ignoring side roads off to the left (to the old KFOR base) and to the right, and you eventually come to the lake. In summer an entrance fee of €1 is charged which goes some way (it is hoped) to clearing the rubbish left behind by the picnickers. Unfortunately the sewage from the illegal buildings is not treated before it goes into the lake so be warned before you swim!

The road continues on past several restaurants, including: the Pyramid Café which is, as the name suggests, shaped like a pyramid; Adriatiku; Restaurant Guri; and further just beyond Orllan village, Milenium 2000 which is on stilts and looks right out onto the lake. Perhaps owing to global warming, the level of the lake has receded recently. However, in true Kosovo fashion such problems are addressed through more building. The restaurants are simply extending their terraces further each time the water retreats!

You can continue on from here to a beach and beyond that to a church and mosque. The road then ceases to be asphalt. If you have a 4×4 then from here you can also go across to Ballaban and on to Keqekolle which brings you back on the main road to the Serbian border and Prishtina – this makes a good, if bumpy, round trip.

There are lots of buses to Orllan from Prishtina bus station, the first leaving at 07.35, then one every hour (usually at 25 minutes past) until the last at 19.25.

🏠 WHERE TO STAY AND EAT

🏠 **Motel Lugu i Tëndafilave** m 044 264 024/147 484. A beautifully decorated hotel, with large French windows, modern bathrooms & fresh white linen. When you are here you feel a lot further away than only 33km from Prishtina. $$$

🏠 **Hotel Residence Milenium 2000** (4 rooms).

Restaurant ⊕ 07.00–24.00. $$$

✗ **Restaurant Adriatiku** m 044 296 222/700 011. With 100 sun loungers & access to a private beach for €2. Restaurant ⊕ 10.00–23.00.

✗ **Restaurant Guri** m 044 505 079/89; ⊕ 10.00–23.00

5

Western Kosovo

Some may say that western Kosovo is really the 'true' Kosovo. Travellers will be rewarded with a region rich in cultural heritage and endowed with fantastic scenery, from the Rugova Gorge to the Mirusha Falls. Many of Kosovo's best highlights are to be found here, including the Visoki Dečani Monastery, Hadum Mosque and the old bazaar in Gjakova, the Serb Orthodox Patriarchate in Peć and traditional kullas in Isniq and Dranoc. This region has always been a multi-cultural mosaic, with sizeable Catholic Albanian, Orthodox Serb and Montenegrin minorities. Much of this diversity was lost during the 1999 war, which hit this area particularly hard. Places like Gjakova, Peja or Junik suffered considerable destruction.

Thanks to the fertile Dukagjini (Metohija) Plain, western Kosovo has traditionally been a wealthy area with a strong sense of local pride shared by everyone coming from 'Dukagjin area'. For passionate mountaineers the region offers endless adventures from the Bjeshkët e Nemuna (Accursed Mountains) at 2,522m to the Junik Mountains (2,656m). This region well deserves an extended day trip, or even better, a long weekend.

PEJA/PEĆ

A day trip to Peja is a must for anyone visiting Kosovo. The town is most famous for being the seat of the Serb Orthodox Patriarchate and for Serbs, Peć (Peja) is seen as the spiritual seat of the Serbian nation. Albanians on the other hand cherish Peja as an important Ottoman trading town and home to Haxhi Zeka, a charismatic leader of the Albanian national movement in the late 19th century. By size of population Peja is also Kosovo's second-largest city. Despite its near total destruction in 1999, you can still get a flavour of the Ottoman market town and discover some beautiful examples of Ottoman-era town houses and *kullas* (fortified tower-like houses). The location of Peja is perhaps its real asset – the mountains rise up behind and spread below it is the fertile plain of Dukagjin (Metohija in Serbian). Cutting into scenic mountains the Rugova Gorge offers great opportunities for hikers, skiers and cave explorers. If there is one thing that both communities agree on, it is that Peja is the city where you can find the most beautiful girls in Kosovo. If you want to go inside any of Peja's monuments then contact Rugova Experience (see page 167) or the municipality at least one day in advance for them to organise you a guide, particularly if you plan to come at the weekend. While the municipality now has a tourist information office in the centre of town, it has limited opening hours and is closed at weekends. A guide is not prohibitively expensive and avoids the frustration of arriving and not being able to get into the sites.

HISTORY Peja's early history has been closely linked with the seat of the Serb Orthodox Church. In 1253, Bulgarian raiders completely destroyed the original seat of the archbishop at Ziča Monastery in inner Serbia, so the decision was taken

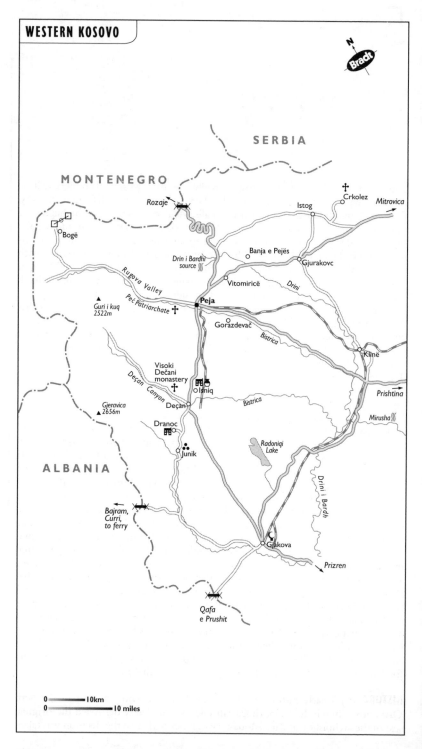

WESTERN KOSOVO

SERBIA

MONTENEGRO

Rozaje

Crkolez

Mitrovica

Istog

Bogë

Drin i Bardhi source

Banja e Pejës

Gjurakovc

Rugova Valley

Vitomiricë

Drini

Peć Patriarchate

Peja

Guri i kuq 2522m

Gorazdevač

Bistrica

Klinë

Visoki Dečani monastery

O Isniq

Prishtina

Dečan Canyon

Bistrica

Gjeravica 2656m

Dečan

Mirusha

Dranoc

Radoniqi Lake

ALBANIA

Junik

Drini i Bardh

Bajram, Curri, to ferry

Gjakova

Prizren

Qafa e Prushit

0 — 10km
0 — 10 miles

to relocate the Patriarchate to a safer place. Located on a plain, on the foot of the panoramic Bjeshkët e Nemuna Mountain (2,522m), protected by the narrow Rugova Gorge, Peja seemed the ideal location. Peja's importance was greatly enhanced by the decision in 1346 to elevate the Serbian archbishop to the rank of patriarch. After the tumultuous early years of the Ottoman advance in the Balkans, the Patriarchate was officially reinstated in 1557. From then on, with minor interruptions, Peja was the residence of the patriarch and the archbishop of the Serb Orthodox Church until the Patriarchate's formal closure in 1766.

In the early years under Ottoman rule, when Peja temporarily lost its importance as seat of the Orthodox Church, it gained prominence as an important market town and trading outpost of Ragusa. Geography worked in Peja's favour. Thanks to its position on the crossroads between Dubrovnik and the eastern part of the Kosovo territory, and with the Bistrica River serving as a natural 'road' connecting Peja with Mitrovica, Peja emerged as the unrivalled economic centre for the region. In the 14th century, Peja had about 12,000 inhabitants and 960 shops.

The most important local family was the Mahmutbegolli – or just Begolli – family. The family claimed direct descent from the medieval Dukagjin family and supplied most of the governors to Peja in the late 16th and 17th centuries. A large fire in the 16th century destroyed most of the Old Town.

In 1958, the communist leadership set out to 'industrialise' the town. The first industries were a leather and shoe company, a wood and furniture company and a gigantic agricultural business, including a sugar factory and brewery. In 1968, the Ramiz Sadiku Factory started producing car parts for the Zastava car plants in Kragujevac. Today, Peja's economy is largely trade and construction based.

GETTING THERE Peja is easily accessible by a regular **bus** service from all of Kosovo's major towns. Buses from Prishtina take about two hours, with departures every 20 minutes starting at 07.30 till 18.30. There are six daily buses from Prizren to Peja (which stop off at Gjakova). For details see the bus timetable in *Chapter 2*, page 60. The main bus station is on Rr Adem Jashari, not far from Haxhi Zeka's mill complex and the OSCE headquarters. The walk to town takes about ten minutes along Rr Adem Jashari which then turns into Rr Mbreteresha Teuta.

In July and August there are several buses a week from Peja to Ulqin (an Albanian-populated town on the Montenegrin coast) via Podgorica (for schedules ask at the main bus station).

By **car**, the trip to Peja from Prishtina takes about two hours. It's a 90km drive on a good, but busy, road which at the time of writing was being upgraded to a dual carriageway. If you are coming from Prishtina the first thing you will come across as you approach Peja is the large industrial complex of the Peja Brewery on the right-hand side and shortly before this there is the Vita milk and Tango fruit-juice factory and the customs terminal. Birra e Pejës is Kosovo's most popular local brew and tastes similar to a Czech pilsner. Keep on the main road until you get to the first roundabout; where you take the left turn (Rr Bill Clinton). At the second roundabout turn left into Rr Mbreteresha Teuta. When the road forks again after about 200m, you can either turn right into Rr General Wesley Clark – taking you straight to the Patriarchate and the Rugova Valley, or left on Rr Mbreteresha Teuta towards the town centre.

GETTING AROUND The easiest way to get around is on foot: all sites are within walking distance and are often tucked away in pedestrian areas, including the Peć Patriarchate provided you don't mind a pleasant half-hour walk across the city. Orientation is relatively easy and it helps that the municipality has been really good

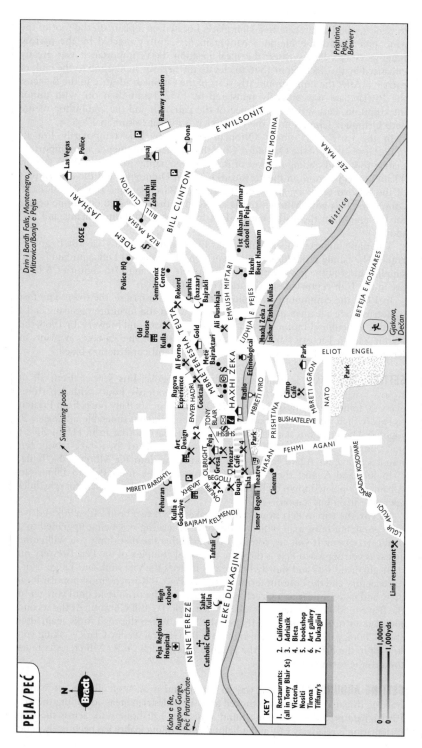

PEJA/PEĆ

152

KEY

1. Restaurants:
(all in Tony Blair St)
Victoria
Nositi
Tirona
Tiffany's

2. California
3. Adriatik
4. Bleta
5. bookshop
6. Art gallery
7. Dukagjini

0 _____ 1,000m
0 _____ 1,000yds

in putting up street signs recently. Watch out, however – Rr General Wesley Clark/Rr Nëne Terezë is a one-way street from the centre to the Patriarchate and Rr Lekë Dukagjini is also only one way from the Patriarchate into town!

There is plenty of parking, for example along Rr Adem Jashari and General Wesley Clark/Rr Nëne Terezë, near Art Design and also in the area near the theatre. For a full day's parking the maximum charge is €1.50.

TOURIST INFORMATION/TOUR OPERATORS

Municipality Tourist Information Right opposite the Hotel Dukagjini; ☏ 039 33 859; e pejatourism@ hotmail.com; www.pejatourism@yahoo.com; ⏰ 08.00–16.00 (closed for lunch 12.00–13.00)

Mon–Fri. An alternative for more information & to organise tours is Rugova Experience (see below).
Rugova Experience For further details, see *Rugova Valley*, page 167.

WHERE TO STAY
Peja does not have many hotels to choose from and there was, at the time of writing, no top-end hotel.

For budget-conscious travellers the cheapest rate at the time of writing was €10 for a single room in the rather dilapidated Hotel Jusaj (see below). A nice alternative to staying in town (especially if you have your own transport) is to try one of the mountain-resort hotels in the Rugova Valley (see page 167), or if your itinerary permits, stay in Deçan or Istog (good budget options) or Motel Nora – especially if you are seeking a good-standard hotel (see *Klina*) – 20km outside Peja.

For something more akin to 'original Albanian' you can also try one of the restored kullas (fortified tower houses) in the Deçan region. (See *Dranoc*, page 184.)

Mid-range $$$

🏠 **Hotel Dukagjini** (16 rooms) Sheshi i Deshmoreve 2; ☏ 039 429 999; e info@hoteldukagjini.com; www.hoteldukagjini.com. This has the best location – right on the river. Previously known as Hotel Metohija & Hotel Royal Arda, the hotel's recent history mirrors that of the town: under Milošević Serb paramilitaries converted it into a casino, then for several years after the war it housed a contingent of Italian *carabinieri* stationed in Peja region. In 2005, it was privatised. After a first renovation it changed hands again & is now owned by the Dukagjini conglomerate. They are undertaking their own renovation works & expansion which will be concluded by end of summer 2010 and the rooms are expected to be greatly improved so that finally Peja has a top end hotel! The brand new indoor bar with the roof's water feature is probably one of the smartest places to go in Peja. There is also a huge banqueting hall with chandeliers. The in-house restaurant serves local food as well as pizza & meat dishes. In summer you can enjoy the nice view from one of the 2 huge outdoor terraces by the riverside.

🏠 **Hotel Gold** (16 rooms) Rr 122/D5 106; ☏ 039 34 571; e hotel_gold@hotmail.com. In a convenient location only 3mins' walk from the old bazaar area. It offers clean rooms with good beds, Wi-Fi throughout the hotel, modern bathrooms & cable TV. No AC. A b/fast buffet is included in the price. There is no restaurant, but the hotel bar features a large-size TV screen (in case you want to watch a football match) & a pub-like atmosphere.

🏠 **Hotel Peja** (10 rooms) In a side alley just off the main square; m 044 406 777; e hotel_peja@ hotmail.com. Tucked away just beside the entrance of the former UN headquarters, near the NLB Bank & 20m from Victoria & Tirona restaurants, this hotel offers clean furnished rooms with modern bathrooms, heating, AC, cable TV; Wi-Fi is being installed. Don't be put off by the office-like atmosphere in the entrance hall. The hotel restaurant only caters for wedding parties during the summer months. The owners speak good German. B/fast is served in a nearby restaurant & we were warned by previous visitors that there might therefore be a bit of a wait.

🏠 **Motel Las Vegas** (5 rooms) Rr Agim Benesijelaj 35; m 044 349 062. Coming from the bus station head 10mins north in the direction of Mitrovica/Banja e Pejës. Basic rooms with bathrooms. AC but no Wi-Fi. Generally the reception & hotel service is a little ropey, but cheaper than the other places in town.

🏠 **Koha e Re/Veranda** www.kohaere.com. Just before the entrance to the Rugova Valley. At the time of writing still just a restaurant, but from 2011 they plan to have more than 20 rooms. Call or check the website. A 15min walk into town, near the Patriarchate.

Budget $$

⌂ **Hotel Dona** (23 rooms) Rr Rifat Begolli 286/A;
\ 039 434 470; m 049 244 207. A few hundred
metres from the train station at the entrance to town,
Hotel Dona offers a good deal for basic comfort. It's a
good place to stop over if you are with your car as
there is parking in front of the hotel. In the ground-
floor restaurant you can grab a pasta dish or risotto
for €3 or a full main course for €5. It's about a
15min walk to town. Simple, clean rooms, all with
bathrooms & TV, are good value but there is no AC.

⌂ **Hotel Jusaj** (24 rooms) Rr 254 7; \ 039 427
631; m 044 139 043; e majorjusaj@hotmail.com
(answered sporadically). No Wi-Fi or internet. The
owner Sylë Jusaj is proud to tell you that this was
one of the first private hotels in former Yugoslavia.
It is the cheapest address in town, but don't expect
much in terms of style or comfort. It's cheap
because about half the rooms share bathrooms &
toilets & only some have AC. Even the more
'expensive' rooms with en-suite bathrooms are poorly
furnished. If you don't mind shabbiness, it's
conveniently located not far from the main bus
station & the train station. Besides budget travellers,
the hotel is also frequented by young couples trying
to get some privacy away from home. Parking
behind the hotel.

✖ WHERE TO EAT

Peja is blessed with a number of nice restaurants dotted across
town. There is a string of good restaurants along the riverside after the main square
and in the vicinity of the police headquarters. Thanks to Italian KFOR and
carabinieri, the local cuisine is very Italianised. Some of the restaurants also serve
traditional dishes from the Rugova area, including oven-baked meat stews (*tavë*),
pogaqe bread (typically served warm), lamb or *suxhuk*, a spicy garlic sausage. Al
Forno is the best address for pizza; Victoria Restaurant has the best salads and fresh
fruit juices. For the nicest ambience try the restaurant Art Design, just behind the
police headquarters.

Mid-range

✖ **Al Forno** Rr Enver Hadri 27; m 044 136 115;
⊕ 09.00–23.00 daily. Right in the centre of town,
Al Forno is very popular with internationals & is
reputedly the best pizzeria in town. The blue-&-red
chequered tablecloths give the place a real *trattoria*
flair – & the thin-crust, oven-baked pizza definitely
passes the Italian test. If you are lazy & don't want
to leave home, you can call up & ask for home
delivery (orders can be placed in English, without
any problems).

✖ **Art Design** Rr Enver Hadri, a side street off Rr
General Wesley Clark, just behind the main police
headquarters; m 044 144 622; ⊕ 08.00–24.00
daily. Definitely the most atmospheric restaurant in
town. Its interior design is a tasteful mix between
stonemasonry & rustic décor. The stone walls blend
in well with the other furniture, & the open stone
fireplace & piano adds extra charm. The food is also
great. Don't be put off by the presence of the
police; it's a popular place for police officers to have
a coffee just across from the police headquarters.

✖ **California Park** m 049 138 470; ⊕ 07.00–
24.00 daily. Off the Sheshi (main square) further up
nearer the park next to Art Design, California Park
is a popular restaurant with pizza & steak dishes.

✖ **Camp Café** Park Karagaç; m 044 825 157;
⊕ 07.00–22.00. Traditional & Italian style food. Set
in the green park surroundings – open in summer
only.

✖ **Cocktail Restaurant** \ 039 428 735; m 044
159 011; ⊕ 08.00-23.00 every day. Nicely
renovated upstairs restaurant with balcony. Set back
from the street. Pizzas, steak & pasta.

✖ **Gresa Pizzeria** Off Rr William Walker, Rr 17
Nentori; \ 039 31 710; m 044 308 362;
⊕ 07.00–23.30 daily. Somewhat dark & dated
Italian-style pizzeria.

✖ **Hotel Dukagjini** Sheshi i Deshmoreve 2; \ 039 429
999; ⊕ 07.00–24.00. Right on the river & very
popular. In addition to the outdoor terrace an
enclosed glass conservatory is being built so you can
see the outdoors & mountains even when it is chilly.
Wi-Fi available. Not just good food but a panoramic
view of the mountains rising up just behind Peja and
definitely one of the smartest addresses in town.

✖ **Koha e Re/Veranda** m 044 505 125/45; ⊕
07.00–24.00. About 50m before the Patriarchate/
Rugova Valley entrance. Huge, professional place with
downstairs restaurant seating 70 & an upper floor for
events & weddings. Large terrace with outdoor seats
overlooking the river. Also owners of Koha 3 which is
near Rugova Experience off Rr Mbreteresha Teuta.

✖ **Limi Restaurant** ⊕ 09.00–24.00 daily, summer
only. Up on the southern hill above Peja with a

fabulous view & a green setting. Traditional fare with *tava* & meat dishes & Italian. Also holds dancing. The music can be a bit cheesy Albanian style but it is worth the experience. To get there go down Hasan Prishtina & then Fehmi Agani, take the right up Brigadat Kosovare & Gura Kuqi. If you don't have a car then you will need to take a taxi.

✖ Nositi Sheshi (main square); ☎ 039 34 434; ☏ 044 372 579; ⏲ 08.00–23.00 daily. Passable restaurant & pizzeria with Italian food.

✖ Semitronix Centre Between Rr Bill Clinton & Rr Mbretresha Teuta; ☎ 039 32 754; ☏ 044 285 345. ⏲ 10.00-23.00 every day. A not uncontroversial

yellow building with green glass. Includes on the top the only revolving restaurant in Peja above the various boutiques with good views of Peja & the surrounding mountains.

✖ Tiffany's Off the Sheshi (main square); ☏ 044 768 147; ⏲ 07.00–24.00. The usual menu of pizza & pasta dishes & serves good coffee & beer. In the past, the Socialist Hunters' Association owned the building & maybe that partly explains the older clientele.

✖ Tirona Off the Sheshi next to Tiffany's; ☏ 044 308 362/246 902; ⏲ 07.00–24.00 daily.

Budget There is a cluster of fast-food places along the river between the Hotel Dukagjini and the area at the far end near the next bridge selling both burgers and *qebabi* (smaller minced meat rolls) served with bread, salad and *ajvar* (a spicy sauce made of red peppers). Some also serve the local speciality *suxhuk*, a spicy garlic sausage.

✖ Ali Dushkaja Rr Amrush Miftari. A popular local fast-food restaurant serving traditional cuisine, including stews, burgers & salads.

✖ Buqja Qebaptore Not far from Rr Lekë Dukagjini. A popular & good kebab shop.

✖ Lala Qebaptore Off Rr Lekë Dukagjini. Fresh meat & yoghurt.

Cakes and sweets

✖ Adriatik Embeltore Off Rr Lekë Dukagjini. This tiny shop serves probably one of the best & most traditional chocolate, meringue & baklava selections in Peja. You can also try their ice cream & *boze* (a traditional corn drink).

✖ Bleta Bleta Embeltore Ice cream, *boze* & desserts right on the Rr Lekë Dukagjini pedestrianised area by the river.

✖ Rekord Bakery Rr Mbreteresha Teuta (formerly Rr 122), at the corner close to the tall, bright-orange shopping centre. A friendly & cosy option for a quick bite for little money. You can try their filo pastries or *burek* stuffed with meat, spinach or cheese. It's also a popular place just to hang out & drink a coffee. From here, it's only a few steps to the old bazaar area.

CAFÉS AND BARS There are plenty of bars and cafés in Peja, maybe not quite as trendy as in Prishtina, but fun to hang out and enjoy a few nice evenings. Most indoor places tend to get smoke-filled in the evenings and crowded. In summer, it's best to enjoy Peja's mild climate in one of the outdoor venues such as in the park area or in the Rugova Valley, if you really want some fresh air. The area along the Bistrica River, in particular the stretch between the Hotel Dukagjini and Rr William Walker, is thronged with bars and cafés, some of them also serving fast food and pizza. While in Peja, you should try the local beer (known as Birra e Pejës) brewed in the now privatised Peja Brewery at the entrance to town. The outdoor terrace of Hotel Dukagjini is a particularly nice place to hang out. For people watching, try one of the bars along the main square.

For summer specials or open-air festivals it's best to ask around at the time of your visit. There have been one-off open-air concerts in the past and occasionally DJs from Prishtina and other towns travel to Peja for special gigs.

☕ Mozart Café Rr Lekë Dukagjini (2mins' walk from the main square on the right). A popular hangout with an outdoor terrace, serving pizza as well.

☕ Radio Café A somewhat eclectic-looking but apparently popular café almost opposite Hotel Dukagjini.

ENTERTAINMENT

Ismet Begolli Theatre This is newly reconstructed off Rr Lekë Dukagjini near the river facing the park. Sadly it shows very few plays.

Jusuf Gervall Cinema/Theatre Rr Hasan Prishtina 73. This is Peja's local cinema & theatre hall restored with Italian funds after the war. Foreign films are shown in their original language with Albanian subtitles. You can check their programme in the information window on the outside wall.

SHOPPING The old bazaar has lost most of its flair following its destruction in 1999 and careless modernisation, but you can still get a flavour of how the Oriental market town of the past when taking a stroll through the network of narrow streets around Bajrakli Mosque. The bazaar area is still packed with shops selling local products, filigree silverware, leatherware or traditional household items like *sofras* (low, round-shaped wooden tables) or *dieppi* (wooden baby cradles). Globalisation has not forgotten about Peja, and many shops are packed with cheap Chinese and Turkish imports.

On the corner of Rr Jashar Pasha there is a small shop selling *dieppi* in different sizes – including a portable 'souvenir' size. These *dieppi* are traditionally passed on from brother to sister. There are also a number of nice, but not cheap, **jewellery shops** along Çarshia e Gjate, the main road from Bajrakli Mosque to Rr Eliot Engel. Budget-conscious travellers should stick with the silver filigree, which is more affordable than the gold. Traditionally, Albanian families spend a small fortune on jewellery on the occasion of a wedding. With all properties in a traditional Albanian household owned communally, the wedding trousseau of the bride was the only valuable property that really belonged to the bride alone (for more information on traditional weddings see *Isniq*, page 179). Jewellery that was given to the bride as a wedding gift thus had the function of an old-age pension. Nowadays, some families spend up to €5,000 on jewellery alone, explaining the high number of jewellery shops.

The most prominent shopping centre in town is the privatised former socialist department store renamed **Mëtë Bajraktari Plaza**. **Semitronix Centre** is a rather garish glass outfit, but aside from some wedding dress shops the other shop tenants seem to have given up and left. It is worth, however, going up in the lift for a drink in the enclosed glass bar on the roof (which apparently revolves – rotating once an hour when there are guests) or on the terrace (the view is better than the food). The huge red building of the **ETC shopping centre** on the main road to Prishtina before the brewery is easy to find. Open every day, it has also become a popular weekend pastime for Peja families to go 'shopping' and meet for coffee or a meal in the shopping mall. ETC also operates free minibuses shuttling between town and the shopping centre, easily recognisable by the red-golden ETC logo. You can flag them down on the street if you see one. Other shopping centres have recently opened along the main Peja–Deçan road.

If you are looking for hiking boots or other shoes, try the **Planinka shoe shop** at the corner of Rr Mbreteresha Teuta and Rr Eliot Engel. They have a wide range of good-quality Slovene shoes to choose from.

In case your shoes fail you, there is a little **shoe-repair shop** located on Rr William Walker. For little money your shoes will receive deluxe treatment.

In **Zahaq village**, about 8km outside Peja on the main Prishtina–Peja road, you will see Albanian carpets and costumes hung up for sale along the road. They are all homemade, using wool from local sheep and natural dye made from plants from the mountains towards Montenegro. A 2m² carpet costs around €100; great as special gifts or souvenirs.

SPORTS AND ACTIVITIES

Roni Fitness Rr Lidhja e Pejës 102. If you are in the mood for a workout indoors, Roni is equipped with running machines & a wide range of modern weights. You can pay a daily rate or arrange for a monthly ticket.

Swimming pools The open-air swimming pools with views of the mountains are to the north side of town. Entrance €1–2.

OTHER PRACTICALITIES There are several **banks** in Peja: ProCredit Bank (*Sheshi i Deshmoreve;* ☎ *039 433 128; Rr TMK & Rr Mbreteresha Teuta;* ⊕ *08.00–18.00 Mon–Fri, 09.00–14.00 SAT*) NLB, ⊕ 08.00-17.00 Mon-Fri and Raiffeisen Bank (*Rr Haxhi Zeka;* ☎ *038 222 222 ext 607;* ⊕ *08.30–17.30 Mon–Fri, 10.00–14.00 Sat*).

The central **post office** is located on Rr Mbreteresha Teuta, just across from Hotel Dukagjini. There is another small post office near the main park area near the road to Gjakova.

A couple of **pharmacies** (*barnatore*) are clustered around the small green area where Rr Mbreteresha Teuta and Rr Tony Blair meet.

There are two smaller health centres close to each other: one on Rr Nëne Terezë on the corner with Rr Bajram Kelmendi and another one on Rr Bajram Kelmendi next to the mosque.

Peja Regional Hospital is at the end of Rr Nëne Terezë, on the right-hand side, just before the Patriarchate.

There are a few **internet cafés** in town, including some on Rr Tony Blair, then there is also **BridgeNet** (⊕ *09.00–24.00 daily; €1 per hr*), with 12 computers tucked away on Rr William Walker, and **NitaNet** (m *044 364 678; €0.60 per hr*), also with 12 computers, is located near the main bus station, across the street from Hotel Jusaj.

A sister branch of the major Prishtina shop **S&B Computers** is on Rr Mbreteresha Teuta opposite the Semitronix Centre.

The **Anadolli bicycle shop (including bike hire)** (*Rr Mbreteresha Teuta 122;* m *049 545 154;* ⊕ *08.00–19.00 Mon–Sat*) is a bit further down Rr Mbreteresha Teuta towards the Semitronix Centre from the main post office, and repairs, sells and rents bikes, with rental available for reasonable prices for one day (€10) or longer. Contact the owner by phone in advance. The incredibly helpful owner is also available out of hours for emergencies. There is a limited stock of spare parts so consider bringing your own, but their mechanical skills look good.

The **Dukagjini Bookshop** (*Rr Haxhi Zeka;* ⊕ *08.00–19.00 Mon–Sat*) is the only one with English or foreign titles. It also has a photocopier, but for more sophisticated copying use the Dukagjini graphic centre on Rr Mbreteresha Teuta near Cocktail and Al Forno restaurants.

At the **Art Gallery Isa Alimusaj** (m *044 142 916*), there is a Peja artist focusing on (often large) oil paintings, who is available for commissioning work.

Travel agencies

Euro Tours ☎ 039 33 285
Exim Tours ☎ 039 33 891

MCM Travel ☎ 039 33 213/34 213
Rusolia Tours ☎ 039 34 127

Taxi numbers

🚕 **Besiana Kasapolli** m 044 327 286
🚕 **London Taxi** m 045/049 668 668. Traditional London taxis!

🚕 **Njaci Taxi** ☎ 039 33 737; m 044 394 888
🚕 **Royal Taxi** ☎ 039 433 433; m 049/044 364 364

Haxhi Zeka was a charismatic Muslim cleric and Albanian national activist living in Peja at the turn of the 19th century. He had also been a member of the League of Prizren and fought for uniting the four Albanian-populated Ottoman districts of Kosovo, Monastir, Ioannina and Shkodra into one province with a large degree of autonomy. In 1893, Haxhi Zeka and Bajram Curri, a former Ottoman officer, led a first armed revolt in western Kosovo. Following a second revolt in 1897, Haxhi Zeka began summoning a gathering of 450 Albanian delegates with the aim of reviving the League of Prizren (see *Chapter 1, National Awakening*, page 11). This meeting is commonly referred to as the League of Peja or Besa-Besë to commemorate its first decision calling for a general truce (*besë*) of all blood feuds. After days of intense discussion, the delegates finally agreed on a list of 12 points declaring their loyalty to the sultan, setting up local committees to oversee the implementation of Albanian customary law (the Kanun of Lek) and calling for Albanian-language education. Haxhi Zeka's final political stroke was leading a revolt against a planned extension of an Austrian railway line from Bosnia to Mitrovica. A year later, in 1902, he was assassinated. Haxhi Zeka's statue can be found today on Rr Eliot Engel just across from the Mëtë Bajraktari shopping centre.

For more information on Peja's cultural heritage you can also contact the Regional Institute for the Protection of Cultural Monuments, Abdyl Hoxhaj (Director) (✆ *039 34 147*), who also gives tours.

WHAT TO SEE AND DO The best place to start your walk through the historic part of town is in front of Mëtë Bajraktari Plaza, the main shopping centre at the corner of Rr Eliot Engel and Rr Tony Blair. Across the square, hidden away behind the petrol station, is the **Regional Ethnological Museum of Peja** (✆ *039 21 446;* m *044 165 232;* ⏱ *07.00–15.30 Mon–Sat, small charge*), housed in a beautiful example of a typical Ottomak *konak* (town house). The permanent collection presented in three rooms includes traditional costumes, cloth, musical instruments and Illyrian handicrafts. Allow about half an hour to visit the museum. At the centre of the square outside the Ethnological Museum is a statue of Haxhi Zeka (1832–1902), a famous Muslim cleric and nationalist activist. His family house, a typical fortified stone house is only a few minutes' walk from the museum along Rr Lidhja e Pejës – **Haxhi Zeka's kulla**. The original building was set on fire in 1999 and only parts of the outer walls have survived. The kulla is still owned (and inhabited) by the Zeka family. After its destruction, the family set out to restore it carefully. Unfortunately, it is not open to visitors. A real jewel of an 18th-century Ottoman *konak*, Haxhi Zeka's *konak*, just behind the kulla, was also torched and destroyed by Serb forces in 1999. The building was under protection in recognition of its great historical value. You can only peek your nose into the rear garden on Rr Jashar Pasha to see what remained of the *konak*. It's not clear yet if funds will be made available for its restoration.

Haxhi Zeka's biggest claim to fame was the convention of 450 Albanian delegates gathered in Peja in January 1899 to conclude what became known as the League of Peja. The delegates, after declaring their loyalty to the sultan, agreed on a manifesto calling for Albanian-language education and the application of Albanian customary law as codified in the *Kanun*. You can also visit the **Haxhi Zeka Mill complex** (*theoretically* ⏱ *07.00–16.00; in future a charge of up to €1 may be taken, but best booked in advance through the municipal tourist information office or Rugova Experience*) near the main bus station. This 19th-century mill has been restored by the Ministry of Culture and converted into a gallery, book fair and exhibition room.

right & below right Brown bear (*Ursus arctos*), and lynx (*Lynx lynx*) can be glimpsed in the Brezovica/Štrpce area, a national park (MK/FLPA) (KW/MP/FLPA) page 4

below left Sharr dogs, a variety unique to Kosovo, are bred in Dragash, where they are used as sheepdogs (GW) page 222

bottom The Kosovo Protection Force (KFOR) was widely rumoured to have been breeding eagles (*Aquila chrysaetos*) and releasing them into the wild (ML/FLPA) page 4

above left Time has stood still in Janjevo, an evocative yet largely abandoned town that is still home to a small Croatian community (GW) page 142

above right Gjakova's 16th-century market still sells traditional goods such as in this saddlery shop (GW) page 186

below The League of Prizren was a famous movement in 1878 to form a wider Albanian state. The movement's original headquarters in Prizren contains a mosque and museum (FBP/DT) page 208

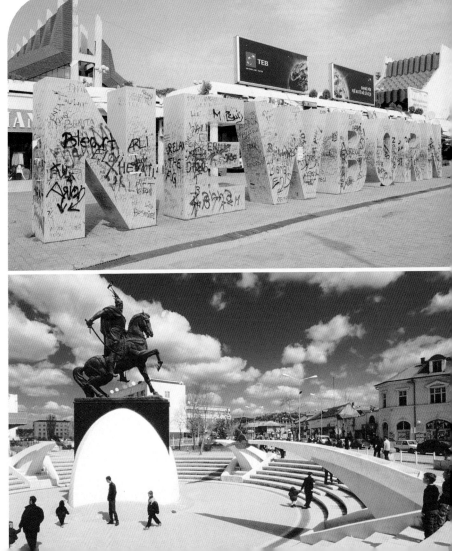

above left Gjakova's Çarshia, a 16th-century market, has recently been restored and continues to offer traditional wares to visitors today (GW) page 189

left Gjakova's Hadum Mosque is a uniquely well-preserved example of Balkan artistry, with an ornate ceiling and wall paintings that hint at local scenes (GW) page 191

below left Prizren has several *tekkes*, including one belonging to the Ra'afi sect (FBP/DT) page 214

below right The Visoki Dečani Monastery's frescoed walls are like a picture Bible, with over 1,000 scenes and figures, and this family tree of the Serbian Nemanjić dynasty (ISA) page 175

above Ura e Fshejt, an Ottoman bridge outside Gjakova, is now the scene of an annual jumping competition (SKS) page 194

above right The Serbian Orthodox Sokolica Monastery is still active today, and the nuns run their own icon-painting school (VK) page 276

right The Church of St Stephen in Velika Hoča is one of five churches remaining in this Serbian village known for its ancient wine- and *raki*-making traditions (GW) page 226

below The Sokolica home of the famous activist and local hero Isa Boletin has recently been restored (AR) page 276

above   **The proud owner of Kukleci Kulla, Isniq** (GW) page 181

below left   **This little boy is dressed up in traditional costume for his *synet* and circumcision ceremony, usually the subject of a big family party** (GW)

below right   **Girls outside a school in Obiliq, central Kosovo** (GW) page 74

right — A Kosovar family celebrating the birth of their child (MC)

below — The *tupan* (drums) and *zurle* (woodwind) musicians at weddings are often members of the Roma community (MO) page 182

bottom — Bosniak women in Gornje Selo (GW) page 231

top images   Kosovo's *raki*-drinking culture is deeply entrenched; the clear, often home-brewed, spirit is sipped at all times of the day (SS). This bottle (GW) is from the Serbian village Velika Hoča, where it has been brewed for centuries and they specialise in inserting wood sculptures into bottles page 64

middle   Peppers — green, red and yellow — are ubiquitous in Kosovo (ISA). They form the base for homemade *ajvar* (MO), a pepper dip traditionally made in autumn page 62

bottom left   *Flija*, a typical Albanian pie made of pancake layers, is cooked over an open fire (A/FL) page 63

bottom right   Macchiato espresso is the drink of choice in Kosovo's towns (VK) page 64

Continuing along Rr Lidhja e Pejes, you arrive at the **Haxhi Beut Hammam** (*Lidhja e Pejës 121*) and the **Haxhi Beut Mosque**, the private endowment of Haxhi Bey. This former Turkish bath has recently been restored with Italian money and converted into an exhibition hall. The precise date of the construction of the *hammam* is not known, but according to an inscription it was reconstructed in 1861. The mosque was heavily damaged and has been restored after the war. Again for access pre-book through Rugova Experience or the municipality. If you turn left after the *hammam*, you pass the old **Albanian-language primary school** on your right. The building was restored in 1999 with funds from the UN Refugee Council and friends of the singer Pavarotti. Take a first left again onto Rr Gazmend Zajmi, and keep a lookout for 'number' 120. Tucked away, there is another beautiful example of an old Ottoman town house, with a richly decorated wooden veranda. On your right, you pass a half-demolished kulla.

Turn right into Rr Jashar Pasha and head straight to **Bajrakli Mosque**, also known as the Çarshia or Market Mosque. The precise date of its construction is not known, but it is believed to have been built in the second half of the 15th century, at the time when Peja was the centre of the Peja sançak (an Ottoman military district). That was also the time when Peja enjoyed its unrivalled role as an important regional trading outpost for Dubrovnik. It is called the mosque 'with the banner' (in Turkish *bajrakli*), because by flying a banner on its brick-layered minaret it determines the time when the other mosques begin their prayers. Thanks to restoration work done by the Italian Intersos Foundation, in 2002, the mosque has preserved its charm. In the surrounding cemetery you can see several beautifully decorated tombstones with floral ornaments and depictions of weapons and other insignia. Some of the tombstones are in the shape of traditional headgear, including turbans, fezzes and the religious hats worn by those who had been on the Hajj (pilgrimage) in Mecca. The two fountains are for Muslim believers for the ritual ablution (the washing of the hands, ears and feet) before praying. Look out for the fountain with symbols of the moon and stars. The mosque's interior is spacious and delicately decorated in blue and golden colours. The ceiling is covered in a floral design.

Peja has always been an important **market** town for the Dukagjini region and the bazaar was at its heart. Once a week, on market days, farmers, shoppers and traders would stream towards the main square around Bajrakli Mosque to sell and haggle their wares as best as they could. Market days were always colourful events. Men dressed in traditional costumes would be selling hand-woven cloths, vegetables, honey, cheese and livestock. Albanian women, dressed in brightly coloured trousers, would be selling hand-knitted stockings, woollen costumes and rugs. Traditional costumes are rarely seen nowadays, except for the occasional man wearing a *plisi* (the traditional Albanian skullcap). The tradition of Peja as a market town, however, continues to this day.

To get a feel for the great loss that has been brought on the Old Town by the near-total destruction of Peja during the 1999 war, you only need to turn into the **Çarshia e Gjatë** – what used to be the main street of the old bazaar. In the past, both sides of the street were lined with traditional houses, small jewellery ateliers and little shops. Much of the hard cash earned abroad by Albanians working in Switzerland or Germany found its way here to pay for expensive gold jewellery for prospective brides. During the 1990s, this street was also nicknamed 'Rr Devisa' for the concentration of moneychangers who would trade in deutschmarks and dinars. Throughout the 1990s, Albanians were using the deutschmark despite the dinar being the official currency. Changing money in those days was a risky but profitable business. In 1999, the entire street was set on fire by Serbian troops and whatever was left in the shops was stolen. In the post-war hurry, cheap new buildings and a new shopping centre replaced the old ateliers. There are still some

Peja in particular, and Kosovo in general, is one of the few places in the world where streets are named after political figures while they are still alive. The choice of names reflects Peja's most recent history. Rr Tony Blair has been named in memory of Tony Blair's efforts to align European and NATO allies behind the decision to bomb Serbia. William Walker, a veteran US diplomat, was the first witness of the Raçak massacre in January 1999 in his function as head of the OSCE-led Kosovo Verification Mission. This mission was set up to guard the ceasefire between Milošević's troops and the Kosovo Liberation Army. On 16 January, Walker publicly denounced the killing of 45 villagers in western Kosovo as a massacre and blamed the Serb security forces. He was immediately declared *persona non grata* by Milošević. His personal account of the Raçak massacre sent shockwaves around the West and paved the way for the Rambouillet talks where Serb and Albanian leaders failed to come to a peace agreement. The Kosovo Verification Mission under Walker was evacuated from Kosovo on 19 March 1999, only a few days before the NATO bombing campaign. Peja also has a NATO Street and one named after the former US secretary of state, Madeleine Albright. Eliot Engel not only has a street named in his honour; there is also an oversized poster with his face on the Mëtë Bajraktari shopping centre (which is also owned by a US Albanian). A Democrat from New York, Engel has been a strong advocate of the Kosovo Albanians' right to self-determination. In the American House of Representatives he is a member of the International Relations Committee and co-chairs the Albanian Issues Caucus.

traditional jewellery shops, but more and more shops revert to selling cheap imports from China. The smell and sound of generators during an electricity outage can make this narrow alley rather unpleasant.

Find your way through the maze of little streets in the bazaar area to get back to Rr Mbreteresha Teuta. Just as you turn left into Rr General Wesley Clark, keep your eyes open; there are two outstandingly beautiful kullas on the right-hand side. You can opt for a quieter walk along Rr Enver Hadri, and by taking the first left you will pass a few more faithfully restored kullas on your way, including the **Kulla e Gockajve** (*Enver Hadri 75;* ❯ *039 34 147; accessible only via a pre-organised tour through the Institute for the Protection of Monuments or Rugova Experience* – see page 167), today housing the Institute for the Protection of Monuments. If you are tired, follow the steps from Rr Enver Hadri to the main square, and stop for a drink or a coffee in any of the cafés. On your left, at the lower end of the square, you will see two of Peja's most prestigious hotels – the former Hotel Metohija, recently reopened as the **Hotel Dukagjini**, and the run-down pink façade of the old **Hotel Korzo** (closed today and the subject of a court dispute, but likely to become commercial premises). Once refreshed, it's best to continue your stroll towards the Bistrica River, taking a right turn on Rr Lekë Dukagjini. Turn right into Rr William Walker, and another impressive kulla can be seen on the left-hand side. Turn left into Rr General Wesley Clark and keep a lookout for three well-preserved Ottoman town houses, set back a little from the road, across the street from the offices of Rugova Experience. Nearby, on Rr Bajram Curri, you can visit Peja's oldest mosque, **Defterdari Xhami**, dating back to 1570. It was also used as a mausoleum for Muhamed Efendi who died in 1624. At your leisure, you can continue your walk along Rr Nënë Terezë, past the Catholic church dedicated to Saint Catherine (Shen Katarina), towards the Patriarchate.

THE PEĆ PATRIARCHATE

HISTORY The Patriarchate is located in an impressive natural habitat, where the Bistrica River comes out of the Rugova Gorge into the fertile plain of Dukagjini (in Serbian, Metohija). Peć (Peja) is seen as the spiritual seat of the Serbian nation and the mausoleum of the Serbian archbishops and patriarchs. In the early Nemanjić period, the seat of Serbian monasticism was in the area around Rasčia north of present-day Kosovo, and the seat of the archbishop was in Ziča Monastery. The decision to relocate the seat to Peć (Peja) was taken after a devastating attack on Ziča by marauding Tatar and Cuman forces in about 1290. The narrow Rugova Gorge offered natural protection and seemed a safer place.

The first church dedicated to the Apostles was built at the beginning of the 13th century by Archbishop Arsenije and was intended as burial place for the Serbian archbishop. In 1346, at the peak of the reign of King Dušan, the Serbian archbishop was raised to the rank of patriarch, hereby cutting all ties with Constantinople. From now on, the Serbian Orthodox Church was fully independent (autocephalous). In turn, Dušan let himself be crowned by the new patriarch and proclaimed first Serbian emperor (tsar).

At the time of the Ottoman conquest of the region, the ecclesiastical administration of the Patriarchate moved to inner-Serbia and the Patriarchate was abandoned. Arsenije II, the last-known patriarch, died in 1463. Grand Vizier Mehmet Sokolli, born into an Orthodox family in Herzegovina but raised at the imperial court, re-established the Patriarchate in Peć (Peja) in 1557. The person he appointed as new patriarch was none other than his own brother Makarije, a monk from Mount Athos.

When the Serbian Orthodox Church regained its seat it was awarded religious jurisdiction over 40 episcopates and the bishops of Gračanica, Vushtrri, Prizren and Peja held the high rank of *metropolitan*.

This favourable shift in relations between the Ottoman Empire and the Serbian Orthodox Church was politically motivated. An Orthodox patriarch reliant on the goodwill of the Ottoman rulers was seen by the Ottomans as a useful way of politically controlling the Orthodox subjects. The Catholics on the other hand were seen as the main enemies of the sultan.

Relations took a downturn when the patriarch, loyal to the pope, 'sided with' the Austrians during their short-lived conquest of Kosovo. When the Austrian troops were defeated and the Ottomans returned in 1690, Patriarch Arsenije fled to Serbia. In the patriarch's absence the monastery was sacked by plundering Tatar troops. The treasury of the Patriarchate had been hidden in Gračanica, but upon its discovery by the Ottomans, it was plundered there in 1688. According to legend, the treasure was so great that nine horses were required to carry it away. The Greek Orthodox Church lobbied the sultan to refuse Arsenije permission to return and seized this chance to appoint their own, subordinate patriarch. For a brief period lasting from 1691 to 1706 there were suddenly two patriarchs: Arsenije, who had fled to Serbia and Kalinik, a second patriarch appointed by a subordinate to the Greek Orthodox Church. The Istanbul-based Greek Patriarchate saw the Serbian dioceses as a source of income to be squeezed. A period of decline and instability gradually slowed down all artistic activity in the Patriarchate and the buildings fell into general disrepair. In 1766, at the order of the sultan, the Patriarchate was officially closed down.

During the 19th century, a new watermill, a representative guesthouse and new stone walls were added to the complex. After 1912, the Serbian patriarchs were once again crowned in Peja. The years 1931–32 saw major restoration work. The latest addition, a new guesthouse, was built in 1981.

5

GETTING THERE You can easily reach the Patriarchate on foot from Peja city centre. It is about a half-hour walk from the main **bus** station. The easiest and fastest way to get to the Patriarchate, however, is to flag down a taxi on the street or call a radio taxi (see *Other practicalities*, page 169). There are **taxi** stands on the main square and on Rr Eliot Engel. It takes about 15 minutes from the city centre, depending on traffic, and costs less than €4 one-way – they should use the meter. Agree on a pick-up time with your taxi driver for the return or call them out. If you are coming by car from Prishtina, take a left turn at the first roundabout (Rr Bill Clinton), and turn left again at the second roundabout (Rr Mbreteresha Teuta). When the road forks after about 200m, turn right and continue on Rr General Wesley Clark until the Italian KFOR checkpoint at the entrance of the Rugova Gorge (right after the Peja Hospital).

The nuns are extremely picky about who they let in. You must show a picture ID card at the Italian checkpoint and hope that the nuns like the look of you. For the past few years, the nuns have refused entry to anyone with an Albanian-sounding name. This can be extremely frustrating if you are travelling with a Kosovar Albanian friend, and surely does not help to improve relations between the communities.

WHAT TO SEE AND DO The monastic complex is surrounded by high stone walls protecting it from sight and against the elevated road leading into the Rugova Gorge. Set in this beautiful mountain scenery, with the sound of the Bistrica River in the background, it is easy to imagine why Serbian archbishops and patriarchs wanted to have their final resting place here. Only the occasional rumbling of a car winding up the Rugova road disturbs the peaceful atmosphere. There is parking just outside the monastic complex. The entrance is through a tall gate: to your left are the monastic living quarters and to the right you see the three-chapel construction of the Patriarchate.

The Patriarchate owes its present appearance to construction works in the 14th century. The ensemble consists of three large churches linked via a common narthex and a chapel. The oldest one, the Church of the Holy Apostles, was built in the third decade of the 13th century by St Sava, the first Serbian archbishop. In the period 1321–24, Archbishop Nikodim added the Church of St Demetrius to the north side of the Holy Apostles Church. His successor, Archbishop Danilo II, added the Holy Virgin Hodegetria Church and the Chapel of St Nicholas along the south side of the Church of the Holy Apostles. The fresco paintings were created from the middle of the 13th century through to the last decade of the 17th century.

The original narthex added by Archbishop Danilo II was a light and elegant structure, but repair works in the 16th century have turned it into a rather heavy edifice. You can access all three churches from the outer narthex. In the narthex, only a few 14th-century frescoes survived including a depiction of the Nemanjić family tree immediately on your right as you enter. Among the other frescoes you can recognise a depiction of the *Last Judgement* and the Church calendar, with one painting for every day of the year. Most other frescoes date back to the period when the Patriarchate was restored in the 1560s with Makarije Sokolovic as its new head.

At the far end, you enter the St Dimitrius Church through a beautiful stone portal. Several 14th-century frescoes survived here, including depictions of Tsar Dušan and impressively realistic portraits of shepherds in the Nativity of Christ. The church's treasure is also stored in this chapel and includes valuable manuscripts, ecclesiastical vestments and a bell from 1432. The oldest frescoes, dating back to the mid 13th century, are in the cupola and supporting arches of the Church of the Holy Apostles in the centre. Along the walls there are 14th-century portraits of Nemanjić rulers. The graves belong to three archbishops who are buried here. Some of the paintings in the Church of the Holy Apostles in the Patriarchate were donated in 1633 by a Christian knight who served in the sultan's army.

A portrait of Archbishop Danilo II, with a model of the monastery in his hands, can be found in the Church of the Holy Virgin Hodegetria. Danilo II's tomb is also located here. Some of the most beautiful 14th-century frescoes are preserved here, including a total of 23 frescoes portraying members of the Nemanjić family. The smaller St Nicholas Church is locked most of the time, but if you are lucky, you will be able to see some 17th-century paintings with scenes from the life of St Nicholas.

OUTSIDE PEJA

THE SOURCE OF THE DRINI I BARDHË (WATERFALLS) The waterfalls are about a 10km drive out of Peja on the road to Montenegro. Follow the signs to Rožaje/Montenegro and about 5km after the village of Novo Sello in the village of Radac you come to a restaurant called Shpella e Bobit and then a second restaurant called Te Arrat with a wooden fence. The path to the falls is off to the left almost directly opposite the turning for Te Arrat. There is no official sign, just sometimes a white notice with 'Drini' written in black pen. This is the name of the river. The falls are a further 2km up the road.

If you do not have your own car you can take one of the fairly infrequent **buses** to Rožaje (the night buses to Ulqin will want the whole fare) or take a **taxi** for about €10.

The falls are quite spectacular – there are three major falls plus a small one. You can walk along the yellow metal fence alongside the irrigation channel for about 3km past the walnut trees in the fields, however the road eventually peters out and you have to retrace your steps.

Where to eat

✕ **Te Arrat ('Walnut') Restaurant** ⋔ 044 150 069/207 813; ⏱ Jun–Oct 24hrs; otherwise 08.00–24.00. In this tastefully decorated wood cabin with clean toilets you can have fresh trout from their troughs outside with rice & vegetables for just €4 or very reasonably priced tasty meat dishes & warm traditional-style Turkish bread. Service is excellent.

This incidentally is the last major restaurant before Rožaje in Montenegro (or rather the last restaurant for nearly 20–30km) – there is a small stone restaurant halfway up the hairpins which serves good chicken! In summer Te Arrat also has an outdoor kebab or meat grill hut for passers-by including the buses on their way to Montenegro.

GORAŽDEVAC Goraždevac village lies to the southeast of Peja, accessible on a bad road turning off the main Peja–Deçan route.

Tucked away in Goraždevac village, one of the few Serbian villages in Peja region, is **St Jeremiah Church**. This is possibly the oldest log-cabin church in Kosovo. According to local legend, it was built in 1737 by the Srbljaci – one of the oldest Serb tribes in this area. The church is built entirely of wood and stone, without any nails. The log walls consist of simple planks and large slabs of stone cover the low roof. The church has not been used since 1936. The last detailed restoration and conservation works were done in 1968. If you want a full tour and a Serbian lunch then contact Rugova Experience (see page 167).

BANJA E PEJËS This small resort village is located about 16km from Peja along the main road to Mitrovica. On your way you pass through several Bosnian villages and then through Vitomiricë village, a village founded by Serb and Montenegrin settlers who were encouraged to move here in the 1920s as part of a large-scale colonisation programme (see *Chapter 1, History*, page 6). At the sign turn left (there is a petrol station at the turn-off) and bend slightly left up the hill towards Banja e Pejës. It's set in a nice and shady forest. Although under communism, when most of the baths and hotels were built, Banja e Pejës was Kosovo's most elegant spa resort, at the time of writing it was a forlorn place lacking investment. This may change soon, now that the spa had been tendered in privatisation. For now, the public spa was still open to visitors for a €2 entrance fee covering hot pools, saunas, massages and swimming pools. It is worth calling ahead to check as there may well be much-needed refurbishment underway.

A better reason to come here is the Hotel Kosova Park (see below), recently opened and set on a hilltop offering an amazing view of the entire Dukagjini Valley. What makes this place special is the creative table arrangement in the forest. Tables are literally built around trees, with little stone paths for the waiters to bring new servings of *flija* baked in the open fire or grilled lamb. It's really a great place for a warm summer evening to chill out and taste your way through the region's specialities.

Where to stay

Hotel Restaurant Kosova Park (20 rooms, 8 villas) m 044 640 008–10; e info@hotelkosovapark.com; www.hotelkosovapark.com. Coming from Peja, turn left at the sign before entering Banja e Pejës; the road first passes a couple of houses before it bends right & slightly uphill to the restaurant. There is parking in front. Thanks to its romantic location, the hotel is also a favourite getaway for couples. The rooms are fully furnished with baths, TV & DVD players. Note that not all rooms have AC. Some Wi-Fi available in the main reception, but it may not function in the cabins. You may want to try one of the log cabins with slightly zany bathrooms (with jacuzzi showers & saunas). At the weekends the staff wear traditional costumes. $

INTO MONTENEGRO Contrary to what your Yugoslav-era map (or even some of the GPS software or online Michelin or similar route maps) might tell you, it is not possible to legally enter Montenegro through the top of the Rugova Gorge. This pre-1999 crossing has been closed, meaning a 250km round trip for Albanians who wish to visit their relatives in Plav on the other side of the border. For this reason there is much talk of reopening the border, although others are concerned about the environmental impact, not least on the monastery site. Unofficially and illegally pedestrians, horses and mountain bikers could still physically cross the border.

There is only one **official crossing** from Kosovo directly into Montenegro (over the high pass into Rožaje). Note this road is extremely dangerous in winter. Lorries still try and use it and jacknife across the road. The road is narrow, so you cannot then pass them in many places, even in a 4×4. Therefore, whenever there is snow you should avoid this border crossing into Montenegro and get a Serbian stamp and enter Montenegro via Serbia and Zubin Potok (see *Practical Information* page 45 for important notes on driving into Serbia and Serbian immigration issues for visitors from Kosovo). You will also need appropriate insurance for Montenegro, which can be bought at the border – approximately €15 for two weeks, and to pay an environmental tax of about €10 (you receive a sticker for your car and a receipt – the payment is valid for a year).

In the summer up to ten **buses** a day (in fact mostly at night to avoid the heat of the day) head from Kosovo through Rožaje down to the Albanian-Montenegrin resort of Ulqin. It can therefore pay to cross the border before 19.00 as between 20.00 and 23.00 it can be extremely busy.

If you are heading for Montenegro by **car** (via the Rožaje crossing) you do not need to go into Peja at all. In fact you can take a right turn about 4km before you get to Peja, following signs for Rožaje and the ring road. In case you missed the turn for Montenegro, continue straight along the main road, turning right at two consecutive roundabouts. This road eventually joins up with the ring road again at a third roundabout further out of town. After a 10km steady climb, the road up to the Montenegrin border consists of 8km of amazing switchbacks and when you finally arrive at the customs point you have stunning views across Kosovo. From the Kosovan border it is a further 10km of uphill climbing through no-man's-land before you get to the Montenegrin wooden cabin isolated border post and a further 10km down to Rožaje Town. For more information on Rožaje and Montenegro see the Bradt guide to Montenegro.

Who this 10km of **no-man's-land** stunning pine wood and alpine meadow scenery belongs to (Kosovo or Montenegro) is not yet clear as the two borders are still not finalised in detail. If you do stop for the views, do not stray much off the beaten path as the area (perhaps deliberately to deter smugglers) has not been cleared of land mines. It is not known exactly how much altitude you gain on this journey, but probably at least 1,500m. Biking the other way back down from the Montenegrin border post down to the Te Arrat Restaurant (see page 163) is 45 minutes to one hour's solid pure downhill adrenalin and you can easily reach speeds of 50–60km/h.

ISTOG (BURIM)/ISTOK
Istog is about 20km east of Peja. The Mokra Mountains rising up high just behind Istog Town offer a beautiful backdrop (you can walk up to the river sources or springs), but there is not much to see in Istog itself. There are really only two things Istog is famous for: Ibrahim Rugova and the Trofta fish farm. Rugova spent his early childhood years in Cerrce village, just outside Istog. For more on Rugova's life see box in *Chapter 3, Prishtina*, pages 128–9. Istog was largely destroyed during the war and much of the Serbian population has left. Rugova's village of Cerrce, for example, was 90% destroyed. The Mokra Mountains, which in the past were used as summer pastures for cattle and sheep for the whole Istog–Klina area, are heavily mined and no longer accessible. In Istog Town, the scars of the war are still visible. New high-rise apartment blocks and café bars sit uncomfortably beside destroyed and burnt out buildings.

There was once a Roman settlement along the Istog River, which also gave the town its name. Several churches were built under the Nemanjić dynasty in the area around Istog, including the Gorioc Monastery high above Istog Town and the monastery dedicated to the Virgin Hvostanska in Vrellë village. As a result of destruction and subsequent repair works, few of the original structures have survived. In the later Middle Ages, the area around Istog fell under different Serbian military rulers (*vojvods*). Under the Ottomans, Istog's economy developed slowly thanks to a few watermills. In 1924, Istog Town was declared the centre of the region and in the 1940s, Istog became an administrative centre during the Italian and then German occupation. Industrial development began in Istog with the construction of the Istog hydro-electric plant that brought electricity for the first time in 1948. Even under communism, Istog's industry was agriculture-based. The two flagship industries were the wood and furniture plant Radusha and the Trofta fish farm.

Getting there
To get to Istog there are direct **buses** from Prishtina every hour (except between 12.50 and 14.00) starting at 09.00 with the last at 19.30. There are also regular buses from Peja.

Where to stay and eat

Hotel Trofta (19 rooms) Rr Bajram Gashi;
📞 039 451 015; m 044 405 869/138 603;
e info@trofta.com; www.trofta.com ⊕ 07.00–
23.00 daily. Turn left after the renovated Serbian
Orthodox church in Istog centre as if you are heading
to Peja. The Hotel Trofta is a great place to stop for
high-quality & fresh fish straight from the in-house
fish farm. The Trofta fish farm's reputation stretches
from the socialist era. The new owners have tastefully
renovated the interior & designed a beautiful garden
area built around a little pond & a nice children's
playground in the back. The view of the nearby
mountains is really beautiful & the water & wooden

roofing keep it cool & shady in summer. Surrounded
by freshwater streams & fishponds you can literally
choose your own fish. The real speciality, naturally, is
trout in different variations, & the Trofta fish soup. All
rooms are fully furnished & centrally heated, with
modern baths. 7 rooms are in the main building &
12 rooms are in 6 bungalows around the pond. There
are heaters installed in the bungalows. $$$

✕ **Freskia Restaurant and Pizzeria** m 044 138
580/276 602; ⊕ 08.00-23.00 daily. A nice outdoor
alternative to Hotel Trofta, with equally great views
of the nearby mountains & a large outdoor garden
area.

Other practicalities There is a **ProCredit Bank** (*Rr 2 Korriku;* 📞 *038 502 641;*
⊕ *08.30–16.00 Mon-Fri and 09.00–14.00 Sat).*

What to see and do

Orthodox monuments in Istog municipality North of Istog Town up the hill there is
a small Serbian Orthodox monastery by the name of **Gorioc** whose origins date
back to the 13th century. Its present-day structure was constructed in the 16th and
18th centuries. According to popular belief, St Nicholas had healed the burnt eyes
of Stefan Dečanski, founder of the Visoki Dečani Monastery, on the same spot
where the St Nicholas Church was later built. It is currently guarded by Spanish
KFOR troops.

West of Istog, there are the ruins of an Orthodox monastery and bishopric
dedicated to **Virgin Hvostanksa,** built at the foot of the Mokra Mountains near
the village of Vrellë, on the road from Gjurakovc to Peja. In 1381, the bishopric
was elevated to the rank of a *metropolitan* and the monastery flourished until the
middle of the 17th century. After the Austrian incursion in 1690, the monastery
fell into disrepair. Its ruins were partially excavated in 1930.

Another Orthodox church in **Gjurakovc** village, south of Istog, is also
dedicated to St Nicholas. After the collapse of its original 14th-century structures,
a local villager by the name of Cvetko rebuilt the church in 1592. The church was
partially burnt and is now also guarded by Spanish KFOR troops.

Crkolez village: Church of St John About halfway from Mitrovica to Peja in Istog
municipality, there is a little church up on the hill in Crkolez village. If you are
coming from Skenderaj, take a right turn halfway between Citak and Rakosh
villages. The unpaved road winds uphill for about 3.5km. Bear left as the road forks,
and after passing several destroyed Serbian houses, turn right towards the church.
It is also only a short taxi ride from Istog – the driver should be prepared to drop
you outside the village.

The Church of St John in Crkolez was built in 1355 as an endowment by a
landlord named Radoslav. The church is set beautifully in an old graveyard
overlooking the Albanian-Serb mixed village and the Dukagjini Plain. The real
treasure is the church's extraordinary collection of fresco paintings preserved on
the walls. The original paintings date back to the 14th century, but a new layer of
frescoes was painted by Radul, a famous Serbian painter, in 1672. The depiction of
the *Last Judgement* is particularly interesting for the representation of different social
ranks among the sinners. The floors of the church are covered in old tombstones,
including the tomb of the church's patron Radislav and later monk John. There is

not much lighting in the church, so bring a torch. It is usually locked but you can ask for the key at the first house just below the church. The nuns may bring you some photocopied material about it. Nowadays, the church is maintained and looked after by the villagers.

RUGOVA VALLEY

For nature-lovers and sporty types Peja region is a true paradise. The Rugova Valley is stunningly beautiful in all seasons and provides a wealth of sporting opportunities that are largely unexplored. Peja's tourism industry is in its infancy, but there is enormous potential. In a few years, the Rugova region may well develop into a real magnet for rural and ecotourism. With peaks of the Accursed Mountains (or Bjeshkët e Nemuna) rising up to 2,560m at Marjashi Peak, there is great potential for skiing (see *Bogë*, page 168), hiking, snowshoeing, paragliding, rock climbing and caving.

The Rugova region covers an area of 32,000ha, encompassing 13 villages at different altitudes between 1,000m and 2,000m above sea level. Far out of reach of the towns, these villages had always enjoyed a special tax status during the Ottoman era in return for maintaining the mountain roads. The narrow gorge along the Bistrica River continues for about 12km from the Patriarchate, then the valley opens up into beautiful mountain scenery stretching all the way to Montenegro. There are 30m-high waterfalls and two lakes at about 1,800m above sea level, and numerous, undiscovered caves dotted around the mountains.

For an easy walk, you can park your car at Rugova Camp, 12km into the valley and start out on the road from there. You can cross the river on the little bridge that is reached after 3km, from where a road winds up into the forest. The only people you will encounter on this path are the wood loggers, driving into the forests to chop wood, legally and illegally. Upon your return you can stop for refreshments at Rugova Camp before heading back to Peja.

TOUR OPERATORS

Era Rr Pandeli Sotiri 78a; ☎ 039 423 122, & Fatos; ☏ 044 161 844; e info@era-group.net; www.era-group.net. The Environmentally Responsible Action Group (Era) also organises awareness raising campaigns & environmental action programmes in the region of Peja as well as hikes, including at least one major trip per year – often into Albania or Montenegro.

Municipality Tourist Information For further information, see *Peja*, page 153.

Orta ☎ 039 362 150; e orta-ngo@gmail.com. This NGO works out of Deçan & Junik & in particular with Cultural Heritage Without Borders. They can organise bike tours & day trips including Deçan, Junik & Gjakova, providing substantial information on the historical & cultural side.

Rugova Experience Rr Mbreteresha Teuta (set back from the road near Koha 3 Restaurant); ☎ 039 432 352; ☏ 044 348 831/049 390 589; e rugovatour@hotmail.com, rugovatour@yahoo.com; www.rugovaexperience.com.

Created by the initiative of an Italian organisation called the Trentino Kosovo Roundtable, Rugova Experience is dedicated wholeheartedly to the promotion & development of ecotourism in the Peja region. As such, it is truly unique in Kosovo. It specialises in organising tailor-made hiking, trekking, climbing & camping tours in summer & winter with groups from 6 to 12 people. For approximately €15 a head you can join a guided trek in the Rugova Valley with a professional mountain guide & picnic lunch, adventure biking tours or, in winter, a day trek on snowshoes (including snowshoe hire) for anything from €20 upwards. A good option to organise any tailor-made tour of Peja & also any trips to the surrounding area, including Rugova, Gorazdevac, Deçan or Junik. Rugova Experience also offers trips to beekeepers & Serbian villages. Syzana Baja & her team arrange transport to the point of departure. Syzana is extremely helpful & will provide you with leaflets & information sheets on all their activities. Enquire by phone or email well in advance.

WHERE TO STAY AND EAT The road winding up along the Bistrica River into the Rugova Gorge has always been a popular place for family weekend luncheons or romantic dinners for two. There are a couple of options to reward yourself after a day of hiking with some fresh fish or a meat grill.

🏠 **Guri i Kuq** (6 houses which can house up to 10 people) Selim Dreshaj; m 044 150 551. High up in the Rugova Valley but accessible by car in summer & by 4x4 in winter, provided conditions are not too bad. Great summer or weekend getaways up in the fresh air amongst beautiful nature. From the houses you can do a small hike up to the lakes at 1,800m, a round trip of 1hr 45mins. $$$

🏠 **Motel Restaurant Gryka** (7 rooms) m 044 148 348. Modern rooms, simply furnished with double beds, baths & TV. A good alternative if you want to base yourself in the Rugova Valley but still want some modern comfort. Also good fish restaurant with own trout ponds & lamb speciality. $$

🏠 **Rugova Camp** (7 bungalows) m 044 281 608/248 270; e info@rugovacamp.com; www.rugovacamp.com. Situated about 13km into the Rugova Valley. The restaurant has a pleasant outdoor area, a large children's playground & basketball fields. You can also rent one of the block hut-style bungalows. Each bungalow has 2 rooms, sharing 1 bath. They are particularly popular with young couples. If you plan to stay longer ask for a discount. $$

✕ **Bjeshka Restaurant** After 12km on the right, Shtupeq i Madh village; m 044 291 394; ⏰ 08.00–23.00

✕ **Pizzeria Guri i Kuqi** After 2km on the left. If you are time-pressed or on foot, it's your first stop in Rugova Valley.

ACTIVITIES There is a local **Shoqata Gjeravica** (Gjeravica Asociation), named after Kosovo's highest peak. The main person is Sali Maloku (m +381 64 478 7016), a passionate mountain hiker. If you speak Albanian or Serbian, see if you can join this group on one of their hikes.

The stunning Rugova Gorge also has a number of well-hidden **caves** that are just waiting to be explored. A group of friends has founded Kosovo's first – and so far only – caving association, **Aragonit Speleo Association**, which is based in Peja. The association runs various projects exploring caves in Kosovo and other extreme sports. For more information and details of their next trip check out their website at www.aragonit-speleo.org, or contact Mentor Bojku (m 044 508 637; e mentorbojku@yahoo.com), or Fatos Katallozi, who currently lives in the UK (m + 44 780 194 7007; e fatoskatallozi@yahoo.co.uk, fatos64@gmail.com).

Vyryt Morina (m 044 217 741) of the **Marimanga Climbing Association** arranges climbing in the Rugova Valley.

Visit to the Rugova water factory (m 044 545 154) Rugova water has become the best-selling mineral water in Kosovo – partly because it is not bottled close to any major settlement and also because it is managed well by Slovenians. You can tour their factory (a visit can also be arranged through Rugova Experience) (see page 167).

Visit to the Drelaj Mill (m 044 142 810) Drelaj village is a short hike from Bogë. Ask the hotel owners or arrange a trip with Rugova Experience (see page 167).

BOGË In the past few years a couple of great places have opened up, largely designed for domestic tourists in the Rugova Valley. For Kosovars facing difficulties with obtaining a visa to travel abroad, this has become an attractive alternative holiday destination. In summer, Rugova is great for hiking and biking; in winter, thanks to recent investment in a ski lift in Bogë, there is now also skiing. Some of the hotels are really cosy, with open fireplaces and cute kitchenettes. If you ever feel like a weekend away with a group of friends, book one of the four–six-person huts right on the slopes in Bogë. You only need to bring yourself – there is ski and bike rental available and a range of restaurants and cafés should you need to warm up.

Getting there To get to Bogë, you must continue for about 28km into the valley (starting from Peja), and turn right at the junction. It's signposted and hard to miss. Turn left to Qokorr (and the summer resort of Guri i Kuq) and right to Bogë. Bogë is 6km away and these last 6km are without asphalt so it's best to be in a 4×4 on the gravel stones, but you can also make it up to Bogë in a normal car, provided there is no ice on the road. The road is more or less maintained in winter, but can be quite messy on weekends, when half of Peja tries to get up on summer tyres. It's best to come early and to leave before everyone else is trying to get down again.

All the hotels up in Bogë can arrange a pick-up from Peja if you don't have transport. Minibuses also drive up and down between Peja and Bogë. It takes about 45 minutes to get there from the beginning of the Rugova Gorge, depending on your driver.

There are plenty of choices for accommodation. At weekends, if there is lots of snow, Bogë can get booked up, but generally you can expect to find something when you arrive.

Where to stay

🏠 **Alpin Resort Rudi** (24 beds in total) m 044/049 127 637, 044/049 125 488; e ylber_rudi@yahoo.com; www.rudigroup.net. Just like its name, Rudi could be anywhere in Austria. The 4 wooden bungalows are designed as self-contained apartments; spread over 2 floors, with 6 beds each, plus a kitchenette, living room & open fireplace. They are really cosy, & great for groups of friends or families for a fun weekend. The owner himself is a keen mountaineer, skier & biker, and will happily arrange special tours for you in summer & winter. $

🏠 **Motel Berati** (11 rooms) m 044 151 565; www.pushimorijaberat.com. All rooms have hot water, electric & gas heating. The friendly Mehmet Mekaj also runs a fruit- & mushroom-gathering co-operative in the Bogë region, so this is a good place to stay if you want to find out about the local flora or to visit and buy some fruits to take back to Prishtina. $

🏠 **Motel Burri** (13 rooms) m 044 420 638/653 601. Motel Burri is walking distance from the slope, just across on the hill opposite. There is an outdoor terrace for sun-admirers & a plentiful *à la carte* menu. Rooms are simple, with double & bunk beds; 2 rooms share 1 communal bath with a shower. $

🏠 **Motel Dardani Ski** (21 beds in total) m 044 275 489. Right on the slopes. You literally fall onto the snow as you exit from Dardani's ground-floor restaurant. Dardani can house 11 people in total. Similar to Motel Burri, rooms are ski-hut-style, with bunk beds & shared baths. A real bargain for a day of skiing! $

🏠 **Motel Gurra** (8 rooms) m 044 278 035. All rooms with heating & hot water. Price includes b/fast & evening meal as there is also a restaurant. $

🏠 **Vila Kodra** (4 villas) m 044 695 488. Villas each sleep 5, with 2 bedrooms each, bathroom & wood heater. $

Private houses for rent Three houses are available, offered by their two owners (✆ *039 31 071;* m *044 139 419/722 996/283 072*); one is on the left (27km from Peja), before you get to Bogë. It's a bit far to walk to the slope, but if you have your own car it is a good alternative if everything else is booked up.

Other practicalities Mobile-phone reception is patchy in the valley, although improving, so don't rely on arranging your accommodation en route. Bogë is not a big place and you are bound to bump into your friends, but it's better to arrange a meeting point and not to rely on 'we'll call when we get there'.

A day-pass for the **ski lift** (🕐 *09.00–16.00*) costs €10. The length of the piste is 1km, and you can choose from three possible routes. In Europe it would be categorised as a 'blue' piste, suitable for beginners but not particularly challenging for good skiers. The bottom part of the slope is lit up at night, so night-time bob sliding is always an option. The lift runs on a generator, so it's independent of the electricity outages at the power plant in Prishtina. If you want to call ahead to check the conditions of the slope, call the lift operator, Bujar Kelmendi (m *044 198 602*), who speaks Albanian and German.

The ski lift also has a small ski-rental business attached. You can get carving skis and boots for €8 a day or older models for €5.

Skiing tuition and rental

Alpin Resort Rudi Also runs a ski rental, where you can get a full set of skis & boots for €7 or a mountain bike for €5, & a ski school. Individual lessons cost €5 per hr, group lessons €4.
Kollqaku m 049 181 8108/522 984. Individual ski instructor. Charges similar to those above.
Skischool Dardani In the same building as the Motel Dardani, you can book a ski instructor for groups from 1 to 5 people. The hourly rate per person for groups with fewer than 5 people is €5, for larger groups €4. A whole day, including 4hrs of ski instruction, is €10. There is a range of skis, snowboards & boots to choose from, both older & newer models. The daily rate for ski rental is €5, for guests of the house or rentals for 1 it's €3 per day. In summer, you can rent mountain bikes for €5 a day.

KLINË/KLINA

Klina municipality, home to about 55,000 people, lies exactly on the fault line between the Dukagjini and the Drenica valleys. It stretches over an area of 308km² of fertile agricultural land. Six rivers wind their way through the municipality, among them the Klina River which lends its name to the municipality. The White Drin, one of Kosovo's most important rivers, cuts through the municipality from north to south before continuing its journey towards Prizren. A third river, the Mirusha, created the area's biggest natural tourist attraction: the Mirusha Waterfalls.

HISTORY The name 'Klina' derives from an ancient Illyrian settlement named Chinna. This name appears for the first time on a map by Ptolomeus dating back to 150–87BC. The ancient Illyrian settlement extended from the left bank of the upper flow of the White Drin (Drini i Bardhë). In the 1st century BC, the territory of Klina and the entire Dardania province came under the rule of the Roman Empire. Various historical records mention a municipal settlement by the name of Dersnik, populated by the Dardan tribe, close to modern-day Klina Town. Profirogonitus writes about Dersnik in AD950, and describes it as a densely inhabited town. Today, Dersnik is just a small village and Klina Town little more than a messy urban agglomeration designed under communism to service the surrounding villages.

For the past half century, Kosovo Albanians formed the majority, but there has always been a sizable resident Serb, Roma and Ashkali minority. Prior to the war, Serbs made up about 10% of Klina's population; most left in 1999 and only few have returned since. The region was heavily affected by fighting, especially the eastern part bordering the Drenica region. There are still many people missing as a result of the war from all communities.

Klina also has a large Catholic Albanian community – the largest in percentage terms in Kosovo – with Catholic churches in Zllakuqan, Budisalc and Doberdoll. That is why Klina is sometimes nicknamed 'little Rome'. Permission to build a new Catholic church in Klina Town was refused by the Serb authorities and was only granted after the war. The tall new church on the outskirts of Klina Town visible from afar was built in 2003. There is also a functioning Serbian Orthodox church in Budisalc village, northwest of Klina, with three resident nuns. Throughout the centuries, Klina's inhabitants engaged in agriculture. The first communist investment was made in the bauxite mine in Volljak, but this was only short-lived and Klina's economy is almost entirely dependent on agriculture.

Klina Town itself is unspectacular. It's a hotch-potch of communist apartment blocks, new high-rise houses built in the past few years, wholesale shops, cafés and barbers. There is an old, unused Turkish bridge as you enter the town on your left. The road from Klina to Peja via Istog is a scenic drive passing through villages and fruit orchards alongside the Mokra mountain range. The apples and plums grown are used to make the local *raki* (a very strong spirit). Klina also has the second-largest lignite deposit in Kosovo, as yet unexplored.

GETTING THERE Klina is 70km from Prishtina, about 1½ hours by car. Follow the signs for Klina on the main road to Peja and turn right at the Klina Bridge. The road takes you straight to the centre of town. If you want to continue your journey towards Istog, bear left at the main roundabout in the centre of Klina.

The easiest way to Klina by bus is to hop on a Peja–bound vehicle and get off at the Klina Bridge. There are usually minibuses waiting for passengers.

WHERE TO STAY AND EAT

🏠 **Motel Nora** (30 rooms) ☎ 039 470 555; m 049 470 555; e info@norahotel.com; www.norahotel.com. The main place to stay in the area, this is not in Klina itself but on the main road between Peja & Prishtina. It is a smart modern hotel (a privatisation success story) with a good restaurant & excellent service. Heating, AC, internet included. Conference rooms for 35–50 people. $$$

🏠 **Motel Restaurant Pisha** Left-hand side along the main road from Klina to Budisalc; newly opened restaurant along the Drini River with a nice outdoor garden & a playground for children.

✗ **Residenca Restaurant and Pizzeria** Right-hand side along the main road from Klina to Budisalc; m 044 607 430/049 222 837. Popular local restaurant, nicely furnished & serving pizza & coffees.

✗ **Café Dollomiti** ETC shopping centre as you enter Klina Town. Popular with local shoppers & youth; serving pizza & ice cream.

✗ **Restaurant Astra** Zllakuqan (10mins' drive from Klina Town); m 044 267 728/235 230. Famous for its garlic chicken, Astra has expanded from a 1-table restaurant only a few years back to what it is today & it is particularly popular in summer with visitors to the Europark swimming pool.

Gjurakovc is between Peja/Istog and Klina. There is little to stop off for in the town itself but the hotel below is a feasible option for an overnight stay.

Hotel Parku (22 rooms) Behind the petrol station; m 044 282 068. Located right at the main turn where the roads from Istog, Klina & Peja meet, you cannot miss it. The rooms are simple & clean, with TV, heating, AC in about half the rooms which each have a bathroom. Wi-Fi in reception, but not in rooms. The ground-floor restaurant is also a popular place to drink coffee & is a hangout for students at the nearby secondary school. In summer, you can sit on the little terrace in front. $

OTHER PRACTICALITIES There is a ProCredit Bank (*Rr Abedin Rexha;* ⊕ *0.830-16.00 Mon-Fri and 09.00-14.00 Sat*) and Raiffeisen Bank (*Sheshi Muje Krasniqi;* ☎ *038 222 222 ext 630;* ⊕ *08.30–16.30 Mon–Fri, 10.00–14.00 Sat*) in the centre of Klina, a post office and a few smaller internet cafés catering mostly to local teenagers, all lined up along the main road leading to the main roundabout in the centre.

If you are heading for the Mirusha Waterfalls, be warned – there is no mobile reception in the area around the falls and only limited coverage near the fish restaurants along the Drini River.

MIRUSHA WATERFALLS

The Mirusha Waterfalls are really worth a visit. They are about 45 minutes to an hour's drive from Prishtina. Coming from Prishtina on the road to Peja, as you head downhill from Gilareva, take a left and follow signs for Gjakova for a further 8km or so. For Mirusha Waterfalls, get **a bus** to Gjakova from Prishtina and ask the driver

Azem Bejta and his wife Shota from Galica village were the military leaders of the *kaçak* revolt, a local rebellion against the Serbian occupation of Kosovo after World War I. The name 'kaçak' derives from Turkish and means 'fugitive'. In many respects, the kaçak rebellion was the forerunner of the UÇK (Kosovo Liberation Army). The kaçak's main area of activities, like that of the UÇK, was in the more mountainous regions around Drenica and Deçan. The forests and mountains provided for ideal cover to hide and launch attacks against Serbian forces and police. The rebellion was directed from the Committee for the National Defence of Kosovo, based in Shkodra in modern-day Albania. At the time of the Paris Conferences, when Europe's map was redrawn in the wake of World War I, the leaders of the National Committee tried unsuccessfully to lobby the European powers to reverse Serbia's occupation. The kaçak rebellion's main demands were the recognition of Albanian-language education and self-administration.

Azem Bejta and his wife Shota operated mainly in the area around Klina and Drenica. They closely escaped a major campaign by the Serb authorities to crush the rebellion in the winter of 1920. In the hope of weakening the Kosovo lobby in Albania, Ahmet Zogolli, the later King of Albania and Minister of Interior at the time, co-operated with the Yugoslav authorities to defeat the kaçak rebellion. In 1922, Azem Bejta was tried *in absentia* by Ahmet Zogolli. In 1924, the Yugoslav authorities staged a surprise attack against Azem Bejta's village, Galica. He died from his wounds on 25 July. This left his widow as the last remaining kaçak rebel. She continued the fight until she was also fatally wounded in July 1927 at the age of 32.

to drop you at the Ujvarat e Mirushës Restaurant. From there it's a half-hour walk to the first waterfalls. For bus times see the bus timetable in *Chapter 2*, page 60.

There are two nice fish restaurants along the White Drin River (Guri i Zi and Restaurant Drini, see below) just before you get to the sign for the waterfalls – the sign is in Albanian, 'Ujvarat e Mirushës'. At the petrol station, turn left.

The path to the falls is unmarked but nevertheless is easy to find; in essence you are just following the flow of the Mirusha River. For most of the way you stay close to the river, but after 15–20 minutes the path turns slightly left over an open field, before rejoining the river. The whole walk takes a good half hour. The walk can be muddy so take good shoes, and there is little shade near the falls so bring cream and a hat. There are small stalls selling drinks near the falls. The first waterfall opens into a natural pool, a popular place to cool down and swim on hot days. It can get crowded in the summer and at the end of the day there is usually quite a lot of rubbish around. The water is fresh, but not as cold as you might expect. Surrounded by rocks on three sides, the sun sets rather early here.

You can continue to climb up to the second waterfall and if you like you can jump back down into the first pool. Take care, however, as the stones are very slippery. Good shoes are essential. The third waterfall is altogether trickier. It is very slippery and the overgrowth gets thicker. If you are into rock climbing you can continue your climbs throughout the total 32km length of the Mirusha Canyon. There are more than a dozen waterfalls as you climb up, but it gets tougher at every level and most people give up at the fourth one. There are also some good caves in the vicinity, best visited with specialists.

WHERE TO STAY AND EAT
Motel Restaurant Drini (15 rooms) m 044 150 779/350 829. The motel is on the right-hand side just after you turn off the road to Peja on your way to Mirusha (also the main road to Gjakova). The local

speciality, naturally, is trout, but they also have a whole range of hefty meat dishes & salads. It's a good place in summer with a nice outdoor terrace. Given the mosquitoes on the river, wear long-sleeved clothes & bring some repellent if you are staying on in the evening. The blue neon interior light is a little off-putting. Rooms are clean but rather small, with baths. The restaurant is open every day until midnight. $$

🏠 **Motel Restaurant Guri i Zi** (14 rooms) m 044 138 845. On the junction of the Peja–Gjakova road. Try to get one of the tables right on the riverside. This restaurant, with its large terraces & gardens, is the nicest place to enjoy your trout after a hike to the Mirusha Waterfalls. All rooms have showers & TV. The restaurant is named after a large rock that you will see sticking out on the road. According to a Gjakovar myth you should go & chip something off the large rock & keep it close to your chest to improve your health. $

✗ **Restaurant Ujvarat e Mirushës** m 044 508 336/049 508 336; e ujevaraemirushes@ hotmail.com; ⏰ 07.00–23.00. This is on the other side of the main road to Guri i Zi & Drini, further along the road to Gjakova, just by the turn-off to the Mirusha Waterfalls — coming from the Prishtina turn-off heading towards Gjakova on your left-hand side. It started as a roadside kiosk but as a testament to entrepreneurial success is now a large red-brick building with some additional balconies & terraces added this year, including a ground-floor one right by the river. It's a good place to buy some drinks before you set off on your walk.

✗ **Villa Park Ujvara** m 044/049 307 512; ⏰ 08.00–23.00 daily. This is further along the Mirusha turn-off from the main road (after Restaurant Ujvarat e Mirushës), so is quieter. There is a large outdoor garden lawn including a playground for children. It's also attractive in winter for its cosy wooden interior with fireplaces. The menu includes fish, pizza & local meat dishes.

DEÇAN/DEČANI

HISTORY Deçan is most famous for the Visoki Dečani Monastery set in the forests of the Deçan Canyon. It's really a masterpiece of Orthodox monastic art, a fusion of styles and maybe the most peaceful and impressive monument in Kosovo today. It's a must-see for anyone in Kosovo because no other monument captures the beauty of Kosovo's cultural heritage like this one. Venerated and protected by all communities, Muslim and Christian, it survived centuries of wars and conflict.

Deçan's more recent claim to fame is closely linked to the Haradinaj family. Ramush Haradinaj was the leading commander of the Kosovo Liberation Army in this part of Kosovo. He ditched his uniform for a suit after the war and founded the Alliance for a Future of Kosovo, coming third in the 2004 elections. In 2004, he became prime minister but was forced to abdicate after 100 days in office in order to face charges of war crimes at the International War Crimes Tribunal for Yugoslavia in The Hague. After his acquittal he returned to Kosovo and resumed politics as head of the AAK, the Alliance for the Future of Kosovo, the third-largest political force in the country.

GETTING THERE AND AWAY Deçan is about 80km from Prishtina, or about 1½ hours' drive. To get to Deçan by **bus** you must first take a bus to Peja or Gjakova. They depart every 20–30 minutes from Prishtina, starting at 06.30 until 18.30 (see the bus timetable in *Chapter 2*, page 60). From there you can catch one of the minibuses shuttling between Peja and Gjakova with stops along the way in Isniq, Deçan and Dranoc. Tell the bus driver that you want to stop in Deçan. The bus trip from Peja takes half an hour. The trip from Gjakova about 40 minutes.

The main bus station in Deçan is on the main square on Rr Dëshmorët e Kombit. From there it's a half-hour walk to the Visoki Dečani Monastery or negotiate a taxi.

In the summer months, there are daily buses to Tirana and to Ulqin on the Montenegrin coast operated by Diona Deçan Travel Agency on Rr Dëshmorët e Kombit 112 (see *Other practicalities* below).

WHERE TO STAY

Hotel Eliza (15 rooms) Along the main road from Peja to Deçan about 200m before Isniq village; m 049 639 891; e info@hotel-eliza.com; www.hotel-eliza.com. This hotel, with AC & bath in every room, is conveniently located for trips to Isniq. $$

Hotel Fis (21 rooms) Rr Sali Çeku. Take a turn into a little side street at the Raiffeisen Bank & as you turn you will spot Hotel Fis on your left. All rooms are fully equipped with bathrooms, TV & balconies. On sunny days, you can enjoy your b/fast on the spacious outdoor terrace & in the evening you may be lucky enough to catch a traditional Albanian wedding party. $$

WHERE TO EAT
For a quick bite it's best to stop in one of the cafés on the main square along Rr Dëshmorët e Kombit where the buses drop you off. There are a couple of fast-food places serving the usual staple of pizza, burgers and coffee.

Gryka e Deçanit 1.5km outside Deçan on the main road to the Visoki Dečani Monastery. A good place to stop before or after your visit to the monastery to try the river fish, grilled or fried, or pizza.

Kroni Jerina m 044 652 441; ⊕ until 23.00 Mon–Sat, until 21.00 Sun. In summer this is a good place to eat for its nice outdoor terrace. Pizza costs €2.

Restaurant Iliria Rr Luan Haradinaj; m 044 133 616. Halfway between Deçan centre & Isniq village. A spacious restaurant decently refurbished with a long menu offering anything from pizza to meat courses.

Te Mulliri Caféteria Rr Dëshmorët e Kombit. For a quick coffee or drink you can stop at this café, tucked away behind the Shabanaj Mill, a few steps south from the main square in Deçan.

OTHER PRACTICALITIES
Banks There are Raiffeisen (🕿 038 222 222 ext 620) and ProCredit (🕿 039 61 201) bank branches along Rr Dëshmorët e Kombit operating 24/7 ATMs. The most central one is located on Rr Sali Çeku, just beside the petrol station.

Fitness centre The building may not be particularly inviting, but for all those keen to work out Deçan even offers a fitness and aerobic centre on Rr Sali Çeku, a couple of hundred metres north from the main square on the left-hand side.

Internet There is a small internet café on the left-hand side of Rr Sali Çeku as you are walking north from the main square.

Shopping Like in every other small town in Kosovo, dozens of family-owned grocery stores sell the basic supplies from drinks to bread and toothbrushes. You can stock up for a picnic lunch if you are planning a hike in the Deçan Canyon. If you are looking for a larger store, a new hypermarket has recently opened halfway up Rr Sali Çeku.

Travel agents
Diona Deçan Travel Agency Rr Dëshmorët e Kombit 112; 🕿 039 061 430; m 044 180 180. In the summer season, Diona travel agency & bus company operate a daily coach schedule to Tirana departing at 06.30 & to Ulqin in Montenegro at 20.30. Return tickets cost €30, one-way €20. They can also help you with any other travel planning.

WHAT TO SEE AND DO Most visitors just pass the town on their way to the Visoki Dečani Monastery, but while waiting for your bus connection you can visit two statues – one of Sali Çeku right in front of the municipality building, and another one of Luan Haradinaj, a brother of Ramush Haradinaj – and a little further on there is another UÇK war memorial, built on top of a burnt-out kulla. This one is actually one of the more tasteful UÇK memorials around.

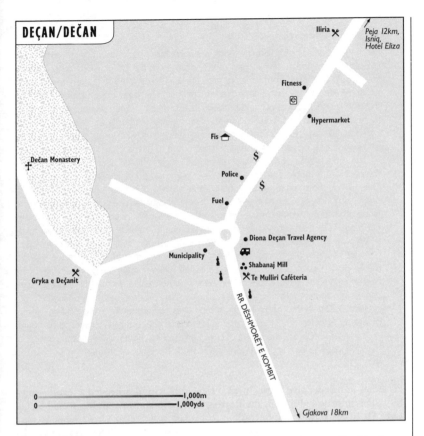

DEÇAN/DEČAN

Iliria ✗
Peja 12km,
Isniq,
Hotel Eliza

Fitness •
🅴

Hypermarket

Fis ⌂

Dečan Monastery †

$

Police •

$

Fuel •

• Diona Deçan Travel Agency
🚐

Municipality •
Shabanaj Mill

Gryka e Deçanit ✗
✗ Te Mulliri Caféteria

RR DËSHMORËT E KOMBIT

0 ————————— 1,000m
0 ————————— 1,000yds

↘ Gjakova 18km

Shabanaj Mill This traditional water-powered mill (*Rr Dëshmorët e Kombit, close to the main square;* ⊕ *10.00–16.00 daily; free entrance*) was severely damaged during the war, but thanks to restoration works done in 2004 by Intersos it now houses the Jeta Women's Association. The women members of the association produce a variety of different handicrafts and souvenirs for sale. In case you need any urgent repairs, you may also ask for tailoring services.

Visoki Dečani Monastery The undisputed highlight and a real must for any visitor to Kosovo is the magnificent Visoki Dečani Monastery, set in the beautiful surrounds of the Deçan Canyon. The monastery is about 2km from Deçan Town, easily accessible by road. Italian KFOR troops guarding the building will ask you for an ID card, but unlike at the Peja Patriarchate, the Dečani monks are very welcoming and it is also possible for Kosovo Albanians to visit the monastery. Take a torch with you to properly see the frescoes as the interior is often very dark. A special highlight is the weekly evensong on Thursdays at 19.00 and the choral church service on Sundays at 08.00. If you can time your visit, it's an unforgettable experience to listen to traditional Orthodox chorals in this amazing setting. The monastery is the endowment of **King Stefan Uroš III**, who ruled over the Serbian lands from 1321 to 1331. His life was marked by grave family disputes. Back in his childhood, he was imprisoned for six years in Constantinople on the orders of his father King Milutin. Upon his return, he inflicted a crushing defeat on the Bulgarians in 1330. His son, Stefan Dušan, displayed exceptional courage and military skills fighting alongside his father in this decisive battle. In 1331, Stefan Dušan spearheaded a revolt against his father, imprisoned him in the fortress of Zvečan and gave orders to kill Stefan Uroš III in his prison cell. According to his last will, Stefan Uroš's remains were buried in the Dečani church and to this day he is venerated as a Serbian saint on 24 November. In memory of his greatest legacy, the endowment of the Visoki Dečani Monastery, Stefan Uroš became known in history as Stefan Dečanski.

Construction of the Dečani church started in Stefan Uroš's reign in 1327 under the guidance of the architectural mastermind Fra Vita, a Franciscan monk from Kotor, in present-day Montenegro. The construction of the church was completed under King Dušan in 1335. He entrusted the exceptionally gifted Archbishop Danilo II with the supervision of the works. The completion of the **fresco paintings** lasted until 1350. They are attributed to a Greek school of painters assembled at King Dušan's court, who painted in Orthodox and Catholic churches along the coast.

The Visoki Dečani Monastery was raided and partially destroyed only once in the early days of the Turkish conquest of the Balkans. Throughout the major part of the **Ottoman era**, the monastery enjoyed the sultan's personal protection, as confirmed by several charters issued by successive sultans extending special privileges to the monastic community and their estates. The sultan's *firmans* (decrees) not only provided for protection, they also guaranteed the monks from Deçan a special tax status. The monastery also enjoyed special protection from the population living in the area, because according to folk belief, the tomb of Stefan Dečanski located in the church's interior had healing powers and was venerated by Orthodox, Catholic and Muslim Albanians alike.

Thanks to this privileged position, the monastery prospered in the Ottoman period. Richly endowed with **agricultural land, vineyards and fruit orchards,** only be cleansed by killing a male member of the offender's family. This led to a situation whereby a victim's family could only restore their honour by 'taking the blood' of the offender's family. The kanun contained strict rules on how to 'take blood'. You could not, for example, kill a person in his home. You could, however, grant a besa – a word of honour – that would be the equivalent of securing a 30-day armistice between two families. Some men would spend decades in their homes for fear of being killed; others were only able to till their fields during the time when a besa was granted. If there was no man in the family who could take blood, women would cut their hair, dress like men and assume the duty to kill. Those women were treated as men and were not allowed to marry. As late as the 1980s, it was estimated that the lives of 17,000 men were threatened by the tradition of blood feuds. A campaign was launched by a group of students together with the Council for the Defence of Human Rights, Kosovo's most active civil society organisation at the time, to reconcile blood feuds. Anton Çetta, a professor at the Albanological Institute, was asked to head the campaign. The year 1990 was declared the Year of Reconciliation. Starting in February, some 500 students and intellectuals would travel to villages to identify families in a blood feud and try to persuade them to grant a public 'pardon' to the family of the offender. Public ceremonies were organised and families invited to 'forgive in the name of the people, youth and the flag' in front of witnesses. The largest public gathering of this kind took place on a plain near Deçan on 1 May 1990 with upwards of 100,000 people in attendance. More than 2,000 disputes were peacefully resolved in the course of the campaign that lasted from 1990 to 1992.

A copy of the Kanun of Lekë Dukagjin in original Albanian and in English can be obtained in the Dukagjini Bookshop in Prishtina for €35 (see page 111).

the monastery sustained a vibrant monastic community. An important school of monastic learning developed here in the 15th and 17th centuries, producing books bound in leather skins as well as elaborately decorated miniatures and a large collection of icons. One of the most valuable books was the *Life of Stefan Dečanski*, written by the scholar Grigorije Camblak. Some of the monks chose to live high up in the hills over the left bank of the Bistrica River in medieval hermitages (inhabited caves).

Disaster struck with a devastating fire that destroyed large parts of the complex in the 17th century. The monastery fell into a period of rapid decline. When Daniel Pastrovich-Kazanegra took over the monastery's priory in 1764, there was only one monk left. Under his energetic administration, a new **iconostasis** was built and the **monastic dwellings** were rebuilt. Daniel is often considered the second founder of the Visoki Dečani Monastery. The importance of the monastery in the history of the Serbian Orthodox Church secured it generous donations during the course of the 19th century. The Serbian prince Miloš Obrenović, for example, donated the construction of a new **refectory** for the monks in 1836 and Prince Aleksandar Karadjorjević financed the lead roofing of the church in 1857. The First Yugoslav government in the late 1930s also financed major restoration works.

A wall surrounds the monastery and as you enter the complex through an impressive gate, a spectacular view opens up in front of you. The church walls are built with carefully hewn blocks of red-purple and light-yellow marble, set against a beautifully composed monastic complex. Take a moment to enjoy this peaceful setting before entering the church itself.

The church is one of the largest medieval Serb structures, 29m in height, with a length of 36m. Its **five-nave structure** is topped with a slim cupola resting on four major pillars. Combining Byzantine, Romanesque and Gothic elements, it

5

The basic form of social organisation in the north Albanian highlands was the clan (*fis*). Belonging to a large clan provided for security and economic survival. Pastoral households needed manpower to manage large flocks and defend their grazing grounds. In the plains of Kosovo, the importance of clans was gradually lost and its place was taken by the extended family. Most Kosovars, however, if you press them, will still know which 'clan' they belong to (eg: Thaçi, Gojani, Kelmendi). In the past, Serbs and Albanians used to live in multi-generational households called *zadruga* (Serbian) or *shtëpia* (Albanian). These households were characterised by several generations living together under one roof, sharing one stove and one budget. In a traditional household, the *zoti i shtëpisë* (the head of the household) takes all the decisions pertaining to communal life, from marriage to the division of labour and family finances. His authority is rarely questioned. Traditionally, every evening the men would meet in the *oda* (men's room) and the head of the household would divide the chores of the next day. All property was held in common, except for a wife's trousseau and a man's gun. After 1945, the *zadruga* died out among the Serbs as a result of rapid urbanisation and industrialisation. Kosovo's low rates of urbanisation (up to two-thirds of Kosovo's population still lives in rural areas), high population growth and large-scale labour migration helped to preserve the patriarchal households. Among rural Albanian families the patriarchal household survives to this day as it provides a safety net and security in the absence of a welfare state. There are also practical advantages in terms of sharing the care for young children and the elderly. The average household size in rural Kosovo – about eight members – has not changed since 1948. This created a situation of high dependency: every Kosovar with a job has to sustain 4.7 family members who do not work. It also contributed to the lowest share of female employment in Europe with less than 10% of women working. The current trends all point towards a slow but steady disintegration of these larger households. Brothers no longer want to share one roof, and brides no longer want to live with their parents-in-law. The ongoing building boom is testimony that Kosovo is changing fast.

reflects the different artistic influences competing at King Dušan's court. Gothic influences came via the Adriatic coast, while the school of Byzantine painters ensured the flow of the latest trends from Constantinople. In its design it is similar to the mausoleum of Stefan Nemanjić in Studenica, in Serbia today, especially the three-part window near the altar, which is decorated with animal creatures and scenes symbolising paradise and hell.

Above the southern entrance of the church you can see an inscription in old Cyrillic about the construction of the church. The western entrance is guarded by two lion figures (one is actually a creature part-lion, part-eagle), with Christ hovering above surrounded by two angels. The artists had never actually seen a lion in their lives!

As you enter the church through its north-facing doorway, you can admire an exceptionally well-preserved and colourful interior covered entirely with more than 1,000 compositions and figures. It is like a splendidly illustrated book of biblical stories for illiterate believers, capturing the spirit of the 14th century. The masters of these fresco paintings are unknown, with the exception of Sergius the Sinful, who inscribed his name on one of the church's pillars.

Christ the Pantokrator is represented in the cupola, surrounded by the prophets. The frescoes on the nave depict the life of Christ. The passion of Christ is painted on the four main pillars supporting the cupola in the centre. Other compositions include scenes from the life of the Virgin, a cycle on the lives of the Apostles as well as the entire story of Genesis starting with the creation of the world on the western side of the arch in the chapel of St Dimitrius and finishing with the construction of the Tower of Babel. In the narthex you can see a Nemanjić family tree and portraits of Emperor Dušan and his family. The paintings are impressive in their love of detail and bright colours.

The carefully carved and painted tomb of the church's founder Stefan Dečanski rests appropriately in the church's centre.

ISNIQ

HISTORY Isniq has always been one of the largest villages in Kosovo with some 6,000 inhabitants. It has a picturesque setting on the fertile Dukagjini Plain at the foot of the Accursed Mountains on the left shore of the Dečani White Drin River. The area is famous for its chestnut trees and the medical plants that grow in the alpine mountains with peaks as high as 2,656m. The local economy was always dependent on agriculture and cattle farming. During the summer months, the entire village would accompany their cattle herds to the summer pastures and cottages at 2,000m. In winter, women would prepare their own wool and produce rugs, clothes, socks and blankets. In the past there were eight mills in Isniq, using water from the local streams. In the 14th century, Isniq village was part of the monastic estate of Dečan, and two local families were trusted with the collection of taxes paid to the monastery from the villagers. Under the Ottomans, the land of Isniq was divided into three *timars* (military estates), each ruled by a different knight. Over the centuries, the village gradually adopted Islam, with many families converting as late as the 18th century. With the growth of the village, each quarter appointed one delegate (*barqe*) as a representative in case of disputes. Local disputes and blood feuds forced many families to leave Isniq and to start a new life elsewhere. Several 'emigrants' from Isniq thus formed other new villages within Kosovo.

GETTING THERE Isniq is located on the main road connecting Peja and Gjakova, at a distance of about 12km from Peja and 2km from Dečan. There are regular shuttle bus services from Peja to Dečan, stopping at Isniq. If you are coming from Prishtina with your own transport follow directions to Peja, but before entering the city turn left, following the signs to Gjakova. At the next T-junction, turn left again. The main road connecting Peja to Dečan is called Rr UÇK; it's a beautiful alley flanked by walnut trees on both sides. In autumn you will find many children selling walnuts on the street. There is a new war memorial near Raushiq village along the way. In Strelle village and near Lebushe village look out for beautifully carved wooden gates.

The Isniq bus stop is on the main Peja–Dečan road. From there it's a 1.2km walk to the centre of Isniq on an asphalt road.

WHERE TO STAY For details of the Hotel Eliza, see *Dečan*, page 173.

OTHER PRACTICALITIES There is an internet café and two small grocery stores on the main square in Isniq village. If you get hungry you can stop there to buy supplies for a picnic lunch. There is no public toilet in the village, but ask politely if you can use a bathroom in one of the shops or the internet café.

The most knowledgeable person on Isniq and the area is Rexhep Maksutaj, who in his daytime job teaches in the Isniq primary school. His book on Isniq, *Isniq through Centuries*, published by Shtëpia Botuese Libri Shkollor in Prishtina in 2002, is an interesting read (available in English and Albanian). You can call or email ahead of your visit and arrange a tour with him, although you may want to find an

Albanian–English speaker to go with you to translate (m *044 348 780;* e *maksutaj@hotmail.com*).

WHAT TO SEE AND DO Once you leave the main Peja–Deçan road, an asphalt road takes you for 1.2km straight into the centre of Isniq village. At about halfway, on your left, there is an old water-run mill owned by the Dervishaj family. It is the only one of five mills in Isniq that has survived. The water from the Isniq Canal comes straight from the mountains and passes Isniq before it joins the Bistrica River in Deçan. There is a small bedroom on the right-hand side for the millers to stay overnight. The two millstones and the old wooden door were part of the original inventory. Look out for the small openings in the walls that were used to position guns to protect the mill.

Where the road narrows, you can spot a beautiful example of a traditional *kulla*. The little wooden structure attached to its outside wall was used as the family's toilet. All the waste would drop down into a little canal that would be channelled into the fields as natural fertiliser.

The two most interesting examples of traditional Albanian kullas that can be visited today are all within a radius of a few hundred metres. As part of a joint Swedish–EU programme launched in 2001, two *kullas* in Isniq – Kukleci and Osdautaj – were restored. From the main square, turn right and after 100m you will see the Osdautaj kulla on your right. To get to Kukleci Kulla, return to the main square and take the path that passes the mosque on the right and follow as it bends to the right until you see Kukleci Kulla on your right-hand side.

Osdautaj Kulla The Osdautaj family has been living in this kulla for almost 220 years. Since its restoration in 2002, Osdautaj Kulla and the Ethnological Museum (⊕ *09.00–15.00 Tue–Sun*) have provided a unique opportunity to learn more about the traditions and colourful past of this region. As you enter the gate, call out loudly for a family member to show you around the complex.

It is best to start your discovery on the top floor where the *oda e burrave*, the men's room, is located. A flight of steep wooden stairs takes you straight up to the third floor. According to tradition, this floor was the exclusive preserve of male members of the family and male guests. The antechamber (*diva hani*) is where the coffee was prepared on the open fire by younger men of the family, who would

---

KULLA

The Albanian word *kulla* derives from the Turkish word for 'tower'. The traditional kulla is a fortified tower, usually two or three storeys high with thick stone walls on a square shape. Some kullas have walls as thick as 1m. The ground floor has no windows to protect it from intruders and was commonly used as a barn for cattle. In most *kullas*, the family's living quarters are on the second floor and the men's guestroom on the third, accessible directly by a small staircase. In peaceful times, families would sleep in separate buildings next to the *kulla*. In the towns in the early 20th century, kullas were increasingly built of brick.

The instability and insecurity of the late 18th and early 19th centuries in western Kosovo in particular led to a real boom in the construction of *kullas*. In some villages like Junik or Dranoc near Deçan, every family would have a *kulla* surrounded by high stone walls. Walking through such villages felt like walking through a medieval town. As unique symbols of Albanian architectural heritage, *kullas* were singled out during the 1999 war as targets for destruction. In Deçan municipality 70 out of 263 *kullas* were almost or totally destroyed and another 161 significantly damaged.

also wash the cups and dishes in the little opening on the side. From here you also have a nice view over Isniq village and of course it was here that the family's defences and guns were positioned.

The *oda e burrave* is really a beautiful example of its kind. The centrepiece of the room is the open chimney. It provided for warmth and was used to make coffee or light cigarettes. Matches were stored in the little opening to the right of the chimney. Coffee, sugar and tobacco were stored in the drawers built into the wall above; bed sheets and cushions for guests were tucked away in the cupboard on the left. The seat immediately to the left of the chimney was reserved for the male elders of the household. On the wall above you can spot a picture of the grandfather wearing traditional dress. The cushion placed just in front of the fire is called the *seqatë* – it was the duty of each new bride to bring one such cushion into the household upon marriage. Prospective brides would also bring the woollen carpets that you can find on the floor in black and red colours as wedding gifts.

As part of the recent restoration works, the animal stables on the ground floor have been converted into an Ethnological Museum. As you enter on your left, you see a traditional dowry, including a decorated chest (*arka*), bridal dresses and hand-knit stockings. In case you were wondering, the little wooden boards were used to wash clothes and the wooden forms were used to keep shoes and the traditional Albanian hat (*plis*) in shape. You can also see the same kind of *qylimi* – carpets – as in the men's room upstairs. In the centre of the room beside the chimney, you can find kitchen utensils used for traditional dishes. Among other things there is a *saq* (a flat dish), used to prepare the national dish *flija*, an indoor cooking stove and the wooden tools used for handling the hot stove (*lakraqë*). The round table in the left-hand corner is called a *sofra*. On very special occasions some families today still eat seated around a sofra on the floor. The right-hand corner of the room is reserved for various tools related to dairy processing.

Kukleci Kulla Kukleci Kulla is one of the oldest *kullas* in the Dukagjini Valley, with parts of the walls dating back 260 years.

For generations this *kulla* has been the home of the Kukleci family. The ground floor (side entrance) was used as stables for animals, the first floor was the family's living area and the third floor was reserved for men and guests. During the war a grenade hit the roof and marauding police destroyed the marble chimney in the guest room. You can still see some of the bullet holes in the door to the stables. The most famous guest who stayed in this *kulla* was the Norwegian anthropologist and human rights activist Berit Backer. In her book *Behind Stone Walls* she captures the lives and social customs of Isniq in the mid 1970s.

Watch your step as you climb up the steep stairs to the top floor. The antechamber is a beautiful example of traditional carpentry works. Special wood, believed to be bullet-proof, is used for the window shutters and the decorative carvings. The toilet is also located on this floor. The openings for the guns pointing straight towards the road are testimony to the fact that *kullas* were built mainly for defensive purposes during a troublesome period in the region's past.

The layout of the *oda e burrave* (men's room) is typical for traditional guest rooms across the Ottoman Empire. The eldest man in the family would sit on the left side of the chimney, while the warm place to the right of the chimney was reserved for the guest of honour. Family members would sit beside the landlord on the left-hand side while guests would line up on the right side – the closer you sat by the warm fire the higher your social rank. Look out also for the layout of the wood panels on the ceiling. The *oda e burrave* is where key decisions affecting the family or the village were taken in elaborate rituals over several cups of Turkish coffee.

A traditional Albanian wedding is truly an unforgettable experience! It is seen as the purpose of life and families do not spare any expense to make the wedding day the most memorable of a young couple's life. Even now, especially in rural Kosovo, engagements and marriage ceremonies follow a strictly defined traditional pattern.

Once a boy reaches marriage age, usually in his mid 20s, his mother, grandmother or sisters start to look out for potential brides. Since marriage is regarded as not just a relationship between a bride and a groom but a union between two families, it is important to find a prospective bride from a family of a similar social standing and with a reputation for trustworthiness and hospitality. The 'ideal' bride – according to custom – had to have many brothers and sisters, her mother must have breastfed all her children, her family had to belong to a different clan and the families had to be separated from each other by at least seven generations. The beauty of the bride is only of minor importance. Once a prospective bride has been identified, the traditional matchmaking process can begin. Traditionally, the boy's uncle (his mother's brother) would be appointed as **misit** or 'matchmaker'. It was the duty of the *misit* to visit the bride's family and to give an account of the boy's family, wealth and ancestors. The boy's family would provide coffee, sugar and cigarettes to the *misit* as presents for the bride's family. According to popular belief, one of the shoelaces of the matchmaker should be untied on his way to the bride's family in the hope that there will be no obstacles on the way. Usually, the matchmaker would have to make several polite visits to the bride's family, before he would be told by the father of the bride to 'await the next day' ('*po e presim ditën e re*') – an indication that the family agreed to the engagement. The next morning, the matchmaker would be invited by the bride's father and in the presence of her relatives, the father of the bride would officially accept the matchmaker's request for the girl's hand. The agreement was sealed by all the men present and drinking coffee together. That night, the matchmaker would bring the good news to the boy's family. Traditionally, the boy's family would fire shots in the air to announce the boy's wedding and offer a pair of socks known as *këputë*, towels or money to the matchmaker to thank him for his services.

The official **'engagement ceremony'** known as the 'word of the bride' ('*fjale e nuses*') traditionally takes place at the boy's house. The matchmaker together with the bride's brothers and uncles are invited to the groom's house. Originally, this important encounter would take place in the special guest room of the house and guests and family members would be seated around the room in strictly hierarchical order. When everyone has been served cigarettes and coffee, two senior members of both families would stand up to congratulate each other and the uncle of the bride would deliver the official 'word of the bride' – her consent to the marriage. Celebrations then continued till the next day and members of the bride's family were given small presents as they were leaving the house. From that day on, the bride starts preparing her dowry (*cejz*) and now being considered 'under the ring', she is expected to behave morally and not move around or socialise too much. In the past, the groom's family had to provide at least 100kg of sheep wool and 100 yards of cotton so that the future bride could prepare all the clothing for herself, her husband and her future children, including also the clothes she would wear when she died. Nowadays, the groom's family may still provide some yarn or wool, but more commonly the groom's family would either send money or the groom's and the bride's mothers together with the bride would purchase all necessary items from bed sheets to clothes and jewellery for the bride. The next stage involved the setting of a wedding date. Usually, the groom's father would visit the bride's family to arrange a date. Until recently weddings were held on Mondays or Thursdays but nowadays they are more commonly set for weekends. In the past most wedding invitations were personally delivered and still today a personal invitation by the head of the household is considered a particular honour. Three days before the actual wedding day, the women in the groom's house start preparing *qyshkek*, a dish made of boiled wheat, water and sugar, while the men start cutting the wood and preparing the guestroom. Some families celebrate so-called women's nights (*kanagjeqi*) attended only by female friends and relatives of the bride a few days before the actual wedding. There is usually a lot of dancing and the bride is expected to show off all her different bridal costumes in the course of the evening.

A **traditional wedding** in the Dukagjini Valley would start the night before with a dinner among male relatives of the bride and groom in the groom's house. On this occasion, gifts were delivered and drums (*tupan*) and woodwind instruments (*zurle*) would accompany the tunes of traditional songs amidst the occasional firing of a gun. Often the *tupan* and *zurle* players at Albanian weddings are members of the Roma community. On the actual wedding day, the wedding procession of the groom's family was led by the *bajraktar* (standard-bearer) carrying the flag. In the past, the bride's carriage was decorated in red rugs whereas nowadays instead of a horse cart families take the nicest car they can find – ideally a Mercedes – and decorate it with flowers and towels. Very often, modern brides are picked up in German or Swiss cars borrowed from a diaspora relative. In summer, rural roads tend to get clogged up by columns of decorated cars, peeping their horns, with children and women leaning out of the windows dancing and singing. If you travel in Kosovo on any Saturday or Sunday between June and September you are bound to meet one of these wedding processions. Once the groom and his relatives arrive at the bride's house, the bride is taken out of the house by her older brother and handed over to the groom. In the past, the groom was not allowed to meet the bride till late in the evening when they were finally introduced to each other in their bedroom. Nowadays young couples generally know each other and the bride and groom celebrate together. The bride, however, is still expected to look down at the floor and keep a stern and sad-looking face throughout the wedding ceremony. A big smile on her face could be misinterpreted as if she is happy about leaving her own family or – even worse – as if she is excited about the wedding night. The moment when the bride has to leave her family and depart with her new husband usually involves a lot of weeping and crying of the bride and her female relatives. The moment she enters her groom's car really marks a watershed in her life. From that moment on, she 'belongs' to her husband's family.

Rather than celebrating separately at the groom's and bride's houses, wedding celebrations nowadays are increasingly held in restaurants or hotels. Many hotels are purpose-built for weddings only and can cater for parties with up to 500 people. Traditional Albanian wedding costumes have also been replaced by white wedding dresses and ever more fancy special effects are copied from Hollywood movies, including fireworks coming out of the wedding cake or special ramps built so the couple can drive to the wedding banquet in their car. You will still find the traditional Roma bands playing catchy tunes on the *tupan* and *zurle* and, as the night progresses and with more *raki* in the blood, the traditional dancing gets faster and more daring. A number of **folk beliefs and traditions** continue to this day. The bride's first step out of the groom's car, for example, must be taken with her right foot. She is also expected to dip her fingers into a plate with honey and touch the doorframe of her new house three times upon entering. Traditionally the morning after, the wedding couple is served a special bread called *kulac*. This bread is prepared on the wedding night in the presence of a young boy wearing three Albanian hats (*plisa*) in the hope that the bride will give birth to male children in the future. The wedding ritual extends also to the first visits of the bride to her former home. One week after the wedding, the groom's father traditionally visits the bride's family together with the bride. After one month, the bride's family is allowed to pick her up for the first time and take her home for a week. In her new home, the new bride or *nuse* is expected to serve coffee to guests and family members until the day she gives birth to a son.

continued overleaf

Taking a closer look, one can actually discover some similarities between traditional Albanian and Serbian weddings in rural Kosovo. In the past, Serb weddings also lasted for one week, starting traditionally on a Monday with Sunday being the main day of celebrations. On the morning of the wedding day, the bride's hair is decorated with gold and her friends and female relatives sing mournful songs marking her departure from her home. The wedding guests from the groom's family also come to take the bride led by a *bajraktar*. It was a custom for the bride's brother-in-law to bring a shoe filled with candies called *bisag* to the bride and pour the candy over her head as a sign of good luck and fertility. As the new bride enters the groom's home, she throws an apple over her head, dips her fingers three times into a bowl of honey and touches the doorframe of her new home. Upon entering her new house, a young Serbian bride would also sit three times on the lap of her new mother-in-law before the official celebrations begin.

DRANOC

There is a beautifully preserved and partially restored historical zone in Dranoc village consisting of *kullas* and traditional stone walls. Dranoc offers a unique Albanian experience: a reasonably priced overnight stay in a traditional *kulla*. Dranoc is also a good base from which to explore the area and to make day trips to Peja, Deçan, Gjakova and Prizren. Dranoc deserves a small detour if you are in the Deçan area.

GETTING THERE Dranoc village is about 4km south of Deçan on the main Deçan–Prizren road. There are regular **buses** between Prizren, Gjakova and Deçan – just tell the driver to stop at the turn-off to Dranoc, from where it's about a 15-minute walk. In Dranoc village, turn left after the 'historical zone' sign.

WHERE TO STAY

Kulla Banakaj (4 rooms & men's room) As part of an effort to set up a regional B&B association, Cultural Heritage Without Borders is also letting out rooms in a second kulla in Dranoc's historical zone as well as a modern house owned by the Mazrekaj family. The family owning Banakaj Kulla is now living abroad for most of the year, so the entire kulla, including 4 bedrooms & the beautiful men's room, is available for guests. $

Kulla e Mazrekajve (4 beds) For reservations please call the current manager Naim on m 044 609 479, or e naim.uka@chwb.org (email checked occasionally). This beautiful example of a typical Albanian *kulla* has been restored since the war & is now managed by Cultural Heritage Without Borders. It is open to visitors or conference organisers in search of a real *kulla* experience. The ground floor has been adapted to a meeting room available for hire. There are 2 bedrooms with 2 beds each on the first floor & sleeping mats in the traditional *oda e burrave* (men's guestroom) on the second floor sleeping up to 8 people comfortably. All rooms share a modern bathroom, including a shower. If staying, however, bring your own eggs & coffee supplies as you can use the common kitchen. $

Mazrekaj home The fully furnished home (as opposed to the *kulla* above) of the Mazrekaj family, inc 4 bedrooms & the men's guest room, is another alternative to the *kulla* if you are looking for a bit more comfort. For reservations call Naim on 044 609 479, or contact e naim.uka@chwb.org.

JUNIK

There is little left to see in Junik today and it's not really worth a stop, unless you want to get a feel for the meaningless destruction inflicted on this region during the last conflict. Before the war, Junik's streets were lined with beautiful stone *kullas* typical of this part of Kosovo. Today, with the exception of the **Oda e Junikut**, a historical *kulla* that was restored with international funds after the war, there is little left to see.

The Oda e Junikut has been in the possession of the Hoxhaj family for generations. It was here in May 1912 that leaders of a local revolt swore a general truce from all blood feuds and took an oath to overturn the Young Turk regime. The representatives included Hasan Prishtina, Isa Boletin, Bajram Curri and Nexhip Draga. From Junik, the rebellion spread to Prishtina, Mitrovica, Vushtrri and Prizren. In 1913, Junik became the centre of the Albanian Resistance Movement (the kaçak rebellion) fighting against the Serbian occupation of Kosovo after World War I and against the division of the Albanian lands. In 1998–99, Junik became an operational centre of the Kosovo Liberation Army.

There is good hiking around Junik but it is best done with a guide because of the continued risk of land mines.

ODA E JUNIKUT Turn right at the main square in Junik and it's the first *kulla* on the left, set aside a little from the main road. You must enter through a gate and if locked, knock on the door and call for a member of the family. The ground floor is currently being prepared for a regional museum on the history of Junik and the building. The top-floor guest room is restored and the family is happy to show it to you. If you arrange your visit in advance, you can meet Abdyl Hoxhaj (m *044 285 385*), the owner of the *kulla* and Director of the Regional Institute for the Protection of Monuments in Peja or with someone he nominates, to ensure that you get in. He can give you the lowdown on the history of the building and tell you more about his great-great-great-grandfather, who was a member of the League of Prizren. The delegates from Junik met in this *kulla* to agree on their common points, before they sent their representative to Prizren in 1878. The high esteem of the family also meant that this *kulla* was the place where the council of the village elders would meet to administer the customary law. Alternatively, make the necessary arrangements to visit through Rugova Experience (see page 167).

If you take the road that leads towards the mountains from the main square, past the police station, you get to an old mill owned by the Gacaferri family. In the past, this mill was used to press wool used for traditional trousers and cloth. The water of the Ereniku stream passing underneath operated the *vajavica* ('the machine to press the wool') – making this the first 'industry' in Junik. During the 1999 war, UÇK set up a temporary operations centre using the electricity generated from the Ereniku stream to operate their computers.

GETTING THERE Junik is southwest of Deçan, about 15km from Deçan Town. After about 10km turn right at Rastavicë village, following signs to Junik. There are **minibuses** from Deçan and Gjakova to Junik, departing near the main bus station.

WHERE TO STAY AND EAT

🏠 **Motel Restaurant Oda e Junikut** (7 rooms) 📞 038 870 333/444; m 044 182 912/160 982; e oda_e_junikut@yahoo.co.uk (answered occasionally). The only hotel in Junik is hard to miss on the main road leading into Junik. This 4-storey hotel's rooms are all fully fitted with baths & TVs & there is a restaurant with an outdoor area open every day from 07.00 to 23.00. No AC or internet. For longer stays it's best to negotiate a special price. The owner speaks French. $$

✕ **Restaurant Junik City** Right on the central square in Junik, next to the Oda e Junikut, this is a rather run-down, smoke-filled local restaurant, with TV running in the background. A plus, however: there is an internet terminal in the corner.

Gjakova lies almost equidistant between Prizren and Peja. Although many internationals never make it to Gjakova, it is really worth visiting for a half or full day, in particular because of the old restored market, mosque, Ethnographic Museum, *madrasa*, bridges and its history. If you live in Kosovo you should be ashamed if you have never spent a day in Gjakova. There are also some of the best restaurants in Kosovo and a much better-priced hotel selection than Prizren and an equally good nightlife. This means that if you are touring Kosovo there is a lot to be said for heading to Gjakova from Prishtina and using it as a base for one or two nights and visiting Peja, Isniq, Deçan, Prizren and the outlying villages, rather than switching hotels between cities. While you can wander round Gjakova on your own, like in Peja it may well be less frustrating and a better use of your time to pre-arrange a tour – for the little extra it costs. This way you should guarantee being able to get into the key buildings, museums and courtyards of the old houses. You can either contact the Institute for the Protection of Monuments (see below) or make an arrangement with Orta NGO (039 362 150; e orta-ngo@gmail.com).

HISTORY Gjakova's current population is around 60,000 (nearly all of which is Albanian), which makes it smaller than Prishtina, Prizren and Peja but in the eyes of Gjakovars it is equally important. Gjakova struggles with the idea that it is a smaller town and in many respects has ideas above its station. This is perhaps because it had a significant role in Yugoslav times when it was known for producing the civil servants and elite that represented the then autonomous Kosovo in the Yugoslav parliament. It was the only place outside Prishtina with a commercial court, a military training camp with an airport, a medical school and district heating facility and its own reservoir of world-class standards funded by the World Bank in the 1970s.

Gjakova always had a very small Serbian population in comparison with other cities and was perceived by the Serbian regime to be a stronghold of Albanian nationalism. In the past, it was home to several prominent Albanian activists who played a role in the Prizren League in the late 19th century. In 1998–99, thanks to its proximity to the Albanian border and the mountainous terrain providing refuge, it became a UÇK stronghold. It suffered badly in the 1999 conflict and was the subject of several civilian massacres. The attractive wooden market which dated from the late 1800s was burnt to the ground in 1999.

Given its strong former communist affiliation, perhaps surprisingly it is and has always been one of the most religiously diverse cities in Kosovo, with more than 20% of the population being Catholic. Furthermore, it has no fewer than seven different dervish *tekkes* (religious buildings), including the headquarters of at least two of such dervish sects.

Before the industrial expansion, like Prizren it was famous for its artisans and guilds who clubbed together to build bridges, including the tannery and tailor bridges. It had a particularly strong leather industry and there is an area of town known as the *Tabak* or *Tophane*, or tannery area. In the surrounding fields, tobacco and fruits were also grown.

Generally, perhaps as a reward for its contribution in World War II, Gjakova did well out of socialism with investment in a brick factory, a production plant for Gorenje appliances and a textile factory. It kept pace with the changes and Gjakova enterprises were among the first to transform themselves into joint-stock entities under the first economic reforms, known as the Markovic reforms, in the early 1990s. Today it has been put on the back burner with privatisation and its industries have languished in inactivity.

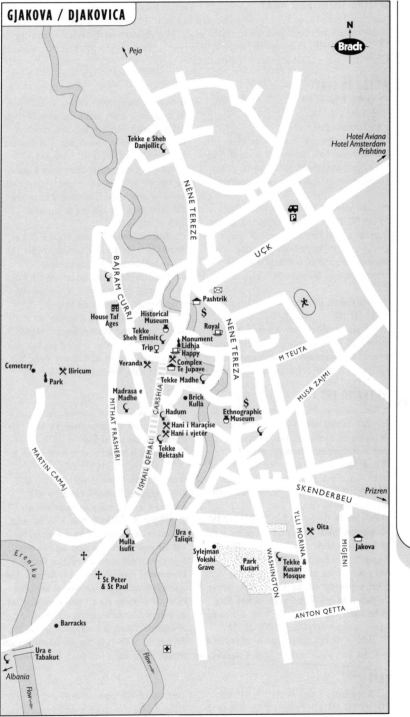

GJAKOVA / DJAKOVICA

Peja

N

Bradt

Hotel Aviana
Hotel Amsterdam
Prishtina

Tekke e Sheh
Danjollit

NËNE TEREZË

UÇK

Pashtrik

Historical
Museum

House Taf
Ages

BAJRAM CURRI

Royal

Tekke
Sheh Eminit

Monument
Lidhja
Happy

NËNE TEREZA

Trip

Veranda

Complex
Te Jupave

M TEUTA

Cemetery

Iliricum

Tekke Madhe

MUSA ZAJMI

Park

Madrasa e
Madhe

Brick
Kulla

MITHAT FRASHERI

Hadum

Ethnographic
Museum

ÇARSHIA

Hani i Haraçise
Hani i vjetër

ISMAIL QEMALI

Tekke
Bektashi

SKENDERBEU

Prizren

MARTIN CAMAJ

Oita

YLLI MORINA

Mulla
Isufit

Ura e
Taliqit

Jakova

Erenik

MIGJENI

St Peter
& St Paul

Sylejman
Vokshi
Grave

Park
Kusari

WASHINGTON

Tekke &
Kusari
Mosque

ANTON QETTA

Barracks

Ura e
Tabakut

Flow

Albania

Flow

GETTING THERE AND AWAY There are frequent **buses** to Gjakova from Prishtina (journey time 1½ to two hours) The first bus is at 08.00 and the last at 21.00. Peja and Prizren are each just 40 minutes away. The **Albanian border crossing** at Morina is 20–30 minutes' drive away (no regular buses). See the bus timetable in *Chapter 2*, page 60, for more information.

WHERE TO STAY

Çarshija Te Jupave (19 rooms) ☎ 039 026 798; m 044/049 129 159; e qarshijaejupave@hotmail.com; www.quarshijaejupave.com. Beautifully decorated rooms with good beds, bathrooms, a central AC & Wi-Fi throughout. Underground parking but there's also parking outside. Prices of rooms vary depending on size. $$$–$$$$

Hotel Jakova (21 rooms) Rr Migjeni 50 (bloku I); m 044 334 746; e hoteljakova@hotmail.com. Not as central as Hotel Pashtrik, but with all facilities although no prizes for the bright-green satin eiderdowns or overall décor. With AC & en-suite bathrooms. Internet downstairs. Wi-Fi is planned. $$$

Hotel Pashtrik (70 rooms) Rr Nëne Terezë; ☎ 039 327 101; m 044 547 101; e hotel_pashtriku@yahoo.com. A modern 1960s–80s' looking hotel. The most central place to stay. Recently privatised & renovated with modern bathrooms & even a refurbished lift. Connected to the city central heating so the rooms are beautifully warm in winter. Wi-Fi in the restaurant & coming soon in the rooms. All rooms with AC although there have been some complaints about the standards of the beds. Best of all there is a 25m swimming pool (the largest indoor pool in Kosovo), a very well-equipped fitness centre & sauna in the basement which can also be used by non-residents for €3 for each facility. There is also a 2-lane bowling alley. Room prices vary according to size. Group discounts available. $$$

Hotel Amsterdam (17 rooms, 1 apt) Rr UÇK, on the road in to Gjakova from Prishtina; m 044 123 003; e hotelamsterdam-ks@hotmail.com; www.hotelamsterdam-ks.info. Not so central & with a bit of a 'shiny' feel. Bathroom & AC, 6 rooms with jacuzzi. Internet available in the lobby. $$

Hotel Aviana (16 rooms) About 5km out of Gjakova on the road from Prishtina; m 044/049 189 173. More of a budget option if you have your own transport, although not shoestring. Rooms have AC & baths (some with jacuzzi). $$

WHERE TO EAT

Hani Haraçise m 045 272 667; ⊕ 08.00–23.00 daily. 200 years old with 50 years as a café. Stunning old building on 2 levels with open courtyard with great summer ambience. Reasonable prices.

Hani i Vjetër Rr Q Bakalli, midway down Rr Ismail Qemali, next door to Hani Haraçise; m 044 236 838/344 719; ⊕ 16.00–23.00. Stunning old wooden building. Reasonable prices.

Pizza Jeta On the road to Peja; m 044 252 500

Restaurant Iliricum Kodra e Cabratit, on top of the hill with a view of the town; ☎ 039 025 067; ⊕ mid-May–Sep daily only. Small museum-type display of traditional crafts inside. Huge outdoor terrace. Very popular with the diaspora in the summer. The place to be seen & good traditional food, pizzas.

Restaurant Oita 1, 2, 3, 4 Rr Ylli Morina & 2 on the bypass out of town; m 044 310 892/122 950; ⊕ 07.00–23.00 daily. Serves pizzas & Italian food & ice cream. More popular with the locals. A bit tacky in layout with rather twee fountains. Not as good as the other options, with poor service, but an alternative if this side of town.

Restaurant Te Jupave End of Rr Ismail Qemali 9; ☎ 039 026 798; m 044 129 159; e carshijaejupave@hotmail.com; ⊕ 07.00–24.00 daily. 2 entrances. Downstairs café & bar with ambience & upstairs quality restaurant with nice plates & napkins. Conference room & bar for events. Fabulous tastefully restored stone & wood building with old wooden doors embedded, beautiful fireplace & possibly the best restaurant toilets in Kosovo. Recommended dishes are the *tava*, in particular *Tave Gjakova*. Try also the different types of bread. Very reasonable prices. You can eat here at less than half the price of Prishtina restaurants.

Restaurant Veranda Rr Ismail Qemali, top end near the *kulla*; ⊕ 09.00–21.00 Mon–Sat. Reasonable prices although now looking a little dreary & run-down.

CAFÉS

Happy Çashija e vogel (market); ☎ 039 022 221; m 044 154 631. Pasticeria & fast food. On 2 floors. Popular with internationals. View of Old Town & river. A good place to get a packed lunch if you

are heading for the ferry to Albania.
Pasticeria Royal Rr Nëne Terezë, 200m away from Hotel Pashtrik; m 044 128 540. Ice creams & cakes.

Trip Top end of Rr Ismail Qemali. Wonderful *kulla* but sadly a tacky interior. There's a quiet terrace at the back.

OTHER PRACTICALITIES The post office is not far from Hotel Pashtrik – diagonally across the main road.

ProCredit Bank is further along Rr Nëne Terezë past the municipality. There is a branch of NLB Bank on Rr Nëne Terezë and a branch of Raiffeisen Bank on the ground floor of Hotel Pashtrik.

Monday is market day.

Useful shops

Bicycle repair shops Blendi, bottom end of Rr Ismail Qemali; m 044 449 436. The owner is Selaimi Sader. He also provides information about the local bike club – run by Fari Duraku (m *044 745* 630), who is based in a café near the Solidarity Flats. No spare parts, so bring your own. Besnik Mehmeti (m *044 328 579*) also runs a bike-repair shop, opposite Park Lirise, Hysni Dobruna. Again, no spares are available, so bring your own.

Carpenter In a side road off Rr Ismail Qemali; 039 328 583; m 044 236 370. Gezim Gola makes traditional chests, including the flour-container/bread-making chests & wooden cribs, & will make to order.

Fishing shop Rr Ismail Qemali, in the market towards the kulla end; m 044 347 012; 08.00–19.00. Fly & rod fishing. Also information on fishing permits & details of the Ereniku Fishing Club in Gjakova.

Motorbike- and bicycle-repair shop Rr Ismail Qemali, halfway up the road; m 044 189 300. All sorts of motorbikes & bikes repaired by Rexhep Argendi & family. Limited spare parts.

Vejsa Saddlery Rr Ismail Qemali; m 044 660 335. Everything from traditional saddles & bridles, dog collars & other leather products. One of the last of over 20 saddlers that used to be in Gjakova.

WHAT TO SEE AND DO As you drive into town from Prishtina, you pass some rather sleazy-looking hotels and discos, followed by the old Shtepia i Mallrave, Cultural House and shopping centre. Coming from Rahovec you pass the big socialist factories either side, including the Mozart chocolate factory where you can buy wholesale-price chocolates. All this gives a rather negative first impression of Gjakova but ignore this, park the car either outside the bus station and walk the ten–15 minutes to the old market or, provided it is not peak diaspora season, drive further in and go across the river leaving the Hotel Pashtrik on your left and park on the riverside at the back of Restaurant Te Jupave. You will need two–five hours to see all the sights, depending on how long you wish to spend at each.

Below we set out a suitable walking tour of Gjakova including the main sights which are all quite close together (see map). The sights which are a bit further afield, including the hill top, require either a lot more time and energy if walking or perhaps resorting to taking a taxi or driving.

Walking tour Start at the top of the **Çarshia** on Rr Ismail Qemali. The Çarshia is the heart of Gjakova. It is a wooden market with small stalls and wooden shutters. From the 16th century, if not earlier, this was the hub of artisans and craftsmen trading around the main mosque. There were leather, metal, cloth and other craftsmen in their wooden shops on the then cobbled streets.

The whole of the Çarshia was set on fire in 1999 and, being constructed of wood, the fire caught on quickly. The Çarshia has been rebuilt in much of the original style and is perhaps one of the most interesting sights in Kosovo. Even today after the advent of the hypermarket and mini market there are small boutiques, mini markets, graphic-design shops, filigree, lace and souvenir sellers. You may want to leave your shopping until after the walking tour as most of the shops stay open until 18.00.

A **Historical Museum** at the top of the Çarshia is planned in the kulla of Abdullah Dreni but is taking time to complete. This would make a good start to a walking tour as it will give you a perspective of Gjakova's history. The museum is being set up by the incredibly enthusiastic historian Moni and passionate archaeologist Bedia, both from the Institute for the Protection of Monuments. If you really want to know more about Gjakova and particularly if you are a large group, consider contacting the institute for a guided tour (✆ *039 022 610;* e *bedirraci@yahoo.com*). Give them enough advance warning to plan translation and their diary as they are often out and about in the field and remember they are not really paid as tourist guides so consider an appropriate 'thank you' for them.

Next to the proposed Historical Museum is one of the seven *tekkes* in Gjakova. **Tekke Sheh Eminit**. For more information on *tekkes*, see box, pages 214–15. The renovated tekke is walled with big wooden doors and the *tyrbe* (grave) on the left-hand side. This is part of the Ra-fai dervish sect which is renowned for intense trances culminating in penetration of the face, in particular piercing the cheeks with skewers, apparently without pain. The *sheh* will be happy to talk to you about the history if he can find time. They hold a festival on 21 March each year but you would be very lucky to get in as it takes place in the small inner courtyard so space is very limited and often reserved for the great and the good, ie: politicians and international visitors such as KFOR.

Further down the road on the corner of the triangle of two roads is the modern stone **Monument to the League of Prizren** (Monument Lidhja) which also had many followers in Gjakova. In the wake of the Berlin Congress of 1878, the Turkish authorities sent Mehmed Ali Pasha from Istanbul to Gjakova to oversee the redrawing of the boundary and to persuade the people to not object to the decision of the Great Powers to hand over Albanian-populated lands around Gusinje and Plav to Serbia. Gjakova became famous for being the place where Mehmed Ali Pasha was shot, apparently on the bridge entering Gjakova. Thereafter the League of Prizren was treated as a risk by the Turkish authorities and members of the League were captured and imprisoned.

Further down the Çarshia road (Ismail Qemali) on the left-hand side is a large renovated stone and light wood building, built in the traditional style which straddles a foot passageway between Ismail Qemajli and the river. This is now the **Çarshija e Jupave complex** – a restaurant, conference/events room and bar and a series of shops. In due course it may have rooms to stay in. It has well-priced traditional food but is also worth visiting just to see the high quality of the renovation. Diagonally opposite its Çarshia side entrance are two restored stone *kullas*, one three-floored building dating from the 17th–19th centuries which belonged to the Batusha family (Abdurrahaman Koshi Kulla) and the other one is restaurant Veranda, a trendy bar with a terrace on the roof in summer.

Opposite the *kullas* is a small two-storey building which was the first Albanian-language school in Gjakova. While there are interesting old houses up the side road between the *kullas* (see below), for now continue with the main sites down the Çarshia road. The next main side turning to the left (east) on this main road is another low tile-roofed *tekke*. This is the **Tekke Madhe (large *tekke*)**, which has a brother *tekke* in Prizren, at the Marash tree. Again you can look round. For more information see box, pages 214–15.

You can now cross the river and head back into the more modern side of town and bear right on to the main Rr Nënë Terezë to visit the **Ethnographic Museum** (🕐 *times vary; entrance* €1 *or* 2). The museum is not so obvious but the best landmark to look or ask for is the municipality building. Directly opposite is a low wall with brick clay tiling and if you go through the door (push hard even if it looks closed – it might be open) behind it is a fabulous-looking building with the upper front room that was used for guest entertaining which is stuck out on four tall, strong wooden pillars. The construction dates from the 18th–20th centuries. The house gives you a good feel for how a well-to-do urban family would have lived at this time.

The house was purchased by the municipality from brothers who received four modern flats in the city in return. Downstairs is a room which is being kept for exhibitions. Up the wooden stairs however are the real treasures, in particular the woodwork. There is one room for offices and then another which has low benches round the outside and most stunning of all, a wooden ceiling with extremely ornate decoration, with each rose petal carved. On the side walls are traditional wooden inset cupboards and on the back wall is a white decorated stone oven which you can see would have been fed with wood from the corridor outside. Inside the second room are various tools and household implements which have been gathered from around the area, including looms for weaving. More interesting perhaps are the wooden decorated implements on the wall which resemble extended butter pats but which were apparently used by women to beat/wash clothes in the river. Also of interest is the wooden implement and the various shaped moulds which were used to make the traditional Albanian hat. This required at least 28 different steps in the making.

Back outside you can take a left off the main street and back to the Çarshia and on the other side of the bridge to the left is the three-storey brick *kulla* **Tasum Beut** which is tucked back behind a car park. This was built in the 19th–20th centuries. It is privately owned and a rare example of this type of architecture. Brick *kullas* were more common in towns, whereas stone *kullas* were found in villages.

Suitably halfway down, and in the centre of the Çarshia is the stunning **Hadum Mosque** which is entered by one of two sets of small gates (if the first set is closed, continue down the street and turn left to the next set of gates). At prayer time in any event you can be sure to get in. The mosque, with its smooth, flat grey stones has ornate ceiling and wall paintings and beautifully decorated doors. Also admire the beautiful gallery behind you as you come in. It was built in 1595 (apparently the building work took nearly 20 years) and is the oldest mosque in Gjakova and the only one that has not undergone irreversible reconstruction or major intervention, thus making it a unique and important example of Balkan artistry. On the top left-side wall is a painting of a town which rather than heralding Mecca seems more to reflect the region and perhaps even be a series of kullas. There are also painted cypress trees. Above the beautifully coloured main door in Arabic it says that the painting work was carried out by the deaf mute Sylejman in 1260 (Islamic calendar). The wooden *hayat* (fencing) enclosing the portico was probably added at the time of the major 1842 restoration and surfaces that had formerly been on the exterior were rendered and painted. In spring 1999, the mosque was set on fire by Serbian forces and the hayat was lost. The top of the minaret was shot off and the upper part collapsed on the library beside the mosque, causing serious damage to at least half of the building. In 2005, a major restoration programme was carried out faithfully under CHWB management. The gravestones as you can see even today are very ornate. This was the place where the great and the good of the city were buried.

Outside the mosque is the library building which was built in the 17th century with a cupola. Sadly all the 2,000 books (150 of which were unique) were destroyed in 1999.

Further down the side road, not so far from the Hadum Mosque are two old houses with wooden porticos allegedly owned by brothers and known as **Hani i Vjetër** and **Hani i Haraçise**. Again these are worth visiting, not just for the good food and courtyard setting, but to admire the traditional outside architecture with the extended balconies and wood pillar supports. They were built in the 17th–18th centuries as a hostel for the market traders to stay in.

Near the Hani is the **Bektashi Tekke** which is often regarded as the fourth faith in Albania proper. For more information see pages 214–15).

Continue on down Ismail Qemali to the end of the bazaar and you will see the old squat **Mosque of Mulla Isufit** with its wood minaret. It is worth a glance if you have time as it retains its traditional mud and wood structure.

Continue further down the main road to the right past the taxi stand to the Catholic part of Gjakova and you come face to face with the large modern yellow church with its PVC windows rising up out of Gjakova from a distance. Opposite this is another church which is still quite modern in style and which seems to be suffering from damp. There have been Catholic churches here, it is believed, since the 19th century and they operated freely under the Turkish Empire. During the war in 1999, the St Anthony Church was taken over and turned into a military facility by the Yugoslav army, hence the restoration.

Nearby if you continue on the road beyond the **Church of St Peter and St Paul** and past the bombed-out **barracks** on the left-hand side parallel with the main road is the stone **Ura e Tabakut** (Tannery Bridge). It spans the river with its 113.5m length and 3.5m height. It was renovated in 2004 and has two different types of arches. This bridge heads towards Albania but unless you have time to explore more countryside you will need to turn back at this point. Now you have two choices, depending on timing. Either you can grab a taxi from the taxi rank at the end of the Çarshia and head up Martin Camaj Road to the Çabrat at the top of the hill (a good idea if you are hungry as the Iliricum Restaurant at the top is excellent), or if you have energy for more sightseeing you can wander the back streets of Mithat Frashteri and Bajram Curri. These and Rr Çabratit (the road leading up to the Çabrat or hill top) have several old-style houses, mostly tucked behind high walls and which you could probably only visit properly by arrangement with the Institute of Monuments or by asking around.

The House of Beqir Haxhibeqiri on Rr Çabratit is an old-style residence with traditional closed-in bay windows and balcony. The inside retains its traditional cupboards, bath area and fireplace. It was built from traditional materials including stones from the river.

The House of Mazllom Zherkës on Rr Çabratit was built and added to between the 17th and 20th centuries, and has a lot of wood decoration.

The **large madrasa (Madrasa e Madhe)** is a centre for Islamic education which trains young *imams* and was founded by Vesel Efendiu in the 17th century, but the building was not completed until 1748. The original buildings were all in stone but were destroyed completely in 1999 and all that remains is a stone stump left symbolically at the corner of the mosque.

Nonetheless, the restoration after the 1999 war, funded by Middle Eastern donors, is on the whole nicely done using wood and traditional building styles and the complex is worth visiting. The mosque is simple with bare walls, the fountain a little kitsch. The dormitory complex around the walls is more traditional. In the corner in the traditional-style tower are two classrooms for the two different year groups. The centre operates with more than 28 students today who come from all over Kosovo, although with a strong bias towards the Drenica region. They learn three languages – Turkish, English and Arabic. The current director of the school is Turkish and there is a lot of contact with Turkey. They are happy for visitors to enter and look around but do so discreetly as students may be studying or praying.

The **smaller madrasa**, further away and today pretty well destroyed, was traditionally also used as a dormitory complex and to host visitors and travellers who needed somewhere to stay. This is no longer possible as the institution now has a solely educational focus.

Up on the hill (Çabrat) It is really worthwhile going up the hill to get a great view of Gjakova in front of you and the mountains behind. You can enjoy this from the Iliricum Restaurant (see page 188). You should go into the Iliricum anyway for a drink as it has an interesting collection of local artefacts.

On the hill next door to the Iliricum is a **World War II memorial building** in a distinctive socialist style – arranged as a circular building with black marble plaques. Unfortunately it has fallen into disrepair and is usually locked.

Better tended, further back towards the hills, are the **graves from the 1999 conflict**. A visit here is very moving as the graves are in mounds above ground, rather than underground and are rather like the styles of the türbe in the tekkes. They are decorated with photos, names, dates and plastic flowers. In some ways the relatives here are the lucky ones as they have somewhere to mourn. Gjakova has a large number of missing people, more than any other single city in Kosovo, with around 500 unaccounted for since 1998–99.

FURTHER OUT OF TOWN If you have more time or are living in Gjakova, then you can visit these additional sights.

Ura e Taliqit/Taliqi Bridge The bridge is situated above the river Krena and is difficult to spot because the modern bridge was built so close to it by the socialist regime, sadly spoiling the view of the old bridge (although arguably the huge piles of rubbish in the river do even greater damage to this). Renovated in 2004 and a protected monument since 1962, the bridge was built in the 17th and 18th centuries and is 21.5m long, 4.05m wide and 5m high, with two types of arches and two types of pillars.

Kusari Mosque and tekke Near the Kusari Park (which incidentally also hosts the grave of League member and Albanian nationalist Sylejman Vokshi). It was built in 1800 and then adapted by the addition of a balcony in 1916. It is traditional mud-brick style, with wooden timber beams.

Just beyond this are the traditional communist flats and a wide-laned smart housing district with its gardens and broad pavements giving an unusual sense of space and order for a Kosovo city.

Tekke e Sheh Danjollit This is off the main road on the left on the way in from Peja. This tekke (one of Gjakova's seven) was built in the 19th century and retains much of the style of the time with its courtyard and meeting room with murals and citations from the Koran.

Gjakova also had two Orthodox churches: one built in 1823 which had many icons and frescoes and a later one from 1992 to 1998 surrounded by large town houses with courtyards and gardens. The former was destroyed in March 2004 and the latter in 1999.

OUTSIDE GJAKOVA

RADONIQI LAKE This lake is designed for water consumption, so quite justifiably, swimming is banned. The lake was built as a result of a World Bank-funded project in 1976 and the dam and filtration designs were near state of the art and still operate well today. The area around the lake is, however, attractive and it is possible to walk a bit in the region (although many of the forest roads peter out so it can be a bit frustrating) and there are one or two small but not spectacular restaurants (for better restaurants try the Guri i Zi fish restaurant further along the main road to Prishtina; see pages 100–3). The lake has none of the buzz or noise of Battlava. To get to Radoniqi you need to take the right-hand north fork out of Gjakova on the main road to Prishtina (as opposed to the left-hand one which goes to Deçan). Take a left at Novo Selo on a road with limited asphalt or ask and go the long way round via Cërmjan and Rakoc villages.

URA E TERZIVE/TAILOR'S BRIDGE This is a longer bridge over the Ereniku River. It has been a protected monument since 1962. It is 8km outside Gjakova on the road to Prizren. Much longer than any of the other bridges – it is 190m long and 3.5m wide, with 11 semi-oval arch openings – it was built at the end of the 15th century and repaired in the 18th century as evidenced by a Turkish stone inscription. The bridge was repaired using funds supplied by the Gjakova Tailors Guild which gives it the name, with further repairs carried out in 1982–84.

URA E FSHEJT Further along on the same road is Ura e Fshejt. Built in the 18th century, it is 37m long, and 18.5m high. It was damaged completely in World War I and again to some degree in 1999, but repaired with funds from the Italian KFOR. The gorge below the bridge is that of the Drini i Bardhë and is quite spectacular and the subject of an annual jumping competition. There is a **fish restaurant** (m *044 477 100/ 045 700 100;* ⊕ *08.00–24.00 daily*) next to the river, and to get the best views of the bridge it is best to go onto their terrace.

ACROSS INTO ALBANIA, BAJRAM CURRI AND THE FERRY There are two border crossings into Albania close to Gjakova. The Qafa e Morinës crossing is more of a main road and you head back towards Junik/Deçan to a pass in the mountains. The road has been upgraded and from the border it is another 20km along a good asphalt road to the town of Bajram Curri and from there to Fierze where you can catch the 08.00 ferry across the north of Albania. In summer there are two ferries a day (the second leaves at 13.00), but it pays to be safe and arrive early as there is often a battle to get on. The ferry in the opposite direction leaves the terminal at 09.30. For more information see the Bradt guide to Albania. The Prushit Qafa crossing on the other hand takes you into an even more rural area with very remote villages and roads.

TRIPS TO THETHI/VALBONA Gjakova is also the best place in Kosovo to start a trip by car to Valbona in north Albania, and from there undertake the beautiful hike of approximately seven hours to the village of Thethi for an overnight stop. This can only be done after May owing to the snow in Thethi. For information on trips starting from Kosovo it is best to contact the Kosova Mountain Federation (for further details, see *Chapter 3*, page 115). For more information on travelling in Albania, see Bradt's *Albania* guide (*www.bradtguides.com*).

6

South Kosovo

The ethnically mixed area of southern Kosovo includes the famous museum city of Prizren and the little-visited but stunningly beautiful mountains of Dragash with its Gorani population. There are attractive Bosnian- and Serb-populated villages with hidden churches in the sheltered Zhupa Valley and the gorge. The road then winds its way up to the high Sharr Mountains bordering Macedonia with the Serb-populated Brezovica ski resort and good walking country. There are also high mountains to the other side of Prizren on the Albanian border, including the infamous Pashtrik. Around Pashtrik is the Has area of Kosovo with its Catholic Albanian villages. The Prizren area with its abundant rivers and fresh water is known for its crafts and agriculture, including Sharr cheese and honey, and we have also included the vineyard towns of Rahovec and Suha Rekë in this section.

While Prizren is on most Kosovo visitors' lists, Dragash, Has and the Sredska villages require more time (possibly the allocation of several weekends if you are based in Kosovo). Rahovec and Velika Hoča are also worth a break in your journey from Prishtina to Prizren or vice versa.

PRIZREN

This is the jewel in the crown of Kosovo and a 'must-see' for any visitor. It has the highest number of preserved Ottoman buildings with their upper storeys jutting out into the narrow cobbled streets. Prizren has not only retained the architecture from the Ottoman era but also many other flavours of Turkey, with the language being widely used, and delicious Turkish food. Many schools in Prizren still teach in Turkish and it is the only municipality where Turkish is an official language alongside Albanian and Serbian so you will see it on street signs and it also appears on tax bills. Several radio stations broadcast in Turkish and there is a weekly Turkish-language newspaper, *Yeni Dönem*.

Prizren is the most ethnically mixed municipality with large numbers of Bosnians and Turks and also Roma, Gorani and Terbesh. The cultural festival Zambak is held in July each year with songs and dancing from different ethnic groups.

Approximately 221,000 people live in the municipality, with between 40,000 and 60,000 in the city itself. It's a young population with the schools operating up to two shifts a day and up to 50 in the class.

The town pretty well escaped damage in the 1998–99 war, but when the Albanians returned in summer 1999 a considerable number of Serbian homes were looted and burnt. Prizren also suffered the most material damage in the riots of March 2004, with 55 houses and eight Orthodox sites damaged. It is therefore the focus of rebuilding efforts today.

The town of Prizren is close to the Albanian border, with mountains on two sides. It has good access to water, with the Bistrica/Lumbardhi River flowing fast through the town and a pleasant sheltered climate.

HISTORY The earliest archaeological find is the so-called *Runner of Prizren* which is a bronze figure of a running girl which may have been attached to a vessel or utensil. A dealer sold it to the British Museum in 1876 and you can still see it there today. According to the museum, the object was possibly made in Sparta between 520BC and 500BC. It may have arrived in Prizren as a gift or loot and been used as a grave-god.

The Romans also made their mark around Prizren and records refer to a **Roman road**, Via Zeta, running from Shkodra to Niš. In 1019, a **Bulgarian outpost** was founded in Prizren and Stefan Nemanjić conquered Prizren briefly in 1189, but after the defeat of 1191, had to give the city back to the Byzantines. In 1208, Prizren was finally seized by Prince Stefan II Nemanjić and incorporated into the Serbian medieval kingdom. In the 13th century, Prizren benefited greatly from King Milutin's ambitious church-building programme with the building of St Bogodorica and Levišja. King Dušan continued this church-building programme with the wealth accrued by the mixed community of traders and artisans from places such as Kotor, Zadar and Dubrovnik. He built the Monastery of Archangels further out in the valley beyond Prizren, St Petar Church in Korisishte and a series of churches around Mushishte about 10km out of Prizren (St Bogodorica, St Simeon and Rusnica). Other churches built around this time in the area include St George in Rečan and the churches in Velika Hoča (5km from Suha Rekë).

Prizren was favourably positioned on a major trade route and developed as a commercial centre supplying the Kosovo region. As a **trading** town on a crossroads, Prizren had always been home to many communities, not only Muslim but also Catholic and Orthodox communities. The exact date of the Ottoman conquest of Prizren is uncertain – it may have been as early as 1455 or as late as 1459. Ahmet Bey, the first Ottoman governor, built a mosque, and there are shops that take his name in the west of the city. By the mid 16th century there were seven or eight mosques, a madrasa, several elementary schools, a *hammam* and a stone bridge. For the Ottomans, Prizren was an important **administrative centre** and they stationed one of the largest Ottoman armies in the castle. Initially Prizren was a *sançak* (military district) under the Skopje (Usküp) *vilayet*. It was upgraded to the status of centre of a *vilayet* in 1843. In 1865, Prizren became the administrative centre of a wider *vilayet* covering Elbasan, Peja, Tetovo, Luma, Gostivar and Niš.

In November 1689, the Austrian imperial army under the command of General Piccolomini entered Prizren to a warm welcome from the Catholic and Orthodox communities, led by Archbishop Pjeter Bogdani. On his arrival General Piccolomini already had a boil under his arm and succumbed to the plague, being buried in the graveyard of St Levišja Church. When the Turks regained Kosovo a considerable part of the population left Prizren for Serbia in fear of reprisals for their co-operation with the Austrians. Such reprisals did ensue, although as it was winter and with the distances involved, fewer Kosovars left than is often made out to be the case (most of the exodus at this time was from eastern Kosovo, nearer to what is now the boundary with Serbia). Pjeter Bogdani himself was in Prishtina where he also died of the plague by the time the Turks had regained control. His body was dragged into the main square, with his mitre on his head, and quartered by way of public punishment for his collaboration.

Life in Prizren steadily improved in the 18th and 19th centuries under the Ottomans. There was a strong tradition of **crafts**, in particular tanners, armourers (with guns exported as far afield as Egypt), metalworkers and filigree. A total of 124 different trades were recorded in the books of the time, divided into eight official professions. The Prizren tanners were particularly important and they enjoyed a privileged status among the guilds, thanks to their close links to the military (who needed their saddles). In the early 18th century, there were 43 tanning shops in Prizren

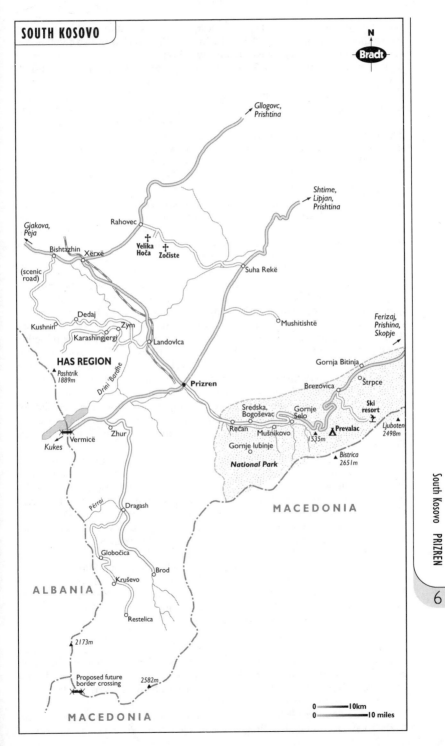

SOUTH KOSOVO

N

Bradt

Gllogovc,
Prishtina

Shtime,
Lipjan,
Prishtina

Rahovec

Gjakova,
Peja

Bishtazhin   Xërxë

Velika
Hoča   Zočiste

Suha Rekë

(scenic
road)

Dedaj

Kushnin   Zym
Karashingjergj   Landovlca

Mushitishtë

Ferizaj,
Prishina,
Skopje

HAS REGION

Pashtrik
1889m

Gornja Bitinja

Drini Bardhe

Prizren

Brezovica   Štrpce

Sredska,
Bogoševac

Gornje
Selo

Ski
resort

Zhur

Rečan   Mušnikovo

Ljuboten
2498m

1535m   **Prevalac**

Kukes   Vermicë

Gornje lubinje

Bistrica
2651m

National Park

MACEDONIA

Përroi

Dragash

Globočica   Brod

Kruševo

ALBANIA

Restelica

2173m

Proposed future
border crossing   2582m

6

MACEDONIA

0   10km
0   10 miles

and 50 in Gjakova. They had their bases near the river, using it for washing the hides which they strung out on wooden racks. In 1863 Prizren's bazaar had 1,200 shops.

In the late 19th century the **Rotull family** in Prizren had a great say in the running of Prizren affairs and in 1875 printed the first dual-language Serbian–Turkish newspaper, called *Prizren*. The population grew steadily and in 1836 it is estimated that there were 26,000 inhabitants in the town. In 1874–75 (by which time Prizren was the capital of the *vilayet*), there were between 30,000 and 40,000 with around 80–90% being Muslim (mostly Albanian), 8,000 or so Serbs (mostly Orthodox), and 2,000 Catholics. The population at that time also included about 2,000 Vlachs (Slavs speaking a Latinised language) known as *Gog* (stonemasons). In the 1860s, they formed their own school teaching in Greek and Serbian and later in Greek only. There were also Turkish, Serbian, Italian and Albanian schools supported by the various governments. Records from the 19th century show that there were 25 mosques in Prizren, 13 inns, eight *tekke* and two *hammams*. The Vlach minority used St Saviour's church which the Serb Orthodox population sought to reclaim in 1869, causing the Vlachs to set fire to the icon screen which was the most distinctively Serb item in the church. Over the years, the Vlachs became assimilated into the Serbian community and disappeared as a minority in Kosovo.

Political life in the region became increasingly unsettled in the late 1800s. As capital of a *vilayet* Prizren's fate was closely tied to the weakening Ottoman Empire. Relations between Albanians and Serbs first soured with the arrival of hundreds of **muhaxhir refugees** (Muslim Albanians) who were expelled from Niš and its surrounding areas in Serbia in the 1870s by the advancing Serbian armies. Albanians were increasingly concerned about the territorial ambitions of Serbia and that they might suffer the same fate as the recently expelled *muhaxhirs*. Formed around a group of leading intellectuals and wealthy landowners, Prizren became the home of the very first national Albanian movement in centuries – the League of Prizren. Prizren was a logical choice for the movement's base as it offered access to foreign embassies for lobbying. The League's diplomatic efforts, however, did not succeed and sensing the League shifting to more violent separatism the Ottoman Empire cracked down on the League's members, imprisoning some in the Prizren Fortress (Kalaja).

In 1913, when Kosovo and Prizren passed to the **Serbian Empire**, multi-ethnic and religious tolerance waned. The mosques were taken over and used as barracks and for munitions. From 1916 until 1918, Bulgarian occupying forces pursued a policy of 'Bulgarianisation' of the Serbs, forcing them to join the Bulgarian Orthodox Church. There was a shortage of food, which caused the deaths of 1,000 of the city's population. Those years also saw the first exodus of Prizren families who migrated to Turkey as part of ensuing treaties between Serbia and Turkey.

This political turmoil also took place against the backdrop of Prizren's economic decline. The opening of the railway line from Thessaloniki to Mitrovica dealt a severe blow to Prizren's position as Kosovo's commercial centre. The new borders between Serbian-occupied Kosovo and Albania also severed traditional trading links and cut off Prizren from its economic hinterland in Albania. Yet Prizren was by no means dead – there were still 1,000 shops in Prizren at this time and agriculture continued to employ around 87% of the population right up to 1930.

The Italian – and later German – occupation of Prizren in the 1940s brought some short-lived revival of traditional trading links with Albania, but after the break between Enver Hoxha and Marshal Tito, Prizren was forced to look east to the rest of Yugoslavia for trade. The final blow – or maybe a blessing – was the decision in 1947 to declare Prishtina the capital of Kosovo.

Under communism Prizren's economy was regenerated to some degree thanks to the food-processing plant Progres, the textile factory Printeks, a metalworking factory Famipa and pharmaceuticals plant Farmakos. Prizren was still a popular tourist destination and the Hotel Theranda became Prizren's top address. As a result of political and economic pressure by the authorities, a large number of Turkish-speaking families from Prizren migrated to Turkey in the period 1953–61. Of all the towns in Kosovo, however, Prizren has best preserved its Ottoman flair. Turkish, alongside Albanian and Serbian, is the third official language, and to this day Turkish is widely spoken in Prizren homes. It is also here that you can get the best baklava (a honey-sweetened nut pastry) in all of Kosovo. Prizren hopes to capitalise on its cultural heritage and is looking to tourism and agriculture to revive the local economy. The planned highway from the Serbian border through Prishtina joining up with the Albanian side to Durrës will greatly improve transport links and place Prizren again in the centre and not the periphery of this corner of the Balkans.

GETTING THERE AND AWAY The bus station no longer has an information telephone number, so to get the schedules you need to go there in person. Prizren is just over 1½ hours' drive from Prishtina (77km).

The first **bus** from Prishtina is at 06.50 (07.50 on Sunday), and the last at 19.45; buses leave every 15 minutes except Sundays when there are about half as many. The first bus from Prizren to Prishtina is at 05.45 and the last at 18.00.

Buses from Prizren to Peja leave every two hours starting at 06.50 until 17.45 and to Gjakova every 30 minutes starting at 06.00 until 16.00. Both services are less frequent on Sundays. There is one bus a day from Prizren to Gjilan at 13.15, and one from Prizren to Mitrovica at 17.00, going on to Novi Pazar, Serbia, where you can change for Sarajevo buses. Buses to Rahovec leave at 06.30, 06.55, 07.15 and 16.10, and to Klina at 06.05 and 12.50.

You can also travel directly to Belgrade (there are three buses a day, at 20.00, 20.30 and 21.00), Albania (departing at 19.30, arriving at 04.00, and goes the long way round even when the new tunnel/road is open, although at the time of writing services in Tirana via the tunnel were starting), and Skopje (departing at 05.30 and 09.00 – these buses go via Suha Rekë, Ferizaj and Kaçanik), and are operated by Vector Tours. The cost is €9 one-way. There is a daily bus to Podgorica, departing at 08.00 and one to Ulgin during the summer, leaving at 18.00. There is also a daily bus to Istanbul, which leaves at 13.00 and arrives the next day at 07.00, operated by Alpar Tourizm (*www.alparturizm.com*), a Turkish company whose representative office is Vector Travel (see travel agents, page 206). The full route is Peja–Prizren–Ferizaj–Skopje–Sofia–Plovdiv–Istanbul. The cost is €40 one-way, €60 return.

There is no direct bus to Prizren from Prishtina Airport but the **private taxi** driver Ibrahim Krasniqi (m *044 202 975/049 202 975;* e *ikrasniqi@yahoo.com*) runs a shuttle service at a cost of €35 one-way per car, taking up to four passengers. He is also available for other journeys in and around Kosovo and Albania/Macedonia. Alternatively a taxi from the airport is €50.

WHERE TO STAY Downtown Prizren has a shortage of hotel rooms and demand almost always exceeds supply, especially during Dokufest, so as an alternative consider staying in Vermicë or the Zhupa Valley, Suha Rekë, Rahovec or even in Gjakova. During Dokufest ther is a campsite for €7 for seven nights (see www.dokufest.org and pages 210–11).

Upmarket $$$$

🏠 **Hotel OK** (20 rooms) 🕿 029 624 769; m 044 131 761; e hotel_ok@hotmail.com. About 8km out of town on the road to Suha Rekë, Prishtina. Brand new, all-mod-cons hotel with indoor swimming pool, gym, large restaurant with outdoor terrace & free Wi-Fi.

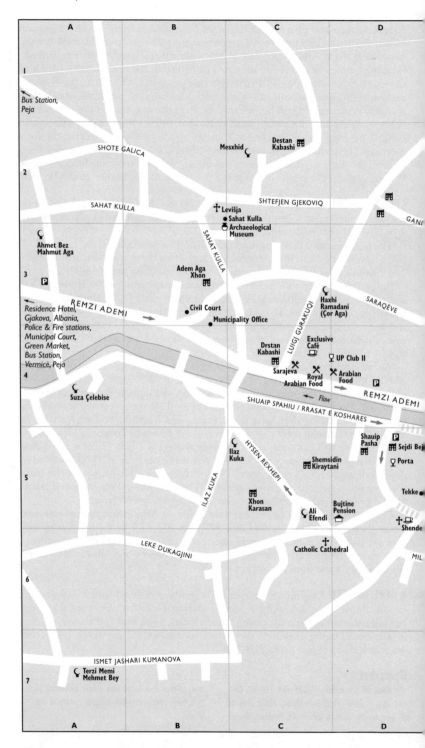

Bus Station,
Peja

SHOTE GALICA

Mesxhid

Destan
Kabashi

SHTEFJEN GJEKOVIQ

SAHAT KULLA

GANI

Levišja
Sahat Kulla
Archaeological
Museum

Ahmet Bez
Mahmut Aga

SAHAT KULLA

Adem Aga
Xhon

P

Haxhi
Ramadani
(Çor Aga)

SARAQËVE

REMZI ADEMI

Civil Court

Municipality Office

LUIGJ GURAKUQI

Residence Hotel,
Gjakova, Albania,
Police & Fire stations,
Municipal Court,
Green Market,
Bus Station,
Vermicë, Peja

Drstan
Kabashi

Exclusive
Café

UP Club II

Sarajeva
Arabian Food

Royal

Arabian
Food

P

Suza Çelebise

SHUAIP SPAHIU / RRASAT E KOSHARES

Flow

REMZI ADEMI

Shauip
Pasha

P

Sejdi Bej

Porta

Ilaz
Kuka

HYSEN REXHEPI

Shemsidin
Kiraytani

Tekke

ILAZ KUKA

Xhon
Karasan

Ali
Efendi

Bujtine
Pension

Shende

LEKE DUKAGJINI

Catholic Cathedral

MIL

ISMET JASHARI KUMANOVA

Terzi Memi
Mehmet Bey

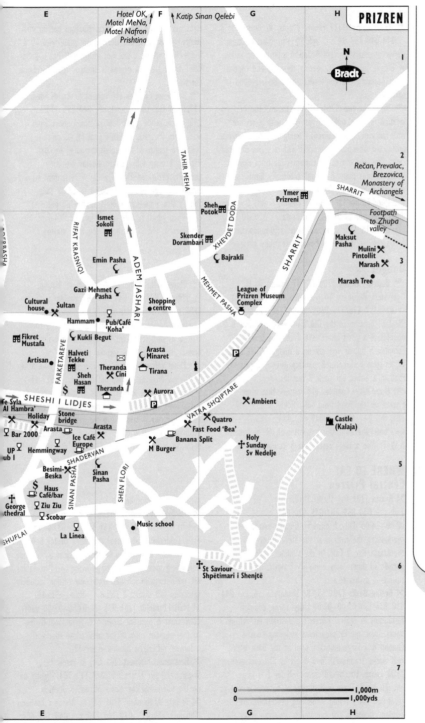

PRIZREN

Hotel OK,
Motel MeNa,
Motel Nafron
Prishtina

Katip Sinan Qelebi

N

Brad

Rečan, Prevalac,
Brezovica,
Monastery of
Archangels

SHARRIT

Footpath
to Zhupa
valley

Ymer
Prizreni

Sheh
Potok

Maksut
Pasha

Mulini
Pintollit
Marash

Ismet
Sokoli

Skender
Dorambari

TAHIR MEHA

XHEVDET DODA

Marash Tree

Emin Pasha

Bajrakli

SHARRIT

ADEM JASHARI

RIFAT KRASNIQI

Gazi Mehmet
Pasha

League of
Prizren Museum
Complex

MEHMET PASHA

Cultural
house

Sultan

Shopping
centre

Hammam

Pub/Café
'Koha'

Kukli Begut

Fikret
Mustafa

Halveti
Tekke

FARKETAREVE

Artisan

Theranda
Cini

Arasta
Minaret

P

Sheh
Hasan

Tirana

Theranda

SHESHI I LIDJES

Aurora

VATRA SHQIPTARE

Ambient

e Syla
Al Hambra'

Holiday

Stone
bridge

Arasta

P

Castle
(Kalaja)

Bar 2000

Arasta

Quatro

Ice Café
Europe

Fast Food 'Bea'

UP
ub I

Hemmingway

SHADERVAN

Banana Split

M Burger

Holy
Sunday
Sv Nedelje

Besimi-
Beska

SINAN PASHA

Sinan
Pasha

SHEN FLORI

Haus
Café/bar

Ziu Ziu

George
thedral

Scobar

La Linea

Music school

SHUFLAI

St Saviour
Shpëtimari i Shenjtë

0   1,000m
0   1,000yds

E   F   G   H

Mid-range $$$

🏠 **Centrum Hotel** (17 rooms, 3 apts) Rr Butinaj 1; ☎ 044/049 153 345; e info@centrumprizren.com; www.centrumprizren.com Beautiful interior decoration by filigree salesman, AC/heating. New top-end central hotel. Restaurant & conference room. Underground parking.

🏠 **Hotel Theranda** [201 F4] (56 rooms) The best location in town, right on the river, with a terrace with fantastic views. Currently being renovated after a protracted privatisation process with a series of court cases. The new owner, an entrepreneur from Prizren, has ambitious plans & should eventually finish the renovation by spring 2011.

🏠 **Hotel Tirana** [201 F4](13 rooms, 1 apt) Opposite Hotel Theranda above NLB Prishtina; ☎ 029 30 818; m 044 216 155; e tirana_hotelpz@yahoo.com. A concrete, socialist-style building centrally placed

right next to the Archaeological Museum but no view. Somewhat old style but clean & adequate with AC & fridge. No parking. B/fast not included. It has a good-value triple room & overall is cheaper than Residence Complex.

🏠 **Residence Complex** (10 rooms) Rr Remzi Ademaj 117 (near municipal court); m 044 255 774/135 298; e residence_pz@hotmail.com. A short 5min walk from the centre. With digital TV, AC, en-suite rooms (6 singles & 4 doubles), including minibar. Popular & often fully booked. Rooms are fairly tastefully decorated. There's a bar & restaurant serving traditional food open from 06.00 to 23.00 daily. There's also a meeting room (capacity 80 persons) & a disco which is only rented for occasional private functions so should not deter you from staying.

Budget $$

🏠 **Bujtine Pension** [200 D5] (7 rooms) Rr M Ugarevic/E Bujtinave 14 (near the Catholic church); ☎ 029 231 628/223 860; m 044 113 252. Pleasant pension in the Old Town with 5 singles & 2 doubles, & a good alternative if the Residence Complex is full or you are on a budget. Wi-Fi, cable TV, en-suite bathrooms & parking directly across the road in a public car park. B/fast included.

🏠 **Hotel Albes Complex** (18 rooms) 4km from Prizren on the road from Suha Rekë. ☎ 029 247 381; m 044 484 104/049 633 133; www.hotelalbes.com. Good rooms with AC, bathrooms & Wi-Fi. Also a large restaurant & conference room.

🏠 **Motel MeNa** (8 rooms) Next to Motel Nafron; ☎ 029 622 373; m 044 304 580. Popular with KFOR troops. Good value at half the price of the Residence Complex in town, with nice rooms & friendly staff & its own restaurant. En-suite bathrooms, central heating, digital TV, AC & secured parking.

🏠 **Motel Nafron** (8 rooms) On the road to Suha Rekë, 5–10mins' drive or 6–8km out of town. ☎ 029 41 840. An alternative if MeNa is full as it is less cosy & has a room for weddings underneath (which means noise, especially in summer) & the heating is only accumulators so it is colder in winter. With modern décor, TV, en-suite bathrooms & parking directly outside.

✖ WHERE TO EAT
Central Prizren

✖ **Arasta** [201 F5] Sheshi Shadërvan; ☎ 029 222 255; m 044 859 887/049 420 049; ⏲ 08.00–24.00 daily. A bustling, friendly restaurant overlooking the river near the Stone Bridge, beside the Arasta Bar & Café. In the summer tables are set outside so diners may enjoy river views. Traditional cuisine – dishes €2–7.

✖ **Besimi-Beska** [201 E5] Rr Shadërvan 56; m 044 230 836; ⏲ 07.00–02.00 daily. Large, popular restaurant in central Prizren's pedestrian district, on 3 floors. Some quirky ornaments including Charlie Chaplin & a large fountain, pool at the back with real ducks. Traditional food & pizzas. There is even a KFOR kebab. The mixed meat dish for 1 is large enough for 2. There is a display of options as you go in, if you fancy trying something new. There are outdoor tables in the summer so you can enjoy the

main-square atmosphere.

✖ **Holiday** [201 E5] Rr Rrasat e Koshares (Shuaip Spahiu); m 044 807 777/151 597; ⏲ 08.00–24.00 daily. Centrally located near the Stone Bridge between the ProCredit & Raiffeisen banks, Holiday is a busy but welcoming spot for dining or enjoying a coffee. Tables are set outside in summer. Traditional cuisine, including speciality fish dishes, & pizzas – dishes €1–10.

✖ **Mulini Pintollit** [201 H3] ⏲ 07.00–23.00 daily. Convenient & pleasant location & good food. Owing to the religious links of the area (close to the site of a former *tekke*), no alcohol is served.

✖ **Restaurant Ambient** [20! G4] Rr Vatrat Shqiptare/Tetori 1; m 044/049 119 964. Slightly up on the hill below the castle. Attractive position.

✖ **Te Syla 'Al Hambra'** [201 E4] Rr Rrasat e Koshares (Shuaip Spahiu); ☎ 029 240 240; m 044 147 604;

⏱ 07.00–23.00 daily. No trip to Prizren is complete without a visit to its most famous *qebaptore*-restaurant. Te Syla started some 40 years ago as a street vendor & as his popularity grew he eventually established this restaurant. Centrally located beside Raiffeisen Bank, near Holiday Restaurant, Al Hambra offers excellent quality & service & is particularly busy during lunch/dinner times & on weekends. Traditional cuisine, speciality meat dishes (kebabs & *pleskavica*) – main dishes €1–5.

✗ **Theranda Cini** [201 F4] Rr Adem Jashari; ⏱ 07.00–24.00 daily. Located on the ground floor of the Theranda Hotel, this newly renovated restaurant offers a range of traditional & Italian dishes.

Fast food

While there is an abundance of fast-food options located around Prizren, a good selection is located on Rr Vatrat Shqiptare (beside the river near Shadërvan). In summer tables are set out beside the river, which makes for a lively yet relaxing atmosphere. Prices at these popular places are generally between €1 and €4.

✗ **Fast Food 'Bea'** [201 F5] Rr Vatrat Shqiptare 28; ⏱ 08.00–24.00 daily. A take-away/diner with excellent food & service, offering a range of pizzas, hamburgers, kebabs/*pleskavica*, sandwiches & salads.

✗ **M Burger** [201 F5] Rr Vatrat Shqiptare 4; m 044 362 995; ⏱ 08.00–24.00 daily. A take-away/diner that also offers a delivery service. Offers a range of pizza, hamburgers, sandwiches & salads.

✗ **Quatro** [201 G5] Rr Vatrat Shqiptare 23; ⏱ 08.00–23.00 daily. A take-away/diner with Turkish flair. Offers a range of Turkish-style pizza, hamburgers & sandwiches.

Elsewhere in Prizren

✗ **Aurora** [201 F4] Rr Adem Jashari (beside the river); m 044 642 185; ⏱ 06.00–03.00 daily. Located opposite Theranda Hotel, this large 2-storey cafeteria-style eatery is a very popular place to eat in or take out. Offers a range of kebabs, pizza, pasta, *burek*, cakes & pastries.

✗ **Royal Arabian Food** [200 C4] (shortly to be renamed – under new management) Rr Remzi Ademi 34, beside the Arabian Food Bakery; ⏱ 07.00–24.00 daily. Offers a range of burgers, sandwiches, pizza, omelettes & salads.

✗ **Sarajeva** [200 C4] Rr Remzi Ademi 36; ⏱ 08.00–21.00 Mon–Sat. Sarajeva is the sister restaurant to Te Syla Al Hambra. Located on the other side of the river near the municipality offices, Sarajeva offers traditional meat dishes (kebabs/*pleskavica*).

✗ **Turkish Rest Akdeniz** Rr Zahir Pajaziti 48 (on the ring road near Ortokol area); m 044 426 496; ⏱ 07.00–23.00 daily. A very popular restaurant/diner that offers a selection of Turkish fast food (*meze*, meat specialities & doner kebabs), & also pizza.

If you are in a hurry, en route to the bus station there are also many *qebapatore*, small diners and cafés along Rr De Rada/Remzi Ademi starting from the civil court.

Bakeries

Arabian Food [200 D4] Rr Remzi Ademi 34; ⏱ 07.00–24.00 daily. This newly established bakery offers a wide range of delicious Jordanian speciality breads, baklava, pastries, cookies & sweets. Well worth a visit & the sweets/cookies would make ideal gifts.

Sultan [201 E4] Rr Saraçet/Farketareve; ⏱ 07.30–23.00 daily. This long-established Turkish bakery, with outlets also in Prishtina, is considered to be the most famous in Kosovo with a range of delicious Turkish cakes, pastries, baklava, cookies & sweets.

Cafés

⎉ **Arasta** [201 E5] Sheshi Shadërvan; ⏱ 08.00–23.00 daily. A bustling, friendly bar/café in a prime location beside the Stone Bridge. In the summer tables are set outside so patrons may enjoy river views.

⎉ **Banana Split** [201 F5] Rr Vatrat Shqiptare 4; ⏱ 07.00–24.00 daily. A popular café & ice-cream parlour offering an array of Gorani speciality cakes & pastries.

⎉ **Exclusive Café** [200 C4] Rr Remzi Ademi 34 (above the Arabian Food Bakery); ⏱ 07.00–24.00 daily. Overlooking the river, this café offers a selection of coffees, teas & cakes.

⎉ **Haus Café/Bar** [201 E5] Rr Besim Ndreca (just off Sheshi Shadërvan); ⏱ 07.00–24.00 daily. A popular café with a vivid atmosphere offering good-quality food & service. Offers a range of pitta-style sandwiches, *burek*, cakes, pastries, baklava & ice creams. Free Wi-Fi.

🛏️**Ice Café Europe** [201 E5] Sheshi Shadërvan 9; ⏰ 08.00–24.00 daily. A popular café, offering a range of cakes, pastries, baklava & ice creams.

Bars

♀️**Bar 2000** [201 E5] Rr Shadërvan (behind Al Hambra Restaurant); ⏰ 09.00–24.00 daily. Popular with the students. Live music on the weekends.

♀️**Hemmingway** [201 E5] Sheshi Shadërvan 62; ⏰ 08.00–24.00 daily. Set in a prime location in the main square, patrons may observe the comings & goings through Sheshi Shadërvan. Free Wi-Fi.

♀️**La Linea** [201 E6] At the top of Rr Sinan Pasha. DJs & live music attracts a hip crowd that are into the Dokufest.

♀️**Makadam** Just off Shadërvan to the left; ⏰ 08.00–24.00. The tables outside are crowded with young people in the summer. 2 floors inside.

♀️**Porta** [200 D5] Rr Pushkataret 13; ⏰ 09.00–24.00 daily. A favourite haunt of university students who like to hang out in either the bar area or the garden outside. 'Broadcasts' Albanian rap music to the surrounding neighbourhood. Live music on weekends with many of the leading Kosovar

🛏️**Shendeti** [200 D5] Rr Shadërvan 39; ⏰ 07.00–23.00 daily. A cosy, friendly atmosphere with good-quality food & service. Offers a range of burek, cakes, pastries, baklava & ice creams. Free Wi-Fi.

bands & entertainers performing there.

♀️**Pub/Café 'Koha'** [201 F4] Rr Sheshi i Lidjes 17; ⏰ 08.00–24.00 daily. This bar/café has indoor/outdoor seating & is a popular meeting point.

♀️**Scobar** [201 E5] Besim Ndreca (just off Sheshi Shadërvan); ⏰ 09.00–24.00 daily. Lively atmosphere. Free Wi-Fi.

♀️**UP Club I** [201 E5] Rr Shadërvan 36; ⏰ 09.00–24.00 daily. This bar/café also has indoor/outdoor seating & is popular with the young trendy set. Free Wi-Fi.

♀️**UP Club II** [200 C4] Rr Remzi Ademi 34 (above the Arabian Food Bakery); ⏰ 20.00–03.00 daily. This disco & bar offers live music on the weekends & is popular with the young trendy set. UP Club is also a member of Facebook.

♀️**Ziu Ziu Bar** [201 E5] Off Shadërvan. Another bar attracting a young & trendy crowd.

ENTERTAINMENT The **Dokufest** (*www.dokufest.com*) is a renowned documentary film festival held in several venues over four or more days each August. For information see the website or contact Prizren municipality.

SHOPPING
Bookshops

Dituria Remzi Ademi 9; 📱 044 131 335; ⏰ 07.00–19.00 Mon–Fri, 07.00–18.00 Sat. Offers a range of educational & general-interest books.
Headway Libraria Rr Sheshi i Lidhjes 17A; 📱 049 139 624; ⏰ 08.00–19.00 Mon–Sat. Offers a range

of local & international books.
Siprint-R Rr Sheshi Shadërvan 1; 📱 044 210 423/113 465; ⏰ 07.00–17.00 Mon–Sat. Offers a ranges of educational, general-interest, local & international books.

Computer shops

Cleon Rr Iljaz Kuka 3; ⏰ 09.00–19.00 Mon–Sat. Sells computer, IT equipment & office supplies.
Eltine Electronics Rr Sahat Kulla 67; ⏰ 09.00–18.00 Mon–Sat. In addition to its computer & electronics sales, it offers business services (scanning, photocopying, fax, printing, etc). It is also an agent

for IPKO phone & internet services.
Media World Computer Shop Rr Rrasat E Koshares (Shuaip Spahiu); ⏰ 09.00–18.00 Mon–Fri, 09.00–14.00 Sat. Sells computers, IT equipment & office supplies.

Food There is a Ben-Af **supermarket** (⏰ *daily*) to the north of town at the Peja roundabout on the ring road. Behind Ben-Af is the newly opened Albi shopping centre (⏰ *daily*). ETC, a major hypermarket/supermarket, is on the road to Vermicë.

Wednesday is **market** day with many traders and farmers from Albania and the villages in the mountains converging on Prizren to conduct business. They usually arrive using various modes of transport ranging from large trucks, cars, tractors, *kombi* (a rotavator with trailer), to horse-drawn carts. Green Market (⊕ *daily*) is located about 3km out of town on the road to Vermicë/Albania with a wide selection of vendors selling food, clothing and household items, and some livestock.

Markets in the Ortokol area sell food, clothing and domestic wares. The market on the road to Prishtina (near the German KFOR camp) sells furniture and livestock. Traffic can be heavy morning and evening on market day, so plan some extra time for a journey around town.

Sports equipment

Sporting Rr Shesi i Lidhjes 2; ☎ 029 222 361; ☎ 029 243 346; m 044 116 368; e sporting_pz@hotmail.com; www.sportingks.com. Road & mountain bikes for sale (distributor for Aprilla & Scott bikes), basic spare parts (including inner tubes, etc), & other sporting gear including weights.

Souvenirs

Souvenirs Prizren has a long history in the art of **filigree**. While a small number of producers still manufacture for the local and export market, there are collections of jewellery and filigree shops located on the outer part of Rr Adem Jashari (to Prishtina) and in the Sheshi Shadërvan.

Krystal souvenir shop Rr Remzi Ademi 36; ⊕ 09.00–18.00 Mon–Sat. Sells a variety of local & imported souvenirs & artefacts.

Souvenir Shop Rr Rrasat e Koshares (Shuaip Spahiu) 10; ⊕ 09.00–20.00 Mon–Sat. Sells a range of interesting local & imported souvenirs.

OTHER PRACTICALITIES

Banks There is a Raiffeisen Bank at Sheshi Shadërvan 38 (☎ *029 630 103*); and also Rr Nёne Terezё 7 (☎ *029 626 257; e prizren-info@ raiffeisen-kosovo.com;* ⊕ *08.00–17.00 Mon–Fri, 10.00–14.00 Sat*). A branch of ProCredit is located at Rr Zhair Pajzati (☎ *029 43 149*).

Car hire Self-drive options in Prizren are limited to one local company.

🚗 **Fargen Rent-a-Car** Mr Alihajdar Bujari; m 044 390 290; e fargen49@hotmail.com

Car repairs

Auto salon 'Muzbeg' Rr L Bukabjini; m 044 149 459; e ertan_mclaron@hotmail.com

Auto servis 'Renault' m 044 200 891

Dry cleaners

Diolen Rr Farketareve; ☎ 029 30 401; m 044 126 524; ⊕ 09.00–17.00 Mon–Sat

Yliza Rr Iljaz Kuka 8; ⊕ 09.00–17.00 Mon–Sat

Gyms and fitness centres

Hidi Gym Rr Iljaz Kuka 22; ⊕ 09.00–22.00 Mon–Sat. A modern, well-equipped gym with a small café. Membership options range from 1 day to 3 months; bring ID if applying for membership. Female members are eligible for a discount. It also has locker & shower facilities.

Internet cafés/telephone kiosk

Dreni Tours Rr Remzi Ademi 36; ⊕ 08.00–18.00 daily. Internet café with business services (scanning, photocopying, fax, etc).

Internet Café Meganet Rr Pushkataret (opposite the offices of the Privatisation Agency of Kosovo (nr 9), & just around the corner from Café Shendeti (Rr Shadervan 39)); ⊕ 08.00–20.00 daily

Ipko Rr Remzi Ademi 30; ⏲ 08.00—19.00 daily. You can also buy IPKO sim & top-up cards from **Eltine Electronics** (*Rr Sahat Kulla 67;* ⏲ *09.00—18.00 Mon—Sat*).
Telephone Kiosk Rr Remzi Ademi 23; ⏲ 09.00—19.00

Mon—Sat. Provides discount call rates to local & international numbers.
Telephon Sheshi Shadërvan 6; ⏲ 08.00—21.00 daily. Services include phone calls, fax, & purchase of scratchcards.

Language schools
Oxford Studio (English Language School) Rr Sheshi i Lidjes (opposite the Headway Bookshop; ☎ 038 554 657; www.oxford-studio.com

Locksmith (key cutting)
There are a number of locksmiths' shops on Rr Sahat Kulla (behind the municipality offices) that provide key cutting and other services.

Silica Service (Rr Sahat Kulla 74; ☎ 029 224 224; m 044 718 484; ⏲ 08.00—18.00 Mon—Sat) also offers a 24hour callout service.

Photocopying shops
There are numerous places around town. Many shops are located around the various court houses and the municipality offices, particularly Rr Sahat Kulla/Rr Remzi Ademi. Usual opening hours are 08.00—17.00 Mon—Sat.

Photography
Fotoshop Feran Rr Suzi Qelebi 58; ⏲ 08.00—20.00 Mon—Sat. Also provides printing services (cards, letterheads, stationery, etc).

Fuji Film 'Xharra' Rr Suzi Qelebi; ☎ 029 231 582; m 044 486 828; ⏲ 09.00—18.00 Mon—Sat

Post office/postal services
DHL Rr Rrasat e Koshares (Shuaip Spahiu) 44; ☎ 029 623 364; m 044 128 739

PTK Main office, Rr Adem Jashari (beside Hotel Theranda); ⏲ 08.00—18.00 Mon—Sat

Religious services
Catholic church Rr Papa Gjon/Rr Pal Paluca. Masses on Sun & holidays at 08.45 & 11.00.

Shoe repairs (cobblers)
Iliza Kuka 6 (beside Yliza dry cleaners); ⏲ 08.00—18.00 Mon—Sat

Tailors
Robaqepese 'Shyki' Rr Remzi Ademi 20; m 044 777 987; ⏲ 09.00—18.00 Mon—Sat. Bespoke dressmaker & seamstress who also sells traditional costumes made locally.

Tailor Rr Pushkataret 17 (in the shopping arcade); ⏲ 08.00—18.00 Mon—Sat. Bespoke tailor with alteration service.

Taxis
🚕 **Blue Taxi** m 044 555 252
🚕 **Fortuna** ☎ 029 630 222; m 044 380 000/334 433

🚕 **OK Radio Taxi** ☎ 029 225 557; m 044/049 333 500/600

There are lots of ranks at Rr De Rada (beside the bus station), Rr Remzi Ademi (near the Residence Complex), Rr Shuaip Spahiu (over the bridge opposite the municipality offices) and Rr Adem Jashari (outside the Hotel Theranda).

Travel agents

WHAT TO SEE AND DO Allow at least a half day to see Prizren. If you wish to go up to the castle and to visit the sights further out from the centre you will need a full day or more. Sredska and Srnica villages need a day for themselves.

True to form, one of the first things German KFOR troops did was to improve the roads and institute a one-way system. While much needed, the one-way system can be confusing for the first-time visitor. Furthermore, because parking is not easy and much of Prizren is pedestrianised or has narrow streets not suited to cars, the best option is to park your car either on the outskirts, eg: the road to Prishtina as you come in or a car park on the Sharr road (if approaching from Prevalac). You can also drive into the centre and park in the car parks at the following locations for a fee: the top of Rr Adem Jashari, near Aurora opposite the Theranda Hotel); Rr Shuaip Spahiu, near the Al Hambra Restaurant; or Rr Bujtinat, opposite the Bujtine Pension. Parking rates are about €0.60 per hour so if you plan to stay longer and particularly if you are staying at any of the out-of-town hotels it can be better to park further out and get a taxi there and back.

Below is a suggested walking tour, commencing from outside Hotel Theranda.

Around the Hotel Theranda Standing by the Hotel Theranda, you have a stark contrast between the communist new buildings of the post office next door, the Hotel Tirana opposite and the old architecture. Opposite the PTK is the **minaret of Arasta Mosque** [201 F4]. After local protests this part of the 1526 mosque was saved when the remainder of the area was made a shopping area in 1960–61.

There is a rather decaying **socialist war memorial** on the river just before the car park and behind the Tirana Hotel with a triangle that is supposed to symbolise Yugoslavia, and a concrete culvert with running water to symbolise life. The story behind this is that it is a memorial to commemorate Nazi victims who were murdered near the riverbank in 1944. There is also a separate UÇK memorial here.

Behind the Hotel Theranda is **Kukli begut/Xhamia e Saraçhanes** [201 E4]. This mosque was built in 1534. The name Saraçhane means 'saddlers' and their market area used to be nearby. Hajredin Kukli Bey was not badly off – he allegedly had 117 shops, six mills and a motel. The mosque has retained much of its character from that date and is linked with the adjacent Halveti Tekke.

The **Halveti Tekke** [201 E4] is more than 350 years old. Prizren is the headquarters for the *tarikat* order in the region with other Halveti branches in Rahovec, Mitrovica and Albania. The dervish ceremonies room is attractive with old wooden cupboards and shelves with the swords of the members, ornate instruments used in the ceremonies and rows of the white felt hats. The black-rimmed hats are used by the more experienced members. Ceremonies are held every Thursday after evening prayers and it is possible to attend as long as you are discreet. You can walk through the pleasant courtyard and past the restored wood fence lattice *türbe* out the other side back towards Hotel Theranda.

Squeezed between the hotel and the *tekke* is an old nobleman's house. This is **Sheh Hasan House** [201 E4], which is one of the few remaining examples of the traditional Ottoman town house, dating from probably the 18th century. It includes the old woodwork lattice room on stilts. Whilst a protected building, it remains inhabited by a large family today. The Museum of the League of Prizren (see pages 210–11) or the Society for the Protection of Monuments can apparently arrange tours of the inside which includes some old wooden ceilings. The side road running down from the Theranda past the BpB Bank from the main road is known as Farketareve, which means 'metalworkers', and a few metres along at the *tekke* entrance there is another old yellow dilapidated house. In the basement is an **ironmongers and artisan shop**. At the back of the shop on the wall is a selection of knives which are carved by the owner from animal bones and horns (this was a Prizren speciality), and he will happily engrave your name on them. For a few euros you have a perfect pocket knife souvenir of Prizren to replace all those Swiss penknives confiscated at the airport. Prizren metalworkers were also famous for gunmaking, screens, decorative door handles and door knockers.

North of the centre If you head away from the river up the Farketareve and round the back of the Kukli Mosque, then behind the post office is the **Gazi Mehmet Pasha Hammam** [201 F4]. These Turkish baths were built in 1573 by Gazi Mehmet Pasha at the same time as the mosque nearby (which also included a madrasa). The baths consisted of separate male and female areas. Each part had a rest room, bath steam room and water-heating room. The *hammam* operated fully until 1926 when the female area was closed. It was then closed completely in 1944 from when it served as a storage and sales area for the agricultural co-operative. Conservation works were carried out when Prizren had a cultural revival in 1968, but it fell into disrepair again and was used partly as a market. It was renovated once more after the war and is now used as an art gallery or venue for artistic functions. The entrance is at the northern end furthest away from PTK opposite the mosque. It is worth trying to get inside as the rooms, while not quite as well preserved as the Skopje Old Town *hammams*, still give you a feel for how the baths once were.

On the other side but close by is the **Emin Pasha Mosque** [201 F3]. This Arabian-style mosque was built much later than the *hammam* – at the same time as many other buildings in 1831 when Prizren was really in its heyday. Its benefactor, Emin Pasha, travelled widely around the Ottoman Empire and his attractive white marble grave is in the grounds. The incongruous glass surround was a recent unfortunate mistake.

Further up the main road to Prishtina (Adem Jashari) on the left-hand side is the Baroque-style house of **Ismet Sokoli** [201 F3], a member of the League of Prizren, dating from the 19th century. Allegedly the stairs inside are wrought iron, made by Prizren craftworkers.

On the main Prishtina road you will also see other remnants of Prizren's crafts – lots of filigree shops. This is also the part of town where the brides-to-be come to shop – there are lots of wedding-dress shops. If you want an Albanian man's white felt hat there is even a shop on one corner selling these. A more modern shopping centre is midway up the street. There is another mosque further up the Prishtina main road – **Katip Sinan Qelebi** from 1591 – but now cross the main road and turn back to the **Complex of the League of Prizren**.

The League of Prizren complex Part of the League complex, with the entrance behind (as opposed to from the riverside) behind the wooden fencing is **Gazi Mehmet Pasha** or **Bajrakli Mosque** [201 F3]. This dates from 1566 and is possibly the most beautiful mosque in Prizren (on a par with Gjakova's Hadum Mosque) with ornate woodwork and detailed blue-and-white paintings. Note the row of seats and individual water fountains for washing. There was also a library here and possibly a madrasa (Islamic school). The term 'Bajrakli' is used for the main mosque which raised the prayer flag as a signal to the other mosques for the time for prayer.

On the other side of Rr Xhevdet Doda, diagonally opposite the mosque entrance, are two houses from the 19th century, **Sheh Potok House** and **Skender**

Dorambari House [201 G2], both of which need renovation. In an even worse state, further along this road, round the corner is the **house of Ymer Prizreni**, a mud-and-wood construction which is crumbling down and just about propped up with some metal supports. Ymer Prizreni was the prime minister in the provisional government created during the League of Prizren. He died at the age of 65, suspected murdered, during political asylum in Montenegro.

You can now come out on to the main road again near the river. At this point you can either cross the bridge if you like to the **Maksut Pasha Mosque** [201 H3] or visit the League of Prizren Museum.

The **League of Prizren Museum** [201 G3] (⏲ *09.00–15.00, 16.30 or later in the summer; entrance €1*) is a complex of buildings on the riverbank reconstructed in late 1999 after being burnt down in March 1999 by the Serbian forces. Unlike many reconstructions, however, it has been done well and is well worth a visit (see also pages 210–11). There are two buildings on either side of the courtyard – the main entrance building and then the smaller two-storey one which fronts the road. The smaller one contains a map of greater Albania but perhaps most interestingly for the English-speaking visitor upstairs in a glass cabinet are copies of letters during the era in English, including some from the foreign office adviser Earl Fitzmaurice to the Earl of Granville commenting on the League, the inhabitants of the area and their religion. In the larger, main building downstairs are traditional Albanian costumes and upstairs are photos of places associated with the League and the Albanian lands at the time, including photos of Tivar (present-day Bar in Montenegro), Shkodra in Albania, Plav in present-day Montenegro as well as photos of embassies in Turkey which were closely associated with émigrés from Niš and the lobbying which was carried on for the Albanian cause. Unfortunately the photos do not have any English-language explanations.

At the far end upstairs amongst ceramic plates of Albanian heroes is a rug which has sewn into it the different types of wool hats of the Albanians – the conical shape for the north and Kosovo and the more rounded one of southern Albania.

Eastern Prizren From the League Museum you can cross the river and walk upstream to the mosque on the corner, **Maskut Pasha Mosque** [201 H3], dating from 1833. The garden of the mosque includes some old graves. The mosque is again linked with a tekke, in this case the Sa'adi tarikat. This *tekke* was founded by the grand *tekke* in Gjakova by Sheh Sulejman Efendi, who is buried in the *türbe* with the inscription which includes a phrase highly apt for Kosovo which always seems to be an interim or temporary state:

> With his citations and ceremonies he has enhanced God's majesty until he came to know the secrets of Sahedin 'that everything in the world is transitory'.

The *tekke* was associated with Albanian separatism and the second League of Prizren. The Sheh Musa Shehzhade Shehu was murdered here in 1944 by Slav communists, and the *tekke* subsequently destroyed in 1950. There are plans to restore the *tekke* on the plateau just above the remaining *türbe*. As you can see the water was diverted to flow through the *tekke* area. The *tekke* had tearooms attached to it next to the Marash tree. This was destroyed by the communist authorities and replaced with a *qebaptore* (kebab shop). The Kosovo Privatisation Agency sought to privatise the rather ungainly building right on the waterfront, but halted the plan amongst howls of protest as the land is regarded as belonging to the *tekke*, having been expropriated at a time when the *tekke* was regarded an enemy of the state. The *tekke* has plans to restore its own tearooms. For now, in lieu of the original tearooms you can find the Marash Café which is just a little further on the right-hand side.

In 1877, Russia declared war against the Ottoman Empire in present-day Bulgaria. Serbia and Montenegro seized this chance to open a second flank and advanced south towards Niš far into Kosovo territory. A weakened Ottoman Empire signed the Treaty of San Stefano with Russia, effectively creating a large Bulgarian state and granting large parts of Albanian-populated lands in Montenegro and south Serbia to Serbia. In response, the Albanian population living in Niš, Vranje, Prokuplje and Leskovac was kicked out forcefully by the victorious Serbian army. Around 50,000 Albanian Muslims – known as *muhaxhirs* (refugees) – flooded into Kosovo. Meanwhile, the Great European Powers led by Bismarck called for a second peace conference in Berlin. France, England and Germany were reluctant to grant Russia and Bulgaria the great spoils of the disintegrating Ottoman European provinces. The revised Treaty of Berlin conceded Niš, Gusinje and Plav to Serbia and Montenegro, but returned large swathes of land to the Ottoman Empire.

The Albanian national leaders were alarmed by the Serbian advance, the expulsion of Albanians and the weakness of the Ottoman Empire. Propelled by this concern, the Albanian leadership in Prizren began to organise for the first time on any significant scale since the Skenderbeg uprising in the Middle Ages. The diaspora, led by the Istanbul-educated Frasheri brothers (Abdyl and Sami) took the lead, and in December 1877, established a 'Committee for Defence of the Rights of the Albanian nation'.

The committee began lobbying for the Albanian cause using diplomatic lobbying via the embassies in Prizren and sending letters to the Great Powers. It soon became clear that diplomacy would not achieve the hoped-for results.

The League's manifesto was written up within the *Kanararname*, or *Book of Decisions*. In Article 1 of this document, the Albanian leaders restated their intention to preserve and maintain the territorial integrity of the Ottoman Empire in the Balkans by supporting the Turkish sultan, calling for Islamic Sharia law (based on the principles of the tekkes), and 'to struggle in arms to defend the wholeness of the territories'.

Article 6 stated: 'We should not allow foreign armies to tread on our land. We should not recognise Bulgaria's name. If Serbia does not leave peacefully the illegally occupied countries, we should send *bashibazouks* (*akindjias*) and strive until the end to liberate these regions, including Montenegro.'

From the Ottoman vilayets of Kosovo and from Bitola they requested the formation of a united Albanian vilayet. The Prizren League created a provisional government with a president, prime minister (Ymer Prizreni) and ministries of war (Sylejman Vokshi) and a foreign ministry (Abdyl Frasheri). Other members included Bajram Curri and Hasan Prishtina.

The committee met several times in Prizren, including in the mosque behind the present-day League building. The League wrote formally to the Berlin Congress in July 1878 and to various diplomats:

> …To annex to Montenegro or to any other Slav state, countries inhabited ab antiquo by Albanians who differ essentially in their language, in their origin, in their customs, in their traditions, and in their religion, would be not only a crying injustice, but further an impolitic act,

The wide oriental tree **Rrapi i Marashit** [201 H3] with a 2m-wide trunk is unique in the Balkans and survives because of the favourable sheltered climate in the valley bend where it stands. The myth from the *tekke* is that there were originally three trees which grew from three pieces of wood taken out of the fire by the founder Sheh Sylejman.

This whole stretch of the river had several mills on it as the river was fast flowing. As if there had not been enough damage done to local sensitivities on this side of the river, the 1990s' authorities also destroyed the 18th-century Shotman which cannot fail to cause complaints, discontent and sanguinary conflicts… notwithstanding their longing to escape the misfortunes which Turkish rule has inflicted on them for five centuries, the Albanians will never submit themselves to any Slav State which Russia may attempt to put forward; race, language, customs (...) national pride, everything, in a word, is opposed to such a state of things; and it is neither just nor prudent to free them from a yoke only to place them under another, which would in no way ameliorate their social position.

Yet despite all the requests sent to heads of state by so many Albanians, Albania was not granted autonomy in any form. Similar to Metternich who once claimed that there was no Italian nation, Bismarck declared that: 'Albania is merely a geographic expression; there is no Albanian nation.'

The League's pleas were ignored and instead Albanian-populated areas like Ioannina in modern-day Greece were given to the Greeks. Having failed therefore to win their claims on a diplomatic level, Albanians set out to redraw the map militarily. Within weeks, the Prizren League had an estimated 16,000 armed members under its control.

At first, the League was supported by Istanbul and even assisted with donated arms. When the League succeeded in effectively bringing all of Kosovo under its control, it was increasingly seen as a threat by the sultan. With military success – the League succeeded in taking back parts of Epirus in northern Greece – the League's national demands increased and instead of autonomy, which may have been tolerated, it demanded complete secession from the Ottoman Empire. In 1878, Mehmed Ali Pasha, a Turkish emissary sent to Gjakova to oversee the redrawing of the boundary as foreseen by the Berlin Congress, was killed. That marked a decisive turning point in the relations between the League of Prizren and the sultan. The Ottoman Empire withdrew its support, believing that the League posed a dangerous threat, and sent an army led by Turkish commander Dervish Pasha to suppress the League. By April 1881, the Ottoman Empire regained control, captured Prizren and crushed the resistance at Ulcinj. There were fierce battles at Slivove, Shtime, Caraleve and Qafa e Dules (which is the hill on the road from Shtime to Prizren). The leaders of the League either fled or they were caught, their families killed, arrested and imprisoned in the Prizren Fortress (as was the case with Abdyl Frasheri). Ymer Prizreni, the League's prime minister, sought refuge in Montenegro where he was then killed under unclear circumstances.

While it was active, the League managed to some degree to bring Albanian national interests to the fore with the Great Powers even if their requests were rejected. This paved the way for the League of Peja of 1899, which enjoyed more foreign support from both Italy and the Austro-Hungarian Empire. The first League of Prizren was also the inspiration for the second League of Prizren which was formed in 1943 and which allied with the Germans to preserve Albanian independence from Yugoslavia. To this day, the formation of the League of Prizren in 1878 and its anniversaries are celebrated by Kosovo Albanians as the moment of their national awakening. It is interesting to think what would have occurred if the League's requests had been heeded by the Great Powers – events in the 20th and 21st centuries might have been quite different.

Mill. Now in lieu of any operating mills, further back towards town and only about 200m from the *tekke* and the tree is the **Mulini (mill) Restaurant** [201 H3], which is on the site of the former mill.

Central Prizren – the south bank It is possible to continue upstream on foot as a pathway has now been built which continues for several miles and makes for pleasant riverside walking or possibly a biking route heading out in the countryside past a sports pitch and swimming pool to the Monastery of Archangels, the Hydroelectric

Museum and Korishte Monastery (see page 216). In the summer this route is full of picnickers, and this is the venue for the campsite during the Dokufest (see page 75).

Assuming you want to stay in town, however, continue back downstream along the river towards the stone bridge and to the cobbled Shadërvan (Fountain Square).

The **16th-century stone–arched bridge** [201 E5] is a well-known symbol of Prizren. In 1979, the swirling storm waters destroyed the bridge and it was painstakingly renovated stone by stone in 1982.

Sinan Pasha Mosque [201 F5], just across the bridge, is regarded as Prizren's main mosque. It takes its name from its founder Sinan Pasha, who built this impressive mosque in 1615. The ruler had the prefix 'Sofi' added to his name in recognition of his wisdom. He had travelled widely, defeating Yemen and being awarded a position in Budapest. The prevailing view is that the mosque is more likely a unique design than a copy of others. The Serbian story is that the mosque was built using stones from the Monastery of Archangels which is further up the river. Other historians say that this is not true based on the analysis of Italian archaeologists in 1941. More controversy arises from the destruction of the mosque by Ivan Vangelov in 1919 when the stones were allegedly thrown in the river. This act of destruction inspired the well-known Albanian poet Ymer Pacari to write the poem *Xhaliët* or 'Vandals', which is said to have been written in a shop opposite. Apparently Ivan Vangelov was killed in revenge. The murals date from about 1628; the porch is a replacement. Make sure you take the time to go inside and note the stonework on the base and top of the pillars.

Continue on from the mosque and up towards the main cobbled Shadërvan. This is still the centre of life in Prizren and fortunately the 1960s' eyesore block in front of the river will be destroyed soon to make way for a park, opening up the view to the river on one side of the square. There are still a few old houses from the late 19th century around the square. There is a proverb: 'he who drinks water from the Shadë rvan fountain will find it hard to leave Prizren'. If you don't fancy sampling the water you can try a *boza* (a traditional semi-alcoholic orange-ish Turkish corn drink) from one of the cafés. There is a good one on the right up the hill opposite the **St George Cathedral** [201 E5]. Construction of this Serb Orthodox cathedral began in 1856 and was completed and decorated in 1887, funded by Serbian merchants in Prizren. The interior of the church was richly decorated and designed with ashlar in different colours, polished onyx, marble panes, fresco paintings by a painter from Debar, and icons. A wooden bell tower was erected in 1903. There were old books and a lot of icons gathered from other churches which had been ruined in 1999. Sadly these were all lost when in the March riots in 2004, the church was first looted and burnt and then aggressive graffiti was put on the walls. The church is now being restored by the Kosovo Government Restoration Programme. There is also another small church opposite St George.

If you are feeling energetic you can take the path to the left-hand side of the church and then switch back left again behind the mosque to go up the road to the castle. If you need sustenance then try Besimi-Beska [201 E5] on Rr Sinan Pasha for a local culinary experience. On the way up to the castle you will pass the **music school** [201 F6] in an attractive building which includes the ballet school Lorenc Antonia which was opened in 1999 and is connected with Tirana. There has been a tradition of music in Prizren for some time, with one of the most famous Kosovo Albanian composers Akil Mark Koci going to music school in Prizren.

You will now pass through an area of abandoned Serb houses which after more than three years of not being lived in, are very much overgrown. Serbs had started to return here, but fled with the March 2004 riots. Until the 19th century, this area was not inhabited and was surrounded by thick woods. Only when Prizren really expanded in that century were smart homes built in this district.

On your right as you ascend, behind KFOR barbed wire is the **Orthodox Church of Hrista Spasitelja** or **St Saviour (Shpëtimari i Shenjtë)** [201 G6]. The church was built in the 14th century in Byzantine style. Then, during the reign of Mahmud Pasha Rotulli in 1882, it was (to the consternation of the local Serb population) designated by the Ottoman authorities for use by the Vlach population. This led to a claim being filed in Istanbul in 1869. The church was returned to the Serbs in 1912, by which time the Vlachs had in any event assimilated into the Serb population. The paintings were done in two phases – first the altar area around 1335 and then the rest of the church around 1348. In 2004 the mob managed to get as high as this church and it baffles the outsider as to how KFOR were unable to stop them given that there is only one access route, but presumably the road was too tight for tanks. Sadly the church was damaged and is now being restored.

The **Holy Sunday Church (St Nedelje/të Dieles së Shenjtë)** [201 G5], built in 1371 by King Marko, is further across on the side of the hill, lower down and nestled against the castle walls. It is now difficult to reach because of the abandoned, overgrown houses.

From the **castle/kalaja** [201 H5] (*entrance free, no barrier or restrictions*) you get a fabulous view of Prizren and out to Pashtrik Mountain and Albania on one side, and if you make your way to the back of the castle there are also views towards Prevalac Mountain and the Lumbardhi River and Zhupa Valley, with the old, Dušangrad upper castle along the riverside about 3km away.

It is not known from exactly when the castle dates but there are suggestions that a castle has existed on this mound since the 6th century. It was used for military purposes until 1912. In the Ottoman period it consisted of an upper town and a lower town with two entrances and it used to include a mosque within its walls which was built in 1805 and renovated in 1828 by Emin Pasha, who also brought back a bell from Smederevo, Serbia as part of the spoils of war from a victory against Serbia. The castle also housed a prison which was used to house Abdyl Frasheri after his participation in the League of Prizren. There were at least four towers.

The base of the castle contains a network of tunnels but after 1938 it was used for water storage as part of the hydro-electric arrangement and Prizren city water system.

You can only safely go back down the same way. When you get to the bottom you can now turn left leaving St George on your right, past a bookshop and head to Kosovo's main **Catholic cathedral** [200 C6]. The cathedral dates back to the 19th century, although there was probably an earlier church on this site (there are plans to construct a new Catholic cathedral in Prishtina). Try your luck – if it's open you can visit.

Continue down the narrow road to the **Ali Efendi Mosque and madrasa** [201 C5] which is on a triangle in the centre of the road. It was founded in 1581 and Ali Efendi, the founder, is buried in the garden. It was used as a Red Cross centre in World War II, which resulted in a fair amount of damage. It is famous for being the place where the 1908 Muslim three-year boycott of Catholic shops began. Further down the road on the left-hand side, behind gates, is the quite attractive **house of Xhon Karasan** [200 C5] and further down still on the corner is the **Ilaz Kuka Mosque**.

The **Suza Çelebise Mosque and bridge** [200 A4] (old stone with a modern top) is further left along the riverbank. The mosque was founded in 1513 and is known for being the centre of poets and literature. It had an extensive library, now destroyed, which was a beautiful latticed wooden building on stilts including Arabic and Iranian books. Suza Çelebi (1455–1534) apparently wrote several thousand poems and his work was known as far afield as Russia. It seems that he studied more than verse and charmed the women that he took back to his village home outside Prizren from countries further east.

Dervish orders or *tarikat* (*tekke*) are particularly strong in western Kosovo, especially in Gjakova and Prizren and also Rahovec. A dervish order or *tarikat* is a group of Muslim followers with a leader who believe in particular in the mystical or ritual element of the religion. Through study, philosophy and rituals, the believers achieve spiritual enlightenment. They often speak of two Korans – an inner meaning and an outer meaning, and poetry, literature and music play a large part.

There are up to 12 different orders including Bektashi, Halveti, Sa'adi, Ri'fai, Mevlevi, Nakshibendi and Kadiri. There is no rivalry between them. Dating back to Ottoman times, *tarikat* orders are usually cross-border, having branches in several countries. The Bektashi order is particularly strong in Albania (it moved its headquarters there after being banned in Turkey as part of Ataturk's secular reforms in Turkey) where in the mid 1960s it was regarded as the fourth religion with more than 30% of Albanians being members. Despite their links with Albanian nationalism, the tarikat are not unique or confined to the Albanian ethnic group, nor are they mono-ethnic. A Skopje *tekke* was led by a Turk and in Mitrovica a Roma was in charge of a *tekke*.

The founder is referred to as *pir*. The leader of each *tekke*, the *sheh*, is a spiritual master (or in a Bektashi *tarikat* a *baba*), generally a knowledgeable person who is regarded as a quasi-living saint. Thus there are rules such as not being able to turn one's back on him. Sometimes the *sheh* is elected but usually the position of *sheh* is inherited, not always directly to the eldest son but to a male in the family who is marked out by the existing *sheh* – this may be a nephew for example. There is generally a hierarchy within the *tarikat*. More knowledgeable members wear a black-rimmed hat rather than the plain white one. In the Bektashi order the *gjysh*, literally 'grandfather', is the superior of the *babas* and is responsible for all the *tekkes* in a certain region. The *gjysh* has passed through the final level of ceremony and wears his white *taj* (special hat) with a green cloth band wrapped around it. Finally, the *kryegjysh* – 'head grandfather', known in Turkish as *dede baba*, is leader of the Bektashi order as a whole, chosen from among all the *gjysh*.

The *tekke* is the building or residence. They are usually in a town with several rooms, including a *misafir odasi* (reception room), *sema hane* (where the prayers take place) and sometimes a women's gallery.

The *türbe* are the graves of the dead *shehu* who are embalmed and revered by the living members through prayers of devotion or the giving of amulets. The *türbe* are usually close by the *tekke* but can be outside the town, for example on mountaintops. On the top of Mount Pashtrik between Prizren and Gjakova on the Albanian border is Baba Sari Salltyk Türbe, which is visited as part of a pilgrimage each year between 1 and 21 August. There are many other practices and ceremonies that share similarity with other faiths, such as a ritual meal (*muhabbet*) and yearly confession of sins to a baba (*magfirat-i zunub*). The *zikr* is the ritual prayer. It occurs at least weekly, usually on a Thursday evening or Friday at 13.00. It involves the reverent repetition of God's name. Forms vary from one *tekke* to another and the participants may go as far as to whip themselves into trances and in the case of the Ra'afi (in Prizren, Rahovec and Gjakova), undertake self-mutilation. They are

Back on the north bank Across the river again is a modern white building which is used by the **municipality** [200 B3]. This was the headquarters of the now bankrupt Bankos Bank. If you take the road to the left just after the OSCE, then on your left you will pass the **house of Adem Aga Xhon** [200 B3] which does not look too special.

Continue on to **Levišja/St Petka Church** [200 B2]. Apparently this predates the arrival of the Slavs in Prizren, dating from the Dardania era. At least seven different building phases have been identified, starting with the Romans and known to stick needles in one cheek and out the other or in the lips, to burn skin and to eat glass. Ra'afi have a ceremony each 21 March lasting about four to five hours. Kosovo does not have the same whirling that is associated with Turkey's dervish dances.

Many *tekkes* do not adhere strictly to all the rules of the Muslim faith – permitting consumption of alcohol and not always observing Ramadan. The Bektashi pray only twice a day (not necessarily in the direction of Mecca) and Bektashi prayers do not always involve prostration. As with other Muslims, most *tarikats* refuse to eat pork. Some *tarikats* drink alcohol and even make their own *raki*. In the case of Bektashis, women participate equally with the men in ceremonies and gatherings, something which again has caused upset with mainstream Islam and in the past fuelled a number of negative rumours about Bektashi *tekkes*. Fasting in Ramadan is not required, but they do fast and abstain from drinking during *matem*, the first ten days of the month during which the suffering and death of Imam Husein is commemorated. During *matem*, they will drink only bitter yoghurt and lentil soup. After matem follows the feast of *ashura* during which a dish is eaten made of cracked wheat, dried fruit, crushed nuts and cinnamon all cooked together. Nevruz, the Persian New Year and birthday of the Prophet Ali, is also commemorated by the Bektashi.

As well as believing in Allah and Muhammad they accord a special place to the Prophet Ali, his wife Fatima and their two sons, Hasan and Hussein. Many Bektashi homes have pictures of the Prophet Ali, considered the manifestation of God on Earth. The Bektashi, like other Shi'ites, revere the 12 Imams, among whom the Prophet Ali in particular of course, and consider themselves descendants of the sixth imam, Jafer Sadik. Naturally, they also revere Haji Bektash as founder of the order.

The tekkes are generally sociable, with the sheh taking on a councillor role and in some instances, prophesying outside the *tekke*. The *sheh* also played a role in solving disputes under the Kanun of Lekë Dukagjini.

With regard to ethics, the Bektashi adhere to the Turkish formula: *eline, diline, beline sahip ol*–'be master of your hands, your tongue and your loins', used during initiation ceremonies. Essentially, this means not to steal, not to lie or talk idly, and not to commit adultery.

The *tarikats* were founded mostly in the 13th and 14th centuries and had close connections with the Ottoman Janissary Corps (army), although the corps were not all adherents. The Kosovo and Albanian *tarikats* have been linked with supporting the Albanian nationalist cause (most recently some *tarikats* supported the UÇK). Naim Frasheri (1846–1900), one of the best-known Bektashi adherents himself, was one of the founders of the League of Prizren. He hoped that the rules could be adopted as part of the new law for an independent Albanian state. He also wrote an introduction to the Bektashi faith and ten spiritual poems, using Albanian terms in lieu of the previous Turkish ones. Unlike Enver Hoxha who banned all religion in 1968, *tekkes* were more or less tolerated under Yugoslav socialism with some police harassment.

Some extracts above are taken from Dr Robert Else's articles on the tarikat *in Albania and the Balkans.*

including renovations in the 9th century. The Slavs converted it into an Orthodox church, and it remains as such to this day. In 1307, it was renovated by Milutin who used a Greek fresco painter. Later during the Ottoman period it was converted again into a mosque (believed to be around 1756) named Promised Mosque/Xhuma Zhami, and a minaret was even put on top of the tower (fragments of this are in the nearby Archaeological Museum). The minaret was brought down in 1923. The church was very badly damaged during the March 2004 riots.

Near the church is the **Sahat Kulla (clocktower)** [200 B2] and the **Archaeological Museum** [200 B3]. While the museum has some interesting pieces it was not open at the time of writing as it was waiting for donor funding to re-establish itself.

It is worth venturing further up the hill as on the corner is the now modern-looking (but old in origin) **Mesxhid Mosque** [200 C2] and, perhaps more significantly, the impressive **nobleman's house of Destan Kabashi** [200 C2], which has retained its style. You might even be able to go inside, although it often seems locked. Concerts are occasionally held inside. There is also an Ethnographic Museum in Prizren but it seems it is not open to the public to drop in; access can, however, be gained via an organised tour.

There is more to see in and around Prizren but this requires substantial walking, a bus or a car.

VERMICË The drive between Prizren and the Albanian border is a common excursion for Prizren families. Most of them head straight for the fish restaurants which start about 8km out of Prizren, shortly before the Albanian border, close to the Fierze Lake which heads into Albania. Vermicë is also the site of an ancient village, including many stone houses with pagan snake, stars, suns and other symbols found on their walls. It is the lowest-lying point in Kosovo at just 250m above sea level.

✘ Where to eat

✘ **Kështjella** Vlashnje, 5km outside Prizren on the main road to Vermicë, after the wholesale market; m 044 607 402/216 070;
⊕ 09.00–23.00 daily. A mixture of reasonably priced meat & fish dishes in a restaurant which may look like a rather twee mock castle on the outside but which is quite cosy indoors with upper wrought-iron balcony.
✘ **Restaurant Iliria** m 044 113 400;
⊕ 08.00-24.00 daily), with 5 acres of gardens, **Restaurant Gurra** and **Restaurant Mifabeli** (m 044 500 650; ⊕ 07.00-24.00 daily) are all restaurants of a similar vein. Good-quality fish at these places, on the left-hand side of the road. Iliria & Mifabeli are particular favourites with the locals.
✘ **Restaurant Liqeni** m 044 113 245;

⊕ 09.00-23.00 daily. The original of the Vermicë restaurants. Directly on the water so hard to match for views.
✘ **Univers** m 044 401 552/414 172;
e universi_vermic@hotmail.com; ⊕ 08.00–23.00 daily. Almost the last of the chain of restaurants before the Albanian border. A front hotel building & then 2 modern glass towers that resemble some astronaut outfit looking out onto funky metal fountains. There is also now a large outdoor swimming pool & a sauna. The towers apparently open up onto the garden in summer, which must make for a pleasant environment, with the flexibility of protection in a rainstorm. Unusually for Kosovo the restaurant is solar powered which may explain the fact it feels slightly cold in winter. 2 large stuffed trout €6.

What to see and do Just 3km outside Prizren in the direction of Morina/the Albanian border is a zoo called 'Shqiponja' with various different kinds of animals including bears. It's very popular with children.

OUTSIDE PRIZREN – ON THE ZHUPA VALLEY ROAD

There are a number of sights no more than 5km from Prizren along the Lumbardhi River.

MONASTERY OF ARCHANGELS This is about 3km out of Prizren along the valley on the right-hand side across an old stone bridge. The monastery was founded by King Dušan who was also buried here in a stone grave. The tomb with its stone relief of the buried person was the first of its kind in this region, inspired by Western models at the time. There was a church in the centre with Dušan's tomb, a refectory (in an unusual cruciform shape), monks' dormitories, a library, hospital and a small church dedicated to St Nicholas, and mosaic floors. Excavation works confirmed that the monastery was richly endowed and no luxury was spared with extensive use of marble and sculptures. Apparently Dušan gave specific instructions that the monastery should benefit from the lead produced in the Trepça mines. The building project lasted from 1343 to 1352 and was inaugurated in 1355 under Prior Jacob, who later became bishop in Serres.

The monastery had fallen into disrepair already in the 15th and 17th centuries and it is not possible to tell how it looked beyond the foundations. According to Serbian narrative, the destruction of the monastery had been ordered by Sinan Pasha and the stones were removed to construct Sinan Pasha Mosque in Prizren. Another theory argues that the monks have simply deserted the monastery and the buildings subsequently fell into disrepair. This latter theory was confirmed by an Italian archaeological visit in 1941 that proved that the stones used in Sinan Pasha Mosque were different from those of the monastery. An effort to restore the monastery – not in its original look but adapted to modern needs – was nearly complete, when the monastery was attacked during the 2004 riots. As before the very recent restoration, the monastery resembles an archaeological site.

HIGH CASTLE/VIŠEGRAD This was quite a substantial castle and the ruins of the walls can still be seen from the road (to the right about 4km coming from Prizren) or better still from Prizren Castle. It is mentioned in Serbian literature as Višegrad, Stanigrad and Dervengrade and on Yugoslav maps as Dušangrad. In Ottoman times it was known as Kiz Kalesi (the girls' castle). There were at least four towers. It was probably constructed before or around the same time as the St Archangel Monastery but was taken over by the Ottoman army after their arrival. One story is that it was then inhabited by citizens of Dubrovnik who left in haste in 1372 with the Ottoman advance.

HYDROELECTRIC MUSEUM Just before the St Archangel Monastery is a small stone building across the bridge which today houses the museum. The first Kosovo hydro-electric power plant was built in 1929 by a firm from Vienna and at its peak produced 220,000kWh. It also worked the water-pumping system for the town (the water for the town is stored in a reservoir under the castle from 1938). The plant operated until the 1970s. The museum (which apparently has no fixed opening hours) also displays other electrical artefacts if you are into engineering and water pumps.

CAVES There are 13 caves at about 960m altitude which were used as hermitages by monks and decorated with fresco paintings. To find them you need a guide and sturdy shoes.

MONASTERY OF ST PETER KORIŠA This monastery is east of Prizren in the village of Koriša. It seems there was a hermitage monastery in the rocks in memory of Peter the hermit from the beginning of the 13th century, as the frescoes have been dated from 1220. At the end of either the 13th century or the beginning of the 14th century, a church was built on the narrow plateau in front of the cave. Nothing is left of the temple itself or really of the refectory buildings. The monks probably moved out in the 1570s. Apparently the site suffered further destruction in 1999.

There was also a church of the Holy Virgin in the village dating from the 14th century which was destroyed in summer 1999.

SCENIC DRIVE OR BIKE RIDE TO BISHTAZHIN VIA ZYM This route can be done either way round and is a more scenic (albeit much longer) alternative to the main Gjakova–Prizren road.

Coming from Prizren you turn off left just opposite Landovica (where you can stop off if you wish to see the large World War II memorial) after going under the railway. The road winds up to Donaj which is a medium-sized town with a small graveyard and *türbe*. Take the steep switchback road about a further 3–5km up to the village of **Zym**. This area is known as the Has region, a mountainous region that straddles Kosovo and Albania. The population has its own distinctive costume (see examples in the Ethnographic Museum in Gjakova (see page 190) and in the League of Prizren Museum (see page 209)), with women wearing wooden bars underneath their skirts which helped carry the milk and other heavy goods. Many of the villages remain Catholic to this day, owing to their relative isolation from zealous imams. The region's biggest claim to fame is the local bakery and filigree tradition. Catholic Albanians, especially those from the Has region, are famous throughout Yugoslavia for setting up bakeries and jewellery shops. Many families from the Has region have migrated to Croatia and all along the Dalmatian coast you can find bakeries and jewellery shops run by Catholic Albanians. The money sent back from the Has region diaspora has financed some of the modern newly renovated houses which are in stark contrast to the crumbling stone to be found elsewhere.

A key reason for travelling up the hill is to see the **traditional-style stone houses** which are hard to find in other parts of Kosovo. The Catholic church on the other hand is striking because it is so modern and very different from Orthodox churches. Pass by the entrance to the church, bearing left uphill leaving the mini market/café on your right, and behind a wall on the left you can see a very old house with a plaque commemorating the Austro-Hungarian occupation. The house is built in the old style with small reinforced stone windows. There is an oven built into the outer wall that backs on to the road. This road then peters out so you may wish to park your car lower down and just walk this last uphill stretch.

There is a large amphitheatre near the school which is used partly to host the **Stefan Gjeçovi poetry festival** on 14 October every year. Stefan Gjeçovi, a well-known supporter of the Albanian language, poet and author was born further across Kosovo in Janjevo (see *Janjevo*, page 142) but died in the village of Karashëngjerg – a derivative of 'St George'. It is worth heading back down the hill and then taking the right turn above the pink civic building to visit **Karashëngjerg**. It is about 4km away down a road through the woods with Muslim graves scattered in the woods. There is another large, modern Catholic church and in the graveyard behind this (the gate is not locked, it is just a difficult catch) a low old stone building which is Stefan Gjeçovi's grave. The graves are also interesting for the Catholic names and the etchings of the men and women in the Has costumes and head veil.

Back down in the bottom of the valley, you can continue on for a further 4–5km to the villages of Romaja, Dedaj and then Kusinin. These are all attractive and you will see women in Terbesh or Has costume. A sight in itself is one of the few remaining working watermills in Kosovo – **the Kushnin Mill**. This is a small, isolated stone building on the left-hand side of the road. It is more than 500 years old and if you are lucky two old men will emerge from the dark who are usually grinding sweetcorn for individuals (whose names are all written onto the bags). They grind the corn into cornflour which is still used for baking bread, broth and a mash-type vegetable dish. You can purchase some from the mill operators. If you peer behind the mill building you will see the wooden channels out of tree trunks which guide the waterfall down into the mill to turn the grindstones.

On from here there is another small village and then about 3–4km further on you suddenly come across the **Restaurant Gurra** in Demjan (m *044 236 318/ 675 333;* ⊕ *08.00-24.00 daily*), a modern wooden building with huge gardens, the river and a trout farm. Trout costs €4. It is very pleasant and makes a good stop before you continue on to **Bishtazhin**. Bishtazhin did have a very old Orthodox church but this was completely destroyed and there is now just a very modern Catholic church, the spires of which can be seen from a distance. From Bishtazhin it is only a couple of kilometres back onto the main Gjakova–Prizren road.

DRAGASH/DRAGAŠ MUNICIPALITY

Dragash municipality is in the sock-like bottom of Kosovo, surrounded by the high Sharr Mountains on two sides and the tall Accursed Mountains of Albania on the other. The only route currently in and out is via Prizren which makes it the least-accessible part of Kosovo and the roads are poor. This is set to change. A border crossing is being opened with Macedonia and Albania and there will soon be road connections between Prizren, Zaplluxhe and Tetovo (Macedonia), and Prizren, Restelica and Strezimir (Macedonia). This area will also pick up tourism with the new road from Merdare to Durrës.

Owing to the distance, too many internationals and tourists miss out on Dragash, which is a great shame as it is really worth the trip. It has possibly some of the most beautiful and unspoilt countryside in Kosovo and no land mines (except on the western border with Macedonia nearest the Tetovo side) which means it is ideal for hiking, with flower meadows, herbs, sheep and stone villages that are stuck in a time warp, with hay carried up and down the hills on horseback. Most of the population survives on **subsistence farming** and is very poor. Recently NGOs have tried to encourage farmers to take up beekeeping. The people are incredibly friendly and welcoming to foreigners, breaking into smiles when they see you on a hike. The only 'problem' with hiking in the area is that you are constantly asked in for coffee by the villagers! Another potential obstacle is the roaming Sharr dogs.

A large percentage of the land in Dragash municipality is owned by the social enterprise, Sharr Prodhimi, which was an agricultural enterprise and which still has several hundred sheep. The Privatisation Agency has been faced with a dilemma – caught between a need to maximise the receipts (which might mean selling off small parcels of land, destined for uncontrolled ugly buildings such as city dwellers' holiday homes) and ecotourism projects which would perhaps offer greater long-term returns for the local economy. The biggest problem, as ever in Kosovo, is how any controlled planning can be enforced. It would indeed be a tragedy if Brod and Zili Potok's rural stone village character was lost and it became littered with scattered half-built brick houses as is the case with Kosovo's central plains.

In addition to sheep farms there are also cattle, horses, cheese-making and beekeeping and a very wide variety of local herbs, including wild calendula, wild raspberries and strawberries. In September it seems like the whole population is out on the hillsides collecting juniper berries which they sell in big bags which are loaded onto the horses and carried down the hill.

GETTING THERE AND AROUND It is very difficult or nigh impossible to explore Dragash by public transport. There are only irregular **buses** from Prizren but most of them only as far as Dragash Town, which take about 30–45 minutes. The Adio Tours (*Dragash office;* m *044 494 064/ 245 085*) company buses from Belgrade to Prizren reach Prizren at 06.00 and 19.30 and arrive one hour later in Dragash. They leave Dragash at 08.00 and 20.30 but priority will be given to passengers going to Belgrade. Minibuses to/from Brod (a further 40 minutes from Dragash)

Today, Dragash is a mixed municipality comprising approximately 60% Albanian and 40% Gorani. There were apparently 16,000 Gorani in the 1991 census, although other estimates today suggest there are only 10,000 left. The word 'Gora' reflects the terrain as it means 'mountain' in Slavic and Gorani are 'the mountaineers'. The Gora or Gorani are Slavic-speaking Muslims believed to have come from Bulgaria or Macedonia across the mountains in the Middle Ages and to have been converted from Christianity to Islam. Their language is a mixture of Serbian, Macedonian, Bosnian and Turkish. They refer to their language as 'Našuski', meaning roughly 'ours'. They have been variously claimed by Bosnians and Serbs and most recently by Macedonia, who even went as far as to move the border posts into Kosovo territory and have granted many Gorani people passports, resulting in even greater emigration. In 2005, an alleged attempt to create a 'Bulgarian national community' among the Gorani occurred, supposedly with the motive of getting Bulgarian EU passports. The general consensus is that they should be treated as a special minority.

It is not uncommon to see Gorani in their local costume which for the women can be quite ornate with embroidered black satin coats, large trousers and headscarves. They also wear chains with gold coins either round their headscarf (if married) or their necks (if single). These are known as *dukati*. Gorani women are more likely to object to photographs than Albanians as traditionally they must ask their husband's permission. They are famous for having some of the best burek and baklava in Kosovo. In the 1980s and 1990s, some Gorani changed their Albanian-sounding names to more Slavic endings and also in the 1990s and in 2004, Gorani confectionery shops in Serbia were attacked during the periods of unrest because of the similarity of their surnames to Albanian ones. The Gorani live in the south and eastern part of Dragash, a region referred to as 'Gora'. Albanians mostly live in the western part referred to as 'Opoja'. Each region is reached by turning down either way down a fork from the mixed town of Dragash (population 4,000) in the centre of the municipality. Gorani also live in the Zhupa Valley.

All parts of Dragash are sparsely populated by comparison with the rest of Kosovo, and given the lack of economic opportunities large numbers – up to two-thirds – of Gorani have worked outside Kosovo, starting in the 1960s. Many of the houses are therefore partly abandoned, with family members returning only in the summer when the roads are full of BG (Belgrade) and NS (Novi Sad) plates as well as cars from further afield such as Germany, Italy or Switzerland. Weddings are common during this time and last several days. The Gorani have a good proportion of their ethnic group in Belgrade (c3,400) and Novi Sad (c600), and strong links there. They run a daily bus service from Dragash to Novi Sad (via Belgrade) and back (see page 50).

Relations between both ethnic groups are good. The Gorani were not involved in any 1998–99 atrocities, keeping to themselves more or less. Schools in Dragash municipality are divided into Albanian and Gorani (similar to Serbian) or Serbian-language classes, but the pupils mix for English and physical education lessons. Until recently, Gorani teachers took salaries from the Kosovo budget and also from the Serbian government. Some Gorani speak Albanian which certainly helps them get on in life in terms of trading their produce in Prizren or beyond.

After a project in the 1960s, the 36 villages were nearly all electrified but water and other infrastructure remains poor. Roads suffer from the winter freeze and the villages are cut off in snow when it is hard for the children to get to school. Many of the Goranis go to secondary schools near Prizren as weekly boarders.

and Dragash or Restelica are ad hoc and relate to market times and no precise times could be given. Because transport is so scarce, **hitch-hiking** is not uncommon, but you would be expected to pay a share and you can negotiate rides for a price with car owners in the villages. The locals cannot afford taxis so there are almost no taxi services. This hitch-hiking method is therefore a feasible way of getting around if you want to walk stretches in the mountains and don't want to have to retrace your steps to get the car. The roads are also quiet enough to **cycle** on, with the downside being the absence of round trips as the roads fork along the valley and often peter out.

WHERE TO STAY

The only hotel in Dragash Town was previously occupied by Turkish KFOR personnel but is now being privatised so if you want a hotel you have to go to Brod. There is no hotel in Restelica.

Motel Arxhena (28 rooms) Brod; m 044 502 368; e info@arxhena.com; www.arxhena.com. This hotel is at the far end of Brod on the river with a huge outdoor terrace & a conservatory that looks over the river where you can sit in winter. There are 9 singles, 9 doubles & 10 triples, with beautiful new beds, bathrooms, TV, internet & tea-making facilities. As with anywhere in Dragash, the food is good. Reservations can also be made online. In the eyes of some, however, the large modern hotel is somewhat incongruous in the peaceful ancient valley. There is a restaurant which is open all year daily. Their speciality is the local meat *katundi*. $$$

There is an informal campsite along the river path just outside Brod (same direction as the restaurant). It is not quite clear what the payment arrangements are for this but the fee is surely not much and given the views, it is a bargain. There is also a hunters' mountain hut, the key of which is kept by the director of Sharr Prodhimi social enterprise which is the main landowner in Dragash.

One of the best options, especially if you are in Zili Potok or Restelica, is to try and stay with a local family for a fee – a bed-and-breakfast arrangement. Hopefully the entrepreneurial Cultural Heritage without Borders people will add Dragash to their list. Failing this, try ringing the municipality of Dragash or Avni (see below) in advance and they may be able to find some accommodation in the village of your choice or you can just risk the drive and hope that you will find something on arrival.

WHERE TO EAT

The inhabitants of Dragash have little cash to spend on eating out, so restaurants are few. There are a couple of options in Dragash Town (one on the right as you come in and one in the cultural house).

Some of the best *burek* in Kosovo is in Dragash municipality and there are plenty of *burektores*. The Gorani also like their baklava so there are also many coffee and baklava shops. Incidentally, many of the burektores and ice-cream stalls in Novi Sad are run by Gorani.

OTHER PRACTICALITIES

There is a branch of Raiffeisen Bank (*Rr De Rada;* 038 222 222 ext 535; ⊕ 09.00–14.00 Mon–Fri) and a ProCredit Bank (*Rr Sheshi i Deshmoreve;* 029 281 010; ⊕ 08.00-16.00 Mon-Fri and 09.00-14.00 Sat).

Both Dragash and Brod have a PTK (*Brod;* 029 285 197; ⊕ 0830-17.00 Mon-Fri).

While there are a few mini markets, the choice is very limited. The signs that this economy is self-sustaining are clear. This is not the part of the world for packet food. If you are on a long weekend hike, come prepared or shop at the major supermarkets such as Ben-Af or ETC in Prizren on the way.

BROD To reach the village, continue on through Dragash, pass the municipality on your left, and go uphill out of town. Carry on climbing and you will leave the now-defunct textile factory of Printeks below on the valley floor on your right (this was privatised but never restarted). The road deteriorates somewhat with many pot-holes. Continue on for 30 minutes, passing fountains on the left-hand side. You will see some turn-offs to other villages to the right but Brod is right at the end of the valley.

Brod is a real treat, with traditional Ottoman buildings as well as stone houses along the river. From now on you are likely to see as many horses as cars and they seem to have priority right of passage through the town, so it is best to park. There is a family which makes cheese in the village and you can buy it directly from their dairy.

Brod has ideal walking opportunities and merits a full weekend of hiking. If you want creature comforts you could spend Friday night in Prizren and then get up early so you can start your walks in time. Even if you don't have the time or energy for a full walk, you should at least make it down to the river that runs through the valley past the new hotel and the hunters' lodge and walk around here to take in some of the fresh air and the dramatic mountain rockfaces.

There is tremendous potential here. Take a look at the big broad mountain opposite the hotel – this would make a great ski mountain. In fact on the other side of this row of hills is Macedonia and Mount Tito, which is the country's largest peak. You can get a good view of it if you climb the hill the other side above Brod. Mount Tito is a peak above the Popova Šapka ski resort.

✖ Where to eat

✖ **Motel Arxhena** See *Where to stay*, above, for details.

✖ **Restaurant Ramce** ⏲ 24 hours. The original restaurateur of Brod is Ardian or 'Avni' (m *029 288 170*). He runs a bar restaurant in town & then in summer sometimes operates a second ad hoc outlet, near the river/campsite about a 3km walk from town along the path, which seats about 100. If you are coming with a group ask Avni to open up especially for you, stay open late, order in food for you or to prepare picnics. He may also be able to arrange accommodation with local families. Avni's summer restaurant serves possibly the best *pleskavica* (fresh minced meat burger) in Kosovo as it seems to come fresh from the cows in the fields next door. There is no doubt that the local yoghurt comes from the cows. Ask any of the children for directions to the restaurant.

Walking routes

Brod to the glacier lake and the sheep shelter (*5–6-hour round trip*) For this walk you need to head towards the campsite/restaurant and hotel and instead of following the river down by the hut you should take the right-hand path which travels up several hundred metres' height from the hut. The path is well marked because of the frequent traffic of horses to the sheep shelter and you just keep on going past the fields of wild raspberries. After 4km or so you will come across a series of waterfalls. Then the road continues right up to the sheep station. This is also used for breeding **Sharr sheepdogs**. Give the station a wide berth to the right as the dogs can be hostile. The lake is just over the hill from the sheep station.

Sharr dogs seem to be a variety unique to Kosovo. They have thick, shaggy hair and while they seem small when young they grow quickly to a tremendous height – even by the age of six months. They are happy in the snow and cold but beware their appetite – they can eat you out of house and home.

From the sheep station it is possible to go back slightly and follow the path over the steep hill to Restelica. You need two–three hours for this. The alternative is to retrace your steps down to Brod.

Brod to Kruševo *(2–2¹/₂ hours)* For this walk you need to head out of Brod past the football stadium and the path next door to the water fountain seat. The path divides after about 30 minutes and you need to take the right-hand fork. You continue round the hill for some time, through hills of juniper berries. After 1¹/₂ hours the vista widens into broader fields and meadows which roll down to Kruševo – the last stretch of this walk is on asphalt.

It is possible to walk up the hill from Kruševo and over back to Brod but the path is hard to find and the route is a very steep climb, although the views from the top across to Macedonia are stunning.

From Kruševo you can also continue down the road for an hour or so to Restelica.

Skiing Right now there are no lifts but unofficial tourism is organised around Zaplluxhe.

RESTELICA Reached after driving through the village of Kruševo, Restelica is the largest town in Dragash, with lots of new houses. Most of the population lives in Italy and returns for July and August only as there is little prospect of work. The road is being asphalted from Dragash and the tarmac is now not far from Restelica (28km from Dragash). It should eventually go the further 18km to the Macedonian border. The Macedonians have a **border post** ready here but the Kosovo side is not yet open so they are reluctant to let many people through as yet. It is 30km from the border to the Macedonian ski resort of Mavrovo. The dramatic barren wilderness, with its backdrop of the Vrsač and Crni Kamen peaks, is interrupted only by a few sheep, Sharr dogs and wolves. The local Gorani will warn you about dangerous Albanians from across the Albanian border who head armed to Macedonia. Our enquiries revealed that these incidences are rare.

The main problem is that as there are huge mountains, and no road between Brod and Restelica, and they are each at the end of separate forks (from Dragash Town), you cannot hop between the two villages in a day as they are more than an hour's drive apart!

There is reputedly a stone *tekke* above the hills in Restelica but you'll need the villagers to point it out. If you get into the older Restelica mosques you can also spot the Arabic writing on the graves inside.

RAHOVEC/ORAHOVAC

HISTORY Rahovec has existed since Roman times as various bronze figures have been found in the area. In the Ottoman era, it was the home of four mosques and four tekkes (Ra'afi, Halveti, Kader and Melami).

At first sight, especially in autumn, Rahovec has a Tuscan feel thanks to the rolling hills and abundant vineyards. Rahovec is most famous for its wine, although sadly many thousands of hectares of vines have turned to scrub through years of neglect. The focus of communist developers in the 1980s was on bulk, low-quality production. There is now some hope that Rahovec wine will become famous again because the two main vineyards were privatised in 2006 and private vineyard owners have also been investing in new vines and attractive product packaging. Some of the grapes, such as Vranac, originate and are commonly found elsewhere in the Balkans but the Prokupacs grape is indigenous to the area (although also found in Macedonia and Albania). Gamay and Smedereveka (a white grape) are also common.

Throughout September and early October vendors line the roads around Rahovec, selling pallets of bargain-price tasty table grapes or more bitter ones better destined for your *raki* home-brew. If you are in Kosovo around the second Thursday of September then you should not miss the **wine festival** in Rahovec Town with traditional costumes, dancing, tastings and displays of the local products. In any event Rahovec town is well worth a visit.

Rahovec's inhabitants are some of the friendliest in Kosovo and on a weekday the town has some air of industriousness about it which might be due to the fact that the fertile soil and abundant water resources from tributaries of the Drini i Bardhë River make the area the greatest provider of Kosovo's agricultural produce. Consequently the markets of Rahovec and Xërxë offer some of the cheapest seasonal wholesale vegetable prices. Rahovec is also famous for its peculiar dialect. The older inhabitants in particular, including ethnic Albanians, speak a Slavic dialect which apparently is Bulgarian in origin.

Rahovec suffered badly after a failed attempt by the UÇK to hold the town against Serbian forces in July 1998. Police and military retaliation turned against the civilian population and reduced large parts of the town to rubble. To this day many Rahovec families don't know the whereabouts of their beloved ones. Now only few Serbs remain in an isolated pocket of town and just about 700 inhabitants in nearby Velika Hoča.

GETTING THERE AND AWAY There are regular **buses** to Rahovec from Prizren (approximately 40 minutes away) and from Gjakova (approximately 20 minutes away). Some buses from Prishtina will also stop at Rahovec. Rahovec is approximately 90 minutes from Prishtina by bus.

WHERE TO STAY AND EAT

⌂ **Hotel Park** (12 rooms, 5 apts) In the centre of town; m 044/049 203 484. Newly renovated with a rather 'shiny' look. Location of the annual wine festival. Prices very cheap. AC & no internet at the time of writing, but it is planned. There's a disco hall downstairs & it seems to be popular for weddings but the rooms fortunately seem far enough away from this. $$

⌂ **Motel Adora** (10 rooms) Xërxë; m 044 242

922/500 799; e hekurani_adora@hotmail.com. $$
⌂ **Motel Kosova** (25 rooms) On the road to Xërxë; m 044 254 841. Spacious, modern, large garden, & good views. Home also to large wholesale market. $$

⌂ **Motel Haxhi Jaha** (4 rooms) Rr UÇK, near the petrol station on the way out of town towards Xërxë; m 044 278 745; ⏰ 08.00–24.00 daily. Specialises in veal & fish dishes. Reasonable prices. $$

OTHER PRACTICALITIES There is a post office at the main crossroads, and a Raiffeisen Bank (*Rr Xhelal Hajda [Rr Toni Mici];* ☏ *029 77 944;* ⏰ *08.00–16.30) Mon–Fri and 09.00-12.00 Sat*), ProCredit (*Rr Xhelal Hajda I;* ☏ *029 277 377*) ⏰ *08.00-16.00 Mon–Fri and Sat 09.00–14.00*) and a branch of NLB further along from the municipality on the way out of town. The cultural centre in town shows exhibitions of local painters (⏰ *08.00–16.00*).

WHAT TO SEE AND DO Approaching Rahovec from Malisheva (heading towards Prishtina), you will come to a crossroads with the post office/PTK on the other side of the road. Turn left here and follow the road uphill. If you take another left before the roundabout and head back north, then on the hillside up a fairly steep paved (rather than asphalt road) next to an abandoned restaurant called Europa with a KFOR sticker, there is an old stone **Sahat Kulla** with a distinctive bell tower in amongst some older, partly abandoned houses. The *kulla* was apparently built in 1815 but the bell was replaced by one from Velika Hoča in 1908, donated by Princess Milica. As the barbed wire and air of sad abandonment suggests, these are mostly Serb-minority homes. There is a sign on one house just higher up beyond OSCE which indicates it was the place where the Rahovec branch of the

Communist Party was founded in 1945. Most people know where the *kulla* is but you can also ask for the OSCE office or military police office which is in the same area. If you can look beyond the fact that the homes are now crumbling, this is one part of Rahovec which has not changed with modern buildings and you can get some sort of feel for how traditional Rahovec might have looked.

Another part that gives you some feel for the Rahovec of the past is the **Halveti Tekke**. This is next to the large twin minaret Arab-style (and funded) mosque which is an inappropriate replacement for the ancient 15th-century Ottoman mosque that once accompanied the *tekke*. Unlike the mosque, the *tekke* has, however, retained much of its character. It is more than 350 years old, having been founded by the son of the founder of the Halveti Tekke in Prizren (see page 207). It was put under state protection in 1973. On 20 July 1998, 300 to 400 people were sheltering in the tekke, hiding from Serb forces. According to one witness interviewed by Amnesty International, Serbian police told the *sheh* that if they did not leave they would enter the *tekke*, but as they were leaving the Serb military opened fire. The next day, the 76-year-old venerated Sheh Muhedini Shehu was shot in the back in the courtyard and killed by Serb paramilitaries. This was the end of a difficult but honourable life which included two spells in prison for a total of 13 years (in 1945 for three years for co-operating with Germans, and in 1955 for 'acts' against the state). In the 1950s and 1960s, in particular, the communist leadership turned against religious authorities. His Yugoslav passport and voting rights were taken away but he was given a diplomatic passport by the Liechtenstein government. You can meet the son of the *sheh* today if you go to the *tekke* and he will show you photos and ask if you wish to sign the visitors' book – visitors include Bob Dole and many of the KFOR commanders and former SRSGs. The nephew of the Sheh Muhedini Shehu is the current *sheh*.

The tekke's courtyard includes the *türbe* or graves of the great and the good of the *tekke* of the past as well as some ancient graves and a water fountain. On the left-hand side of the courtyard is a 400-litre clay *pitos* (Roman-style pot), which was used to store grain or wine and at the back on the ground is an old stone *stella* (large stone). Its Latin inscription suggests it dates from Roman times and the main point of note is the decorative vines which suggest that wine must have been around in the Rahovec area for some considerable time. Amazingly, despite being ransacked in 1998, much of the library remains and is stored upstairs in the *tekke*, including 25 writings declared as being under special protection.

The younger **Melami Tekke** is lower down in town. This is where Sheh Hilmi Maliqi (1865–1928) established an Albanian-language school. The *tekke* was hit by a projectile during the Serb shelling in summer 1998, which fortunately only damaged the roof.

A renowned Kosovar-Albanian American bought the largest **vineyard** and undertook to invest more than €5 million, rebranding the vineyard Stone Castle Vineyards. It is possible to tour his vineyard with the chance to taste the different wines (and also *raki*) from the area. For further information, contact the vineyard (\ 029 76 051/3; e *info@stonecastlewine.com; www.stonecastlewine.com*). In any event there is a shop (⊕ *07.00–17.00 Mon–Sat*) outside the factory where you can buy the wine at near wholesale prices.

To reach the vineyard, take the road out of town towards Xërxë/Gjakova for about 3km and on the right-hand side you will see the tall aluminium vats and the towers of the other successful former social enterprise, the cooling system company, Termosistemi. The vineyard offices are on the opposite left-hand roadside before a small Serbian church.

An alternative *raki* and winemaker with a 100-year tradition is Faik Vucitërna (m *044 204 379 for tours/sales*). You can also tour and do tastings with the Eko

Vineyard owned by the Hoxha family. Ring in advance (m *044 200 823*). If you want a completely authentic, if slightly less sophisticated, experience then visit Ismet's cellar. **Ismet Metbala** (m *044 697 077*) has been making his own *raki* and wine for more than 20 years and has for the last few years been selling to KFOR and other visitors who can find his cellar which is tucked away under his house. You can go there to see the vats and then he will bring out a variety of different *rakis* and wines to taste, as well as the non-alcoholic grape juice. A particular one to try is the sweet *raki*, which he says is popular with women. Ismet is also a great storyteller. He will inform you why his son is nicknamed Gandhi and about his work in Serbia. To make the most of this, however, take someone with you who can translate from Albanian. To find the house, go to the area of the town not far from the kulla at Rr Hadija Spahija 26 and ask the kids for 'te Ismet'. Bring some strong bags and/or boxes to carry all your purchases!

OUTSIDE RAHOVEC

VELIKA HOČA/HOGË MADHE Velika Hoča is a Serbian village of approximately 700 inhabitants about 8km from Rahovec in the direction of Suha Rekë. It includes a cluster of very historical buildings and has its own atmosphere and pace which is quite distinct from the rest of the area and nearby Rahovec. It is well worth a visit, although getting into the historical buildings can be a little difficult as the Serbian population is quite suspicious about any visitors. Having said that they have geared themselves up to the Swiss KFOR visits with signs advertising the local *raki* and honey brew. Wine has been brewed here since Roman times, as proved by two jars which have been unearthed. At the end of the 20th century, there were 62 wine cellars in Velika Hoča. In 1198, Stefan Nemanjić gave the land to the Hilandar Monastery and the area developed into an important spiritual centre. It was also a place in which various wealthy families lived and through which traders came on the trading route from Prizren to Raska. It declined in the Ottoman era when the main seat switched to Rahovec. Velika Hoča is under Ahtisaari protection. Documents note at least 12 churches, although there are fewer remaining today.

Getting there and away There is no public transport from Prishtina, Prizren or Rahovec to Velika Hoča. You could get a taxi from Rahovec for about €6 (a local Albanian taxi may be reluctant to enter the village but can drop you at the turn-off which is only a five-minute walk into the village).

To get to Velika Hoča, follow the road uphill out of Rahovec town and then bear left towards the Muslim graveyards either side of the road. Continue on for a few kilometres until the first unmarked turning right downhill. At the time of writing there was a European Agency for Reconstruction sign at the entrance. The village cannot be seen at the turn-off as it is tucked down below.

Buses do run from Prizren via Velika Hoča and Prishtina to Belgrade once a week. For further information, call the agency **Erhan Trans** (m *049 190 915*).

Where to stay and eat There is a national restaurant in Rahovec town below St Stephen's Church. Ask for directions. It is also possible to stay with local villagers.

There are plenty of places where you can buy locally brewed *raki* and honey. The speciality is the *raki* in bottles with wooden carvings inside with the words 'Kosovo' or even 'KFOR'. Look out for the signs in German at the kiosks.

What to see and do You can spot the bell tower of **St Jovan Monastery (St John the Baptist)** as you descend into the village — it is on the left-hand side on a small hill. To enter the church you need to knock on the door of the monastery buildings. It was built in the 14th century but the frescoes were added in the 16th century. Fragments of the 14th-century fresco decoration have been preserved on the southern wall of the nave and in the altar apse. The rest of the mural decoration dates from the 1580s. The iconostasis is composed of several parts dating from different epochs. The royal doors are probably from the 16th century. On the left of the door is the *Last Judgement* and above the door is a fresco of the birth of St Jovan.

There is also a war memorial below the church on the left-hand side as you enter the village. While KLA war memorials are common throughout Kosovo, it is unusual to see a memorial to Serb deaths in the 1999 conflict.

The **Church of St Nicholas** and its graveyard is situated above the village and was built and painted in 1345. It is a simple one-nave building. It has been assumed that the construction of the church was funded through Gradislav Sušenica. Fragments of the original 14th-century frescoes have been preserved on the western wall, including one which shows three Jews being burnt in a furnace! The church was restored in the 16th century, about 1577, when it also got new mural decoration and icons but these are in St Stephen's Church (see below). The present icon is the work of Petar Filipović from Galičnik, dated 1825–26.

The **Church of St Stephen** is the one with the triple-arched turret near the village centre (which is itself unusual). It can be reached either through the house and courtyard of the priest through a double wooden door which can involve some investigation and negotiation, or by going down the side road down the hill and entering from the door at the back. It dates from the 14th century but was repainted in the 16th century. It contains icons brought from other destroyed churches.

The **Visoki Dečani Monastery wine cellar**, which was used to produce wine as part of the Visoki Dečani Monastery estate, is probably the most impressive building in the village and was recently restored by Cultural Heritage Without Borders. It is opposite St Stephen's, behind a wall. The monastery building dates from 1851. It was built to house large barrels 5m high and 4m wide. Again, negotiating entrance is difficult but it can probably be arranged through Father Milenko at St Stephen's or if you plan well enough in advance through Cultural Heritage Without Borders.

The **Serai House** is a former communal building, another which has been restored by the wonderful Cultural Heritage Without Borders. Unfortunately there doesn't seem to be any way to get inside. Serai was derived from the local word designating a manor. The Serai House was built by Effendi Shane, an owner of feudal property in Velika Hoča. The building used to house the municipality office between 1912 and 1941.

The **memorial tower of Lazar Kujundzić** is the *kulla*-like tower building in the village. The story is that Lazar Kujundzić was a Serb official who was staying with his companions when *en route* from Kuršumilja in present-day Serbia (near Kopaonik) to Macedonia. He was put up by Lam Uka, an Albanian who promised not to betray him to the Turks, however the Turkish army crept in while they slept and fired shots through the wooden ceiling. Some of the group were murdered outright and the remainder jumped out of the window but were killed. The tower was then set on fire. Apparently this event was so strong in local memory that in 1936 the population built an equivalent tower on the site of the previous one and Lazar Kujundzić's body is buried in a sarcophagus in the basement. The **Hadžispasić House** is an important building because it shows the real residential architecture that existed in Velika Hoča for the merchants and aristocracy of the day. It was built between 1830 and 1835, and renovated in 1860. The house was designed on a typical scheme adopted for houses from the suburban zone of Prizren. The interior boasts some beautiful wooden carved ceilings so you are in for a treat if you can manage to enter it with a tour group or otherwise. There is also a so-called 'Jerusalem Chamber', which is a wooden shrine-like centre in a room to which the men were traditionally brought. It included the items brought from the pilgrimage to Jerusalem such as prayer scrolls. There are other heritage houses in the village but none as well preserved as this one. There is also a watermill in the village.

ZOČISTE Zočiste village and monastery is about 4km further on towards Suha Rekë from Velika Hoča. The village was mixed prior to the 1999 conflict and houses have been built ready for Serbian returnees. The monastery entrance is immediately on your right and is guarded by KFOR to whom you must give your ID to get through the barbed wire. The bell tower can be seen from above. The **monastery** was blown up and completely destroyed in 1999 but is now in the process of restoration using funds from Belgrade. The bell tower and living quarters have been tastefully rebuilt, as has the small central church, including a genuine slate roof and stone. Some of the stones from the original church have been put in the side wall in front of the church. The monastery dates from the 14th century (there was apparently a written document mentioning it in 1327), and was renowned as being a place of healing for all the local communities, including Albanians. It contained relics of what was believed to be Damina/Kozma.

XËRXË Around 5km from Rahovec is another agricultural town and home to one of the most successful Kosovo businesses to date, M&Sillosi — a mill and pasta producer, which after privatisation is expanding into potato chips and other snacks. The factory is easy to spot with its large metal branded towers.

Continuing past Xërxë on the road from Rahovec to Gjakova is a beautiful Turkish-era stone bridge, **Ura e Fshejt**, running parallel with the main road (see page 194).

Further on to the right is the town of **Bishtazin** and a modern Catholic church with tall spires.

SUHA REKË/SUVA REKA/THERANDË

HISTORY Suha Rekë is another agricultural centre, with a recently privatised vineyard with good development potential. In the past, Schweppes drinks were bottled here but the licence was revoked. There is not much to see in Suha Rekë, but it is a cheaper alternative to staying in Prizren itself.

The 'cellar' of the Suha Rekë drinks plant is the dappled-looking concrete building in the centre of town. You can stop off here if you wish to see or learn about *raki* in the making, although at the time of writing because of a change of ownership, no concrete information could be given.

The Orthodox church in Suha Rekë from the 14th century is now destroyed.

WHERE TO STAY AND EAT

🏠 **Hotel Rozafa** (20 rooms) Off the main road in the centre; ☎ 029 72 067; 📱 044 184 235; ℮ hotelrozafa@hotmail.com; www.hotelrozafa.com. Modern hotel set back from the road, with central heating which isn't always on. Right now the best bet in town & quite passable. Free internet use downstairs. $$

✗ **Restaurant Kulla** On the main road, in the centre of Suha Rekë, just in front of Hotel Rozafa; 📱 044 184 357; ⏰ 07.00–24.00. Stone building, nice, cosy atmosphere with a front terrace. Very reasonably priced traditional food or place to stop for a drink.

OTHER PRACTICALITIES There are branches of NLB, ProCredit (\ *029 271 243;* ⏰ *09.00–16.00 Mon–Fri and 09.00–14.00 Sat*) and Raiffeisen (*Sheshi Brigada 123;* m *044 306 306;* ⏰ *08.30–16.30 Mon–Fri*).

There is also a Ben-Af supermarket on the main street and PTK, at the Prishtina end of the town. The bus station is also at this end of town.

OUTSIDE SUHA REKË

Mušutište churches Mušutište and Povoljane villages are nestled against the tall hill on the way from Prishtina to Prizren on the left-hand side. Mušutište was a major religious centre from the 14th century, with a big church built in 1315, but this is now completely destroyed and the other churches in the same area are also just ruins.

ZHUPA VALLEY

The Zhupa Valley is possibly the most scenic 'drive' in Kosovo. You can start either at the Shtime end or from Prizren. The road is good asphalt and is never too busy, but passing places are limited. Coming from Prizren you will pass through the steep dramatic sides of the Lumbardhi Gorge, the Monastery of Archangels, the Hydro-electric Museum and the castle on your right. After a few kilometres, the picnickers from Prizren become fewer in number and the signs are in Serbian as you approach the Bosnian and Serbian villages. In 2003 Zhupa Valley was dubbed 'returns valley', owing to the number of successful returns of refugees. The villages are often high up and not easily accessible with stone houses and villagers subsisting on agriculture. It can be hard for the children to get to school in the winter. For sightseeing purposes, the valley can be divided into four areas – the initial sights of the monastery, the Sredska district with its churches up to Prevalac Mountain, the busier ski-resort villages of Brezovica and Štrpce, and then the Siriniça group of villages. We describe them below in the order in which they are reached.

SREDSKA DISTRICT The mountain villages in this area have been known as a district since the Middle Ages, including in the donation charter of King Dragutin to the Hilandar Monastery in 1276–81, then again at the time of the Monastery of Archangels. The villages are mostly Serbian, with some resident Bosniaks (particularly in Rečan) and Gorani (for example in Lubinje). Most village churches date from the mid 16th to the early 17th centuries and have been constructed at the initiative of and with funds from the villagers themselves. There was then a second wave of construction in the wake of reforms in the later years of the Ottoman Empire between 1865 and 1875.

Where to stay and eat
Rečan village

🏠 **Madera** m 044 275 855/165 977; ⏰ 08.00–23.00 Thu–Tue. Located on the main road in the centre of the village, beside the river, this cosy & welcoming restaurant offers a wide range of delicious traditional Bosnian cuisine, including delicacies such as brain, tripe, 'calf's lockets' & 'shouting bedlam'. Dishes €1–6.

✗ **Pizzeria Kapricosa** ⏰ 08.00–23.00 daily. Again on the main road in the centre of the village, beside the river, this is a modern-style restaurant on 2 floors with splendid views of the snowcapped mountains. Offers a range of traditional & Italian cuisine. Dishes €1–5.

Continuing a few kilometres from Rečan in the direction of Sredska, there are a number of restaurants and motels nestled in the hillside with spectacular views over the countryside and mountains. This is a very popular location for family outings, especially on weekends, so traffic to/from Prizren is quite busy, particularly in summer.

Between Rečan and Sredska

⌂ **Finlandia Motel and Restaurant** (9 rooms) m 044 237 784/049 389 191; www.finlandia.weebly.com. After spending 20 years living in Finland, the proprietor Fejzula Hoxha returned to Kosovo to realise his ambition to design & build this elaborate complex with no expense spared. Recently opened, the main building offers 2 dining areas, open from 09.00 to 23.00 daily, offering a range of traditional & Italian cuisine (kebabs are the speciality). Dishes €3–8. There is also a large seminar/function room & a bar. Outside, the pond & water features weave their way through the gardens beside the terraced dining area. On the top floor of the main building there are 4 double rooms, 2 triples & 1 apartment. A little bit more expensive but much nicer than Hotel Elegance. $$$

⌂ **Hotel Elegance** (6 rooms) m 044 199 308. A basic hotel where the cleanliness & service standards are not great, but if you are tired & on a budget it is an option, being the first main hotel coming from Prizren & walking distance to dinner at Villa Park Restaurant. Rooms have very basic bathrooms but no AC. $$

✗ **Villa Park Restaurant** m 044 656 427; e vilapark@live.com; www.vilapark.com; ⊕ 09.00:23.00 daily. On the right-hand side

coming from Rečan or Prizren just before Sredska & after Hotel Elegance, this is a newly built timber complex with no expense spared. The inside is cosy in winter & in summer the tables outside are close to the trout ponds. The food is delicious & incredibly reasonably priced with trout at just €5. Other dishes €3–10. There is a good selection of Kosovo & international wines & the owner plans to expand the collection in the wine cellar that is being built. Outside there is a children's play area & terraces with water features. It makes a good break from visiting churches or is an alternative to eating in the noisier Prizren if you are heading down the Zhupa Valley. Make sure you bring mosquito repellent if you are dining outside in the evening, however.

⌂ **White House Hotel and Restaurant** Continuing to Sredska, on the right-hand side is this ostentatious establishment. The architecture is unique – neoclassical Greek meets Kosovar opulence. In spite of this there are elaborate garden features & splendid views of snow-capped mountains. Unfortunately, at the end of 2009, these premises were closed on account of the owner's financial difficulties, & there is no indication when it may reopen. In the meantime, it remains a spectacle & curiosity for locals & visitors alike.

Prevalac

⌂ **Hotel Sharri** (20 rooms) 20km from Prizren, 1,200m above sea level & not far from Lubinje village below; m 044 662 674; ⊕ 07.00–24.00. Top-level hotel with beautiful views & large garden. Conference room with 200 seats, video beam system & new sound system. There are VIP rooms with a separate lounge & also 1- or 2-bed villas. Rooms have AC, minibar, TV, hairdryer & room service. Wi-Fi, jacuzzi, laundry & dry-cleaning service, business centre. 2 restaurants. $$$

⌂ **Koha Hotel and Restaurant** (2–3 rooms) m 044 126 571. A budget option at the top of the Prevalac Pass. Prices vary according to the season. $

Å **Campsite Prevalac Pass** Has power & water connections, but there are no showers, & it gets crowded in Jul/Aug. It is not certain how long it will remain open as the politicians who have built their illegal second homes there are not too keen on the site. $

What to see and do

Sredska Church of St George This is in the middle of the village by the road. It is a tiny church which was apparently a family chapel, and is interesting for the quality of the frescoes which are believed to date from 1530. Maybe the painter was practising for a monastery assignment because they seem to be out of proportion to the modesty of the church, with depictions of exceptional warriors.

Sredska Church of the Holy Virgin The church was probably built in 1646–47 with the contributions of the villagers whose names are mentioned in the inscription. The frescoes include the *Passion of Christ*, *Last supper* and various saints. A small belfry was added in the 19th century.

Bogoševci, Church of St Nicholas The church probably dates from the 16th–17th centuries. Situated near the riverbank, and containing some preserved paintings depicting the Holy Archangel and St Paraskeve.

Drajčiči To get here you have to turn to the right up an unasphalted road on switchbacks uphill from Sredska. The **Church of St Nicholas** is believed to have been built in the 16th century and is slightly different in style from other local churches, with a rounded apse.

Mušnikovo Church of the Holy Apostles Mušnikovo is about 10km from Prizren and 3km on from Sredska. The church is up on the right-hand side of the road coming from Prizren up a side road. It was built and painted in 1563–64 and extensively renewed in the second half of the 19th century. The paintings apparently were done by an artist who learnt some of his styles in Greece and there are Greek inscriptions as well as a representation of St Peter and St Paul in an embrace. The paintings nearer the altar are not so impressive. Stone flags and a dome were put on during the renovations in 1962.

Gornje Selo Gornje Selo is a very attractive village a further 3–4km on from Mušnikovo nestled at the bottom of the steep road up (if coming from Prizren) to Prevalac. There are lots of traditional stone houses crumbling because their mortar is made of mud and from the water running down after each annual snowmelt. The population includes Albanians, Bosnians, Gorani and Serbs, although many houses, particularly the ones at the far top end of the village beyond the beautiful renovated stone school, are abandoned. You can keep following the path up past the school for several kilometres through the houses and on up the hill as a walk to the top of Prevalac. The attractive little **Church of St George** is across the river and halfway up the hill with a small cemetery. Try and get someone to open up because the wall paintings include a cross and birds and are attractive. Unfortunately the mosque is a modern replacement.

Prevalac Pass (1,535m) The road snakes back up to Prevalac. Before getting to the top you may want to pull over safely and take a picture of Gornje Selo below you with its stone houses and mosque gleaming in the sun. When you get to the top of Prevalac, the peace of the countryside may be broken by the army of day trippers who have all congregated in the same spot with their litter and noise. There is a campsite here but it has no real facilities other than toilets, nor is it tranquil. There is also (in winter) a small beginners' ski lift, a couple of mountain huts and restaurants and in summer, plenty of kebab vans.

BREZOVICA

GETTING THERE AND AWAY At the time of writing there were still no buses between Ferizaj (the nearest major town) and Štrpce or Brezovica – the best you could do was to get a *kombi* from Ferizaj to Ferije/Firaja, which is the last Albanian town on the hill, and to Štrpce (where the road bump and former checkpoint was), and get off there. An alternative if you are coming from Prishtina is to ask one of the travel agencies, as many **buses** run from Kosovo's main towns during the ski season and on weekends. Certainly getting back from Brezovica to Prishtina during the skiing season should not be a problem as there are plenty of buses up and the ski lifts are usually full of young Kosovars. It takes about one hour 45 minutes to get from Prishtina to Brezovica.

It is also possible that there are buses from Prizren, at least in the summer and winter seasons as Prevalac is a popular spot.

WHERE TO STAY The former Breza Hotel, which is on the right as you come into town from the Shtime direction, is occupied by KFOR and the Lahor and Junior hotels are occupied by internally displaced persons (refugees) from inside Kosovo. There are, however, several choices. The main decision you have to make is whether to stay in Brezovica town down below or 8km uphill near the slopes. If you are skiing two days then it is generally preferable to be up at the slopes to save the trek down and up. Remember that electricity supply is limited in both Brezovica and Štrpce because for political reasons the local Serbs do not wish to pay electricity fees to KEK. Therefore KEK has categorised this area as Zone C, which means that Štrpce and surrounds only get electricity when there is enough for the rest of Kosovo. This can be anything from one to three hours a day, to four hours on and two off. In any event it means that while the hotels have generators, hot water and heating can be somewhat limited. Therefore bring lots of warm clothes with you and be ready to forgo that hair wash until you get back to Prishtina or Prizren! If you want a bit more luxury over the weekend then you either have to pay for the Woodlands Hotel on the slopes or drive further and stay in Hotel Sharri (see page 230) at the top of Prevalac (on snowy days in the winter this is only an option if you have a 4×4).

On the slopes

Woodland Hotel (30 rooms) m 044/049 444 448; e info@woodlandhotel-kos.com; www.woodlandhotel-ks.com/. This is the luxury option for Brezovica. As a result it can often be full in peak season on Fri/Sat nights. A rather incongruous red colour on the outside. The Queen's Room is 50m², with jacuzzi & a view of the ski lifts. Other rooms are 2 or 3 beds with bathroom & TV, but perhaps the best luxury for Brezovica is the 24hr electricity & hot water! For Kosovo the prices are high, however, with rooms nearly €70, making this the most expensive hotel outside Prishtina. Wi-Fi. Restaurant. $$$

Hotel Molika (100 rooms) ✆ 029 070 310/452; often only during the season. This is the big Yugoslav hotel up top. Rooms have a bathroom. Generally warm but basic with sporadic hot water. Still not privatised! $$

Hotel Sara (30 rooms, 100 beds) ✆ 029 070 653; ⊕ during the season only. This is the yellow hotel slightly further below the Molika. They also organise ski lessons. Prices are reasonable & the rooms are adequate. $$

Mountain Hotel/Buan (4 rooms/apts) ✆ +381 64 356 4235/049 545 922. This is a very small hotel/restaurant with pleasant owners, operating a double lift. The apartments have a sit-in kitchen & are nice, quiet & pleasant. $$

In town

Hotel Narcis (300 beds) ✆ 029 70 333. This Yugoslav hotel must have been really something in its heyday when Brezovica was renowned for being the best place to ski in Serbia. There is a huge lobby & restaurant. The rooms are clean & the staff mean well although the service standards hark back to the same socialist era as the décor. $$$

Motel Ljuboten (2 rooms, 5 apts) ✆ 029 073 030; www.brezovica-ski.com. This is a pleasant hotel in a new-looking wooden hut just as you turn up to the ski resort road, so still down in town. The hut, combined with a great restaurant, is cosy with a fire, simple décor, a wide selection of wines & simply delicious food, including trout, pork, beef & of course pickled peppers. Frequented by Serbs & Albanians alike. Good service. $$

If you are planning on staying longer, it is also possible to rent a house or rooms in a house much more cheaply and usually this is more pleasant than the hotels. Ask in any of the ski shops or restaurants for information.

WHERE TO EAT
On the slopes

Braça Restaurant ⊕ 09.00–22.00 during the season only. This is tucked down the slope slightly near the funicular. It is a very reasonably priced, cosy, friendly restaurant with a fire, wooden tables & absolutely delicious fresh food (you can see the kitchen) & great service. The çorba (soup) is filling & superb, the meat platter has tasty pork & the soft

cheese & *kajmak* should be tried. The pancakes are also good. If not driving back down the road, try *srpski caj*, which is a tea with *raki*, or the hot wine.
✕ **Pizza Tina's** ⊕ 09.00–22.00 during the season only. Lively, friendly hangout in a wooden hut of the Serbian & Albanian younger ski & snowboard crowd but 'oldies' also welcome. Filling pizzas & hot chocolate. Can get a bit stuffy & smoky.

✕ **Restaurant Mala Brunara** ➘ 045 560 058; ⊕ 10.00–21.00. Halfway up the road near the wooden weekend houses. Tables outside right next to the stream. Try the fish. The owner has been there for more than 40 years. **Mountain Hotel/Buan** See *Where to stay*, above.
✕ **Woodlands Hotel** See *Where to stay*, above.

In town
✕ **Motel Ljuboten** See *Where to stay*, above.

OTHER PRACTICALITIES   For banks or ATMs you have to go to Štrpce (3–4km away).

WHAT TO SEE AND DO
Ski resort   Most people come to Brezovica for the skiing. Brezovica has snow from December to the end of April and is higher up than Kopaonik and has better snow than Popova Šapka or Mavrovo. There are six basins in Brezovica. The height of the resort is from 1,718m at the ski hotels and base of the lifts, to 2,522m. Before you get too excited – yes, Brezovica has tremendous potential and could be a truly fabulous ski resort but it is currently a victim of Kosovo's political situation and international dithering, resulting in a ski resort stuck in a time warp, suffering from serious under-investment. It desperately needs some major capital spent on the lifts and on general slope maintenance. There are about 11 lifts in varying states of decay but at the moment only two chairlifts ever run regularly, together with a T-bar on a crowded beginners' slope. In the eyes of the Serb government the ski resort belongs to the company Inex in Belgrade and should not be privatised and the local Serbs feel (or at least felt) obliged to toe this line, although it seems to have got them nowhere. The Kosovo Privatisation Agency on the other hand tendered the resort for privatisation in 2005 and received some interest, but the process was put on hold after the UN became twitchy about the political fallout. They are rumoured to be trying again in 2010.

To ski in Brezovica you have to adjust your expectations as Brezovica really is like no other ski resort. Despite being a Serb area, lots of Albanians visit. Many do not have enough money to ski or to buy the equipment so many just come on a day trip scantily clad. They slide around in the snow and ride the lift once up and down, giggling and shivering in their jeans and often even high heels. For them this is a special trip and they certainly seem to have a great day out.

A manager of a Western ski resort might suffer a heart attack at the absence of safety arrangements as the crowds congregate right on the pistes intermingled with sleds and teenagers shooting down the slope out of control on pieces of plastic. Furthermore, as if to create a target for the sledgers and skiers rather like a skittle alley, the local vendors set up stalls of food, drink and beer right at the bottom of the piste next to the chairlifts. Again, try not to wince too much when the couple on the lift in front throw the waste from their food and drink into the snow below. The operating slopes include one beginners' slope and one steep black/red run on the front of the double chair and a red on the backside. The pistes are neither marked, nor groomed.

For all these reasons and the absence of snow patrols, helmets are a good idea and while there is great **off-piste skiing** to be had, small avalanches are not unheard of. Go with a friend and bear in mind that there is no real rescue service and limited health care. The lifts have to be switched to the generators when the power stops so be prepared to be suspended in mid air for quite long periods and wear appropriate clothes.

Also, remember that in the Balkans queuing is unheard of, which can be frustrating. As Kosovo's middle class has grown, the volume of young Kosovars who can afford a day out skiing and boarding has grown, and in 2009–10, the crowd at the bottom (as mentioned – it is no queue!) was considerable – involving waits of more than an hour and quite painful pushing and shoving into a bizarre metal door arrangement. In any normal place this might be seen as a recipe for crush injuries. It is no place for an impatient person. Once (or if) you have come to terms with all of this, then because of the good snow and challenging runs Brezovica is a great place to ski for experienced skiers, although not so good for beginners. Internationals who work in Prishtina are very grateful to have a resort less than two hours' drive away for only €11!

To drive up the 8km from the village to the resort you ideally need snow tyres with chains or a 4×4 as the road can be very slippery. It is also badly maintained. During the ski season there is usually a fee for entering the car parking area which is approximately €1.50 per car and then €1 for each person in the car. Sundays tend to be busier than Saturdays and the parking can extend down the hill a long way and be quite chaotic. Weekdays are beautifully quiet, but occasionally the lift staff may be reluctant to open the lifts. Ring the Molika Hotel ahead on a weekday to find out if there is a group staying. If this is the case then they may be opening the lifts and you might have your best midweek day out.

Prices are cheap, with day **ski passes** only €11. Weekend passes are also available. Beginners' and towbar lift passes can be bought for €1, and if you are a pedestrian but just want to ride the chairlift, it costs €2 for a round trip. To hire skis or board and boots costs €10 per day. There is a good choice of kit (both good-quality skis and snowboards) at several outlets (you must leave ID), including one in the Molika Hotel, next to the ski-pass booth, and another lower down near the top of the car park. If the lifts close early (or do not open) for whatever reason you do not get your money back on the pass or skis so it pays to wait and see if the lifts really will open. Weather permitting, lifts should open between 09.00 and 10.00 and close at 15.00.

If you are staying overnight, you may wish to move your car at the end of the day up the hill towards the hotels where it should be slightly safer.

The Brezovica/Štrpce area, being a national park, also has good walking and is worth visiting for the countryside. The park is also replete with herbs, birds and wild animals – bear, chamois, roe deer, wild boar, marten, lynx and grouse, to name but a few, and of course the rivers are full of trout.

ŠTRPCE/SHTERPCË

HISTORY Štrpce has a 65% Serbian majority, with the remainder mostly Albanian. The centre is Štrpce town but the municipality also includes Brezovica. Inter-ethnic relations have generally been good. Income is solely from agriculture and tourism and the Brezovica ski resort.

Turkish records from 1455 mention the village having 65 households and a shrine. The town is not large but is quite pleasant with some older stone buildings and attractive churches.

GETTING THERE AND AWAY Ask for Brezovica (see above) except that you need to get off the bus in Štrpce town.

WHERE TO STAY AND EAT If you turn down the road which goes quite steeply downhill at the side of the municipality building there is a junction at the end of the road. On the left before the bridge is the Hotel Lovac.

🏠 **Hotel Lovac** (10 en-suite rooms, 2 apts) ☎ 029 070 700; e triumph@email.co.rs. Rooms are cheap. Internet, AC & heating. $

🏠 **Hotel/Restaurant Karpa** (4 rooms) ☎ 029 070 218. Further round from Hotel Lovac, on the river (not across the main bridge). Follow the road & line of the river round from Hotel Lovac past a semi-derelict factory, construction site & market area; Restaurant Karpa is then on the other side of the river across its own dedicated small bridge. It has its own terrace on the river & a fish restaurant which is very pleasant in summer. Rooms have no bathroom. $

✕ **Restaurant Lipa** ⊕ 08.30–23.00. This is up the road from the police station & includes a nice outdoor terrace.

OTHER PRACTICALITIES Štrpce has a Raiffeisen Bank (⊕ 08.30–16.30). ProCredit is also on the main road, with an international ATM.

There is also a Serbian post office (near the municipality) and a PTK.

WHAT TO SEE AND DO

Štrpce Church of St Nicholas Built and decorated in 1576–77 with donations from the villagers, the church houses original paintings, and has a deacon. Restored in the 19th century, adding a belfry, icons and more paintings. The church's icons are believed to assist fertility, and it is still visited today by women wishing to conceive.

On the top hill is **Steti Petka Church**, which is apparently mentioned in the Serbian gospels.

Sirinic district This set of villages on the Shtime side of Štrpce, on the north slopes of the Sharr Mountains, were like the Sredska villages mentioned in the Hilandar Monastery charter. Most villages had their own shrines, but as they were usually made of mud, wood and stone not all survived. A 19th-century traveller counted 11 shrines in eight villages. Today only four really remain. Usually the villagers funded the paintings.

Donja Bitinja The church at Donja Bitinja, about 2km on from Štrpce (turn left off the highway before the single church), has decorative paintings from a village artist. The church retains the icon representing the vision of the Prophet Eliah dated 1635–36, which could be a throne icon judging by its dimensions.

Continue on up the hill for another 2–3km to **Gornja Bitinja**, with good views. The frescoes state that a Jelena was the patron of the paintings and that Nikodin Prtušin donated a watermill, forest and meadow to the church in 1592.

Gotuvuša village Back down, and another 2km along the road, is Gotuvuša village with the Church of St Nicholas. There are two churches in the village. The older one has the village cemetery and is dedicated to St Savoir, but it is also known as St Dimitrios. There are only parts of paintings left depicting the Great Feasts, angels and Emmanuel. Based on the dates of other paintings, it is assumed they date from the 1570s.

WALKING NEAR ŠTRPCE

The following are all marked on the Brezovica Tourist Map (a pre-1999 1:50,000 map) that the hotels may have. The paths can also be found on the KFOR map (see page 61).

LJUBOTEN PEAK (2,498m) (*c20km round trip & a steep 1,500m climb*) This climb, which is a dawn to dusk affair and is not for the faint-hearted, offers good views towards Thessaloniki and straight down to the mountain huts above St Selo near Tetovo in Macedonia. The ascent is from Gotuvuša village, following the logging road after the top church, past the Zidovnica archaeological remains on your right, then up 1km from the village to Mršejci at 1,104m. Next, continue round in a curve (skirting the hill) on the track to Kaluerov Kamen Cave on your right to a ridge called Preslap, then to Cvetkov grob at 1,782m. From then on it is more or less straight up to 2,061m and then a further gradual climb before you arrive at the summit. It's worth taking a guide as the ridge may have some land mines.

BISTRICA PEAK (2,651m) (*c17km round trip & a steep 1,100m climb; estimated time: 5–7hrs return*) From Prevalac there is a walking trail up to Bistrica Peak. To get there, walk up the paved gravel/asphalt road opposite the Koha Restaurant parallel to the skilift and behind the campsite, in a southerly direction. Do not follow the paved road all the way, however. You will come to a three-way junction (the paved road bears right; straight ahead is the track you want and to the left is a smaller, narrower track which heads downhill). You must go uphill at all times! After about 4–5km of steep uphill climbing with some false summits you will come to the top of another intermediate peak (Pavlov kam) at 2,081m with a waterfall on your right and from then on the walk is steeper still on a ridge known as Velika planina for a further 3km. Take care as Bistrica's summit is right on the Macedonian border. Crossing is illegal and the behaviour of the border guards unpredictable. There may also be mines on the border from the 2002 Macedonian conflict or the 1999 Kosovo conflict – do not go any further than you have to.

There is an old Yugoslav path behind Prevalac up to the Prilinjska peak and along the ridge opposite Bistrica, but the path now crosses straight through a cluster-bomb site. This may now be cleared but we do not recommend experimenting.

AROUND THE SKI LIFTS There is a good walking path in a loop which goes right round the tops of the ski lifts at Brezovica.

Northeast to the glacier lake Livadčko Go to the top of the far left lift and, imagining you were getting off, take the left path northeast directly across about 2km to Tumba Peak at 2,346m. Standing on the top of this peak you can look down towards Macedonia, and you can see the glacier lake – Lake Livadčko, or Štrbačko, a good sheltered spot for wild camping. From this peak you follow a left-hand circular curve towards the east and then north about 1km and drop about 500m to Demir Kapija. You are then on the same level as the ski hotels (they are now southwest of you), directly above Štrpce. You can choose to either walk back round the hills on the paths to the ski hotels or follow the marked track straight down to Štrpce.

Southwest to the glacier lake Jažinačko Go to the top of the far right double chairlift, imagine you were getting off, and turn right, or southwest. Go slightly uphill and then down into the neighbouring valley and up again onto the next hill (a steep climb) so that you are then standing parallel with the top of the ski lift on the neighbouring hill. The lake is at the southern end of this second valley – a direct horizontal line from the ski lifts two valleys away. From there you can head down the paths to the left of the river to Gornje Sija and Donja Sija through the woods (you can also reach the lake by coming up this way). Have faith and you will emerge in Preslap at the end of the logging tracks. The major track on the left takes you to Prevalac. Stay straight and head downhill on the footpath and you end up a few kilometres west of Brezovica town.

BREZOVICA TO ST PETER'S CHURCH CAVE (*7–8km each way; estimated time: 4hrs*) If you fancy a different view and a less steep walk then try going up the tributary valley northwest out of Brezovica village in the direction of Radonava Mala and Vrbeštica villages – the latter has an archaeological site (Groki Grad) on the right of the valley. There is also one cave on the right after Straški Most at 1,106m and another one on the left higher up close to Jama Mijatoviči at 1,272m. Continue until the road peters out and then hike a further 1–2km to Crkvena Pecina (church cave). This is a well-type cave with 57m of corridors and it was used as a hermitage. The only problem is that as this walk is in a valley with steep sides a round trip is not feasible and you have to retrace your steps.

DONJE BITINJA TO SUŠICE BACK TO DONJE BITINJA ROUND TRIP (*About 15 km; estimated time: 4hrs*) This walk is not too strenuous and fits nicely into a morning or afternoon. It can be done even in early spring when the higher mountains have snow on them so are not passable. The views across the fields to the mountains on the opposite valley are stunning and for several hours you are up high. Park the car at Donje Bitinja which is about 3–4km before Štrpce when driving from Ferizaj/Brod. If travelling by bus, alight at that point. You will see a track going up the hill to the right of the village which is used for logging tractors. The name of the hill to ask for is Mužiljak. Continue until about 1,250m altitude. You can then either take the lower track or the higher one. You will see Gornja Bitinja (the next village) in the valley below and then you continue along the track which winds now through the beech trees. After about two hours you need to drop down to Sušice village through the meadows. The six–eight houses in this village are nearly all made of traditional stone and some are abandoned. From Sušice to Gornje Bitinja and back to Donje Bitinja the road is asphalt. Gornja Bitinja is about 4–5km downhill from Sušice. Unlike Sušice and Donje Bitinja, which are Serb villages, this was a mixed village and while the mosque and the church still sit side by side, clearly there were frictions and there are many identical bare red-brick small post-war rebuilds, some of which are inhabited and some not. It is then another 5–8km back to Donje Bitinja, past the farms, haystacks and fruit trees either side of the road.

Once you have absorbed the views of Prevalac, leave the crowds behind – you will find this is easy as they do not go far. It becomes quiet again as you descend the 6–8km, towards Brezovica, which is the next inhabited village.

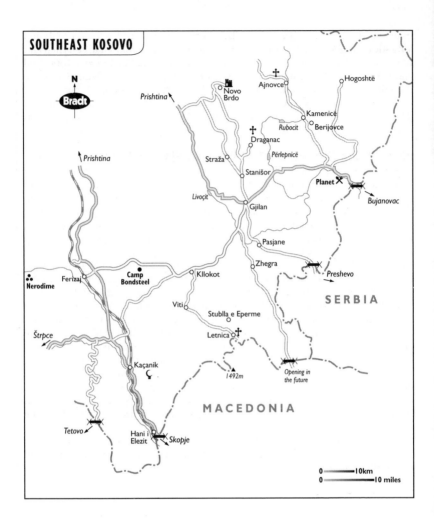

SOUTHEAST KOSOVO

N

Bradt

Prishtina

Novo Brdo

Ajnovce

Hogoshtë

Kamenicë

Rubocit

Berijovce

Draganac

Përlepnicë

Straža

Prishtina

Stanišor

Planet ✕

Livoçit

Bujanovac

Gjilan

Pasjane

Zhegra

Camp Bondsteel

Nerodime

Ferizaj

Kllokot

Preshevo

SERBIA

Viti

Stublla e Eperme

Štrpce

Letnica

Kaçanik

1492m

Opening in the future

MACEDONIA

Tetovo

Hani i Elezit

Skopje

0 ━━━10km
0 ━━━10 miles

7

Southeast Kosovo

HISTORY

The area of southeastern Kosovo (excluding Kaçanik, Hani i Elezit and Ferizaj) as a whole is often referred to as Anamorova, the area closest to Kamenicë is known as Gollap, and that closest to Macedonia is known as the Karadak region or Malesi Shkupit (the Black Mountains of Skopje). The people were referred to historically as Izmorniku. During the Ottoman era, the Gjilan area as a whole fell under the *vilayet* of Prizren and at times Prishtina and Skopje. The Kaçanik area has always been part of the Skopje *vilayet*.

In the Middle Ages, by far the most important town in Kosovo was the mining city of Novo Brdo. Today it is nothing more than a dying hamlet. The silver and gold attracted traders from Dubrovnik, and large numbers of Saxon miners tolerated by the Ottomans. A combination of technical mining problems, reduced investment in equipment, and higher taxes eventually led to the town's decline in the late 17th and 18th centuries.

As the importance of Novo Brdo declined, Gjilan to the south developed as the new regional centre. It is not known exactly when it was formed – stories say around 1750 when an inn was set up and by the early 18th century there were some 200 houses. Gjilan benefited from being on a trading route from Shkodra via Prizren to Niš, and likely then, as now, villagers brought in their agricultural wares to trade.

Kaçanik was a smaller town founded by Sinan Pasha and its size remained pretty constant, with primarily a military role and a pass-through trading function until the development of the Sharr factories in the 1930s.

Both Albanians and Serbs in the area participated in the failed 1689 Austrian uprising against the Turks, suffering large losses from its foot soldiers trapped and abandoned in the Kaçanik Valley. A further 1910 uprising also proved to be fruitless.

Nearby Viti municipality is predominantly rural. Its small pockets of Croat and Catholic Albanians living in the area of Letnica, a well-known pilgrimage site, also date back to the times when the mountains bordering Macedonia were mined for silver.

Ferizaj grew in importance after the completion in 1874 of the railway line connecting Skopje and Thessaloniki, which passed through the town. Under communism, several key factories were added, including the sunflower oil factory and the pipe factory. After 1999, Ferizaj grew rapidly thanks to the nearby US camp of Bondsteel and the influx of villagers from the surrounding area.

GEOGRAPHY

The countryside of the Gjilan area is undulating, rather than steep, with the highest hills on the Macedonian border. There is some particularly fertile farmland around Gjilan and Viti and, like elsewhere in Kosovo, agriculture was the main source of income for this area before the war, with most parts cultivated, leaving only small woods. This is the main orchard fruit area of Kosovo, and Kravarica was traditionally famous for its cherry trees. NGOs have also encouraged the replanting of apple trees around Gjilan.

Many villages near the Serbian border around Kamenicë are now abandoned and there has been the usual population shift from the countryside, especially to larger towns like Gjilan.

The main river in the Gjilan area is the Morava e Binçes. There are two artificial lakes near Gjilan – Lepenic and Prilepnicë – built to collect water for the town, although now only Prilepnicë really functions. Three rivers run through Gjilan itself – the Dobusha, Banjska and Stanishorka. They then join together in the village of Malisheva and run to the Morava River 6km outside Gjilan.

The Kaçanik countryside on the other hand is much steeper with a dramatic gorge. The main rivers in the Kaçanik area are the Lepenc, which runs on to Skopje and the Nerodime River. Ferizaj is famous for its bifurcation (see page 251).

Both the Kaçanik and the Gjilan areas are rich in stones and minerals and there are several large quarries (including a big granite one known as Morava e Binçes between Gjilan and Kamenicë, and also large cement and limestone factories in the Kaçanik/Hani i Elezit Valley.

There are large reserves of kaolin in the Gjilan/Kamenicë areas. Kaolin is used in ceramics, medicine, bricks, coated paper, as a food additive, in toothpaste, as a light-diffusing material in white incandescent light bulbs, and in cosmetics. Recently, it is also being used as a specially formulated spray applied to fruits, vegetables and other vegetation to repel or deter insect damage. A traditional use is to soothe an upset stomach, but the most common use overall is in the production of paper, as it is a key ingredient in creating 'glossy' paper (but calcium carbonate, an alternative material, is competing in this function). The Gjilan and border area near Bujanovac and Medvedja is also rich in spas and hot springs, attracting several new water-bottling companies, such as Dea, which have set up since the war. The Dea factory can be reached by following the sign off the road from Prishtina. The factory seems incongruously modern with glass houses over the springs. You can fill up your own bottles at a public spring near the factory.

The Gjilan area is prone to earthquakes and in 2003, a quake was sufficient to destroy several houses and led to the demolition of the old mosque in town.

GJILAN/GNJILANE

Although there is relatively little to see, Gjilan still has a fairly pleasant feel to it, with plenty of cafés and bars thronging with young people. The town has rather a civic air about it as a result of serious planning and Yugoslav social investment in the 1970s and 1980s. The results of this can still be seen – as you enter from Ferizaj you pass the textile, tobacco and radiator factories to your right. In the 1980s, each house in the planned grid-system housing estate to the north, known as 'Gavran', was set back from the road with its own garden; however, now many gardens are built over and the houses have grown upwards and outwards.

From 1970 to the 1990s, the region was very much linked with factories and business in Bujanovac, which now lies across the Serbian border, and Kumanovo across the Macedonian border.

Along with Gjakova, Gjilan had some of the most profitable factories in Kosovo, including the battery factory, textile factory (now abandoned), the tobacco factory (which restarted and then stopped owing to the global financial crisis), and the domestic radiator factory (which still exports to much of Yugoslavia and has more than two-thirds of the Kosovo market).

The population and size of Gjilan and the surrounding area has grown post-1999 to around 133,000, including more than 12,000 Kosovo Serbs. They mostly live in the villages and come in regularly by bus to sell their wares at the market in the side street near the church. You can often see the black-headscarved women collecting their pensions at the banks and Serbian is spoken on Gjilan's streets.

The city suffered from a fire in 1830, so nearly all the buildings (except the mosque) date from after that point.

GETTING THERE AND AWAY There are **buses** approximately every 20 minutes to/from Prishtina (€1.50 – the first bus is at 06.30 and the last bus from Prishtina to Gjilan is at 21.00; the last bus from Gjilan to Prishtina is at 19.30), and every 20 minutes to/from Ferizaj (€2 – the first bus is at 06.20 and the last bus from Ferizaj is at 19.30; in the other direction the last bus is at 19.20). There is one direct bus to Prizren, at 08.00.

There are also regular buses to/from Bujanovac in Serbia if you are entering Kosovo this way from Serbia (it is possible to get off a train in Bujanovac and transfer easily to the bus station). Buses from Gjilan to Bujanovac leave at 06.45, 09.00, 10.30, 11.00, 11.45, 12.15, 14.45, 15.15, 16.30, 17.15 and 19.00. There are also buses to Preshevo at 10.00, 10.45, 13.00, 14.10, 17.00, 18.00 and 18.30.

Taxis from Bujanovac to Gjilan are about €20 – you need to find an Albanian driver. Remember if you leave Kosovo through Serbia that you need a Serbian entry stamp (the other direction is fine – see *Chapter 2, Getting there and away*, page 46). It is about 45 minutes to an hour from all these places to Gjilan.

GETTING AROUND The **bus station** is only a five–ten-minute walk into town. Even if you are driving, the bus station **car park** (or the hospital car park) may well be a good place to leave your car as the centre is best explored on foot. There are also various signed parking places in the centre for about €1 a day (€0.50 a half day).

WHERE TO STAY Gjilan lacks a top-end hotel and a budget hotel. The only real option in town is the mid-range Hotel Kristal. There are some new motels on the outskirts of town.

Hotel Planet (18 rooms) A few kilometres out of town on the road to Bujanovac; 028 032 4432; m 044 501 700; e info@planet-gjilan.com; www.planet-gjilan.com. Smart rooms. AC & Wi-Fi. Opening in 2010, with rooms attached to the restaurant. $$$

Hotel Kristal (45 rooms) Rr Skenderbeu; 028 032 0466; m 044 370 881; e info@hotelkristal.biz; www.hotelkristal.biz. As central as it gets (this is the centre!) & pretty well the only address in town. Privatised & renovated, with double glazing which blocks out the street noise. Central heating, AC & Wi-Fi. Conference hall for up to 100. The restaurant is still a bit communist in style. There is an outdoor terrace to watch the world go by, overlooked by the war-hero statues. Some rooms en suite, some use on-floor communal bathrooms, some so-called 'apartments' (designed really for families with 1 room with double bed & 1 room with 2 beds & bathroom for use by the 2 rooms). Range of prices, depending on the room. $$

WHERE TO EAT AND DRINK

Bujana Restaurant On the left-hand side 2–3km out of town on the road to Ferizaj; m 044 376 928; e restaurantbujana@hotmail.com; ⊕ 07.00–23.00 daily. Huge restaurant. Good food (including some traditional fare) & service, & a pleasant garden – if a slightly tacky stone castle-style frontage.

Donati Rr Mulla Idrizi, 200m from Hotel Kristal down the side street; m 044 540 009; ⊕ 07.00–23.00. Wonderful lasagne, good pasta & salads. Outdoor & indoor seating, including a wood-stove heater in the winter. Also a nice atmosphere for evening drinks. Music is light & good to listen to.

Popular with locals & internationals alike.

🍴 **Embeltore Bezi** Rr Dardania; m 044 692 666; ⏲ 06.00–23.00. Traditional place for coffee & cakes with great, reasonably priced homemade pastries, baklava & other sweet goodies.

🍴 **Embeltore Gogi** Rr Dardania 22; m 044 178 255; ⏲ 08.30-19.00 Mon-Sat. Alternative cake shop further along from Bezi.

🍷 **Hani i Mbretërve** Rr Beqir Musliu; m 044 77 077; ⏲ every day from 11.00 umtil late. Pizza pub. Large bar, nice evening atmosphere. At the time of writing was undergoing renovation.

✗ **Ideal 2** On the right-hand side 3km out of town on the road to Prishtina; m 044 177 500/290 690; ⏲ 07.00–24.00 daily. Not quite up to the standard of the Planet & Bujana. While the outdoors is done well, with huge space & fountains, the indoors looks a bit plastic & ragged at the edges. Pizza bias.

✗ **Planet Restaurant** About 6km out of town on the road to Bujanovac, near Kmetovc; ☎ 028 324 432; m 044 501 700/134 073; ⏲ 07.00–23.00. One of the large, attractive garden restaurant complexes that have sprung up around Kosovo. Especially popular with families & the diaspora in the summer when it serves fresh fruit. Try also the traditional *tavë* & *flija*

dishes often cooked by women in traditional dress.

✗ **Restaurant Center** Rr Dardania, near Hani i Mbretreve; m 044 888 4354; ⏲ 07.00–24.00. Italian cuisine. Popular with internationals.

✗ **Restaurant Elegant** On the outskirts of Zhegra village. Garish orange-&-yellow-painted building but a big garden & places for children to play.

✗ **Restaurant Karadak** m 044 132 693; ☎ 08.00–24.00 daily. 15–20km out of town towards the Macedonian border so is really an excursion in itself (see *Zhegra* below). Trout farm.

✗ **Restaurant Lura** Rr Xh Washington; ☎ 028 322 232; m 044 132 628; e rest.lura@hotmail.com; ⏲ 07.00–23.00 daily. On the way out of Gjilan towards Bujanovac, but not too far. Large restaurant with terrace, specialising in pizzas, steaks & emphasis on fresh food.

✗ **Restaurant Valli Ranch** m 044 369 365; e info@valiranch.com; www.valiranch.com; ⏲ 07.00–23.00. Out in the country at Përlepnicë 8km out of town, with beautiful views of the mountains & plenty of animals to entertain the children. Creating their own French wine cellar.

✗ **Route 66** Rr Beqir Musliu; ⏲ 08.00–23.00. Popular fast-food restaurant.

CAFÉS AND BARS The main venue for the under-25s is a string of small bars with names such as Picasso or Times on Zija Shemsiu, just near the secondary school. They change hands frequently so we have not given any listings. They are noisy and smoky but are 'the place to be seen', particularly in the summer when the diaspora cruise up and down with their smart cars from Switzerland.

If you are older or wish for quieter venues, try the alternative area for pubs, west of the Beqir Musliu complex of streets.

Try also **Hani i Mbretërve** (⏲ 08.00–24.00 daily) on Rr Beqir Musliu (see *Where to eat and drink* above). The **Royal Billiards** (⏲ 09.00–24.00) is a pleasant pub with fruit machines at the back and a large billiard table (€0.30 a game).

ENTERTAINMENT The **theatre** is on Rr Skenderbeu – attend in person to find out about plays. Theoretically, performances are held twice a week at 20.00 for €1 and once a week for children at an earlier time, but not during August or September. The cultural festival of Flaka e Janarit is also held here. The theatre has a café which seems to be a popular place to hang out.

SHOPPING Most people would go to Prishtina for a serious shop but if for some reason you are stuck in Gjilan, here is a selection:

General

Green market Down the road, left of the Hotel Kristal, between the hotel & the Shtepia I Mallrave.
Agmia Centre Newer shopping centre just outside Gjilan with supermarket, trendier clothes and electronics shops. Perhaps most importantly there's a branch of the Sporting shop which sells gym, tennis,

football, Scott and other bikes and bike gear. m 049 419 920; info@sportingks.com www.sportingks.com. They can also order sports gear for you.
Mobi In Rr Prishtina. Modern, German furniture shop.
Serbian market Near the church, an ad hoc market

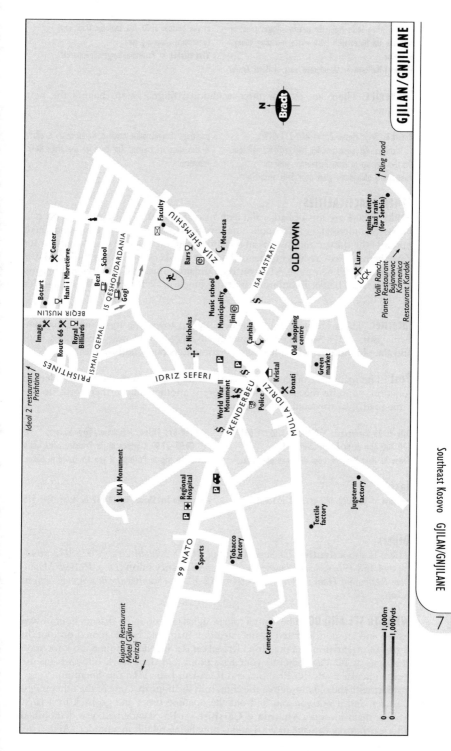

on Wed when Serbs from the nearby villages come in with the UN buses with fresh wares, including honey & cheese.

Shtepia I Mallrave Rr Skenderbeu, east of Hotel Kristal

at the bottom of Rr Zija Shemsiu. Traditional communist shopping mall.

Viva market Rr Prishtina. Large supermarket.

Souvenirs There are two or three traditional filigree shops behind the new mosque.

Botart Rr Beqir Musliu 3; m 044 231 019; e mxhemali@yahoo.com, loli_wecke@hotmail.com. On the way up to Hani Restaurant, with an unassuming aluminium glass door. Sells attractive

paintings (Impressionist, modern, watercolours & oils) & also runs art courses. The base for the artist NGO community.

OTHER PRACTICALITIES

Banks There are lots of banks and cash machines in the centre of town. NLB is on Rr Skenderbeu, near the police station. Raiffeisen is also on Rr Skenderbeu, opposite the theatre and there is an ATM opposite the popular strip of bars on Rr Zija Shemsiu. ProCredit is on the road behind Rr Skenderbeu, near the World War II monument. There is an ATM on Rr Dardania, outside Café Bezi and outside Hotel Kristal. Banka Ekonomike is at the junction of Rr Zija Shemsiu and Rr Skenderbeu.

Internet There are numerous internet cafés in town, the most substantial one being **Jini** on Rr Adem Jashari, down from Zija Shemsiu near the music school and the old mosque, which has over 20 computers but loud(ish) music.

Post The main post office is on Zija Shemsiu, just up from the Rr Skenderbeu junction, opposite the new mosque. There is another one further north up the same road, near the faculty of education.

DHL Rr 28 Shadervani; ☏ 028 021 250; m 044 120 300. Also at Rr Fehmi Ladrovci 6.
Fedex Rr Haki Myderizi, near the small post office;

m 044 873 993; e fedexkosova@gmail.com; ⊙ 08.00–21.00. A branch of the Prishtina office which saves the trip to Prishtina if you are based in Gjilan.

Taxis

🚖 **Bini** ☏ 028 022 480; m 044 255 003

🚖 **Radio Taxi Shaqa** ☏ 028 032 0235; m 044 515 151

Others

There is also a **dentist** (*Dr Shpend A Aliu, Rr 28 Nentori 244;* ☏ *028 032 9043;* m *044 158 396;* e *shpendaliu@yahoo.com*), and a **beauty salon** (*Diva, Rr Beqir Musliu, near Restaurant Hani i Mbreteve;* m *044 338 504;* e *beautycentrediva@gmail.com*) in town.

WHAT TO SEE AND DO The central tourist sights take no more than an hour or two to see and are concentrated in one area (see map) and best explored on foot. In terms of orientation, use the Hotel Kristal on Rr Skenderbeu (but also known on the signs as Rr Pavaresise) as your base point and then work outwards up the perpendicular roads (Rr Prishtina and Rr Adem Jashari/Rr Zija Shemsiu).

Start with the old mosque or the church, in the hope that one or the other might be open and if not you can find out the opening times and go back to it later.

The main mosque, **Xhamia e Çarshisë** on Rr Skenderbeu, was demolished after earthquake damage in 2001 and is now being rebuilt in a modern Arab style.

However, the other old mosque, known as **Xhamija e Medreses**, remains intact with its minaret. It dates from the 14th century and has separate doors for women and men. The name suggests it was formerly associated with an Islamic school although there is no sign of this now. The interior includes some simple frescoes but the wooden pillars which seemingly support the whole roof are probably the most noteworthy feature. There are some old graves outside. Across from the mosque is the **music school** which is one of the older remaining buildings in Gjilan dating from the 1800s. Next door, from the same era, is a recently restored building used by the **municipality** in a rather garish orange colour with a modern interior. It is possible to go inside.

If you stand in this area and imagine the streets with trees and cobbled stones you can get some feel for how Gjilan appeared in the past. Unfortunately the cobbles have now all been asphalted over.

To get to **St Nicholas Church** you have to walk up Rr Prishtina and take the second right-hand turn. The local Serbs use the churchyard as a safe-ish place to park their Serb-plated cars (mostly with the old registrations of 'GL'). On market days the side street is thronged with Serbian women with headscarves and men with their *kepis* selling their local wares, including cheese, honey, spicy peppers and other vegetables at reasonable prices.

The gates to the church are marked with a cross and open with a push. To get into the church you need to knock on the doors of the building with the barbed wire in front of the gates, or go through the gates to the far building in the corner across the car park. While not that old, dating from 1861, the church is unusual for a Kosovo Orthodox church. Firstly, there is a series of galleries with latticed wood (see also the Pasjane church below) with an airy feel. Secondly, the Greek architect has used some Byzantine styles, eg: in the buttresses to the galleries. The ceiling frescoes were done by Gjilan citizens who were all involved in various trades. Unfortunately the tops of the arches on the side walls are now cracked – either from the 2003 earthquake or from the 2001 hand-grenade attack and the building is therefore in urgent need of repair. Other paintings were commissioned by the artist from colleagues. Service times are shown on the door.

The Cubic-style statue on the corner of Rr Skenderbeu and Rr Prishtina is one of the few remaining **World War II memorials** in Kosovo.

People-watching in Gjilan is probably more important than its buildings, and to get a feel for modern Albanian society a trip to the **cluster of cafés on Zija Shemsiu** is a must. At any time between 10.00 and the evening, this area will be heaving with young Kosovars from the ages of 13 to 25, strolling at least four or five abreast on the pavement, often with linked arms. Here more than in many parts of Kosovo, the young age of the population hits home. The youth descend from the schools and Education Faculty further up the hill but also come in from out of town to hang out. This is the place to be seen to chat with your mobile phone, to play on the internet with your friends and to catch up on the gossip. Things get more serious in the summer when the road is clogged with diaspora cars as the young Kosovars back from Switzerland show off their possessions, the young women from Gjilan and the villages strut their stuff in the hope of a ticket out of Kosovo and just about everyone catches up with who is marrying whom.

A more sedate over-30s' social life is further up behind the stadium, where there are cake shops on what is known as the road near the school and also pizzerias in the Beqir Musliu housing estate.

There is a cultural festival in Gjilan every January known as the **Flaka e Januarit** which includes poetry, literature and plays. For more information contact the municipality.

PASJANE This is a friendly Serbian village about 5–8km south from Gjilan with an attractive church and bell tower from 1861 (the same date as the Gjilan church and there are some common characteristics, eg: the gallery). The outside does not look old, but the frescoes inside are beautiful, including an unusual and bright one of a well-attended burial which is drawn across the gallery wall below the gallery. The gallery is also quite beautiful with the wood lattice. The red-brick bell tower is in itself fascinating – with an enormous stork's nest on the top. The priest lives around ½km away in the main village, so to get in you need to head there and ask. The third building is the church town hall which is often used for celebrations.

The local festival is 19 August, and rumour has it that the stork is always gone by then, as he dislikes the noise.

To get there leave Gjilan by taking the one-way road to the right of Hotel Kristal, then take the right-hand fork at the large yellow-ish Arab-style mosque. Leave the textile factory on your left. Drive out through the new suburbs of large houses built with money sent back from the Swiss diaspora and through the village of Velkenicë with the LBG meat factory and RC Cola depot on your right, go over the Morava River and the next village you come to is Pasjane. The church is off to the left along an unasphalted road.

STANIŠOR This village is 6km out of Gjilan on the road north to Novo Brdo, situated above and beyond a large quarry. The Sveti Georgia Church is on the hill, reached by a 300m climb, with attractive frescoes. The old Byzantine tomb in town seems to have been destroyed.

STRAŽA This village is a further 5–7km from Stanišor. Continue on from Stanišor on the road below the church on the hill leaving the new quarry on your left-hand side and climbing uphill. Pass the initial '1 May' shop, then continue on to the next one and take the left fork down then with a sharp uphill section. The stone 16th-century St Petka Church is atop the hill but is often closed.

PËRLEPNICË The main reason to come to Përlepnicë, 8km from Gjilan, is the Vali Ranch, a splendid place with 24 horses, donkeys, llamas, chickens, turkeys and ducks. You can ride the horses at the riding school from 07.00 to 19.00 – One hour is €10. There's also minigolf and a restaurant (see *Where to eat and drink*, pages 241–2).

DRAGANAC Again on the same road north of Gjilan to Novo Brdo, continue on through Stanišor and beyond for a further 6km or more until the first main right-hand turn at the point where there is a new outdoor restaurant with fountains being built and a restored warehouse-looking building on the right at the turn. Continue up the hill (no asphalt), and take the left-hand fork after 2km. Continue on, and Draganac Monastery is another 2–3km. The frescoes of the Church of Holy Archangel Gabriel (dating from 1868) are not really worth the out-of-the-way trip, and the monastery has a rather mixed feel to it with its hotch-potch of modern buildings (including the pink-painted bell tower). The old dilapidated quarters at the back are being replaced by more modern ones at the front. At the time of our visit there were only a few monks who had all come from Serbia proper.

Draganac can also be reached from Bostan/Novo Brdo by taking the road down by the St Bogdorovica church and then taking the right-hand fork and continuing on for 6km.

HISTORY AND GEOGRAPHY Novo Brdo was at one time the largest city in Kosovo with over 40,000 people, including a large community of people from Dubrovnik who had their own councils and even German-speaking miners (known as Saxons) who named the town 'Neuberg'. Historians have found a statute in Latin dating from the 12th century, in which Novo Brdo was already granted special status. The town had its heyday in the 15th and 16th centuries. Records from the 15th century reveal at least four Jewish families who traded with Skopje (where there were over 3,000 Jews) and Thessaloniki. This importance came from the silver mine. Silver was mined for the manufacture of coins, ornaments and silver spoons and sent as far afield for minting as present-day Dubrovnik and, during the Ottoman Empire, to Istanbul. In 1580, the mine produced more than 935kg of silver annually.

The castle itself was built in the time of Prince Lazar in the 13th century and fortified under the orders of Sinan Pasha in the 14th century. Apparently the population successfully resisted one siege in 1412 and held out for between 15 and 30 days before capitulating against the Turks after another siege in 1455. The Turks then took over the town and continued the mining. Because of the importance of Novo Brdo's silver for the sultan's treasury, Novo Brdo was granted special exemption from the *devsirme* (the forced recruitment of Christian boys every seven years by the Janissary Corps) and the miners enjoyed special rights, including the right to elect their own governing councils. They were also exempted from the poll tax levied on non-Muslims and all other extraordinary taxes levied in times of war.

The Saxon church in Novo Brdo was converted into a mosque, but Islamisation only happened slowly in mining towns like Novo Brdo with their large foreign communities protected by special privileges. In 1488, Novo Brdo had 38 *mahallas* (neighbourhoods), all of them Christian. In 1525, there were 42 Christian *mahallas* and only four Muslim *mahallas*; by 1544, there were still only five Muslim *mahallas*.

Little remained of Novo Brdo 'town'; in fact today the town itself consists of only three blocks of dilapidated flats, a disused social centre, a post office, the municipality centre and a few houses. The village of Bostan follows on from Novo Brdo. The attractions are the old fortress remains and the view.

The whole place has an air of a mining ghost town. The mine became part of the Trepça complex in 1991–92, but it has not operated for over ten years. Already in the 1990s it was losing money and today the old rusty cable cars are swinging eerily in the wind.

Novo Brdo is now a municipality in its own right (albeit one of the smallest in Kosovo). The population of the whole municipality is only 3,900, with about 61% of the population being Albanian and the remainder mostly Serb. This is compared with a pre-1990 population of 54% Serb.

The surrounding area is hilly with very little agriculture directly near the mine – it is mostly silver birch woods and bracken. You should be careful of walking close to the mine area or to the north of the mine as there are several uncovered mine shafts. There is much better walking or biking from Novo Brdo to the south towards Gjilan or east towards Kamenicë.

GETTING THERE AND AROUND Because the area has so few people and many of those are Serbs who do not move around Kosovo much, getting there is difficult without a car. There are three direct **buses** (signed 'Artanë'), leaving at 07.30, 13.00 and 15.30 from the Prishtina bus station. The more frequent buses between Gjilan and Prishtina will stop on request at the Novo Brdo turn-off on the main road, but from there it is a good 10km undulating (but mostly uphill) walk to Novo Brdo itself. From the Prishtina road ignore the first right-hand turn and continue on the main road. There are no regular buses direct from Gjilan but infrequent buses for the Serb population to/from Kamenicë and there may be **ad hoc minibuses** from Gjilan on market day in Gjilan. Probably the best option if you are pushed for time is a **taxi** from Kamenicë or Gjilan (approximately €15).

When you reach the blocks of flats in Novo Brdo, to get to the castle and mine you need to take the first left uphill after the post office (PTK) and the school and continue uphill for a further 2–3km.

WHERE TO STAY AND EAT For food and hotels, head to Gjilan, Kamenicë, Prishtina or Gračanica, although there is a new rural tourism project organised by CARE (a British NGO), ICEED and the Dutch government, where you can stay in any of 14 bed-and-breakfast venues (housing up to 25 people in total) for €11 a night in summer and €13 in winter (m *044 465 471;* e *rural.tourism.nb@gmail; www.tourism-novobrdo.com*). They can also organise traditional dinners/lunches if you book in advance and there is a room for training/seminars.

ACTIVITIES The rural tourism project also organises mountain biking, paintball (up to ten people), motor-cross, billiards and table tennis. One suggestion we have is to hire a bike and head down to Përlepnicë for the lake and ranch (see above), maybe taking in Draganac along the way as this is a very quiet route. Save some energy for the trip back, however!

OTHER PRACTICALITIES There is a **post office** in town near the flats. For the **police station**, continue on the road past the flats, passing by the castle turn-off and on beyond the municipality (3km from the flats), tucked behind the low-lying now mostly abandoned houses.

WHAT TO SEE AND DO The ruins of the **castle** are the obvious draw. It is possible to walk round on a small path (bring good shoes). This takes ten–15 minutes. It is a popular picnicking spot in the summer with beautiful views across the countryside. The castle consists of two 'rings' and the walls are in varying states of repair.

The **mosque** just outside the castle is very old – probably 14th century–with half the stone minaret left, and some stone walls. To get in you need to ask around beforehand when down in the town.

There are also some remains of a 14th-century church close to the mosque.

The **mine** itself is also worth a look from above with an eerie ghost-town atmosphere, particularly on a misty day. The buildings and the area of the mine are unsafe and the police make regular checks for theft.

The **Bostan church** (St Bogdorovica), which dates from 1868, also merits a visit. Turn down the road opposite the municipality building. The key is kept by the Roma caretaker at the house within the walls. There are some simple frescoes. A much older church which dates from Novo Brdo's heyday is now only ruins higher up on the other side of the road to the municipality.

KAMENICË/KOSOVSKA KAMENICA

Kamenicë (approximately 20,000 inhabitants) is one of the rare places in Kosovo where Serbs and Albanians really mix, both socially and at work. The current population is approximately 82% Albanian and 17% Serbian with a small number of Roma. There are about 63,000 people in the wider municipality.

There is little known about Kamenicë's early history – its origins seem almost entirely rural and the town did not really develop until after World War II when it experienced a rapid expansion. The name Kamenicë itself derives from the word 'stone' and in the area are plenty of quarrying opportunities, including considerable magnesite reserves at Strezofc 14km outside Kamenicë, but also granite, marble and kaolin reserves. Traditionally, ceramic plates were also made in the town.

Kamenicë joins in with Gjilan by participating in the traditional three-day festival **Flaka e Janarit** in January. There is also a book fair once a year in October.

GETTING THERE In most instances you will need to change buses in Gjilan. There are buses at 07.10, 10.10, 12.10, 14.30, 16.00, 18.00 and 19.15 from Gjilan.

WHERE TO STAY AND EAT

Hotel Jehona (9 rooms) m 044 222 519/766 661. Situated 400m above the town & serving wood-oven pizzas. Panoramic views with woods behind it. A modern hotel, completed in 2006. Reasonably priced. $$

Sugarfree dance club m 044 504 4011. Includes live performances. Entrance €2–3.

ENTERTAINMENT The Cultural House 'Isa Kastrati' has films for €2 on Thursday and Friday at 17.00 and an amateur theatre, Alexander Mosiu, which shows three plays a year.

OTHER PRACTICALITIES Both Raiffeisen and ProCredit banks have branches in town.

WHAT TO SEE AND DO The Sveti Nikola Church dates from 1862, with its frescoes painted from then until 1906. It is generally open for visiting. Other sites around Kamenicë include **Berijvoce** – a Serb area immediately outside Kamenicë with a 14th-century church – and **Ajnovce**, also majority Serb, about 10km due north of Kamenicë, with a 14th-century monastery.

FERIZAJ/UROSEVAČ

Ferizaj is a victim of the great Kosovo population shift from the villages to the towns and the lack of urban planning or enforcement. Assisted by fortune-seekers who have descended from the villages in the hope of jobs at the US Camp Bondsteel, the town has sprawled and now includes a plethora of construction companies and seedy motels which line the main Skopje–Prishtina road for several kilometres. If this initial and representative flavour of Ferizaj does not deter you, then to see the centre you must turn off the highway before the flyover to reach the centre of the town.

Ferizaj is a relatively new town, starting with a cluster of houses after the railway was built in 1873. In addition to some desolate former industrial yards waiting to be redeveloped into doubtless yet more housing stock, there is some active industry – a sunflower oil factory (although the sunflowers in the fields between Prishtina and Ferizaj have gone), a metalworking factory, and a pipe factory.

GETTING THERE AND AWAY Ferizaj is 35km south of Prishtina and a similar distance from Gjilan and Skopje. There are regular buses to/from Skopje, Prishtina and Gjilan. Buses run every 15 minutes from Ferizaj to Prishtina starting at 06.30 (€1.50) and every 15 minutes in the other direction. The last bus from Ferizaj to Prishtina is at 19.30.

Buses from Ferizaj to Gjilan (€2) start at 06.00 and are then every 20 to 30 minutes with the last leaving at 19.30. Buses from Ferizaj to Skopje (€4) are at 07.00, 10.07, 10.40, 11.15, 15.10, 16.20, 17.07 and 18.07.

WHERE TO STAY AND EAT

⌂ **Hotel Bolero** (12 rooms) ☏ 029 032 7048; ⬜ 044 394 999. On 4 floors, restaurant terrace with a good view. Modern rooms with en suites & Wi-Fi, but no AC. $$

⌂ **Hotel Ujëvara** About 3km out of town on the road Epopeja e Jezercit – just along from the bifurcation point (see below); ⬜ 044 142 360; ⏱ 08.00–24.00 daily. A pleasant restaurant, mini zoo & swimming pool complex with views of the Sharr Mountains, waterfalls & trout in troughs. There may be rooms available in future, but at the time of writing they were not ready.

✖ **Restaurant Gjyla** Rr Dëshmorët e Kombit; ⬜ 044 219 431/224 198; ⏱ 11.00–21.00 Mon–Sat. A 'not-to-be-missed' restaurant favoured by the political elite. This is tucked at the end of the road (which peters out into a track) on the west side of the railway tracks. The high quality of the traditional Albanian fare & hot homemade bread here almost makes Ferizaj worth visiting just for this. The open fire makes for a cosy setting in winter. Unfortunately there is no garden for the summer. No menu; the chef will let you know what the specialities are – the veal & lamb are recommended. Very reasonable prices.

✖ **Restaurant Syri** ⬜ 044 120 433; ⏱ 07.00–24.00. On the main Dëshmorët e Kombit drag. A decent pizza restaurant.

OTHER PRACTICALITIES The post office is on Rr Dëshmorët e Kombit (☏ 029 020 134).

A branch of Raiffeisen Bank is also located on Rr Dëshmorët e Kombit, along with ProCredit at No 74, a further branch of which is at Rexhep Bislimi 36A (☏ 029 021 108; ⏱ 08.00–17.00).

A bicycle- and motorbike-repair shop **Tranzit Moto Centre** is at Rr Sylemani Avni Nuha (President of the Kastrioti and National Cycling Clubs of Kosovo) (☏ 038 129 027/027 430; ⬜ 044/049 323 111/044 657 743; e kastrioti-bike@hotmail.com, tranzit10@hotmail.com).

A fishing shop is on the corner of the main market street.

WHAT TO SEE AND DO There is not much to see in Ferizaj. You can park your car on the road for €0.20 per hour near the municipality building and walk around – probably no more than an hour is needed. First, however, to get to the municipality you must cross the railway tracks which split Ferizaj on a north–south axis. Venture beyond the bus station and the clutter of *kombis* and taxis and there is a rather unassuming modern **municipality** building facing a large marble open square. Formerly there was an enormous socialist statue on the square.

Next to the municipality building is a more traditional and pleasant-looking red-and-yellow painted **library** with reading rooms, an internet centre and in addition to the Albanian books a good collection of English novels and reference books, presumably donated by US army wellwishers. You can explore inside. Next door to the library is an **art gallery** and **city museum**, although despite dozens of visits to Ferizaj, both of these always seem to be firmly closed behind metal grilles.

On the other side of the main square, behind the shiny central hotel, the orange-painted **Orthodox church** and bright white modernised **mosque** – in a rare moment of tolerance for Ferizaj – share the same yard. The church is firmly closed behind gates and sandbags and has a strong air of neglect about it. In front and along the back streets of Ferizaj there are ad hoc market stalls with tinny cassettes and CDs of traditional music, matches and candles.

There is a carnival on 14–15 June each year.

You will, however, likely want to quickly escape the traffic, noise, markets and crowds of Ferizaj. Fortunately there are good bus and train links to the rest of Kosovo and to the nearby countryside, including the Sharr Mountains and Brezovica ski resort.

NERODIME This village is 6km west of Ferizaj. This is the point of 'bifurcation' which as all good Kosovar schoolchildren learn is unique in Europe. The Nerodikima River divides and flows in two different directions – one part towards the Aegean Sea and the other towards the Black Sea in Bulgaria. Nerodime was also important from a Serbian historical perspective. It was here that King Milutin died in 1321 and Stefan Dušan was crowned in 1335. Stefan Dečanski also spent a considerable period here when he was drawing up his charter and designs for the Visoki Dečani Monastery. Nerodime was home to a large park and palace, as well as the Church of the Assumption (Monastery of S Uroš). The St Archangel Monastery in Nerodime, dating from the 13th century, was unfortunately destroyed in summer 1999. Trading rights negotiations took place in the palace with traders from Dubrovnik, including negotiations on the Novo Brdo silver trade (see *Novo Brdo*, page 247).

PETRIČ FORTRESS There were two medieval towns here on the tops of the two adjacent hills above the river mouths: Veliki (large) Petrič – and Mali (small) Petrič. Each had fortresses which are only ruins now and hard to find. They lie to the west of Ferizaj near the village of Gornja Nerodime. Their purpose was to protect the palace of the rulers at Nerodime. Allegedly Veliki Petrič was a substantial five-cornered fortress with underground corridors. The palace had a strategic position as it was on the route from Prizren. Reputedly Stefan Dušan captured his father Stefan Dečanski here and sent him to prison in Zvečan Castle.

CAMP BONDSTEEL Camp Bondsteel is located off the road between Viti and Ferizaj. Named after a Vietnam medal holder, James L Bondsteel, this is not a town but is essentially the size of one, with the only genuine Burger King and Anthony's Pizza in Kosovo, three gyms and two chapels, and the Laura Bush education centre with links to Maryland and Chicago universities. There is a helicopter landing zone and a prison which includes non-US military prisoners, allegedly not just from Kosovo, although no-one is sure. This was the largest purpose-built military installation by the US since the end of the Vietnam War, catering for approximately 7,000 US personnel in KFOR. It is a major employer and source of contracts for the Ferizaj area.

The camp stretches across several acres (specifically 360,000m²), with a perimeter of 9km. During construction, more than 150,000m³ of earth had to be moved. With its thick steel fence and nine watchtowers it is clearly visible from a distance, particularly at night from the powerful floodlights. While the UN emphasised its temporary status and erected containers which were still temporary seven years on, the US bedded down early and the camp has an air of permanence. Soldiers live in purpose-built SEA huts (the name stemming from where they were invented in southeast Asia) with air conditioning, heating, electricity and TVs. The camp was forced to build its own sewage-treatment arrangement for lack of a local sewage network.

Unless you are a US VIP or you have an invitation, you will struggle to gain access even with a US passport and even then you are unlikely to be able to shop in the attractively priced duty-free shops known as PX-es. For many Kosovars Camp Bondsteel will most likely remain an American mystery.

VITI/VITINA

Viti is a rural backwater tucked away on the slopes of the Karadak Mountain and stretching over the plain of the Morava River. If you have time on your hands and want to explore a bit of rural Kosovo, then Viti is a good destination. It is also home to Kosovo's most famous Catholic pilgrimage site located in Letnica village (see page 253). Every August, the festivities around the Assumption draw thousands of visitors from Kosovo and Croatia. If you make it to Viti you will also be rewarded with some beautiful natural scenery stretching over rolling hills and the plain of the Morava river valley. Viti municipality, like Gjilan, has also preserved its multi-ethnic character. Its 60,000 inhabitants are a patchwork of Albanian and Serb, Muslim and Catholic with a small and shrinking Croat minority.

HISTORY Archaeological findings suggest that this region has been inhabited since the 7th century AD. A Byzantine document from 1019 first mentions a fortified castle in Binqe village and other records from 1455 speak of 104 families living in this area. In the 13th century, Viti was part of the medieval Serb kingdom of Rascia and in the 15th century it was ruled from Novo Brdo. After the Berlin Congress in 1878 and the withdrawal of the Ottoman armies from the area around Niš in south Serbia, refugees known as *muhaxhirs* or *cerkez* settled here in large numbers. Cerkez Sadovine village is still named after them. Following the collapse of the Ottoman Empire and the Serbian occupation, most of the large estates owned by Turkish-Albanian feudal landowners were broken up on the pretext of agricultural reforms and reallocated to Serb and Montenegrin settlers. Many Turkish-speaking families escaped to Turkey in those years. During World War I, this region was occupied by Bulgarian troops and again in the 1940s, the border between the Bulgarian and Italian zones of occupation ran right along the Morava River. The mainstay of Viti's economy has always been agriculture. There was no industry until the 1970s, but even then, communist industrialisation brought little more than a mineral water-bottling plant, a textile plant and some agro-processing. Some of the earliest 'Yugoslav guestworkers', arriving in Germany back in the 1960s, came from Viti. There are many villages like Lubishte village, on the slopes of the Karadak Mountain, which has one-quarter of its population living abroad (mostly in Switzerland) and most of the cash circulating in the village is sent home from Germany or Switzerland.

GETTING THERE If you have a **car**, take the main Prishtina–Skopje highway heading south. You have two choices. You can turn off to Viti at Ferizaj, 35km south of Prishtina, following signs to Gjilan. This road takes you past Camp Bondsteel, the largest US military base in the Balkans. After the Orthodox church in Kllokot, turn right towards Viti Town.

Alternatively, you can also go beyond Ferizaj (coming from Prishtina), following signs for Viti. The road makes a sharp loop left before turning east towards Viti. If you choose this second route, you will pass a unique war memorial commemorating a local UÇK hero in Sadovine village. Continue straight for Viti Town.

There are no direct **buses** from Prishtina. By bus it's best to catch a ride to Ferizaj or Gjilan and to change there to a local line to Viti. Buses from Gjilan are hourly, starting at 06.10 until 19.10. For the whole bus journey from Viti to Prishtina allow one–two hours, depending on how good your connection is.

WHERE TO STAY AND EAT While there are a couple of hotels in Viti itself, they are nothing to write home about and you are better off staying in Gjilan or Ferizaj or if you want somewhere more upmarket, Prishtina. There are a number of fast-food restaurants and Italian outfits along the main streets and around Viti's central square. The best bet is always a pizza, as they are quick, inexpensive and generally good quality.

✗ **Kalaja** Bar frequented by young people on the right-hand side of the square; ⊕ 08.00–23.00. Usually packed with high-school students & youngsters people-watching & hanging out.

✗ **Restaurant Drenica** On the left side of the square, serving local, hefty meat courses & very popular with the locals.

✗ **VIP Bar** Next door to the Kalaja. Same opening hours.

OTHER PRACTICALITIES There is a branch of ProCredit Bank on Rr Adam Jashari on the main square (✆ *028 036 1610*) and also a Raiffeisen (✆ *038 222 222 ext 780;* ⊕ *08.30–16.30 Mon–Fri, 10.00–14.00 Sat).*

Internet cafés are plentiful and scattered all over Viti Town and even in the villages.

WHAT TO SEE AND DO Viti Town is largely a 1960s' creation with some socialist apartment buildings, a cultural centre and a centrally located department store. There is nothing charming about the town, but there are plenty of restaurants and cafés. The main attraction in Viti municipality is the Catholic Letnica village and the surrounding hillsides where you can walk, bike and see some beautiful, but abandoned, stone houses.

LETNICA/LETNICË

HISTORY A long time ago, the Karadak mountain range was an important mining centre, luring experienced Saxon miners and traders from Dubrovnik. Their legacy lives on in place names like Shashare village (Sasari meaning 'Saxons'). The descendants of these Saxons, Croat and Albanian miners still live in villages like Letnica and Stublla e Eperme. During the Croatian war of independence starting in 1991, Kosovo's small Croat minority was increasingly exposed to pressure by Serb hardliners. Most of Viti's Croats were pushed to resettle to houses abandoned by Serbs in western Slavonia. Only a handful of Croat families remain, mostly the elderly. Villages like Shashare or Vernakolle, close to Letnica, resemble ghost towns today.

Letnica's church (Të Ngriturit e Zojës se Bekuar në qiell/Church of the Black Madonna/Zoja e Cernagorës) is visible as soon as you enter the village. It sits elevated on a little hill at the far end of the village. There is parking along the little side path up to the gate. From here you have a nice view over Letnica village. It's a sleepy, quiet place. Only about 32 mostly elderly Croats, 22 Albanian Catholic families and 33 Albanian families who came here as refugees during the 2001 conflict in Macedonia, live in Letnica today. The abandoned stone houses give the village an eerie feel, but they are still beautiful to look at.

A first church was probably built here in the 14th century, at a time when Letnica must have been a small, but thriving mining centre. In 1584, Ottoman records show some 500 Christian families living in the area. In 1737, the church underwent major repairs and was reconstructed again in 1866. The latter building was damaged during an earthquake and construction of the present-day structure was started in 1928 and completed in 1934.

Three times, so it is said, the Madonna appeared in Letnica urging the villagers to construct a church. The main attraction today is a 300-year-old **Black Madonna Statue** (called the Mother of God – Crnogorska), made of blackened wood, hence its name, which according to local belief can help childless families. The Madonna is venerated by Christian and Muslim couples alike. Another legend surrounds the miraculous travel of the Black Madonna Statue from its original location in Skopje across the Karadak Mountain to the church in Letnica.

On 14–15 August, Letnica church hosts a two-day festival attracting close to 30,000 believers, including many Croats who have left Kosovo in recent years.

Some of the diehard Letnica fans walk to Letnica barefoot, without shoes, sometimes for kilometres. Visitors come from the neighbouring countries, and in recent years, 25 NATO army chaplains, 1,300 NATO soldiers stationed in Kosovo and other high-level political representatives, also attended the festival. The whole village turns into a campsite and picnic area: tents are put up in the garden of the church and on surrounding fields. Those who booked well in advance can take up a room in the purpose-built guestrooms next to the church.

The festivities begin with a mass at 11.00 on 14 August. This mass is held to commemorate the blessing of the current church building in 1931. In the evening of the 14th, there is another church service in the Croatian language at 17.00 and in Albanian at 18.00. At 19.00, the Black Madonna Statue is carried ahead of a procession that starts at the church and leads through Letnica village. The night of 14–15 August, candles are lit and people try to stay awake. The next day, at 06.00, the day starts with an Albanian-language mass, followed by a Croatian service at 09.00 and the main mass at 11.00, in both the Albanian and Croatian languages. After the mass, the Black Madonna Statue is taken for another procession through the village. During the festivities, believers try to touch the Madonna with their jewellery and hope to catch a piece of the Madonna's cloth that is cut in pieces and distributed to all attendants.

GETTING THERE To get to Letnica, you must drive around the main square in Viti Town, cross the river at the Serbian church (Steta Petka), turn right around the secondary school, and then straight in the direction of the Serbian-populated village of Verbovc. In Verbovc, bear right and continue straight on the asphalt road until you get to Letnica. On your way, you pass a few examples of beautifully carved and painted wooden farm gates.

A **taxi** ride from Viti Town to Letnica costs €4; there are taxi stops along the main square and near the bus station.

WHERE TO STAY There is nowhere really to stay in Letnica, so it's best to do Letnica as a day trip either from Prishtina or Gjilan.

WHERE TO EAT Follow the Letnica River as it bends round the church to the end of the village. On your way you pass an old mill still owned by Froke Dokic, an elderly Croat miller.

Trofta Restaurant m 044 262 502; ⊕ 11.00–23.00 daily. Nicely located at the end of the village. They serve fried trout for €3.50, but it's slightly on the oily side. There is a playground for children & you can set off for a pleasant digestive walk up into the hills.

WHAT TO SEE AND DO **Stublla e Eperme** is a nicely kept Albanian Catholic village up on the hill (you must turn before you get to Letnica), offering good views over the surrounding countryside. In Stublla everything seems to be called 'Jozef'. There is a nice restaurant called Jozefi (m *044 245 328/323 025*), with a terrace, just below Saint Jozef Church.

Shashare and Vernakolle villages, close to Letnica, are set on rolling hills and are good destinations for walking or mountain biking. They are completely abandoned, so you must bring your own food and drinks.

Kllokot, now a separate municipality formed under the Ahtisaari plan, is famous for its natural mineral water that is both bottled and used for the Kllokot spa, built under communism. The spa was privatised a few years ago (the water is now sold under the label 'Jeta') and a private spa hotel was also built (see below). To get there, use the Ferizaj–Gjilan bus line (see *Gjilan, Getting there and away*, page 241).

Kllokot is a Serb-populated village and has an Orthodox church at its centre. There was once an Orthodox monastery dedicated to the Archangel in Buzovik village, but it was burnt down and mined in 2001.

The village of **Sadovinë e Jerlive**, the first one you see if you are coming from Ferizaj, has its own local war memorial dedicated to Bajram Sylejmani and Gursel Sylejmani, two brothers and UÇK fighters. This memorial is a village initiative and is being maintained by volunteer gardeners. It is incredibly kitsch, but carefully looked after.

Spa

Nena Naile Spa Pools (534 rooms) ☎ 028 038 5101; 📱 045 385 555/044 666 006; www.nenanaile.com. There are 3 buildings – one with 3 medical pools & VIP apartments (each with a jacuzzi), & a second one with 2 larger pools. There's also a conference room for 80 people & 2 large restaurants with free Wi-Fi. The setting is quite pleasant with good views of the Sharr Mountains. Various therapies are offered including magnet therapy, electrotherapy, thermotherapy, saunas & massages.

KAÇANIK/KAČANIK

Most Kosovar visitors just drive through Kaçanik and from the road one might be deceived into thinking that it has nothing to offer as you can only see the white dust clouds of the Lepenci marble factory (formerly part of the Sharr empire and still the main employer in town – see *Hani i Elezit*, page 256). It is worth, however, turning off the road to visit – the town is tucked below the road, straddling the Lepenci River and the railway tracks.

HISTORY The name Kaçanik apparently derives from the word *kacanlar* which means 'fugitives' in Turkish, referring to the bandits hiding in the Kaçanik Gorge and launching regular raids on trade caravans and travellers passing through this narrow point. Traders passed through Kaçanik from the 16th century on their way to the Turkish district of Üsküp (Skopje), also known as Nahije. There was an old *han* (guesthouse for traders) at the bottom of the hill and there is an old tombstone dating from this time which has been placed in the white modern shopping centre. In both world wars, Kaçanik was part of the Bulgarian zone of occupation.

Kaçanik and Hani i Elezit are renowned for their piety and during the Ramadan fast the teahouses of Kaçanik are thronged with men gathering for the traditional Iftar meal (the breaking of the fast at dusk). The population is almost entirely Albanian and Serbs are reluctant to return for fear of reprisal acts as Kaçanik had experienced several civilian massacres during the 1999 conflict.

GETTING THERE AND AWAY Buses leave for Prishtina at 06.00, and 07.40, 08.00, 09.00 and 12.00 to Ferizaj. Buses leave Ferizaj from 07.20, and then every 20 minutes until 19.45.

WHERE TO STAY AND EAT The only hotel options are the rather dubious but clean and reasonably priced motels on the main Skopje–Prishtina road.

Pizzeria Krapi, 'crappy' by name, but not by nature (*krapi* means 'carp' in Albanian!), and **Bulevardi Ismail Raka** both offer similar fare overlooking the river in the centre of town.

WHAT TO SEE AND DO The main sight in Kaçanik and definitely worth stopping to go inside is the **mosque**. This is one of the oldest and most attractive in Kosovo, founded by Sinan Ali Pasha in 1594 (see *Prizren*, page 212). Its paintings and old blue window frames are preserved, although the upper prayer floor can no longer be used and the wooden pillars are in need of repair.

On the other hand, the hotel sadly no longer functions (it may be privatised once a land ownership dispute is settled). It sits atop a mound where there was a former Turkish **castle** founded by Sinan Pasha in the 15th century (attractive parts of the old stone walls remain). There are no remains of the *han* or *hammam*.

AROUND KAÇANIK

Between Kaçanik and Hani i Elezit the countryside and gorge become increasingly dramatic and beautiful and this is the most attractive stretch of the cross-Kosovo (north–south) train ride.

If you are travelling by road, on the left-hand side there is a turn-off with an ancient Turkish bridge (this marks the old road to Skopje). Close by was another large Turkish fortress with up to 30 buildings constructed by Sinan Pasha in the 15th century overlooking the Lepenci River, but now all the stones have been removed so there is nothing to see and the site is difficult to find.

HANI I ELEZIT In common with many border towns Hani i Elezit has a rather gloomy or seedy feel to it, which is not helped by the looming shadow of the coke-powered cement factory. Sharr, founded by General Djanković (which is another name given to the border town area) was one of the largest social enterprise conglomerates in Kosovo and is the only real employer both in Kaçanik and in Hani i Elezit. It had three main factories – Sharr cement in Hani i Elezit, Lepenci producing marble, and Silcapor, producing building insulation blocks. Unfortunately the factories continue to pollute the rivers but provide critical employment, export revenue and freight for the railways. There are believed to be substantial rock reserves in the whole Hani i Elezit and Kaçanik region.

There is no real reason to stop here other than for border business or to use the train station. There was a former horseshoeing/stabling venue (hence the name 'Han') and this can now be visited only by accessing the tight security of the Sharr cement factory – but there is little or nothing left beyond a few bricks.

✖ WHERE TO EAT
✖ **Pizzeria Alba** On the main road on the right-hand side coming from the border just on exiting Hani i Elezit; m 044 420 730. Good pizzas & a possible stop.

OTHER PRACTICALITIES There is a Raiffeisen Bank **ATM** outside the Sharr cement factory.

8

Northern Kosovo

The region stretching north from Vushtrri to the border with Serbia is richly endowed with valuable minerals and metals. Whoever held the keys to this strategic area controlled the access route to the Kosovo plains. The region comprises Vushtrri, a former Ottoman administrative centre that in the past surpassed Prishtina in splendour and wealth, parts of the poor and heavily war-afflicted Drenica region, the famous mining town of Mitrovica – today divided by the Ibar River into an Albanian south and Serb north, the stunningly beautiful Zubin Potok Lake and the historic Banjska Monastery.

VUSHTRRI/VUČITRN

Vushtrri can look back on an eventful history as a Roman settlement and an Ottoman administrative centre, but only few traces of this exciting history are visible today. Located just off the main Prishtina–Mitrovica route, it makes for a convenient stop if you have some time on your hands or just want to take a break. But don't be disappointed; you will need a lot of imagination to appreciate Vushtrri's important role in Kosovo's history. The majority of Vushtrri's 100,000 inhabitants struggle to make ends meet on subsistence agriculture and small-scale trade. Today, Vushtrri's only pride is the police school set up in 2000 which has since trained more than 7,000 Kosovo police officers.

HISTORY In antiquity, the area of Vushtrri was the seat of a Roman city by the name of **Vicianum**. Its development was closely linked to its location on an important Roman communication route connecting Niš to Skopje via Ulpiana. In AD518, a major earthquake destroyed Skopje and greatly damaged the ancient city of Vicianum. Much time passed before Vushtrri could regain its regional importance. In the course of the 12th century, Vushtrri became known as Vëlcitërn and formed part of the Nemanjić kingdom ruling over Kosovo. Prince Lazar, according to local legend, built Vushtrri's first church in what is today the village of Samodrezhë. The two most important monuments – Vushtrri Castle and the nine-arched bridge over the Sitnica River – were both built in the 14th century and reflected Vushtrri's growing importance as a **trading outpost for Dubrovnik** (formerly known as Ragusa). Close ties with Dubrovnik secured Vushtrri access to the European markets.

In 1445, as the Ottoman conquest of the Balkans was nearing its completion, an **Ottoman garrison** was positioned in Vushtrri. A few years later, Vushtrri became the administrative centre of a newly formed Vushtrri *sançak* (a military district) covering the eastern half of Kosovo, including Prishtina. Vushtrri at the time had a majority Christian population and only 47 Muslim households. The high concentration of Ottoman soldiers and administrators accelerated the spread of Islam, first among the urban population and gradually also in the villages. Vushtrri also gave birth to two prominent 'Ottomans' from Kosovo: Evlija Celebia,

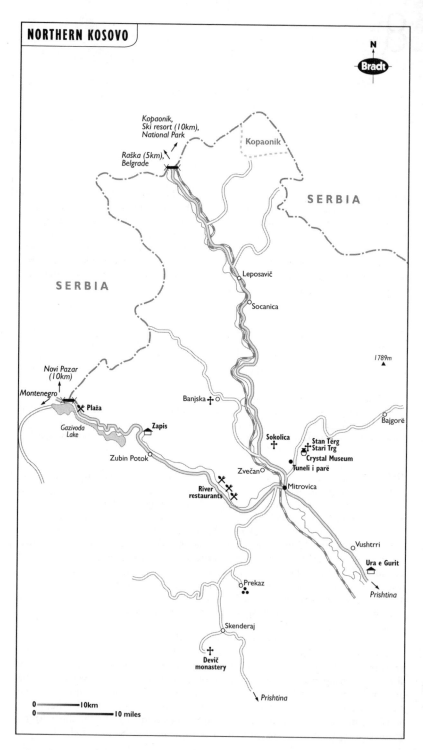

NORTHERN KOSOVO

N

Bradt

Kopaonik,
Ski resort (10km),
National Park

Raška (5km),
Belgrade

Kopaonik

SERBIA

SERBIA

Leposavič

Socanica

1789m

Novi Pazar
(10km)

Montenegro

Banjska

Bajgorë

Plaža

Gazivoda
Lake

Zapis

Sokolica

Stan Tërg
Stari Trg

Crystal Museum

Zubin Potok

Zvečan

Tuneli i parë

Mitrovica

River
restaurants

Vushtrri

Ura e Gurit

Prekaz

Prishtina

Skenderaj

Devič
monastery

Prishtina

0 ————10km
0 ————10 miles

an Ottoman travel writer from the 16th century, and Hasan Prishtina, a prominent Albanian national activist in the early 20th century. In 1868, Vushtrri was merged with the newly created *vilayet* (province) of Prizren and the seat of the Ottoman administration was moved to Prishtina. This ushered in the rapid decline of Vushtrri, from Kosovo's largest and most important town in the 16th century to a provincial backwater. The opening of the Skopje–Mitrovica railway line in 1874 gave the town a short-lived economic boost, but could not halt its decline. The greatest loss for Vushtrri as an urban centre was the **mass migration** of its Turkish-speaking community. With the collapse of the Ottoman Empire and the incorporation of Kosovo into the First Yugoslavia, there was tremendous pressure on the Turkish-speaking population of Kosovo to declare themselves as Turks and migrate to Turkey. The authorities were keen that they should leave – politically, the authorities hoped that this would help change the ethnic balance in favour of Serbs, and for economic reasons, they wanted to break up the large estates owned by Turkish-speaking landowners. A large number of Vushtrri's 'Turks' left in the years before and after World War I. Vushtrri, which for centuries had been a vibrant Ottoman trading town and urban centre, thus lost its economic and intellectual urban elite. In turn, more than 1,000 Serb and Montenegrin colonists were settled in the area of Vushtrri and given 9,974ha of land. During World War II, Vushtrri was part of the German zone of occupation. In fact, it was in Vushtrri where the German and Italian authorities signed the agreement that granted Germany the exclusive exploitation rights of the Mitrovica mines. Under communism, Vushtrri's flagship company was Llamkos, a steel galvanising plant. It has recently been privatised and has now resumed its position as the region's most important employer and one of Kosovo's largest exporters.

GETTING THERE AND AWAY Vushtrri lies on the main road that connects Prishtina and Mitrovica. There are **buses** to Mitrovica every 15 minutes departing from Prishtina bus station, with the first at 06.30 and the last at 20.30, most of which stop in Vushtrri (the so-called 'Express' buses go straight to Mitrovica and will only let you off on the road near Vushtrri, meaning you have to walk to town). See the bus timetable in *Chapter 2*, page 60.

There are two turns into the city: both lead directly into the town centre. If you take the first turn coming from Prishtina, the road winds through an area which has seen rampant building construction in recent years, being formerly a Serb-populated area. It passes by an Orthodox church that was torched and severely damaged in the conflict, and then arrives straight in the town centre.

WHERE TO STAY AND EAT There are some cafés and local restaurants in Vushtrri Town, and a few decent petrol-station restaurants along the main road, but the real highlight if you are in the area is Hotel Ura e Gurit, out of town on the way to Prishtina.

⌂ **Hotel Kalaja and Restaurant** (32 rooms, 11) Along the Prishtina–Mitrovica highway; ☎ 028 527 120; m 044 506 606/487 487; www.hotelkalaja.com. The hotel offers clean rooms & spacious apartments with jacuzzis. The price of the rooms depends on the size; all rooms have en suite bathrooms & free Wi-Fi. The restaurant is open from 07.00 to 24.00 daily. $$–$$$$

⌂ **Hotel Ura e Gurit** (18 rooms) Muxhunaj, Vushtrri; ☎ 028 572 750; m 044 606 044; e info@ uraegurit.com; www.bajraktari-ks.com. This hotel (opened in 2005) & restaurant is a pleasant surprise with its tasteful décor & great food. The owner of the hotel has lived in Germany for many years & the hotel has something of an Elizabethan style to it. The interior, however, is more authentic, a mix of stone & wood, decorated with typical Albanian rugs & hand-woven pillows. It's cosy & inviting. There is also a small collection of handmade Albanian crafts for sale at the reception. The hotel rooms are nicely furnished

& clean, with baths & TV and some rooms have AC. Free Wi-Fi. In summer there is a nice outdoor garden area. $$$

⌂ **Swiss Wellness Park** Visible on the right-hand side along the Prishtina–Mitrovica highway, before approaching Vushtrri; m 044 510059/069; ⏱ 08.00–24.00 daily. This newly opened wellness centre has one of the very few covered swimming pools in Kosovo (15m x 8m). Besides the pool & fitness centre, guests can dip into jacuzzis, enjoy the sauna & solarium, or sign up for a massage and aromatherapy. Physiotherapy on appointment only (see above for mobile) ⏱ 08.00–12.30. Afterwards, you can refresh at the restaurant, serving Italian-style pizza, risotto & fish dishes. There is also a large selection of wines. The restaurant seats up to 60 & can be booked for special occasions. Regular entrance (for 3hrs) covering towels, swimming pool, fitness centre, sauna & jacuzzi is €10 pp, or €5 for children aged up to 12 years.

SHOPPING There are three new shopping centres along the main Prishtina–Mitrovica road, including ETC and Emona, each with their own in-house pizzeria and café, and an Albi shopping centre. In the centre of town, between the cultural centre and the municipality, you can also find another modern shopping centre featuring several local restaurants. The open-air market is just behind, next to the ruins of the old *hammam*.

OTHER PRACTICALITIES There is a post office, a branch of ProCredit Bank (*Rr Dëshmorët e Kombit*; ☏ 028 572 663) and an ATM close to the castle's ruins.

WHAT TO SEE AND DO It's quite amazing how little there is to see in Vushtrri given the town's interesting past. It is difficult to imagine that Vushtrri was once Kosovo's largest city, a thriving market town and the administrative centre of eastern Kosovo. In the 16th century, Vushtrri boasted a mosque constructed on the order of Sultan

ARRIVAL OF A NEW FORCE: THE KOSOVO LIBERATION ARMY

The Kosovo Liberation Army (KLA or UÇK – in Albanian, Ushtria Çlirimtare e Kosovës) made its first public appearance at the funeral of a teacher who had been killed during a police raid in Skenderaj in December 1997. Three masked men with automatic rifles declared at the funeral, attended by around 20,000 people, that the Kosovo Liberation Army would continue to fight for Kosovo's freedom. This announcement came at a time of escalating violence in the region and growing frustration with the LDK-led non-violent resistance movement. The UÇK received a lot of support especially in areas like Skenderaj and its numbers swelled quickly. The looting of state weapons' depots in Albania in 1997 flooded the region with small arms and other weapons, many of which ended up in Kosovo. In the early days the UÇK was organised regionally on a village or extended family basis, lacking any form of central command. Its tactics consisted of guerrilla ambushes and hit-and-run attacks on Serb security forces and police. Serbia responded with a dramatic build-up of its forces and prepared for a major Drenica offensive in spring 1998. The first Drenica massacre took place on 28 February 1998. Police and helicopters surrounded the home of the Ahmeti family in Likoshane village and killed 13 family members plus neighbours who happened to be in the house. In a similar assault on the Nebiu family in Qirez village Serb forces killed another 13 unarmed civilians, some in police custody. On 5 March, military assault vehicles and tanks surrounded the walled compound of the Jashari family in Prekaz village. After three days of fighting and shelling, a total of 56 bodies were buried, including 41 members of the Jashari family, 11 of them being children younger than 16. The fierce-looking Adem Jashari thus became a hero of the Kosovo Liberation Army and is being promoted by war veterans' associations as a symbol of Kosovo's fight for independence.

Murat II, a Turkish bath, several *tekkes* belonging to different dervish orders and numerous elegant guesthouses. The communist makeover in the 1950s and 1960s, however, succeeded in extinguishing any trace of this Ottoman past.

The two highlights of Vushtrri, the **ruins of the 14th-century castle** and the stone bridge, are both in a sorry state and in need of urgent repair. The castle's ruins are on Rr Dëshmorët e Kombit, the main street passing through the centre. You can see parts of the walls, but that's it. In the 15th century, the castle was the seat of the Branković ruling family, a vassal of the Ottoman sultan. It was here in the castle that Gjuragj Branković signed a special trade agreement with a legate from Venice in 1426.

The nine-arched **stone bridge** is a little further along on Rr Wesley Clark. Be warned, though – it's a curious sight. In the past it spanned the Sitnica River that passed through the town, but diversion of the river resulted in a bridge without a river. Unfortunately, the field surrounding the bridge is covered in fly-tipped waste. Major restoration works of the bridge are being planned and may give some dignity back to this 14th-century monument. The old Turkish bath (*hammam*) on Rr Mic Sokolli is in no better state; its walls are grown over and crumbling and it's not accessible for visitors.

SKENDERAJ/SRBICA

Skenderaj municipality is the heart of the Drenica region, historically the poorest region of Kosovo. The vast majority of the population depends on subsistence agriculture, made worse by the poor quality of the soil and high population density. Around 98% of Skenderaj's 65,000 inhabitants are Albanian. There was no investment in this region until the 1970s and the Yugoslav state was effectively absent. Hardly any roads were paved: in wintertime many of the 52 villages were completely cut off, there was no sewage system and no telephone lines. The only industries to speak of were a brick factory, a textile factory and an ammunition plant. In the early 1990s, Milošević shut them all down with the exception of the ammunition plant. It continued to operate until 1998 and was then converted into a military base. Poverty was widespread and the only way to survive for most families was emigration. During the 1990s, the state was only visible in this region in the form of uniformed police and the military. Against this background, the Kosovo Liberation Army (UÇK) could draw on large support among Skenderaj's impoverished population.

As a centre of UÇK activities, Skenderaj was hit hard during the war. In response to UÇK attacks, Serb forces launched a first major Drenica offensive in February 1998. Large numbers of villagers took to the forest to escape the systematic destruction of their homes. In the course of 1998 and spring 1999, 3,528 houses – 40% of all homes – were destroyed, 6,000 people were permanently injured and around 2,000 children lost parents. Today, 14,000 people depend on social assistance provided by the state.

WHERE TO EAT AND DRINK

✗ **Ben-Af** Bd Adem Jashari; ⊕ 07.00–23.00 daily. Right down town in the pedestrian zone, Ben-Af Restaurant (located in the shopping centre of the same name) is a popular & cheap option for lunch, dinner & coffee. It's self-service, & you can choose from a wide selection of hot dishes, including pizza, desserts, & a salad bar.

✗ **Number 5** Rr Iljaz Kodra (near the main bus station); m 044 238 859/555 522; www.nura5.com; ⊕ summer 07.00–24.00 daily; winter 08.00–23.00

daily. Spacious & modern restaurant located inside another shopping centre. On the menu you can find Italian-style dishes as well as some Albanian cuisine. Free Wi-Fi.

♀ **Classic Bar** Bd Adem Jashari; ⊕ summer 08.00–24.00; winter 08.00–22.00. Comfy & modern bar with leather chairs & small tables & a popular place to hang out for coffee & beer with friends at any time during the day. There is also free Wi-Fi & a Facebook group called 'Classic Bar'.

OTHER PRACTICALITIES The Ben-Af shopping centre is best for shopping. There is also a Pro Credit Bank on Adem Jashari Square (✆ *028 582 600*), and local branches of Raiffeisen Bank and NLB.

WHAT TO SEE AND DO The region's two main sites capture its troubled history. In Prekaz i Poshtem, you can visit the Adem Jashari Memorial and just 5km out of Skenderaj Town, there is the Serb Orthodox Devič Monastery, dating back to the Middle Ages but destroyed and burnt during the March 2004 riots and currently not accessible to visitors.

Adem Jashari Memorial The Adem Jashari Memorial (⊕ *daily; entrance free*) is located in his home village in Prekaz i Poshtem, a few kilometres out of Skenderaj Town, and is an interesting place to visit to better understand the Adem Jashari myth and its place in the process of defining a new Kosovo identity. The memorial is Adem Jashari's family complex, as it was left after the shelling and burning by Serb forces. It consists of two destroyed homes and the cemetery where the 56 victims of the assault are buried. You can walk over scaffolding and look at the destroyed houses, but besides this there is not much else to see. There is a small information office at the entrance where you can buy postcards and publications on Kosovo, the conflict and the Jashari family.

Getting there and away Follow the main road to Skenderaj Town and near the mosque turn left at the sign towards Prekaz i Poshtem. The road has recently been paved and decorated with streetlights. You can easily spot the memorial and the cemetery across the street. There is parking at the entrance.

By **bus**, you must first catch a ride to Skenderaj, either by taking a bus *en route* from Mitrovica to Peja or by taking one of the Prishtina–Skenderaj buses. From Skenderaj you must get a minibus or taxi to Prekaz i Poshtem.

Special event On 5, 6 and 7 March of every year as part of the Epopeja e UÇK-se festivities (a commemorative celebration of the Kosovo Liberation Army) a series of special events is organised at the Adem Jashari complex. On 5 March, there is an official commemoration organised by the Kosovo Security Force (the former Kosovo Protection Corps) and attended by senior politicians and party activists. The event is marked by long speeches and lots of flag raising. More interestingly, on the night of 6 March, huge fires are lit in Prekaz i Poshtem at the Adem Jashari Memorial complex and in other places in Drenica to commemorate the war and the heroes of the Kosovo Liberation Army.

Devič Monastery The monastic complex is located 5km south of Skenderaj Town. The exact date of its construction is not known, but its name derives from the tomb of Joanikije Deviki, a local saint, who was buried here in 1430. The cult of this local saint elevated the church to the rank of a monastery. In 1578, the monastery was restored and new cycles of frescoes were painted on the interior. Throughout the 16th and 17th centuries, the monastery was reputed for its writing school. It was heavily damaged during both world wars, but restored again in 1950. Right after the war, UÇK forces occupied the monastery before handing it over to KFOR. In March 2004, during the two-day-long riots, Albanian protestors burnt and looted the building. Today, only a very small community of nuns still lives in the monastery. At the time of writing, it was not accessible to visitors.

Adem Jashari was born on 28 November 1955 as one of eight children of the Jashari family. His father Shaban Jashari had worked as a teacher, but was accused of national agitation and banned from his job in 1952. His oldest son Rifat migrated to Switzerland in 1969 and sent money back to the family living in Prekaz. His second son worked for the Skenderaj ammunition factory until he was fired from his job in 1990. Adem himself had five children, but never worked a proper job. In 1981, Adem Jashari participated in the mass protests (see *Chapter 1, History*, page 24). In December 1991, Serbian police surrounded the village of Prekaz looking for Adem Jashari and his brother. On that occasion, they were able to escape to Switzerland with the help of Jakup Krasniqi, a former political prisoner-turned LDK activist, then UÇK's first spokesperson and Speaker of the parliament in an independent Kosovo. In 1993, Adem returned to plan the formation of a Kosovo Liberation Army. In July 1997, he was sentenced *in absentia* to 20 years in prison. On 7 March 1998, he and 55 family members, including small children and grandparents, were killed in their home in Prekaz. The cult surrounding his 'heroic martyrdom', fostered by supporters of the Kosovo Liberation Army, resulted in comparisons with Kosovo's Che Guevara. He is usually portrayed with his characteristic wild hair and beard, wearing a military uniform and a Kalashnikov. Enjoying a hero's glory, his disputed role as underground activist, émigré and police assassin is rarely challenged. The memorial in Prekaz celebrates him in as defender of the Albanian fatherland and his portrait decorates numerous wall calendars and buildings, the most prominent being the Boro Ramiz Youth and Sports Palace in Prishtina.

MITROVICA REGION

The Mitrovica region, including Mitrovica, Zvečan, Leposavić and Zubin Potok has a combined population of about 120,000. Compared with the rest of Kosovo it is sparsely populated and predominantly rural and mountainous, with the Rogozna Mountains to the east and the Kopaonik Massif to the northeast. The three northernmost municipalities have Serb majorities, with only small pockets of rural Albanian communities. Precise population figures are hard to get given the lack of, and the politicisation of, census data, but best estimates put the number of Serbs living in this area at fewer than 50,000. This region is characterised by two key features: the Ibar River, and its exceptional wealth in mineral reserves. The Ibar River, with a total length of 276km, rises in Montenegro and flows into the Zapadna Morava near Kraljevo. In Kosovo, it passes through the artificial Gazivoda (also known as Zubin Potok) Lake in the northeast, cuts through Mitrovica and then makes a sharp turn north towards Zvečan and Leposavić. For millennia this region has generated wealth thanks to its deposits of gold, silver, lead and zinc. The valuable mineral reserves exploited here have financed the Roman, Bulgarian, Serbian, Ottoman and Yugoslav 'Empires'. This region, with a history going back to 3000BC, has a number of interesting attractions. For one, there is the politically divided town of Mitrovica dominated by the spooky ruins of the industrial giant Trepça. Then there are the Banjska and Sokolica monasteries, two beautiful examples of Serbian Orthodox art and the ruins of Zvečan Castle. For nature lovers, there is also Zubin Potok Lake, offering great swimming, hiking and biking opportunities in a beautiful setting.

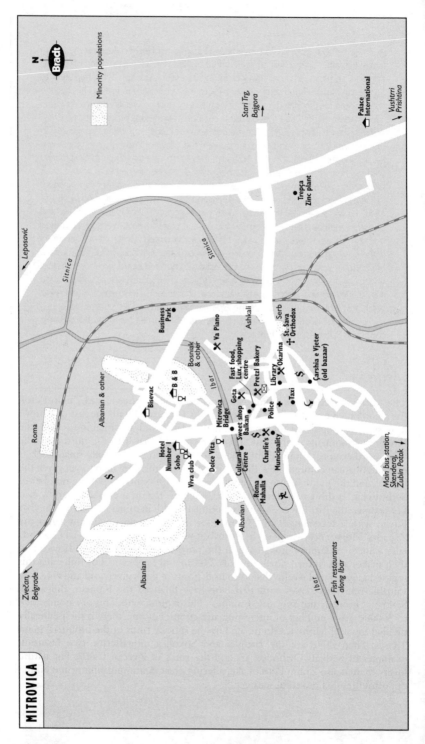

MITROVICA

Minority populations

Roma

Albanian & other

Albanian

Albanian

Zvečan,
Belgrade

Leposavić

Sitnica

Sitnica

Business
Park

Bisevac

B & B

Hotel
Number 1
Soho

Dolce Vita

Viva club

Cultural
Centre

Sweet shop
Balkan

Roma
Mahalla

Mitrovica
Bridge

Gota

Municipality

Charlie's

Police

Taxi

Va Piano

Fast food,
Lux, shopping
centre

Pretzl Bakery

Library

Okarina

Ashkali

Serb

St. Sava
Orthodox

Çarshia e Vjeter
(old bazaar)

Trepça
Zinc plant

Palace
International

Stari Trg,
Bajgora

Vushtrri,
Prishtina

Main bus station,
Skenderaj,
Zubin Potok

Fish restaurants
along Ibar

Ibar

Ibar

Bosniak
& other

Bradt

264

Mitrovica has been in the international headlines since 1999 as Kosovo's most difficult trouble spot. The famous bridge that was rebuilt with French government money after the war, instead of bridging the Serbian and Albanian divide across the Ibar River, has become the symbol of the town's division.

Ironically, prior to the war Mitrovica had been the most ethnically integrated town in Kosovo. It was a town with a strong local identity built around the Trepça conglomerate, which once provided employment for more than 20,000 people. There was shared pride in the town's football club that once made it into the Yugoslav First Division. The language on the street was a mix of Albanian and Serbian and almost everybody switched comfortably between the two. The Yugoslav authorities made a conscious effort to combine ethnicities in socialist housing blocks so neighbourhoods in Mitrovica were highly mixed. The war in 1999 and the subsequent forced expulsion of Albanians and Serbs from their respective homes in the north and south part of the city created an artificial division that did not exist before. North Mitrovica used to have an Albanian majority and many houses and apartments in the north are still owned by Albanians. Equally, there was a strong Serb and Roma community living in what is today the southern part of the city, evidenced by the Orthodox church and cemetery in the south. For the time being, many Albanians and Serbs are fearful of returning to their homes on the 'other' side. Yet the political and ethnic division of the town is not absolute. There are still about 2,000 Albanians living in the northern part of the city in the Miners' Hill neighbourhood and in apartment blocks close to the Ibar River. Shops and small cafés located in a multi-ethnic area known as Bosnjak Mahalla, located in the north, are frequented by Albanians and Serbs alike. Besides the main bridge, there are in fact two other bridges where people regularly cross the Ibar River, plus the main Mitrovica–Zvečan road used frequently to go north and south by car. Despite political tensions, members of both communities do cross regularly and in recent years there have even been some returns of Roma families to the south and Albanian families moving back to their rebuilt homes in the north. However, the source of tensions remains the fact that, for hardliners on both sides, Mitrovica has become the symbol of their cause. The fallback option of Serb extremists had always been to retain the north of Kosovo, the area north of the Ibar River, regardless of Kosovo's status. Immediately after the war, so-called 'bridge watchers', armed gangs with criminal connections and close links to Milošević's former security apparatus, emerged on the northern side 'guarding' the bridge. Albanian hardliners, feeding on frustration with UNMIK's inability to rein in Belgrade-financed parallel security and governance structures operating freely across Kosovo, continued to dream of retaking north Mitrovica by force. Conflict has thus been simmering in a territory not larger than a few square kilometres. In March 2004, a false rumour that Serbs had chased Albanian children into the Ibar River sparked unrest across Kosovo. The resulting March Riots left 19 people dead and more than 3,000 displaced. In the month following Kosovo's declaration of independence, Serb protestors stormed the UN-run courthouse in north Mitrovica and burnt down the customs posts on the border with Serbia. The government in Belgrade has since been reinforcing its parallel structures in northern Kosovo, and continues to challenge the authority of Prishtina and the EU-funded rule of law and police mission.

Yet the vast majority of Mitrovica's 85,000 inhabitants, Albanians and Serbs alike, remember the days when Mitrovica was a proud and economically vibrant town. Given some political rapprochement between Belgrade and Prishtina and given better economic opportunities, Mitrovica may one day again become a town united – and not divided – by its river.

HISTORY   Three symbols capture the troubled history of Mitrovica best. The Miners' Monument in commemoration of the town's centuries-long mining tradition, the Zvečan smelter, a monument to the Trepça conglomerate, and the bridge spanning the Ibar River that has now become a symbol of Mitrovica's division.

The name 'Mitrovica' derives from St Dimitrius, the patron saint of a church built in the 8th century on the lower slopes of Zvečan Castle. The name of this medieval settlement became Dmitrovica, which later changed to Mitrovica.

Two rivers meet in Mitrovica, the Ibar and the Sitnica, and there have been settlements along these riverbeds dating back to 3000BC. With the **arrival of the Romans** in the 1st century BC, Mitrovica was integrated in a network of military routes spanning the Balkan Peninsula. Just outside Mitrovica, in Lushte village on the road to Peja, there was a small Roman settlement and in the city itself, Roman sarcophagi and remains of temples dedicated to Jupiter and Juno have been discovered during the construction of the railway station.

The **strategic importance** of Zvečan Castle made this a hotly contested region. Whoever controlled the castle effectively controlled the northern access to the Kosovo plains. After the Romans came the Slavs, then the Byzantines and, in the 9th century, Mitrovica region was incorporated into the Bulgarian kingdom under Tsar Simeon. In 1185, the Nemanjić rule extended to include Mitrovica and Stefan Nemanjić immediately ordered the reconstruction of Zvečan Castle. The Kosovo mines, in particular the mines in Novo Brdo where the royal mint was located, effectively financed the expansion of the Serbian Medieval Kingdom.

In 1399, a **Turkish garrison** was placed in Zvečan to guard the north. Mitrovica quickly developed into an important garrison town and attracted a large influx of Turkish traders, soldiers and administrators. The old Ottoman town developed on the right bank of the Ibar River with a bazaar at its centre, a mosque and a *hammam* (today's regional museum). As a garrison town, Mitrovica's economy was mostly geared to provide for the needs of the soldiers, including saddlers and armsmiths. In those years, Mitrovica had about 2,500 inhabitants, but compared to nearby Vushtrri or Banjska, its importance was mainly military.

Mitrovica's breakthrough came with the **construction of the railways** in 1873–78 connecting Mitrovica with Skopje and Thessaloniki. The main purpose of the railway was to ensure that troops could be moved quickly to Mitrovica. As the last stop on the railway line, Mitrovica soon became an import and export centre. The new wealth immediately trickled down into the local economy. The roads were paved with stone slabs (*kalldrëm*) and the number of artisan and trading shops increased rapidly. By about 1890, when Mitrovica was joined with the Prishtina sançak, it had a population of about 7,000 inhabitants. In recognition of its strategic importance, Russia and Austria-Hungary opened consulates in the town. The end of the Ottoman Empire ushered in dramatic changes. The inter-war period was marked by the large-scale exodus of Mitrovica's Turkish-speaking population and the cautious beginning of Mitrovica's **industrialisation**. In 1926, Radomir Pasic, a Belgrade industrialist, sold the exclusive rights to mineral exploitation in Stan Tërg to the English company Selection Trust Ltd. The newly established company Trepça Mines Ltd reported profits of £200,000 in 1935. In the 1940s, under German occupation, Kosovo's mines supplied 40% of Germany's lead consumption and produced the batteries used in the German submarine fleet. In Tito's Yugoslavia, Trepça grew into an industrial giant with 22,885 employees in 1988. At its peak, the **Trepça conglomerate** combined more than 40 mines, battery plants, knife- and cutlery-making plants and seaside hotels for its workers. Trepça financed the construction of apartments in Mitrovica and Stan Tërg, the Trepça football club, the stadium and various cultural associations. For all intents and purposes Mitrovica was a one-company town built around the Trepça complex.

Economically, the conglomerate started to make losses in 1984, but under the Yugoslav system these losses could be covered by cheap loans from state banks and cash infusions from the Yugoslav Development Fund. Trepça's business collapsed with the rise of Milošević. A first major strike broke out in May 1988. In February 1989, in protest against the proposed constitutional amendments that were intended to revoke Kosovo's autonomy, 1,300 Albanian Trepça miners called for an eight-hour strike followed by a march on Prishtina. Milošević responded with mass dismissals. From 1989 to 1991, employment in the Trepça mines in Mitrovica shrank from 13,261 to 7,000, including only 1,200 Albanians. During the 1990s, Milošević appointee, Novak Bjelič pursued a policy of major asset stripping and outright theft. The company was spared destruction during the bombing campaign, but technical failures and fire did great damage to the zinc smelter, the accumulator factory and the fertiliser plant located in the south. On 14 August, British parachutes shut down the lead smelter in Zvečan on environmental and health grounds. The Trepça complex was thus placed into the hands of the UN which in turn passed all responsibility to the Kosovo Trust Agency, now replaced by the Kosovo Privatisation Agency. In late 2004 and early 2005, the mines slowly restarted operation and the Stan Tërg mine reopened. In the interest of avoiding social unrest, thousands of workers, Serbs and Albanians, continue to receive direct payments financed by the Kosovo budget. Trepça's ores and mining licences undoubtedly have a value in today's commodity market and there have been several interested suitors, although the mine did suffer from the global downturn in 2007– 10. Trepça's privatisation has been bogged down in discussions between internationals and the Kosovo government and creditors have brought claims in the courts although there is currently a moratorium on enforcement. As things stand, it is likely that litigation will eventually force the government's hand.

Without Trepça, Mitrovica's economy is struggling. In the northern part of town, the economy is entirely dependent on public-sector jobs and money transfers from Belgrade, financing about two-thirds of monthly cash incomes. The south is hit hard by the collapse of Trepça and the lack of viable economic alternatives. The continued economic and political insecurity keeps Mitrovica in an uncomfortable limbo.

SECURITY Mitrovica is certainly the most volatile and politically tense place in all of Kosovo. Organised unrest and political protests do happen occasionally. Especially in north Mitrovica, where hardliners try to keep a firm grip on power, the situation can be tense at times. As a rule, as long as you stay away from protests and demonstrations, there are few risks involved for any traveller or foreign national. You may get asked by police officers to show your ID when crossing the main bridge. At the time of writing, the situation in and around Mitrovica was calm and given the high presence of international police and NATO troops in the area, the situation is expected to stay under control. In general, tensions tend to increase at election times, in March or around holidays such as the independence anniversary on 17 February or Serbian National Day on 28 June. To be on the safe side, you can check with the local police for an accurate situation analysis at the time of your visit. The police headquarters is just before the bridge in the south on Rr Mbreteresha Teuta.

We advise visitors to take note of the following practical issues:

- In the south, Albanian is the language on the street while in the north everybody speaks Serbian. Be aware that (only in Mitrovica) some people may get upset if addressed in the 'wrong' language. If you are unsure what language to use, it's best to try your luck in English or German.

8

- It is, generally speaking, not a good idea to drive with KS plates (or Albanian plates) into the Serb-dominated north of Kosovo. If you have a hire car or your own car with these plates then you should take them off before you enter the Serb area. Driving without plates may seem peculiar but is common practice by the north Mitrovican inhabitants who do not have Serb plates. Foreign plates, eg: Macedonian, Bosnian, French, UK, Italian, Bulgarian, are fine.
- In South Mitrovica the euro is the official currency, while in the north prices are commonly listed in Serbian dinar, although payment can usually be done in either dinar or euro. There are international ATMs operated by ProCredit Bank and Raiffeisen in both parts of the town along the main street crossing the bridge over the Ibar. See Practicalities below for more information.

GETTING THERE AND AWAY There are regular **buses** every 15 minutes from Prishtina to Mitrovica. The journey takes approximately one hour.

As an alternative, you can also wave down any of the **taxi vans (kombi)** heading towards Mitrovica. *Kombis* stop right in front of the market in Mitrovica, while regular buses will drop you off at the main bus station on Rr Mbreteresha Teuta a few minutes' walk from the bridge. For timetables, contact Mitrovica bus station (📞 *028 539 075;* m *044 722 713*).

Be warned that Mitrovica bus station is a dingy place with no infrastructure at all.

From Peja to Mitrovica, buses depart at 08.15, 09.25, 12.25, 13.25, 16.20 and 18.25. For more information, see the timetable in *Chapter 2*, page 60.

By **car** from Prishtina, just follow the signs for Mitrovica heading north along the main road. Soon after Vushtrri, you will see the industrial ruins of the Trepça complex on your left. Take a left turn following signs to Mitrovica, turn right immediately at the T-junction (the Serb Orthodox cemetery is on your right), and keep heading straight (over the railway tracks) into downtown Mitrovica. There is paid parking all along the main roads or private parking in some of the side streets.

From **north Mitrovica** there are **minibuses** to most major Serbian towns departing every hour and coaches every hour, from 08.00 to 13.00 direct to Belgrade, but make sure you have a stamp (see page 46).

In the evenings, there is a daily **coach** leaving north Mitrovica to Sarajevo via Novi Pazar at 19.15 (close to the first traffic light on the main road extending from the bridge to Zvečan).

GETTING AROUND There are three main bridges plus the Mitrovica–Zvečan road connecting south and north Mitrovica. There is actually a lot of movement between north and south and the city is not 'divided' as such. There is, however, no direct bus line linking north and south Mitrovica and some taxis may be reluctant to cross the river for fear of being exposed on the 'other side' by their licence plates. Cars in south Mitrovica have the standard KS licence plates, while in the north many cars kept their old KM (Kosovska Mitrovica) licence plates, or have none at all. It's truly an unusual sight to see so many cars without any plates! Just in case, be prepared that you may have to cross the bridge on foot.

In the south, taxis are parked in the area around the market or you can call any of the following numbers: Radio Taxi Albani (m *044 384 600/700*); Radio Taxi Mitrovica (📞 *028 23 403;* m *044 626 222/+381 63 700 3636*); Taxi Nori (m *044 103 600*); Radio Taxi Caci (m *044 384 500*) and Radio Taxi Nardi (📞 *028 535 595;* m *044/049 331 330* 📞 *+381 65 504 0603*).

In the north, taxis are lined up along the main road extending from the bridge towards Zvečan. One friendly driver who will also do runs up to Kopaonik ski resort for €50 is Zoran Dordević (📞 *+381 63 802 5109/028 424 475*).

Most taxi drivers will accept payment in euros, but it's best to agree on a price before taking off. If you want to climb to Zvečan Castle expect to pay €2; a round trip to Banjska Monastery costs around €5.

🏠 WHERE TO STAY
South Mitrovica

🏠 **Palace Hotel International** (42 rooms, 3 apts with jacuzzis) Shupkovc, Mitrovica; m 044/049 214 000; e info@hotelpalace.org; www.hotelpalace.org. Located a few kilometres out of town on the main road towards Prishtina, this is Mitrovica's best hotel if you have your own wheels or don't mind taking a taxi. The rooms are decent & clean, all with showers & satellite TV. The restaurant is open every day, serving à la carte until 21.00. In summer, you can sit outdoors in the garden beside the children's playground. There is a shared computer connected to the internet & a printer free of charge for hotel guests, & free Wi-Fi. There are also 2 conference rooms, equipped with projectors & screens. On the top floor there is a sauna (for up to 4 people), a massage room & a solarium. Sauna & massage are €20 for 1hr, €10 for the solarium. In summer, the ground floor is mainly used for weddings or disco nights featuring local singers & bands. $$–$$$$

North Mitrovica

🏠 **Bisevac Motel** (25 rooms) Ul Knjaz Miloš (extension of the 2nd bridge); ☎ 028 422 025/38; m +381 63 815 2147. A rather dingy place with old furniture & minimally equipped bathrooms, including showers. If you are travelling in a larger group, you can ask for one of the rooms with 5 or more beds. This hotel is not recommended for women travelling alone. $$

🏠 **Hotel B&B** (11 rooms) Ul Lola Ribara; ☎ 028 423 688. Named after its 2 owners, Bato & Blaso, this is another centrally located hotel in a new building with modern bathrooms. The overall style & leather-cushioned doors make you feel a bit like you are in a 1960s' James Bond movie. The adjacent restaurant serves food till 23.00. $$

🏠 **Hotel No 1** (8 rooms, 4 apts) Ul Sutjeska; ☎ 028 425 359; e info@northcity.com; www.northcity.com. Conveniently located near the bridge & right in the most happening neighbourhood, No 1 is the best choice for anyone looking for a place to stay in north Mitrovica. The rooms are modern & clean, all with showers & TV. The 4 apartments are equipped with little kitchenettes, including a fridge, office desk & a sitting area. If you are planning to stay for longer, try to negotiate a special price with the owner Markovic Tihomir. $$

✖ WHERE TO EAT
South Mitrovica

✖ **Charlie's** Rr Mbreteresha Teuta; m 044 676 464; ⏰ 07.00–24.00 daily. A popular place frequented by internationals & Kosovars alike, serving salads, pasta & different meat dishes. At lunchtime it can get very crowded. If you really want to make the owner happy, just add another Charlie Chaplin picture or photo to his collection. Free Wi-Fi & good coffee.

✖ **Gota Restaurant** Rr Arta; m 044/049 447 466; ⏰ 07.00–23.00 daily. Frequented mostly by internationals & local curry lovers. Best known for its Mexican & curry dishes. In summer, the large outdoor terrace is a very nice meeting place. There is also home delivery & take-away, as well as free Wi-Fi.

✖ **Okarina Restaurant** Rr Ali Pasha Tepelena (main road as you enter town); m 044 146 252; ⏰ 08.00–24.00 daily. A cosy place downtown just across from the Mitrovica Museum. The interior is a rustic mix of traditional Albanian cushions, wooden panelling & stone decorations. The garden is nice & cool even in hot summers, thanks to a little fish pool. Pizza comes right from the wood stove or you can choose one of the traditional Albanian oven-baked dishes & starters. Courgettes oven-baked in a cheese sauce are an all-time favourite!

✖ **Va Piano** Rr Kemajl Ataturk; m 044 383 250; e info@eurotex-ks.com; www.eurotex-ks.com; ⏰ 07.00–24.00 daily. Tucked away in the old industrial zone (using parts of the premises of a now-privatised textile factory), Va Piano's grilled fish, pizza & traditional Albanian meat dishes are worth the 5-min drive from the centre. Especially in summer, the spacious outdoor garden area is peaceful & inviting.

Bakeries and cake shops

'Pretzl Bakery' (the famous no-name bakery opposite the police station); ⊕ 06.00–22.00 daily. There are usually long queues in the morning for the house speciality – wood-oven baked salty pretzelss. Best served hot. The bread is also the best in town.
Sweetshop Balkan Rr Mehe Uka (between the bridge & Lux shopping centre); ⊕ 09.00–22.00 daily. A popular place with excellent sweets, from cakes to baklava.

North Mitrovica

✕ **No I** Ul Sutjeska; ☎ 028 424 903; e info@northcity.com; www.northcity.com; ⊕ 07.00–23.00 daily. The best address in north Mitrovica for a nice meal & to try some traditional Serbian food. The open chimney, stone walls & traditional décor give the place a warm & cosy feel that make you forget the political tensions on the bridge just a few minutes' walk away. Thanks to its reputation as 'the' best place, it is here that local politicians & international officials meet to strike a new political deal over a glass of homemade *slivovica* or a dish of roasted beans. Ask for the specials like *prebranac* (roasted beans with sausage), *sarma* (stuffed cabbage) or *punira paprika* (stuffed peppers).
✕ **Visitor** Zvečan (just across from the main taxi stand). A *qebaptore*, famous for its *cevapcici*, definitely the best fast food around.

Fish restaurants along the Ibar River

There are a few recently opened fish restaurants along the Ibar River on the road to Zubin Potok. Follow the signs for Podgorica and Zubin Potok. These restaurants make a good stop for lunch or dinner, especially with children thanks to their spacious gardens and playgrounds. You can also take a digestive stroll along the river after your meal. At the time of writing, the top four were the following:

✕ **Ibri Restaurant** Koshtovë-Mitrovica (along the Ibar River on Zubin Potok road); m 044 196 399. Nicely set up with a huge children's playground. You can literally pick your own fish from the outdoor fish basins.
✕ **No Name** Koshtovë-Mitrovica; m 044 157 302/307 234. Recently opened, also directly on the riverside.
✕ **Qetesia** Koshtovë-Mitrovica (9km out of town); m 044/049 164 232; www.qetesiarestaurant.com; ⊕ 09.00– 24.00. Beautiful garden with a lake & a large playground for children. The best choice for fish in the area – the house speciality is grilled trout. Free Wi-Fi.
✕ **Top Fashion** Koshtovë-Mitrovica (first restaurant along the Ibar River on the Zubin Potok road; m 044 173 910/+381 63 873 1876; ⊕ 08.00– 24.00 daily. An unusual name for a fish restaurant, but that's because the owner also runs a clothes store in Mitrovica with the same name. The round-shaped interior has a huge tree hovering in the air above a couple of traditional Albanian *sofra* tables (floor-level round tables) & wooden stools. No worries if you are of the tall sort & prefer normal seating there's plenty. In summer it's particularly nice to sit in the garden. A small bridge right in front of the restaurant also leads across the Ibar River. The specialities include the traditional *flija*, various *tava* dishes &, of course, trout.

WHERE TO DRINK

Both in the north and south, the bar scene is concentrated in one main street. In the south it is the Çarshia e Vjeter (the old bazaar); just turn right into the busy alleyway at the corner of Hotel Adriatik (under construction at the moment) next to Raiffeisen Bank. In the north, the street where nightlife is happening is Ulica Sutjeska, a side street off Sumadija Square.

South Mitrovica

Times have really changed in the **Çarshia e Vjeter (old bazaar)** and instead of jewellery ateliers or arms smiths, the street is packed with young people and a string of bars.

Cafés and bars

⊑ **Ma Belle** Rr Afrim Zhitia; ☎ 028 535 536; ⊕ 07.00–23.00. Nice modern coffee house serving sandwiches & cakes. Free Wi-Fi. Delivery service.
♀ **Okarina Pub** Rr Ali Pasha Tepelena (right next to Okarina Restaurant); m 044 595 083; ⊕ 07.30–23.00 daily. A popular pub & the best choice for a cool beer in the evenings or a quiet coffee during the day. Also free Wi-Fi.

Before the conflict there had been a settlement of an estimated 7,000 Roma on the south bank of the River Ibar. After NATO arrived, Albanians set the buildings on fire in revenge for the Roma's perceived collaboration with the Serb regime. The Roma were driven out of their homes despite the presence of KFOR. They were moved to refugee camps in the north on land near Trepça mine tailings (waste). These were never meant to be permanent homes but years passed and despite several NGOs trying to work on the Roma return to the south, 700 remained in the camps and others took refuge abroad or in Belgrade.

In 2004, Mitrovica residents were tested by the World Health Organisation for levels of lead in their blood. The levels were all above the average but they were a particular cause for concern in the Roma camps. The WHO demanded immediate evacuation. UNMIK and the Ministry of Returns of the Kosovo government linked the issue with return to the Roma mahalla. Others feared that the issue was so acute, and return would take too long, pointing to deaths from lead poisoning in the camp and irreversible deformation of the children who formed a large proportion of the residents of the camp. UNMIK was blamed for allowing the residents to remain in the camps so long. Analysis was carried out into whether it was really the soil and water that caused the problem or whether the lead poisoning arose from the practice of illegal lead smelting which many Roma families carried out (sometimes even using the same pots for water-carrying, washing and cooking).

The issue hit the headlines across the world, including articles in the *Herald Tribune*, *The Guardian*, and German newspapers. There were calls for the removal of UNMIK's immunity and analysis of whether Trepça could be sued. UNMIK went into panic mode and coded cables flew backwards and forwards from New York. Every institution and acronym seemed to be involved, but few would come up with hard cash as six years after the conflict the previously free-flowing cash was drying up fast.

The Roma diaspora put pressure on the Roma not to return to the mahalla in the south, fearing this would be used as evidence that Kosovo was safe now, triggering their forced return from Germany and other western European countries.

Furthermore, some of the Serb community did not want to see success in returns and to give credit to the Kosovo government. Tempers were frayed, but eventually the EU and other donors found some funds and action was taken to move the high-risk individuals to other camps and in early 2007, more than seven years after their expulsion, the first few Roma families were able to return to the former Roma mahalla across the river where social housing and private houses have been rebuilt as part of an ongoing large-scale Kosovo government and donor-funded returns project.

While the Kosovo government was keen for the return to succeed, the problems of this one project begs the question of how they and the international community will address the social and housing problem for the anticipated forced return of tens of thousands more Kosovar Roma, Ashkali and Egyptians (RAE) who previously lived in Kosovo and who are now in Montenegro, Germany and Serbia. These RAE may find themselves, like the Roma from the Roma mahalla, passed from pillar to post.

North Mitrovica and Zvečan

♀ **Exponto** Ul Karadjordeva 4 (Zvečan). At the time of writing this was the most happening place on Fri/Sat. The party generally picks up from midnight until early morning. The DJs mix the best of Yugo-Rock with electro beats.
♀ **Soho** Ul Sutjeska (first left, off Pizzeria No 1);

m +381 63 866 0245. A popular hangout. In summer there are live bands occasionally; on Mon blues night & every Sun Whisky Dan (Whisky Day) – 1 shot of whisky for €0.50.
♀ **Song** Ul Sutjeska (second floor of Hotel No 1). New club attracting a nice young crowd, but open only

every other night. DJ nights on Wed, mainly house & Latino, & Fri sometimes rock & jazz concerts. ♀ **Viva Club** Ul Sutjeska; m +381 63 804 0633/+381 64 509 6666; e vivakm@yahoo.com.

Since its opening in 2004, it's become a popular hangout in the evenings for the younger crowd. In summer, there is also a small outdoor terrace. It's easy to recognise by its bright-orange décor.

SHOPPING For souvenirs there is a cute shop on the corner of Çarshia e Vjetër Street, between the *hammam* (museum) and Raiffeisen Bank. Here you can get old postcards and various other souvenirs.

OTHER PRACTICALITIES There is an internet café right next to the Lux shopping centre on Rr Mehe Uka in south Mitrovica and one more on Çarshia e Vjeter, the little street next to Raiffeisen Bank.

Banks ProCredit, NLB and Raiffeisen have branches on both sides of the Ibar. ProCredit Bank is on on Rr Mbreteresha Teuta (✆ *028 530 235/532 236; ⊕ 08.00–16.00*) and in Ul Knjaz Miloš (✆ *028 424 601; ⊕ Mon–Fri and 09.00–14.00 Sat*). The Raiffeisen headquarters is in the south on the main road as you enter the town (*Rr Ali Pasha Tepelena; ✆ 038 222 222 ext 555; ⊕ 08.30–17.30 Mon–Fri, 10.00–14.00 Sat*).

NLB also has several branches including on Mbretnesha Teuta and next to the municipality in the north (⊕ *08.00–17.00 Mon-Fri*).

Pharmacies There are a couple of pharmacies close to the health centre on Rr Agim Hajrizi.

WHAT TO SEE AND DO The first impression as you approach Mitrovica is the ghastly view of the dilapidated industrial site left off the main road coming from Prishtina. But don't be discouraged; Mitrovica is definitely worth a visit, if only to walk across the famous Mitrovica Bridge and to see with your own eyes how ridiculous the artificial division of the town really is. A visit to Mitrovica is more about the experience than about any particular historical site, with the exception maybe of the Ethnological Museum in the old *hammam*.

Old Mitrovica The old Ottoman part of town developed on the right bank of the Ibar River, in what is now referred to as south Mitrovica. The bazaar with its narrow streets and small ateliers stretched out between the main mosque and the *hammam*, now housing the Regional Ethnological Museum. As an important garrison town, it was a military leader, Gazi Isa Bey, who supervised the construction of the main mosque, the clock tower, a *madrasa* (religious school) and a guesthouse. The quarter that developed around these sites is still called the Gazi Isa Bey *mahalla* (quarter). Different quarters developed around the old city centre, including the quarter of refugees (*muhaxhirs*) who settled here after their expulsion from south Serbia in 1878, the Potok quarter and the Varosh quarter. Little has remained from those days. New constructions compete with old shop fronts in the bazaar area. The **Serb Orthodox church** built in 1896 and dedicated to St Sava is surrounded with barbed wire and closed to visitors. Restoration works are being planned. The nearby **Catholic church** is almost hidden from view.

The 18th-century *hammam* used to house the **Ethnological Museum of Mitrovica**, but the building's ownership is disputed and it is currently closed to visitors. The Ethnological Museum and its collection of traditional costumes, jewellery and other everyday items, were looking for a new home at the time of writing. The 'newer' part of the Old Town spreads out between the main street and the river along Rr Agim Hajrizi and Rr Mehe Uka. This part of town has been completely transformed under communism, with only the occasional building dating back to the 1930s, including the former Russian consulate building on Rr Kemajl Atatürk. This is now the 'city centre' in the south, and the area to go out and be seen. The best restaurants in town are all concentrated here (see *Where to eat*, pages 269–70).

North Mitrovica To grasp just how small North Mitrovica is, it is best to tour it on foot. The bridge was refurbished with French government money in 2001 and is usually guarded by Kosovo police who occasionally check your ID cards. Walk across the main bridge for the experience. If you continue your walk up along the main street you get the impression of being in a time warp. North Mitrovica definitely has a much stronger 'post communist' feel to it than any other place in Kosovo. The cars are old and cranky and still use the old Yugoslav number plates with KM (for Kosovska Mitrovica) or none at all. Some of the shops appear unchanged from their worst days under communism – with empty shelves covered by a thick layer of dust. Trg Sumadija (Sumadija Square) is considered the 'city centre' in the north, but it is in essence no more than a road crossing. It is here, however, that the best bars and restaurants in town are concentrated and where it is most lively in the evenings. The patchy painting of the socialist apartment blocks was an initiative of Michael Steiner, a German UNMIK chief. He hoped to 'cheer up' Mitrovica with a bit of colour. Well, you can judge for yourself whether it worked. If you turn left you arrive at Pizzeria No 1, undoubtedly the best address in town, and further along on Ulica Sutjeska you have a string of nice bars. If you continue straight on the main road, you can turn left on the road that winds uphill towards the newly constructed **Serbian Orthodox church** and the Miners' Monument. The **Miners' Monument** was put up by the communist regime in commemoration of a miners' strike during the German occupation. You can easily recognise it by its strange U-shape, almost like a huge soup bowl. If you keep walking the main road takes you straight to Zvečan.

Zvečan/Zveqan Zvečan is a residential suburb of Mitrovica, a sleepy, quiet place. There are two sites worth visiting: Zvečan Castle and the Zvečan lead smelter.

The conical-shaped hill overlooking both Mitrovica Town and Zvečan has always been of great strategic importance. It provides for extensive views along the Ibar River Valley to the north and far to the south over the Kosovo plain. Its natural shape made it an ideal place to construct a castle. There was already a medieval settlement on the slopes of the Zvečan Castle hill from the 6th to the 8th centuries. In those years, a church dedicated to St Dimitrius gave the town its first name 'Dmitrovica'. The unique strategic position of the Zvečan Hill inspired a first Roman fortification, which was later expanded under the Byzantines. Under Bulgarian rule, from the 9th to the 11th centuries, a new castle was constructed using the old Roman stones and Byzantine walls. Historical records mention **Zvečan Castle** for the first time in connection with border clashes between the Serb and Byzantine armies in the 1090s. Under Stefan Nemanjić, the castle was once more restored and fortified. Legend tells that Stefan Nemanjić ordered a special thanksgiving prayer to be held in the Church of St George on top of the castle to celebrate a victory over the Byzantines in 1170. The first Turkish garrison in Kosovo was stationed in Zvečan in 1399 to protect entry into Kosovo from the north. The strategic position of Zvečan was once more tested during the Austrian invasion in 1688. The Austrian general Piccolomini set out to conquer Mitrovica, Banjska and Zvečan, but the imperial forces were beaten back from Zvečan and withdrew under heavy bombardment. In the 18th century, the fortress was eventually abandoned.

There are several routes up to the castle, but no marked paths. It's definitely worth the hike for the view of Mitrovica and the surrounding area and great for pictures and picnics, but the last part is very steep and can be slippery, so make sure you have good shoes. The shortest and most direct route sets out from Mali Zvečan (Little Zvečan), a small settlement literally behind the hill, halfway on the back route between Zvečan and Mitrovica. The easiest way to get there is by taxi from north Mitrovica to Mali Zvečan. The journey should cost no more than €2. An asphalt road leads halfway up the hill and ends at a Serbian cemetery. From there you can set out along the trodden paths zig-zagging up around the hill. The other, slightly longer, route is from Zvečan itself. If you are on foot, you must turn at the first roundabout and take the cobbled stone road uphill towards the castle. The first part takes you through a residential area. The actual hike starts at TV Most (the local Serb TV and radio station). If you want to save time, take a taxi to TV Most, and set out from there. Again, there are no signs, so just take it slowly and follow the paths you see. On the top of the hill, you can see remains of the Church of St George, a cistern and a tower.

Zvečan smelter The skyscraping lead smelter of the Trepça company in Zvečan is the first thing you see when you are approaching Zvečan from any direction. It is a symbol of Trepça's past glory and its troubled history. You cannot enter the company's grounds, but driving past is good enough (or looking down from Zvečan Castle) to get a grip of its dimensions. The smelter dates back to 1938 when Trepça was owned by the British firm Selection Trust Ltd. The lead produced here was exported to all of Europe and provided a good source of income, first for the British, then the Germans in the 1940s and later for the Yugoslav economy. After a brief shutdown during the aerial bombing campaign in 1999, the smelter resumed its activities in August 1999. The plant was fully under Serbian control, and operated with the tacit tolerance of UNMIK authorities. UNMIK's greatest worry was the environmental hazard represented by the plant. Lead levels in the air were about 125 times higher than those deemed acceptable by European Union standards. In the early morning of 14 August 2000, 900 British, French and Pakistani KFOR troops cordoned off the area and launched a raid on the Zvečan smelter from helicopters. The smelter was shut down and placed under UN administration. Workers of both ethnicities in Trepça continue to receive pro-forma salaries and stipends mostly for cleaning-up and maintenance works. In a twist of fate, it was British parachutes shutting down a smelter built by a British company.

OUTSIDE MITROVICA

TREPÇA AND STAN TËRG/STARI TRG Trepça and Stan Tërg are about 10km northeast of Mitrovica in a long-stretched valley surrounded by rocky hills. The history of these two settlements is closely linked to the region's mineral reserves and the history of the Trepça conglomerate. To get there, turn left at the T-junction after the turn to Mitrovica, and follow the signs for Stan Tërg.

Records first mention 'Trepice' in 1303, as a mining settlement and home to a Catholic parish. The Catholic Church was permitted under the patronage of Ragusan merchant colonies and Saxon miners. In fact, these 'so called' Saxons were actually Germans from Transylvania. They were encouraged to settle in the Serbian territory because of their mining expertise, and allowed to practise their own faith, run their own courts and preserve their language. The combination of Saxon miners and Ragusan merchants created a boom in the trade with silver, gold and lead and thus greatly benefited the Serbian treasury. There is an old **Saxon church** you can visit in Stan Tërg, dating back to the 13th century.

In 1455, under Sultan Mehmet II, the Trepça mines started to produce exclusively for the Ottoman Empire. From then on, the silver and mineral wealth of the mines was used to finance the expansion of the Ottoman Empire and to fill the sultan's coffers. The Ottoman sultan also granted special privileges to the miners to retain the **Saxon colony**. Miners had special rights, including the right to elect their own governing councils and they were exempted from the poll tax on non-Muslims (levied on the head of the household) and all other extraordinary taxes levied in times of war. Regular **trade fairs** developed in Trepça, attracting artisans and silversmiths from afar. The **Mazic Mosque** in Stan Tërg was also built in the 16th century. Over the years, the ore became increasingly depleted and Trepça's **silver mines** stopped producing by 1642. Trepça subsequently contracted in size and importance.

With the collapse of the Ottoman Empire, Kosovo's mining industry was slow to develop properly and did so only thanks to foreign investment. In 1926, a British company by the name of Selection Trust Ltd was granted the exclusive rights to exploit the minerals at Stan Tërg. In 1938, Selection Trust Ltd started the construction of the Zvečan smelter and integrated the Kopaonik mine from Leposavić into the Trepça company. The German army also greatly benefited from the Trepça mines. During the 1940s, a daily train load of 500 tons of lead and zinc concentrate was transported directly to munitions factories in Germany. In the 1980s, the Trepça mines contained more than 70% of Yugoslavia's **mineral reserves** and were among the top exporters of Yugoslavia.

From the 1960s to the 1980s, Trepça's productivity rapidly declined while its employment increased. Ore production in Stan Tërg had dwindled to insignificance and the funds pouring into Kosovo from the Yugoslav Development Fund were squandered on subsidising the Trepça conglomerate.

The majority of Albanian miners were dismissed following a first miners' strike in February 1989 and a general strike on 3 September 1991 (see *Chapter 1, History*). In 1989, 3,400 miners employed in Stan Tërg lost their jobs overnight. Almost every family was affected by the **mass dismissals**. Once home to a strong and highly respected mining community, the Mitrovica Valley became poor and despondent. In the 1990s the mine struggled with the sanctions and corruption. Since the end of the conflict mining did restart in 2005 and the mine is still currently operating but awaiting a solution to its financial situation (see page 22). Sometimes pre-scheduled VIP visitors are taken the 1,000m down into the shaft via the lift, but it is not a trip for the claustrophobic.

Getting there   There are regular **buses** departing every hour from 07.00 to 19.00 from the market (opposite the main mosque) of south Mitrovica, stopping in Tuneli i Parë and Stan Tërg. There are also **minibuses** you can flag down along the way. The fare is €0.40. If you share a **taxi**, it's €1 a head or €5 if you travel alone.

Other practicalities   The **post office** in Tuneli i Parë is open 08.00–15.00 Monday–Friday. There is also a small **family health centre** in case of emergency.

What to see and do   The **Crystal Museum of Trepça** (*Stan Tërg, near the Trepça mines (up the ramp across the bus stop, the first building to the right)*; m *044 906 477;* ⊕ *09.00–13.00 daily; entrance €0.50/2.50 students/adults*). The Crystal Museum is a curiosity and a must for anyone interested in valuable specimens of crystals in all forms and shapes. Over the years an impressive collection of crystals, quartzes and other minerals has been assembled from the Trepça mines. In terms of the collection, this museum ranks among the top 100 mineralogical museums in the world. In terms of presentation, however, it is really poor. Time has stood still since its first opening in 1965. To get the most out of a visit, contact Vjollca Meha, the very knowledgeable and helpful director of the museum, on the above mobile number, and arrange a special tour.

Group visits of more than five people must be by appointment. The museum is just starting in a new purpose built facility.

Hiking From Bajgora village, further along from Stan Tërg where the road becomes a dirt track, there are good hiking options and a very good restaurant.

✕ **Dodona Restaurant** Bajgora-Mitrovica; ☎ 028 555 975; m 044 245 227; ⊕ 09.00–24.00. A beautiful location at the top of a mountain, this restaurant is a popular weekend getaway for families from Mitrovica in both summer & winter. Serving traditional Albanian specialities like *flija*, *mantija* & various oven-baked clay-pot dishes, the food & the view are definitely worth the 30-min drive up the mountain (the quality of the road is really good). You can enjoy the view of the mountains from every table & in summer the outdoor garden & playground for children is especially nice. In winter, the restaurant operates 2 ski lifts: I for kids & I for adults. There is also free Wi-Fi.

SOKOLICA There is a faded yellow sign in Cyrillic for Sokolica Monastery along the main road connecting Mitrovica and Zvečan shortly after the Mitrovica turn-off if you continue north on the main road when coming from Prishtina. The road winds uphill through a village and then continues for another 5km on gravel. A beautiful hillside view opens up over the Ibar Valley and the peaks of the Kopaonik Massif to the northeast. The road takes you to a peaceful and quiet valley known for the Sokolica Monastery and the house of Isa Boletin.

Sokolica Monastery (⊕ *10.00–16.00 Sun–Fri, cleaning day Sat*) You'll quickly understand why this place was chosen for a monastery. Clinging to the hillside overlooking Boletin village, it's a peaceful location and thanks to recent restoration works the monastic complex is in a very good state. The monastery is guarded by Greek KFOR troops who may check your ID, but at the time of writing Albanians were allowed to enter. The actual name of the church is Bogorodicin Pokrov, but it is known as 'Sokolica' after the hill at whose foot it is located. Its claim to fame is the *Sokolica Virgin*, a sculpture of the Virgin and the Child cut in stone and dating back to the 13th century. The statue is originally from Banjska Monastery where it was a central piece of the sculptural decoration. It is rumoured to have been brought to Sokolica to escape successive Turkish raids on the Banjska Monastery. It was discovered in Sokolica by Rastko Petrovica, a Serbian poet, in 1920. It then became known as the *Holy Peasant Woman in Kosovo*. The *Sokolica Virgin* has been a venerated object of folk belief. Villagers, especially childless families, prayed to the *Sokolica Virgin* and traditionally covered her in garments and jewellery. This folk belief was shared by all faiths, Christian and Muslim alike. To this day, childless couples travel from as far afield as Belgrade for the Virgin's blessing. Thanks to the arrival of the statue, what was once a small church was elevated to the rank of a monastery. The monastery is still active today, and the nuns run their own icon-painting school. The nuns of Sokolica have also painted some of the icons in the church. The small church is right in front of you as you enter the monastery complex. Watch your head when you enter, the doors are very low. The frescoes are currently being restored.

Isa Boletin complex Right across from the Sokolica Monastery you see the home of Isa Boletin, a famous Albanian national activist living at the turn of the last

Isa Boletin's family came from Isniq, in Deçan region, but had to leave the area to escape a blood feud. The family then settled in Boletin village, close to Mitrovica, and took the name Boletin. Isa Boletin's career reflects the instability and rapid changes that took place in this part of Europe at the turn of the last century. At first, Isa Boletin had been employed as a guard for the Serbian Orthodox community in Mitrovica region in 1898–99. He was even honoured for his services by the Serbian consul. In 1902, he was appointed head of the sultan's personal 'Albanian guard', an assignment that took him to Istanbul. In 1903, a joint proposal was presented to the sultan by the Russian and Austro-Hungarian consuls in Mitrovica calling for the disarmament of the population and the creation of foreign-supervised gendarmes. This plan caused bitter protests, including an attack by more than 2,000 protestors on the Ottoman garrison in Mitrovica led by Isa Boletin. In the course of this revolt, the Russian consul was shot.

The news that Sultan Adulhamit had been deposed by the Young Turks in 1909 came as a shock to Isa Boletin. His entire career, his rank and privileged position depended on close relations to the sultan. Out of self-interest, he turned against the Young Turks. In 1910, Isa Boletin and Idriz Seferi took the lead in co-ordinating a large-scale uprising against the Young Turks in Kosovo. The Albanian rebels under Idriz Seferi's command succeeded in blocking the railway lines but the Young Turks' army soon outnumbered the rebels. Boletin was able to escape, but most of his fellow rebels were imprisoned or hanged. Another revolt erupted in western Kosovo in 1912. Isa Boletin was among the Albanian leaders who decided on a 12-point list of demands at a meeting in Junik, near Deçan. The rebels swiftly mustered a force of 45,000 armed men and took control of Kosovo and all major towns. Faced with this threat, the sultan eventually agreed to concede the right to Albanian-language education and a degree of self-rule. But before this agreement could be implemented, the tide turned against the Albanian national movement. In October 1912, Serbian troops marched into Kosovo's territory and routed the Ottoman army. Once more, Isa Boletin assumed a key role in putting up a first line of defence against the advancing Serbian armies. As one of his last actions, Isa Boletin travelled to the Peace Conference in London to lobby for the unification of all Albanian lands. When Mitrovica fell, Isa Boletin fled to Albania. A few years later, in the course of World War I, Isa Boletin was killed in a shootout as the Austrian army advanced into Montenegro.

century. The building has recently been restored and is planned to reopen as a museum soon.

BANJSKA As the name suggests (*banjska* meaning 'bath'), Banjska was an important spa resort and its thermal springs at temperatures of 31–54°C were sought after by patients suffering from rheumatism and various skin diseases. In the Ottoman era, Banjska developed into an important border town of the Vushtrri vilayet and the Bosnian vilayet. There was also a customs point levying duties on all caravans passing through Banjska. At the time when Ottoman travel writer Evlija Çelebivisited in the 1660s, he described the spa town of Banjska with its 300 houses made of brick as an important caravan stop.

Getting there Banjska Monastery is located 16km from Mitrovica along the Banjska River. There is a marked turn to Banjska on the main Mitrovica–Leposavić road. Take a sharp left and continue on the road until you get to Banjska village. The monastery is located above the village at the end of the road.

There are regular bus connections from north Mitrovica and Zvečan to Banjska leaving from the main road close to Sumadija Square. Alternatively, a taxi ride from north Mitrovica to Banjska costs €5 – it's best to ask the taxi driver to wait in Banjska for your return.

Banjska Monastery (*Entrance free; short sleeves/shorts not allowed*) The Monastery of Banjska is an endowment of King Milutin and was constructed in the years 1312–16. King Milutin was one of the most active patrons of the Serbian Orthodox Church, and is rumoured to have built 40 churches during his 40-year reign. Banjska Monastery was special, as it was intended as his burial place. King Milutin consciously wanted to imitate the final resting place of the founder of the Nemanjić dynasty in Studenica in modern-day Serbia. The church was dedicated to Saint Stephen, the patron of the Nemanjić family. The Nemanjić rulers made it one of the largest estates of the time, not only building the monastery itself, but also endowing it with 75 villages, nine summer pastures, 500 shepherd families and other valuable assets. The sheer size of the complex reflects the grand design of King Milutin. According to the king's wishes, a massive defensive wall surrounded the complex, including a fortified tower modelled on Mount Athos, a string of monastic dwellings and a refectory. At the gate, according to Byzantine tradition, there were stone seats for the poor to receive food distributed by the monastery on special occasions. The dining hall in the refectory was decorated with stone carvings and the walls were covered in frescoes. The top floors of the monastic dwellings were used as sleeping rooms by the monks.

The design of the church is greatly influenced by the Romanesque architecture that could be found along the Adriatic Coast. Typical for Italian Romanesque buildings, the church's façade was decorated in neatly cut three-coloured stones. King Milutin had gathered some of the best coastal masters at his court, and in the case of Banjska it was none other than the experienced Fra Vita from Kotor who took charge of the overall design (Fra Vita was also the mastermind behind the Visoki Dečani Monastery). The church itself was built on top of the ruins of the 13th-century seat of the Banjska diocese.

Unfortunately, successive reconstruction works have fundamentally changed the original appearance. Only a few remnants of the old church are still visible in the present-day edifice. All the brick parts of the church's structure have been added during restoration. The most important sculpture, the *Sokolica Virgin*, has been moved to Sokolica Monastery (see *Sokolica*, page 276). Little remains of the celebrated wall paintings in the church. Only a few fresco fragments have been preserved in special frames.

LEPOSAVIĆ/LEPOSAVIQ

The southern edges of the Kopaonik mountain range (in Albanian known as Shala e Bajgorës) offer a beautiful and untouched landscape, ideal for hiking or mountain biking.

Leposavić town is an uninteresting former mining town sporting the usual mix of socialist buildings, banks, restaurants and small shops. It also houses a couple of faculties from the parallel Serbian-language Prishtina University. The Kopaonik mines were started in 1927 with the arrival of English geologists who rediscovered the region's lead and zinc reserves. Over the years, more mines were opened in Belo Brdo in 1937, in Cernac in 1968 and in Zuta Perla in 1971. The flotation in Leposavić was built in 1971 and also formed part of the Trepça conglomerate.

GETTING THERE There are regular **bus** connections from north Mitrovica and Zvečan to Leposavić. At the time of writing the **train** services from Hani i Elezit,

Prishtina or Fushë-Kosova were suspended, but they may soon be resumed. See page 50.

WHERE TO STAY The nicest hotel in the area is actually in Lešak, near the border with Serbia.

Octan Motel Next to the petrol station, 1km north of Lesak, on the left side of the main road; ↘ 028 88 414. Doubles, triples & apartments available. All rooms with central heating, hot shower, basic TV & minibar. Simple but clean, with parking outside. No b/fast served at the motel, so most guests go to the nearby bakery in Lešak. $$

OTHER PRACTICALITIES The main road in Leposavić Town is 24 November, a 90° turn from the main entry and exit road. There you can find several ATMs, a Serbian **post office**, **pharmacy**, **health centre** and a couple of fast-food **restaurants**.

If you want a **taxi** to drop you off for a hike, you can call Pink Taxi (↘ *028 84 555*) or OK Taxi (↘ *028 84 500;* m *+381 64 403 8038*).

WHAT TO SEE AND DO
Hiking and biking The main attractions around Leposavić are the Rogozna Mountains to the west and the southern slopes of the Kopaonik Mountains to the east. There are several attractive bike routes or walking possibilities in this area. Since it is a Serbian-majority municipality, the area was spared the conflict in 1999 and there is no risk of mines (except on the Podujevo side). A nice drive (or for really fit bikers a possible cycling route) is the road up to Belo Brdo, at an altitude of about 1,300m in the Kopaonik Mountains. There is a possible tour on a path setting out from Dren along the road up to Belo Brdo and coming down via Ostrace and Lešak. It's a stiff uphill climb and very long drag, but the scenery is beautiful. Alternatively, you may want to explore the Rogozna side. There is a small path just before the border at Ibarsko Postenje village (across the Ibar River) leading up to Trebice, a small mountain village at 850m. KFOR is using these routes for reconnaissance trips, so they are relatively well maintained.

AROUND LEPOSAVIĆ

SOCANICA/SOCANICË With the arrival of the Romans in the 1st century BC, the **second-most important Roman city after Ulpiana** (see *Chapter 4*, page 138) was Socanica, 30km north of Mitrovica near present-day Leposavić. Attracted by the silver and lead reserves in the Kopaonik Mountains, the Romans settled here and founded a municipium that stretched over an area of 30ha. Archaeological findings confirm that there was a Roman forum, a basilica and numerous houses dating back to the time of Emperor Hadrian in AD136. Unfortunately, the archaeological remains are currently buried underground and therefore not visible.

Socanica (Socanicë) today is a small village set on the slopes of the Kopaonik Mountains. There are still a number of traditional hay barns and old stone houses. If you like to venture into the hills, you can follow the main road that leads uphill through Socanica village to a small **monastery** on the top. It is signposted and easy to find. The monastery is still active. There are picnic tables outside from where you can enjoy a nice view back over the Ibar Valley and the surrounding hills.

ZUBIN POTOK: GAZIVODA LAKE

Zubin Potok is best known for Gazivoda Lake, Kosovo's largest and most beautiful lake. It is a manmade lake built as part of the Ibar-Lepenc hydro system supplying

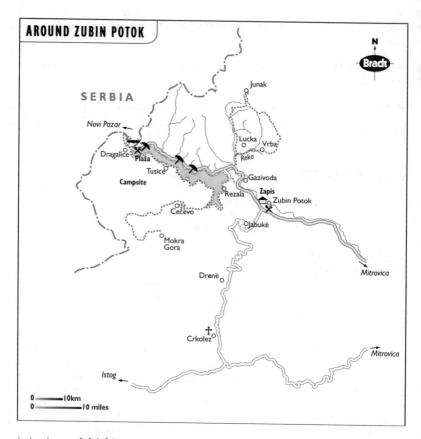

irrigation and drinking water to north and central Kosovo. The northernmost part of the lake extends over the border into Serbia.

Its panoramic setting amidst the Rogozna Mountains makes it one of Kosovo's main natural attractions. The lake stretches over a length of 24km and offers great swimming, walking and mountain-biking opportunities. There are several little beaches along the lake; just park your car at road level and walk down. Just before the border, there is a small beach and a restaurant where you can also rent a boat (see *Plaža Restaurant*, below). A quieter beach where you can camp unofficially is across the other side of the dam from Zubin Potok Town between Tusice and Dragalice. Unfortunately, litter is a problem everywhere.

The best route for walking or mountain biking goes along the southern edge of the lake. After crossing the dam (also a great viewpoint for the entire lake), turn right and follow the path along the lake (if you turn left at that T-junction you get to a viewpoint looking back on Zubin Potok). The first part is still asphalt but then it gets patchy, and in winter very icy. You can bike along the entire length of the lake and return via Serbia on the other side. Don't forget your passport, and most importantly, make sure you have the required Serbian-entry stamp that allows you to cross over into Serbia. It's a beautiful tour, but very demanding. For a great view, you can also take the route up to the top of Mokra Mountain. To get there, take the path up to Cecevo village and left around the mountain. The view from the top is spectacular.

There is another KFOR-permitted route east of the lake, closer to Gazivoda. The route goes via Lucka Reka to Vrba and up to Junake and from there back to

Lucka Reka. It's very steep, but your efforts are rewarded with a fantastic view back over the lake.

WHERE TO STAY

⌂ **Hotel Zapis** (4 rooms, 2 apts) Zubin Potok; ☎ 028 460 993; m +381 63 858 0308. Situated just outside Zubin Potok on the main road to Gazivoda, the hotel's rooms are simple & decently furnished. $$

Houses to rent on Gazivoda Lake There are a few houses to rent on the small beach 1km before the border right on the lakeshore. One of them belongs to Milan from Zvečan. It's fully furnished and has a terrace overlooking the lake. For reservations call m +381 63 807 5477.

WHERE TO EAT

✕ **Jedno Mesto** If you enter Zubin Potok from Mitrovica, Jedno Mesto is immediately on the first street left. Most famous for its huge pancakes filled with cheese, meat or jam.

✕ **Plaža Restaurant** Just before the border crossing to Serbia; m +381 63 855 0810; ⊕ 09.00–21.00 daily. A cosy place, all in wood with open fires, offering a full range of Serbian cuisine including hefty pork dishes & a good serving of *slivovica*, of course. It's popular with border police & customs officials, as it is just about the only place around. There is outdoor & indoor seating, & in summer you can take a swim at the restaurant beach. If you are lucky, you can rent a little boat for a ride on the lake.

OTHER PRACTICALITIES In Zubin Potok village you can find internet, a Serbian post office and a small health centre.

Appendix 1

LANGUAGE

ALBANIAN Albanian is in the Indo-European group of languages, but is unique in that it is not affiliated with another language. There are two varieties – Gheg (spoken in Kosovo and northern Albania) and Tosk (spoken in southern Albania). The differences are apparent and recognisable but not so great – speakers of the two understand each other without problems. The differences are perhaps similar to those between an American and an Englishman at most. Since the advent of satellite television and increased interaction between Albania and Kosovo, the differences have narrowed somewhat. Albania is more influenced by Italian whereas Kosovars have greater influences from German, with words such as *knapp* or *rückwerts* having crept into the language. There are many foreign words in the language including English, Latin, and French words, eg: *trottoir* for pavement, and if in doubt you can always try using the foreign word. One difference between Gheg and Tosk that is apparent to even a foreigner is that Tosks tend to speak faster and in a higher pitch whereas Gheg speakers tend to sound more masculine with a lower pitch and more rounded (albeit sometimes less articulated) words, and they also speak slightly slower. Furthermore, in Gheg, many words seem abbreviated and the 'ë' sound in the middle of the word is not pronounced as an open sound, but as a deeper 'a'.

Albanians will proudly tell you that they have 36 letters and how difficult their language is to learn. They are so used to foreigners speaking English and German, that they are surprised to hear someone speaking Albanian and therefore may not always have tuned their ear to recognise any mispronunciation. Do not despair, but try again. Invariably they will switch back to English/German as it seems unnatural for them not to try to speak a foreigner's language. For them, conversing with a foreigner in Albanian is an alien experience. If you do manage to master Albanian you will open many doors through a mixture of heartfelt admiration and pride and taxi drivers will effuse for the whole journey and everyone wants to know how long it took you to learn and where. Since so few foreigners master Albanian, Albanians cannot usually guess from your accent where you are from.

The main problem with learning Albanian is a complex grammar, plus the fact that some words seem unrecognisable and therefore are difficult to remember. The upside is that the language is phonetic (words are spelt how they are said, unlike English, and with one exception the pronunciation of letters does not vary depending on word position). Another positive is the fact that the Albanian language has a limited vocabulary – it often has only one word where English or German has several eg: *keq* means 'bad', 'awful', 'dreadful' and 'wrong'. Therefore if you can persist with learning the language, you will find that it gets much easier after a while. There is a lot of dialect or street talk in Kosovo which can be difficult to grasp and Albanian rap songs are largely unintelligible to even the most linguistically skilled foreigners. Educated Kosovars will be able to switch to literary Albanian to help you understand. A great way to improve is to watch films with subtitles on Digital cable TV.

There are relatively few books which are of use in learning Albanian. Probably the best is *Routledge's Colloquial Albanian*, written by Isa Zymberi. This has a very grammatical bias however and gets difficult almost too quickly, so many readers give up at Chapter 8. If you can get hold of them (as they are both out of print) then use either *Learning Albanian in a Short Period of Time* by Bahri Beci and Merita Bruci, a bargain for €10 including CD – at the time of writing available at Buzuku or *Mësoni Shqip* by Çezar Kurti published by Legas in Tirana. The best dictionary is the *Oxford Albanian–English Dictionary*, but it is only available in the one language direction. You can download free flashcards on the 'Before you know it' website at www.byki.com.

The alphabet and pronunciation Albanian is spelt how it is pronounced (it is phonetic) and the pronunciation does not depend on the position in the word. It has 36 letters and some letters that are pronounced differently from English.

b, c, d, f, g, j, h, k, m, n, p, s, t, sh, v, xh, z are pronounced like the initial English sounds in 'book', 'church', 'dog', 'foot', 'goal', 'kit', 'mime', 'nine', 'pit', 'sip', 'ship', 'stop', 'tin', 'van', 'judge' and 'zoo'.
zh is pronounced like the 's' in 'pleasure'.
nj is pronounced like the 'n' in 'new'
th and dh are pronounced like 'think' and 'they'.
l is like 'leaf' or 'long' whereas double l ie: 'll' is pronounced like the final sound in 'bill' or 'hall'
r is rather like the Scottish pronunciation of 'r'; 'rr' is trilled
c is pronounced like 't' and 's' together
x is pronounced like 'd' and 'z'
q is like the 'tu' in 'mature'
gj is like the 'du' in 'endure'
ë is not not usually pronounced at all when it is at the end of a word and at the beginning is like the 'a' in 'around' when short and the vowel of 'burn' when long.
e is like 'get' or 'dead' or 'set'
a is like the vowel in 'cut'
u is like the English 'bush' when short and 'moon' when long
y does not exist in English – it is like the French 'une' or German 'ü'
o is like 'hot' when short and 'thought' when long
ç as in 'church'

In general the stress falls on the last word of a phrase and on the last stem of a compound word and on the last syllable of a polysyllabic word.

Words and phrases Expressions and phrases followed by a (g) indicate the Gheg dialect version which you will hear more often in Kosovo than the literary alternative, although Kosovars will understand both.

Essentials

Good morning	*mirëmëngjes* (until about 11.00)
Good afternoon	*mirëdita*
Good evening	*mirëmbrëma/ mirëmrama (g)*
Goodnight	*natën e mirë*
Hello	*tung* or *tungatjeta* (short for *tungjatjeta* (which is almost never used) or *përshëndetje* (very formal)
Goodbye	*Tung! Mirëupafshim* (more formal)
My name is …	*Emri im është* or *Unë jam …*
What is your name?	*Si quheni?/ Qysh e ki emnin (g)*
Where are you from?	*Prej nga jeni?*

I am from	Unë jam nga
... England	... Anglia
... Scotland/Wales/Ireland	... Skocia/ Uells/ Irlandë
... America	... Amerika
... Germany	... Gjermania
... Switzerland	... Zvicra
... France	... Franca
... Italy	... Italia
... Sweden	... Suedia
... Netherlands	... Holanda
... Canada	... Kanada
... Spain	... Spanja
... Austria	... Austria
Where do you live?	Ku banoni?
Are you visiting/working?	A keni ardhur për vizitë/ punë?
I am a tourist	Unë jam turist
How are you?	Si jeni? (or sometimes A jeni lodhë)
(literally 'are you tired?')	Qysh je (g)
Are you Albanian/Serbian?	A je shqiptar/ serb?
Pleased to meet you	Më vjen mirë që u takuam
Thank you	Faleminderit/ faliminerës (g)
Please	Ju lutem
Don't mention it	S'ka përse
Excuse me/I'm sorry	Më fal (ni)
Cheers!	Gëzuar!
yes	po
no	jo
good/bad	mire/ keq
ok	në rregull
of course	natyrisht
I don't know	Unë nuk e di
I don't understand	Nuk kuptoj/ S'kuptoj
I don't speak Albanian	Unë nuk flas shqip
Do you speak English?	A flisni (dini) Anglisht?
... German	... Gjermanisht
... Serbian	... Serbisht
... French	... Frëngjisht
Please would you speak more slowly	Ju lutem mund të flisni më ngadalë?
What did you just say?	Qysh? (g) Si thoni?
Do you understand?	A më kuptoni?
Is it possible ...?	A eshtë e mundur ...?
Wait!	Prit!
Don't	Mos
I want to make a phone call	Dua te bëj një telefonatë

Questions

How?	Si/ qysh? (g)
What?	Çfarë?
Where?	Ku?
What is it?	Çfarë është kjo?
Which?	E cila?
When?	Kur?
Why?	Pse?

Who?	*Kush?*
How much?	*Sa kushton?*

Numbers

0	*zero*
1	*një/nji (g)*
2	*dy*
3	*tre*
4	*katër*
5	*pesë*
6	*gjashtë*
7	*shtatë*
8	*tetë*
9	*nëntë/nandë (g)*
10	*dhjetë/dhetë (g)*
11	*njëmbëdhjetë/njimdhetë (g)*
12	*dymbëdhjetë/dymdhetë (g)*
20	*njëzet*
21	*njëzetenjë/njizetenji (g)*
30	*tridhjetë*
40	*katërdhjetë/katërdhetë (g)*
50	*pesëdhjetë/pesëdhetë (g)*
60	*gjashtëdhjetë*
70	*shtatëdhjetë*
80	*tetëdhjetë*
90	*nëntëdhjetë*
100	*njëqind*
1,000	*njëmijë/njijë (g)*

Time

What time is it?	*Sa është ora?*
today	*sot*
this evening	*sonte*
tomorrow	*nesër*
yesterday	*dje*
morning	*mëngjes*
evening	*mbrëmbje*
now	*tash*
and then/afterwards	*pastaj/masanej (g)*
early	*herët*
later	*më vonë/ma vonë (g)*
in … minutes	*për … minuta*

Days

Monday	*e Hënë*
Tuesday	*e Martë*
Wednesday	*e Mërkurë*
Thursday	*e Enjte/e Ejte (g)*
Friday	*e Premë*
Saturday	*e Shtunë*
Sunday	*e Diellë/e Diel (g)*

Months of the year

January	*Janar*
February	*Shkurt*
March	*Mars*
April	*Prill*
May	*Maj*
June	*Qershor*
July	*Korrik*
August	*Gusht*
September	*Shtator*
October	*Tetor*
November	*Nëntor/ Nandor (g)*
December	*Dhjetor/ Dhetor (g)*

Getting around
Public Transport

I'd like…	*Unë dua…*
…a one-way ticket	*… nje biletë vetëm vajtje*
…a return ticket	*… nje biletë vajtje-ardhje*
I want to go to…	*Unë dua të shkojë në …*
How much is it?	*Sa kushton?*
What times does it leave/arrive?	*Në sa ora niset?*
When is the next bus?	*Kur vjen autobusi tjeter*
I want to get off	*ka zbritje*
What time is it now?	*Sa është ora?*
The bus/train has been …	*Autobus/ tren është …*
… delayed	*… vonuar*
… cancelled	*… anuluar*
ticket office	*sportel*
timetable	*orari*
from	*nga*
to	*te*
bus station	*stacioni i autobusëve*
railway station	*stacioni trenit*
airport	*aeroport*
bus	*autobus*
minibus	*kombi*
train	*tren*
plane	*aeroplan*
boat	*barkë*
car	*veturë/ kerr (g)*
by foot	*në kembë/ në kamb (g)*
4×4	*kerr me katër rrota*
taxi	*taksi*
motorbike/moped	*motoçikletë*
bicycle	*biçikletë*
arrival	*arritja*
departure	*nisja*
here	*këtu*
there	*atje*
bon voyage!	*rrugë të mbarë!*

Private transport

Is this the road to…?	A *është kjo rruga për në …?*
Where is the petrol station?	*Ku është pompë benzines?*
Please fill it up	*Mbushem plotë ju lutem*
I'd like … litres	*unë dua … litra*
diesel	*naftë*
unleaded petrol	*benzinë pa plumb*
my car has broken down	*Më është prishur vetura*

Geography

road	*rruga*
crossroads	*kryq*
centre	*qendër*
roundabout	*rrethi*
boulevard	*bulevard*
bridge	*ura*
square	*sheshi*
mountain	*bjeshkë*
hill	*kodra*
river	*lumë*
border	*kufiri/kufini (g)*
town	*qytet*
village	*fshat/katund (g)*
neighbourhood	*Llagja/mahalla*

Road signs

give way	*stop*
danger	*rrezik*
entry/entrance	*hyrje*
no entry	*nuk lejohet hyrja*
exit	*dalje*
detour	*devijacion*
one way	*njëdrejtimësh*

Directions

Where is it?	*Ku është ai/ajo?*
How far is it to …?	*Sa larg është …?*
Is it near/far?	*Ai është afër/larg?*
Go straight ahead	*Shko drejt përpara/vetem e drejtë*
Turn left	*kthehumajtas*
Turn right	*kthehunë të djathtë*
… at the traffic lights	*… në semafor*
… at the roundabout	*në rrethi*
north	*veri*
south	*jug*
east	*lindje*
west	*perëndim*
behind	*prapa*
in front of	*përpara*
opposite	*përballë*
near	*afër*
far	*larg*
here/there	*këtu/atje*

beginning	*fillim*
end	*fund*
turning	*kthejsa*

Signs

entrance	*hyrja/hymja (g)*
exit	*dalja*
open	*hapur*
closed	*mbyllur*
toilets – men/women	*banjo – (wc) burrat / (wc) gratë*
information	*informacion*
no smoking	*Mos pi duhani*

Accommodation

Where is a cheap/good hotel?	*Ku është një hotel i lire? / imirë?*
Could you please write the address?	*A mund të shkruani adresën?*
Do you have any rooms available?	*A keni një dhomë?*
I'd like...	*Unë dua ...*
... a single room	*... njëshe (teke)*
... a double room	*... dyshe*
... a room with two beds	*... një dhomë me dy shtretër*
... a room with a bathroom	*... nje dhomë me banjo*
How much is it per night/person?	*Sa kushton për një natë/person?*
Where is the toilet/bathroom?	*Ku është banjo?*
Is there water?	*A ka ujë?*
Is there electricity?	*A ka rrymë?*
Is there a generator?	*A keni gjenerator?*
Do you have air conditioning?	*A keni klimë?*
Do you have internet/wireless?	*A keni internet/wireless?*
It's off/there's none	*s'ka*
It doesn't work	*s'punon*
shower	*dush*
towel	*peshkir (g)*
floor (storey)	*kat/i*
stairs	*shkallë*
Is breakfast included?	*A është i përfshirë mëngjesi?*
I am leaving today	*ssot do të shkoi*

Food and drink

restaurant	*restorant*
breakfast	*mëngjesi*
lunch	*dreka*
dinner	*darka*
waiter	*kamarier*
Do you have a table for ... people?	*A keni një tavolinë për ... njerëz?*
... a children's menu?	*... një menu për fëmijë*
I am a vegetarian	*Unë jam vegjetarian*
I don't eat meat/fish	*Unë nuk ha mish/peshk*
Do you have any vegetarian dishes?	*A keni ushqim vegjetarian?*
Please bring me a fork/knife/spoon/ a second plate	*Ju lutem, më sillni njëpirun/thikë /lugë /një pjatë të dytë*
Please may I have the bill?	*Faturën (llogarinë), ju lutem*

Basics

bread	*bukë*
butter	*gjalpë*
cheese (white/yellow)	*djathë (të bardhë/kaqkaval)*
oil (olive oil)	*vaj (ulliri)*
vinegar	*uthull*
pepper	*biber*
salt	*kripë*
sugar	*sheqer*
soup	*supë/çorba*
pasta	*makarona*
chocolate	*çokollatë (g)*
dessert	*ëmbëlsirë*
ice cream	*akullore*

Fruit

fruit	*pemë*
apples	*mollë*
bananas	*banane*
grapes	*rrush*
oranges	*portokall*
pears	*dardha*
watermelon	*bostanë*
yellow melon	*pjepër*

Vegetables

vegetables	*perime*
aubergine	*patligjanë i zi*
broccoli	*brokoli*
carrots	*karotë*
garlic	*hudhër*
onion	*qepë*
peppers	*speca*
potato	*patate/krompir*
tomatoes	*domatë/patligjanë*
salad	*sallatë*
beans (broad beans)	*pasul*

Fish

salmon	*salmon*
trout	*troftë*
tuna	*tuna*

Meat

beef (veal)	*mish viçi*
chicken meat	*mish pule*
pork	*mish derri*
lamb	*mish qengji*
sausage	*suxhuk*
kebabs/meatballs	*qebapa*

Drinks

beer	*birrë*
coffee (espresso/Turkish)	*kafe (espresso/ Turke)*
large macchiato	*makiato e madhe*
(espresso with milk & froth)	
small macchiato	*makiato e vogël*
(espresso with a dash of milk froth)	
orange juice	*portokall* or *jus*
apple juice	*lëngë mollë*
milk	*qumësht/ tamël (g)*
black tea	*çaj (i zi)*
water	*ujë*
still water (bottled)	*(shishe) ujë pa gas*
sparkling water	*ujë mineral me gas*
tap water	*ujë të thjeshtë*
wine (red/white)	*verë/ ven (g)*
a glass (a bottle) of	*një gotë (shishe) verë të*
red (white) wine	*zezë (të bardhë)*
ice	*akullë*

Shopping

I'd like to buy	*Dua të blej …*
Can/May I …?	*A mundem?/ A muj (g)?*
How much is it?	*Sa kushton?*
I don't like it.	*Nuk më pëlqen*
I'm just looking	*Vetem po kerkoj*
It's too expensive	*Ajo është shumë e shtrenjtë*
I'll take it	*Unë do të blej*
Please may I have …	*Më jepni ju lutem …*
Do you accept (Can I pay with)	*Mund të paguaj me*
… credit cards	*kartë krediti*
… debit cards	*debitkartë*
more	*më shumë*
less	*më pak*
smaller	*më e vogël*
bigger	*më e madhe*
I don't have small change	*S'kam tima*
Do you have (small) change?	*A keni tima?*

Communications/facilities/landmarks

I am looking for …	*Unë jam duke kërkuar për …*
When is … open?	*Kur hapet …?*
bank	*bankë*
post office	*zyrë postare, postë*
church	*kishë*
mosque	*xhami*
bridge	*urë*
embassy	*ambasada*
café	*kafe*
internet café	*Internet kafe*
ATM /cash machine	*bankomat*
supermarket	*supermarket*
restaurant	*restorant*

290

Emergency

Help!	*Ndihmë!*
Call a doctor!	*Thërrisni një doktor*
Please help me	*Ju lutem më ndihmoni*
There's been an accident	*Ka patur një aksident*
hospital	*spitali*
Accident and Emergency clinic	*emergjenca/urgjenca*
I'm lost	*Unë kam I humbur*
Go away	*Largohu!*
police	*polici*
fire	*zjarr*
ambulance	*ambulancë*
thief	*vjedhës*
I am ill	*Jam i/e sëmurë (male/female)* or *smutë (g)*

Health

diarrhoea	*diarre*
nausea	*të përzier*
doctor	*mjek*
dentist	*stomatolog/dentist*
prescription	*recetë*
pharmacy	*barnatore*
paracetamol	*paracetamol*
antibiotics	*antibiotikët*
antiseptic	*antiseptik*
tampons	*tamponë*
condoms	*kondom*
contraceptive	*kontraceptive*
I am ...	*Unë jam ...*
asthmatic	*astmatik*
epileptic	*epileptik*
diabetic	*diabetik*
I'm allergic to	*Unë jam alergjik ndaj*
penicillin	*penicilinë*
nuts	*arra*
bees	*bletë*
I have pain in my ...	*Unë kam dhimbje ...*
stomach	*stomaku*
ear	*veshi*
tooth	*dhëmbi*

Travel with children

Is there ...?	*A ka një ...*
... a children's menu?	*... menu për fëmijë*
... a highchair?	*... karrige për fëmijë*
Do you have ...?	*A keni ...*
infant milk formula	*qumësht formule*
nappies	*pampers*
baby wipes	*palloma te laqta*
dummy/pacifier	*biberon*
playground	*shesh lojërash*

AI

Family

Are you married?	*A jeni i/e martuar?*
No, I am single	*Jo, jam beqar-e/vetëm*
Yes, I am married	*Po, jam i/e martuar*
Do you have children?	*A keni fëmijë?*
No, I do not have children	*Jo, nuk kam fëmijë*
Yes, I have children	*Po, kam fëmijë*
How is your family?	*Si e ke familjen?*

Other

my/mine/ours/yours	*i/im/ime; i e imja; i e jona, i e juaja*
and/some/but	*dhe/disa/por*
this/that	*kjo/që, ky, kjo, se, që*
expensive/cheap	*shtrejtë/lirë*
open/closed	*hapur* or *çel (g)/mbyllur* or *mshel (g)*
ready	*gati*
busy/quiet	*i/e zënë/l qetë*
slow/fast	*ngadalë* or *kadal (g)/shpejt*
beautiful/ugly	*bukur/shëmtuar*
a lot	*shumë*
a little	*pak*
big/small	*i/e madh/ i/e vogël*
full/empty	*plotë/ zbrazët*
hot/cold	*ngrohtë* or *nxehtë/ftohtë*
old/new	*vjetër/të reja*
good/bad	*mire/keq*
early/late	*herët/vonë*
hot/cold	*nxehtë/të ftohtë*
difficult/easy	*veshtirë orshtirë (g)/lehtë*
boring/interesting	*i mërzitshëm/interesant*
by yourself/alone	*vetëm*
together	*bashkë*
with/without	*me/pa*
outside/inside	*jashtë/brenda*

Common Albanian phrases and questions

Mirëserdhët/Mirë së vini	Welcome
Mirë se ju gjeta	May I have found you well! (response to '*mirëserdhët*')
Shëndet/Shnet (g)	Bless you! (to someone who has sneezed)
Shëndet paç/Shnet paç (g)	the response to the above
Urime!	Congratulations!
S'ka problem!	No problem!
Puna e mbarë	May your work go well (when somebody is working)
Mbarëpaç	the response to the above
A jeni lodhë? (g)	Are you tired/how are you?
A po ju p...	Do you like...

SERBIAN Serbian is a Slavonic language in the same family as Slovenian, Macedonian and Bulgarian. Serbo-Croat is the traditional name for what was formerly regarded as a shared language with Croatia and Bosnia-Herzegovina. However, since these countries became independent they are now identifiably separate languages – Serbian, Croatian and Bosnian (with Montenegrin joining in) – although the speakers understand each other and read each other's books and newspapers without much adaptation. In Kosovo you arguably find variants of all three spoken: Croatian in Janjevo and Letnica, Bosnian by the Bosniaks and Serbian by the Serbs. As for the Gorani, theirs is a variant of their own with much Macedonian. In any event, all three groups include some Turkish words in their dialect.

Recommended books (with accompanying CDs) for learning Serbian are Routledge's *Colloquial Croatian and Serbian* by Celia Hawkesworth, *Teach Yourself Serbian* (probably less heavyweight and an easier start) and the very comprehensive, grammar-orientated two books from the Serbian Language Institute which are hard to find on the internet and really only available in Belgrade bookshops. See also the 'before you know it' series on the internet (*www.byki.com*), a good way to learn vocabulary.

Pronunciation and alphabet Serbo-Croat has two alphabets – Cyrillic (almost all official documents are in this) and Latin. Tonal stress is almost never complicated with the stress on the last syllable. Generally, however, the pronunciation is not as complex as the grammar – there are three genders and the nouns decline.

Unusual pronunciations are:

c	as ts
č	as **ch**urch
ć	like **c**iao
dž	as in **j**et
đ	as in **dy**
h	as in Scottish lo**ch**
j	as in **y**es
lj	like **ly**
nj	as in on**i**on
s	like **s**it
š	like **sh**ut
u	like sh**oo**t
z	**z**ebra
ž	plea**s**ure

Essentials

Good morning	*Dobro jutro*
Good day/afternoon	*Dobar dan*
Good evening	*Dobro veče*
Good night	*Laku noć*
Hello	*Zdravo*
Goodbye	*Do viđenja/ćao*
My name is…	*Ja se zovem…*
What is your name?	*Kako se zovete?*
I am from …	*Ja sam iz …*
… England	*… Engleske*
… Scotland/Wales/Ireland	*… Škotske/Velsa/Irske*
… America	*… Amerike*
… Germany	*… Njemačke*
… Switzerland	*… Švajcarske*
… France	*… Francuske*

... Italy	*... Italije*
... Sweden	*... Švedske*
... Netherlands	*... Holandije*
... Canada	*... Kanade*
... Spain	*... Španije*
... Austria	*... Austrije*
Where do you live?	*Gde živite?*
Are you visiting/working?	*Da li ste posetilac/ radite?*
I am a tourist	*Ja sam turista*
How are you?	*Kako ste?*
Are you Albanian/Serbian?	*Jeste li Albanac/ Srbin?*
Pleased to meet you	*Drago mi je*
Thank you	*hvala*
Please	*molim*
Don't mention it	*nema problema*
Cheers!	*Živeli!*
yes	*Da*
no	*Ne*
good/bad	*dobar/ loš*
OK	*u redu*
Of course	*naravno*
I don't know	*neznam*
I don't understand	*Ne razumem*
Do you speak English?	*Govorite li engleski?*
I don't speak Serbian	*ja ne govorim srpski*
I am	*Ja sam*
... a foreigner	*... stranac*
... German	*... Nemac*
... Serbian	*... Srbin*
... French	*... Francuz*
Please could you speak more slowly?	*Molim vas da govorite sporije?*
What did you just say?	*Šta ste upravo rekli?*
Do you understand?	*Da li razumete?*
Is it possible?	*Da li je moguće?*
Wait!	*Sačekajte!*
Don't	*Ne*
I want to make a phone call	*Želim da telefoniram*

Questions

How?	*Kako?*
What?	*Šta?*
Where	*Gde*
What is it?	*Šta je to?*
Which?	*Koji?*
When?	*Kada?*
Why?	*Zašto?*
Who?	*Ko?*
How much (does it cost)?	*Koliko košta?*

Numbers

0	*nula*
1	*jedan*
2	*dva*

3	*tri*
4	*četiri*
5	*pet*
6	*šest*
7	*sedam*
8	*osam*
9	*devet*
10	*deset*
11	*jedanaest*
12	*dvanaest*
20	*dvadeset*
21	*dvatdesetjedan*
30	*trideset*
40	*četrdeset*
50	*pedeset*
60	*šesdeset*
70	*sedamdeset*
80	*osamdeset*
90	*devedeset*
100	*sto*
1000	*hiljadu*

Time

What time is it?	*Koliko je sati?*
Today	*danas*
This evening	*večeras*
Tomorrow	*sutra*
Yesterday	*juče*
Morning	*jutro*
Evening	*veče*
Now	*sada*
And then/afterwards	*a onda/posle*
Early	*rano*
Later	*posle*
In ... minutes	*za ... minuta*

Days

Monday	*ponedeljak*
Tuesday	*utorak*
Wednesday	*sreda*
Thursday	*četvrtak*
Friday	*petak*
Saturday	*subota*
Sunday	*nedelja*

Months

January	*januar*	July	*juli*
February	*februar*	August	*avgust*
March	*mart*	September	*septembar*
April	*april*	October	*oktobar*
May	*maj*	November	*novembar*
June	*juni*	December	*decembar*

Getting around
Public transport

I would like a …	Želim …
… one-way ticket	… kartu u jednum pravcu
… return ticket	… povratnu kartu
I want to go to …	Želim da odem u …
What time does it … leave/arrive?	Kada … polazi/dolazi?
I want to get off!	Želim da sišem!
What time is it now?	Koliko je sati?
The bus/train has been …	autobus/voz je …
delayed	odložen
cancelled	otkažan
ticket office	biletarnica
timetable	red vožnje
from	od
to	do
bus station	autobuska stanica
railway station	železnička stanica
airport	aerodrom
What time is the next bus?	kada polazi sledeći autobus?
bus	autobus
train	voz
boat	brod

Private transport

car	auto
on foot	pešice
4×4	pogon na četiri točkat
Taxi	taxi
motorbike/moped	motorcikl/moped
bicycle	bicikl
arrival	dolazak
departure	odlazak
here/there	ovde/tamo
Bon voyage!	Sretan put!
Is this the road to …?	Da li je ovo put za …?
How do I get to …?	Kako mogu da dođem do …?
Where is ….?	Gde je …?
the petrol station	Bezinska stanica
the church/monastery	crkva/manastir
Please fill it up	molim vas napunite ga
I'd like … litres	hteo bih … litara
diesel	dizel
unleaded petrol	bezolovni bezin
My car has broken down	moj auto se pokvario

Geography

road/street	ulica
crossroads	raskrsnica
centre	centar
roundabout	ringišpil
boulevard	bulevar

bridge	most
square	trg
hill/mountain/peak	brdo/planina/vrh
river	reka
border	granica
village/town	selo/grad

Road signs

give way	propuštanje puta
danger	opasnost
entry/entrance	ući/ulaz
no entry	zabranjen ulaz
exit	izlaz
detour	zaobilazni put
one way	jednosmerna

Directions

Where is …?	Gde je …?
go straight ahead	Pravo
turn …	skrenite …
left	levo
right	desno
at the traffic lights	na semaforu
at the roundabout	na kružnom toku
How far is it to …?	koliko je daleko do …?
near	blizu
far	daleko
up/down	gore/dole
under/over	ispod/iznad
north	sever
south	jug
east	istok
west	zapad
behind	iza
in front of	ispred
opposite	naspram
near	blizo
far	daleko
beginning	početak
end	završetak
turning	skretanje

General signs

entrance/exit	ulaz/izlaz	УЛАЗ/ИЗЛАЗ
open/closed	Otvoreno/zatvoreno	ОТВОРЕНО/ЗАТВОРЕНО
information	informacije	ИНФОРМАЦИЈЕ
prohibited	zabranjeno	ВАБРАЊЕНО
toilets	toaleti	ТОАЛЕТИ
men	muški	МУШКИ
women	ženski	ЖЕНСКИ
danger	opasnost	ОПАСНОСТ
arrival	dolazak	ДОЛАЗАК

departure	*polazak*	ПОЛАЗАК
No smoking	*zabranjeno pušenje*	ЗАБРАЊЕНО ПУШЕЊЕ
No entry	*ulaz zabranjen*	УЛАЗ ЗАБРАЊЕН

Accommodation

Where is a cheap/good hotel?	*Gdje je jeftin/dobar hotel?*
Could you please write the address?	*Možete li molim vas da napišete adresu?*
Do you have any rooms available?	*Da li imate soba na raspolaganju?*
I'd like ...	*hteo bih ...*
a single room	*jednokrevetnu sobu*
a double room	*dvokrevetnu sobu*
a room with two beds	*sobu sa dva kreveta*
a room with a bathroom	*sobu sa kupatilom*
How much is it per night/person?	*Koliko košta noćenje/po osobi?*
Where is the toilet/bathroom?	*Gde je WC/kupatilo?*
Is there water?	*Imate li vode?*
Is there electricity?	*Imate-li struju?*
Is there a generator?	*Imate li generator?*
Do you have air conditioning?	*Imate li klima ujređaj?*
Do you have internet/wireless?	*Imate li internet/bežični*
It's off/there's none	*isključeno je/nema tu*
It doesn't work	*ne radi*
shower	*tuširanje*
towel	*peškir*
floor (storey)	*sprat*
stairs	*stepenice*
Is breakfast included?	*Je li doručak uključen u cenu?*
I am leaving today	*Ja odlazim danas*

Food and drink

food	*hrana*
restaurant	*restoran*
tavern	*konak, konoba*
breakfast	*doručak*
lunch	*ručak*
dinner	*večera*
waiter	*konobar*
Do you have a table for ... people?	*da li imate sto za ... ljudi?*
A children's menu	*meni za decu*
I am a vegetarian	*ja sam vegetarijanac*
I don't eat meat/fish	*ja ne jedem meso/ribu*
Do you have any vegetarian dishes?	*Imate li vegetarijanska jela?*
Please bring me ...	*molim vas, donesite mi ...*
a fork/knife/spoon	*viljuška /nož/kašika*
plate	*tanjir*
bottle	*flaša*
glass	*čaša*
cake	*kolač, torta*
drink (noun)	*piće*
fish	*riba*
fish soup	*riblja čorba*
Please may I have the bill?	*Račun molim! / molim vas mogu li obijem račun?*

Basics

bread	*hleb*
butter	*puter*
cheese	*sir*
eggs	*jaja*
honey	*med*
(olive) oil	*(maslinovo) ulje*
vinegar	*sirće*
pepper	*biber*
salt	*so*
sugar	*šećer*
soup	*čorba*
pasta	*pasta*
chocolate	*čokolada*
dessert	*desert*
home-made	*domaće*
ice cream	*sladoled*

Fruit

fruit	*voće*
watermelon	*lubenica*
apples	*jabuka*
bananas	*banana*
grapes	*grožđe*
oranges	*pomorandža*
pears	*kruška*
yellow melon	*dinja*
strawberry	*jagoda*
plum	*šljiva*

Vegetables

vegetables	*povrće*
salad	*salata*
broccoli	*brokoli*
carrot	*šargarepa*
garlic	*beli luk*
onion	*crni luk*
pepper	*biber*
potato	*krompir*
tomato	*paradajz*

Meat

meat	*meso*
beef	*govedina*
chicken	*piletina*
pork	*svinsko meso*
lamb	*jagnetina*
veal	*teletina*
ham	*šunka*
sausage	*kobasica*
grilled	*sa roštilj*
roasted meat	*pečeno meso*

kebab/meatballs	ćevapi/ ćufte
veal soup	teleća čorba

Drinks

beer	pivo
coffee	kafa
large macchiato	veliki makijato
small macchiato	mali makijato
orange juice	đus
apple juice	sok od jabuka
milk	mleko
tea (black)	čaj (crni)
tea	čaj
water (mineral)	voda (kisela voda)
wine (white/red)	vino (belo/ crno)
cup	šoljica
a bottle	boca
red/white wine	crno/ bielo vino
mineral /tap water	mineralna/ kisela voda
ice	led
plum brandy	šljivovica

Shopping

I'd like to buy ...	hteo bih da kupim ...
Can/may I ...?	mogu/ smem li da
I don't like it	ne sviđa mi se
I'm just looking	samo gledam
It's too expensive	previše je skupo
I'll take it	uzeću je
Please may I have ...	molim vas mogu da dobijem
Do you accept (Can I pay with ...)	da li primate / mogu li da platim sa ...
... credit/debit card	... kreditnom karticom
more/less	više/ manje
smaller/bigger	manja/ veća
I don't have small change	ja nemam sitno
Do you have (small) change	da li imate sitno?

Communications/facilities/landmarks

I am looking for ...	ja tražim za ...
When is ... open?	Kada je otvoren?
café	Kafić
Internet cafe	internet kafe
ATM/cash machine	bankomat
supermarket	supermarket/ samoposluga
bank	banka
post office	pošta
chemist (pharmacy)	apoteka
discount	popust
shop	radnja
market	pijaca
money	novac
cheaper	jeftinije

Emergency

Help!	*Pomoć!*
Call a doctor!	*Požovite lekara!*
Please help me!	*Molim vas pomožite mi*
There's been an accident	*tamo je bio udes*
hospital	*bolnica*
accident/emergency clinic	*nesreća/ambulanta*
I'm lost	*izgubio sam se!*
Go away!	*Odlazite!*
police	*policija*
fire	*vatra*
ambulance	*Hitna pomoć*
thief	*lopov*
I am ill	*ja sam bolestan*

Health

health	*zdravije*
diarrhoea	*proliv*
nausea	*mučina*
cold	*prehlada*
doctor	*lekar*
dentist	*zubar*
prescription	*recept*
pharmacy	*apoteka*
paracetamol	*paracetamol*
antibiotics	*antibiotik*
antiseptic	*antiseptički*
tampons	*tamponi*
condoms	*kondomi*
contraceptive	*kontraceptivni*
sun block	*krema za sunčanje sa zaštitnim faktorom*
I am ...	*ja sam ...*
asthmatic	*astmatičar*
epileptic	*epiletpičar*
diabetic	*dijabetičar*
I'm allergic to ...	*alergičan sam na ...*
penicillin	*penicilin*
nuts	*orase*
bees	*pčele*
I have a pain in my ...	*imam bolove u ...*
stomach	*stomaku*
ear	*uvo*
tooth	*zub*

Travel with children

Is there ...	*da li postoji ...*
a children's menu	*meni za decu*
a highchair	*visoke stolice*
Do you have ...	*da li imate ...*
infant milk/formula	*mleko za odojčad /formule*
nappies	*pelenje*
baby wipes	*vlažne maramice za bebe*

| dummy/pacifier | lažna/cucla |
| playground | igralište |

Family

Family	porodica
Are you married?	Da li ste oženjeni?
No, I am single	Ne, ja sam neoženjen
Yes, I am married	Da ja sam oženjen
Do you have children?	Da li imate dece?
No I do not have children?	Ne ja nemam decu
Yes, I have children	Da, imam decu
How is your family?	Kako je vaša porodica?

Other

my/mine/yours	moj/moj/tvoj
and/some/but	i/neki/ali
this/that	ovo/taj
expensive/cheap	skup/jeftin
open/closed	otoreno/zatvoreno
ready	spreman
busy/quiet	zauzet/tiho
slow/fast	polako/brzo
beautiful/ugly	lepo/a/ružan
a lot	puno
a little	malo
full/empty	pun/prazan
hot/cold	toplo/hladno
old/new	stari/novi
good/bad	dobar/loš
early/late	rano/kasno
difficult/easy	teško/lako
boring/interesting	dosadan/zanimliv
by yourself/alone	samo/a/po sebi
together	zajedno
with/without	sa/bez
outside/inside	izvan/unutrašnja

Appendix 2

ALBANIAN AND SERBIAN PLACE NAMES

ALBANIAN	SERBIAN
Deçan	Dečani
Dragash	Dragaš
Ferizaj	Uroševac
Fushë-Kosova	Kosovo Polje
Gjakova	Djakovica
Gjilan	Gnjilane
Gllogovc (Drenas/Drenica)	Glogovac
Istog	Istok
Kaçanik	Kačanik
Kamenicë/Dardan	Kamenica
Klinë	Klina
Leposaviq	Leposavić
Lipjan	Lipljan
Malisheva	Mališevo
Mitrovica	Mitrovica/Kosovska Mitrovica
Novobërdë	Novo Brdo
Obiliq/Kastriot	Obilić
Pejë	Peć
Podujeva/Besian	Podujevo
Prishtina	Priština
Prizren	Prizren
Rahovec	Orahovac
Shterpcë	Štrpce
Shtime	Štimlje
Skenderaj	Srbica
Suha Rekë/Therandë	Suva Reka
Viti	Vitina
Vushtrri	Vučitrn
Zubin Potok	Zubin Potok
Zveçan	Zvečan

Appendix 3

BOOKS The violent breakup of Yugoslavia and NATO's intervention sparked a lot of literature on the region and Kosovo in particular. Further, subsequent to 1999 numerous reports, studies and doctoral theses have been written on Kosovo by academics, journalists and think tanks from around the world. The list of titles, books and internet sites below is a good starting point for anyone planning a trip or short stay in the region – it is not intended to be exhaustive.

Books specifically on Kosovo

Backer, Berit *Behind Stone Walls* Dukagjini Publishing House, 2003. The most vivid account of traditional Albanian village life based on the life-long research on Isniq village near Peja by the passionate Norwegian anthropologist Berit Backer.

Bieber, Florian and Daskalovski, Dizas *Understanding the War in Kosovo* 2003. A series of insightful, probing short essays from authors in Belgrade and international academic institutions about the Serbian Albanian and independence question. A good read if you want to understand more than the basic history and go right behind the origins of the 1999 conflict.

Clark, Howard *Civil Resistance in Kosovo* Pluto Press, 2000. The best account on Kosovo in the 1990s, including detailed descriptions on the parallel Albanian government and education system. Very readable and highly recommended.

Independent International Commission on Kosovo *Kosovo Report* Oxford University Press, 2000

Gowing, Elizabeth, *Keeping Bees in Kosovo, Travels in Blood and Honey* 2010. An account of an international working in Kosovo who takes time to learn Albanian language and culture. Available on Amazon.

Judah, Tim *Kosovo: What Everyone needs to Know* Oxford University Press, USA (September 29, 2008). A compelling summary of Kosovo's recent history and its path to independence.

Judah, Tim *Kosovo: War and Revenge* Yale University Press, 2002. Judah is one of the leading journalists and commentators and a specialist in Balkan affairs. He is also the author of the book *The Serbs: History, Myth and the Destruction of Yugoslavia (see below)*.

Kelmendi, Migjen and Desku, Arlinda *Who is Kosovar? Kosovar Identity* Java, 2005. This publication of essays debating Kosovar identity is a first in Kosovo's post war history.

King, Iain and Mason, Whit *How the World Failed Kosovo* 2006. First-hand account written by former UN employees about the success and failure of Kosovo's unique nation-building experiment.

Malcolm, Noel *Kosovo a Short History* Pan Macmillian, 1998. This is not short (356 pages) but that can be the only criticism. Noel Malcolm is possibly the only international historian who has tried to really investigate the Kosovo history back from the early days without being clouded by his own origins. Tremendous research and widely regarded as 'the Bible' on Kosovo history. Has been translated into Albanian and has won wide respect from Kosovars for his depth of insight and research.

Maksutaj, Rexhep *Isniq Through Centuries* Shtëpia Botuese Libri Shkollor, 2002. Interesting account of customs and rites in Western Kosovo.

OSCE Kosovo Verification Mission *Kosovo/Kosova As Seen, As Told Parts I + II* 1999. Based on interviews with refugees and victims of the war, this is the best account of what actually happened in Kosovo in 1998 and 1999.

Peace Research Center *Confrontation or Coexistence* 1997. Interesting compilation of articles on different angles of the Kosovo problem.

Petritsch, Kaser, Pichler *Kosovo Kosova* Wieser Verlag, 1999. An illustrated account of Kosovo's history available in German and Albanian.

Sherifi, Remsije *Shadow Behind the Sun* 2007. Stories of a Kosovar refugee on arrival in the UK, winner of Scottish book prize.

Sullivan, Stacy *Be Not Afraid for you have Sons in America* 2004. An extremely readable true account of how a Brooklyn roofer diaspora helped ferry arms into Kosovo and persuaded the US to join in the war.

Vickers, Miranda *Between Serb and Albanian: A History of Kosovo* Hurst & Company, 1998. A vivid history of Kosovo, particularly strong on the 20th century, taking the reader up to the emergence of the Kosovo Liberation Army in 1997.

Weller, Mark *Contested Statehood: Kosovo's Struggle for Independence* Oxford University Press, 2009. A detailed history of what really happened behind the scenes from an international law perspective.

Zogiani, Salih *Albanian Anecdotes* 2006. Compilation of stories and Albanian tales.

Interesting articles

European Stability Initiative (ESI) *Cutting the Lifeline: Migration, Families and the Future of Kosovo* 2006. A detailed narrative of village and family life in today's Kosovo and a critical assessment of migration, rural development and family structures. Available in English, Albanian and German on www.esiweb.org.

European Stability Initiative (ESI) *The Lausanne Principle: Multiethnicity, Territory and the Future of Kosovo's Serbs* 2004. A carefully researched analysis on the Kosovo Serb community, the prospect for returns and for a multiethnic Kosovo. An English, Albanian and Serbian version can be downloaded on www.esiweb.org.

European Stability Initiative (ESI) *People or Territory? A Proposal for Mitrovica* 2004. Drawing on a detailed study of the political economy of Mitrovica region, this policy proposal is enlightening for anyone trying to understand the politics of Mitrovica today in English, Albanian and Serbian language on www.esiweb.org.

Iniciativa Kosovare për Stabilitet (Kosovar Initiative for Stability) *Reconstruction National Integrity System Survey – Kosovo* 2007. A good overview of Kosovo's post-war institutional landscape and assessment of successes and failures of donor intervention. Available on www.iksweb.org.

International Crisis Group *UNMIK's Kosovo Albatross: Tackling Division in Mitrovica* 2002. A good introduction for first-timers to understand the Mitrovica conundrum. Available on www.crisisgroup.org.

International Crisis Group *Collapse in Kosovo* 2004. The most detailed account of what happened during the 2004 March riots. Downloadable on www.crisisgroup.org.

World Bank *Kosovo Poverty Assessment* 2005. A detailed study on the nature and extent of poverty in Kosovo, available on www.worldbank.org/kosovo.

Books on Albanians

Gawrych, George *The Crescent and the Eagle: Ottoman Rule, Islam and the Albanians 1874-1913* I B Tauris & Co, 2006.

Jacques, Edwin, *The Albanians: An Ethnic History from Prehistoric Times to the Present* McFarland & Company, 1994. The author has lived among the Albanians for a big part of his life as a missionary. The book has been translated into Albanian and by some local historians is considered among the best books written by foreigners for Albanians.

Pettifier, James and Vickers, Miranda *The Albanian Question Reshaping the Balkans* I B Tauris & Co, 2007. A good read for anyone trying to disentangle the regional dimension of the Kosovo conflict.

Schwandner-Sievers, Stephanie and Fischer, Bernd J *Albanian Identities: Myth and History* Hurst & Company, 2002. A compilation of articles on Albanian myths, national identity and religion.

Books on Yugoslavia and the Balkans

Allcock, John *Explaining Yugoslavia* Hurst & Company 2000. A concise account of the Yugoslav system, including a detailed account of Yugoslavia's unique economic system.

David, Rieff, *A Bed for the Night, Humanitarianism in Crisis* Vintage Books 2002. Readable, if perturbing insight about whether humanitarian organisations have lost sight of their purpose.

Glenny, Misha, *The Fall of Yugoslavia: The Third Balkan War* Penguin Books, 1992. Glenny is a journalist and specialist on Eastern Europe and Southern Europe and international organised crime. As a BBC correspondent he reported on the crisis in Yugoslavia in the late 1980s and early 1990s as the Central European correspondent.

Glenny, Misha *The Balkans: Nationalism, War and the Great Powers 1804-1999* Granta Books, 1999. Misha Glenny and Mark Mazower take very different approaches to the modern history of the Balkans. Glenny, a journalist, offers a long but lively narrative of war, politics and people, with generalisations used to help make sense of that. Mazower, a historian, offers a short but insightful account of long-term processes and trends, with details used to illustrate those. Both seem reasonably objective – neither is himself in the grip of any nationalist fervour – and both provide references, an index, and an excellent selection of maps (essential for following the complexities of border changes).

Jelavich, Barbara *History of the Balkans, Volumes I + II* Cambridge University Press, 1994 (reprinted). The textbook on Balkan history.

Judah, Tim, *The Serbs: History, Myth and the Destruction of Yugoslavia* Yale University Press, 2000. Judah lived in Belgrade from 1990 to 1995, reporting for the London *Times* and the *New York Review of Books*. Here the author provides a perspective on the Bosnian war in particular but also on the Serbs as a nation and their politicians.

Kaplan, Robert *Balkan Ghosts* 1994 (out of print). Attractive writing style. A 1990s journey through the Balkans with an insightful account of the region's troubled history.

Lampe, John R *Yugoslavia as History: Twice there was a country* Cambridge University Press, 2000 (2nd edition). Detailed and very readable account of the break-up of Yugoslavia in light of its troubled history.

Lebor, Adam *Milosevic: A Biography* Bloomsbury, 2002. This book gets behind the personal character of Milosevic, his family relationships and upbringing and tries to understand the psyche of an individual who after Hitler's demise is arguably accountable for the highest number of deaths in Europe.

Little, Allan and Silber, Laura *The Death of Yugoslavia* BBC Paperback. The best account of the Yugoslav wars.

Mazower, Mark *Salonica City of Ghosts* HarperCollins, 2004. A fantastically written history of Thessaloniki. Highly recommended to every occasional Thessaloniki-weekender.

West, Rebecca *Black Lamb and Grey Falcon* Canongate Books, 1993. Yugoslavia in the 1930s, wrong in places but an engaging, opinionated style.

WEB RESOURCES
News links

www.b92.net The most respected of Serbia's news channels. Includes news reports in Serbian and English. Is followed not just by Serbs, but also by Albanians, and you get a good insight on the Serbian angle on stories in Kosovo. Serb and English.

www.balkaninsight.com English language news by the Balkan investigative reporting network

www.gazetaexpress.com A local express newspaper. Albanian language only.

www.kohaditore.com Possibly Kosovo's most serious and respected newspaper (Albanian only). See also **www.koha.net** which is the related site for the sister TV station, which is more light-hearted in outlook.

www.zeri.info Kosovo's second serious newspaper (Albanian language only).

www.kosovapress.com This news agency was founded during the Kosovo war to mainly inform people about the war zones where the press could not penetrate.

www.kosovalive.com Mostly subscription only and Albanian language only. Well-respected enough to be commonly quoted by the BBC.

www.newkosovareport.net A somewhat simplistic and pro Kosovo propagandist English language site but with some useful news and nice cultural articles.

www.rtklive.com Kosovo's publicly funded broadcaster, showing in three languages.

www.telegrafi.com One of the pure online Albanian language news sites with a lot of material and hits.

www.shkabaj.tk Compilation of most Albanian-language online news (Albanian only but great for further links to international online news).

Travel websites

www.beinkosovo.com Well designed website by an entrepreneurial young group of Kosovars working in the tourist industry.

www.hotelskosova.com Some hotels are listed here.

www.kosovaguide.com A new USAID funded site to promote travel tips and tours in Kosovo

Government links

www.assembly-kosova.org Kosovo Assembly

www.ks-gov.net Kosovo Government

www.pm-ksgov.net Kosovo Prime Minister's Office

www.mafrd-ks.org Ministry of Agriculture, Forestry and Rural Development of Kosovo

www.ks-gov.net/masht Ministry of Education Science and Technology

www.ks-gov.net/mem Ministry of Energy and Mining

www.mmph.org Ministry of Environment and Spatial Planning

www.mfe-ks.org Ministry of Finance and Economy, including tax information

www.ks-gov.net/mpms Ministry of Labor and Social Welfare

www.ks-gov.net/mshp Ministry of Public Services

www.mti-ks.org Ministry of Trade and Industry

www.mtpt.org Ministry of Transport and Post – Telecommunication

www.ks-gov.net/ESK Statistical Office of Kosovo – thin but basic statistics including birth, deaths, employment. Hopefully will improve with time.

www.unmikonline.org/regulations/index.htm UNMIK Official Gazette

Municipalities

www.decani-komuna.org Municipality of Deçan/Dečane

www.komuna-dragash.org Municipality of Dragash/Dragaš

www.ferizaj-komuna.org Municipality of Ferizaj/Urosevač

www.gjakova-komuna.org Municipality of Gjakova/Djakovica

www.gjilani-komuna.org Municipality of Gjilan/Gnjilane

www.kamenica-komuna.org Municipality of Kamenica

www.istogu.com Municipality of Istog/Istok/Burim

www.junik-komune.org Municipality of Junik

www.komuna-kacanik.org Municipality of Kacanik

www.komuna-kline.org/al/history Municipality of Klina
www.lipjan-komuna.org Municipality of Lypjan/Lipljan
www.leposavic.org Municipality of Leposaviç/Leposaviq
www.malisheva.org Municipality of Malisheva
www.mitrovica-komuna.org Municipality of Mitrovica
www.peja-komuna.org Municipality of Peja/Peć
www.podujeva-komuna.org Municipality of Podujeva/Podujevo/Besiana
www.prishtina-komuna.org Municipality of Prishtina/Priština
www.prizreni-komuna.org Municipality of Prizren
www.suhareka-komuna.org Municipality of Suhareka/Suva Reka/Theranda
www.shtime-komuna.org Municipality of Shtime/Štimlje
www.komuna-viti.org Municipality of Viti/Vitina
www.kk-vushtrri.org Municipality of Vushtrri/Vučitrn

Business links

www.amchamksv.org American Chamber of Commerce, Kosovo.
www.cbak-kos.org Central Banking Authority of Kosovo (CBAK). Details of banks, insurance companies, inflation and lending rates
www.eciks.org Economic Initiative for Kosovo. Promotes foreign investment.
www.kosovo-eicc.org Euro Info Centre.
www.ero-ks.org Energy Regulator.
www.kosovo-mining.org Independent Commission for Mines and Minerals (ICMM). Includes some good maps for sale and the place to go if you fancy being part of the silver rush!
www.seerecon.org Joint World Bank/European Commission Site – southeastern European news, including energy sector.
www.oek-kcc.org Kosovo Chamber of Commerce. Focus more on local businesses but well respected and with AmCham (see above) one of the few organisations really trying to get their voice heard in a difficult economic climate.
www.usaidkbs.com Kosovo Business Support. Supports construction and agricultural business sectors.
www.pak-ks.org Privatisation Agency of Kosovo. How to buy a piece of Kosovo.

Public utilities

www.kek-energy.com Kosovo Energy Corporation (KEK). Includes all the energy timings, how/where to pay your bill.
www.kosovorailways.com Kosovo Railways Train timetable and information.
www.ptkonline.com Post and Telecommunications of Kosovo (PTK). Very detailed information on post (see also www.postaekosoves), philately and everything you need to know about your phone.
www.airportpristina.com Prishtina International Airport – flight times, airport information.
www.unmikcustoms.org UNMIK Customs. If you need to get things into the country.

Think tanks and other institutions

www.balkansunflowers.org Balkan Sunflowers. Interested in hands-on volunteers.
www.esiweb.org European Stability Initiative
www.birn.eu.com Balkan Investigative Reporting Network – news and media
www.chwb.org/kosovo Cultural Heritage NGO
www.iksweb.org Kosovo Stability Initiative
www.crisisgroup.org International Crisis Group
www.gapinstitute.org Institute for Advanced Studies
www.kipred.net Kosovo Institute for Policy Research and Development

www.kfos.org Kosovo Open Society Institute – Soros Foundation
www.kcsfoundation.org Kosovo Civil Society Foundation
www.gmfus.org/balkantrust Balkan Trust for Democracy
www.sfera-institute.com Institute for Social and Policy Studies
www.riinvestinstitute.org Riinvest – Institute for Development Research
www.balkanspeacepark.org Cross-border Peace Park Project (Montenegro, Albania, Kosovo)

Radio and music
www.dardamedia.com What's on in the clubs and theatres of Kosovo.
www.blueskylive.com Radio Blue Sky
www.radio-dukagjini.com Radio Dukagjini
www.kimradio.net Radio KIM
www.radio-kosova.com Radio Kosova
www.radioplusi.com Radio Plus
www.radiotema.net Radio Tema
www.radio21.net Radio21
www.albasoul.com Albanian Music, history and more.
www.yu4you.com/eng/international Internet store for Balkan music.

International organisations
www.dfid.gov.uk/countries/europe/kosovo.asp Department for International Development (DFID)
www.eulex-kosovo.eu – European Union Rule of Law Mission
www.delprn.cec.eu.int European Commission Liaison Office to Kosovo
http://ec.europa.eu/enlargement/potential-candidates/kosovo Official European Commission Enlargement portal on Kosovo.
www.eumm.org European Union Monitoring Mission (EUMM)
www.un.org/icty International Criminal Tribunal for Yugoslavia
www.ico-kos.org International Civilian Office, EU Special Representative
www.nato.int/kfor NATO Kosovo Force (KFOR)
www.osce.org/kosovo OSCE Mission in Kosovo
www.stabilitypact.org Stability Pact for South Eastern Europe
www.kosovo.undp.org United Nations Development Programme (UNDP)
www.unhcr.org United Nations High Commissioner for Refugees (UNHCR)
www.unmikonline.org United Nations Mission in Kosovo, including all UNMIK legislation
www.unosek.org United Nations Office of the Special Envoy of the Secretary-General for the status process for Kosovo (UNOSEK)
www.usaid.gov/locations/europe_eurasia/countries/ko United States Agency for International Development (USAID)

Bradt Travel Guides

www.bradtguides.com

Africa

Access Africa: Safaris for People with Limited Mobility	£16.99
Africa Overland	£16.99
Algeria	£15.99
Angola	£17.99
Botswana	£16.99
Cameroon	£15.99
Cape Verde Islands	£14.99
Congo	£15.99
Eritrea	£15.99
Ethiopia	£16.99
Gambia, The	£13.99
Ghana	£15.99
Johannesburg	£6.99
Madagascar	£15.99
Malawi	£15.99
Mali	£14.99
Mauritius, Rodrigues & Réunion	£15.99
Mozambique	£13.99
Namibia	£15.99
Niger	£14.99
Nigeria	£17.99
North Africa: Roman Coast	£15.99
Rwanda	£14.99
São Tomé & Principe	£14.99
Seychelles	£14.99
Sierra Leone	£16.99
Sudan	£15.99
Tanzania, Northern	£14.99
Tanzania	£17.99
Uganda	£16.99
Zambia	£17.99
Zanzibar	£14.99
Zimbabwe	£15.99

Britain

Britain from the Rails	£14.99
Go Slow: Devon & Exmoor	£14.99
Go Slow: Norfolk & Suffolk	£14.99
Go Slow: North Yorkshire: Moors, Dales & more	£14.99

Europe

Abruzzo	£14.99
Albania	£15.99
Armenia	£14.99
Azores	£14.99
Baltic Cities	£14.99
Belarus	£14.99
Bosnia & Herzegovina	£14.99
Bratislava	£9.99
Budapest	£9.99
Bulgaria	£13.99
Cork	£6.99
Croatia	£13.99

Cyprus see North Cyprus	
Czech Republic	£13.99
Dresden	£7.99
Dubrovnik	£6.99
Estonia	£14.99
Faroe Islands	£15.99
Georgia	£14.99
Greece: The Peloponnese	£14.99
Helsinki	£7.99
Hungary	£15.99
Iceland	£14.99
Kosovo	£15.99
Lapland	£13.99
Latvia	£13.99
Lille	£9.99
Lithuania	£14.99
Ljubljana	£7.99
Luxembourg	£13.99
Macedonia	£15.99
Malta	£12.99
Montenegro	£14.99
North Cyprus	£12.99
Riga	£6.99
Serbia	£15.99
Slovakia	£14.99
Slovenia	£13.99
Spitsbergen	£16.99
Switzerland Without a Car	£14.99
Tallinn	£6.99
Transylvania	£14.99
Ukraine	£15.99
Vilnius	£6.99
Zagreb	£6.99

Middle East, Asia and Australasia

Bangladesh	£15.99
Borneo	£17.99
China: Yunnan Province	£13.99
Great Wall of China	£13.99
Iran	£15.99
Iraq: Then & Now	£15.99
Israel	£15.99
Kazakhstan	£15.99
Kyrgyzstan	£15.99
Lake Baikal	£15.99
Maldives	£15.99
Mongolia	£16.99
North Korea	£14.99
Oman	£13.99
Shangri-La: A Travel Guide to the Himalayan Dream	£14.99
Sri Lanka	£15.99
Syria	£15.99
Tibet	£13.99
Yemen	£14.99

The Americas and the Caribbean

Amazon, The	£14.99
Argentina	£15.99
Bolivia	£14.99
Cayman Islands	£14.99
Chile	£16.95
Colombia	£16.99
Costa Rica	£13.99
Dominica	£14.99
Grenada, Carriacou & Petite Martinique	£14.99
Guyana	£14.99
Nova Scotia	£14.99
Panama	£14.99
Paraguay	£15.99
St Helena	£14.99
Turks & Caicos Islands	£14.99
Uruguay	£15.99
USA by Rail	£14.99
Yukon	£14.99

Wildlife

100 Animals to See Before They Die	£16.99
Antarctica: Guide to the Wildlife	£15.99
Arctic: Guide to the Wildlife	£15.99
Central & Eastern European Wildlife	£15.99
Chinese Wildlife	£16.99
East African Wildlife	£19.99
Galápagos Wildlife	£15.99
Madagascar Wildlife	£16.99
New Zealand Wildlife	£14.99
North Atlantic Wildlife	£16.99
Pantanal Wildlife	£16.99
Peruvian Wildlife	£15.99
Southern African Wildlife	£18.95
Sri Lankan Wildlife	£15.99
Wildlife and Conservation Volunteering: The Complete Guide	£13.99

Eccentric Guides

Eccentric Australia	£12.99
Eccentric Britain	£13.99
Eccentric Cambridge	£6.99
Eccentric London	£13.99

Others

Something Different for the Weekend	£9.99
Weird World	£14.99
Your Child Abroad: A Travel Health Guide	£10.95

WIN £100 CASH!
READER QUESTIONNAIRE

Send in your completed questionnaire for the chance to win £100 cash in our regular draw

All respondents may order a Bradt guide at half the UK retail price – please complete the order form overleaf.

(Entries may be posted or faxed to us, or scanned and emailed.)

We are interested in getting feedback from our readers to help us plan future Bradt guides. Please answer ALL the questions below and return the form to us in order to qualify for an entry in our regular draw.

Have you used any other Bradt guides? If so, which titles? . . . .
. . . .

What other publishers' travel guides do you use regularly? . . . .
. . . .

Where did you buy this guidebook? . . . .

What was the main purpose of your trip to Kosovo (or for what other reason did you read our guide)? eg: holiday/business/charity etc.. . . . .
. . . .

What other destinations would you like to see covered by a Bradt guide?
. . . .

Would you like to receive our catalogue/newsletters?

YES / NO (If yes, please complete details on reverse)

If yes – by post or email? . . . .

Age (circle relevant category) 16–25   26–45   46–60   60+

Male/Female (delete as appropriate)

Home country . . . .

Please send us any comments about our guide to Kosovo or other Bradt Travel Guides. . . . .
. . . .
. . . .
. . . .

Bradt Travel Guides
23 High Street, Chalfont St Peter, Bucks SL9 9QE, UK
✆ +44 (0)1753 893444 f +44 (0)1753 892333
e info@bradtguides.com
www.bradtguides.com

CLAIM YOUR HALF-PRICE BRADT GUIDE!

Order Form

To order your half-price copy of a Bradt guide, and to enter our prize draw to win £100 (see overleaf), please fill in the order form below, complete the questionnaire overleaf, and send it to Bradt Travel Guides by post, fax or email.

Please send me one copy of the following guide at half the UK retail price

Title	Retail price	Half price
...	....	....	....

Please send the following additional guides at full UK retail price

No	Title	Retail price	Total
...	....	....	....
...	....	....	....
...	....	....	....

Sub total ....
Post & packing ....
(£2 per book UK; £4 per book Europe; £6 per book rest of world)
Total ....

Name ....

Address ....

Tel .... Email ....

☐ I enclose a cheque for £........ made payable to Bradt Travel Guides Ltd

☐ I would like to pay by credit card. Number: ....

Expiry date: .../... 3-digit security code (on reverse of card) .....

Issue no (debit cards only) .....

☐ Please add my name to your catalogue mailing list.

☐ I would be happy for you to use my name and comments in Bradt marketing material.

Send your order on this form, with the completed questionnaire, to:

Bradt Travel Guides KOS2
23 High Street, Chalfont St Peter, Bucks SL9 9QE
✆ +44 (0)1753 893444   f +44 (0)1753 892333
e info@bradtguides.com   www.bradtguides.com

NOTES

Index